1970
- The CRTC imposes regulations mandating that AM radio programming include at least 30 per cent 'demonstrably' Canadian content, and that FM radio programming include 10–30 per cent 'demonstrably' Canadian content
- Named for the first president of the CRTC, Pierre Juneau, the Juno Awards are established to recognize excellence in Canadian music
- Dogged by controversy, the Trans Continental Pop Festival, a.k.a. the Festival Express, finally kicks off at Toronto's CNE Grandstand on 27 June
- Crosby, Stills, Nash, and Young, *Deja Vu* ('Helpless', 'Ohio')
- The Guess Who, *American Woman* ('American Woman', 'No Time', 'No Sugar Tonight/New Mother Nature')
- Gordon Lightfoot, *If You Could Read My Mind* ('If You Could Read My Mind')
- Lighthouse, *One Fine Morning*
- Joni Mitchell, *Ladies of the Canyon*
- Anne Murray, 'Snowbird'
- Mashmakhan, 'As the Years Go By'
- Neil Young, *After the Gold Rush* ('Tell Me Why', 'After the Gold Rush', 'Don't Let It Bring You Down', 'Cripple Creek Ferry', 'Only Love Can Break Your Heart')

1971
- The Bells, 'Stay Awhile'
- Leonard Cohen, *Songs of Love & Hate* ('Last Year's Man', 'Famous Blue Rain Coat')
- Crowbar, 'Oh What a Feeling'
- Five Man Electrical Band, 'Signs'
- Joni Mitchell, *Blue* ('Carey', 'River', 'Little Green')
- The Poppy Family, 'Where Evil Grows'

1972
- Neil Young, *Harvest* ('Heart of Gold', 'Old Man', 'The Needle and the Damage Done')

1973
- Bachman-Turner Overdrive, *Bachman-Turner Overdrive II* ('You Ain't Seen Nothin'' Yet', 'Let It Ride')
- Edward Bear, 'Last Song'
- Stompin' Tom Connors, *Stompin' Tom and the Hockey Song* ('The Hockey Song')
- Skylark, 'Wildflower'

1974
- Bachman-Turner Overdrive, *Not Fragile* ('Takin' Care of Business', 'Second Hand')
- Beau Dommage, *Beau Dommage* ('La complainte du phoque en Alaska')
- Leonard Cohen, *New Skin for the Old Ceremony* ('Chelsea Hotel #2', 'Who by Fire', 'Take This Longing')
- Harmonium, *Harmonium*
- Terry Jacks, 'Seasons in the Sun'
- Joni Mitchell, *Court & Spark* ('Help Me', 'Raised on Robbery')

1975
- Rita MacNeil, *Born a Woman*
- Neil Young, *Tonight's the Night* ('Tonight's the Night', 'Borrowed Tune')

1976
- The Band plays its farewell concert, 'The Last Waltz', at the Winterland Ballroom in San Francisco
- Patsy Gallant, 'From New York to LA'
- Harmonium, *L'heptade*
- Gordon Lightfoot, 'The Wreck of the Edmund Fitzgerald'

1977
- Rolling Stones guitarist Keith Richards is arrested in Toronto for narcotics possession
- Burton Cummings, 'Stand Tall'
- Rush, *A Farewell to Kings* ('Closer to the Heart')
- Max Webster, *High Class in Borrowed Shoes*

1978
- Dan Hill, 'Sometimes When We Touch'
- Anne Murray, 'You Needed Me'

1979
- Bruce Cockburn, *Dancing in the Dragon's Jaw* ('Wondering Where the Lion's Are')
- Teenage Head, *Teenage Head*
- Triumph, *Just a Game* ('Lay It on the Line')
- *The Wall*, by Pink Floyd, just one of many albums produced by Canadian Bob Ezrin

1980
- Rough Trade, 'High School Confidential'
- Teenage Head, *Frantic City*

1981
- April Wine, *The Nature of the Beast* ('Just between You and Me')
- Chilliwack, *Wanna Be a Star* ('My Girl')
- D.O.A., *Hardcore 81*
- Loverboy, *Get Lucky* ('Turn Me Loose', 'Lovin' Every Minute of It')
- Rush, *Moving Pictures* ('Tom Sawyer')

1983
- Bryan Adams, *Cuts Like a Knife* ('Cuts Like a Knife', 'The Best was Yet to Come')
- Corey Hart, *First Offense* ('Sunglasses at Night', 'It Ain't Enough')
- Men without Hats, 'The Safety Dance'
- Platinum Blonde, *Standing in the Dark* ('Standing in the Dark', 'It Doesn't Really Matter')

1984
- Launch of MuchMusic, 'the nation's music station'
- Bryan Adams, *Reckless* ('Summer of 69', 'Run to You')
- Bruce Cockburn, 'If I Had a Rocket Launcher'
- Kim Mitchell, *akimbo alogo* ('Go for Soda')
- Honeymoon Suite, 'New Girl Now'

1985
- Corey Hart, *Never Surrender* ('Never Surrender', 'Boy in the Box')
- Northern Lights, 'Tears Are Not Enough'
- Platinum Blonde, *Alien Shores*
- Skinny Puppy, *Bites*

Continued at the back…

ROCK

A Canadian Perspective

Larry Starr   Christopher Waterman   Jay Hodgson

OXFORD

UNIVERSITY PRESS

OXFORD
UNIVERSITY PRESS

70 Wynford Drive, Don Mills, Ontario M3C 1J9
www.oupcanada.com

Oxford University Press is a department of the University of Oxford.
It furthers the University's objective of excellence in research, scholarship,
and education by publishing worldwide in

Oxford   New York

Auckland   Cape Town   Dar es Salaam   Hong Kong   Karachi
Kuala Lumpur   Madrid   Melbourne   Mexico City   Nairobi
New Delhi   Shanghai   Taipei   Toronto

With offices in
Argentina   Austria   Brazil   Chile   Czech Republic   France   Greece
Guatemala   Hungary   Italy   Japan   Poland   Portugal   Singapore
South Korea   Switzerland   Thailand   Turkey   Ukraine   Vietnam

Oxford is a trade mark of Oxford University Press
in the UK and in certain other countries

Published in Canada by Oxford University Press

Copyright © Oxford University Press Canada 2009

The moral rights of the author have been asserted

Database right Oxford University Press (maker)

First Published 2009

Library and Archives Canada Cataloguing in Publication

Starr, Larry
Rock : a Canadian perspective / Larry Starr, Christopher Waterman, Jay Hodgson.

ISBN 978-0-19-542761-5

1. Rock music—Canada—History and criticism. 2. National
characteristics, Canadian. I. Waterman, Christopher Alan, 1954–
II. Hodgson, Jay, 1976– III. Title.

ML3534.6.C2S796 2008   781.660971   C2008-903600-X

Cover image: S-E-R-G-O/iStockphoto

This book is printed on permanent (acid-free) paper ∞.
Printed and bound in the United States of America.

1 2 3 4 — 12 11 10 09

CONTENTS

             Punk, Funk, and Disco   250
             The Outlaws: Progressive Country   250
             'I Shot the Sheriff': The Rise of Reggae   256
             'Psycho Killer': The Dawn of Punk and New Wave   264
             'Tear the Roof off the Sucker': Funk Music   279
             'Night Fever': The Rise and Fall of Disco   282
             'Droppin' Science': Hip-Hop and Rap   294
             Discussion Questions   301

Chapter 7   MuchMusic, Mega-Stars, and Mega-Events: Rock in the 1980s   302
             Canada Enters the Eighties   302
             The Early 1980s: Record Recession   303
             The Sudden Rise of Music Videos   305
             The Global Record Industry: Horizontal Integration   310
             Digital Technology and Popular Music   311
             Now Playing on MuchMusic   314
             A Tale of Three Albums: *Thriller, Born in the U.S.A.*, and *Graceland*   335
             Prince, Madonna, and the Production of Celebrity   344
             Discussion Questions   357

Chapter 8   Alternative Currents: Rock in the 1990s   358
             The Meaning(s) of 'Alternative'   359
             Up from the Underground: Hardcore, Indie, and Alternative Rock   361
             In Search of Canada: The Tragically Hip   383
             Rap City: Rap in the 1990s   390
             Techno: Dance Music in the Digital Age   406
             The Years of the Canadian Women: Shania Twain, Céline Dion,
                Sarah McLachlan, and k.d. lang   409
             Discussion Questions   418

Chapter 9   What Just Happened? Rock in the 2000s   419
             The Rise and Fall of World Music   422
             'World' as 'Roots': Canadian Definitions   431
             Electronica at the Turn of the Century   434
             Music and Technology in the Twenty-First Century   437
             Canadian Indie and Post-Rock   445
             Discussion Questions   450

             Appendix: Internet Resources   451
             Glossary   461
             Bibliography   467
             Index   471

BOXES

PREFACE

▮ From the Publisher

Oxford University Press is proud to release *Rock: A Canadian Perspective*, the first and only rock music text to provide meaningful coverage of Canada's crucial contributions to the history of rock 'n' roll. Tracing the development of the genre from its roots to the present day, the text is unique in its detailed examination of the ways that rock music has shaped and reshaped Canada's culture since World War II. The text also looks at key episodes in our nation's history—such as the Cold War, prairie populism, the rise of the CRTC and 'CanCon', Quebec's Quiet Revolution—and assesses the role these and other developments have had on shaping Canadian popular music.

Written in a highly accessible style, *Rock: A Canadian Perspective* engages students with a balance of musical analysis and social context. Students will learn not only how and why rock music has changed, but also how its sound has changed over time. Rich in pedagogy and beautifully designed, this text is certain to appeal not just to students and instructors but to fans of Canadian music as well as anyone who wants to develop a critical appreciation for rock music.

■ **Uniquely Canadian.** The first and only text to survey the history of rock and popular music from a Canadian perspective, the text gives Canadian students an engaging, exclusive overview of how rock has evolved in this country.

■ **Up-to-date.** Material on present-day Canadian Indie Rock and on Aboriginal, Asian, and World music genres, as well as an updated section on music and technology, ensure that students are exposed to current and relevant insights into the present and future of rock music.

■ **Insightful discussion of technology.** Focusing on the relationship between technology and North American popular music, *Rock: A Canadian Perspective* helps students understand how changes in technology have shaped pop and rock.

■ **Unique approach.** The authors draw a connection between culture and the changing sounds of popular music. The result will encourage students to think on a deeper level about how rock music has evolved in relation to cultural change.

Listening Chart: 'You Oughta Know'

Music and lyrics by Alanis Morissette and Glen Ballard; performed by Morissette et al.

FORM	LYRICS	DESCRIPTIVE COMMENTS
A-a	I want you to know . . .	Close-miked and 'dry' vocals start the song, backed by Ballard's syncopated snare drum sample and high-end guitar frequencies quietly in background.
-b	An older version of me . . .	Electric bass enters, followed by a full drum kit; 'breakbeat' sample; lead guitar enters; high-end guitar frequencies continue in background.
-c	'Cause the love . . .	Pre-chorus section; rhythm guitar enters; vocals are close-miked and doubled, and panned far left and far right along the stereo spectrum.
Chorus	And I'm here . . .	Vocals centred, and treated as in 'A-a' and 'A-b'; distorted electric guitar plays straight eighth notes, and electric bass subdivides the beat with a basic sixteenth-note pulse.
A-a	You seem very well . . .	As in 'A-a'.
-b	Did you forget about me . . .	As in 'A-b', but with more active accompaniment from the electric bass, which at times plays in the 'slap-and-pop' style.
-c	'Cause the love . . .	Pre-chorus section repeats, as in 'A-c'.
Chorus	And I'm here . . .	Chorus repeats.
B	Bridge Oooooh . . .	Breakdown section, featuring vocalizations doubling a melody played on electric guitar; strummed whole notes from the electric guitar are panned far left and far right along the stereo spectrum; drums enter to signal return to chorus.
A-c'	'Cause the joke . . .	As in 'A-c', with slight variation in lyrics.
Chorus (x2)	And I'm here . . .	Chorus repeats twice and fades out.

■ **Guided Musical Discussions.**
Musical analysis and listening charts for dozens of tracks give students an opportunity to fine-tune their ears for different rock sounds.

Daniel Lanois created some of the most influential avant-garde rock and pop records of the 1980s and 1990s. © Lynn Goldsmith/Corbis.

■ **Comprehensive.** The text balances discussion of rock history with interesting anecdotes and musician profiles, providing students with a detailed and comprehensive treatment of rock's history from the milestones to the finer details.

Chapter Eight

Alternative Currents:
Rock in the 1990s

Throughout the 1990s, the marketplace for popular music continued to metastasize into hundreds of named genres, each correlated with a particular segment of the listening audience. Among these were:

- classic rock (Tragically Hip, Tom Cochrane)
- alternative rock (Sloan, Alanis Morissette)
- foxcore (Bif Naked)
- hardcore (D.O.A.)
- country rock (Blue Rodeo)
- new country (Shania Twain)
- alternative country (k.d. lang)
- roots rock (Cowboy Junkies)
- alternative roots (Be Good Tanyas)
- First Nations pop (Kashtin, Susan Aglukark)
- Celtic pop (Great Big Sea)
- alternative Celtic (Ashley MacIsaac)
- techno (Ti Tiga)
- rap (Maestro Fresh Wes)
- novelty pop (Moxy Früvous)

The 1990s saw a splintering of genres that exceeded anything previously experienced in rock. While many of these styles sprung 'from the ground up', as it were, nurtured

What Just Happened? Rock in the 2000s   847

Broken Social Scene: A collective that launched the Canadian indie rock explosion and is in part responsible for the success of the renowned indie label, Arts & Crafts. Chris Weeks/WireImages.

The band's second release, the David Newfeld-produced *You Forgot It In People* (2003), proved their breakthrough. Including the hit song 'Stars and Sons', eventually featured on the Academy Award-nominated film *Half Nelson* (with a breakout performance by London, Ontario, native Ryan Gosling), the record received the 2003 Juno for Alternative Album of the Year. Later that year, a collection of 'B' sides, entitled *Bee Hives*, was released. Two years later the band released their third record, *Broken Social Scene*, which prompted a slight breakthrough in the US. To promote the album, the band performed on *Late Night with Conan O'Brien*, performing '7/4 (shoreline)'. This album garnered another Juno for Alternative Album in 2006, after which point the group said they were going on hiatus following the end of their US tour in November. Since then, the group has spun off into numerous solo projects, the collective's best known alumnus now being Leslie Feist, whose second release, *The Reminder* (2007), ranked as one of the best-selling and most critically acclaimed albums of 2007.

Arts & Crafts

Most subsequent releases by ex-members of Broken Social Scene, and all of the group's albums save their debut, have been released on the Arts & Crafts label, which was established by Jeffrey Remedios in 2002, a friend of the band then working as the head of promotions for Virgin Music. Certain that Broken Social Scene and other

■ Outstanding design.
Modern and clean, the stunning full-colour design engages students while highlighting and supporting pedagogical features, making it sure to appeal to today's student.

---

462   Glossary

by numerous off-beat syncopations. Breakbeats were often sampled from moments on dance-oriented records, called 'breaks', when all harmonic and melodic activity ceased, leaving just the rhythm section or drums exposed. Once the purview of hip-hop DJs, breakbeats have become common in almost every subgenre of rock, save the more veridically oriented subgenres (i.e., punk, folk, and heavy metal).

bridge A passage consisting of new, contrasting material that serves as a link between repeated sections of melodic material. A bridge is sometimes called a 'release' (see discussion of AABA song form in Chapter 2).

cadence A melodic or harmonic event that signals the end of a musical line or section, or of the piece as a whole.

call-and-response A musical form in which a phrase performed by a single musician (the 'call') is answered by a contrasting phrase performed by a group of musicians (the 'response'), as was done, for example, among field workers and on prison chain gangs. In African-American music and related genres the call is typically improvised, while the response is repeated more or less exactly.

Canadian country A style of country music performance, typically particular to musicians born and raised in Canada. The genre typically reflects Canada's regional dialects and manners of speaking, and is generally sung in a lower-pitched, less nasal, and more clearly enunciated style than American country music. Most Canadian country songs also tend to be clearly based in folk styles of composition and performance, and thus typically enjoy greater crossover success than other varieties of country music.

CanCon A shorthand reference for Canadian content regulations, first established in 1970, whereby radio and music TV stations are required to play a certain percentage of Canadian songs, 'Canadian'

being defined according to several criteria, including music and lyric composition, producer, and artist(s) (see Chapter 5).

chansonnier [...]
often of a [...]
minimal [...]
i.e., only [...]

chansons eng [...]
topical lyri [...]
ent pitches.

chord The s [...]

chorus A re [...]
consisting o [...]
is repeated [...]
ically follow

coda The 'ta [...]
tion, typica [...]
complete se [...]
piece to its [...]

composer A [...]
music. Alth [...]
often is, us [...]
popular so [...]
applied to t [...]
formally no [...]

counterculture [...]
opposition [...]
trary to tha [...]
term is mor [...]
ues and life [...]
late 1960s a

counterpoint [...]
pendent m [...]
one another

cover version [...]
version' ref [...]
all subsequ [...]
formed by t [...]
that origin [...]
except its c [...]
of rock 'n' [...]
frequently [...]
by black a [...]
formers ha [...]
the cover v [...]
inal record

---

84   Rock: A Canadian Perspective

▌Discussion Questions

1. Why might it be better to consider rock 'n' roll an 'implosion' rather than an 'explosion'?
2. We know that Alan Freed was a relentless promoter of what [...] roll' music, and that he was hounded by controversy for his e[...] acteristics of the kind of rock 'n' roll that Freed promoted wer[...] parents and public officials, both in musical and social terms?
3. Why do historians consider the 'cover version' one of the mo[...] *dents* for the rise of rock 'n' roll? What are some current exam[...] sions? Do listeners tend to value a 'cover version' differently f[...] an 'original' song? Why do you think that is?
4. We know that many of the more important white R&B acts a[...] tral Ontario. In your opinion, is there something about t[...] sounds distinctly Canadian? How might white R&B have sou[...] it emerged from, say, Halifax or Quebec?
5. We know that the displacement of radio by television opened [...] for baby boomers to fill with rock 'n' roll music. Has anythin[...] since then?
6. Ronnie Hawkins had to lie to get Canadian bands work in Ca[...] think that is? How have attitudes towards domestic culture c[...] same in Canada since Hawkins's time?
7. What role did the CHUM charts play in fostering the notion of [...] ket with distinct tastes and preferences? Should we consider [...] part of our national heritage?

---

456   Appendix

▌Government Arts Institutions

CRTC: www.crtc.gc.ca/eng/welcome.htm
Provides a number of useful links. An explanation of how the MAPL system works is provided (crtc.gc.ca/eng/INFO_SHT/R1.htm). Researchers can also gain access to an on-line repository of related decisions, notices, and orders; news releases; and speeches given (crtc.ca/eng/documents/htm). Useful information concerning government regulations for the implementation of Canadian content laws can be found on the same site (crtc.gc.ca/eng/cancon.htm). Finally, under 'Statutes & Regulations' (crtc.gc.ca/eng/statues.htm), researchers can find text for a number of statutes and regulations, helpfully organized according to 'Acts', 'Regulations (Broadcasting)', 'Regulations (Telecommunications)', and 'Directions to the CRTC'.

Canadian Heritage Fund: www.canadianheritage.gc.ca/index_e.cfm
An overview of the policies established and enforced by the Canadian Heritage program. The site can be difficult to navigate but provides useful information on funding policy under the heading 'Arts and Culture'. Provides links to information on a number of funding programs for Canadian music, including: Canada Council for the Arts, Canada Music Fund, Canadian Broadcasting Corporation, Music Policy and Programs, etc.

FACTOR (Foundation Assisting Canadian Talent on Recordings): www.factor.ca
Provides information on the historical development of FACTOR, its programs, composition of competition juries, information on applications, and an advertisement for upcoming live events.

▌Country, R&B, and Traditional Music

Canadian Country Music Association: www.ccma.org
Provides an overview of the Association, information on Country Music Week, the Canadian Country Music Hall of Fame (see above), and information for members. Also provides links to the official sites for country music stars, and listings for upcoming country music events.

CJTM: Canadian Journal of Traditional Music: cjtm.icaap.org
Provides an on-line collection of all current and past issues of the *Canadian Journal of Traditional Music*. Also provides submission guidelines for interested authors.

■ Pedagogically Rich. A glossary, an annotated list of Web resources, and discussion questions for every chapter help enhance student understanding of the material presented in the book.

■ **Robust ancillary suite.** A companion website features a complete instructor's manual and student study guide, allowing students and instructors alike to enhance their use of the text.

■ **FREE subscription to Grove Music.** Students who purchase the text get a free subscription to Grove Music Online, a Web-based music resource with access to over 50,000 articles, 20,000 biographies, audio examples, links to related websites, and much more.

■ **iMix song list.** All of the songs referenced in the text are included in an iMix song list available for purchase through iTunes™.

From the Author

What follows is not an exhaustive history of rock music composed and performed by Canadian musicians. Rather, it is a survey of rock's history that takes into account some of the unique ways in which Canadians have used the rock genre to reflect their own interests and needs. In other words, it offers a Canadian perspective on the historical development of rock music. It was for this reason that I chose to title this book *Rock: A Canadian Perspective*.

The fact that it is an adaptation of a textbook called *American Popular Music: The Rock Years* seems entirely appropriate. After all, Canadian rock itself began as an adaptation of what was—if only for a short while, in the mid-1950s—a distinctly American musical idiom. Even today, the academic literature on rock music is dominated by American events and issues. That focus may seem lopsided, but it is not surprising. Rock 'n' roll was an American invention. Most Canadian listeners care deeply about the rock music made by American musicians, and most Canadian musicians hope to be heard by American listeners. To reflect this complicated dynamic, I have tried to broaden the usual American perspective on rock's history by looking at the same developments from another, often very different, point of view.

Canadians have had a unique relationship with rock music ever since it first crossed the border. Rock has had a profound influence on Canada, musically, culturally, and economically. And Canada's distinct political and economic character, in turn, has had a profound influence on the rock genre. This give-and-take remains a crucial tension in Canadian popular culture. Canadian history complicates many of the stories now so often told about the rock tradition. Continental solidarity and Cold War paranoia, prairie populism and Western alienation, the struggles of First Nations peoples, fears of Americanization, the Quiet Revolution and linguistic politics, the rise of left-nationalism, the rise of the New Right—these are only a handful of the issues, events, and ideas that have affected the way Canadians make and listen to rock 'n' roll. They are important to understanding the evolution of rock in Canada because they were, and are, important to the people who took rock to the forefront of Canadian popular culture and have kept it there.

Finally, I know that many still find the concept of a national identity—let alone a distinctly Canadian identity—questionable. All I can say is that I have always heard something distinctly Canadian in music made by the Tragically Hip, Gordon Lightfoot, the Guess Who, Buffy Sainte-Marie, Ian and Sylvia, Anne Murray, Feist, k-os, Maestro Fresh Wes, Avril Lavigne, Robert Charlebois, Nelly Furtado, Neil Young, Joni Mitchell, Leonard Cohen, Susan Aglukark, Gilles Vigneault, Kashtin, BTO, Our Lady Peace, Chantal Kreviazuk, Sum 41, and all the other Canadians who have topped the charts at home and abroad with their rock, or rock-oriented, songs. Many Canadians agree with me. I don't think they are dupes or victims of false consciousness. Most Canadians care deeply about Canadian identity, and Canadian rock music is an important component of that identity. In writing this adaptation, I hope I have given their perspective a hand in shaping another 'official' history of the rock tradition.

▌ Acknowledgements

I owe a great many people thanks for their encouragement, friendship, and support while I worked on this book. First, I must thank my wife and son, Eva and James Georg (the strongest little boy in the world); this work took much time away from them, and they were patient and understanding throughout. I could not have done this without them. I also owe much thanks to my colleagues in the Popular Music Studies Department at the University of Western Ontario, especially Bob Toft, who was incredibly supportive and continually offered me great advice. Thanks also to Henry Klumpenhouwer and Mickey Vallee, at the University of Alberta, for the conversations about rock over the years; I learned much from both of you. Members of my family also went above and beyond the call of familial duty: my mother and brother, Beverley and Jonathan, kept me working, constantly asking me how the adaptation was shaping up; my father, James, was a credibly skeptical sounding board for many of the ideas I pursued in this text, spending long breaks from our manly regimen of marathon biking on a bench at Couchiching Park talking about Canadian history and rock; my sister, Corrina, hammered many unwieldy passages into shape for me; and my brothers, Tyler and Big John, offered their support from afar. I would also like to thank a number of people at Oxford for their patience and assistance during the planning and writing stages—in particular Katherine Skene and Jennifer Charlton, both of whom were indispensable, Janna Green for her work in obtaining permissions for many of the lyrics cited in this text, and Richard Tallman for his crucial, and insightful, criticisms and suggestions. Likewise, I am indebted to my reviewers for their insightful criticisms on earlier drafts of this adaptation, especially Norman Stanfield and Kristi Yri. And, of course, I owe an extra big thanks to Sharron O'Brien for bringing this project to my attention in the first place.

Jay Hodgson
London, Ontario
May 2008

LYRIC CREDITS

A HARD DAYS NIGHT by John Lennon and Paul McCartney. Northern Songs/Sony/ATV Tunes LLC. All rights on behalf of Northern Songs/Sony/ATV Tunes LLC administered in Canada by Sony/ATV Music Publishing Canada. All rights reserved. Used by permission.

ALL REVVED UP WITH NO PLACE TO GO written by James Steinman, published by Edward B. Marks Music Company (BMI).

ALL TOUCH BY ROUGH TRADE Courtesy of Mummy Dust Music Ltd (SOCAN).

BLACK DAY IN JULY words and music by Gordon Lightfoot. © 1968 (renewed) Moose Music, Ltd. All rights reserved. Used by permission from Alfred Publishing Co., Inc.

BLACK NIGHT words and music by Jessie Mae Robinson, copyright © 1951 Aladdin Music Publications. Copyright © renewed MPL Communications, Inc. All rights reserved.

BLOWIN' IN THE WIND (Special Rider Music) by Bob Dylan, copyright © 1962 by Warner Bros. Inc. Copyright renewed 1990 by Special Rider Music. All rights reserved. International copyright secured. Reprinted by permission.

BOBCAYGEON by The Tragically Hip. Songs of Peer Ltd.

BORN IN THE U.S.A. by Bruce Springsteen, copyright © 1984 Bruce Springsteen (ASCAP). All rights reserved. Reprinted by permission.

BORN IN WATER by The Tragically Hip. Songs of Peer Ltd.

CHARLIE BROWN words and music by Jerry Leiber and Mike Stoller. Copyright © 1959 Sony/ATV Music Publishing LLC. Copyright renewed. All rights administered by Sony/ATV Music Publishing LLC, 8 Music Square West,

Nashville, TN 37203. International copyright secured. All rights reserved.

CHELSEA HOTEL NO. 2 by Leonard Cohen. Stranger Music Inc./Sony/ATV Songs LLC. All rights on behalf of Strange Music Inc./Sony/ATV Songs LLC administered in Canada by Sony/ATV Music Publishing Canada. All rights reserved. Used by permission.

CHOO CHOO CH' BOOGIE words and music by Vaughn Horton, Denver Darling, and Milton Gabler, copyright © 1945 (renewed) RYTVOC, Inc. All rights reserved.

CHOTEE by Bif Naked. Words and music by Beth Hopkins and X-Factor. © 1998 Tay/Kar Music and Alex Arundall Publishing Designee. All rights on behalf of Tay/Kar Music administered by WB Music Corp. All rights reserved. Used by permission from Alfred Publishing Co., Inc.

COCNUT CREAM by The Tragically Hip. Songs of Peer Ltd.

DIARABY By Ali Farka Toure, copyright © World Circuit Music Ltd/PRS (admin. by ICG). All rights reserved. Used by permission

DISCO SUCKS by D.O.A. Joe Keithley, Prisoner Publishing, SOCAN.

DON'T BE CRUEL words and music by Otis Blackwell by Elvis Presley. Copyright © 1956; renewed 1984 Elvis Presley Music (BMI). All rights for Elvis Presley Music administered by Cherry River Music Co. International copyright secured. All rights reserved.

DON'T THINK TWICE, IT'S ALL RIGHT by Bob Dylan, copyright © 1963 by Warner Bros. Inc. Copyright renewed 1991 by Special Rider Music. All rights reserved. International copyright secured. Reprinted by permission.

DOO WOP (THAT THING) by Lauryn Hill Obverse Creation Music Inc./Sony/ATV Tunes LLC. All rights on behalf of Obverse Creation Music Inc./Sony/ATV Tunes LLC administered in Canada by Sony/ATV Music Publishing Canada. All rights reserved. Used by permission.

ELEANOR RIGBY by John Lennon and Paul McCartney. North Songs/Sony/ATV Music Publishing Canada. All rights on behalf of Northern Songs/Sony/ATV Tunes LLC administered in Canada by Sony/ATV Music Publishing Canada. All rights reserved. Used by permission.

THE FACE OF LOVE Words and music by Nusrat Fateh Ali Khan, David Robbins, and Tim Robbins, copyright © 1995 Woman Music Ltd and Robbins Egg Music. All Rights for Woman Music Ltd assigned to EMI Virgin Music Ltd. All rights for EMI Virgin Music Ltd in the United States and Canada controlled and administered by EMI Virgin Songs, Inc. All rights reserved. International copyright secured. Used by permission.

FIFTY MISSION CAP by The Tragically Hip. Songs of Peer Ltd.

THE FUTURE by Leonard Cohen. Stranger Music Inc./Sony/ATV Songs LLC. All rights on behalf of Stranger Music Inc./Sony/ATV Songs LLC administered in Canada by Sony/ATV Music Publishing Canada. All rights reserved. Used by permission.

GET UP STAND UP words and music by Bob Marley and Peter Tosh. Copyright © 1974 Fifty-Six Road Music, Ltd, Odnil Music, Ltd, Blue Mountain Music, Ltd, Songs of the Knoll, and Embassy Music Corporation. Copyright renewed. All rights in North America administered by Fairwood Music USA (ASCAP) on behalf of Blue Mountain Music, Ltd and throughout the rest of the world by Fairwood Music Ltd (PRS) on behalf of Blue Mountain Music, Ltd. International copyright secured. All rights reserved.

GOD GIVETH—BILL TAKETH by D.O.A. Joe Keithley, Prisoner Publishing. SOCAN.

GOODNIGHT IRENE words and music by Huddie Ledbetter and John A. Lomax. TRO-© Copyright 1936 (Renewed) 1950 (Renewed) Ludlow Music, Inc., New York, NY. Used by permission.

GOOD VIBRATIONS by Brian Wilson and Mike Love, copyright ©1966 Irving Music, Inc. (BMI). Copyright renewed. Used by permission. All rights reserved.

THE HARDER THEY COME by Jimmy Cliff © 1972 Island Music Ltd. Copyright renewed. All rights administered in the US and Canada by Universal—Songs of PolyGram Int., Inc. (BMI). Used by permission. All rights reserved.

HIGH SCHOOL CONFIDENTIAL by Rough Trade. Courtesy of Mummy Dust Music Ltd (SOCAN).

THE HOCKEY SONG by Stompin' Tom Connors. Song lyrics to 'The Hockey Song' reprinted by permission. Copyright © Crown Vetch Music (A division of Stompin' Tom Ltd) c/o Morning Music Ltd.

HOLIDAY IN CAMBODIA by Jello Biafra, East Bay Ray, Klaus Flouride, and Bruce Slesinger, copyright © 1980. Published by Decay Music (BMI). Administered by Bug. All rights reserved. Used by permission.

HOOCHIE COOCHIE MAN by Willie Dixon, copyright ©1964, ® 1992 Published by Hoochie Coochie Music (BMI). Administered by Bug. All rights reserved. Used by permission.

HOTEL CALIFORNIA by Don Henley, Glenn Frey, and Don Felder, copyright ©1976 (renewed) Cass County Music/Red Cloud Music (BMI)/Fingers Music (ASCAP). All rights reserved. Used by permission.

HOUND DOG words and music by Jerry Leiber and Mike Stoller. Copyright © 1956 Elvis Presley Music, Inc. and Lion Publishing., Inc. Copyright renewed, assigned by Gladys Music and Universal Music Corp. All rights administered by Cherry Lane Music Publishing Company, Inc. International copyright secured. All rights reserved.

I'M AGAINST IT words and music by Jeffrey Hyman, John Cummings, and Douglas Colvin, © 1978 WB Music Corp. and Taco Tunes. All rights administered byWB Music Corp. All rights reserved. Used by permission from Alfred Publishing Co., Inc.

PSYCHO KILLER words by David Byrne, Chris Frantz, and Tina Weymouth. Music by David Byrne © 1976 (renewed) Index Music, Inc. (ASCAP) and Bleu Disque Music Co., Inc. (ASCAP). All rights administered by WB Music Corp. (ASCAP). All rights reserved. Used by permission from Alfred Publishing Co., Inc.

QUEBEC, MON PAYS by Raymond Levesque. Unidisc Music.

RAPPER'S DELIGHT by Bernard Edwards and Nile Rogers. Sony/ATV Songs LLC/Bernard's Other Music. All rights on behalf of Sony/ATV Songs LLC administered in Canada by Sony/ATV Music Publishing Canada. All rights reserved. Used by permission.

SHAKE, RATTLE AND ROLL words and music by Charles E. Calhoun. Copyright © 1954 by Unichappell Music Inc. Copyright renewed. International copyright secured. All rights reserved.

SH-BOOM (LIFE COULD BE A DREAM) words and music by James Keyes, Claude Feaster, Carl Feaster, Floyd McRae, and James Edwards. Copyright © 1954 by Unichappell Music Inc. Copyright renewed. International copyright secured. All rights reserved.

SHEENA IS A PUNK ROCKER words and music by Jeffrey Hyman, John Cummings, Douglas Colvin, and Thomas Erdelyi, ©1977 (renewed) WB Music Corp. and Taco Tunes, Inc. All Rights Administered by WB Music Corp. All rights reserved. Used by permission from Alfred Publishing Co., Inc.

SIXTY MINUTE MAN words and music by William Ward and Rose Marks. Copyright © 1951 by Fort Knox Music Inc. and Trio Music Company. Copyright renewed. International copyright secured. All rights reserved. Used by permission.

STAIRWAY TO HEAVEN by Led Zeppelin. Warner Bros. Music Corp.

STAY AWHILE by Jackie Ralph and Cliff Edwards.

SUPERMAN'S DEAD written by R. Maida/A. Lanni. Copyright © 1997 under Zenith Publishing (SOCAN)/Catchit Songs (SOCAN)/Lanni Tunes (SOCAN)/Sony ATV Music Publishing Canada (SOCAN). All rights reserved.

SUPERMAN SONG by Brad Roberts © 1992 Dummies Prod., Inc. All rights administered by Universal–PolyGram Int. Publ. Inc. (ASCAP). Used by permssion. All rights reserved.

TIME OF THE PREACHER words and music by Willie Nelson. © 1976 Full Nelson Music, Inc. All rights controlled and administered by EMI Longitude Music. All rights reserved. International copyright secured. Used by permission.

UNDERWHELMED by Andrew Scott, Chris Murphy, Jay Ferguson, and Patrick Pentland © 1993 Universal Music Corp. and Two Minutes for Music Ltd (SOCAN). All rights administered by Universal Music Corp. (ASCAP). Used by permission. All rights reserved.

WHO AM I (WHAT'S MY NAME)? Words and music by Calvin Broadus, William Collins, George Clinton, Garry Shider, Jerome Brailery, Mose Davis, Bernard Worrell, and David Spradley. Copyright © 1993 WB Music Corp., Suge Publishing, Bridgeport Music, Inc. (BMI)/Southfield Music, Inc. (ASCAP). All rights on behalf of itself and Suge Publishing Administered by WB Music Corp. All rights reserved. Used by permission.

YESTERDAY by John Lennon and Paul McCartney. Northern Songs/Sony/ATV Music Publishing Canada. All rights on behalf of Northern Songs/Sony/ATV Tunes LLC administered in Canada by Sony/ATV Music Publishing Canada. All rights reserved. Used by permission.

YOU CAN CALL ME AL by Paul Simon, copyright © 1985 Paul Simon. Used by permission of the publisher: Paul Simon Music.

YOU CAN'T HURRY LOVE by Edward Holland, Lamont Dozier, and Brian Holland. © 1965, 1966 (renewed 1993, 1994) Jobete Music Co., Inc. All rights controlled and administered by EMI Blackwood Music Inc. on behalf of Stone Agate Music (a division of Jobete Music Co., Inc.). All rights reserved. International copyright secured. Used by permission.

YOU OUGHTA KNOW by Alanis Morissette and Glen Ballard © 1995 Universal Music Corp., Songs of Universal, Inc., Aerostation Corp., and Vanhurst Place Music. All rights for Aerostation Corp. administered by Universal Music Corp. (ASCAP). All rights for Vanhurst Place Music administered by Songs of Universal, Inc. (BMI). Used by Permission. All rights reserved.

Introduction

The Post-War Context

The advent of rock 'n' roll music in the mid-1950s brought enormous changes to Western popular music, and then to world popular music. Musical styles that, from a marketing standpoint, had remained on the margins of pop music began to infiltrate and, eventually, to dominate the centre completely. Rhythm and blues and country and western records were no longer necessarily directed to specialized and regionalized markets; they began to be heard in significant numbers on mainstream pop radio, and many could be purchased in music stores that catered to the broadest general public. The impact of these changes is still being felt today.

The emergence of rock 'n' roll was surely an event of great cultural significance as well. Because of its importance, we must be careful not to mythologize it or to endorse common misconceptions about it. The following issues in particular demand our attention: first, rock 'n' roll was neither a 'new' style nor was it any single style of music; second, the era of rock 'n' roll does not mark the first time that popular music was written specifically to appeal to young people; and, finally, rock 'n' roll is certainly not the first popular music to bring black and white popular styles into close interaction. In fact, the designation 'rock 'n' roll' was introduced as a commercial and marketing term, for the explicit and sole purpose of identifying a new target audience for musical products—nothing more or less.

This new audience was dominated by those born into the so-called 'baby-boom' generation at the end of and immediately following World War II. It was a much younger audience than had ever before constituted a target market for music, and it was a large audience that shared some specific and important characteristics of group cultural identity. These were kids growing up in the 1950s—a period of economic stability and prosperity, but also a time when many pursued a sometimes stifling ideal of 'normalcy' that was defined in socially and politically conservative terms.

The Baby Boom, Baby Boomers, and Post-War Canada

Between 1944 and 1946 about 300,000 Canadian women—more than 25 per cent of the country's entire female workforce—voluntarily left or were pressured to resign from their wartime jobs. Veterans subsequently took advantage of an occupational right-of-return, which stipulated that any man who left work for active duty during the war must have an equivalent job made available to him on his discharge. Relationships put on hold until the end of the war, and new relationships forged during the war, were legitimized in the traditional way: each year between 1945 and 1955 more than 250,000 Canadian couples married, making the marriage rate for those years the highest on record in Canada. Added to this number were the country's many new war brides, over 40,000 of whom became naturalized citizens in 1946 alone. These newlyweds had children faster and younger than any other group in history, typically conceiving in less than two years of their wedding day, when both parents were still between 22 and 24 years of age. Thus, the live birth rate in Canada rose from a historical low of 227,000 in the mid-1930s to 338,000 in 1956; and it did not stop rising until 1959, when more than one in five Canadian women gave birth, making Canada's the highest sustained birth rate in the industrialized world. In all, the population of Canada catapulted 29.6 per cent between 1949 (13.5 million) and 1959 (17.5 million), the largest jump ever recorded in one country within a single decade.

Children born at this time, dubbed 'baby boomers' by historians, were historically fortunate—they were born at a time of unprecedented prosperity and abundance (indeed, the boomer mantra 'all you need is love' must have seemed maddeningly privileged to those who came of age during the Great Depression and World War II). During the 1950s the Canadian gross national product more than doubled, from $16.8 billion in current dollars to $36.8 billion, making Canada's the second largest economy in the world, after only the United States. Social scientists on both sides of the Atlantic began to use the term 'post-scarcity' to describe North American society; and some, such as the University of Toronto's soon-to-be world famous media theorist, Herbert Marshall McLuhan, wondered aloud what people would do when, in the not-too-distant future, automation made work obsolete. Douglas Owram, a historian of the baby boom in Canada, explains the effect that this prosperity, and the so-called 'long-wave optimism' accompanying it, had on boomers:

> Few generations grew up in such prosperous times. The quarter-century after the Second World War brought the Western world some of the most sustained economic growth in history. People—both parents and children—went from year to year expecting things to improve. Although occasional recessions caused worry, and many individual lives did not reflect the prosperity of the times, the good fortune was broadly based. A growing economy, an improving set of governmental social programs, and a wide dispersion of wealth meant that the average Canadian citizen benefited. As a result the baby boomers became the best-fed, best-educated, and healthiest generation in Canadian history. Boomers did not have to struggle for survival and could afford to worry less about economic security.

Thus the generation could turn its attention to its own sensibilities. The boomers' sense of self was due, in no small part, to the fact that they had the luxury of being free to think about such things. (Owram, 1996: x)

Prosperity in Canada was geographically isolated, however. Only a few regional economies actually boomed: Montreal, the 'golden horseshoe' region from Oshawa through Toronto to St Catharines, Victoria, Vancouver, Halifax, and Ottawa. The rest of Canada, but especially its rural and prairie regions (which still housed over half the country's population), could only look on as the country's main urban centres prospered. In fact, so many moved to so few cities in Canada during World War II that, in 1944, Parliament passed a law officially outlawing migration to Vancouver, Victoria, Ottawa, Hull, Toronto, and Montreal (Pound, 2005: 441; Owram, 1996: 11). A stark regional divide thus emerged, which has characterized the Canadian cultural landscape ever since—'haves' in the major cities of British Columbia, Ontario, and Quebec, and 'have-nots' in the rest of the country.

Nonetheless, it seems that laws against moving to particular cities went unenforced, as Canadians continued to move to cities like Toronto, Vancouver, Montreal, and Winnipeg throughout the 1940s and 1950s. This intense and sudden agglomeration of population and wealth into only a few urban centres, coupled with a massive spike in live births, combined to create a strong demand for new and affordable housing. These new houses, built in 'prefabricated cities' beyond the urban fringe—that is, in suburban regions—transformed the urban landscape almost literally overnight. No less than 70 per cent of all single-dwelling homes built in the 1950s were located in one of these suburban areas, and they generally looked the same: single-story, two-bedroom, one-bathroom dwellings on 50-foot x 100-foot lots, costing roughly $11,000 but requiring only a 10 per cent down payment (5 per cent for returning veterans). Couples moved to these suburbs in droves. Outside Ottawa, for instance, in two census tracts south of Carling Avenue and west of Maitland Street, a population equal in number to the original population of these two tracts moved in each year between 1956 and 1960, expanding the total population from 5,000 to over 25,000 in less than five years; meanwhile, the suburb of Hamilton Mountain, minutes from downtown Hamilton, grew from a population of 12,000 to 50,000 between 1955 and 1960; and North York, now a part of greater Toronto, expanded by a staggering 1,075 per cent between 1951 and 1961, surpassing the population of any Maritime city in the process (Owram, 1996: 54-83).

Canada's suburbs were not just prefabricated cities, as critics called them, but also cultures unto themselves. Most obviously, suburban culture was 'filiocentric', or child-centred, a term coined by social scientist William Whyte to describe the 'dictatorial effect' he felt boomers were already having not just on their parents' lives but on the culture in general by the mid-1950s. Birth control continued to be officially illegal both in Canada and in the United States, and sexual contact outside of wed-lock was strongly discouraged; suburban parents were thus expected to be (and gen-erally were) married, matrimony remaining basically the only avenue available for proving maturity, and confirming one's sexuality, to peers (the latter was particularly important since the only officially legal sexuality was one that existed within the con-text of a traditional marriage). Furthermore, two-parent families were expected to survive on only one income, which father was assumed to provide through work in the city while mother tended the kids and home.

During leisure hours families shopped at shopping malls, which sprang up around the country beginning in 1949. The first such malls were built in Norgate and Dorval, outside of Montreal, and then in West Vancouver. When they were not out shopping, parents were expected to educate themselves on the vagaries of child-rearing. Indeed, it is not exaggerating to say that child-rearing, and babies in general, comprised a majority portion of Canadian culture in the 1950s. Dr Benjamin Spock's *The Common Sense Book of Baby and Child Care*, which famously advocated a 'permissive' approach to child-rearing, sold over 5 million copies across the nation that decade, meaning that roughly one in three Canadian households owned a copy of the book; at the same time, child psychologists such as William Blatz regularly filled Toronto's Massey Hall to capacity for evening lectures. CBC radio, and eventually CBC televi-sion, featured regular broadcasts from the likes of the University of Toronto profes-sor and self-professed 'child expert', S.R. Laycock, on how best to avoid becoming a 'bossy' or 'lazy' parent, and local and national newspapers transcribed and reprinted their advice the next day.

Canada: A Middle Power

Despite the outward appearance of peace and prosperity, the 1950s were an extremely anxious decade. Canada became a so-called 'middle power', wedged both geographi-cally and diplomatically between the United States and the Union of Soviet Socialist Republics as both countries engaged in an ever-intensifying nuclear arms race and bout after bout of diplomatic sabre-rattling. Though Cold War hostilities between America and Russia arguably commenced well before World War II had ended, and though Canada was never more accommodating of socialism than was the United States—Canadian authorities incarcerated 'left radicals' by the hundreds throughout the 1930s, 1940s, and 1950s—Canada did not officially enter the Cold War until September of 1945, when Igor Gouzenko, a cipher clerk at the Soviet embassy in Ottawa, turned over documents elucidating the particulars of a Soviet spy ring in Canada and the United States. The discovery of espionage at the highest ranks of Canadian government sent the press into a frenzy, sparking the first political scandal of the post-war era.

That World War III could erupt at any time, and with a nuclear volley over Canadian skies, struck many Canadians as a distinct possibility. For some, in fact, Canada itself had become nothing less than an American military installation: the famous Distant Early Warning (DEW) Line, a string of more than 20 radar posts built along the 70th parallel in the Canadian Arctic to warn Americans of incoming nuclear missiles from Russia, was established in the 1950s, as were the so-called 'Pinetree' and 'Mid-Canada' Lines, situated along the 50th and 55th parallels, respectively. As cultural critic Greg Potter explains, 'for Canada, pinned between irascible superpowers waiting to see who'd blink first, the possibility that some Troika-tanked Bolshevik in Siberia might drunkenly reverse the coordinates and drop the Big One on Spuzzum, Tuktoyaktuk, or Chibougamau was very real, indeed' (Potter, 1999: 9–10).

Thus did boomers come of age amid fears of Cold War espionage and, more dramatically, an impending nuclear holocaust. To this day many boomers still vibrantly recall the safety drills they practised as children at school in the event of a nuclear strike; students were told to seek refuge beneath their desks with their hands crossed over their heads and their eyes closed, since the flash of an exploding nuclear bomb was thought to be instantly blinding. 'I remember when I was a kid of 11 or 12, I had dreams of mushroom clouds wiping out civilization', recalls Red Robinson, the Vancouver disc jockey credited with introducing many Canadians to rock 'n' roll. 'My generation thought the whole world could go up any day—it was a threat that was there all the time' (cited in Potter, 1999: 10).

Anti-Communism, Continental Solidarity, and Americanization

Not surprisingly, Canada entered a period of intense anti-communism in the 1950s. In the United States, Senator Joseph McCarthy headed Senate hearings in the 1950s to root out Communists and 'fellow-travellers' in America, as had the House Un-American Activities Committee in the late 1940s, which resulted in the blacklisting of many entertainment personalities suspected of involvement with left-wing groups. In Canada, Prime Minister Mackenzie King convened an investigatory commission on 5 February 1946 endowed with enormous powers to subvert civil liberties under the War Measures Act (Pound, 2005: 443). This commission arrested and interrogated Canadians with 'questionable' politics by the dozens, most of whom had had some form of political or personal association with Igor Gouzenko. A number of Canadians were eventually convicted, including a nuclear physicist, a clerk in the Department of External Affairs, secretaries at various government offices, and, most famously, Canada's only Communist member of Parliament, Fred Rose of the Labour Progressive Party (Pound, 2005: 446; Gillmor et al., 2001: 219).

Anti-communism served a symbolic purpose in Canada that was probably not readily apparent to the outside world. Put simply, through anti-communism

Canadians expressed their solidarity with Americans, and, at the same time, a rejection of British colonial culture. Though by 1960 more than half of all Canadians still claimed British or Irish heritage, and 32 per cent more claimed French heritage, most were demonstrably eager to cut ties with Canada's colonial past. Much more than simply an attitude or an approach to art in Canada, modernism—a fetish for the new—thus suggested autonomy, sovereignty, and a new post-colonial identity for the country and its citizens.

Mackenzie King thus pursued a program of 'continental solidarity', seeking to align the country's political, cultural, and economic policies with those of the United States; and French Canadians in particular lauded the program, seeing it as a certain end to British dominance in Quebec. Openly assailing what he called 'the last badges of British colonialism', King asked Canadians to, among other things, adopt a new and 'distinctly Canadian' flag; expunge the word 'Dominion' from all public documents, including the Constitution, which was still kept in England; and end the referral of constitutional amendments to British Parliament for approval (Archbold, 2002: 61; Igartua, 2006: 30–5). Pundits and political scientists followed suit, many going so far as to propose an 'open' or 'integrated' border with the United States, most often called a 'Customs Union' (an eerily similar suggestion was made by analysts immediately following the 9/11 terrorist attacks in 2001).

While some nationalists publicly decried 'continental solidarity' as a ruse to distract Canadians from their ongoing annexation by the United States, a process they called 'Americanization', few would heed the warning publicly until almost a decade later, when anti-Americanism became as fashionable with boomers as anti-communism had been with their parents. At the outset of the Cold War the threat of Soviet expansion simply overwhelmed worries about cultural and economic sovereignty. And, in any event, for a majority of Canadians, annexation by their neighbour to the south was clearly preferable to annexation by their 'godless' neighbour just across the North Pole.

▌Rock 'n' Roll Teenagers—North and South

As we shall see, rock 'n' roll exacerbated nationalist tensions in Canada. Some heard in rock 'n' roll's raucous rhythms 'continental solidarity', while others heard only 'Americanization'. But arguably the most important factor of all for Canadian and American boomers was their identification as a unique generational peer group, one that transcended nationality as they were growing up. Told by advertisers and 'experts' alike that they were unique on an almost daily basis, boomers quickly developed a sense of self-identification as 'teenagers' (this category was not necessarily limited to young people between the ages of 13 and 19; many 10–12-year-olds participated fully in 'teen' culture). Naturally, such a group, from a young age, had to have its own distinctive emblems of identity, including dance steps, fashions, ways of speaking, and music.

The prosperity of the 1950s gave these young people an unprecedented collective purchasing power, while the decade's political and military anxieties imparted a sense of now-or-never urgency to their lives—that they should enjoy themselves now because their parents' generation could force it all to a violent, crashing end at any given moment. Millions of North American teenagers spent their allowances, and revenue from after-school and weekend work, on leisure and entertainment products geared especially to their tastes and sensibilities. By 1958, teenagers comprised over 75 per cent of the record-buying market in North America, and they almost unanimously preferred rock 'n' roll to other kinds of music. What resulted was an increasingly volatile give-and-take between products and trends prefabricated for teens by the adult commercial culture and products and trends chosen and developed unpredictably by members of the new generation themselves.

Rock 'n' roll music was at the centre of this dynamic. It emerged as an unexpected musical choice by increasing numbers of young people in the early to mid-1950s. It then became a mass-market phenomenon exploited by the mainstream music industry in the later 1950s. And, eventually, it was to some extent reclaimed by teenagers in the 1960s as they grew old enough to make their own music and, thus, to assume some form of control over its production and marketing.

Chapter One

Pre-History of Rock 'n' Roll, 1944–1955

The decade leading up to the emergence of rock 'n' roll is often described as a period of musical stagnation or, at best, a prolonged gestation. In fact, the decade after World War II was one of the most interesting, complicated, and dynamic eras in popular music history. The entertainment industry grew rapidly after the war, and in 1947 record companies achieved retail sales of over $214 million, finally surpassing the previous peak established in 1921. This growth was supported by the booming post-war economy and by a corresponding increase in the disposable income of many North American families.

Most of the hit records of the late 1940s and early 1950s were romantic songs, performed by crooners—sweet-voiced singers who used the microphone to create a sense of intimacy—with orchestral string backing. The sentimentality of these songs can be gleaned from their titles: 'Prisoner of Love' and '(I Love You) For Sentimental Reasons' (1946), 'My Darling, My Darling' and 'You're Breaking My Heart' (1949), 'Cold, Cold Heart' and 'Cry' (1951), 'No Other Love' and 'You You You' (1953), all of which were Number 1 pop hits. These romantic vocal records were interspersed on the hits chart with catchy, lighthearted novelty songs, including Number 1 hits such as 'Woody Woodpecker' (Kay Kyser, 1948), 'The Thing' (Phil Harris, 1950), 'I Saw Mommy Kissing Santa Claus' (Jimmy Boyd, 1952), and 'The Doggie in the Window' (Patti Page, 1953).

Big-band swing, the dominant jazz-based popular music style of the World War II era, was also supplanted by the romantic 'easy listening' or 'mood music' of Jackie Gleason, Montovani & His Orchestra, and Toronto native Percy Faith, whose 'Theme from A Summer Place' was the best-selling record of 1960 and earned the ex-CBC orchestra leader a Grammy award for Record of the Year in 1961. These records typically featured string orchestras and choruses, with an occasional light touch of the exotic—i.e., maracas, castanets, a harpsichord, or a vaguely Latin rhythm—and they soon became a mainstay of Muzak, a corporation dedicated to supplying businesses with recorded music designed to subliminally encourage worker productivity.

The Top 40 and Market Saturation:
The Industrial Basis of Musical Conservatism

The roots of this musical conservatism are not difficult to pinpoint. Alongside cultural and political factors, the economics of the music industry played a crucial role in establishing a conservative trend. For the first time during the post-war decade we can clearly see a phenomenon that has helped to shape the development of North American popular music ever since: a constant tug-of-war between the efforts of the music business to predict and control the public's consumption of music and the periodic eruption of new musical fads, usually based in youth culture. In general, the centre of the music business, like most other economic sectors at the time, became increasingly routinized after World War II. Music became a 'product' sold in 'units', and listeners were 'consumers'.

The idea of Top 40 radio programming, a clear example of the industry's attempt to control the uncertainty of the marketplace, was developed in the early 1950s by Todd Storz, a disc jockey in Omaha, Nebraska. Storz observed teenagers dropping coins in jukeboxes and noticed that they tended to play certain songs repeatedly. He applied this idea to radio programming, selecting a list of 'Top 40 hits'—40 because that was how many records the average jukebox held at the time—which he then played repeatedly. The idea spread quickly and many stations adopted the same format. The ability of radio stations to control the public's exposure to new records, and the fact that programmers and disc jockeys generally maintained final say in which records they put on the Top 40, led to the practice of **payola**, which entailed record companies giving gifts to disc jockeys who put their records on the air (by the mid-1950s this profitable practice had come under legal scrutiny through 'antitrust' and 'unfair competition' legislation).

The increasingly rapid turnover of hit songs on the radio and jukebox, which the Top 40 paradigm encouraged, meant that record companies started producing many more records than the public was willing to buy. The big record companies began to compete by saturating the market, sometimes sending as many as 100,000 copies of a new record to stores with a guarantee that storekeepers could return all of the discs they didn't sell. This is clearly not a sound business strategy, and it adversely affected the overall quality of pop music in the early 1950s—one record company executive rather honestly referred to this technique as 'throwing a lot of shit at the wall to see if anything sticks'.

In general, though, the major record companies of the post-war period—RCA-Victor,

Columbia, Decca, and a new Los Angeles-based company called Capitol Records—experienced considerable growth, even while the genres they regarded as marginal began to influence their primary demographic. Country and western music, for instance, expanded its audience during World War II, and this trend continued well into the 1950s. The market for rhythm and blues also expanded as a result of post-war prosperity—the income of the average black family tripled during the war—and a growing (though still small) white audience, whose musical conversion had been prepared by the swing era. This market was supported, as well, by a new generation of music publishers and independent record labels devoted to manufacturing country and western and rhythm and blues records, such as Chess in Chicago, Aladdin and Specialty in Los Angeles, Atlantic in New York City, King in Cincinnati, Sun in Memphis, and Duke/Peacock in Houston.

Music Technology in the Post-War Era

The country and western and rhythm and blues genres also received a significant boost from the introduction of new technologies for the reproduction and transmission of musical sound and visual images in the 1930s, 1940s, and 1950s. Magnetic tape recording, developed by the Germans and Japanese during the 1930s and brought back to North America by military personnel returning from active duty in World War II, offered a number of advantages over the established means of recording music: it was better able to capture the full range of musical sounds than the older process of recording directly onto 'master' phonograph discs; and it allowed musicians to re-record over the unsatisfactory parts of previous performances and to add—or 'overdub'—layers of sound to a recording (the best-known innovator in this field was the guitarist/inventor Les Paul, who designed his own eight-track tape recorder and began in 1948 to release a series of popular recordings featuring his own playing, overdubbed to sound like an ensemble of six or more guitars).

By the late 1940s recording studios were using audiotape rather than 'transcription discs' to produce most recordings, and some artists, but notably the popular crooner Bing Crosby, began to use tape to pre-record their 'live' appearances on radio. In 1948 the Ampex Corporation, backed by Crosby, introduced its first tape recorder, a machine that soon became a mainstay of the recording industry. The next year, 1949, saw the introduction of a two-track recorder that could record simultaneous inputs from two microphones and thus produce stereo effects. While tape recorders were not initially successful as a home consumer item, their advantages for recording were felt immediately in the music industry.

The post-war era also saw a fierce competition over new disc technologies, known as the 'Battle of the Speeds'. In 1948 Columbia Records introduced the twelve-inch long-playing (LP) disc. Spinning at a speed of $33^1/_3$ revolutions per minute (rpm), the LP could accommodate more than 20 minutes of music on each side, a great improvement over the three- to four-minute limitation of 78 rpm discs. In addition, the LP was made of vinyl, a material at once more durable and less noisy than the shellac used to make 78s. Interestingly, although the long-playing disc opened the possibility of longer uninterrupted records—a great advantage for fans of classical music and Broadway musicals—most pop music LPs remained 'albums' of three-minute performances. This suggests that what, from the engineering point of view, had seemed to be a technological restriction—specifically, the three-minute limit of 78 rpm phonograph records—had long since become a musical convention. To this day, in fact, most pop songs are still no longer than four minutes in length, and most radio and music television stations are still reluctant to broadcast tracks totalling more than four or five minutes, though no technological reason exists for this to be the case.

Responding to Columbia's innovation, the RCA-Victor Corporation introduced yet another new disc format in 1949: the seven-inch 45 rpm single. The '45', as it was called, which was actually close to the old 78 rpm in overall recording time, required a special mechanical record changer that fit the large hole at the centre of the disc. However, the new technology had at least one definite advantage over the LP from a consumer's viewpoint. Using a record changer the listener could load a stack of singles onto the record player, thus preprogramming a series of favourite songs, each of which would begin less than 15 seconds after the end of the previous record. This meant that consumers could focus their spending power on their favourite records, rather than buying a prepackaged series of songs by a single artist on an LP, pointing the way forward to present-day digital technologies that allow consumers to program specific tracks in any order they choose.

The so-called 'battle of the speeds' was ultimately resolved by a technological compromise, in which turntables were set up to accommodate all three existing formats (78, 45, and $33^1/_3$). LPs continued to serve as a medium for albums of pop songs and longer musical works such as Broadway cast recordings, while the 45 became the favoured medium for distributing hit singles, with the 'flip side' of the 45 almost always providing the young consumer with a pleasant or not-so-pleasant surprise, since the 'flip' or 'B' side was a song by the same artist that had not received airplay. Only rarely would the 'B' side later become a Top 40 or even Number 1 hit, as happened with Elvis Presley's 'I Was the One', on the flip side of 'Heartbreak Hotel'.

Radio broadcasting was also affected by technological change in the post-war period. In addition to the older AM (amplitude modulation) broadcasting technology that had dominated radio since the early 1920s, the post-war period saw the rapid growth of FM (frequency modulation) broadcasting. FM radio, which used higher frequencies than AM, had better sound quality and was not as easily subject to electrical disturbances such as lightning. The first commercial FM radio broadcast took place in 1939, and by 1949 around 700 FM stations were operating in North America alongside more than 1,000 AM stations. By the late 1950s FM was being used for stereo broadcasting. We will now consider some of the musics that these AM and FM radio stations were broadcasting at the time, each of which comprises a distinct musical tributary of the rock 'n' roll tradition.

Urban Folk Music

During the early 1950s a new genre of popular music called 'urban folk' appeared on the pop charts. This genre combined a number of seemingly contradictory tendencies: it was inspired by rural folk music yet performed by urban intellectuals; while embracing populist and presumably anti-commercial values, it generated millions of dollars in profits; many urban folk records were seemingly harmless singalongs, designed to invite audience participation, yet only a few years after the initial burst of public interest in this music some of its best-known practitioners were persecuted for their political beliefs. And the record industry really didn't know what to do with the music. Was it 'folk music'? Was it 'country and western'? Was it 'novelty' music? Nobody was sure.

The first urban folk group to achieve commercial success was the Weavers, a quartet led by the singer, banjo player, and political activist Pete Seeger (b. 1919). The Weavers developed a repertoire based on American and international folksongs, and performed at union rallies, college concerts, and urban coffeehouses. The group was 'discovered' at a New York City nightclub by Gordon Jenkins, the managing director of Decca Records, and between 1950 and 1954 they placed 11 records in the Top 40. However, their success was short-lived, and it remains difficult to gauge what impact the group might have had if they had been allowed to sustain their early success—three members of the group, including Seeger, were accused of being Communists during the early 1950s, even though their main accuser later admitted that he had fabricated the charges and went to prison for perjury. Unwilling to maintain relations with suspected Communists, Decca dropped the group, and they never again appeared on the pop charts. Seeger, however, continued to play a leading role as a champion of folk music and a social and environmental activist in the United States, eventually earning the moniker 'America's tuning fork' in the 1960s for his efforts.

The Weavers' singalong version of 'Goodnight, Irene', composed by the Louisiana-born musician Huddie Ledbetter (a.k.a. Leadbelly, 1889–1949), was their most successful record, reaching Number 1 on the pop charts in 1950. Of course, this was not folk music in any strict sense—Leadbelly had been recorded first by the Library of Congress folksong collectors, John Lomax and his son, Alan, in a southern prison in the early 1930s, and accompanied his own raw singing with a blues guitar; on the Weavers' commercial recording of 'Goodnight, Irene', in which the lyrics had been somewhat 'sanitized', the Weavers were accompanied by the orchestral arrangement of Gordon Jenkins, who also worked with Frank Sinatra, Nat 'King' Cole, and other pop stars. Despite their folksy informality, 'Goodnight, Irene' and the Weavers' other hits are pop records—no more, no less. And they ultimately helped to define a niche in the popular music market for folk-based popular music, including the later work of the Kingston Trio; Joan Baez; Peter, Paul, and Mary; Buffy Sainte-Marie; Gordon Lightfoot; Ian Tyson and Sylvia Fricker (Ian and Sylvia); Murray McLaughlin; Bruce Cockburn; and, of course, Bob Dylan.

Leadbelly, the composer of 'Goodnight Irene'. Courtesy Library of Congress.

Weavers (Pete Seeger, Lee Hays, Fred Hellerman, Ronnie Gilbert). Courtesy Library of Congress.

Listening To the Weavers' 'Goodnight, Irene' (1950)

'Goodnight, Irene' is a perfect illustration of one of the oldest and most enduring of all musical forms: the **strophic** song. In a strophic song, a musical unit—which may be of any length, but typically is rather short—is heard and then repeated again and again, to changing words. The term 'strophic' is derived from the literary term, **strophe**, indicating a poetic unit that contains a certain number of lines, usually with a set pattern of meter and rhyme. The vocal **melody**, which is the pattern of pitches and rhythms to which the words are sung, remains the same in a strophic song for each of the poetic strophes in the song's lyrics.

Strophic songs are found in virtually all types and styles of music, including the folk music traditions of many countries, and particularly in the blues and early 'hillbilly' musics of the American rural South. They also appear in all the periods of popular song. It is easy to understand why this is true. Strophic songs, because of the repetitive nature of their music, are easy to learn and to remember. They can also readily be used by performers to encourage listeners to participate by singing along; in fact, the Weavers habitually concluded their public performances with 'Goodnight, Irene', urging their audiences to sing with them. Strophic songs can also be almost infinitely adapted, lending themselves to the spontaneous alteration of lyrics and to the creation of new poetic strophes to fit new occasions, new contexts, new performers, and new audiences—since everybody, presumably, either knows the tune to begin with or else can learn it in short order.

In 'Goodnight, Irene' each strophe may be divided into two parts: the **verse**, in which the words change from strophe to strophe; and the **chorus**, in which both the music and the words remain the same. This offers a source of variety and interest within the strophic form, as each strophe presents one section that remains consistent and completely predictable, and another section in which the words change, revealing a new event or twist in the developing story. Again, it seems obvious why this verse-chorus arrangement became a favoured approach to strophic form. The Weavers' recording of 'Goodnight, Irene' clearly preserves a feeling for the basic verse-chorus strophe while using the catchy chorus melody independently as a hook at the beginning of the record and as a means to facilitate a fade-out effect at the end. This formal arrangement is outlined here:

'Goodnight, Irene': Outline of the Form

INTRODUCTION: [brief instrumental introduction]
CHORUS: *Irene, goodnight . . .*
[instruments, background voices repeat the chorus tune]

Strophe 1:
> VERSE: *Last Saturday night . . .*
> CHORUS: *Irene, goodnight . . .*

Strophe 2:
> VERSE: *Sometimes I live . . .*
> CHORUS: *Irene, goodnight . . .*

Strophe 3:
> VERSE: *Stop ramblin'. . .*
> CHORUS: *Irene, goodnight . . .*
> [chorus is repeated, fading out]

A closer look at the chorus of 'Goodnight, Irene' will help introduce some basic concepts of melody and rhythm. The chorus may readily be subdivided into four phrases, that is, four brief melodic patterns separated from one another by breathing spaces (pauses or rests) in the vocal line:

Irene, goodnight, [vocal pause]
Irene, goodnight, [vocal pause]
Goodnight, Irene, goodnight,
Irene, [brief vocal pause]
I'll see . . . dreams. [vocal pause]

Each phrase varies in pitch content — sometimes going higher and sometimes lower—in patterns that mimic the natural inflections of spoken words (phrases that 'sing' naturally are generally a hallmark of effective songwriting). As is typical of most speech, the vocal melody tends to fall in pitch at the ends of phrases. Some phrase endings seem musically more conclusive than others; in the chorus of 'Goodnight, Irene' this is true of the second and fourth phrases, both of which end on the same pitch. When the melody reaches such a temporary stopping point, what we might call the end of a musical 'sentence', musicians call this a **cadence**. The feeling of cadence will almost always be reinforced by events in the harmony, or the **chord** structure, of the music accompanying the melody, and this is certainly true in 'Goodnight, Irene'.

Attentive listening will reveal that each of the verses in 'Goodnight, Irene' is constructed analogously to the chorus. Even though the melody for the song's verses is obviously not the same as the melody for its chorus, each verse also may be divided into four phrases, with clear cadences occurring at the ends of the second and fourth phrases.

We have considered melody, harmony, and form, but have left out what is probably the most basic of all musical elements: rhythm, that is, the movement through time that, in fact, shapes melody, harmony, and form. In most popular music, the passage of time is marked by regular rhythmic pulses or beats. Beats are equal measurements of musical time; when you tap your foot or your finger to a tune, you are sensing and indicating its beats. In 'Goodnight, Irene' the musical instruments start to articulate the beats shortly after the song begins, and this regular beat then persists right through to the fade-out. All beats are not equally intense, however, and a larger, regular rhythmic pattern is created by the significant accent given to every third beat: *One*, two three; *One*, two three; *One*, two three; etc.

These groups of three beats, defined by the recurring accents, are called measures or bars. The three-beat bars—or, triple meter—of 'Goodnight, Irene' evoke the rhythm of the waltz, a dance whose popularity dates back to the nineteenth century. It may also be noticed that the phrases of the vocal melody in this song all extend over a span of four bars. Thus, a great consistency characterizes the rhythmic patterns of this song at every level: a regular beat; constant three-beat measures; phrases that are all four bars in length (with cadences occurring regularly at the end of every other phrase); four-phrase verses and four-phrase choruses, producing in turn uniform eight-phrase strophes. Such regularity is typical of popular music, since it results in easily remembered, reassuringly predictable patterns that lend themselves readily to singing and dancing. Of course, too much regularity results in boredom, so most popular records tread a fine line between what is predictable and what creates novelty and interest. In the Weavers' 'Goodnight, Irene' the interest aroused by the changing words of the verses is reinforced musically by having a different member of the group sing each verse.

The Folk Genre in Canadian Popular Music

Folk music followed a different trajectory in Canada than in the United States, and reflected a distinct set of circumstances. While groups such as the Travellers obviously aped the style of the Weavers, scoring probably their biggest hit with a cover of Woody Guthrie's 'This Land Is Your Land', urban folk music was identified much less with leftist politics in Canada—though it was, indeed, a mainstay at union rallies and strikes—and more with the 'mosaic' concept of Canadian culture. Though this association may seem self-evident to Canadian readers by now, its origin has as much to do with marketing as with anything else. In 1922, Victoria Hayward, an author from Bermuda, used the image of a 'mosaic' to describe the 'patchwork' of churches and land she saw out her window on a cross-Canada railway trip. John Murray Gibbon, a publicity agent for the Canadian Pacific Railway (CPR), took up Hayward's image and transformed it into a marketing ploy. With the help of anthropologist Marius Barbeau of the National Museum of Canada, who was an inveterate popularizer of the traditional music he and others collected for the Museum, Gibbon organized a series of music and arts festivals celebrating Canada's 'cultural mosaic' at each of the CPR's 'flagship' hotels.

Folk music was given an important boost in Canada by Samuel 'Sam' Gesser of Montreal, who, in 1950, opened a Canadian arm of Moses Asch's influential Folkways Records label. Between 1950 and 1965, Gesser produced and financed roughly 100 records for the label. Gesser initially focused on traditional folk fare, releasing a series of records chronicling many regional traditions in Canada, with such titles as: *Songs and Dances of Québec*; *Folk Songs of Newfoundland*; *Folk Songs of the Canadian North Woods*; *Indian Music of the Canadian Plains*; *Songs and Ballads of Northern Saskatchewan and Northern Manitoba*; *Folk Music from Nova Scotia*; *Folk Songs of Ontario*; *Songs from Cape Breton Island*; *Nootka Indian Music of the Pacific Northwest*. By the mid-1950s, however, Asch had begun to record more modern urban folk records. Most notably, Asch recorded Quebec's Alan Mills—already a popular folksinger on CBC radio's *Folk Songs For Young Folks* and *Songs de Chez Nous* programs—whose 'I Know an Old Lady Who Swallowed a Fly' (1951) became a standard of the urban folk genre, covered by the likes of Burl Ives; Peter, Paul, and Mary; and numerous others. Mills's recordings of the Newfoundland song, 'I's the Bye', and the rebellion-era lament 'Un Canadien Errant', are also classics of the genre. The significance of the records Gesser made to the development of the idea of a Canadian culture probably cannot be overstated. As Brenda Dalen, a music historian at the University of Alberta, explains:

> When Gesser embarked upon his association with Folkways, Newfoundland and Labrador had just joined Confederation (1949); Canada boasted a population of 14,009,429 (1951); the flags flown were the British Union Jack and the Red Ensign (until the adoption of the Maple Leaf flag in 1965); and 'O' Canada' was yet to be proclaimed the official national anthem (1967). The Folkways recordings document the history of the Canadian folk music revival of the 1950s and 1960s—roughly parallel to but far less politically motivated than its American counterpart—and furnish evidence of burgeoning nationalism in the years leading to 1967, the centennial of Confederation.

Pop Crooners

By 1946 the main focus of popular attention had shifted away from celebrity bandleaders of the swing era, such as Benny Goodman, Count Basie, and Glenn Miller, and towards a new generation of crooners. Many of the top singers of the post-war era, including Frank Sinatra, Perry Como, Nat 'King' Cole, Frankie Laine, and Rosemary Clooney, started their careers singing in front of big dance bands during World War II. By the early 1950s these pop stars had been joined by a younger generation of vocalists who specialized in sentimental ballads, novelty numbers—cheerful, disposable songs that often resembled advertising jingles—and crooner-style **cover versions** of country and western and rhythm and blues hits. These vocalists were promoted to the expanding teenage audience, even though, as Douglas Owram notes, their 'crooning did not distinguish [them] in form or content from artists appealing to adults.'

The American Federation of Musicians' 'recording ban' of 1942–4, which was a boycott on any and all recording sessions by members of the AFM in protest over poor compensation for jukebox and radio play, encouraged a number of big-band singers to begin recording under their own names, sometimes with choral accompaniment. Those singers with the most entrepreneurial savvy, or the best business agents, were able to parlay this opportunity into long-lasting success. In addition, the music industry's mastery of cross-media promotion on radio, film, and television reached new heights. Following in the footsteps of Bing Crosby, many of the biggest singing stars of the post-war era also became film stars—Frank Sinatra and Doris Day, for instance—or hosted their own television shows (e.g., Perry Como and Nat 'King' Cole).

Frank (Francis Albert) Sinatra (1915–98) was one of the first big-band singers to take advantage of changes in the music business. Born into a working-class Italian family in Hoboken, New Jersey, Sinatra attracted public attention in 1935 when he appeared as a member of a vocal quartet on a popular radio show called *Major Bowes' Amateur Hour*. From 1937 to 1939 he worked as a singing waiter at the Rustic Cabin, a nightclub in New Jersey; although the job paid little, Sinatra wisely kept it because the place was wired for radio broadcasts, which is to say, his nightly performances could be broadcast on the radio. In 1939 the bandleader Harry James hired him, and later that same year he joined the Tommy Dorsey Orchestra.

Frank Sinatra: the ultimate cool 'saloon singer' in the 1950s. Frank Driggs Collection.

Promoted on radio, at the movies, and in the press—including biographical comic books aimed at high school-age females—Sinatra's popularity soared, culminating in the first documented case of modern pop hysteria, the so-called 'Columbus Day Riot' of 1944. The occasion was a return engagement at the Paramount Theater by Sinatra and the Benny Goodman band, and 30,000 people—including thousands of teenage girls, called 'bobbysoxers'—showed up to claim tickets. The Paramount could seat only 3,600, and many fans refused to leave after the first show, triggering a riot among fans lined up outside the theatre.

In a sense Sinatra was the direct predecessor of the teen idols of the rock 'n' roll era, and of the Beatles after them. Falling into a 'Sinatrance', young women cried, screamed, and tore their hair. They followed the singer everywhere, fighting for pieces of his clothing and treating his used cigarette butts as sacred objects. The press and public bestowed nicknames on Sinatra: he was 'Swoonatra', the 'Sultan of Swoon', and, simply, 'The Voice'. Although Sinatra's popularity took a nosedive in the early 1950s, largely as a result of well-publicized difficulties in his personal life, his success in later years was in no small part due to the connection his audience perceived between his voice and his personality, each involving a delicate balance between emotionalism and rationality, deep feeling and technical control.

 ## Listening To Frank Sinatra's 'Love and Marriage' (1955)

'Love and Marriage' introduces us to another venerable form in North American popular music: the four-section AABA form. Songs constructed along these lines typically have sections of equal length, three of them presenting identical (or nearly identical) music to usually different words, while one—the 'B' section—presents new words and new music. The repetitions of the 'A' music assure that the song will quickly become familiar to the listener, while the 'B' section offers some musical variety within the form. The principles behind this formal strategy seem obvious enough: state an effective musical idea to 'hook' the listener; restate it, usually with new words, in order to fix it in the listener's mind; then sustain attention with a deviation from the established pattern; and conclude with the gratifying return of the now-familiar basic idea. It is not surprising that many songwriters have turned to AABA organization for the construction of memorable songs.

It is a simple matter to hear the AABA organization in 'Love and Marriage',

especially since each of the 'A' sections begins with identical words—the words of the title, which thus serve as a recurring musical and verbal hook. After a brief instrumental introduction, the song proceeds as follows. After the completion of the AABA form, an instrumental interlude presents the 'A' music again, after which Frank Sinatra re-enters and sings the last two sections—'B' and 'A'— once more. A brief instrumental passage ends the recording.

A   *Love and marriage, love and marriage, go together . . .*
A   *Love and marriage, love and marriage, it's an institute . . .*
B   *Try, try . . .*
A   *Love and marriage, love and marriage, go together . . .*

'Love and Marriage' is typical of AABA songs of this period insofar as it is organized rhythmically in regular four-beat bars grouped into sections of eight-bar length. We may also call attention to a few formal subtleties that lend interest and distinction to this particular example of the AABA song form. The music of the second 'A' section is indeed identical to that of the first 'A', with one small but important exception—it ends on a different pitch from the first. This is significant because, as a result of this alteration in the vocal melody (and in the accompanying chord), there is a cadence at the end of the second 'A' whereas there was no cadence concluding the first 'A'. In a sense, the first 'A' section sets up the second 'A', then, which in turn musically rounds off the first.

The beginning of the 'B' section is marked by a particularly striking change in the harmony that helps to set the music of this section strongly apart. In fact, the 'B' section in an AABA form is frequently called a **release** or, even more commonly, a **bridge**, presumably because it links two 'A' sections. The final 'A' section of 'Love and Marriage' restates not only the music but also the words of the opening section. Monotony is decisively avoided, however, for two reasons. First of all, this concluding section is extended beyond the expected eight bars to reach a length of eleven bars. Second, unlike the first 'A' section, the concluding section does reach a cadence (although we are, effectively, forced to wait for it), so it provides a definitive feeling of conclusion to the overall form. Because of the differences among the three 'A' sections in 'Love and Marriage', the form is perhaps best represented as AA^{I}BA^{II}.

Although AABA seems initially to represent a formal conception very different from that of the strophic song, a brief glance at the earlier history of popular song in North America establishes a link between them. The employment of AABA song forms was at its height in the first half of the twentieth century, especially in the 1920s, 1930s, and 1940s. This period is frequently called 'the golden age of **Tin Pan Alley**', named for the area in New York City where music publishing was centred, and where the great songwriters of this period, such as Irving Berlin and George Gershwin, plied their trade. Many Tin Pan Alley songs were in fact written in a strophic verse-chorus form; however, a favoured form emerged for the chorus in these songs, and that was the 16- or 32-bar AABA arrangement (with equal sections of four or eight bars, respectively). What happened over time, as these songs gained wide currency through multiple performances and arrangements, is that their verses came increasingly to seem optional or even dispensable, and the choruses alone endured. One of the reasons this might have occurred is that a 16-bar or especially a 32-bar chorus with an interesting internal form has sufficient substance by itself to sustain a performance or a recording; for a demonstration of the validity of this idea, we need look no further than the Sinatra recording of 'Love and Marriage', which shows no traces of a verse. The increasingly free-standing choruses of Tin Pan Alley songs were often called **refrains**, and this term proves useful to distinguish them from the choruses in strophic songs that are almost always performed with their verses.

It should not surprise us that 'Love and Marriage' employs a form inherited from the heyday of Tin Pan Alley, since the men who wrote the song, Sammy Cahn and James Van Heusen, as well as Frank Sinatra himself, began their careers in the 1930s. Indeed, the style of this recording would probably have struck many young listeners in 1955 as 'old-fashioned', especially since rock 'n' roll was beginning to achieve prominence at the time. Still, there remains reason enough to believe that the creators of this record wanted it to have a certain contemporary edge: the arrangement is unquestionably upbeat, and Sinatra does not burden this hymn to the traditional values of domesticity and monogamy with any feeling of excessive reverence (in fact, his delivery of the lyrics seems at points to take on an almost ironic quality). Certainly, the concluding instrumental gesture—a deliberately deflated, off-kilter rendering of a musical cliché—is designed to leave the listener smiling, if not chuckling.

While few post-war crooners were able to match Frank Sinatra's artistry or longevity, this does not mean that the so-called 'Sultan of Swoon' faced no serious competition. Despite the very small number of black artists on the pop charts in the early 1950s, it could be argued that the greatest post-war crooner—in both musical and commercial terms—was a black musician named Nathaniel Coles (a.k.a., Nat 'King' Cole) (1917–65).

Nat 'King' Cole performs in a nightclub, 1954. Courtesy Library of Congress.

Cole was born in Montgomery, Alabama, and his family moved to the South Side of Chicago when he was four years old. His father was pastor of a Baptist church, and young Nat was playing organ and singing in the choir by the age of 12. He made his first record in 1936 with the Solid Swingers, a jazz band led by his brother, Eddie Cole. A year later he moved from Chicago to Los Angeles and formed his own group, the King Cole Trio. A brilliant piano improviser in his own right, Cole influenced later jazz pianists such as Montreal-based Oscar Peterson and Bill Evans.

Nat 'King' Cole was by far the most successful black recording artist of the post-war era, placing a total of 14 records in the Top 10 between 1946 and 1954. Along with the Mills Brothers and Louis Jordan, Cole was one of the first black musicians to regularly 'cross over' to the predominantly white pop charts. Although he continued to record a range of material—including jazz performances with the King Cole Trio—Cole's biggest commercial successes were sentimental ballads, accompanied by elaborate orchestral arrangements: '(I Love You) For Sentimental Reasons' (1946); 'Nature Boy' (1948); 'Unforgettable' (1950); his biggest hit, 'Mona Lisa' (1950), which sold over five million copies; and 'Too Young' (1951), perhaps the first teenage love ballad.

Country Music

Perhaps no genre is so thoroughly identified with the American South and Southwest as country and western—the industry's new title, coined in the 1930s, for what it once called 'hillbilly' music. Though accurate, this association sometimes proves so compelling that historians overlook the key role a few Canadians played in the genre's development, and the popularity and support country music has traditionally enjoyed in Canada, particularly in the country's prairie and maritime regions. Country music is arguably just as essential to Canadian prairie culture as it is to the culture of the American South and Southwest, both being equally defined in terms of cattle ranching and the cowboy ethos in national and international mythologies; and a majority of Canada's most internationally successful country singers—including Wilf Carter, Hank Snow, Anne Murray, and Stompin' Tom Connors—initially hailed from the Canadian Maritime provinces, particularly Nova Scotia and Prince Edward Island, before making their way south to the United States.

A product of the fusion of Appalachian folk music—itself a descendant of numerous but primarily Scottish and Irish folk traditions—and rural blues, which occurred during the first half of the twentieth century in certain regions across North America, country music initially flourished in Canada in Ontario, Quebec, British Columbia, and the Atlantic provinces, regions where rural folk culture remained vibrant well into the twentieth century. In fact, few outside of Quebec realize the popularity country music has traditionally enjoyed in that province. Soldat Lebrun was probably the first Québécois country singer to enjoy long-term popularity, but he was soon joined by the likes of Ti-Blanc Richard, Jean Carignan, and Tex Lecor. The stand-out star of the post-war era in Quebec was undoubtedly Wille Lamothe, however, whose first record for RCA-Victor—'Allo! Allo! Petit Michel' (1946)—sold over 200,000 copies in Quebec alone, as did his second, 'Je Chante A Cheval' (1946). Lamothe would go on to work with the likes of Jean Grimaldi, Gene Autry, Buck Owens, Bill Anderson, and Ferlin Husky, and he appeared at the Grand Ole Opry in Nashville in 1967.

As was the case with their peers in other musical fields, Canada's anglophone country singers enjoyed little, if any, institutional support in their native country. Canada's culture industry was simply not yet developed to the point that it could compete with the compensations offered by its American counterpart. After all, despite how much it boosted the arts and humanities in Canada, the Royal Commission on National Development in the Arts, Letters and Sciences (the Massey Commission) of 1949–51 failed to provide a single penny for Canadian country musicians (see Chapter 3). With a few remarkable exceptions—including George Wade, Don Messer, Tommy Hunter, Don Wade, and, more recently, Stompin' Tom Connors, Rita MacNeil, Jann Arden, and Corb Lund—Canadian country musicians, as a matter of course, have had to travel south to the United States to earn a decent living by their craft. Such was certainly the case with Canada's two country music pioneers: Nova Scotia's Wilf Carter and Hank Snow.

Wilfred Arthur Charles Carter was the first Canadian country singer to achieve international success. Born in Port Hilford, Nova Scotia, in 1904, Carter moved to Calgary in 1923, where he worked as a 'trail-rider' cowboy for the Canadian Pacific Railway, providing entertainment for dances and tourist parties travelling through the Rockies. After appearances on Calgary radio performing the distinct 'echo' or 'three-in-one' style of yodelling he soon became famous for, Carter was invited to record two original songs as part of an audition for RCA-Victor in Montreal: 'My Swiss Moonlight' and 'The Capture of Albert Johnson'. The label was so impressed with Carter's audition that they released the record without any alterations, and it soon became a massive success—establishing both Carter and country music as mainstays in the Canadian market.

Carter soon became famous in the United States, thanks largely to broadcasts he made beginning in 1935 for WABC in New York City, under the pseudonym 'Montana Slim'. Broadcasts for CBC radio in Canada, and for CBS and NBC in the United States, followed soon after. Tragedy struck in 1940, however, when Carter, at the height of his career, suffered a debilitating back injury in an automobile accident. He did not perform again until 1949. Years later, when he performed at the Canadian National Exhibition Fairgrounds in 1969, Carter faced crowds of over 70,000 people, and by then his legend as a pioneer Canadian country singer was well established.

Hank Snow (born Clarence Eugene Snow) is probably the only Canadian who can claim to have rivalled and, ultimately, bettered Carter's successes in the US. A native of Brooklyn, Nova Scotia, Snow moved to Halifax at age 16, taking with him the guitar he purchased from an Eaton's catalogue only two years before. After performing at local clubs and bars, a successful radio appearance brought Snow to the attention of executives at RCA-Victor in Montreal (the same label that signed Carter only a few years before), who signed the singer to an exclusive recording contract. Though his records from this time are aesthetically successful, it was only after Snow agreed to host a weekly radio show on CRBC that he achieved national notoriety as a country singer in Canada. American radio stations soon picked up Snow's broadcasts, and Snow promptly resigned from the CRBC and moved to Nashville, Tennessee, which was fast becoming the country music capital of North America. Adopting the title of 'Singing Ranger', Snow performed at the Grand Ole Opry in 1950, marking the first time that a Canadian singer set foot on the Opry stage. Snow eventually became a regular on the show, and he even played a hand in convincing the Opry's directors to allow a young singer named Elvis Presley to perform. In August of 1955 Snow introduced Presley to Colonel Tom Parker, with whom Snow established the management team Hank Snow Attractions to manage Presley; though their relationship was short-lived—Snow was ousted by the more business-savvy Parker in less than a year—for a short while in the mid-1950s a cowboy singer from Nova Scotia managed the future 'King' of rock 'n' roll.

By then, of course, Snow was already a well-established country star. In 1950, the same year he debuted at the Opry, Snow released 'I'm Movin' On' (1950). The record remains one of the most successful singles in county music history, staying at Number 1 on the American country music charts for nearly six months. Snow followed with seven more Number 1 records, including 'I've Been Everywhere', by now a country standard, 'Buy Me a Rose', and 'Hello Love', the latter recorded when Snow was 61 years old, making him the fifth oldest singer to take Number 1 on the country charts—after Dolly Parton, Kenny Rogers, Johnny Cash, and Willie Nelson. Though he eventually immigrated to the United States, Snow often made a point of promoting his Canadian and Nova Scotian heritage. In 'My Nova Scotia Home', for instance, an original song he recorded in 1964, Snow takes listeners on a tour of what he still calls the Dominion of Canada, only to show them that no place within that Dominion quite compares to his Nova Scotian home:

> There's a place I'll always cherish, 'neath the blue Atlantic skies
> Where the shores down in Cape Breton bid the golden sun to rise
> And the fragrance of the apple blossoms sprays the dew-kissed lawns
> Back in dear old Nova Scotia, a place where I was born
> The Scotian and the Ocean Limited, and the Maritime Express
> Their mighty engines throbbing, make their way towards the west
> And the sturdy fishin' schooners, sways so lazily to and fro
> Nova Scotia is my sanctuary, and I love her so.
>
> For across the great Dominion, I have traveled far and wide
> Where the shores out in Vancouver, kiss the blue Pacific tide
> I have crossed the snowcapped Rockies, saw the wheat fields' golden blaze
> Headed back to Nova Scotia, where contented cattle graze.
>
> Where the pretty Robin Red Breast, seeks its loved ones in the trees
> And the French dialect in old Quebec, keeps callin' out to me
> It seems to say, be on your way, there's a welcome at the door
> Where the kinfolks are a-waiting on that gay Atlantic shore.

Down through beautiful New Brunswick and across the P.E.I.
To the rock-bound coasts of Newfoundland, I'll love them till I die
But if God came here on Earth with us and asked if he could rest
I'd take him to my Nova Scotia home, the place that I love best.

In the United States, as country music's core audience moved north, west, and upward socio-economically into the urban middle class in the years immediately following World War II, the 'mainstreaming' of country music continued apace. Pop artists such as Bing Crosby ('Sioux City Sue', Number 3 on the pop charts in 1946) and Tony Bennett ('Cold, Cold Heart', Number 1 in pop in 1951) had huge successes with adaptations of country material. Since the 1920s the New York-based music industry had underestimated, and often seemed embarrassed by, the popularity of styles rooted in southern folk traditions. By 1950, though, when a pop-style rendition of the country song 'Tennessee Waltz' by country crooner Patti Page became the fastest-selling record in 25 years, record company executives had no choice but to acknowledge that country music was 'off the porch' and into the living room.

Patti Page (b. 1927 in Oklahoma) sold more records than any other female singer of the early 1950s. She had success with love songs ('All My Love', Number 1 pop in 1950) and novelty items like 'The Doggie in the Window' (Number 1 pop in 1953),

The Canadian Country Style

Wilf Carter and Hank Snow created what many historians and critics now call the 'Canadian country' style. An influence on countless country singers, most notably the late Johnny Cash, 'Canadian country' reflects certain of Canada's regional dialects and manners of speaking, and is generally sung in a lower-pitched, less nasal, and more clearly enunciated style than American idiolects. Though songs about boozing, brawling, lovers, and failed loves are not entirely absent from the repertoire, most 'Canadian country' songs are based in the tradition of European and North American folk ballads; they consequently cross over with greater ease and frequency to the pop charts. In fact, one of the most obvious distinguishing characteristics of 'Canadian country' is that it is historically made by musicians and songwriters who are also popular with urban folk audiences: Anne Murray, Gordon Lightfoot, Ian and Sylvia, Shania Twain, the Be Good Tanyas, the Corb Lund Band, and k.d. lang, to name only a few. The fact that most country radio stations in Canada are also considerably more flexible than their American counterparts in terms of programming undoubtedly also plays a key role here—Canadian country music stations regularly play urban folk records, for instance, alongside more traditional country fare, which has led to an ongoing cross-pollination in Canada between country and urban folk styles.

but her biggest hit was 'Tennessee Waltz'. Page's version of the song—previously recorded by one of its writers, Grand Ole Opry star Pee Wee King—held Number 1 position on the pop charts for 13 weeks in 1950, and eventually went on to sell more than six million copies. In some ways this was a record that pointed back towards the nineteenth century—a sentimental **waltz** song packed with nostalgic references to the South. However, the popular appeal of this record was also apparently boosted by two technological innovations: the use of multi-track tape recording, which allowed Page to sing a duet with herself, and the fact that this was one of the first songs to be issued as a 45 rpm single. 'Tennessee Waltz' helped make Mercury Records into a major label, spawned a rash of cover versions by other artists, and served notice that a pop-styled approach to country and western music could not only penetrate but actually dominate the mainstream.

Patti Page, May 1956.
© Bettmann/CORBIS

In some ways, the range of country music styles during the post-war era resembled contemporaneous developments in rhythm and blues: *country crooners* specialized in a smooth, pop-oriented style; *bluegrass* musicians focused on the adaptation of traditional southern music in a package suitable to the times; and *honky-tonk* musicians created a hard-edged, electronically amplified style featuring songs about the trials and tribulations of migrants to the city, and about the instability of gender roles and male–female relationships during a period of intense social change.

Honky-Tonk

Honky-tonk music—sometimes called 'hard country' or 'beer-drinking music'—conveyed the sound and ethos of the roadside bar or juke joint. During the Great Depression of the 1930s, the oil fields of Texas and Oklahoma had provided a lucrative (and rare) source of steady, well-paid work, attracting thousands of men from the American Southwest and farther afield. With the repeal of Prohibition in 1933, the formerly illegal drinking establishments that serviced these men multiplied and became a major source of employment for country and western musicians. These 'honky-tonks', as the people who frequented them called them, provided relief from the daily pressures of work in the oil fields, in the form of drinking and dancing; the practice of going from bar to bar on a Saturday night is still called 'honky-tonking'. By the post-war period, thousands of these rowdy nightspots emerged across the American Southwest, ranging from small, dimly lit dives to big, neon-lit roadhouses.

Country and western music, both recorded and performed live, was crucial to the profitability of honky-tonks; and, in turn, the honky-tonk itself came to exert a significant influence over the genre. Many honky-tonks featured colourfully glowing (and loud) jukeboxes, and 'old-time' country records about family and the church seemed out of place in the new setting. Musicians thus began to compose songs about aspects of life directly relevant to their patrons—family instability, the unpredictability of male–female relationships, the attractions and dangers of alcohol, and the importance of enjoying the present. When the rural past was referred to, it was usually through a veil of nostalgia and longing, as though something terribly important about humanity had been misplaced by the process of urban industrialization.

Honky-tonk vocal styles were often directly emotional, making use of '**cracks**' in the voice and stylistic features borrowed from blues and jazz singing, such as **melismas** and **blue notes**. Like urban blues musicians such as Muddy Waters, country musicians adapted traditional instruments and playing techniques to the rowdy atmosphere of the juke joint. The typical instrumentation of a honky-tonk band included a fiddle, a steel guitar, a 'takeoff' (lead) guitar, a string bass, and a piano. Guitars were typically electronically amplified, and the musicians played with a percussive, insistent beat—sometimes called '**sock rhythm**'—well suited to dancing.

When today's musicians talk about playing 'good old country music', they are most often referring to the post-war honky-tonk style rather than to the folk music of the rural South. Honky-tonk stars such as Ernest Tubb, Hank Williams, Lefty Frizzell, Hank Snow, George Jones, and Webb Pierce dominated the country and western charts during the early and mid-1950s. Although their fortunes declined somewhat after the emergence of rock 'n' roll—especially a country-tinged variety of rock 'n' roll called rockabilly—honky-tonk music remains the heart and soul of modern country music.

GROVE MUSIC

Canadian Readers: To activate your **FREE six-month subscription to Grove Music Online**, go to the following website and follow the instructions there for entering your code printed in the bottom right corner of this page: *https://ams.oup.com/order/GRMRACPSCRIP*

Please note that your personal six-month subscription will start as soon as you enter your code. If you have any trouble activating your subscription, please contact our Customer Service support at: *oxfordonline@oup.com*

Grove Music Online
is the ultimate authority on all aspects of music.

Comprehensive and Authoritative

▌ Over 50,000 articles on all aspects of music, written by 6,000 leading international experts
▌ More than 20,000 biographies—from sopranos to saxophonists; from pop stars to pianists
▌ Broad coverage of musical styles and traditions worldwide—from the Aboriginal music of Australia to the Zarathustran music of ancient Persia
▌ Updated regularly

Invaluable

▌ Over 500 Sibelius-enabled audio examples covering styles and people—from harmony to Handel
▌ Over 3,000 links to related websites, including sound archives and illustrations
▌ Detailed works-lists for a vast range of composers
▌ In-depth bibliographies
▌ 3-D interactive images of musical instruments
▌ Extensive lists of additional research resources

Wide Range of Search Options

▌ Choose to search the full text by category—biographies, bibliographies, links, contributors, or works-lists
▌ Search for people by nationality, occupation, birth or death date, or birth place
▌ Search works-lists by type, title, or city and date of performance

88OA-GQN9-0SMW-EVZI

Hank Williams

Hank Williams (1923–53) was the most significant honky-tonk singer and songwriter to emerge during the immediate post-war period. Williams wrote and sang many enormously popular songs in the course of his brief career; between 1947 and 1953 he amassed an astounding 36 Top 10 records on the country charts, including such Number 1 hits as 'Lovesick Blues', 'Cold, Cold Heart', 'Jambalaya (On the Bayou)', and 'Your Cheatin' Heart'. These hits, along with many other Williams songs, have remained long-term country favourites and are now established 'standards' of their genre. In addition, his songs were successfully covered by contemporary mainstream pop artists, thus demonstrating the wide-ranging appeal of the new country material ('Cold, Cold Heart' helped launch the career of Tony Bennett when the young crooner scored a huge success with it in 1951, the track taking Number 1 on the pop charts for six weeks).

Hank Williams represented for post-war country audiences the enduring myth of the hard-living, hard-loving rambler. Although the details of Williams's life seem, in retrospect, custom-designed for legendary status, it is important to realize that these were the actual facts of his life: born into crushing poverty in Alabama, this son of a sharecropper learned to make his way at an early age by performing on the street, learning a great deal from a black street singer named Rufe 'Tee-Tot' Payne. By the time he was 16, Williams, now called 'the Singing Kid', had his own local radio show; shortly thereafter he formed a band, the Drifting Cowboys, and began touring throughout Alabama. Enormous success came to Williams by the time he was in his mid-twenties, but it did not come without its problems. By 1952 he was divorced, had been fired from the Grand Ole Opry for numerous failures to appear, and was seriously dependent on alcohol and painkillers. He died on New Year's Day 1953 at age 29, having suffered a heart attack in the back of his car while en route to a performance.

Hank Williams performs, while Chet Atkins—soon to be a hugely influential figure in country music himself, as a guitarist and producer—looks on admiringly. Ernie Newton is playing bass. Courtesy of Country Music Hall of Fame and Museum.

Listening To Hank Williams's 'I'm So Lonesome I Could Cry' (1949) and 'Hey Good Lookin'" (1951)

A brief look at two of the most famous songs written and performed by Hank Williams will demonstrate his debts to country music traditions, as well as the progressive elements in his music. 'I'm So Lonesome I Could Cry' is a timeless lament that builds clearly on earlier models in both its words and its music, while 'Hey, Good Lookin'" is an almost startling anticipation of the style that, in the later 1950s, would come to be called rockabilly.

Like the song 'Goodnight, Irene', 'I'm So Lonesome I Could Cry' evokes the flavour of 'old-timey' country music with its waltz-like triple metre and its straightforward strophic structure. The lyrics, too, refer to traditional country images. The 'wide open spaces' are called up with images of birds, of the moon going behind the clouds, and of the 'silence of a falling star' that 'lights up a purple sky', while the presence of a 'midnight train . . . whining by' affirms Williams's ties to the spirits of the 'hobo' ramblers who came before him. Against the steady rhythmic backdrop of guitars and bass, the sound of the fiddle asserts Williams's kinship with earlier country music. On the other hand, the prominent steel guitar throughout the arrangement created a sense of modernity for Williams's audience, and assured that the essence of his music would be a feeling of utter immediacy.

Like much of the finest rurally based music, 'I'm So Lonesome I Could Cry' is structured to capitalize on the regional characteristics of the singer-composer's performance style. The abundance of sustained vowel sounds placed on the downbeats of measures, as in '*Hear that lonesome whippoorwill*' and '*The silence of a falling star*', draws out the characteristic twang of Williams's accent, and lends a particular expressivity to the actual sound of the lyrics that underlines their dark emotional content. Williams's drawl also leads him naturally to delay somewhat the full force of those vowel sounds, so that he seems rhythmically behind the beat. Again, this beautifully reinforces the mournful essence of the song—as if it is a constant effort for the singer to rise to the high notes on those vowels (and this makes the fall in pitch that marks the end of every phrase in the song seem that much more inevitable, and that much sadder). When he approaches the end of the song, the almost-break in Williams's voice as he sings '*and as I wonder where you are*' is heartbreaking; there seems to be no separation between the singer and the song, or between the sound of his 'country' voice and the meaning of its expression.

Along with a few of Williams's other records, the jaunty 'Hey, Good Lookin'" was actually something of a minor 'crossover' hit for him (Number 29 pop, but Number 1 on the country chart for eight weeks in 1951). This should not be surprising, given its danceable character and its pop-friendly 32-bar AABA form, borrowed from Tin Pan Alley models. With its prominent steel guitar and fiddle parts, not to mention the character of Williams's vocal work, there's still no mistaking the record's basis in country music. What is most arresting here, however, is the specific targeting of a youthful audience. The lyrics address cars, dancing, and young romance, and the use of terms like '*hot-rod Ford*', '*soda pop*', '*go steady*', and '*date book*' create what would, in roughly five years, come to be called 'teen-friendly' material.

In a sense, 'Hey, Good Lookin'' came a little too early, and Hank Williams died much too young. Had Williams been able to bring this same song, or something like it, to a savvy record producer in late 1955 or early 1956—a producer aware of the immediate cultural impact being made by the young Elvis Presley or Carl Perkins, say—Williams's name might well have been added to the rockabilly roster, perhaps even close to the top of it. As it is, his early death leaves us pondering what might have been.

▌Rhythm and Blues

Of all the popular music styles bearing a direct influence on the development of rock 'n' roll, the Canadian contribution to rhythm and blues was initially most peripheral. That said, a few R&B musicians of note made their home in Canada during the 1950s—pianist Cy McLean in Toronto, and drummer Johnny Wiggins, leader of the Four Soul Brothers, and trumpeter Billy Martin in Montreal. Furthermore, a number of singers from Toronto made pivotal contributions to the genre during the mid- and late 1950s in the form of so-called 'white R&B' (i.e., the Four Lads, the Crew Cuts, and the Diamonds), but they produced protean rock 'n' roll records more than anything else and, thus, warrant consideration in relation to that genre in the next chapter.

During the early development of R&B, Canadians probably played their most important role as loyal, record-buying listeners. A number of American R&B stars toured Canada in the 1940s and 1950s, including Louis Jordan, Amos Milburn, and Bill Doggett, indicating their knowledge of the market and their desire to develop and expand it. In fact, they would be successful enough in raising awareness of American R&B in Canada that, by 1960, more than half of all bands playing in the Toronto area, and in Montreal, considered themselves R&B bands. Prominent nightclubs that emerged in the 1960s in Toronto, such as the WIF (West Indies Federation) Club, Le Coq D'Or, and Rompin' Ronnie Hawkins's The Hawk's Nest, attest to the existence of a vibrant R&B scene in Toronto then; and there were equally vibrant R&B scenes in Montreal and Vancouver.

Although *Billboard* adopted 'Rhythm & Blues' (R&B) as a new designation in 1949 for what had formerly been called 'race records', in some ways the commercial logic underlying the category didn't change. Like the older term, 'rhythm and blues' described music performed almost exclusively by black artists and produced in the main (at least at first) for sale to black listeners. Far from a single style of music, this supposedly 'new' genre was actually a loose cluster of older styles, each rooted in southern folk traditions. The top R&B recordings of the late 1940s and early 1950s included swing-influenced 'jump bands', Tin Pan Alley-style love songs performed by blues and jazz crooners, various styles of urban blues, and gospel-influenced vocal harmony groups.

The reappearance of small independent record labels—so-called 'indies'—during and just after the war provided an outlet for performers who had been traditionally ignored by major record companies such as Columbia, RCA-Victor, and Capitol. The development of portable tape recorders made record producers and studio owners out of entrepreneurs who could not previously have afforded the equipment necessary to produce master recordings. Each company was centred on one or two individuals, who located talent, oversaw the recording process, and handled publicity, distribution, and a variety of other tasks. These label owners worked the system in as many ways as time, energy, and ingenuity allowed. They offered payola to radio DJs to promote their records on the handful of stations that played black music. They visited nightclubs to find new talent, hustled copies of their records to local record store owners, and occasionally attempted to interest a major label in a particular recording or artist with crossover potential. By 1951 there were over 100 independent labels in the US slugging it out for a piece of the R&B market, though few lasted more than a few months.

Indie owners often put their names down for composer credits on songs they recorded, and thereby often earned more royalties from a given song than the actual composer. In the post-war era the importance of composers' credits was based on the fact that mainstream pop artists and record companies often tried to cash in on the potential popularity of an R&B recording by creating their own (sometimes almost indistinguishable) versions of it. Although the most famous examples of this practice involve white musicians (and major record companies) exploiting songs first recorded by black artists (and independent record companies), the profit motive led to a variety of interactions, including pop versions of hillbilly songs and black versions of Tin Pan Alley songs. In general, this practice—called 'covering' or making 'cover versions' of original songs and recordings—was crucial to the increasing crossover success of genres such as the blues and jazz, which until the later 1950s were coded in the broader North American culture as basically the purview of black musicians.

Jump Blues

Jump blues, the first commercially successful category of rhythm and blues, flourished during and just after World War II. During the war, as shortages made it more difficult to maintain a lucrative touring schedule, the leaders of some big bands were forced to downsize. They formed smaller combos, generally made up of a rhythm section—bass, piano, drums, and sometimes guitar—and one or more horn players. These jump bands specialized in hard-swinging party music, spiced with humorous lyrics and wild on-stage performance antics.

The most successful and influential jump band of the post-war era was the Tympany Five, led by Louis Jordan (1908–75), an Arkansas-born saxophone player and singer who began making records for Decca in 1939. Jordan was tremendously popular with black listeners and, like Nat 'King' Cole, was able to build an extensive white audience during and after the war. But Jordan himself regarded Cole as being in 'another field', namely, the pop field. Although Cole enjoyed greater financial success, in the end Jordan had a bigger impact on the future of popular music, inspiring a number of the first rock 'n' roll artists. As the rock 'n' roll pioneer Chuck Berry put it, 'I identify myself with Louis Jordan more than any other artist' (Shaw, 1986: 64). James Brown, the 'godfather' of soul music, was once asked if Louis Jordan had been an influence on him: 'He was everything', Brown replied (Chilton, 1994: 126).

The fact that his music appealed to an interracial audience should not lead us to assume that Jordan's career was unaffected by racism. An article published in 1944 described what was to become a standard practice for booking popular black musicians in the segregated American South: 'Due to the Louis Jordan band's popularity with both white and colored audiences, promoters in larger cities are booking the quintet for two evenings, one to play a white dance and the other a colored dance' (ibid., 107). As R&B artists like Jordan began to attract a more diverse audience, the separation between white and black fans was maintained in various ways. Sometimes, white R&B fans sat in the balcony of a segregated theatre or dance hall, watching the black dancers below in order to pick up the latest steps. At other times a rope was stretched across the middle of the dance floor to 'maintain order'. Then, as at other times, the circulation of popular music across racial boundaries did not necessarily signify an amelioration of racism in everyday life.

'Choo Choo Ch' Boogie' was Louis Jordan's biggest hit, and it exemplifies key elements of the jump blues style of R&B. Released in 1946 by Decca, the song topped the R&B charts for an amazing 18 weeks, reached Number 7 on *Billboard*'s pop hit list, and sold over two million copies. 'Choo Choo Ch' Boogie' was co-written by Milt Gabler, Jordan's producer, and two country and western musicians who worked at a radio station in New York City. The title of the song draws a parallel between the motion of a railroad train—a metaphor of mobility and change long established in both country music and the blues—and the rocking rhythm of boogie-woogie music. (Boogie-woogie, a style of piano music that originated in black communities in the American Southwest during the 1920s and then triggered a national craze during the 1930s, provided an important link between rhythm and blues and country music during the post-war period, a connection that we shall see proved extremely important in the formation of rock 'n' roll.)

The song's lyric (see box) describes a situation that would have been familiar to many North Americans, particularly ex-GIs returning to the United States and Canada during the post-war economic downturn of 1946, when jobs were temporarily scarce and the future seemed uncertain. The song brings back a character from the Great Depression era—the poor but honest hobo, hopping freight trains and travelling from city to city in search of work. The protagonist arrives home, weary of riding in the back of an army truck, and heads for the railroad station. His initial optimism is tempered as he searches the employment notices in the newspaper and realizes that he does not have the technical skills for the few positions that are open; African-American listeners may have interpreted the line 'the only job that's open needs a man with a knack' as a comment on the employment practices of the many businesses that favoured white over black veterans. Despite his misfortune, however, our hero remains cheerful, and the lyric ends with an idyllic description of life in a shack by the railroad track.

Listening To Louis Jordan's 'Choo Choo Ch' Boogie' (1946)

While obviously very different in musical style from, say, 'Goodnight, Irene', Louis Jordan's recording of 'Choo Choo Ch' Boogie' is actually quite similar in musical form. It, too, is a strophic song with three verse-chorus strophes. The fact that both of these songs share this basic form illustrates how useful and flexible a formal conception the strophic song with verses and a chorus can be.

One of the most immediately apparent and important differences between 'Choo Choo Ch' Boogie' and 'Goodnight, Irene' is that the rhythm of the former is based on regular *four-beat bars*, as opposed to the regular triple meter of 'Irene'. That is to say, the rhythmic accents in 'Choo Choo Ch' Boogie' create the following steady pattern:

One, two three, four; **One**, two, three, four; **One**, two, three four; and so on.

(By far the most common meters found in all styles and periods of American popular music are quadruple meter, triple meter, and duple—a simple **One**, two—meter.) The four-beat bars of 'Choo Choo Ch' Boogie' are arranged into two-bar phrases; each phrase corresponds to one line of the lyrics, as may be seen in the listening chart below. The verses are all 12 bars (six phrases) in length, while the choruses are all eight bars (four phrases) in length, and this in turn creates consistent strophes of 20 bars each.

All this is hopefully straightforward enough to hear and to understand, but it is now important to pause briefly over the *internal form* of the 12-bar verses. This runs the risk of becoming slightly technical, but these verses exemplify the musical pattern of the 12-bar blues—an arrangement of rhythm and chords that has been employed so extensively in North American popular music, especially in the rock era, that it demands our attention here.

Technical Note: 12-Bar Blues
'Twelve-bar blues' refers to a particular arrangement of four-beat bars. The bars are themselves grouped in phrases of two or four, with characteristic chord changes occurring at certain points. The issue of harmony in the 12-bar blues is a complex one, especially since the chord progressions in a form as widespread and diverse as the blues will by no means be absolutely systematic or consistent from case to case. Still, the 12-bar blues does tend to be marked by specific chord changes at particular points, and our present example— 'Choo Choo Ch' Boogie'—offers a con-

veniently straightforward illustration of these changes in each of its verses (the important thing to remember is that the chord changes in 12-bar blues need not be limited only to these typical ones).

If we call our starting chord the 'home' chord (musicians would call it the **tonic**), this chart shows the most important, typical points of change in the 12-bar blues pattern:

BARS:	1	2	3	4
CHORDS:	↑ 'Home' (Tonic)			
BARS:	5	6	7	8
CHORDS:	↑ Change 1 (Subdominant)		↑ 'Home' (Tonic)	
BARS:	9	10	11	12
CHORDS:	↑ Change 2 (Dominant)	↑ Change 1 (Subdominant)	↑ 'Home' (Tonic)	

Note that the chords at 'changes' 1 and 2 are different from one another; thus, there are three essential chords that define the skeleton of the musical structure. Musicians call the chord at bar 5 the **subdominant**, and the chord at bar 9 the **dominant**. These are the same three chords that define the harmony in the verses of 'Choo Choo Ch' Boogie', and they occur at precisely the rhythmic points shown above. To illustrate specifically, here is what happens in the first verse; the numbers of the bars in the diagram below show where the accent (the ***One***) of the bar in question falls, and the chord changes always occur on the accented beats (remember to count the four beats in each bar!):

BARS:	1 2
LYRICS:	*Headin' for the station with a pack on my back*
CHORDS:	**Home (tonic)**

BARS:	3 4
LYRICS:	*I'm tired of transportation in the back of a hack*
CHORDS:	**[Home (tonic)]**

BARS:	5 6
LYRICS:	*I love to hear the rhythm of a clickety-clack*
CHORDS:	**Change 1 (subdominant)**

BARS:	7 8
LYRICS:	*And hear the lonesome whistle, see the smoke from the stack*
CHORDS:	**Home (tonic)**

BARS:	9 10
LYRICS:	*And pal around with democratic fellows named Mac*
CHORDS:	**Change 2 (dominant)**

BARS: 11 12
LYRICS: *So take me right back to the track, Jack.*
CHORDS: **Home (tonic)**

'Choo Choo Ch' Boogie' integrates the 12-bar blues progression into a verse-chorus strophic structure. Verses in 12-bar blues form alternate with the eight-bar choruses. Additional variety is created in the recording by the employment of purely instrumental episodes: an introduction; a concluding 'tag'; and passages following the first and second occurrences of the chorus (see the listening chart). The instrumental introduction follows the chord pattern of the 12-bar blues; the horns (a trumpet and two saxophones) imitate the sound of a train whistle, while the rhythm section (piano, bass, and drums) establishes a medium-tempo rhythm. (This infectious four-beat dance rhythm, common in Louis Jordan's recordings, is also sometimes called a *shuffle*.) After the introduction a verse is sung by Louis Jordan, backed by riffs (repeated patterns) in the horn section. Then a chorus, also sung by Jordan, is followed by a 12-bar blues piano solo. The whole sequence of verse-chorus-instrumental solo is then repeated (with a 20-bar saxophone solo, representing both verse and chorus, instead of a piano solo). A third strophe is sung, and a slight variation at the end of this chorus leads into the concluding 10-bar tag.

Listening Chart: 'Choo Choo Ch' Boogie'

Music and lyrics by Milt Gabler, Denver Darling, and Vaughan Horton; as performed by Louis Jordan's Tympany Five

FORM	LYRICS	DESCRIPTIVE COMMENTS
Instrumental Introduction		12-bar blues. During the first four bars, the horns imitate the sound of a train whistle.
Verse 1	*Headin' for the station with a pack on my back* *I'm tired of transportation in the back of a hack* *I love to hear the rhythm of a clickety-clack* *And pal around with democratic fellows named Mac* *So take me right back to the track, Jack.*	12-bar blues.
Chorus	*Choo choo, choo choo, ch' boogie* *Woo woo, woo woo, ch' boogie* *Choo choo, choo choo, ch' boogie* *Take me right back to the track, Jack.*	8 bars.

Piano Solo		12-bar blues.
Verse 2	*You reach your destination, but alas and alack* *You need some compensation to get back in the black* *You take the morning paper from the top of the stack* *And read the situations from the front to the back* *The only job that's open needs a man with a knack* *So put it right back in the rack, Jack*	12-bar blues.
Chorus	**[as before]**	8 bars.
Saxophone solo		20 bars (12-bar blues + 8-bar 'chorus').
Verse 3	*Gonna settle down by the railroad track* *And live the life of Riley in a beaten-down shack* *So when I hear a whistle I can peep through the crack* *And watch the train a-rollin', when it's ballin' the jack* *Why, I just love the rhythm of the clickety-clack* *So take me right back to the track, Jack.*	12-bar blues.
Chorus	**[as before]**	8 bars.
Tag: Instruments (with brief vocal interjection)		10 bars.

Blues Crooners

If jump bands represented the 'hot' end of the R&B spectrum, the 'cool' end was dominated by a blend of blues and pop singing sometimes called the *blues crooner* style. The most successful blues crooner of the late 1940s and early 1950s was a soft-spoken Texas-born pianist and singer named Charles Brown (1922–99). His smooth, sensitive, somewhat forlorn vocal style—sometimes called 'cocktail singing blues'—attracted attention, and he began to develop a national reputation with the release of 'Drifting Blues', one of the top-selling R&B records of 1945 and 1946.

'Black Night', one of Brown's most successful records, held the Number 1 position on the R&B charts for 14 straight weeks in 1951. The fact that 'Black Night' did not show up on the pop charts can in part be attributed to the record's dark mood, slow tempo, and sombre lyrics:

Nobody cares about me, ain't even got a friend
Baby's gone an' left me, when will my troubles end?
Black night is falling, oh how I hate to be alone
I keep crying for my baby, but now another day is gone.
I've got no one to talk with, to tell my troubles to
Don't even know I'm living since I lost you

Black night is falling, oh how I hate to be alone
I keep crying for my baby, but now another day is gone.
My mother has her troubles, my father has his, too
My brother's in Korea, and I don't know just what to do
Black night, black night is falling, oh how I hate to be alone
I keep crying for my baby, but now another day is gone.

In formal terms, 'Black Night' is a 12-bar blues, although the very slow tempo can make it hard to hear the overall structure of the song at first. It also exemplifies the continuing importance of the blues in black popular music—not only as a musical form but also as an emotional state and a perspective on the world. After 1952 Brown's blues ballad style became less popular—the urban black audience's tastes shifted towards more hard-edged singers, perhaps reflecting the growth of active resistance to racial segregation.

Chicago Electric Blues

A very different urban blues tradition of the post-war era, Chicago electric blues, derived more directly from the rural Mississippi Delta tradition of artists like Charley Patton and Robert Johnson, whose music was originally released on 'race records' back in the 1920s and 1930s. In fact, a number of famous blues musicians played crucial roles in shaping the Chicago electric blues sound, including Willie Dixon, B.B. King, Lightning Hopkins, Muddy Waters, and Koko Taylor. Chicago was the terminus of the Illinois Central railroad line, which ran up through the Midwest from the Mississippi Delta, years later to be immortalized in the urban folk classic, 'City of New Orleans' (1972), written by Steve Goodman. Although Chicago's black neighbourhoods were well established before World War II, they grew particularly rapidly during the 1940s, as millions of rural migrants came north in search of employment in the city's industrial plants, railroad shops, and slaughterhouses, and to escape the repressive conditions of the segregated South (this movement north-ward is sometimes called 'The Great Migration'). The South Side's nightclubs were the centre of a lively black music scene that rivalled New York's Harlem and Central Avenue in Los Angeles. The musical taste of black Chicagoans, many of them recent migrants from the American South, tended towards rougher, grittier styles, closely linked to black folk traditions but also reflective of their new, urban orientation.

   The career of Muddy Waters (McKinley Morganfield) (1915–83) exemplifies these developments. Waters was 'discovered' in the Mississippi Delta by the folk music scholars John and Alan Lomax, who recorded him in the late 1930s for the Library of Congress; Waters apparently had some difficulty in getting copies of these record-ings, but when he did they were played on jukeboxes in the Delta and became regional hits. In 1943 he moved to Chicago and found work in a paper mill while continuing to work as a musician at nightclubs and parties. In response to the noisy crowds, and to the demand for dance music, Waters soon switched from the acoustic

Listening To Muddy Waters's 'Hoochie Coochie Man' (1954)

'Hoochie Coochie Man'—composed by Willie Dixon (1915–92), Chess Records' house songwriter, bass player, producer, and arranger—is an excellent example of Muddy Waters's Chicago electric blues style. The song was Waters's biggest hit for Chess Records, reaching Number 3 on the R&B charts in 1954 (although none of Waters's recordings crossed over to the pop charts, his music was later to play an important role in inspiring rock musicians such as Eric Clapton and the Rolling Stones, the latter adopting their name from one of his songs in tribute). This recording neatly encapsulates Chicago electric blues during the mid-1950s, with its loud volume and dense textures, its buzzing, growling tone colours, and its insistent beat. 'Hoochie Coochie Man' is also an example of a common variation on the blues form: a 16-bar blues. The first eight bars of the song feature a technique called stoptime, in which the beat is suspended in order to focus attention on the singer's voice; in essence, this is equivalent to the first four bars of a 12-bar blues, made twice as long by application of the stoptime technique. Then the regular pulse is re-established, and the last eight bars are played. Because the lyric of the stoptime section changes each time (like a verse), while the words in the second eight-bar section are repeated (like a chorus), the song combines the blues form with a strophic verse-chorus structure.

The lyric of 'Hoochie Coochie Man' is essentially an extended boast, related to the 'toasts' of the urban African-American subculture of gangsters, pimps, and drug dealers—fantastic narratives emphasizing the performer's personal power, sexual prowess, and ability to outwit authority:

I got a black cat bone, I got a mojo too
I got the John the Conkaroo, I'm
gonna mess wit' you
I'm gonna make you girls lead me by
my hand
Then the world'll know the hoochie
coochie man

The song's lyric draws a direct link between the personal power of the singer—quintessentially expressed through sex—and the southern folk tradition of mojo, a system of magical charms and medicines, including the black cat bone and John the Conqueror root. This image of supernatural power applied in the service of personal goals was ultimately derived from the cultures of West Africa, and it tapped a common reservoir of experience among Waters's listeners, many of whom were not many years removed from the folk culture of the rural South. In essence, the lyric of 'Hoochie Coochie Man' is an argument for the continuing relevance of deep traditional knowledge in a new urban setting, and it is easy to see why this would have been an attractive message for recent urban migrants. 'Hoochie Coochie Man' can also be heard as a direct ancestor of contemporary 'gangsta rap' recordings, which project a similar outlaw image as a response to the challenging conditions of urban life.

to the electric guitar (1944) and eventually expanded his group to include a second electric guitar, piano, bass, amplified harmonica ('blues harp'), and a drum set. During the late 1940s and early 1950s he was the most popular blues musician in Chicago, with a sizable following among black listeners nationwide.

Waters's approach to the blues is different from that of blues crooners like Charles Brown. Like many of the great Mississippi guitarists, Waters was a master of the **bottleneck** slide guitar technique. He used his guitar to create a rock-steady, churning rhythm, interspersed with blues **licks**, which were counterpoised with his voice in a kind of musical conversation (what musicians call a 'call-and-response'). The electric guitar, which could be used to create dense, buzzing tone colours (by using **distortion**) and long sustained notes that sounded like screaming or crying (by employing **feedback**), was the perfect tool for extending the Mississippi blues guitar tradition. Waters's singing style—rough, growling, moaning, and intensely emotional—was also rooted in the Delta blues. And the songs he sang were based on themes long central to the tradition. On the one hand were loneliness, frustration, and misfortune ('I Feel Like Going Home' and 'Still a Fool'), and on the other, independence and sexual braggadocio ('Just Make Love to Me' and 'Mannish Boy').

Vocal Harmony Groups

Another important thread in the tapestry of post-war rhythm and blues was the *vocal harmony group*. Although this tradition is more often called 'doo-wop' now, the earliest performers did not use this term. Many of these vocal groups were made up of high school kids from the black neighbourhoods of cities such as New York and Washington, DC, and interviews with the singers indicate that these groups served a number of functions—a means of musical expression; an alternative or adjunct to urban gangs; and a route to popularity and social mobility. Few members of these groups initially saw singing as a way to make a living, but in the early 1950s this perception changed rapidly after the first vocal R&B groups achieved widespread and concrete commercial success.

The vocal harmony group most responsible for creating a new, harder-edged sound more closely linked to black gospel music was the Dominoes, led by vocal coach Billy Ward, a strict disciplinarian and savvy entrepreneur. In 1950 Ward started rehearsing with a number of his most promising students. Their first big hit was 'Sixty Minute Man', recorded in New York City and released by the independent label Federal Records in 1951. A large part of the song's popularity was due to its lyric, which catalogued the singer's lovemaking technique in some detail:

There'll be fifteen minutes of kissin',
Then you holler please don't stop
(GROUP: *Don't stop!*)
There'll be fifteen minutes of teasin'
And fifteen minutes of pleasin'
And fifteen minutes of blowin' my top!

The combination of a naughty lyric, rocking dance rhythm, and bass lead vocal caught the attention of the R&B audience, and 'Sixty Minute Man' held the Number 1 spot on the R&B charts for 14 weeks during the summer of 1951. It was also one of the first vocal-group R&B records to cross over to the pop charts, where it reached the Number 17 position—doubtless without the assistance of AM pop radio.

But it was the Dominoes' next big hit, 'Have Mercy Baby', that pushed vocal-group R&B firmly in the direction of a harder-edged, more explicitly emotional sound. Recorded in Cincinnati, Ohio, and released by Federal Records in 1952, 'Have Mercy Baby' was the first record to combine the 12-bar blues form and the driving beat of dance-oriented rhythm and blues with the intensely emotional flavour of black gospel singing. The song's commercial success (Number 1 R&B for 10 weeks in 1952) was in large part due to the passionate performance of the Dominoes' lead tenor, Clyde McPhatter (1932–72), a former gospel singer from North Carolina. McPhatter, the son of a Baptist preacher and a church organist, was like many other R&B musicians insofar as the black church played a major role in shaping his musical sensibility. While in formal terms 'Have Mercy Baby' is a 12-bar blues, it is essentially a gospel performance dressed up in R&B clothing. With a few changes in the lyrics—perhaps substituting the word 'Lord' for 'baby'—McPhatter's performance would have been perfectly at home in a black Baptist church anywhere in America. The sheer intensity of McPhatter's plea for redemption—you can actually hear him weeping during the fadeout ending—spoke directly to the core audience for R&B, many of whom had grown up within the African-American gospel music tradition.

To be sure, this mixing of church music with popular music was controversial in some quarters, and McPhatter and later gospel-based R&B singers faced occasional opposition from some church leaders. But in retrospect the post-war confluence of the sacred and secular aspects of black music, and its commercial exploitation by the music business, seems almost inevitable. Although it did not appear on the pop music charts, 'Have Mercy Baby' attracted an audience among many white teenagers, who were drawn by its rocking beat and emotional directness. In addition, the Dominoes were featured on some of the earliest rock 'n' roll tours, which typically attracted a racially mixed audience. Although McPhatter soon left the Dominoes to form a new group called the Drifters, the impact of his rendition of 'Have Mercy Baby' was profound and lasting—the record is a direct predecessor of the soul music movement of the 1960s, and of the recordings of Ray Charles, James Brown, and Aretha Franklin.

Women and Gender in R&B: Ruth Brown and Big Mama Thornton

Like many other genres of popular music, rhythm and blues played an important role as a stylized medium for enacting sexual politics. This was particularly important during the post-war period, as black families came under the disintegrating pressures of social change and individuals sought to cope with the sometimes alienating experience of urban life. We have already seen several portrayals of male identity in R&B, including Charles Brown's dejected lover and Muddy Waters's magically charged mojo man.

Here we examine briefly images of male–female relationships in the work of two influential female R&B singers, Ruth Brown and Willie Mae 'Big Mama' Thornton.

Ruth Brown (b. 1928), also known as 'Miss Rhythm', was born in Virginia. As a child she participated in two streams of the black church tradition, the AME (African Methodist Episcopal) and Baptist denominations. In musical terms, the Methodist services she attended were relatively restrained, with the accompaniment of a piano and big church organ, while the Baptist ceremonies, held in a rough-hewn country church, were often ecstatically emotional and featured only hand clapping and tambourine as accompaniment. Both of these streams can be detected in Brown's later work, which ranged from crooner-style ballads to jump band blues songs.

Circa 1955: Promotional headshot of American R&B singer **Ruth Brown.** Photo by Frank Driggs Collection/Getty Images.

Although her parents initially resisted the idea of her singing outside the church, Brown began her professional career at the age of 16 and in 1949 signed with the new independent label, Atlantic Records. Chart figures suggest that Ruth Brown was the most popular black female vocalist in America between 1951 and 1954, and it is said that she almost single-handedly kept Atlantic Records alive during its precarious early years. The song with which Ruth Brown was most closely associated was 'Mama, He Treats Your Daughter Mean', which held the Number 1 position on the R&B charts for five weeks in 1953 and reached as high as Number 23 on the pop charts. Brown, the daughter of a respectable, churchgoing family, did not feel comfortable with the song at first:

That tune, I didn't want to do. I thought, when I first heard it, 'That's the silliest mess I have ever heard.' At that time, I wasn't having too much of a problem [with men], so I felt like, 'What is she talking about, Mama he treats your daughter mean. . . . Mama, the man is lazy, almost drives me crazy.' I wasn't dealing with that kind of a lifestyle, so it didn't make sense to me. (Deffaa, 1996: 35)

According to Brown, the song was recorded quickly, without much rehearsal, and its crossover success on the R&B and pop charts came as something of a surprise. The form of 'Mama, He Treats Your Daughter Mean' is an example of the blending of blues and Tin Pan Alley-derived forms. The song's 'A' section (*Mama, he treats your daughter mean . . .*) is a 16-bar blues. Unlike Muddy Waters's (and Willie Dixon's) 'Hoochie Coochie Man', though, the 12-bar form here is expanded by adding four extra bars in the middle of the song. The 'B' section (*Mama, he treats me badly . . .*) is also 16 bars in length. The band plays the song at a medium tempo, with the horns (saxophones and trumpets) riffing behind the singer. Certain characteristics of Brown's vocal style are clearly evident on this record, including a warm, somewhat husky tone, a strong rhythmic feeling, and the little upward squeals she places at the ends of words such as '*mama*', '*man*', and '*understand*'. This fits the somewhat complaining tone of the song, in which a young woman turns to her mother for help in dealing with a good-for-nothing lover. One of the most memorable features of the recording—and a link to the church music of Brown's youth—is the solo tambourine, which starts the record and continues throughout.

Brown was paid less than $70 for recording the song, in addition to a promised royalty of 5 per cent of sales. As was often the case in the R&B business, she received few of her royalties, since the cost of studio time, hiring musicians, and the songwriters' royalties were charged to her account. One of the biggest stars of the post-war era, Brown ended up leaving the music business entirely for a decade and working as a domestic servant in order to raise her children. She was rediscovered in the 1970s and worked to publicize the plight of older rhythm and blues artists who had been denied their share of profits by record companies. In the 1980s she appeared in the Broadway show *Black and Blue* and won a Tony award in 1989.

Big Mama Thornton (1926–84), born in Montgomery, Alabama, was the daughter of a Baptist minister. She began her professional career as a singer, drummer, harmonica player, and comic on the black vaudeville circuit, and she later settled in Houston, Texas, where she worked as a singer in black nightclubs. Her imposing physique and sometimes malevolent personality helped to ensure her survival in the rough-and-tumble world of con artists and gangsters. One producer and songwriter who worked with Big Mama described her in vivid terms (in the liner notes to the 1992 MCA release *Big Mama Thornton: Hound Dog/The Peacock Recordings*):

In rehearsal she'd fool around, pick up one of those old microphones with a heavy, steel base with one hand and turn it upside down with the base in the air and sing like that. She was a powerful, powerful woman. She had a few scars, looked like knife scars on her face, and she had a very beautiful smile. But most of the time she looked pretty salty.

In the early 1950s Thornton arrived in Los Angeles and began working with Johnny Otis (Veliotes), a Greek-American drummer, promoter, bandleader, and nightclub owner who lived in the black community and was a major force in the R&B scene. Looking for material for Big Mama to record, Otis decided to consult two white college kids who had been pestering him to use some of the songs they had written. After hearing Thornton's powerful singing, Jerry Leiber and Mike Stoller ran home and composed a song that they felt suited her style: 'Hound Dog'. The combination of Leiber and Stoller's humorous country-tinged lyric, Johnny Otis's drumming, and Thornton's powerful, raspy singing produced one of the top-selling R&B records of 1953: Number 1 for seven weeks (this was the first hit written and produced by the team of Leiber and Stoller, who were to become a major force in early rock 'n' roll music).

Of course, most people today know 'Hound Dog' through Elvis Presley's version of the song, recorded by RCA-Victor in 1956. If you are familiar only with Presley's version, then the original recording may come as something of a revelation. From the very first phrase (*You . . . ain't . . . nothin'. . . but a houn' dog . . .*), Thornton lays claim to the song, and to our attention. Her deep, raspy, commanding voice, reprimanding a ne'er-do-well lover, projects a stark image of female power rarely expressed in popular music of the 1950s. The bluntness of the lyric is reinforced by the musical accompaniment, which includes a bluesy electric guitar, a simple drum part played mainly on the tom-toms, and hand clapping on beats 2 and 4. The tempo is relaxed, and the performance is energetic but loose.

The basic form of 'Hound Dog' is a 12-bar blues with an AAB text, in which the first line of each verse ('A') is repeated ('A' again), and the verse concludes with a contrasting line ('B'). The opening verse of Big Mama's performance illustrates this form clearly:

A   *You ain't nothin'*
     You ain't nothin'
B   *You can wag your tail . . .*

Each line of the text corresponds to four bars of music, yielding a total of 12 bars for each verse (this 12-bar form with AAB text is often referred to as the 'standard' blues form, although, as we have already seen, popular musicians often rework the structure of the blues to suit their own expressive purposes). The band adds a few extra beats here and there in response to Thornton's phrasing, another feature that links this urban recording to the rural origins of the blues. The final touch, with the all-male band howling and barking in response to Big Mama's commands, reinforces not only the humour of the record but also its feeling of informality, the sense that these are not distant pop stars but people you could know and maybe even party with.

Although both records are intended to create a humorous effect, the defiant attitude of 'Hound Dog' does make an interesting comparison with the complaining tone of 'Mama, He Treats Your Daughter Mean', a quality that Ruth Brown herself apparently did not find particularly appealing. Both songs were composed by men and sung by women; and both implicitly rely on the 'offstage' presence of a male persona—a lazy, deceitful jerk. But the similarities between the two songs and performances end there.

'Hound Dog' was designed specifically to fit Thornton's strong, rough-hewn persona. 'Mama', written by professional tunesmiths with no particular singer in mind, presents the image of a female narrator unable to deal with the male problem in her life. One woman expresses her frustration with cute little squeals, the other growls in anger. One gossips, the other threatens to inflict physical harm. One—we might imagine—is a somewhat spoiled middle-class teenager, the other an older woman from a working-class background. Of course, these are stylized images, exaggerated for dramatic effect—but it is their very exaggeration that allows them to convey popular conceptions of sexuality and gender identity in a particular place and time.

▌Red Robinson Broadcasts R&B: The Birth of Rock 'n' Roll

R&B was given perhaps its biggest push in Canada by a teenager from Vancouver named Red Robinson. Through good timing and luck, Robinson secured his own radio show in 1953, on CJOR in Vancouver, while he was still a high school student. Between 1950 and 1955 radio endured what some critics call 'a fallow period'—the medium's so-called 'golden age' (1925–50) had ended and it had yet to be 'reborn' as the primary medium for rock 'n' roll (1955–present). Between 1950 and 1955 radio thus suffered neglect in many markets, so much so that Red Robinson could broadcast R&B records, which only a short while before had been almost entirely ignored by programmers if they were not deemed 'obscene'.

Red Robinson and **Elvis** backstage at a show that Red emceed, 31 August 1958. Photo property of Red Robinson Management Ltd.

In 1953 the 16-year-old Robinson became the only Canadian DJ regularly pro-gramming R&B records. Thus did he enter the ranks of an exclusive group of DJs: George 'Hound Dog' Lorenz (Buffalo), Dewey Phillips (Memphis), Hunter Hancock (Los Angeles), and, of course, Alan Freed (Cleveland and New York). Within two years, Robinson had become the first DJ in Canada to program rock 'n' roll records on a regular basis; and he was first to broadcast Elvis Presley records. Robinson would go on to emcee an Elvis Presley concert, and later a Beatles concert, at Vancouver's Empire Stadium, having already become a symbol of rock 'n' roll music and culture in British Columbia by 1957. A testament to his popularity, Robinson once invited all of his listeners to join him at the Kitsilano Showboat amphitheatre on Vancouver's historic English Bay for a 'rock 'n' roll record party', and an estimated 10,000 fans attended, prompting press from as far afield as Toronto and the US Northeast to send investigative reporters to British Columbia to 'find out what the hell this kid was doing', as Robinson himself remembers. With the benefit of historical hindsight, we now know that Robinson was introducing the country to rock 'n' roll music, through the medium of rhythm and blues.

Discussion Questions

1. The development of an industry for popular music in North America seems inextricably tied to the development of a record industry. In fact, many argue that popular music, and especially the rock tradition, is a genre of music primarily made and heard by sound reproduction (i.e., radio, stereos, iPods, etc.). Is this still the case? Could the rock industry have developed without recording technology? Why is rock particularly conducive to the process of making and hearing music recordings?

2. We learn in this chapter that the notion of Canada as a 'cultural mosaic' has proven useful to marketers since at least the 1920s, and that folk music has often been treated by marketers as an exemplary soundtrack of that mosaic. Is this still the case? Can you think of any distinctly Canadian folk repertoires? What makes them distinctly Canadian? Are elements of folk music used by pop and rock musicians today? Can you think of some examples?

3. What about Frank Sinatra's image and sound in the 1940s proved so appealing to his fans? Are acts like the Beatles the direct descendants of Frank Sinatra, given the hysteria he inspired, or does Sinatra represent something entirely unique?

4. We know that Canadian country musicians often 'cross over' onto the pop charts in Canada and abroad. Anne Murray and Shania Twain are two good examples of musicians with this ability. Can you think of other examples?

5. Why do historians consider Hank Williams's honky-tonk songs examples of 'country' music? What all do we mean when we say that a song is an example of 'country' music? On the other hand, what criteria make a song 'rhythm and blues'? How are genre categories more than categorizations of music?

6. Having heard Louis Jordan's 'Choo Choo Ch' Boogie', listen to Big Mama Thornton's 'Hound Dog' and Big Joe Turner's 'Shake, Rattle, and Roll'. Why do we classify these recordings as examples of jump blues as opposed to rock 'n' roll per se?

Chapter Two

Rock 'n' Roll Erupts, 1954–1960

While he didn't coin the term 'rock 'n' roll', Alan Freed (1922–65) was almost certainly the first disc jockey to use it for commercial purposes. In the early 1950s Freed watched throngs of white teenagers line up to buy R&B records by black artists at Leo Mintz's Record Rendezvous record store in downtown Cleveland, Ohio. The spectacle inspired Freed to play R&B records, which he called 'rock 'n' roll records', on his *Moondog Show* nighttime radio program; and when the show became a massive success, he began to promote concert tours featuring black 'rock 'n' roll' artists playing to a young and racially mixed audience, which he called 'rock 'n' roll revues'. These endeavours brought Freed international recognition as the champion of a novel genre called 'rock 'n' roll'.

Freed undoubtedly derived the term 'rock 'n' roll' from the many references to 'rockin'' and 'rollin''—sometimes separately, sometimes together—he heard on R&B records from the 1940s and 1950s, and on race records dating back to the 1920s. Among the relevant records that Freed and his audience would have known was the late 1940s R&B hit 'Good Rockin' Tonight', recorded by a number of different artists but a hit for its composer, Roy Brown; and the huge 1952 hit by the Dominoes, 'Sixty Minute Man', discussed in the last chapter, features the salacious lyric: 'I rock 'em, roll 'em, all night long, I'm a sixty minute man.' The terms 'rock' and 'roll' are clearly associated in these and other songs with the sex act. However, like the similar original implications of the word 'jazz'—a reference to the jasmine perfume worn by sex-trade workers in turn-of-the-century New Orleans—these implications quickly faded, and 'rock 'n' roll' soon referenced only a particular musical and cultural phenomenon.

Disc jockey **Alan Freed** in Cleveland.
Courtesy Library of Congress.

In 1954 Freed moved from Cleveland to station WINS in New York City, taking the term 'rock 'n' roll' with him. Once there he continued to promote black musicians to white audiences, often in the face of serious resistance. In 1957, for instance, a TV show Freed sponsored was cancelled after the black teenage singer Frankie Lymon was shown dancing with a white girl; and the next year, in 1958, Freed himself was arrested for anarchy, and incitement to riot, after a fight broke out at one of his 'rock 'n' roll revues' in Boston. In the early 1960s Freed was publicly prosecuted for accepting **payola**—the illegal practice, common throughout the music industry, of paying bribes to radio disc jockeys in order to get certain records played more often—while promoters like Dick Clark, who handled mostly white acts in the more lucrative field of television, escaped prosecution relatively unscathed. Freed was subsequently black-balled, and he died a few years later, a broken man.

Whatever his indiscretions, Alan Freed was clearly in the vanguard of an increasing number of disc jockeys who wanted to capture the new and large audience of young radio listeners and potential record buyers, and who consequently embraced the term 'rock 'n' roll' as a catch-all to refer to practically any kind of music pitched to that audience. In fact, it would not be exaggerating to say that the 1950s basically invented the teenager as a commercial and cultural entity, and that rock 'n' roll music—along with television and, to some extent, movies—played an essential role in that invention. This included records that previously were marketed solely to R&B and country music fans, along with an expanding group of hybrid records that drew freely on multiple stylistic influences, including those associated with the mainstream Tin Pan Alley style. Strange as it now seems, in the early heyday of rock 'n' roll the likes of Chuck Berry, Pat Boone, Fats Domino, Paul Anka, the Everly Brothers, and Elvis Presley were all lumped together with hundreds of other seemingly unrelated acts as 'rock 'n' roll singers' because they all had records being listened to, and purchased by, large numbers of teenagers.

This was a period of remarkable heterogeneity on radio and on the record charts. An astonishingly eclectic group of musicians could be heard jostling each other on Top 40 radio stations and nudging each other on the pop charts. In the resulting marketing confusion, rock 'n' roll records appeared on different, previously exclusive charts simultaneously. The culmination point of this trend occurred early in 1956, when Carl Perkins's 'Blue Suede Shoes' and Elvis Presley's 'Heartbreak Hotel' made chart history by climbing to the upper reaches of the country and western, R&B, and pop charts—all at the same time! From this point on, one thing about rock 'n' roll was clear: as a genre, rock 'n' roll was totally different from anything that came before it, and nothing would be the same after it.

Technology and the Rise of Rock 'n' Roll

Technological developments played a crucial, if often overlooked, role in the rise of rock 'n' roll to the historical fore. Until the mid-1950s the entertainment hub of most Canadian households was as it had been for decades—a single radio set or, less common, a single record player, usually centrally located in the living room. Access to music in the home was predominantly a matter of family taste and adult arbitration, with adults typically maintaining final say over what was heard. Radio stations and record labels thus catered to the broadest possible market, consciously eschewing any types of music that might irritate the very generational divisions they would so obviously exploit only a few years later when they started to broadcast rock 'n' roll.

As television began to penetrate the domestic sphere, however, radios and record players were rapidly displaced. Once the central focus of family rooms, these technologies were banished to suburban rumpus rooms, bedrooms, and basements—far away from parents' watchful eyes. Thus, TV's rapid dominance of the North American entertainment industry enabled so-inclined Canadian broadcasters to broadcast certain records, but especially R&B records from the United States, which had been deemed unfit for broadcast only a few years before. Sensing opportunity, and noting that it was primarily boomers who 'tuned-in' to their regular broadcasts, radio stations and record labels targeted adolescents in tandem, and eventually established radio sets and record players as essential appliances in the boomer bedroom (89,000 record players sold across Canada in 1955 alone; two years later, in 1957, more than 270,000 sold).

For the first time in history an entire generational cohort acquired unprecedented access to, and control over, recorded and broadcast music in the home, and at roughly the same time. Boomers also enjoyed unprecedented access to music outside of the home. Developments in the materials commonly used to make radios allowed manufacturers to create ever more durable and, thus, more portable generations of radio receivers as the decade progressed; and while car radios were still a luxury during the first half of the 1950s, more than half of all Canadian cars were wired for sound by decade's end—by which point more than half of all Canadian households owned a car. Add to this the cheap and durable transistor radio sets that Sony introduced to the North American market in 1957, which were designed for, and marketed specifically to, the baby-boomer demographic, with over one million units sold in the next two years alone, and boomers emerge as the most thoroughly 'wired-for-sound' generation yet seen.

TV programming also played an important role in the rise of rock 'n' roll. Musical variety shows, such as NBC's *Your Hit Parade*, became a regular feature of television programming when national broadcasters first took to the air. *Your Hit Parade*, which many border-dwelling Canadians picked up on their TV sets between 1950 and 1959, presented elaborately choreographed and arranged 'covers' of the seven top-rated songs of each week, sung by featured vocalists. Canadian Gisele MacKenzie was a regular on the program between 1953 and 1957, and she was able to parlay her new-found celebrity into a Top 5 hit in 1955, 'Hard To Get'. Once rock 'n' roll penetrated the charts, however, the musical programmers of *Your Hit Parade* quickly found themselves out of their depths; vocalist Snooky Lanson's weekly performances of Elvis Presley's 'Hound Dog' (1956), for instance, are still generally agreed to have hastened the show's demise.

By 1956 Elvis Presley had appeared on *The Dorsey Brothers Stage Show*, *The Milton Berle Show*, *The Steve Allen Show*, and, probably more importantly, twice on *The Ed Sullivan Show*—all of which could be seen across North America. The next year, in 1957, the teenage dance and deejay show *American Bandstand* was retooled and broadcast to a continental audience, becoming a pre-eminent weekly showcase for new pop music stars, and a source for teenagers to learn the 'latest' songs, fashions, and dance steps, at least insofar as these were expressed among white Philadelphia teenagers. Given the relative cheapness of the so-called 'dance and deejay' format and the growing influence of the teenage demographic, imitations of *American Bandstand* emerged by the dozens on television screens across Canada, and a number of already existing shows such as CBC-TV's *Cross-Canada Hit Parade* began to exclusively program rock 'n' roll music.

Cover Versions and Early Rock 'n' Roll

In musical terms, one of the most important precedents for the rise of rock 'n' roll was a commercial and musical phenomenon known as the 'cover version'. In the broadest sense this term simply refers to the practice of recording a song that has previously been recorded by another artist or group. However, critics usually use the term in a more restricted, and sometimes pejorative, sense—specifically, to refer to a version, or even an exact copy, of a previously recorded performance, often involving an adaptation of the original's style and sensibility, and usually aimed at 'cashing in' on its success.

The practice of 'covering' often worked in both directions. Country and western and rhythm and blues musicians have always recorded their own stylized covers of each other's songs, and by the mid-1950s it was common practice for them to cover Tin Pan Alley songs that had previously been popularized by the likes of, say, Frank Sinatra, Nat 'King' Cole, or Rosemary Clooney. In fact, Sid Nathan, owner of King Records in the 1950s, made it his label's policy that its country and western and rhythm and blues musicians should record cover versions of each other's songs as often as possible; and, on other labels, artists such as Ray Charles, Ivory Joe Hunter, Billy Ward and the Dominoes, and Moon Mullican regularly crossed genres.

This all said, the most notorious examples of cover versions—and the most important for understanding the rise of rock 'n' roll—involved white pop performers covering the work of black rhythm and blues musicians. This was a relationship not simply between individual musicians but also between competing institutions, since the underlying motivation for covering a song typically involved a major record company wanting to capitalize on the musical discoveries of a small independent record label. Here the practice takes on a new significance, as the element of financial profit is introduced, and issues of social inequality are involved. In such contexts, the influence of one tradition or style on another can also be seen as a kind of musical appropriation, and borrowing becomes something akin to stealing.

To better understand this phenomenon, let's look at a specific example. In 1947 a black singer and pianist named Paula Watson recorded a song called 'A Little Bird Told Me' for the independent label Supreme. Watson's version of the song, released in 1948, reached Number 2 on the R&B charts and made an impact on the pop charts, peaking at Number 6. This early 'crossover' hit attracted the attention of Decca Records, which immediately issued a cover version of the song performed by a white pop singer named Evelyn Knight. Knight's version reached Number 1 on the pop charts, in large part owing to the promotional power of Decca Records and to the fact that white performers enjoyed privileged access to radio and television.

The tiny Supreme label sued Decca Records, claiming that its copyright to the original had been infringed. In this case the crux of the matter was not the song per se—its author, Harvey Brooks, collected composer's royalties from both record companies. Supreme claimed that Decca had stolen aspects of the original record, including its arrangement, texture, and vocal style. Although Evelyn Knight had indeed copied Paula Watson's singing precisely, to the point that it fooled many musical experts brought in as witnesses, the judge ultimately decided in favour of the larger company, ruling that musical arrangements were not copyrighted property and therefore not under legal protection. This decision affirmed the legal principle that the song, published in sheet music, was a copyrightable form of intellectual property, but that individual interpretations or arrangements of a given song could not be protected by the law. This meant the continuation of an older conception of music's legal status—visually biased, focused on the written document—in an era when records, rather than sheet music, were the dominant means of transmission.

The 'Little Bird Told Me' decision opened the floodgates for not only individual cover versions of songs but entire genres predicated on the practice of creating cover versions. The so-called 'white R&B' genre, imported directly to the United States from central Ontario beginning around 1952, was almost entirely based on the custom, and it emerged well before the breakthrough of what some historians now rather smugly call 'clean teen' or 'schlock rock' music (both titles refer to a subgenre of rock 'n' roll, popular in the late 1950s, which was comprised of sanitized cover versions of R&B songs made by white pop singers such as, most famously, Pat Boone). Before looking at rock 'n' roll, then, we should first pause to look at the 'white R&B' genre, for a number of reasons. First, it is arguably the last genre of popular music to precede rock 'n' roll on the pop charts, and thus it influenced many early rock 'n' roll musicians simply by being one of the pop styles most often heard on the radio at the time they were creating rock 'n' roll; second, it eventually came to be regarded as an important subgenre of rock 'n' roll; and, finally, it is the first major popular music trend to emerge from Canada in the post-war period, though we shall see that it was produced almost entirely in the US.

▎White R&B

One of the best-known 'white R&B' groups was the Four Lads. Established in 1947, the quartet—lead tenor Jimmy Arnold, second tenor and arranger Bernie Toorish, baritone Frank Buseri, and bass Connie Cordarini—met as students at St. Michael's Cathedral Choir School in downtown Toronto, where they studied vocal technique under John Ronan, a Domestic Prelate and Protonotary Apostolice of the Catholic Church of Canada. In 1949 the Lads debuted on CBC radio's *Canadian Cavalcade*, hosted by Elwood Glover, and they subsequently achieved widespread popularity in central Canada and in the US Northeast. A booking on *The Perry Como Show* in 1950 led to a contract with Columbia Records and a move to New York City.

The Four Lads worked at first behind the scenes for Columbia. With arrangements by Toorish, then only 19, the Lads backed Johnny Ray on his two biggest hits of 1952—'Cry' and 'The Little White Cloud'—and they backed Frankie Laine on the Toorish original 'Rain, Rain, Rain' (1954). The Lads' first solo release, 'Mockingbird' (1953), sold better than expected, but it was their follow-up, 'Istanbul (Not Constantinople)', which officially launched the group into stardom: the record, a Top 10 hit, was certified gold in 1953 (and as a testament to the song's staying power, the American novelty act They Might Be Giants scored a hit with their own cover of the song almost four decades later, in 1990). Of the 20 more records the Four Lads recorded for Columbia in the 1950s, no less than 15 reached the Top 40, including 'Skokiaan' (1954), 'Standing on the Corner' (1956), 'Who Needs You' (1957), and the million-selling singles 'Moments To Remember' (1955) and 'No, Not Much' (1956).

Also students of John Ronan at St. Michael's Cathedral Choir School in Toronto, and inspired by the success of the Four Lads, the Crew Cuts formed in 1952. Comprised of tenors Pat Barrett and Johnnie Perkins, baritone and arranger Rudi Maugeri, and bass Ray Perkins, and initially calling themselves the Four Tones, the Otnorots ('Torontos' spelled backwards), and the Jordonaires, the group played a number of church variety shows around Toronto and appeared regularly on Barry Nesbitt's CKFH radio show, before an appearance on *The Gene Carroll Show* in Cleveland, and a backstage meeting with Bill Randle (a disc jockey on Cleveland's WERE), led to a contract with Mercury Records in Chicago. At Randle's suggestion, the group renamed themselves 'the Crew Cuts'—becoming the first rock 'n' roll outfit to establish a connection between hairstyle and music.

In 1954 the Crew Cuts recorded the Top 10 Maugeri-Barrett original 'Crazy Bout You Baby'. Thus the group seemed poised to become not only successful performers but successful songwriters, too. However, at the insistence of their label, Mercury Records, they followed with a string of pop cover versions of R&B songs. The strategy paid off, and clearly satisfied a particular demand—between 1954 and 1957, the group scored 11 more Top 40 placements. The Crew Cuts are best remembered for their cover version of the Chords' 'Sh-Boom', though, which took Number 1 on the pop charts in 1954 and was the second-best-selling record of the year.

The Diamonds—the last 'white R&B' group we consider, and perhaps the most successful—were formed in 1952 by Phil Levitt and Ted Kowalski while they were

Listening To the Crew Cuts' 'Sh-Boom' (1954)

The Crew Cuts' 'Sh-Boom' is one of the most famous cover versions of the early rock 'n' roll era. In fact, its original recording by the Chords is often cited as one of the very first rock 'n' roll records. Certainly, the Chords' 'Sh-Boom' is a prime example of the R&B vocal harmony style and, as a Top 10 pop hit, was also one of the first records to demonstrate the huge appeal that style could have for a mass audience. It also illustrates how the presence of unexpected 'novelty' elements in the arrangement of an otherwise ordinary tune can help create an extraordinary pop record.

'Sh-Boom' is basically a standard AABA love ballad, whose sentimental lyrics and stereotypical chord changes would suggest, on paper, either a slow R&B ballad or grist for some latter-day pop crooner's mill. However, the Chords made the striking decision to treat the song as an up-tempo number and to add some novel touches to the arrangement. Among these touches were: an **a cappella** vocal introduction; the incorporation of brief passages of **scat singing** (nonsense syllables), borrowed from the jazz genre, at strategic points in the performance; a long and sizzling instrumental break, in the form of a saxophone solo—accompanied by the vocal group's rhythmic scat singing in the background—right in the middle of record; and an unexpected ending on the term 'sh-boom' itself, intoned by the group on an especially rich chord.

There are novel touches in the Crew Cuts' arrangement as well. As shown in the outline below, their version begins with scat singing. In the middle of the record, though, instead of a saxophone solo, there are two brief sections of group nonsense-syllable singing—each of which is punctuated by an isolated, loud, and humorous kettledrum stroke. Towards the end of the song there are not one but two 'false' endings (see below). Arguably, all these effects tend to push this version into the category of a full-fledged novelty record, whereas the Chords' version comes across as an up-tempo R&B record with some novel aspects.

In terms of singing style, the Crew Cuts are obviously crooners. The alternation between phrases where a solo voice takes the lead and phrases sung by the full group produces some agreeable variety in their arrangement, but there is really no difference in vocal coloration between the two, that is, the group passages are, in effect, 'crooning times four'. In contrast, the Chords' vocal arrangement is typical of an R&B approach insofar as it exploits differences in vocal **timbre** among the group's members, as well as the opposition between solo and group singing. This is heard most clearly in the 'B' section (bridge) of the Chords' version, where the lead is taken by a solo bass voice that presents a strong contrast to the sound of the lead tenor heard in the first two 'A' sections. And the Chords' general approach throughout is rougher in sound than that of the Crew Cuts, underlining the much more aggressive rhythmic feeling of their recording as a whole.

Comparing the Chords' and the Crew Cuts' Versions of 'Sh-Boom'

The Chords	The Crew Cuts
Introduction (group a cappella, then band enters)	**Introduction** (scat singing)
A ('Life could . . .'; tenor lead)	**A** (tenor lead)
(Scat singing interlude)	**A** (tenor lead)
A ('Life could . . .'; tenor lead)	**B** (tenor lead, then full group)
B ('Every time . . .'; bass lead)	**A** (tenor lead)
A ('Life could . . .'; full group)	**Group 'nonsense' singing**
(Scat singing interlude)	(Two sections, each the length of an 'A' section, punctuated by kettledrum strokes.)
Sax Solo (with group 'doo-wop' sounds in background; this is the length of two 'A' sections)	**B** (full group)
A (full group; same words as first 'A' section)	**A** (full group, then tenor lead; same words as first 'A' section).
	(Scat singing interlude, leading to first 'false' ending, then to:)
	A (full group, then tenor lead; same words as the second 'A' section).
(Scat singing interlude, leading to sudden ending with the full group)	('False' fadeout leads to sudden loud conclusion with the full group.)

students at the University of Toronto (partnered in a land surveying class, Levitt allegedly discovered Kowalski's vocal abilities while listening to him catcall passing coeds). Levitt and Kowalski recruited Dave Somerville and Bill Reed, and the group was complete. Calling themselves the Diamonds, the quartet initially found success on Toronto radio, performing regularly on a number of CBC shows throughout the mid-1950s. It was while rehearsing at CBC studios, in fact, that Nat Goodman, a well-known musician from Toronto, first heard the group and decided to manage them. The pairing was propitious—Goodman immediately booked the group at the Alpine Village Club in Cleveland, where local disc jockey Bill Randle heard them perform and, as he had done with the Crew Cuts the year before, introduced them to executives at Mercury Records.

At the insistence of Mercury Records, the Diamonds repeated the formula the Crew Cuts employed, creating cover after cover of black R&B hits for their predominantly white pop audience. In so doing they drew heavily from their primary influence and mentors—a black gospel group from Detroit called the Revelaires—who gave the Diamonds singing lessons whenever they toured Ontario. An early example of cross-marketing in rock 'n' roll, the Diamonds briefly attempted to cash in on the smash success of the Marlon Brando film *The Wild One*, released in 1954, with one of their first records for Mercury, 'Black Denim Trousers & Motorcycle Boots', but turned their attention back to making cover versions of R&B songs soon after.

The Diamonds scored their first hit in 1956 with a cover of Frankie Lymon and the Teenagers' 'Why Do Fools Fall in Love?' They next covered the Gladiolas' 'Little Darlin'', which became the sixth best-selling single of 1957 and stayed for eight weeks at Number 2 on the *Billboard* pop charts before being certified gold. They next recorded possibly their most popular record, 'The Stroll', which set off a minor dance craze across North America, and became one of the best-selling records of 1958 (an original song composed specifically for the group by Clyde Otis at the suggestion of Dick Clark, 'The Stroll' peaked at Number 4 on the pop charts and was certified gold). Later that same year, in November, they reached the Top 10 once more with 'Silhouettes', and recorded another cover, 'Words of Love', which brought the song's composer, Buddy Holly, his first significant publishing royalties; and they performed with the likes of Elvis Presley, Perry Como, Tony Bennett, Steve Allen, and Jimmy Dean on short tours of America, and starred in the popular rock 'n' roll movie, *The Big Beat*.

The Rock 'n' Roll Business in Canada

The popularity of the 'white R&B' genre notwithstanding, Canadian rock 'n' roll musicians were at a distinct disadvantage in the 1950s. Compared to the United States, Canada was simply too small a market to encourage the development of a domestic industry for rock 'n' roll. In 1958 there were 5 million more American teenagers (19 million) than there were Canadian citizens (14 million). Not surprisingly, then, the Canadian music industry was almost wholly dependent on foreign investments. Columbia and RCA-Victor, for instance, which were two of only three 'major' labels with offices in Canada during the 1950s, functioned as wholly subsidiary distributors of American product, while Capital Records Canada, the Canadian arm of Britain's EMI, distributed primarily British releases.

Other than a few notable exceptions, rock 'n' roll records sold in Canada were almost exclusively produced for American and British companies by American and British artists, who reaped the majority of profits to be had. Foreign firms came to look on Canada as a moderate, though reliable, satellite market for rock 'n' roll; for instance, the country could be depended on for sales of over 200,000 copies of Elvis Presley's 'Hound Dog' in 1956, while *Love Me Tender*, Presley's first film, set attendance records at cinemas across the nation. In fact, popular music accounted for roughly 90 per cent of all records sold in Canada in the 1950s, but fewer records were sold nationally than in some American states.

Very few records were actually made in Canada during the rock 'n' roll era. The Beau-Marks 'Clap Your Hands', recorded in 1959 and released by Quality Records in 1960, was the first rock 'n' roll record produced entirely in Canada to chart abroad (the Asteroids' 'Shhhhh Blast Off' and 'Don't Dig This Algreba', both released in 1958 on Halifax's Rodeo Records, have the distinction of being Canada's first domestically produced rock 'n' roll records). And there was little possibility that the group would support the single with the release of a domestically produced LP, since most Canadian labels active at the time—such as Yorkville, Red Leaf, Revolver, Quality, and Sparton—had resources to produce only 45 rpm singles.

All this began to change in 1960, when two labels turned their attention to domestic talent, namely, Sparton of Canada and Quality Records. Sparton of Canada was primarily a record manufacturing subsidiary of the American company Sparks-Worthington; based in London, Ontario, the imprint quickly established itself as the pre-eminent Canadian presser and distributor for Columbia Records between 1939 and 1954, after which point it became the Canadian distributor for ABC-Paramount, Disneyland, and Hifirecord. Sparton began to issue 45s of domestic talent on its own Sparton of Canada imprint in the mid-1950s, including records by the likes of Paul Anka, Cliff McKay, Ward Allen, Joyce Hahn, and Jimmy Namaro—though these records were still recorded in the US. Quality Records, established in 1950 by George Keane, followed suit. Starting in 1960, with the release of the Beau-Marks' 'Clap Your Hands', the label used profits made from distributing various American lines, most notably MGM and Mercury, to produce wholly Canadian-made records—that is, records recorded and pressed entirely in Canada—by such performers as the Beau-Marks, Harmonium, the Guess Who, and Albert Hall.

Notwithstanding the best efforts of Quality and Sparton, however, development of domestic talent in Canada was a slow and difficult process in the 1950s—if anything like artist development could even be said to have existed in Canada at all. Musical trends still typically followed the American lead, sometimes as much as a year later, and the notion that Canadian popular culture was just a pathetically obvious imitation of American culture slowly took root. Though this situation would become extremely contentious just under a decade later, it was mostly uncontroversial during the height of the rock 'n' roll era—which is not to say that people didn't complain about it. It was simply understood that, as Douglas Owram explains, with regard to the development of rock 'n' roll, 'Canada was hardly at the forefront.'

The rise of rock 'n' roll thus heralded 'the beginning of an exodus', as Gregg Potter describes it. 'With no infrastructure to nurture or support a popular music industry in Canada, artists simply had no choice but to bolt.' Due to the evident absence of a culture industry infrastructure in Canada to nurture domestic rock 'n' roll, the country became an exporter of talent more than of culture, specifically, to the US—part of a broader trend called 'the Brain Drain'. The effects of this so-called 'Brain Drain' are still felt today, especially in prevailing attitudes towards Canadian culture within Canada itself. Even now, with the international successes of so many Canadian popular musicians, it still sometimes seems to take success abroad to convince many Canadians of an artist's worth. Of course, we should note that Canada's pronounced regionalism and its sheer geographic size also play a significant role in fostering this attitude. As Michael Godin explains, in the 1950s:

> every city in the country developed on its own and what was going on in Vancouver wasn't going on in Toronto or Montreal. Artists could become big stars in their own market but because of the lack of an infrastructure, there was no crossover from market to market. As a result, they had to go to the States to sign with record companies, which would then get their product out in Canada through regional distributors like Quality and Sparton.

Canadian radio also followed the American leader, as it were, though with a decidedly more conservative approach to programming. While Red Robinson introduced British Columbians to American R&B on his weekly 'rock 'n' roll' show for CJOR in Vancouver, which attracted an estimated 53 per cent of the provincial listening audience during the height of Robinson's popularity, listeners from Manitoba to Quebec in the early fifties had no choice but to find the likes of George 'Hound Dog' Lorenz of Buffalo's WKBW on the dial if they wanted to hear rock 'n' roll. Of course, there was reciprocity: in an ironic twist, due to an elitist and racist programming policy that left entire regions of the United States with no R&B records on the radio, Windsor radio station CKLW eventually came to dominate the Detroit airwaves with its R&B-friendly broadcasts during the mid- and late 1950s. But such exceptions were exceedingly rare, and they inevitably proved the rule of American broadcasting dominance in central and eastern Canada.

This all changed in May of 1957, when 1050 CHUM-AM in Toronto became the first Canadian radio station to adopt a 24-hour rock 'n' roll format. Given that Toronto was the largest English-speaking city in Canada, CHUM's effect was instantaneous—rock 'n' roll records sold more units in Canada almost immediately after they were broadcast on the station, and especially if they were put into heavy rotation. CHUM also began to release its own Top 40 record chart, which was the first to track radio play and record sales within Canada. The so-called 'CHUM Chart' soon became 'both a barometer and an ECG for the Canadian pop-music industry', as Gregg Potter

The Beau-Marks Take Flight

Long before punks in New York City, London, and Vancouver claimed to invent so-called 'Do It Yourself' or 'DIY' rock 'n' roll, a group of musicians from Montreal—called variously the Del-Tones, the Bomarcs, and the Beau-Marks—were busy inventing the tradition. Comprised of pianist and vocalist Joey Frechette, guitarist Ray Hutchinson, bassist Mike Robitaille, and Gilles Tailleur on drums, the Beau-Marks first formed as a rockabilly outfit called the Del-Tones in 1958. Immediately, they established themselves as a group entirely uninterested in 'major' label representation—within a year of forming they had recorded, pressed, and distributed their first single, the Frechette originals 'Rockin' Blues'/'Moonlight Party', completely in Montreal. In 1959 they changed their name to the Bomarcs, after the nuclear-tipped anti-aircraft missiles Prime Minister Diefenbaker controversially requested (and then refused) from the US, before changing it once more to the bilingually punning Beau-Marks.

In 1960 the Beau-Marks, with 'Clap Your Hands', became the first Canadian group—and their label, Quality Records, became the first domestic label—to hit the Top 40 with a rock 'n' roll record produced entirely in Canada. Quickly securing the Number 1 position on the CHUM charts (see below), the single was licensed to Shad Records in the United States, where it reached Number 29 on the *Billboard* pop chart and 15 on *Cashbox*. The band next recorded a French-language version of the song, called 'Frappe Tes Mains', for release in Quebec and France; and they insisted that liner notes for their subsequent LP release, called *The High Flying Beau-Marks*, be printed both in English and French, reflecting their bilingual upbringing and day-to-day life in Montreal. At the same time the group toured central and eastern Canada and the northeastern United States, garnering a moderate though never substantial following in the process. Appearances on *American Bandstand* and on CFTO-TV's *Hi-Time Dance Party* led to five more Top 40 hits in Canada—'Billy, Billy Went A Walking' (Number 39 CHUM, 1960), 'Classmate' (Number 4 CHUM, 1961), 'Little Miss Twist' (Number 17 CHUM, 1962), 'Lovely Little Lady' (Number 17 CHUM, 1962), and 'The Tender Years' (Number 18 CHUM, 1962)—but the group never again cracked the Top 40 in the United States.

Besides being the first rock 'n' roll band to score an international hit with a record produced entirely within Canada, the Beau-Marks were also one of the first bands to record mostly their own songs, and to record a 'live' album. Ten of the 11 songs on their first LP, *The High-Flying Beau-Marks* (1960), were original compositions; and the band's second release, *The Beau-Marks In Person* (1962), was recorded live at Toronto's Le Coq d'Or nightclub (the album reflects the eclecticism of early rock 'n' roll, featuring two jazz standards, 'When the Saints Go Marchin' In' and 'For Me and My Gal', and covers of Ray Charles's proto-soul 'What'd I Say?' and Hank Snow's country standard 'I'm Movin' On'). The Beau-Marks disbanded in 1963, when their third LP, the simply titled *Beau-Marks*, and their follow-up single, 'Stay with Me', failed to chart anywhere in the world.

puts it, and it reinforced the notion that Canadians were culturally distinct—at least insofar as their listening preferences demanded independent tracking. To name but one relevant example, Jerry Lee Lewis's 'Whole Lotta Shakin' Goin' On' is often touted by critics and historians as one of the most successful and significant records in rock 'n' roll history because it topped the pop, country, and R&B charts simultaneously in the US, but it failed to crack even the Top 10 on the CHUM charts, peaking at Number 13 on 22 July 1957 before quickly slipping off the charts altogether—Elvis Presley's '(Let Me Be Your) Teddy Bear' was Number 1 that week, followed by tracks from, among others, Johnny Mathis, Patti Page, Little Richard, and Pat Boone.

Early Rock 'n' Roll on the Country Side: Bill Haley, Elvis Presley, Buddy Holly

The first American subgenre of rock 'n' roll to breach the CHUM charts in a significant way was **rockabilly**, the quintessential rock 'n' roll music from the country side of the pop music world. A portmanteau of 'rock' and 'hillbilly' first designed to insult the southern rockers who primarily performed it, 'rockabilly' emerged to international prominence during the mid-1950s. That it first appeared in the southern US is not especially surprising. Rockabilly was, after all, 'a country man's song with a black man's rhythm', according to Carl Perkins, one of the genre's most famous pioneers; and, as we noted in the last chapter, both country and western and rhythm and blues remain geographically and conceptually linked with the American South and Southwest.

Though Elvis Presley and Sam Phillips at Sun Records typically get much of the credit for creating rockabilly, if not rock 'n' roll, a number of musicians preceded them in fusing country and western with rhythm and blues. By the late 1930s, Moon Mullican, the Delmore Brothers, Tennessee Ernie Ford, and the Maddox Brothers and Rose had already made a number of so-called 'hillbilly boogie' records, all of which mixed country vocals and instrumentation with a boogie-woogie bass line and rhythmic sensibility. Meanwhile, Bob Wills and his Texas Playboys and future rock 'n' roll star Bill Haley and His Saddlemen mixed country and western and big band swing into a new musical hybrid called western swing. And, as we noted in Chapter 1, the honky-tonk genre in general, but particularly the variant played by Hank Williams and the Perkins Brothers Band, was another important precursor.

Bill Haley and His Comets were the first to reach a mainstream pop audience with a fusion of country and western and rhythm and blues—a fusion they called 'rock 'n' roll'. In fact, perhaps the most famous example of a rock 'n' roll cover version is Bill Haley and His Comets' cover of 'Shake, Rattle, and Roll', a song composed in 1954 by Jesse Stone, the black producer and talent scout for Atlantic Records (Stone published the song under the pseudonym Charles Calhoun).

Haley followed the success of 'Shake, Rattle, and Roll' with the equally successful 'See Ya Later, Alligator' (Number 6, 1956). However, he and the Comets attained their unique status in pop music history when their record of 'Rock Around the

Bill Haley and His Comets shake up a crowd at the Sports Arena, Hershey, Pennsylvania, 1956. Courtesy Library of Congress.

Listening To Big Joe Turner's and Bill Haley & His Comets' 'Shake, Rattle, and Roll' (1954)

'Shake, Rattle, and Roll' is a 12-bar blues, with a repeated section that functions like a chorus (*Shake, rattle, and roll . . .*). The original recording of the song, released by Atlantic in 1954, is in the jump blues style. It features Big Joe Turner (1911–85), a 43-year-old vocalist who had begun his career as a singing bartender in the Depression-era nightclubs of Kansas City, and who sang with various big bands during the swing era. Turner was one of Atlantic's early stars, and his recording of 'Shake, Rattle, and Roll' not only held Number 1 on the

R&B charts but also crossed over onto the pop charts, where it reached Number 22.

Turner's crossover hit soon caught the attention of executives at Decca Records, and of a former western swing band-leader named Bill Haley (1925–81). Haley would seem an unlikely candidate for the first big rock 'n' roll star, but in the early 1950s he was seeking a style that would capture the enthusiasm of the growing audience of young listeners and dancers, and he accurately sensed which way the wind was blowing. He dropped his cowboy image, changed the name of his accompanying group from the Saddlemen to the Comets, and in 1953 wrote and recorded a song, 'Crazy, Man, Crazy', that offered a reasonable emulation of dance-oriented black R&B. The record, released by a small indie label, rose as high as Number 12 on the pop charts.

In 1954 the Comets were signed by Decca Records, where they worked in the studio with A&R (artists and repertoire) man Milt Gabler. Gabler, who had produced a series of hit records with Louis Jordan and His Tympany Five (see Chapter 1), helped to push Haley's style further in the direction of jump blues—'I'd sing Jordan riffs to the group that would be picked up by the electric guitars and tenor sax', he later said.

The same year he signed with Decca, Bill Haley recorded a rendition of 'Shake, Rattle, and Roll' that was clearly indebted to Turner's original, but that also departed from it in significant ways. While Turner's version features a band made up of veteran jazz musicians, playing a medium-tempo shuffle rhythm, the Haley recording emphasizes guitars rather than saxophones, and has a rhythmic feeling more akin to western

swing than to jump blues. One of the most obvious differences between the two versions lies in the song's text. The original lyric, as composed by Jesse Stone and embellished by Turner, is full of fairly obvious sexual references:

Well, you wear those dresses, the sun come shinin' through . . .
I cain' believe my eyes, all that mess belong to you
I'm like a one-eyed cat, peepin' in a seafood store . . .
Well I can look at you till you ain't no child no more

Presumably because these lyrics would have proved too wild for AM radio, and might have offended many in the predominantly white pop music audience, Haley sang a bowdlerized (censored) version of the song:

Wearin' those dresses, your hair done up so nice . . .
You look so warm, but your heart is cold as ice.
I'm like a one-eyed cat, peepin' in a seafood store . . .
I can look at you till you don't love me no more

That the 'one-eyed cat, peepin' in a seafood store' survived the censor's blade is surprising, since it is a fairly obvious double-entendre reference to the male and female sexual organs. The person charged with rewriting the lyric may have been a bit too square to catch the sexual reference, a fact that must have delighted those who knew the original version.

The other major difference between Turner's and Haley's versions of 'Shake,

Rattle, and Roll' is the level of profit generated by the two records. In fact, this is not the most egregious example of a white band and major record company reaping profits from a song originally recorded by black musicians for an independent label—both versions appeared on the pop charts, and each sold over a million copies. But while Haley built on his early hit success, going on to become the first 'king' of rock 'n' roll music, albeit self-crowned, Turner was never again able to score a Top 40 pop hit or a Number 1 R&B hit. Atlantic sought to promote the middle-aged blues shouter to the teen audience for rock 'n' roll, but his time had passed. As Turner himself claimed, and as even just a quick listen to his version of 'Shake, Rattle, and Roll' bears out, 'rock 'n' roll' was just another name for the same music that Big Joe Turner had always sung—but he got 'knocked down' in the traffic of a newly crowded scene.

Clock' became the first rock 'n' roll record to reach Number 1 on the pop charts; it stayed in the top spot for eight consecutive weeks during the summer of 1955, and eventually sold over 22 million copies worldwide. The track, written by Max C. Freedman and Jimmy DeKnight, was actually recorded in 1954, and was not a big hit when first released. But when the record was prominently featured in the opening credits of the 1955 film *Blackboard Jungle*, which dealt with inner-city teenagers and juvenile delinquency, it soon achieved massive popularity—and forged an enduring link that has connected teenagers, rock 'n' roll, concerns about juvenile delinquency and the influence of popular culture on young people, and the film industry. The following year, 1956, the 'B' movie, *Rock Around the Clock*, which featured Bill Haley and His Comets, as well as DJ Alan Freed and such other performers as the Platters and Freddie Bell and the Bellboys, successfully capitalized on the success of Haley's hit single and became the first rock 'n' roll movie, establishing a genre that before long would include films starring Elvis Presley and, a decade later, the Beatles.

Though his claim to have 'invented' rock 'n' roll deserves little credibility, Haley was certainly an important popularizer of the genre. He paved the way for the widespread acceptance of many more artists working in the genre, not the least of whom was Elvis Presley, who remains arguably the real 'King' of rock 'n' roll.

Elvis Presley: The Sun Years

The biggest star of the rock 'n' roll era—and arguably in the entire history of rock 'n' roll—was, of course, Elvis Presley (1935–77). Born in Tupelo, Mississippi, Presley was the only child of a poor family (his twin brother was stillborn), and his musical tastes were obviously shaped at a young age by the white gospel music he heard at church, by radio broadcasts of country music and rhythm and blues records, and by the popular crooners of the post-war era, especially Dean Martin.

As a teenager Presley moved to Memphis, Tennessee, when he took a job as a truck driver and nurtured his ambition to become a singing film star. While in Memphis, in 1954, Presley came to the attention of Sam Phillips, the owner of Sun Records. A small independent label in Memphis, Sun specialized in rockabilly records, and had already scored a few regional hits before Elvis arrived. Phillips teamed Presley with two musicians from a local country band called the Starlite Wranglers—Scotty Moore (b. 1931) on electric guitar and Bill Black (1926–65) on string bass—and together they made a series of records, each of which had an R&B cover version on one side and a country song on the other.

In essence, Sam Phillips was 'fishing', using Elvis Presley as bait, trying to see if he could develop a single artist who could sell to both white and black audiences. In his

The young **Elvis Presley** in action, 1956. Courtesy Library of Congress.

Listening To Elvis Presley's 'Mystery Train' (1955)

In 1953 Herman ('Little Junior') Parker (1927–71)—a singer, songwriter, and harmonica player who achieved some success with his rhythm and blues band, Little Junior's Blue Flames—recorded a tune called 'Mystery Train' for Sam Phillips at Sun Records. The song received little attention at the time of its release, but at some point the young Elvis Presley must have noticed it, for he recorded it early in 1955 while he was also at Sun. Examining these two versions of 'Mystery Train' will assist us in understanding the developing synergy between rhythm and blues and country music that led to the phenomenon called rock 'n' roll.

'Mystery Train' as a composition is credited to Junior Parker and Sam Phillips. It is unlikely, however, that Phillips played any role in the song's composition; what more likely happened is that Phillips was given songwriting credit as a form of payment. In any event, the record features a strophic 12-bar blues structure—at least in its original version—with one harmonic irregularity: some strophes begin on the subdominant chord rather than on the tonic, so that the first two four-bar phrases of these particular strophes are harmonically identical.

Both Parker's original performance and Presley's cover version are individually fine recordings. What is most remarkable, however, is how different they are from one another. Although Presley obviously learned a great deal from listening to Parker, and to dozens

of other fine rhythm and blues artists, Presley's 'Mystery Train' is arguably less a traditional cover version than a complete reconceptualization of the song— a reconceptualization that reflects both Presley's distinctive self-awareness as a performer and his emerging, if implicit, ideas regarding his listening audience and how to engage it.

Junior Parker's original 'Mystery Train' is a darkly evocative record with obvious roots in rural blues and in R&B. The train was a favourite subject and image for country blues singers, and the spare, non-linear lyrics in Parker's song are clearly aligned with country blues traditions. In the first strophe, the '*long black train*', with its '*sixteen coaches*' taking the singer's '*baby*' away, paints a funereal picture. By the time we reach the third and final strophe, however, the train is bringing '*baby*' back to the singer, and the mood has brightened. But that brightening is darkened by the certainty already communicated in the second strophe— the train that took her away will '*do it again*'. Thus, Parker articulates a rather world-weary view characteristic of the blues, asserting that any triumph over adversity can only be temporary and that life is a cycle of misfortunes offering, at best, only periodic relief.

Furthermore, Parker's band constitutes a fairly typical rhythm and blues lineup for its time: electric guitar, acoustic bass, piano, drums, and saxophone. The 'chugging' rhythm conveys a perfect sense of the train's steady, inexorable momentum. The saxophone is confined basically to long, low notes that evoke the train's whistle, while an additional atmospheric touch is added at the end of the recording, with a vocal imitation of the sound of the train's brakes as it finally comes to a stop, an event marked by the concluding guitar chord and the cessation of the 'chugging' rhythm.

Elvis Presley's 'Mystery Train', recorded when the 'hillbilly cat' was barely 20 years old, conveys a breathless sense of intensity, excitement, and enthusiasm (listen to Presley's spontaneous-sounding, triumphant 'whoop' at the end of the recording) that makes for a totally different experience from that offered by Parker's rendition. The much faster tempo of the Presley record is, of course, a decisive factor, but it is only the most obvious of many reasons that may be cited for the essential transformation 'Mystery Train' undergoes here. There is little, if any, attempt at naturalistic evocation of the train by Presley's band, which consists simply of electric guitar, acoustic guitar, acoustic bass, and drums—no sax, no piano. One might hear a train-like rhythm in the pattern of the drumsticks, but the speed of the recording encourages one to imagine a roller coaster rather than a train (especially by 1955 standards). In fact, unlike Parker's record, Presley's version focuses on the singer rather than the train. Parker's protagonist seems ultimately at the mercy of the train, which has taken away his 'baby' and will do so again, even if it occasionally brings her back, but Presley's vocal performance portrays a youthful confidence in control of its own future (obviously American racial politics played a key role in how each singer relates to the concepts of 'freedom' and 'destiny' engendered by the song).

Presley's 'Mystery Train' presents significant alterations to Parker's original in the internal structuring of both the words and the music. In the lyrics to the second strophe, Presley makes a crucial substitution, asserting that while the train took his '*baby*', '*it never will again.*' As if to emphasize this essential change, Presley repeats this second strophe, with its altered lyrics, at the end of his record, so that now there are a total of four strophes, three of which look towards the return of his '*baby*', while only one (the first one) emphasizes her departure. As Presley turns the departure into a one-time occurrence, the song assumes a linear narrative shape that it did not have in Parker's original version. Even more importantly, this revision of the lyrics expresses and underlines the singer's feeling of control over the situation—definitely not an attitude traditionally associated with the blues. Moreover, in Parker's 'Mystery Train' the instrumental break occurs between the second and third strophes, emphasizing, and allowing the listener to ponder, the singer's assertion that the train is going to take his '*baby*' again; in contrast, the instrumental break occurs after the third strophe in Presley's version, leaving the singer's words '*she's mine, all mine*' resonating in the listener's ears.

While Parker's 'Mystery Train' follows the standard format of a 12-bar blues in the rhythmic arrangement of all its phrases and strophes, Presley's version is highly irregular by comparison. Many of the phrases in Presley's 'Mystery Train' are longer than they 'should' be—if we attempted to notate his performance in terms of a 12-bar blues paradigm, we would find ourselves constantly having to add 'half-bar' extensions (two extra beats) to many phrases. While there seems to be a general pattern formed by these extensions throughout the first three strophes, Presley breaks free of even this suggested pattern in his final strophe, extending one of the phrases yet further than before, while constricting another. In fact, one of the truly remarkable things about this 'Mystery Train' is that Presley's band was able to follow the apparent spontaneity, and consequent unpredictability, of his phrasing—especially given the breakneck speed of the performance.

With all these differences, we should not ignore Presley's obvious debts to the blues and rhythm and blues traditions on 'Mystery Train', especially as they are represented in Parker's original composition and recording. It is not difficult to hear strong aspects of what Sam Phillips called 'the Negro sound and the Negro feel' in Presley's performance, particularly in his vocal performance, with its strong regional accent, and the frequency of blue notes and melismas. Of course, these characteristics are traditional points of intersection between black blues and white country traditions in general, rather than examples of strict imitation. What is important to understand is how Presley emphasized these common elements to form a style that sounded significantly 'blacker' (particularly to white audiences) than that of virtually any other white singer who had so far emerged in the post-war era, even as he incorporated vocal effects more specifically associated with white traditions (i.e., the stuttering, **'hiccuping'**

effect heard in lines like *'comin' dowhown the li-hine'* or *'she's mine, a-hall mine'*). Even the kind of rhythmic freedom that we have observed in Presley's 'Mystery Train' reflects practices common in African-American music, although one would have to go back to rural blues recordings to find anything comparably irregular, as most rhythm and blues records were tied to the kind of regularity in phrasing that was usually expected in music designed to be suitable for dancing.

This observation brings us to our final point. In sum, Elvis Presley's 'Mystery Train' is unique in our experience of cover recordings thus far because it is more aggressive and 'raw' than the original on which it was modelled. But the freedom and rawness of Presley's version is not primarily in the service of a vision that seeks to return us to the original flavour and context of rural blues. Rather, Presley's 'Mystery Train' is the expression of a young white singer who is looking with optimism towards an essentially unbounded future, flush with new possibilities for stylistic synthesis that would help assure both intensely satisfying personal expression and an unprecedented degree of popular success. Unlike Parker's 'Mystery Train', which is the expression of a man working knowledgeably within a tradition that both defines and confines the outlines of his music, and of his world view, Presley's 'Mystery Train' offers a totally new kind of ride—a ride without immediately apparent limits or preconditions. No wonder so many other young singers, and a remarkably large group of young adults, wanted to climb aboard.

early live appearances Elvis was billed as 'the King of Country Bop', an attempt to indicate his idiosyncratic combination of black and white influences. The last record that Elvis made with Sam Phillips—just before he signed with RCA-Victor and went on to become a national celebrity—was a cover version of an R&B song called 'Mystery Train', and it is this recording that we examine in some detail (see p. 57).

Elvis Presley: The RCA-Victor Years

When RCA-Victor bought out Presley's contract from Sam Phillips in late 1955, at the then-extravagant price of $35,000, the label set about consciously trying to turn the 'hillbilly cat' into a mainstream performer without compromising the strength of his appeal to teenagers. In this they were assisted by two major players: first there was Presley's manager, Colonel Thomas Parker, who saw to it that Presley was seen repeatedly on television variety shows and in a series of romantic Hollywood films; second was RCA's Nashville **producer**, Chet Atkins, who saw to it that Presley's records for the label were made pop-friendly, according to Atkins's standards. (In the 1960s Atkins became the producer most credited with developing the 'Nashville Sound' of pop-oriented country music. Both succeeded beyond anyone's expectations. Although Presley's television performances were denounced by authorities as vulgar because of the singer's hip-shaking gyrations, the shows were attended by hordes of screaming young fans and were admired on the screen by millions of young viewers. And Presley's records racked up astronomical sales as he dominated the top of the pop charts steadily from 1956 into the early 1960s, quickly establishing himself as the biggest-selling solo artist of rock 'n' roll, and then as the biggest-selling solo recording artist of *any* period and style—a title he still held at the beginning of the twenty-first century.

Presley's biggest hit, 'Don't Be Cruel', topped the charts for 11 weeks in the late summer and fall of 1956, eventually yielding pride of place to another Presley record, 'Love Me Tender', which was a reworking of the American Civil War ballad, 'The Ballad of Aura Lee', recorded especially for the 1956 film, *Love Me Tender* (a Western romance, not a rock 'n' roll movie). 'Don't Be Cruel' is based on the 12-bar blues (see listening chart). Presley's vocal is heavy with blues-derived and country inflections; we hear a striking regional accent, and the occasional 'hiccuping' effect (*'baby, it's just you I'm a-thinkin' of'*), even as the strong **backbeat** throughout evokes the rhythm and blues genre. Imposed on all these diverse and intense stylistic elements is a wash of electronic **reverb**—an obviously failed attempt by the engineers at RCA's Nashville studios to emulate the distinctive (and decidedly low-tech) '**slap-back**' echo sound of Presley's previous recordings on Sun Records. There is also the sweetening sound of the backing vocal group, the Jordanaires, whose precise 'bop, bops', and crooning 'aahs' and 'ooos' are doubly rooted in white gospel music and in the most genteel and established mainstream pop style. Whether this odd amalgam is deemed to work as a source of stylistic enrichment, or whether listening to Presley and the Jordanaires together on this record seems like listening to the Chords and the Crew Cuts *simultaneously* performing 'Sh-Boom' (see the preceding discussion of cover versions) will obviously be a matter of personal taste. It can never be known how much the Jordanaires added, or if they added at all, to the appeal of this and many other records Presley made with them for RCA. But the commercial success of these records was unprecedented, and their mixture of styles was yet another indication of the extent to which the traditional barriers in pop music were falling down.

Presley's extraordinary popularity established rock 'n' roll as an unprecedented mass-market phenomenon. His reputation as a performer and recording artist endured up to his death in 1977 at the age of 42—and continues beyond the grave.

Listening Chart: 'Don't Be Cruel' (1956)

Music and lyrics by Otis Blackwell and Elvis Presley; as performed by Elvis Presley, vocal and guitar, with the Jordanaires and backing instrumentalists. Though not generally known as a songwriter, Presley was credited as co-author of several of his early hits for RCA.

FORM	LYRICS	DESCRIPTIVE COMMENTS
Instrumental introduction		Repetitive *guitar* hook, *strong backbeat* (four bars long).
Verse 1	*If you know . . .*	12-bar blues structure, arranged *to suggest* a verse-chorus pattern, with the first eight bars constituting the verse and the chorus.
Chorus	*Don't be cruel . . .*	
Verse 2	*Baby, if I . . .*	12-bar blues structure, with an extension added (six bars in length) to the chorus.
Chorus +	*Don't be cruel . . .*	
extension	*Why don't want...*	
Verse 3	*Don't stop a-thinkin' . . .*	12-bar blues structure, plus extension (as before).
Chorus +	*Don't be cruel . . .*	
extension	*Why should we . . .*	
Verse 4	*Let's walk up . . .*	12-bar blues structure, plus extension (as before).
Chorus +	*Don't be cruel . . .*	
extension	*I don't want . . .*	
Concluding + chorus	*Don't be cruel . . .*	
Additional extension	*Don't be cruel . . .* *I don't want . . .*	

Graceland, Presley's home in Memphis, Tennessee, is now a public museum dedicated to his memory and it is visited by upwards of 600,000 people annually, as Paul Simon would evocatively describe in his 1986 song of musical and spiritual pilgrimage, 'Graceland', in his album of the same name. Presley gave strong performances and made fine records at many points throughout his career, and he starred in many movies, notably the rock 'n' roll movies *Jailhouse Rock* (1957) and *King Creole* (1958). But it cannot be denied that Elvis Presley's principal importance as a musical influence and innovator—like that of Chuck Berry, Little Richard, and Fats Domino, as we shall shortly see—rests upon his achievements during the early years of rock 'n' roll. In 1956 Presley cut a handful of records that literally changed the world for himself and for those around him, and the unbridled exuberance of his live performances at that time was the model for every white kid who wanted to move mountains by strumming a guitar, shaking his hips, and lifting his voice.

Though Elvis never toured overseas—it is rumoured that his manager, Colonel Tom Parker, feared that he would be denied re-entry to the US given that Parker was not an official citizen of the United States—he did tour Canada in 1957 (Parker would not have needed a passport to cross the border into, and back from, Canada in those days). The tour was extremely controversial. Over 25,000 fans peacefully packed Maple Leaf Gardens in Toronto to see the King of rock 'n' roll perform, but an equal number rioted at one of his shows in Vancouver, overwhelming the police and storming the stage in a violent display that only confirmed for local authorities that rock 'n' roll was a dangerous and damaging influence on Canadian youth. In Ottawa, where Presley also played, he was forced to defend himself against charges laid by the Separate School Board that he was vulgar, and that his records should be banned from Ottawa schools; and he could only look on helplessly as some students were expelled from school for attending one of his concerts. Indeed, it would not be until a few years later, when Presley was overseas fulfilling military service duties in Germany, that rock 'n' roll took root in any discernible shape inside Canada.

Rock 'n' Roll in Canada: Rompin' Ronnie Hawkins

According to Neil Young, 'the great Canadian dream is to get out.' One artist who bucked that trend was Rompin' Ronnie Hawkins. Born and raised in Huntsville, Arkansas, Ronnie Hawkins enjoyed some success as a rockabilly singer in the United States before he moved to Canada in the late 1950s and almost single-handedly established a domestic rock 'n' roll scene there. In fact, Hawkins followed a south-to-north path already tread by the likes of Harold Kudlets, a booking agent from Hamilton, and his friend Harold Jenkins (a.k.a. Conway Twitty). On Twitty's advice, Kudlets attended a Hawkins performance at a nightclub in Buffalo in 1958 and, immediately after the show, invited Hawkins to play The Grange nightclub in Hamilton. Hawkins subsequently decided to stay in Canada, hoping to find the success that had eluded him stateside by becoming 'a big fish' in 'a little Canadian pond'.

Rompin' Ronnie Hawkins: One of the only artists who fought to keep his career in Canada.

Hawkins actually fought to stay in Canada. Failing to secure a contract at Sun Records earlier in the decade, opting instead for a contract with the even smaller Roulette Records, Hawkins enjoyed minor success in 1958 with 'Mary Lou' and '40 Days'. However, he refused to return to the more lucrative American market to promote the records, and Roulette promptly dropped the singer from its roster. Undeterred, Hawkins established himself as a dominant force in Canadian rock 'n' roll, and though he never made the *Billboard* Top 20, he scored six Top 10 hits on the CHUM charts between 1959 and 1965: 'Mary Lou' (Number 6, 1959), '40 Days'

(Number 4, 1959), 'Southern Love' (Number 7, 1959), 'Cold Cold Heart' (Number 9, 1961), 'Bo Diddley' (Number 8, 1963), and 'Bluebirds over the Mountain' (Number 5, 1965).

Besides his own musical accomplishments, Hawkins was also an important mentor to young Canadian rock 'n' roll musicians (ex-members of the Hawks, his backing band, include the Band, Janis Joplin's Full-Tilt Boogie Band, Dominic Troiano, David Foster, Duane Allman, and David Clayton-Thomas, to name only a few). When his entire backing band left for the States in 1960—save fellow Arkansan Levon Helm—Hawkins repopulated the group with Canadian musicians, including a Jewish-Mohawk guitarist and vocalist from Toronto named Robbie Robertson, multi-instrumentalist Garth Hudson (from Windsor), bassist Rick Danko (from Simcoe County), and keyboardist Richard Manuel (from Stratford). This group, subsequently renamed the Band, is widely considered the most successful backing band in rock 'n' roll history, eventually backing Bob Dylan on his earliest 'electric' tours of the United States and England in 1965 and 1966 and on some of his most influential recordings, including *Planet Waves* (1973), *After The Flood* (1973), and *The Basement Tapes* (1967/1975).

Hawkins and the Band, then called 'the Hawks', together established themselves as a fixture on Toronto's burgeoning Yonge Street rock 'n' roll and R&B scene. Between 1960 and 1964 they played the numerous rock 'n' roll and R&B venues that lined Yonge Street on an almost nightly basis, but were most often seen at Yonge Street's Le Coq D'Or nightclub and, on its second floor, Hawkins's own The Hawk's Nest. In 1963 the group recorded covers of two Bo Diddley songs, 'Who Do You Love' and 'Bo Diddley', for Quality Records. The single reached Number 8 on the CHUM charts but failed to crack the American Top 200, at which point the Hawks renamed themselves Levon & the Hawks and then the Canadian Squires—a name they soon felt compelled to amend to simply the Squires because, in their opinion, the term 'Canadian' in their name had badly hurt their chances at radio play in both Canada and the United States—and set off on their own.

Hawkins probably deserves even more credit than he currently receives for developing a domestic rock 'n' roll scene within Canada. According to Hawkins, a 'garrison mentality' obviously prevailed in Canada in the early 1960s, which held that domestic talent was second-rate, specifically in comparison to groups from the United States. As Hawkins remembers:

> In the late fifties up in Canada, the musicians were in the same shape that we had been in earlier in Memphis. Most of them were starving to death because agents wouldn't book a Canadian group because they said that club owners felt that a Canadian band wouldn't draw in Canada. That's a bunch of bullshit and everybody knew it. I used to loan different bands my car, which still had American plates on it, and fool the agents and club owners by saying the band came from Memphis or Nashville. They'd pull up and play and when they went over big we'd tell them they were from Scarborough . . . Tennessee. (Cited in Melhuish, 1983: 23)

Sun Records after Elvis

At first glance, Phillips's decision to sell Elvis Presley's contract seems a monumental error. Such is the benefit of hindsight, however. At the time of the sale, things were anything but clear. Sam Phillips was convinced that, in Carl Perkins, he had an artist on the Sun roster who would eclipse Presley, and he needed the money from the sale of Presley's contract to properly capitalize the label anyway. In fact, whether or not Sun could even have survived had Phillips not sold Presley's contract is debatable.

The son of a southern sharecropper with remarkably eclectic musical tastes, ranging from rural blues through Baptist gospel to hillbilly boogie, Carl Perkins did not disappoint Parker. His first release for Sun, 'Blue Suede Shoes', reached Number 2 on the *Billboard* Top 10, and went on to become Sun Record's best-selling record to date. When Presley's first release for RCA-Victor, 'Heartbreak Hotel', kept Perkins from taking Number 1, the rock 'n' roll world had the beginnings of a legendary rivalry on its hands. Sadly, however, Perkins was almost fatally injured in a car crash en route to taping an episode of *The Perry Como Show* later that year, and he never again entered the Top 40.

With Presley gone, and his primary competition injured, Sun Records looked to Jerry Lee Lewis to fill the void. Lewis's first record for the label, 'Whole Lotta Shakin' Goin' On', topped the pop, country, and R&B charts simultaneously in the United States. His follow-up, 'Great Balls of Fire', was gold certified, topped the pop and country charts, and reached Number 3 on the R&B charts (the track peaked for three weeks at Number 2 on the CHUM charts). Lewis's next three records—'You Win Again' (1957), 'Breathless' (1958), and 'High School Confidential' (1958)—all went gold, at which point Lewis began to command $10,000 per performance. However, when news broke that his third marriage was to his 13-year-old cousin, Myra Gale Brown, Lewis's popularity took a nosedive, and the singer never again reached the Top 20 in North America.

Buddy Holly

Buddy Holly (Charles Hardin Holley) (1936–59) offered an image virtually the opposite of Lewis's intense, aggressive, suggestively sexual stage persona. Here was a clean-cut, lanky, bespectacled young man—obviously nobody's idea of a matinee idol, but one who certainly knew his way around a guitar and a recording studio. The Texas-born Holly began his career with country music but soon fell under the influence of Presley's musical style and success, and formed a rock 'n' roll band called the Crickets.

Holly's first record in his new style, 'That'll Be the Day', rose to Number 1 on the pop charts in late 1957, and established his characteristic and highly influential sound. 'That'll Be the Day' combined elements of country, rhythm and blues, and mainstream pop in the kind of synthesis that typified rock 'n' roll in a general sense, but that nevertheless projected a distinctive approach and sensibility. Holly's vocal style—full of country twang and hiccups, along with expressive blue notes—projected that mixture of toughness and vulnerability that forms the essence of both fine country singing and fine blues singing. The Crickets' instrumental lineup of two electric guitars (lead and rhythm), electric bass, and drums provided an intense support for Holly's voice, and during instrumental breaks, Holly's lead guitar playing was active, riff-based, and hard-edged in a way that reflected the influence of Chuck Berry. 'That'll Be the Day' is structured like a typical pop song, alternating verses and choruses of eight bars each; but when it comes time to provide an instrumental break, the Crickets play a 12-bar blues pattern. This works because important aspects of both vocal and instrumental style throughout the record are based on blues- and rhythm and blues-derived elements. On some later records, like 'Oh, Boy!' and 'Peggy Sue', Holly used a 12-bar blues structure for the song itself.

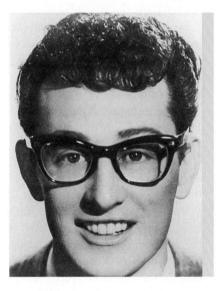

Buddy Holly. Frank Driggs Collection.

Buddy Holly's career was tragically cut short at the age of 22, in the crash of a small plane in an Iowa cornfield during a snowstorm. Also killed were two other prominent rock 'n' roll personalities on tour with Holly: the promising 17-year-old Chicano singer and songwriter Ritchie Valens ('La Bamba'), and the Big Bopper (J.P. Richardson), whose lone hit was 'Chantilly Lace'. Holly's death—and its sad significance to the future course of rock 'n' roll—would later be memorialized in Don McLean's 1972 elegiac classic, 'American Pie', as 'the day the music died'. A measure of Holly's importance for later pop music, the Beatles modelled their insect-based name, their four-piece instrumental lineup, and aspects of their vocal style on the Crickets—and through the Beatles, of course, this influence was passed on to innumerable bands. Holly was also, like Chuck Berry, an important rock 'n' roll songwriter; in addition to the songs already mentioned, he wrote and recorded 'Everyday', 'Not Fade Away', 'Rave On', and numerous others, most of which became increasingly popular in the years after his death and were covered by rock bands.

Furthermore, Holly's experiments with arrangements and studio effects looked forward to some of the recording techniques of the 1960s; he frequently used double-tracking on his recordings—a technique in which two nearly identical versions of the same vocal or instrumental part are recorded on top of one another, foregrounding that part so that it seems to come right out of the speaker at the listener—and some of his last records used orchestral strings.

Early Rock 'n' Roll on the R&B Side: Chuck Berry, Little Richard, Fats Domino

We will represent the rhythm and blues-based side of rock 'n' roll with three of the most successful rock 'n' roll artists ever to have played: Chuck Berry, Little Richard, and Fats Domino. All three achieved their successes recording on independent labels, thus demonstrating the great importance of the 'indies' to the popularization of rock 'n' roll. Domino recorded for Imperial, a Los Angeles-based concern headed by Lew Chudd that also issued records by the important R&B electric guitar stylist Aaron 'T-Bone' Walker; Little Richard worked for Specialty Records, Art Rupe's Hollywood label, which had on its roster such R&B stars as Percy Mayfield, Lloyd Price, and Guitar Slim; and Berry recorded for Chess, the Chicago label owned by the Chess brothers, Leonard and Phil, which also served as home for an impressive list of blues-based artists such as Muddy Waters, Howlin' Wolf, and Willie Dixon, along with other rock 'n' rollers including Bo Diddley and the Moonglows.

Chuck Berry

Charles Edward Anderson ('Chuck') Berry (b. 1926) burst precipitously onto the pop music scene in 1955 with his first record, 'Maybellene'. It was a novel synthesis that did not sound precisely like anything before it, and it introduced listeners to an already fully formed style of songwriting, singing, and guitar playing that would exercise a primal influence on virtually all the rock 'n' roll to follow.

Berry was born in California but grew up in St Louis, where he absorbed blues and rhythm and blues styles. He was one of the first black musicians to consciously forge his own version of these styles for appeal to a mass market—and he was almost certainly the most successful of his generation in this effort. Like many other black musicians, Berry also knew country music, and he found that his performances of country songs in clubs appealed strongly to the white members of his audience. He put this knowledge and experience to good use: 'Maybellene' was distantly modelled on a country number called 'Ida Red'. Nevertheless, the primary elements of 'Maybellene' trace their roots clearly to rhythm and blues: the thick, buzzing timbre of Berry's electric guitar; the blue notes and slides in both voice and guitar; the socking backbeat of the drum; and the form, derived from 12-bar blues structures.

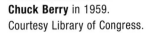

Chuck Berry in 1959.
Courtesy Library of Congress.

Listening To Chuck Berry's 'Maybellene' (1955)

What made 'Maybellene' sound so startlingly new? The explosive tempo, for one thing. While bands occasionally may have played for dancing at a tempo like this, no vocal-based rhythm and blues had ever gone at this pace. But Berry pulls it off, articulating the words with clarity and remarkable force. This brings up another essential aspect of the record's novelty and appeal—the lyrics. 'Maybellene' provides an original and clever description of a lovers' quarrel in the form of a car chase, complete with a punning invented verb form, humorous details, and a breathless ending in which the singer catches Maybellene in her Cadillac at the top of a hill—an ending that still leaves listeners room to imagine a wide range of sequels. And what could reach out to a young audience more effectively than a story featuring both cars and sex appeal?

In addition, we shouldn't miss the implied class distinction the lyrics make between Maybellene, in her top-of-the-line Cadillac Coupe de Ville, and the narrator, in his more humble, middle-class, but eminently functional 'V-8 Ford'. As the singer/narrator chases and finally catches the Cadillac (and Maybellene), there is a sense of the underdog's triumphing in the race, and the boastful claim of the first verse, that nothing could outrun his V-8 Ford, is vindicated. Cars have long been an important status symbol in North America—a song recorded by Bessie Smith in 1928, for instance, more than a generation before Berry composed 'Maybellene', called 'Put It Right Here (Or Keep It Out There)', described the singer's sexually underperforming lover as follows: *'Once he was like a Cadillac, now he's like an old worn-out Ford.'*

All the basic ingredients that would inform a string of successive, successful Chuck Berry records are present in 'Maybellene'. These elements became his trademarks: an arresting instrumental introduction for unaccompanied electric guitar; relentless intensity produced by fast tempo and loud volume; formal and stylistic elements strongly related to earlier rhythm and blues music; and witty lyrics, clearly enunciated and designed to appeal to the lifestyle and aspirations of Berry's young audience.

Form

The form of 'Maybellene' is clearly based on the 12-bar blues. The chorus adheres to the traditional 12-bar structure in every respect: three four-bar phrases; standard chord pattern; and even a traditional three-line poetic arrangement where the second line is a repetition of the first. But the verses, while 12 bars long, completely suppress chord changes, and thus feature no harmonic motion, remaining on the 'home' (or tonic) chord throughout while the voice delivers rapid-fire lyrics using brief, repetitive patterns of notes. Ironically, by eliminating chord changes and restricting melodic interest in the verses, Berry turns what could have been a static, purely strophic form into something more dynamic. Instead of a string of standard 12-bar blues stanzas, we hear an alternating verse-chorus structure that allows Berry to tell his story, and to build his song, in a more exciting way.

The stripped-down music of the verses focuses all attention on the lyrics—which is appropriate, as it is the verses that relate the ongoing progress of the car chase. Their repetitive melodic formulas allow Berry to concentrate on articulating the densely packed words; the continuous verbal activity more than compensates for the lack of musical variety. Actually, the verses build enormous tension, so that when the choruses at last bring some chord changes—basic as they are—there is a feeling of release and expansion. The pace of the lyrics also slows down momentarily for the choruses, which reinforces this effect of expansion and allows Berry to lean expressively on the crucial name 'Maybellene'. Yet, while the choruses provide variety and release, they create tension of another sort, as they postpone the continuation of the story being told in the verses. This same effect is created on a larger scale by the instrumental break before the final verse: variety and release on the one hand (and an opportunity for Berry to showcase his considerable guitar chops), along with a real sense of racing along down the highway, but tension and postponement of the story's climax on the other.

The Song/The Recording

In Chuck Berry's 'Maybellene', the song is the recording. When people think of or cite 'Maybellene', they are referring to Berry's original recording of it, which remains the ultimate, and really the only important, source material. The culture of rock 'n' roll centred to an unprecedented extent on records—records played on the radio, records played at dances, records purchased for home listening. Studio recordings thus increasingly came to represent the original, primary documents of rock 'n' roll, often preceding and generally taking precedence over any live performances of the material. Young people went to hear rock 'n' roll stars perform the hits they already knew from the records they heard and bought; on the internationally broadcast television program *American Bandstand*, singers came without accompanying bands and lip-synched their songs while their records played in the background. The issuing of sheet music was becoming an afterthought, an ancillary to the recording. In many future discussions, consequently, we will be discussing the song and the recording as one, rather than as separate entities.

The record opens arrestingly with the sound of Berry's hollow-body electric guitar playing a blues lick that literally sizzles with sonic energy. The impact of 'Maybellene' is in no small part due to the infectious rhythmic **groove** and texture established by Berry and a gifted group of sidemen, including the great blues composer and bassist Willie Dixon, who was an integral part of Muddy Waters's recordings for Chess Records; Jerome Green, playing maracas; and pianist Johnny Johnson, who may well have played a role in the creation of Berry's songs. Some credit for the overall sound of the recording must also go to Phil and Leonard Chess, who in their years of recording Chicago blues musicians such as Muddy Waters and Howlin' Wolf had learned how to stay out of the way of a good recording. They sometimes offered advice but never tried to radically alter a musician's style for commercial effect.

Amid the numerous elements borrowed from rhythm and blues and urban blues, we may hear in 'Maybellene' a prominent, very regular bass line, alternating between two notes on beats 1 and 3 of each bar (the tonic and dominant of the chord, respectively). The rhythmic feel of this bass line is stylistically much more suggestive of country music than of anything found typically in rhythm and blues, and its presence here points to Berry's knowledge of country music and to what Berry himself has identified as the country origins of 'Maybellene'. As we shall see repeatedly, rock 'n' roll music is often based on a synthesis of widely diverse stylistic elements.

Listening Chart: 'Maybellene'

Music and lyrics by Chuck Berry; as performed by Chuck Berry and His Combo

FORM	DESCRIPTIVE COMMENTS
Instrumental intro	Solo electric guitar 'hook' establishes characteristic sound (suggesting auto horns) and tempo.
Chorus	12-bar blues.
Verse 1	12 bars, without any chord changes; very fast pacing of lyrics.
Chorus	As before.
Verse 2	As in verse 1.
Instrumental break	Two successive 12-bar sections.
Chorus	As before.
Chorus	As before.
Verse 3	As in verse 1.
Chorus	As before.
Instrumental coda	Fades out.

After the success of 'Maybellene', Chuck Berry went on to write and record other excellent rock 'n' roll songs that became more and more explicit celebrations of American teenage culture and its music. 'Roll Over Beethoven' (1956) praises R&B at the expense of classical music; 'School Day' (Number 8 pop, Number 1 R&B, and Number 16 on the CHUM charts in 1957) describes drudgery relieved by an after-school trip to the 'juke joint', at which point the record becomes literally an advertisement for itself and an anthem for the music it represents; 'Rock and Roll Music' (Number 8 pop, Number 6 R&B, also in 1957) articulates the virtues of its subject, as opposed to the limitations of 'modern jazz' or a 'symphony'; 'Sweet Little Sixteen' (Number 2 pop, Number 1 R&B in 1958) wittily describes the young collector of 'famed autographs', coping with growing up, for whom a rock 'n' roll show becomes—in her mind, at least—a national party where all the 'cats' want to dance with her.

Berry's consummate statement on rock 'n' roll mythology is doubtless 'Johnny B. Goode' (Number 8 pop, Number 5 R&B, and Number 6 on the CHUM charts in

1958). Here he relates the story of a 'country boy' who 'never learned to read or write so well' (Berry's autobiography states that the 'country boy' was originally a 'coloured boy', but he opted to make his tale less racially fixed, recognizing the diversity of his audience and the potential universality of his myth). The boy's mother predicts his coming success as a bandleader—as one of pop music's greatest verbal puns embodies the dream of every teenager with a guitar and a wish to succeed as a rock 'n' roller—with parental approval and appreciation, no less.

The Electric Guitar

It is almost impossible to conjure up a mental image of Chuck Berry—or Buddy Holly, or Jimi Hendrix, or Randy Bachman—without an electric guitar in his hands. Certainly one of rock 'n' roll's most significant effects on popular music was its elevation of the electric guitar to the position of centrality. The development of the electric guitar is a good example of the complex relationship between technological developments and changing musical styles. Up through the end of World War II, the guitar was found mainly in popular music that originated in the American South (blues and hillbilly music), and in various 'exotic' genres (Hawaiian and Latin American guitar records were quite popular in the 1920s and 1930s). Because of its low volume, the acoustic guitar was difficult to use in large dance bands, and it was equally difficult to record. Engineers began to experiment with electronically amplified guitars in the 1920s, and in 1931 the Electro String Instrument Company (better known as Rickenbacker) introduced the first commercially produced electric guitars. Laid across the player's knees like the steel or Hawaiian guitars used in country music and blues, these instruments were called 'frying pans' because of their distinctive round bodies and long necks. By the mid-1930s the Gibson Company had introduced a hollow-body guitar with a new type of pickup—a magnetic plate or coil attached to the body of the guitar, which converts the physical vibrations of its strings into patterns of electric energy. This pickup later became known as the Charlie Christian pickup, after the young guitarist from Texas (1916–42) who introduced the guitar into Benny Goodman's band and helped to pioneer the modern jazz style called *bebop*. Despite Christian's innovations, though, few of the popular big bands introduced the instrument, and none allowed it to play a prominent role.

The *solid-body electric guitar* was developed after World War II and was first used in rhythm and blues, blues, and country bands—the country musician Merle Travis (1917–83) had one designed for him as early as 1946, and blues musicians such as T-Bone Walker (1910–75) and Muddy Waters were also recording with electric guitars by the late 1940s. The first commercially produced solid-body electric guitar was the Fender Broadcaster (soon renamed the Telecaster), the brainchild of Leo Fender and

George Fullerton. This model, released in 1948, featured two electronic pickups, knobs to control volume and tone (timbre), and a switch that allowed the two pickups to be used alone or together, allowing the player to create a palette of different sounds. In 1954, Fender released the Stratocaster, the first guitar with three pickups, and the first with a 'whammy bar' or 'vibrato bar'—a metal rod attached to the guitar's bridge that allowed the player to bend pitches with the right and left hand. Fender's most successful competitor, the Gibson Company, released a solid-body guitar in 1952, christening it the Les Paul in honour of the popular guitarist who helped to popularize the new instrument and the use of multiple-track tape recording. The first widely popular electric bass guitar, the Fender Precision Bass, was introduced in 1951.

Little Richard

The centrality of records to the culture of rock 'n' roll didn't negate the significance of live performances. Indeed, live performances disseminated via the new mass medium of television, or on the movie screen, assumed a new importance for performers of rock 'n' roll music, and individual artists and vocal groups sought to cultivate visual characteristics or mannerisms that would set them apart from others and encourage listeners to remember them. Chuck Berry may have had his famous 'duck walk' as a stage device. But no performer in the early years of rock 'n' roll was as visually flamboyant as Little Richard.

Little Richard in 1957. Frank Driggs Collection.

Richard Wayne Penniman ('Little Richard') (b. 1932) spent several lacklustre years as a journeyman rhythm and blues performer before hitting the pop charts early in 1956 with his wild performance of what would become his signature song, 'Tutti-Frutti'. Art Rupe, Richard's manager, sent Richard and producer Robert 'Bumps' Blackwell to New Orleans to record with famed houseband leader Dave Bartholomew, and noted engineer Cosimo Matassa, at Matassa's J&M Studios in 1956. After a frustrating day, in which nothing of value was produced, Blackwell overheard Richard playing an obscene song he called 'Tutti Frutti'. It was instant love for Blackwell, who nevertheless felt compelled to call in a local songwriter named Dorothy LaBostrie to 'clean up' the lyrics.

Based on the 12-bar blues, 'Tutti-Frutti' alternated nonsense choruses ('*Tutti-frutti, au rutti, a-wop-bop-a-loom-op a-lop-bam-boom!*'—and variants thereof) with non-specific but obviously leering verses ('*I got a gal named Sue, she knows just what to do*'), all delivered by Little Richard in an uninhibited shouting style complete with falsetto whoops and accompanied with a pounding band led by Little Richard's equally uninhibited piano. The record reached Number 21 on the pop charts in 1956. In retrospect, it seems surprising that records like 'Tutti Frutti' and its even more successful—and more obviously salacious—follow-ups, 'Long Tall Sally' (see listening chart) and 'Good Golly Miss Molly', got played on mainstream radio at all. It must have been assumed by programmers that Little Richard was a novelty act and that therefore nobody would pay attention to, or understand, the words of his songs. But teenage listeners in the 1950s certainly understood that Little Richard embodied the new spirit of rock 'n' roll music in the most extroverted, outrageous, and original way.

Any doubts on the matter would surely have been resolved by seeing Little Richard's performances in any of the three rock 'n' roll movies in which he appeared during the two years of his greatest popular success, 1956–7: *Don't Knock the Rock* (featuring Bill Haley, a sequel to *Rock Around the Clock*), *The Girl Can't Help It*, and *Mister Rock 'n' Roll*. Heavily made up, with his hair in an enormous pompadour, rolling his eyes, playing the piano while standing and gyrating wildly, Little Richard epitomized the abandon celebrated in rock 'n' roll lyrics and music. Both the sound of his recordings and the visual characteristics of his performances made Little Richard an exceptionally strong influence on later performers; the white rockabilly singer-pianist Jerry Lee Lewis was inestimably in his debt, and in the 1960s the English Beatles and the American Creedence Clearwater Revival—along with many other bands—played music whose roots could readily be traced back to Little Richard. Moreover, the lingering (and carefully crafted) ambiguity of Little Richard's sexual identity—available evidence suggests that he was bisexual—paved the way for the image of performers such as David Bowie, Elton John, and Prince.

Our representative example of Little Richard's music is 'Long Tall Sally' (see listening chart). Like most of Little Richard's songs, this one is built on the 12-bar blues. Like Chuck Berry and other artists who came out of rhythm and blues to seek pop stardom, Little Richard adapted the 12-bar blues structure so as to reflect the more traditionally pop-friendly format of verse-chorus. Here, the first four bars of each blues stanza are set to changing words, forming verses, while the remaining eight bars, with unchanging words, function as a repeated chorus. This simple but surprisingly effective formal arrangement is reflected in both identical and varied ways in many rock 'n' roll songs of the period; for examples of variations on this structure, see the listening charts for Elvis Presley's 'Don't Be Cruel' and for the Coasters' 'Charlie Brown'.

Listening Chart: 'Long Tall Sally' (1956)

Music and lyrics credited to Enotris Johnson, Richard Penniman, and Robert Blackwell, as performed by Little Richard and unidentified band

FORM	LYRICS	DESCRIPTIVE COMMENTS
Verse 1	*Gonna tell Aunt Mary . . .*	Underlying rhythmic and chord structure is that of the 12-bar blues, with the first four bars constituting the verse and the final eight bars the chorus; loud and flamboyant vocal style throughout.
Chorus	*Oh, baby . . .*	
Verse 2	*Well, Long Tall Sally . . .*	12-bar blues pattern persists throughout the song.
Chorus	*Oh, baby . . .*	
Verse 3	*Well, I saw Uncle John . . .*	
Chorus	*Oh, baby . . .*	
Instrumental break		Two 12-bar blues sections; intense saxophone solo reflects mood of the vocal.
Verse 2 — Chorus — Verse 3 — Chorus		
Conclusion	*We're gonna have some fun tonight . . .*	Extended chorus-like section; 12-bar blues structure.

Fats Domino

Antoine 'Fats' Domino (b. 1928), a singer, pianist, and songwriter, had been an established presence on the rhythm and blues charts for several years by the time he scored his first large-scale pop breakthrough with 'Ain't It a Shame' in 1955 (Number 10 pop, Number 1 R&B). In this case, mainstream success was simply the result of the market's catching up with Domino; there is no significant stylistic difference between his earlier rhythm and blues hits and his rock 'n' roll bestsellers like 'I'm in Love

Again' and 'I'm Walkin''. Domino himself remarked that he was always playing the same music, that they called it 'R&B' first and 'rock 'n' roll' later, and that it made no difference to him—although it surely did make a difference to him when the rock 'n' roll market catapulted his record sales into the millions and eventually made him the second best-selling act of the 1950s, right behind Elvis Presley.

Domino was born in New Orleans and grew up bathed in the rich and diverse musical traditions of that city. His distinctive regional style best exemplifies the strong connections between rock 'n' roll and earlier pop music. Jazz was a strong early influence on him, along with the R&B piano style of Professor Longhair (1918–80; real name Henry Roeland Byrd) and the jump blues style of trumpeter Dave Bartholomew's ensemble. Bartholomew became Domino's arranger, producer, and songwriting partner, and their collaboration produced a remarkable string of consistently fine and successful records. Their 'New Orleans' sound—also shaped significantly by the engineering work of Cosimo Matassa at Matassa's J&M Studios—was also widely admired and imitated among musicians; Domino played piano on hit records by other artists, and Little Richard recorded in New Orleans to use the city's distinctive sidemen and, thus, to capture some of the city's rock 'n' roll magic (Little Richard's 'Long Tall Sally' is modelled directly on Domino's 'Ain't It a Shame', both in formal layout and musical arrangement).

Given his strong links to tradition, it is not surprising that Fats Domino recorded a number of standards—in contradistinction to artists like Chuck Berry and Little Richard, who concentrated on novel songs and styles to appeal to their new audience. In fact, Domino's 1956 remake of 'Blueberry Hill' proved to be his most pop-

Fats Domino and his band, in a scene from the 1958 movie *The Big Beat*. Courtesy Library of Congress.

ular record, reaching Number 2 on the pop charts and topping the R&B charts. 'Blueberry Hill' was a Tin Pan Alley tune that had originally been a big hit in 1940 for the Glenn Miller Orchestra (with vocal by Ray Eberle). Domino preserved his own R&B style when performing 'Blueberry Hill' and other standards, however, thus bringing a new kind of musical hybrid to mass-market attention, and with this phenomenon a new and important musical bridge was crossed. We might say that, rather than 'crossing over' himself, Domino made the music 'cross over' to him. Smooth Tin Pan Alley crooning and uninflected urban diction were replaced by Domino's rhythmically accented full-throated singing in his characteristic New Orleans accent—and it certainly wasn't the sound of a sweet band backing him or shaping his own piano accompaniment.

Songwriters and Producers of Early Rock 'n' Roll

The relatively clear lines of division between songwriters and performers that characterized the world of mainstream pop music until around 1955 no longer held up in the early years of rock 'n' roll as the new hybrid musical form gained mainstream success. This is because the roots of rock 'n' roll lie with rhythm and blues and country and western music, areas of activity where performers often wrote their own songs and, conversely, songwriters frequently performed and recorded their own works. Of the five early rock 'n' roll stars we have discussed in detail, only Elvis Presley did not regularly write his own material. This diminishing importance of the independent songwriter represented another major shift brought about by the rock 'n' roll revolution; it eventually came to be expected that performers would be the composers of their own songs, and this led to a correspondingly stronger identification of artists with specific material. Here lie the origins of the mystique of the pop music personality as not merely an interpreter but, rather, a creator, a mystique that came into its own in the later 1960s.

None of this meant that important non-performing songwriters ceased to exist, of course. As we shall see in the next chapter, the early 1960s actually brought a renewed emphasis on songwriting as an independent craft, prior to the heyday of songwriting bands like the Beatles and songwriter-performers like Bob Dylan. And with the increasing importance of the recording itself as the basic document of rock 'n' roll music, another behind-the-scenes job grew steadily in importance in the later 1950s and the early 1960s: that of the record producer. Producers could be responsible for many things, from booking time in the recording studio to hiring backup singers and instrumentalists, to assisting with the engineering process. Essentially, though, the producer was responsible for the characteristic sound of the finished record, and the best producers left as strong a sense of individual personality on their products as did the recording artists themselves. When the producer and the songwriter were the same person (or persons), his or her importance and influence could be powerful indeed.

This was certainly the case with the most innovative songwriting/producing team of the early rock 'n' roll era, Jerry Leiber and Mike Stoller (both born 1933). Leiber and Stoller were not recording artists, but they were already writing R&B songs when they were teenagers. Eventually they wrote and produced many hits for Elvis Presley, and they did the same for one of the most popular vocal groups of this period, the Coasters; they also produced and did occasional writing for the Drifters, and the elaborately produced orchestral sound of these records in the early 1960s was possibly even more influential than Leiber and Stoller's previous records had been in the later 1950s. The team constructed what they called 'playlets' for the Coasters, that is, scenes from teenage life in the 1950s distilled into brilliantly funny rock 'n' roll records. Like many by Chuck Berry, the Coasters' hits were specifically about, and for, their intended audience—teenagers. An examination of 'Charlie Brown' will enable us to appreciate in detail this targeting of the teenage audience, alongside the vocal artistry of the Coasters and the behind-the-scenes writing and production artistry of Leiber and Stoller.

Pat Boone, Paul Anka, and 'Clean Teen' Rock 'n' Roll

As we noted earlier in this chapter, there were a number of reasons why Canadians who wanted to participate in the rock 'n' roll boom were compelled to travel south to the United States to find work, not least being the almost total absence of any rock industry infrastructure in Canada. But there were also cultural impediments involved, which worked against the development of such an infrastructure. To begin with, as noted earlier, Canada simply lacked the market size to justify the expenditures of capital required to launch a 'major' record label devoted to developing and fostering a national market for domestic rock singers and musicians. But, as we shall see in next chapter, rock 'n' roll was almost wholly identified with American mass culture in Canada, which lacked the same kind of prestige that British popular music, and the Western art music tradition, shared (this is not surprising given Canada's demographics in the 1950s, a time when Britain was the starting point for over 80 per cent of all immigrants to Canada).

Listening To the Coasters' 'Charlie Brown' (1958)

'Charlie Brown' presents an indelible portrait of a ubiquitous figure: the class clown. Although such a song topic would probably not have occurred to anyone prior to the 1950s, it certainly made an effective choice at a point when, for the first time ever, the biggest market of potential record buyers consisted of school kids—most junior high schoolers, high schoolers, and even elementary schoolers likely knew at least one 'Charlie Brown' in their classes. And the specific time period and culture of the 1950s is evoked through a sparing but telling use of then-current slang terms like 'cool' and 'daddy-o'.

From the first arresting vocal hook—'*Fee fee, fie fie, fo fo, fum*'—the record brims with unrelenting high energy. Like Chuck Berry, the Coasters were adept at delivering a dense, cleverly worded text very clearly at a fast tempo. The intensity of the Coasters' vocal style owes much to R&B, although certain comic effects—like the low bass voice repeatedly asking, '*Why's everybody always pickin' on me?*' and asking, '*Who, me?*' in the bridge—suggest roots going back to much earlier stage routines, and the low bass voice was already a staple element of rhythm and blues group singing style. Highly effective are the contrasts between passages that are essentially vocal solos, with occasional and minimal contributions from the rhythm instruments at the start of each 'A' section, and the subsequent passages where the full band offers a steady accompaniment and the saxophone engages in a call-and-response with the vocal group.

Form

'Charlie Brown' combines aspects of two different formal designs we have seen in previous musical examples. The song reveals its mainstream pop roots in its overall AABA structure. But the 'A' sections are each 12-bar blues stanzas. Furthermore, each 'A' section divides the 12 bars into a little verse-chorus structure of the type we have seen in 'Long Tall Sally' and 'Don't Be Cruel.'

The song's most direct kinship is with 'Long Tall Sally': four bars of verse, followed by eight bars of chorus. The kinship is that much more marked because of an additional similarity between the two: in both 'Charlie Brown' and 'Long Tall Sally' the 12-bar blues stanzas start off with vocal solos, and a continuous full accompaniment does not join until the chorus portions at the fifth bar of

the structure. The 'B' section, in contrast, is eight bars in length, providing a harmonic and rhythmic release from the succession of blues structures.

The Song/The Recording

As songwriters, Leiber and Stoller always had an interest in mixing elements derived from rhythm and blues music, which they knew well and loved, with elements derived from mainstream pop. This interest is evident in the form of 'Charlie Brown' itself, as we have discussed, but it may also be heard in certain details. For example, the 12-bar blues stanzas in the song are noticeably lacking in blue notes; Leiber and Stoller wrote a simple pop-oriented melody and just directed the bass singer to speak his solo line. But as producers, Leiber and Stoller brought in King Curtis, a Texas-born rhythm and blues saxophonist, to play on the record. In his 12-bar instrumental break Curtis emphasized blue notes, jumping in front of and behind the beat in a complex manner evocative of stuttering (this style, as much indebted to country hoedown music as to R&B, was also used successfully by the country and western saxophonist Boots Randolph). Curtis's 'yackety sax' sound links the Coasters' record to both rhythm and blues and country music—and it creates a humorous, almost goofy effect perfectly suited to the comic tale of Charlie Brown.

Apart from the sparkling clarity of the recording, there is only one prominent production effect in 'Charlie Brown': the artificially high voices in the bridge on '*Yeah, you!*' This effect was produced by playing a tape of normal voices at double speed, a device that was popular on novelty records at this time. Here we see the modest beginnings of the kind of artificial studio effects that would be found on more and more rock 'n' roll records as producers took increasing advantage of increasingly sophisticated recording studios and techniques.

Listening Chart: 'Charlie Brown'

Music and lyrics by Jerry Leiber and Mike Stoller; as performed by the Coasters with accompanying band (King Curtis, sax solo)

FORM	LYRICS	DESCRIPTIVE COMMENTS
A (verse)	*Fee, fee, fie, fie, fo, fo, fum,* *I smell smoke in the auditorium!*	12-bar blues stanza, divided into 4-bar verse (vocal solo) and an 8-bar chorus with full accompaniment and call and response between the voices and the saxophone.
(chorus)	*Charlie Brown, Charlie Brown,* *He's a clown, that Charlie Brown.* *He's gonna get caught . . .* *'Why's everybody always pickin' on me?'*	
A (verse)	*That's him on his knees, I know that's him,* *Yellin' 'seven come eleven' down in the* *boys' gym.*	As before.
(chorus)	*Charlie Brown . . .*	
B	*Who's always writing on the wall?* *Who's always goofin' in the hall?* *Who's always throwing spitballs?* *Guess who? ('Who, me?') Yeah, you!*	Bridge section.
A (verse)	*Who walks in the classroom cool and slow?* *Who calls the English teacher 'Daddy-o'?*	As before.
(chorus)	*Charlie Brown . . .*	
Instrumental break		12-bar blues stanza, constructed exactly like the 'A' sections, but with the voices absent and the saxophone freely improvising over the rhythmic and chordal structure; blue notes are noticeable in the sax solo.
Repetition of final A section		
Instrumental fade-out		

The older generations in Canada seemed positively appalled by rock 'n' roll, but perhaps not simply because of its libertarian *Zeitgeist*. This may have had as much to do with the fact that the genre was taken by many Canadian politicians, and by adult Canadians generally, as the soundtrack to Americanization. Continental integration—economically and culturally—has ever been a much ballyhooed political goal for some people in post-war Canada, as it has been the *bête noir* for others, and deep fears of 'Americanization' through cultural colonization have traditionally been at play in the country's political discourse.

Nonetheless, according to most chroniclers of the 1950s, rock 'n' roll was becoming dangerously acceptable, if not 'sanitized', by the end of the decade. Within roughly 18 months, in 1958 and 1959, a number of lawsuits, mishaps, and personal tragedies forced the genre's edgiest stars to the sidelines: Carl Perkins was seriously injured in an automobile accident; Elvis Presley accepted induction into the United States Army, serving in Germany until 1960; Little Richard was ordained and joined the ministry, and he publicly denounced rock 'n' roll as satanic; Jerry Lee Lewis was pilloried by the press over his marriage to his 13-year-old cousin; Chuck Berry was arrested for violation of the 1910 Mann Act, which made the interstate transport of a female for 'immoral purposes' a criminal offence, and sentenced to four years in prison; Ritchie Valens, Buddy Holly, and J.P. 'Big Bopper' Richardson died in a plane crash; and the rock 'n' roll business was publicly scandalized by the 'payola hearings'.

But the process of the 'sanitization' of rock 'n' roll was aided by another phenomenon, the rise of so-called 'clean teen' singers such as Pat Boone. Born Charles Eugene Patrick Boone in Nashville, Tennessee, in 1934, Pat Boone claimed to be a descendant of Daniel Boone, the famous American pioneer. Beginning his recording career in 1954, Boone's cover of Fats Domino's 'Ain't It a Shame' for Dot Records the next year—a song he often introduced to audiences as 'Isn't It a Shame', decrying Domino's 'poor grammar'—broke the *Billboard* Top 10 and established Boone as an international superstar (it also led to Domino's first Top 10 hit, when his own version of the song followed Boone's cover version up the charts).

Boone was the most prolific cover artist in the history of popular music; to this day no singer has recorded more covers than Boone. That he most often covered records by black R&B artists, and enjoyed success primarily on white pop radio stations with those covers versions, speaks to the racial divisions that still characterized the rock 'n' roll world in the 1950s, despite the genre's much trumpeted promise of integration. In fact, the rise of the 'clean teen' genre probably had as much to do with the division of labour between songwriters and singers that still dominated major record production in the 1950s as it did with rampant racism in the pop music industry. As Michael Godin, former vice-president of A&M Records in Canada, explains:

> You have to look back at the previous era in music to understand it. The big acts of the day, like Tony Bennett, Frank Sinatra and Doris Day, were not songwriters. The functions of the performing artist and the songwriter were very distinct. The idea that, 'Hey I write, record and perform my own songs' didn't really develop until the late 1960s. People weren't stealing ideas from other people and

incorporating them into their own songs. They were covering an existing song that had already come out. I think there is a tremendous misuse and misinterpretation of the term 'ripped off'. If somebody took a Willie Dixon song like 'Little Red Rooster' and re-recorded it, they weren't stealing it. It's not as if people stole songs and claimed they wrote them and took the publishing. In many instances, they were adding to the songwriter's coffer. (Cited in Potter, 1999: 27)

While the 'clean teen' genre was obviously not as innocent as Godin describes it, it was also not wholly malicious. In fact, it was business—nothing more or less. Cover versions sold well, so labels followed their usual business strategy of the time and saturated the market with as many covers as could be produced, until they failed to sell any more.

Paul Anka

Perhaps no 'clean teen' idol of the 1950s, and perhaps no pop singer in general, enjoyed such long-term success in the popular music industry as Canada's Paul Anka; and perhaps no other singer of the late 1950s so easily bridged the gap between the popular mainstream and rock 'n' roll. Born and raised in Ottawa, Ontario, Anka's career as a singer and songwriter officially began in 1956, when his father lent him $100 to showcase his songs for record labels and music publishers in Hollywood, California. Remarkably, the 15-year-old was able to generate some interest in his songs and, in September 1956, he recorded 'I Confess' (1956) with the Cadets for Saul and Jules Bihari's Modern imprint. The single failed to chart, however, and Anka was soon headed home, having failed to secure a long-term contract.

In May of 1957 Anka made it back to the United States—specifically, to New York City—and eventually secured an audition for Don Costa, a well-known producer and arranger at the prestigious ABC-Paramount label (Costa had cut his teeth as a session guitarist for the likes of Bucky Pizarelli and Vaughn Monroe before producing and arranging records for, among others, Frank Sinatra, Eydie Gorme, Lloyd Price, the Rover Boys, and, of course, Paul Anka). Costa signed Anka on the spot and, within six months, the two made popular music history when their debut single, 'Diana'—a sentimental ballad written for Diana Ayoub, Anka's old babysitter— reached Number 1 on the CHUM charts in August, and Number 1 on the American Top 40 in September, before selling over 10 million copies and becoming the second best-selling record of all time, after only Bing Crosby's 'White Christmas'.

Anka would earn the sobriquet 'the baby-faced Midas of Rock 'n' Roll', given to him by *TV Guide* in 1962, and over the next three years, from 1958 to 1960, he scored no less than nine Top 10 hits in Canada and four more in America, with rock 'n' roll 'classics' like 'You Are My Destiny' (Number 7, 1958), 'Lonely Boy' (Number 1, 1959), 'Put Your Head On My Shoulder' (Number 2, 1959), and 'Puppy Love' (Number 2, 1960) (the latter two songs were written about another 'teen idol' with whom Anka had a brief, public affair: ex-mouseketeer Annette Funicello). Anka was likely the first truly global pop star of the early rock 'n' roll era, becoming the first North American pop singer to perform behind the Iron Curtain, and he toured Europe, Japan, and

Australia (the latter was with Buddy Holly, for whom he wrote 'It Doesn't Matter Anymore', one of Holly's biggest hits). Anka broke all previous attendance records during an engagement at the Olympia Theater in Paris, and he appeared regularly on numerous American television shows, including *American Bandstand, The Ed Sullivan Show, Dick Clark's Saturday Night Show, Hullabuloo, The Perry Como Show*, and the *Tonight Show*, for which he eventually wrote the theme song.

Paul Anka: 'Clean Teen' idol of the 1950s. The Canadian Press.

Unlike most teen idols, Anka was able to reposition himself in the popular music market when the initial surge of his popularity receded. In 1962, the first year he failed to reach the Top 20 in either Canada or the United States, Anka smartly purchased all of his masters from ABC and signed a new contract with RCA. Having witnessed the Beatles perform when he toured England earlier that year, Anka became convinced that the days of the rock 'n' roll 'teen idol' were numbered, and he set about rebranding himself as a nightclub singer. This was a serious gamble, as no rock 'n' roll singer had shifted career paths so quickly, or so drastically, before. Nonetheless, in June of 1962 Anka became the youngest person to perform New York's Copa Cabana club, and lineups around the block were reported each night he was there. Later that same year Anka became the first rock 'n' roll singer to perform at a casino in Las Vegas. Over the course of the next two decades, Anka almost single-handedly invented the so-called 'Las Vegas–Lake Tahoe' circuit, and he played a key part in establishing a particular repertoire of songs closely associated with that circuit, including 'My Way' and 'She's a Lady', which were regularly sung by the likes of Frank Sinatra, Tom Jones, Wayne Newton, Sammy Davis Jr, and Englebert Humperdinck.

Discussion Questions

1. Why might it be better to consider rock 'n' roll an 'implosion' rather than an 'explosion'?

2. We know that Alan Freed was a relentless promoter of what he called 'rock 'n' roll' music, and that he was hounded by controversy for his efforts. What characteristics of the kind of rock 'n' roll that Freed promoted were controversial for parents and public officials, both in musical and social terms?

3. Why do historians consider the 'cover version' one of the most important *precedents* for the rise of rock 'n' roll? What are some current examples of 'cover versions'? Do listeners tend to value a 'cover version' differently from a recording of an 'original' song? Why do you think that is?

4. We know that many of the more important white R&B acts emerged from central Ontario. In your opinion, is there something about the repertoire that sounds distinctly Canadian? How might white R&B have sounded differently if it emerged from, say, Halifax or Quebec?

5. We know that the displacement of radio by television opened up a cultural space for baby boomers to fill with rock 'n' roll music. Has anything similar happened since then?

6. Ronnie Hawkins had to lie to get Canadian bands work in Canada. Why do you think that is? How have attitudes towards domestic culture changed/stayed the same in Canada since Hawkins's time?

7. What role did the CHUM charts play in fostering the notion of Canada as a market with distinct tastes and preferences? Should we consider the CHUM charts part of our national heritage?

Chapter Three

From Rock to Pop in Canada, the Rise of *Chansons Engagés*, and the Arrival of the Beatles, 1958–1964

The period from 1958 to 1964 is often described as a fallow time in the history of rock 'n' roll. By 1958 a number of important rock 'n' roll musicians had died, were seriously injured, were imprisoned, felt compelled to retire for personal reasons, or, as with Elvis Presley, were in military service—a series of unfortunate events that left a gaping void at the centre of the rock 'n' roll universe. Moreover, rock 'n' roll music had been identified by some Canadian politicians as not just a product but also a tool of 'Americanization'. The country, it seemed, was being annexed by Americans on every level, and rock 'n' roll was central to the culture wars. As Robert Bothwell explains:

> From every jukebox playing popular music, for every watcher of *American Bandstand* or *Trans-Canada Hit Parade* (playing American songs, though with Canadian performers), the sound of a common North American experience burst forth. Popular music sounded the same in Chicago, Vancouver, Moose Jaw, or Toronto, and Canadians rushed to buy the latest records and the latest styles that American pop stars produced. . . . Canadian parents worried, and Canadian pundits pondered: was rock 'n' roll uniquely bad, or was it just the most recent example of a deplorable and inevitable drift of the young into American mass culture? (Bothwell et al., 1993: 160–1)

'Americanization' didn't just monopolize the cultural conversation about popular music in Canada during the late 1950s, however. It also monopolized the political conversation. In 1957, when a series of oil pipeline contracts were granted by the Canadian government to American interests, a general agreement took root in Canada's business community that Louis St Laurent and his Liberal government had become entirely 'too friendly' with American Big Business; and a groundswell of so-called 'prairie populism', and some straightforward anti-Americanism, swept John G. Diefenbaker—a Tory lawyer from Saskatchewan—into the office of Prime Minister. Almost as soon as Diefenbaker took office, though, Canada was plunged into its worst recession of the post-war era. Thus, the project of cultural autonomy, which 'Dief the Chief' had promised on the campaign trail, was quickly jettisoned—it was simply cheaper to continue importing American programming than it was to finance Canadian productions.

Nonetheless, an infrastructure for popular music in Canada slowly took shape at this time. Numerous rock 'n' roll variety shows took to the airwaves on both the CBC and, beginning in 1961, on the newly founded CTV network; radio stations began to play Canadian records, even if they didn't chart in the United States; Quality Records, Tartan, and Sparton of Canada—only three of the many 'indie' labels that became active in the 1960s—released some of the country's first entirely homemade rock 'n' roll records; and Bobby Curtola, a pop singer from Port Arthur (Thunder Bay), Ontario, became Canada's first totally domestic pop star, breaching the CHUM Top 40 no fewer than 19 times between 1960 and 1965 without once making it to the Top 40 in the United States.

Meanwhile, in America, at least four major trends emerged that would prove crucial to the historical development of rock 'n' roll as the decade progressed:

- a new kind of social dance developed, inspired by 'The Twist' and a spate of other dance-oriented records, which gave rock 'n' roll its first set of distinctive movements and social customs;
- boomers began to assume positions of power in the music industry themselves, as writers and producers of rock 'n' roll songs;
- the Tin Pan Alley system of production was reinvented to suit these new rock 'n' roll entrepreneurs at the Brill Building in New York City, at Gold Star Studios in Los Angeles, and at Motown headquarters in Detroit; and, finally,
- new stylistic possibilities (and cultural contexts) for rock 'n' roll began to emerge from California, spearheaded by Brian Wilson and the Beach Boys, which prefigured the 'westward migration' of North American culture in general, and the American culture industry in particular, that occurred later in the decade.

From Rock to Pop: Solo Pop Singers in Canada

If critics are correct to suggest that, as Gregg Potter puts it, Canadians 'like their artists to go away and come back after they've become stars somewhere else', then

Bobby Curtola was the exception who proved this rule in the early 1960s. Curtola became a massive pop star in Canada without leaving the country, and without achieving a similar level of success anywhere else in the world. Curtola's career began typically enough: he started a high school rock 'n' roll band called Bobby & the Bobcats, before he ventured off on his own to record 'Hand In Hand With You' for Tartan Records, a local Port Arthur imprint, in 1959. Tartan's owners—the songwriting team of Basil and Dyer Hurdon—offered Curtola a management contract, which he accepted. The Hurdons subsequently wrote all of Curtola's major hits during the early 1960s, and they produced all of his hit records, including 'Fortune Teller' (1962), 'Aladdin' (1962), 'Three Rows Over' (1962), 'Indian Giver' (1965), 'Hitchhiker' (1965), and 'Mean Woman Blues' (1965).

Only 18 years old at the time of his major pop breakthrough, Curtola outperformed a majority of pop singers in Canada almost as soon as he began singing professionally. His rendition of 'Fortune Teller', for instance, which Tartan released in 1962, sold over two million copies in less than one year, and established the young singer as English Canada's first homegrown 'teen idol' in the process. 'There really was Curtola-mania', remembers Vancouver DJ Red Robinson:

> He was good-looking, he could sing, and he proved that you could have hits in Canada without Canadian-content regulations. We were all looking for a Canadian hero at the time and he was the one. There had been Paul Anka but he went south. Half those people standing onstage today wouldn't even be there if it wasn't for what Bobby Curtola did. And he stayed home in Canada—that was the thing.

Actually, Curtola was only one of numerous Canadian pop singers who dominated the pop charts in Canada during the early 1960s. Jack Scott, a Toronto native and label mate of Paul Anka's at ABC-Paramount, scored an impressive string of Top 40 pop hits both in Canada and the US between 1958 and 1960, including 'Two Timin' Woman' (1958), 'Leroy' (1958), 'My True Love' (1958), 'With Your Love' (1958), 'Goodby Baby' (1959), 'What in the World's Come Over You' (1960), and 'Burning Bridges' (1960). Les Ericson, Les Voght, and Terry Black enjoyed similar levels of success in Vancouver—Black eventually scored two hits for local 'indie' Arc Records with 'Unless You Care' (1964) and 'Poor Little Fool' (1965)—while Will Millar, a regular at the Depression Folk Club in Calgary, scored a few hits in Alberta before he formed the future Irish Rovers in 1963 (the group debuted at the Purple Onion club in San Francisco and then returned to Canada to host what would become one of the highest-rated television shows in Canadian television history). Shirley Matthews and Shawne Jackson held court in Toronto's burgeoning R&B scene, and Matthews eventually scored a Top 10 hit in the summer of 1964 with her only record, 'Big Town Boy'.

By 1956 most 'major' American record labels had already begun their search for 'the next Elvis'. RCA-Victor was perhaps most successful in this quest, securing Elvis himself from Sam Phillips; Columbia signed Johnny Cash and Carl Perkins away from Sun Records; Capitol signed Gene Vincent, who had greater success in the United Kingdom than in the United States; and MGM hired Conway Twitty. Quebec was not immune to this impulse. Almost immediately after Elvis broke in the province, Yvan Dufresne, a local entrepreneur from Montreal, began a search for 'the Québécois Elvis', eventually finding Michel Louvain, who was then only 19 years old. Louvain's first record, 'Lison' (1957), sold 80,000 copies in Quebec alone in 1957, establishing Louvain as the province's first teen idol (he was followed by Donald Lautrec, Pierre Lalonde, Ginette Reno, and Michelle Richard, daughter of the country singer, Ti-Blanc Richard (see Chapter 1). Louvain would continue to dominate record sales in the province until at least the mid-1970s.

Meanwhile, Robert Goulet, a French-Canadian pop singer from Alberta, was busy garnering international acclaim for his singing. Born in Lawrence, Massachusetts, Goulet spent most of his youth in Girouxville, Alberta. While still a teen, however, Goulet's mother moved the family to the provincial capital of Edmonton. Shortly thereafter, Goulet secured work as a broadcaster at CKUA, a local radio station, and he made his professional debut singing with the Edmonton Symphony Orchestra; he also appeared on numerous CBC television shows, including *Pick The Stars*, *The Consul*, *Sunshine Town*, *The Lady and The Logger*, and *Take The Woods* before he embarked on his career as a solo singer.

Robert Goulet, at the height of his popularity, on *The Ed Sullivan Show*, 11 September 1966. CBS Photo Archive/Getty Images.

While auditioning for a variety show in Toronto in 1960, Goulet met librettist Alan Jay Lerner and composer Frederick Loewe. They offered the young singer the role of Lancelot, opposite Richard Burton and Julie Andrews, in their hit musical *Camelot*; the original cast soundtrack, which featured more than one Goulet solo, stayed at Number 1 on the *Billboard* Top 40 albums chart for several weeks. Goulet capitalized on the show's popularity by securing appearances on *The Danny Thomas Show* and *The Ed Sullivan Show*, establishing himself as a household name across North America almost literally overnight. Not surprisingly, then, the crooner's debut album, *Sincerely Yours*, entered the Top 10 on both sides of the border, based largely on the strength of the hit single 'What Kind of Fool Am I?' The record would go on to earn Goulet a Grammy for Best New Artist of the Year in 1962.

On CBC-TV, vocalists such as Juliette Augustina Sykes, or 'Our Pet Juliette' as she was better known, commanded viewers in the millions, while Bert Pearl (singer and pianist for the extremely successful *Happy Gang*), Tommy Ambrose, Don Messer, and Don Wade all garnered similarly large followings as hosts of their own musical variety shows. From Manitoba came Ray St Germain, who capitalized on his brief stint as co-host with Lenny Breau of CBC-TV's *Music Hop* to position himself as Canada's pre-eminent rock 'n' roll spokesperson for the country's Métis community with songs like 'I'm Mighty Proud I'm Métis' and 'The Métis'. And on the new CTV network's *After Four*, 'youth lifestyle' experts shared the stage with performers such as Bobby Curtola and the show's house band, the Big Town Boys.

Chansonniers, Chansons Engagés, and the Rise of Separatism

Meanwhile, in Quebec, something much less 'pop' but no less popular was happening. A group of politically engaged pop singers, called **chansonniers**, emerged to the cultural fore, propelled to political and cultural relevance by the events of the so-called Quiet Revolution of the early 1960s—a political and economic awakening in Quebec, begun with the election of Jean Lesage as provincial Premier. In fact, a strike at CBC-TV's francophone network in 1959 set the stage for the Quiet Revolution. The strike unceremoniously closed a key avenue for the transmission of Québécois culture—broadcasting of Québécois music, art, and poetry was shut down almost literally overnight. As the strike wore on, without an end in sight, a group of *chansonniers*—including Raymond Lévesque, Jean-Pierre Ferland, Claude Léveillée, Clemence Desrochers, Herve Brousseau, Jacques Blandet, and Andre Gagnon—opened a *boîte à chanson*, or café, on Crescent Street in Montreal called Chez Bozo, after a popular song by Felix Leclerc entitled 'Bozo'. Calling themselves Les Bozos, the club owners doubled as a house band. Les Bozos quickly achieved widespread popularity in Quebec, establishing the *chansonnier* as 1960s Quebec's principal musical figure in the process.

Inspired by the success of Chez Bozo, not to mention Les Bozos, a number of entrepreneurs opened *boîtes à chansons* across Quebec. These provided an ideal proving ground for Quebec's youngest generation of *chansonniers*. *Chansonniers* were typically offered week- and month-long residencies at these cafés, as opposed to nightly engagements; thus, they were afforded long-term exposure to a large and loyal following, even as the younger generation of singers learned their craft on-stage. Gilles Mathieu, for instance, opened a *boîte à chansons* in Val-David, called La Butte à Mathieu, where Raymond Lévesque took up his first residency. Renée Claude first played a *boîte à chanson* in Quebec City called, appropriately, Boîte à chanson; and Gilles Vigneault got his start singing at L'Arlequin in Montreal. And as they achieved the financial security to match their popularity, many *chansonniers* opened *boîtes à chansons* of their own: Claude Léveillée opened no less than 50 in his lifetime, including Le Chat in Montreal; Tex Lecore opened La Poubelle, and Raymond Lévesque opened Le P'tit caporal, in Montreal; Raoul Roy opened Le Pirate in St-Fabien-sur-Mer.

By the time the strike at CBC was over, popular music occupied a new-found position of power in Québécois culture. Not simply a place for residencies, the *boîtes à chansons* quickly became a provincial touring circuit, thanks largely to the work of entrepreneurs such as Guy Latraverse. The *chansonniers* who travelled the *boîtes à chansons* circuit began to sing original songs, often about Quebec's quest for a national identity, the province's position within Confederation, and the concept of a distinctly Québécois culture.

The *Chansons Engagés*

By 1964 the *chansonniers* had created their own genre, known as ***chansons engagés***. These were urban folksongs with topical lyrics set in French and, eventually, *joual*— a Québécois slang form that borrows liberally from English—about the place of Quebec, and of the Québécois, within Confederation. Almost all were set in strophic form, and they generally featured only a strummed acoustic guitar or piano for accompaniment. Melodies were created to be easy to learn and remember, allowing listeners to concentrate on learning and comprehending a song's text, though traditional French folk melodies were recycled with much less frequency in Quebec than were traditional British and Irish folk melodies in anglophone urban folk communities active in Ontario, Vancouver, and New York. Thematically, *chansons engagés* most often promoted and celebrated the notion of a Québécois culture, even as they helped to create that culture; and many songs denounced the alleged sufferings and humiliations of francophones in anglophone Canada. These themes clearly animate Félix Leclerc's lament, 'L'Alouette en colere', for instance. In the song, Leclerc—'an inspiration for younger generations of Quebec *chansonniers* concerned with issues of identity and Quebec nationalism', according to Elaine Keillor (2006: 233)—tells the obviously allegorical tale of an 'enraged', 'dispossessed', and ultimately 'humiliated son' who finds himself sentenced to a lifetime of menial labour because 'his mother tongue' is 'not recognized' even 'in his own country'. Eventually, 'the big neighbour from across the river' must subdue the enraged French Canadian, 'breaking' his 'kidneys and his back and his head and his nozzle and his wings'. Raymond Lévesque's 'Québec, mon pays' provides another example:

When I was in (British) Columbia visiting friends
I wanted to buy a gift to give to my Margot
I shopped around the stores searching for something in beaver
But since I spoke canayen everywhere they were kicking me out
It's then that I understood that Quebec is my country

When I was in Alberta where I was selling sofas
I became interested in the immigrant Québécois
I had dinner with some Berniers who told me—goddamn!—
That over there our students did not have the right to their schools
It's then that I understood that Quebec is my country

When I was in Saskatchewan where I was building cabins
I met a girl that seemed nice and fun
I took her to the hotel; I took off my straps [and] she ran off
That's not how it works in Lac Saint-Jean
It's then that I understood that Quebec is my country

When I was in Manitoba in 1940 as a soldier
Obviously we were training only in English
But at night in the cantina in front of a little beer
If we spoke French, gee, they made a big fuss about it
It's then that I understood that Quebec is my country

When I was in Ontario where I was chopping wood
I was working as hard as the English, the goddamned!
And one day, I discovered that for the same work
They were paying me less and they were treating me like cattle
It's then that I understood that Quebec is my country

When I came back home I opened up the radio
I heard Claude Léveillé who sang with tears in his voice
Everywhere people spoke French
Everywhere people were nice
Nobody insulted me—Damn I felt good
It's then that I understood that Quebec is my country

The principal representative of the *chansons engagés* movement in Quebec was undoubtedly Gilles Vigneault. Born and raised in Natashquan, Quebec, Vigneault graduated from Laval University in 1953 and took a number of jobs—he worked as a prospector, sailor, librarian, and French and math teacher, among other things—before rocketing to fame in the late 1950s as a songwriter and then, in the early 1960s, as a singer-songwriter (albeit with obviously limited vocal abilities). While performing at *L'Arlequin* in Quebec City in December of 1958, Vigneault met a well-known *chansonnier*, Jacques Lebrecque, whose subsequent renditions of two Vigneault compositions, 'Jos Monferrand' and 'Jos Hebert', became instant classics in the genre. During his next residency, at the Boîte à chansons in Quebec City, Vigneault debuted two more original *chansons*—'Jean du Sud' and 'La Danse à St-Dilon'—both of which gained widespread popularity and cemented the singer-songwriter's position as the foremost *chansonnier* in the blossoming movement.

More than any other *chansonnier* active during the 1960s, Vigneault used his music as a political forum. Through his songs, Vigneault celebrated Québécois culture and advocated political independence for the province, even if he approached these subjects somewhat obliquely. In Vigneault's best-known song, for instance, 'Mon Pays' (1964), images of a typically harsh winter in northern Quebec allegorize the province's isolation form the rest of Canada, an allegory, it seems, that most Québécois readily understood: 'Mon Pays' served as an unofficial national anthem for Quebec until Vigneault was commissioned by the Parti Québécois to write an official anthem, 'Gen du Pays' (1976), which was sung at the PQ's electoral victory in 1976. 'Mon Pays' was commissioned by the National Film Board of Canada for Arthur Lamothe's *La Neige a fondu* (1965), and it won Vigneault the Prix Felix Léclerc in 1965 and top honours at the Sopot Song Festival in Poland later that same year, where it was sung by fellow Quebec *chansonnier* Monique Leyrac.

Despite the continued popularity of *chansonniers* like Vigneault, Lévesque, and Leyrac into the mid-1970s, by roughly 1967 the *boîtes à chansons* had become an endangered species in Quebec, as had the *chansons engagés* genre. A new rock-oriented approach to popular song was developing in the province, led by Robert Charlebois (see Chapter 4). For now, we turn our attention to concurrent developments in folk music in English-speaking North America.

▌Urban Folk and the Urban Folk Revival

The early 1960s was a period of explosive growth for acoustic urban music across North America. The baby boomers were reaching college age, demonstrating increasing cultural and political interest and awareness, and they represented an expanding audience both for tradition-based folk music and for newly composed 'broadsides' on the issues of the day (i.e., American and Canadian foreign policy, the testing and stockpiling of nuclear arms, racial bigotry and civil rights, the status of North America's Native peoples, etc.). Encouragement and a sense of history were provided by elder statesmen of the genre, such as Pete Seeger, whose careers in turn were reinvigorated by interest from boomers. By 1962 even the extremely popular Kingston Trio—whose acoustic folk repertoire almost always stayed within the safe bounds of tradition—ventured to record Pete Seeger's poignant anti-war song, 'Where Have All the Flowers Gone', unexpectedly scoring a pop hit with it. This attests to the increasing politicization of the urban folk movement at this time; and the success of 'Where Have All the Flowers Gone' doubtless paved the way for that of Dylan's 'Blowin' in the Wind', as performed by Peter, Paul, and Mary, the next year.

Within the community of urban folk musicians and listeners, rock 'n' roll was often typecast as a commercial and crassly manipulative genre. Thus, urban folk followed an independent course throughout the early 1960s, remaining an acoustic guitar-based genre aloof from the new styles and the large-scale changes that characterized much of the pop music of the time. The dour liner notes to the hugely successful first album by Peter, Paul, and Mary (1962) say it all, exhorting readers, 'No dancing, please!' But by 1967 electric instruments and drums had joined Peter, Paul, and Mary's acoustic guitars, and they were in the Top 10 singing—somewhat ironically, but with a firm bid for continuing relevance—'I Dig Rock 'n' Roll Music' (the record featured Canadian Skip Prokop, eventually of the 13-piece rock orchestra Lighthouse, on drums).

The individual most responsible for this shift was not Peter or Paul or Mary, but the man who had written their biggest acoustic hit, 'Blowin' in the Wind' (1963). He was also the man who almost single-handedly dragged urban folk music—with some people kicking and screaming—into the modern rock era. His name was Robert Zimmerman, though he remains better known by the moniker of his stage persona, 'Bob Dylan', which he legally adopted in 1962. But before there could be Bob Dylan there had to be Joan Baez, the first young star of the urban folk movement.

Joan Baez

Baez remains best known for her crystalline soprano singing voice and her distinctively rapid vibrato, and for the numerous causes in whose service she put her singing career. The daughter of a renowned physicist, Albert Baez, Joan Baez spent the better part of her childhood in various cities and towns across America, France, Switzerland, Italy, and the Middle East. As she has noted in several interviews, she never considered becoming a musician until she was almost 18 years old, when she accompanied her aunt to a Pete Seeger concert and was immediately inspired to pursue a career as a folksinger.

In 1958 Albert Baez accepted a position at the Massachusetts Institute of Technology, and he relocated his family once more to the Boston area. Joan subsequently enrolled at Boston University and, within a year, was playing concerts in the Cambridge area. Her residency at the Club 47 Mount Auburn in Harvard Square, and a record called *Folksingers 'Round Harvard Square*, which she and two of her friends made in the cellar of a friend's house, led to some local notoriety. But it was a chance meeting with Bob Gibson and the then reigning queen of urban folk, Odetta, that got Baez an invitation to perform at the 1959 Newport Folk Festival, where Gibson and Baez sang duets of 'Virgin Mary Had One Son' and 'We Are Crossing the River'. Their performance led to offers from a number of record labels, including Columbia, but Baez ultimately opted for a contract with Vanguard Records, which was a smaller label that she felt would afford her greater artistic licence.

Baez's first album, *Joan Baez*, was recorded in only four days in the ballroom of the Manhattan Towers Hotel in New York City, and was released in 1960. A collection of mostly folk ballads and blues, with the odd children's song and a Spanish folksong ('El Preso Numero Nueve') thrown in for good measure, the record was sparsely arranged, featuring only Baez's voice and acoustic guitar throughout. Despite its almost ascetic production values, the record nonetheless sold well, and it even managed to crack the American Top 100. Baez's next release, *Joan Baez Vol. 2* (1961), was certified gold the same year it was released, and garnered for Baez an appearance on the cover of *Time* magazine as the burgeoning urban folk movement's brightest star. Next the rebellious singer once more bucked convention, recording two 'live' albums of traditional folksongs, as well as songs written by such other folksong revivalists as Bob Dylan, Malvina Reynolds, and Phil Ochs: *Joan Baez in Concert, Part 1* (1962) and *Joan Baez in Concert, Part 2* (1963).

As a celebrity singer, Baez updated the figure of the folksinger-as-activist that Woody Guthrie and Pete Seeger popularized during the Great Depression and later. She championed the non-violent civil rights activism of the Reverend Martin Luther King well before her peers, beginning in 1958; and in 1962 and 1963 she withheld exactly 60 per cent of her income tax—the portion reserved for military spending—in protest over what was still only a 'police action' in Vietnam. Openly bisexual, Baez would also become an outspoken advocate for gay rights later in her career.

On her first fully national tour of America in 1963, which included free performances at numerous civil rights rallies and non-violent protest actions, Baez 'introduced' her new protege (and lover) Bob Dylan to audiences at each performance. The endorsement was resounding, and Dylan's star soon eclipsed Baez's. The two lovers would reign for the next 18 months as the 'king and queen' of urban folk, until Dylan rather brutally, and without explanation, rejected Baez for his future wife, Sara, while he and Baez were on tour together in Britain (the episode was captured for posterity by rock documentarian D.B. Pennebaker in his classic 1964 rockumentary, *Don't Look Back*). After her split with Dylan, Baez enjoyed a rare Top 10 hit in the UK with her subdued rendition of Phil Ochs's already subdued 'There But For Fortune' (1964), and a Top 40 hit in America in 1971 with a cover of Robbie Robertson's 'The Night They Drove Ole Dixie Down'. After these two hits Baez receded from the pop charts entirely, though she continues to perform.

Bob Dylan

Joan Baez's contemporaries in the urban folk scene included such gifted performers as Buffy Sainte-Marie, Gordon Lightfoot, Ian Tyson and Sylvia Fricker, Phil Ochs, Judy Collins, Tom Paxton, and Ramblin' Jack Elliot, to name only a few. Most noteworthy, however, was Bob Dylan, who first established himself as an acoustic singer-songwriter in New York City in the early 1960s. Dylan stood out from his contemporaries for two basic reasons: first, there was the remarkable quality of his original songs, which reflected from the beginning a strong gift for poetic imagery and metaphor and a frequently searing intensity of feeling, sometimes moderated by an almost cruel sense of irony; and, second, there was Dylan's own unique, if occasionally quirky, style of performance, which eschewed the deliberate and straightforward homeliness of the Weavers, the smooth and pop-friendly approaches of the Kingston Trio and Peter, Paul, and Mary, and the lyrical beauty of Joan Baez and Judy Collins—all in favour of a rough-hewn, occasionally aggressive vocal, guitar, and harmonica style that demonstrated strong affinities with rural models in blues and earlier country music.

In fact, Dylan's performance style was sufficiently idiosyncratic in the context of the urban folk scene, which took root first in Boston's Cambridge Square but then more forcefully in New York City's Greenwich Village and Washington Square Park, to keep him from becoming truly pop-marketable for years. His early songs were introduced to Top 40 audiences by other performers: Joan Baez, Peter, Paul, and Mary, Sonny and Cher, and numerous other performers who scored massive pop hits with Dylan songs in the early and mid-1960s. Still, it could be said that Dylan's own performances serve the distinctive intensity of his songs more tellingly than the inevitably sweeter versions of other singers.

Bob Dylan as urban folkie (c. 1964)
Courtesy Library of Congress.

Alias Bob Dylan

According to rock critic Stephen Scobie, aside from any one song in particular, 'Robert Zimmerman's first and most lasting artistic contribution is Bob Dylan himself.' What Scobie means by this is that the singer-songwriter now known as 'Bob Dylan' is actually a stage persona—no less theatrical or 'put on' than, say, Reginald

Dwight's 'Elton John' persona—concocted by a teenager from Hibbing, Minnesota, some time in the late 1950s, after having already been 'Elston Gunn' in his first professional gig, as a pianist on tour for Bobby Vee for a few months in 1959 (history-of-rock.com/bobbyvee; popentertainment.com/vee.html). One thing that is different about the Bob Dylan persona, however, is that nobody knows for certain—or, perhaps, nobody will say—precisely how it came to be, including Bob Dylan himself. In Martin Scorcese's recent study of the folksinger, *No Direction Home*, Dylan himself claims not to remember anything about the decision to change his name. Yet, in Dylan's own memoirs, *Chronicles Vol. 1*, he suddenly seems to recall changing his name after a series of events that, earlier in his career, he explicitly and repeatedly had denied ever happened. To be clear, this is not to suggest that Bob Dylan is a liar, or that he was any less sincere than his colleagues. Rather, it is simply a warning that historians must be careful in their dealings with a historical figure such as Bob Dylan, in large part because he has demonstrated so often in his career his talent for self-invention and self-mythologization.

Probably the best-known story about how Bob Dylan got his name has the young singer-songwriter naming himself after the famous Welsh poet, Dylan Thomas. But Dylan himself has flatly denied this on a number of different occasions. Another explanation has Dylan taking his name from an uncle named 'Dillon' on his mother's side of the family—but his mother's family name is Stone. Yet another explanation, shared by most Dylan biographers, posits Marshall Matt Dillon of TV's *Gunsmoke* as Dylan's primary inspiration; a café owner's mistaken spelling on a sign advertising a performance by 'Dylan' rather than 'Dillon' is said to have inspired the young folksinger to change the spelling. Yet another explanation comes from Dylan himself. In his recent memoir, *Chronicles*, Dylan claims that he considered the name 'Robert Allyn', in honour of a sax player he knew named David Allyn, before finally deciding on 'Bob Dylan' after seeing—not reading—a book of poems by Dylan Thomas. Whatever the case, it should be noted that Dylan Thomas was widely popular among young people in the United States during the 1950s and early 1960s and became mythologized as the embodiment of the poet living on the edge, both for the cadence and power of his poetry and for his dissipated, hard-drinking lifestyle, which led to his death in 1953 while he was on tour in the US.

The source of Dylan's name, however, is ultimately irrelevant. What is significant is simply that Bob Dylan, the folksinger-songwriter, went to enormous lengths to disguise his real identity and family history, even as he was openly disdainful of rock 'n' roll musicians whom he deemed guilty of artificiality and superficial pandering. If anything, then, as the critic David Hajdu writes, 'the irony of Robert Zimmerman's metamorphosis into Bob Dylan lies in the application of so much elusion and artifice in the name of truth and authenticity.'

In fact, Dylan spent his first few years in Greenwich Village 'trying on' a number of different identities. First there was Bob Dylan the 'Woody Guthrie jukebox'—a young performer so enamoured with his hero that some in the audience considered his earliest performances trite and overly derivative. Then came Bob Dylan the cowboy from Gallup, New Mexico, followed by the ex-carnival roustabout Bob Dylan, and, finally, Bob Dylan the last living descendant of the Sioux Nation ('I remember he solemnly gave us a demonstration of Indian sign language, which he was obviously making up as he went along', recalls fellow musician Dave Van Ronk). In an interview that appeared in *Newsweek* in November of 1963, Dylan told the influential critic Robert Shelton that he was an orphan, precisely as his parents—Abe and Beatty Zimmerman—sat a few blocks away waiting in the crowd assembled for their son's debut performance at Carnegie Hall. However, none of Dylan's 'creation myths' were as absurd as the so-called 'gigolo story', which he told to Robert Shelton in 1966: 'Sometimes we'd make 150 or 250 dollars a night', Dylan explained. 'Cats would pick us up, and chicks would pick us up, [and] we would do anything you wanted so long as you paid.' By 1966, though, Dylan was well known as a performer, and one has to assume that the young, and often playful, singer-songwriter was pulling Shelton's leg, as it were. It is not without reason that Dylan is portrayed in Don McLean's 'American Pie' as 'the Jester'. Nor was it purely accidental that Bob Dylan played a character named 'Alias', a mostly sullen, silent sidekick to Kris Kristofferson's Billy the Kid in the 1973 western, *Pat Garrett and Billy the Kid* (for which Dylan did the score, including 'Knockin' on Heaven's Door'), or, for that matter, that the 2003 film written for and starring Dylan was titled *Masked and Anonymous*.

Hammond's Folly: Dylan at Columbia Records

Signing a record deal with Columbia Records in 1961 to work with the label's legendary producer, John Hammond, Dylan did not initially fare well in the pop market with his first two records, *Bob Dylan* (1961) and *The Freewheelin' Bob Dylan* (1963). Thus, he became known around Columbia headquarters as 'Hammond's folly'. However, these records have since come to occupy a significant place in the rock canon, and they aptly summarize the musical tendencies of the urban folk movement in general, for which Dylan would soon replace Baez as the genre's primary figurehead.

One such tendency or 'convention', which can be easily heard in Dylan's early folk repertoire, is the notion that songs should be 'musical broadsides' about ongoing political struggles. In fact, Dylan's earliest songs for Columbia constitute a kind of historical record of the American civil rights movement in the early 1960s. His first protest song, 'The Death of Emmet Till', details the race killing of Emmet Till in Mississippi in 1955 (Till was shot in the head and dumped in the Tallahassee River after he bragged to strangers at a bar that he had a white girlfriend); 'Talkin' John Birch Society Blues' targets and ridicules the John Birch Society, an outfit dedicated to uncovering 'Reds' and 'Commies' in America; 'With God On Our Side' satirizes American military policy from the country's inception to its involvement in Vietnam; 'The Times They Are A-Changin'' served as a kind of catch-all anthem for the civil rights movement in general; 'Oxford Town' detailed the violent conflict that erupted after James Meredith, an African-American, enrolled at the University of Mississippi in 1962; and 'The Lonesome Death of Hattie Carroll' surveyed the terrible murder

of a black mother who died after being struck in the head with a cane by a belliger-
ent customer at a hotel bar in Baltimore ('when I order a drink I want it now, you
black bitch!' the patron allegedly yelled as he hit her).

Almost as quickly as he entered the political arena, however, Dylan withdrew from
it. By 1963 he had played his last protest demonstration, and he had written his last
protest song. Historians are of at least three minds as to why this is so. Some argue
that Dylan felt he had exhausted the civil rights movement as a market, and so he
turned his attention to the resurgent rock 'n' roll market. Still others argue that Dylan
considered the left to be as conformist and power-hungry as the forces they claimed
to 'counter' on the right, an explanation that Dylan himself is supposed to support
in the concluding lyrics to one of his first 'psychedelic blues' songs, 'Maggie's Farm':

> *Everybody tells me to be just like I am*
> *But everybody wants me to be just like them*
> *They say sing while you slave and I just get bored—*
> *I ain't gonna work on Maggie's Farm no more!*

This explanation seems all the more likely given that 'Maggie's Farm' was the song
Dylan used to debut his 'electric' sound at the Newport Folk Festival in 1965, to
resounding catcalls and boos. Still others insist that the blame lay with a rather para-
noid reaction to the assassination of President John F. Kennedy on 22 November
1963, Dylan coming to believe that he himself had become a target, given his prominence in the American left.

Listening To Bob Dylan's 'Blowin' in the Wind' (1963)

As a songwriter, Bob Dylan was introduced to many pop fans through a
series of covers by Peter, Paul, and
Mary, but most notably via their rendition of Dylan's 'Blowin' in the Wind'
from 1963. To this day, in fact, the song
remains one of Dylan's best-known.

The opening strophe of 'Blowin' in
the Wind' clearly reveals Dylan's gift for
concise, evocative, and highly poetic
lyric writing:

> *How many roads must a man walk*
> *down*
> *Before you call him a man?*

> *Yes, 'n' how many seas must a white*
> *dove sail*
> *Before she sleeps in the sand?*
> *Yes, 'n' how many times must the*
> *cannon balls fly*
> *Before they're forever banned?*
> *The answer, my friend, is blowin' in*
> *the wind,*
> *The answer is blowin' in the wind.*

The three successive questions build
in specificity and intensity. The first
question could imply many different
things having to do with maturity and
experience. The image of the 'white

dove' in the second question is one traditionally associated with the idea of
peace. With the third question, the subject of war becomes inescapable, and it
becomes clear that Dylan is asking, in
three different ways, just what it will
take before humankind develops the
maturity to put an end to war. What
ultimately makes 'Blowin' in the Wind'
so poignantly effective, though, is that
Dylan leaves the answer—and even the
issue of whether or not there is an
answer—entirely up to the listener (the
refrain *the answer is blowin' in the wind*
returns to the deliberate ambiguity of
the opening question). Thus, Dylan
encourages his listeners to think about
important social and political issues,
and in a particular way, but without
preaching. This strategy of simply asking questions effectively sets up the two
additional strophes of the song, which
are similarly structured as three increasingly pointed questions followed by the
same ambiguous refrain:

> *How many times must a man look up*
> *Before he can see the sky?*
> *Yes, 'n' how many ears must one*
> *man have*
> *Before he can hear people cry?*
> *Yes, 'n' how many deaths will it take*
> *till he knows*
> *That too many people have died?*
> *The answer, my friend, is blowin' in*
> *the wind,*
> *The answer is blowin' in the wind.*
>
> *How many years can a mountain*
> *exist*
> *Before it's washed to the sea?*
> *Yes, 'n' how many years can some*
> *people exist*
> *Before they're allowed to be free?*

> *Yes, 'n' how many times can a man*
> *turn his head,*
> *Pretending he just doesn't see?*
> *The answer, my friend, is blowin' in*
> *the wind,*
> *The answer is blowin' in the wind.*

Dylan's avoidance of any specific political agenda in 'Blowin' in the Wind' is
typical of many of his best protest songs
from this point in his career as a songwriter. One could even say that this is a
source of continued strength for his
songs, as it ultimately assures their continued relevance, despite changes in the
political climate. As is the case with
many of the finest folksongs—whether
traditional or newly composed—the
melody of 'Blowin' in the Wind', which
Dylan adapted from the traditional
African-American slave song, 'No More
Auction Block', provides a simple, functional, and immediately memorable setting for the words. In this strophic form,
notice how the melody makes each of
the three questions hang unresolved; a
final feeling of cadence in the melody is
delayed until we reach the 'answer' on
the last word of each strophe.

It is illuminating to compare Peter,
Paul, and Mary's cover of 'Blowin' in the
Wind' with Dylan's own performance
from *The Freewheelin' Bob Dylan* (1963)
LP. The folk trio performs the song with
a touching sincerity and simplicity; the
various questions posed in the lyrics are
sung by different numbers and combinations of voices, at varying levels of intensity, while the 'answer' is always provided
by Mary Travers's gentle yet plaintive
solo voice. One might initially find
Dylan's rendition monochromatic in
comparison. But his syncopation of the
melodic line—a performance approach

utterly lacking in the Peter, Paul, and Mary interpretation—throws rhythmic weight on the most pointed words in the song (such as, in the opening stanza, 'be*fore* they're *for*ever *banned*'). The resulting feeling of angularity, reinforced by the intense and 'unpretty' or rough-hewn timbre of Dylan's voice, arguably presses the listener to ponder the lyrics that much more seriously.

In addition to writing impressive musical broadsides, Dylan also quickly distinguished himself as a composer of more intimate but highly original songs about human relationships. Indeed, one hesitates to call a song like 'Don't Think Twice, It's All Right', from *The Freewheelin' Bob Dylan*, a 'love song'. If anything, the song captures an ambivalent or conflicted feeling about a previous heartache, which constitutes a rather more complex and mature approach to the vagaries of romantic love than was often heard in popular music at the time. The song is clearly an expression of regret over a failed relationship, but exactly how Dylan ultimately feels about the relationship remains, in classic Dylan style, entirely unclear. Does he mean it when he says 'it's all right', or is that simply bravado in the face of heartache? Or is Dylan being sarcastic? As is usually the case, it is difficult—if not impossible—to say. In any event, Dylan's gift for irony, to which we have previously referred, is exemplified memorably in the song's concluding lyric:

Now I ain't sayin' you treated me unkind
You could've done better but I don't mind
You just kind of wasted my precious time—
But don't think twice, it's all right.

Until now we have been stressing the innovative character of Dylan's songwriting, but he also maintained important ties with folk traditions as well. Many of his original compositions were modelled—either implicitly or explicitly—on the musical and poetic contours of pre-existing folk material. This is not to say that Dylan 'stole' the music for some of his best-loved songs; it was a convention of urban folk music that songwriters set new lyrics to old melodies, so that listeners could focus on the lyrical content of a song without distraction. Nonetheless, as we have already noted, the music of 'Blowin' in the Wind' is adapted from a traditional African-American slave song. And other examples of this practice abound in Dylan's early folk repertoire: 'Masters of War' (1963), a bitter indictment of the military-industrial complex, is based on the folk ballad 'Nottamun Town', which Dylan learned from fellow folksinger Bob Davenport while on tour in Britain in 1962; on that same tour, Martin Carthy, an English folksinger whom Dylan met after a performance at The Troubadour, taught him 'Scarborough Fair', parts of which appear in 'Boots of Spanish Leather'; and later that same night, Dominic Behan taught Dylan 'The Patriot Game', a song he used as the basis for 'With God On Our Side' (1963).

One of Dylan's most famous broadsides, 'A Hard Rain's A-Gonna Fall' (1963)—about the Cuban Missile Crisis of 1963, according to Dylan himself—is sung to the tune of the traditional English folk ballad 'Lord Randall'. But the similarities between the two songs do not end at the level of melody: both employ a strophic formal pattern, in which each strophe opens with a pair of questions addressed by a mother to her son, followed by the son's answers, and always ending with the same concluding line. Of course, we must stress that Dylan is never merely a mimic, and 'A Hard Rain's A-Gonna Fall' introduces a highly original structural device that has no parallel in 'Lord Randall', which we shall call the 'variable strophe': strophes of widely varying lengths, depending on the number of times a particular—in this case, the third—melodic phrase is repeated to changing words (the son offers anywhere from five to 12 answers to the individual questions posed by his mother in Dylan's song). Variable strophes are found in a number of Dylan's finest songs—most notably 'Mr. Tambourine Man' and, as we'll see in the next chapter, 'Like a Rolling Stone'—and they represent perhaps Dylan's single most lasting musical contribution to the rock tradition as a songwriter.

Yorkville Village: 'Your Last Stop on the Way to Somewhere Else'

While urban folk music flourished across Canada in the late 1950s and early 1960s, the cafés and coffeehouses of Yorkville Village in Toronto were the genre's geographic and cultural epicentre. Bordered by Bloor Street to the south, Davenport Road to the north, and Avenue Road and Yonge Street to the west and east, Yorkville Village was home to a thriving community of creative artists, student activists, and counterculture bohemians throughout the 1960s. As historians Robert Bothwell and J.L. Granatstein explain:

> Toronto's Yorkville was the centre of the action. Clubs, coffee houses, drugs, loud new music, boys with long hair, and a sudden sexual freedom created by the availability of the birth control pill all combined to create a special time and place. Older Canadians were not amused, seeing old values crumbling before their eyes. There were police confrontations with young protesters and Toronto's City Council tried its best to shut down Yorkville. It failed just as the city fathers did in Vancouver, Montreal and every city in North America. (Bothwell and Granatstein, 2000)

A surprisingly large number of Canada's pop music elite called Yorkville Village home in the 1960s, even if only for a short while. Residents included Neil Young, Joni Mitchell, Gordon Lightfoot, Buffy Sainte-Marie, David Clayton-Thomas, John Kay, Denny Doherty, Zal Yanovsky, Murray McLaughlin, and Bruce Cockburn, to name only a few. This is not entirely surprising since, at its peak, Yorkville Village was home to over 30 different coffeehouses and nightclubs, including some of the country's most famous: the Riverboat, the Mynah Bird, the Purple Onion, the Village Corner Club, the Half Beat, and the 71. Work was plentiful for folksingers in Yorkville like no other place in the country. In fact, as historian Martin Melhuish explains, if you were a Canadian folksinger in the 1960s, 'Yorkville was more than likely your last stop on your way to somewhere else.'

In Yorkville in 1965, coffee houses and jazz clubs such as The Mynah Bird were popular hangouts. N. James/Toronto Star.

Buffy Sainte-Marie: More Than 'Pocahantas with a Guitar'

Though she spent most of her life in the United States, Buffy Sainte-Marie has always maintained a close connection with Canada. Born on the Piapot Cree reserve in the Qu'Appelle Valley of Saskatchewan, the future musician, composer, educator, visual artist, and social activist was orphaned at a young age, and was adopted by Albert and Winifred Sainte-Marie, who brought Sainte-Marie to live with them in Maine and, later, Massachusetts. She graduated in the top 10 of her class at the University of

Massachusetts in 1962 with a degree in teaching and Oriental Philosophy, and would eventually go on to earn a Ph.D. in Fine Arts. During a return trip to the Piapot Cree reserve in Saskatchewan where she was born, Sainte-Marie was ceremonially adopted by the youngest son of Chief Piapot, Imu Piapot. A profoundly significant moment in her life, Sainte-Marie's adoption by Imu Piapot strengthened the singer-songwriter's resolve to use her music to advocate for First Nations rights.

By 1962, Sainte-Marie had already embarked on a successful career as a folk singer-songwriter. In keeping with her concern for First Nations life and culture, she made a point of performing at Native reservations as well as the more traditional folk venues such as coffee houses and concert halls. A regular of the Greenwich Village scene in New York, and of the Yorkville Village scene in Toronto, she often performed alongside folk's future elite, such as Leonard Cohen, Joni Mitchell (who Sainte-Marie introduced to future manager Eliot Roberts), and Neil Young. Sainte-Marie quickly gained a reputation as a gifted songwriter with broad appeal—her songs have been covered by artists as diverse as Chet Atkins, Janis Joplin, Taj Mahal, Elvis Presley, Barbara Streisand, Neil Diamond, Cher, Bobby Darin, Bobby Bare, Roberta Flack, and the Boston Pops Orchestra. Her debut album, *It's My Way!* (Vanguard, 1964), included 'Universal Soldier', Sainte-Marie's response to the horror she experienced when she witnessed wounded soldiers returning from Vietnam in 1963. British pop-folk star Donovan would take this song to the British and American Top 40 a short while later. For her efforts, in 1964 Sainte-Marie was named *Billboard*'s Best New Artist.

Sainte-Marie followed her debut success by releasing five more albums in quick succession: *Many a Mile* (1965), *Little Wheel Spin and Spin* (1966), *Fire & Fleet & Candlelight* (1967), *I'm Gonna Be a Country Girl Again* (1968), and *Illuminations* (1969). Though her material was by no means restricted to any one subject in the

Buffy Sainte-Marie, speaking at a forum prior to the 1998 Convocation at the University of Regina. She received an honorary Doctor of Laws degree from the university in 1996. University of Regina Photography Department.

1960s—if anything, her albums from the 1960s attest to the remarkable heterogeneity of subject matter in the singer-songwriter's ouevre—many of Sainte-Marie's compositions from the mid- to late 1960s and early 1970s represent early inroads made by a First Nations activist into the world of popular song. Tracks such as 'My Country 'Tis of Thy People You're Dying' (see below), and her concept album from 1974, *Native North American Child: An Odyssey*, remain hallmarks of the activist movement in pop culture. In fact, so incendiary were some of Sainte-Marie's songs that they earned her a spot alongside the likes of Eartha Kitt and Taj Mahal on a list composed by American President Lyndon B. Johnson of artists whose music 'deserved to be suppressed' (creative-native.com/biograph.htm).

As the 1960s became the 1970s, Sainte-Marie began to challenge prevalent stereotypes of First Nations peoples in North American culture. The most pernicious (and prevalent) of these stereotypes, according to Sainte-Marie, was the romantic 'Pocahantas-with-a-guitar' image of First Nations pop and folk musicians, which she countered in large part through her pioneering embrace of music synthesis technologies in the later 1960s. The singer used a Buchla synthesizer, which was an early modular synthesizer first built in 1963 by Don Buchla on a commission from composers Ramon Sender and Morton Subotnik, to record *Illuminations* as early as 1969. Only the year before, in 1968, Sainte-Marie had shocked many of her listeners when she released an album of country songs, *I'm Gonna Be a Country Girl Again*, embracing a music that was still generally associated with cowboy culture; recorded in Nashville, the album features such veteran session musicians as Grady Martin, Floyd Cramer, and the Jordanaires. Sainte-Maire was also an early pioneer of the digital movement in pop, becoming one of the first pop musicians to use Macintosh computers to record her music as early as 1981.

More recently, Sainte-Marie has taken up posts as an adjunct professor of digital music at various colleges, helped to found the 'Music of Aboriginal Canada' category of the Juno awards, and won an Academy Award in 1982 for 'Up Where We Belong', which she co-composed with Will Jennings and ex-Wrecking Crew arranger and ex-husband, Jack Nitzsche (the winning recording featured Joe Cocker and Jennifer Warnes, and was prominently positioned on the soundtrack for the Richard Gere film, *An Officer and a Gentleman*). As one critic summarized her accomplishments:

Buffy Sainte-Marie virtually invented the role of Native American international activist pop star. Her concern for protecting indigenous intellectual property, and her distaste for the exploitation of Native American artists and performers, has kept her in the forefront of activism in the arts for forty years. (creative-native.com/biograph.htm)

The Yorkville scene scored what was probably its biggest hit in 1963, when Ian and Sylvia debuted the Ian Tyson original 'Four Strong Winds'; Bobby Bare would take the song to the Top 10 of the CHUM charts in December of 1964. Joni Mitchell, perhaps Canada's most successful female singer-songwriter of the rock era, debuted her wildly successful 'Both Sides Now' and 'The Circle Game' while she was still a resident of the village; and the latter song was a response to Neil Young's 'Sugar Mountain', which he performed often during his stay in Yorkville. As well, Buffy Sainte-Marie's 'Universal Soldier', a major hit for Donovan in Britain, was one of the first songs of the still burgeoning anti-war movement to come from the Yorkville district. And Sainte-Marie also positioned herself as an important advocate for North America's Aboriginal peoples, her best-known protest songs on the topic being 'My Country 'Tis of Thy People You're Dying', 'Soldier Blue', and 'Now That the Buffalo's Gone'. In the former song, from her *Native North American Child: An Odyssey* LP, Sainte-Marie outlines a series of complaints about the ongoing mistreatment of Amerindians, including their representation in films, their mistreatment at residential schools, their erasure from official history books, and the ongoing threat of assimilation. The record is arguably one of the first to explore these themes.

With a refrain that clearly plays on the American patriotic song, 'My Country 'Tis of Thee', Sainte-Marie's parody begins with a dispassionate survey of what the singer insists is an emerging awakening of interest in the actual lives of North America's Native peoples, in express opposition to the image favoured in Hollywood cowboy-and-Indian Westerns from the time:

> *Now that your big eyes have finally opened*
> *Now that you're wondering how must they feel*
> *Meaning them that you've chased across America's movie screens*
> *Now that you're wondering 'how can it be real?'*
> *The ones you've called colourful, noble and proud*
> *In your school propaganda*
> *They starve in their splendour?*
> *You've asked for my comment, I simply will render—*
> *My country 'tis of thy people you're dying*

Next, Sainte-Marie addresses the issue of residential schools from the Aboriginal perspective. Residential schools predate Confederation in Canada, though they spread in number after the Indian Act of 1876 obliged the Canadian government to 'provide an education' for Aboriginal peoples in Canada, and to 'assist with their integration into the broader Canadian society'. Located in every province and territory of Canada save Prince Edward Island, New Brunswick, and Newfoundland, the histories provided in residential schools stressed European over Native North American educational concerns, and, according to Sainte-Marie, resulted in a general erasure of Amerindians from history:

> *Now that the longhouses breed superstition*
> *You force us to send our toddlers away*
> *To your schools where they're taught to despise their traditions*
> *Forbid them their languages, then further say*

That American history really began
When Columbus set sail out of Europe, then stress
That the nation of leeches that conquered this land
Are the biggest and bravest and boldest and best.
And yet where in your history books is the tale
Of the genocide basic to this country's birth
Of the preachers who lied, how the Bill of Rights failed,
How a nation of patriots returned to their earth?
And where will it tell of the Liberty Bell
As it rang with a thud o'er Kinzua mud
And of brave Uncle Sam in Alaska this year?
My country 'tis of thy people you're dying

In the song's third strophe, Sainte-Marie details more 'war crimes', including the early use of biological warfare in the United States. Indeed, the British had used smallpox-infected blankets in an attempt to kill the Mi'kmaq in Nova Scotia more than a century prior to the events described in the song:

Hear how the bargain was made for the West:
With her shivering children in zero degrees,
Blankets for your land, so the treaties attest
Oh well, blankets for land is a bargain indeed,
And the blankets were those Uncle Sam had collected
From smallpox-diseased dying soldiers that day.
And the tribes were wiped out and the history books censored,
A hundred years of your statesmen have felt it's better this way.
And yet a few of the conquered have somehow survived,
Their blood runs the redder though genes have paled.
From the Grand Canyon's caverns to craven sad hills
The wounded, the losers, the robbed sing their tale.
From Los Angeles County to upstate New York
The white nation fattens while others grow lean;
Oh the tricked and evicted they know what I mean
My country 'tis of thy people you're dying

Though the song can hardly be said to end on a hopeful note, Sainte-Marie concludes the song with a call for change, acknowledging at least the possibility that some listeners may come to understand that '*their poverty's profiting you*':

Now that the pride of the sires receives charity,
Now that we're harmless and safe behind laws,
Now that my life's to be known as your heritage,
Now that even the graves have been robbed,
Now that our own chosen way is a novelty

Hands on our hearts we salute you your victory,
Choke on your blue white and scarlet hypocrisy
Pitying the blindness that you've never seen
That the eagles of war whose wings lent you glory
They were never no more than carrion crows
Pushed the wrens from their nest, stole their eggs, changed their story
The mockingbird sings it, it's all that he knows.
'Ah what can I do?' say a powerless few
With a lump in your throat and a tear in your eye
Can't you see that their poverty's profiting you?
My country 'tis of thy people you're dying

Perhaps it comes as no surprise to realize that Sainte-Marie is alleged to have been blacklisted in the US during the late 1960s and 1970s.

▌Producers, Arrangers, and Early Sixties Ephemera

Besides urban folk music coming to the fore in the late 1950s and early 1960s, at a time of great social unrest in North America, at the more 'popular' end of the pop–rock spectrum a number of changes could be seen: young baby-boomer producers and arrangers arrived on the scene, dance fads, like 'the stroll', came and went, a major new sound came out of Detroit, and a mellow yet upbeat sound appeared out of California.

The Twist and Social Dance

'The Twist' began its popular career inauspiciously, as the 'B' side of a single produced by the veteran rhythm and blues group, Hank Ballard and the Midnighters. Ballard was convinced that he had written a smash hit with 'The Twist', a teen-oriented rock 'n' roll song using a 12-bar blues structure; it celebrated a simple hip-swivelling dance step that was gaining some popularity among young African Americans. But the decision-makers at Ballard's indie label, King Records, didn't agree. The label promoted the other side of the record instead—a perfectly fine but more old-fashioned R&B ballad called 'Teardrops on Your Letter'.

Somebody at Parkway Records—another indie label headquartered in Philadelphia—must have paid serious attention to that 'B' side of 'Teardrops on Your Letter'. Since Parkway was based in Philadelphia, its artists had particularly easy access to *American Bandstand*, the teenage 'dance party' show hosted by Dick Clark. Thus, Chubby Checker, an 18-year-old chicken plucker turned singer on the Parkway roster, cut a cover of Hank Ballard's 'The Twist' for Parkway in 1960, which *American Bandstand* and Parkway promoted all the way to Number 1 on the pop charts in the US; the track went to Number 2 on the CHUM charts, kept from Number 1 by Elvis Presley's 'It's Now or Never'. The next year, in 1961, 'The Twist'

In 1961 everybody did the twist! Teenagers on *American Bandstand*. Courtesy Library of Congress.

Chubby Checker (centre), with country singer **Conway Twitty** (left) and *American Bandstand* host **Dick Clark**. Courtesy Library of Congress.

shot back up the charts to top the Top 40 on both sides of the border. This feat—scoring Number 1 on two separate chart runs—has been accomplished by only two records in the history of the pop charts; that the other one is Bing Crosby's 'White Christmas' gives some indication of the extraordinary level of popularity of both the twist as a dance and 'The Twist' as a record.

The twist was essentially an individual, non-contact 'free-form' dance, without any real steps. Although it was generally done by a boy-and-girl couple facing one another, there was no inherent reason why it had to be restricted to this format; it could be performed by any number of people—including one—in any dance floor pattern, and in any gender combination. Soon adults of all ages, classes, and races were doing the twist, along with teenagers. In turn, the dance's popularity and widespread acceptance brought rock 'n' roll music to a significantly broader audience than ever before; thanks largely to the broad demographic appeal of the twist, rock 'n' roll became an accepted fact of North American social life. As Douglas Owram (1996) explains:

> The Twist and other crazes of the early sixties demonstrated how ideas could reach out and galvanize youth. Fad after fad, dance after dance, swept across the continent, transmitted by Dick Clark and by hundreds of radio shows to parties and high-school gyms. Dances invented in Philadelphia or Los Angeles in July would be well known in Toronto or Edmonton by September. By then, of course, a new dance was surfacing in California. Finally, by the early 1960s, rock and roll had overcome all resistance. Only the most diehard of parents now tried to prevent their teenagers from listening to rock. This victory of teenage culture over adult resistance demonstrated something only dimly understood at the time—if the youth culture of North America wanted something, it would be very hard to resist. The infrastructure of the youth rebellion was in place long before the youth knew they wanted to rebel.

Clubs called *discotheques*—dedicated to the twist and other free-form dances that followed in its wake (i.e., the pony, the mashed potatoes, the monkey, and countless others)—sprang up across North America in the wake of Chubby Checker's success. One of the most famous of these clubs, New York's Peppermint Lounge, gave its name to one of the biggest hits of early 1962, 'Peppermint Twist', recorded by the club's house band, Joey Dee and the Starlighters. Live rock 'n' roll shows began to include female 'go-go' dancers along with the singing acts. And, in the later 1960s, these dancers also began to be featured—with or without their clothes—in clubs where pre-recorded rock music was played.

Many other popular songs of the early 1960s were dance-oriented. To cite only a few examples: Chubby Checker recorded 'Let's Twist Again' in 1961; teenager Dee Dee Sharp cut a duet with Chubby Checker, 'Slow Twistin'', as well as 'Mashed Potato Time' (both 1962) and 'Do the Bird' (1963); songwriter Carole King tapped her babysitter, Little Eva (Eva Narcissus Boyd), to record her song 'The Loco-Motion' in 1962; and the Motown group the Miracles sang about 'Mickey's Monkey' in 1963. For the most part, these dance songs were catchy and functional, and they tended not to break new musical or lyrical ground. Simple verse-chorus forms predominated. Nonetheless, a few of these songs have retained the affection of a large public for a surprisingly long time. Chubby Checker, for instance, joined with the rap group the Fat Boys in a successful revival of 'The Twist' (subtitled 'Yo, Twist!') in 1988; and 'The Loco-Motion' was a Number 1 song for the hard-rock group Grand Funk in 1974 and for the Australian singer Kylie Minogue in 1988.

Phil Spector and Philles Records

As we have seen, many teenagers achieved success as recording artists in the early years of rock 'n' roll. At the age of 17, Phil Spector (b. 1940) had a Number 1 record as a member of a vocal group, the Teddy Bears, whose hit song 'To Know Him Is To Love Him' he composed and produced (Spector also played guitar and piano on the record, which was the first one he ever made!). It may initially seem surprising, then, that Spector elected to emulate 'behind the scenes' songwriters and producers such as Jerry Leiber and Mike Stoller, with whom he apprenticed, rather than performers like Chuck Berry and Buddy Holly. Nonetheless, by the early 1960s, Spector had established himself as a songwriter-producer, working behind the scenes of rock 'n' roll rather than in its spotlight.

Phil Spector in 1965. Courtesy Library of Congress.

By the time he was 21, Spector was in charge of his own independent label, Philles Records—and he brought a new depth of meaning to the phrase 'in charge'. Working with personally selected songwriters—and often serving as a collaborator in their writing—and with hand-picked vocalists, instrumentalists, arrangers, and engineers, Spector supervised every aspect of a record's production. His level of involvement, and his obsession with detail, became legendary; consequently, a Philles record has a distinctive kind of sonority, tied more closely to Spector's personal talents and vision than to the contributions of other songwriters, technicians, or, even, of the actual performers.

Spector's sound, called the 'Wall of Sound' by critics, was at once remarkably dense and remarkably clear. He achieved this effect by having multiple instruments—pianos, guitars, and so forth—double, triple, and sometimes even quadruple each individual part in the arrangement, and by using huge amounts of echo, all the while carefully controlling the overall balance of the record so that the vocals were pushed clearly to the front. The thick texture and the presence of strings on these records led them to be called 'teenage symphonies'. A perfect example is the Ronettes 'Be My Baby', to be discussed in detail shortly. However, Spector explored many different types of sound textures on his records, and a record like the Crystals' 'Uptown', also discussed below, has a decidedly different and more intimate—while no less impressive—impact.

In general, Spector preferred to work with vocal groups, and his output as a producer helped assure—as a result of both its quality and its influence—that the early 1960s were a 'golden age' for rock 'n' roll vocal groups. To list the songwriters with whom Spector worked is to list some of the most prodigious talents of the early 1960s, including the teams of Carole King and Gerry Goffin, Barry Mann and Cynthia Weil, and Jeff Barry and Ellie Greenwich. For these and many other aspiring songwriters of the time, New York's Brill Building (at 1619 Broadway) served as a base of operations, where they worked in little cubicles with pianos, all packed tightly together, turning out songs for a large number of artists and (mostly indie) labels. The successful songwriters were often working with a number of different artists, producers, and labels at the same time, and consequently could hope to have several hits on the charts simultaneously; the regular work at a stable location and the promise of considerable royalty income made this type of work seem both more reliable and more potentially lucrative than that of performers.

Like Spector, a large proportion of the Brill Building songwriters tailored their output to vocal groups and many of the resulting records remain classics of their period. The Drifters performed 'Save the Last Dance for Me' by Doc Pomus and Mort Shuman (Number 1, 1960), 'Up On the Rood' by Goffin and King (Number 5, 1963), and 'On Broadway' by Mann and Weil and Leiber and Stoller (Number 9, 1963); the Shirelles—one of the first successful girl groups—recorded 'Will You Love Me Tomorrow?' by Goffin and King (Number 1, 1961); the Dixie Cups sang 'Chapel of Love' by Barry and Greenwich and Spector (Number 1, 1964); and the list could go on and on. Talented hopefuls flocked to the Brill Building. In addition to those already mentioned, Neil Diamond and Neil Sedaka both got their start as writers there.

Phil Spector retired from steady writing and production work in 1966, after Ike and Tina Turner's 'River Deep, Mountain High' failed to chart. But he has periodically resurfaced to work on special projects that attract his interest. The best-known of these projects involved the Beatles; he worked on the last album released by the group, *Let It Be* (1970), and then assisted individual members with solo albums throughout the early and mid-1970s, including George Harrison's *All Things Must Pass* and John Lennon's earliest solo efforts. More recently, Spector was arrested for the murder of Lana Clarkson, an ex-model he met at a bar and brought back to his house, though his first trial ended in a hung jury on 26 September 2007 (Spector is currently seeking a new lawyer for his retrial, which is set to start late in 2008).

Listening To Two Phil Spector Productions: The Ronettes' 'Be My Baby' (1963) and the Crystals' 'Uptown' (1962)

'Be My Baby', composed by Phil Spector, Ellie Greenwich, and Jeff Barry, performed by the Ronettes (Number 2, 1963); 'Uptown', composed by Barry Mann and Cynthia Weil, performed by the Crystals (Number 13, 1962)

'Be My Baby' was one of the biggest hits among the many produced by Spector, and it remains a favourite to this day on 'oldies' radio. With its employment of a full orchestral string section, pianos, an array of rhythm instruments, and a background chorus behind the lead vocal, it is an opulent 'teenage symphony' and a fine illustration of Spector's 'wall of sound' at full tilt. To be sure, the arrangement and production give this record its individual and enduring character. As a composition, the song itself is a simple if effective vehicle, expressing the most basic romantic sentiments in a straightforward verse-chorus framework. But the listener is hooked from the first, as an aggressive, distinctive rhythmic pattern on the solo drum gives the record its beat from the outset and draws us immediately into the song. (Notice also the spectacular effect achieved by the surprise recurrence of this drum introduction just before the final repetitions of the song's chorus; this sudden crack in the wall of sound has an explosive impact.)

'Uptown' is an earlier, very different Philles record (one of the first to be issued) that serves well to illustrate another aspect of Spector's production talents. 'Uptown' is a song quite unlike 'Be My Baby', and Spector appropri-ately provided it with a highly individual arrangement and production. Although 'Uptown' uses orchestral strings and percussion effects in as sophisticated a manner as 'Be My Baby', the earlier song conveys a much more open, spacious feeling, as if illustrating in sound the relief experienced by the protagonist when he leaves work each evening and goes uptown.

'Uptown' deals with class inequalities and economic injustice; the fact that it does this gently makes it no less remarkable for 1962, when pop songs on such subjects were virtually non-existent. (These subjects would have been regarded as appropriate for urban folk music at this time, but not for the pop market; see Chapter 4.) The hero of the song works downtown, where he 'don't get no breaks', and it is only when he comes uptown in the evening to his lover's 'tenement', where they 'don't have to pay much rent', that he can feel like a 'king' with the world 'at his feet'. The contrast between downtown and uptown is captured in the music as well. The downtown sections are in a **minor** key (also unusual for this period), while the uptown sections move to a **major** key. Note, also, the striking effect of the flexible tempo of the opening section on the record, which helps establish the unusual atmosphere and functions as a kind of atypical **hook**, by setting up a high degree of anticipation in the listener. The suspense is relieved when a steady tempo is established at the first occurrence of the word 'uptown'.

Spector recorded 'Uptown' in New York. Given his own New York background, which he shared with the songwriters Mann and Weil, it is hard to escape the conviction that 'Uptown' is indeed about New York, where uptown and downtown Manhattan exemplify the economic and class distinctions depicted in the lyrics. Furthermore, given the many Spanish-sounding features of this recording, one suspects that the specific uptown location is probably New York's Spanish Harlem, a largely Puerto Rican enclave that had gained pop music notoriety just a year before the release of 'Uptown' through a song actually called 'Spanish Harlem'—a Top 10 hit for Ben E. King that was co-written by Phil Spector himself.

Several factors contribute to the general Latin feeling of 'Uptown'. (Like so much pop music, 'Uptown' is concerned with the general evocation of an 'exotic' locale, not with any kind of ethnomusicological accuracy. The exotic stylistic effects in 'Uptown' are actually not specifically characteristic of Puerto Rican music at all.) The ornate guitar figures heard as accompaniment to the opening verse are obviously reminiscent of flamenco guitar style. The prominent use of castanets (also present in 'Be My Baby', but just as part of the wall of sound, not as a specifically evocative presence) for percussion and the general rhythmic feeling of Latin American dance throughout the record (aspects of *baion* rhythm in the accompaniment, and aspects of Cuban *bolero* rhythm in the song's melody) also contribute strongly to the exotic coloration of 'Uptown'. We dwell on this because 'Uptown' has to serve as the basic example here of an important trend—the incorporation of Latin American elements into the fabric of 1960s rock 'n' roll. The trend is also clearly evident in 'Spanish Harlem' and in many records of the early 1960s by the Drifters (the most famous of which is 'Save the Last Dance for Me').

Philles Records helped establish a new and important model for the production and marketing of pop records. Many indie companies, mimicking the practice of major labels with earlier styles of pop music, rushed as many records as they could into the rock 'n' roll market, often without much thought for quality control, hoping only for the occasional hit. In contrast, as would be expected from the description provided above, Phil Spector turned out an exceptionally small number of records—about 20 in a two-year period—an astoundingly large percentage of which were hits. The increasingly high-profile of record producers through the later 1960s and up to the present—one need only think of George Martin's work with the Beatles, Quincy Jones with Michael Jackson, personality producers such as Brian Eno and Daniel Lanois, or Nigel Godrich with Radiohead and Beck, to name only a few—is a direct outgrowth of Spector's contribution and notoriety. And when today's bands labour painstakingly for a year or more over the studio production of a disc, they are demonstrating, knowingly or not, Spector's legacy at work.

It is also significant that Spector's own preferred recording venue was Gold Star Studios in Los Angeles. This was an early indication of the coming 'westward migration' away from New York City to Los Angeles as the dominant power centre of the pop music industry. The studio musicians with whom Spector worked regularly at Gold Star Studios came to be known as the 'Wrecking Crew'; individually and collectively, they made essential contributions to a remarkable number of hit records from the 1960s on. Among the best known of these musicians are Hal Blaine, drummer; Carol Kaye, bass; and Jack Nitzsche, arranger and percussionist.

Berry Gordy Jr and Motown

Meanwhile, in Detroit, Berry Gordy Jr (b. 1929) was busy creating his own songwriting/producing/marketing organization along lines directly analogous to Philles Records. But Motown—named after the 'Motor town' or 'Motor city' (i.e., Detroit, the automobile production capital of America)—came to be a success story that surpassed even that of Philles. In fact, Motown records would go on to become the most profitable black-owned business in all of North America, in all history, by the early 1980s. Indeed, while Motown may not have been the first black-owned record label—that distinction belongs to Black Swan, opened in 1921—it was certainly the most successful.

Gordy was determined to keep all of the creative *and* financial aspects of the business under African-American control—which effectively meant under *his* control. This worked because Gordy had an uncanny ability to surround himself with first-rate musical talent in all areas of the record-making process and to maintain the loyalty of his musicians for substantial periods of time. It also worked, of course, because Gordy had a shrewd head for business and a keen ear for hits. Unlike the music of earlier black-owned record companies, Motown's was not directed primarily at a black audience. Gordy unapologetically used Motown to make an African-American pop music addressed to the widest possible listening public. The only segregation Gordy permitted his product was geared to age—like rock 'n' roll itself, Motown's music was designed to cut across divisions of race, region, and class, but it definitely was, as the label itself proclaimed, 'the sound of young America'.

The unique genius of Gordy—and of his entire Motown organization—was the ability to create a black music aimed right at the commercial mainstream, that somehow never evoked the feeling, or provoked the charge, of having 'sold out'. With remarkably few exceptions, Motown records avoided direct evocations of earlier rhythm and blues forms and styles; 12-bar blues patterns are strikingly rare, as are the typical devices of doo-wop, or of anything suggestive of the 1950s sounds of R&B-oriented rock 'n' rollers like Chuck Berry, Fats Domino, and Little Richard. Yet, a generalized blues or gospel manner nonetheless remained a defining characteristic of Motown's performers; sometimes it could be very subtle, as is often the case with William 'Smokey' Robinson, and other times it was much more overt, as is the case with Martha Reeves. And this 'manner' proved sufficient to give a definite African-American slant to the pop-structured, pop-flavoured songs that were characteristic of Motown.

Like Phil Spector, Berry Gordy Jr started his career as a songwriter (he co-wrote a number of pop and rhythm and blues hits performed for Jackie Wilson in the late 1950s), although, unlike Spector, Gordy did not perform on records. Motown, which began its operations in 1959 but at first grew very slowly, was reaching its commercial peak just at the point when Spector folded Philles in 1966. The Motown model was strikingly similar to that employed by Philles: tight quality control on all levels of creation and production, and concentration on a small number of records to yield a high proportion of hits. It is impossible to determine direct influence, one way or the other, between the Philles and Motown organizations; it seems to be a case of two remarkable talents having similar ideas, and similar success, at around the same time. However, Gordy's organization was noticeably larger in its scope and ambition than Spector's.

From the beginning, Gordy planned a group of labels rather than just one. Records under the Motown, Tamla, Gordy, and Soul banners were all issued from Gordy's Detroit headquarters, and each label boasted its own roster of hitmakers. Furthermore, whereas Spector was essentially interested only in the records themselves, Gordy specifically chose and developed his recording artists to be charismatic and sophisticated live performers, complete with characteristic modes of dress and distinctive stage choreography—not to mention strict codes of conduct both on and off stage that apparently were enforced quite vigorously. There were complaints about the 'iron hand' with which Gordy ruled his roost, just as there were complaints about Spector's passion for control. But there can be no doubt that Gordy's active encouragement of his artists to be more than just recording acts made it possible for both individuals and groups from the organization to develop long-term careers. It is no accident that groups like the Supremes and the Temptations are significantly better known to a wide public than are the Crystals or the Ronettes, or that individuals like Smokey Robinson and Diana Ross were able to win the kind of name recognition that enabled them eventually to branch off from the groups with which they initially were associated—the Miracles and the Supremes, respectively—and to forge hugely successful solo careers.

Motown records from the early 1960s exemplify the rock 'n' roll trends of their time. Among the biggest of Motown's early hits were 'Please Mr. Postman' by the Marvelettes (Number 1, 1961), a quintessential girl group record, and 'Do You Love Me?' by the Contours (Number 3, 1962), a hard-driving dance record that linked success in romance to the ability to perform then current popular dance steps such as the twist and the mashed potatoes (the Contours' 'Do You Love Me?' found renewed chart success in 1988, on the strength of its prominent employment on the soundtrack of the movie *Dirty Dancing*, which is set in the early 1960s). By the mid-1960s a more complex, occasionally lush sound came to characterize Motown's productions. Surely, the Temptations' 'My Girl' (see the 'Listening To' section) is as much a 'teenage symphony' as any of Phil Spector's most elaborate offerings. Just like Spector, however, Motown never lost touch with a danceable beat, and although the Supremes' 'You Can't Hurry Love' (see the 'Listening To' section) has a much more sophisticated sound and arrangement than 'Please Mr. Postman' from five years earlier, both records share an irresistible groove. Gordy's touch seemed never to falter, and his organization steadily increased its share of the hit record market throughout the 1960s; in the year 1970 alone, Motown and its affiliated labels placed 16 records in the Top 10 and scored seven Number 1 records (out of the year's total of 21 Number 1 songs).

Motown's headquarters in Detroit (which Gordy named 'Hitsville, USA') served as a magnet for a spectacular array of talented individuals, some of whom did session work or even office work until they finally managed to get the attention of Gordy. Among performers, Gordy—like so many other producers—tended to favour vocal groups, although he did have important solo acts from early on, such as Marvin Gaye, Mary Wells, and Stevie Wonder, and did eventually wean some solo performers from the groups that they fronted. Important Motown groups not yet mentioned include Martha (Reeves) and the Vandellas, Junior Walker and the All Stars, the Four Tops, Gladys Knight and the Pips, and the Jackson Five; the last-named group made their first record for Motown in 1969, when lead singer Michael was all of 11 years old, and their string of hits for the label helped assure Motown's fortunes well into the 1970s.

Gordy's organization was also blessed with remarkable songwriting and production talent, and Gordy would often have his teams of songwriting producers compete for the privilege of working with particular hot recording acts. Among the most famous of these Motown writing/production teams were Eddie Holland–Lamont Dozier–Brian Holland; Norman Whitfield and Barrett Strong; and Nickolas Ashford and Valerie Simpson. Smokey Robinson was unusual among the earlier Motown artists in being both a performer and a songwriter/producer; he furnished material not just to his own group, the Miracles, but also to Mary Wells, the Marvelettes, and the Temptations. Later on, in the 1970s, Marvin Gaye and Stevie Wonder also took on writing and production responsibilities for their own records.

Finally, but certainly not least in importance, Motown had a sterling house band, the so-called Funk Brothers, in every sense a match for Phil Spector's Wrecking Crew in assuring that the highest level of instrumental musicianship was always present to back up and inspire the vocal performers. Bass player James Jamerson, drummer Benny Benjamin, and keyboardist Earl Van Dyke were among the most important contributors to the Motown sound. In fact, though records were seldom kept on who exactly played on which Motown record, it is estimated that the Funk Brothers played on more Number 1 records than any other group in history. The remarkable achievements and camaraderie of the Funk Brothers and the history and Detroit demise of Motown are told in the excellent 2002 documentary, *Standing in the Shadows of Motown*, an oral and musical history of the musicians who made Berry Gordy's Motown projects so successful.

In 1971 Berry Gordy moved the Motown headquarters to Los Angeles, at last joining the 'westward migration' that had been playing an important role in pop music and culture generally since the early 1960s. We now turn our attention specifically to California, to surf music, and to Brian Wilson—who did more than any other single person to make California the new focus of rock 'n' roll mythology.

Listening To the Motown Sound

'My Girl', composed and produced by Smokey Robinson and Ronald White, performed by the Temptations (Number 1, 1965); 'You Can't Hurry Love', composed by Holland–Dozier–Holland, produced by Brian Holland and Lamont Dozier, performed by the Supremes (Number 1, 1966)

'My Girl' is a moderate-tempo love ballad. As a composition, it is a song of sweetly conventional romantic sentiment in a straightforward verse-chorus form. But as a recording, it is lifted emphatically beyond the ordinary by the Temptations' thoroughly engaging performance and by Motown's spectacular production values.

From the outset, the arrangement hooks the listener: a repeating solo bass motive establishes the beat, over which a lead guitar enters with a memorable melodic figure. Both of these instrumental hooks are also used later on in the recording, so that they are firmly fixed in the listener's mind after one hearing of the song. Then the drums and lead voice enter, followed subtly by background vocals; by the time the first chorus is reached, brass instruments are present in the accompaniment, to which are then added orchestral strings. The cumulative layering of sounds gives a sense of steadily increasing passion and intensity to the song, as the singer's words metaphorically detail his feelings for his 'girl'. The second verse brings new brass fanfares in response to the lead vocalist's calls. There is a sumptuous instrumental interlude before the third (last) verse, dominated by strings, which play a new melodic figure over the song's character-istic chord progressions. Then, as a final intensifying gesture, a dramatic upward key change takes place just before the concluding verse and chorus.

If 'My Girl' showcases the brilliance of Motown's arranging and producing staff, 'You Can't Hurry Love' demonstrates that Motown's writers could also come up with clever, innovatively structured pop songs. The listening outline below conveys the intricacies of this Holland–Dozier–Holland composition, although the most casual hearing of the record will affirm that—as with so much of the finest pop music—catchiness was absolutely not sacrificed to the cause of sophistication.

The opening 'A' section of 'You Can't Hurry Love' is extremely short—just half the length of each of the ensuing 'B' and 'C' sections. The function of this 'A' is at first unclear, both because of its brevity (is it a kind of introduction? or is it a very short verse?) and because of its similarity to the music of the 'B' section; the basic chord progressions underlying both 'A' and 'B' are virtually identical, even though their vocal melodies differ. 'C' brings a striking chord change and another change of melody, which might initially suggest a kind of bridge section. But when 'A' fails to return after 'C', and instead 'B' and 'C' alternate with one another, we seem to be in an unorthodox verse-chorus type of situation, in which we hear the first verse ('C') after the chorus ('B'), and in which the words of the chorus aren't always exactly the same. Just when a pattern seems to have been established, 'A' unexpectedly returns with a vengeance. Instead of proceeding right to 'B', it is played twice through, creating a composite section that is now as long as 'B' or 'C'. Then, in the most clever formal manoeuvre of all in this already complex song, an ambiguous section is inserted, as the composers take advantage of the chord progression shared by 'A' and 'B'; with minimal melodic activity from the voice, which keeps '*waitin'*', we can't tell for sure which of the two sections we're actually hearing! The instruments tease us briefly here by playing the melodic motif associated with 'B' ('*you can't hurry love*'). But the voice holds back until we're at the top of the chord progression again, at which point it finally begins a proper, full repetition of 'B', and at this point the record begins to fade out.

All this play with form would be just so much intellectual busy work if it didn't reflect on the meaning of the song. 'You Can't Hurry Love' is a song about the importance of waiting. Formally, the song keeps us guessing—waiting for clarification of the functional relationships among the different sections. When the 'A' section at last returns, it keeps us waiting extensively for 'B' and its restatement of the song's essential message. On the level of detail, notice also in the second and third 'B' sections how the lead vocalist avoids or postpones singing the words '*you can't hurry love*', again forcing the listener to wait. This makes the final 'B' that much more of a release of tension, as it behaves in an expected manner at last.

Like all the great Motown hits, 'You Can't Hurry Love' submerges its many subtleties beneath an irresistible pop-friendly surface. Maybe this is why you don't tend to find it, or other Motown records, the subject of discussion when matters turn towards innovative aspects of 1960s music. Still, any list of the significant music of this period that omits a record like 'You Can't Hurry Love' is surely missing something important.

The Supremes (Diana Ross is on the right). Frank Driggs Collection.

Listening Outline: 'You Can't Hurry Love'

FORM	LYRICS
Instrumental intro	
A	*I need love . . .*
B: b	*You can't hurry love . .*
B	*You can't hurry love . . .*
C	*But how many heartaches . . .*
B: b	*(You can't hurry love—) no . . .*
b	*How long must I wait? . . .*
C	*No, I can't bear . . .*
B: b	*(You can't hurry love—) no . . .*
b	*You can't hurry love . . .*
Brief instrumental break	
A	*No, love, love don't come easy*
A	*for that soft voice . . .*
A or B	*I keep you waitin' . . .*
B: b	*You can't hurry love . . .*
B	*You can't hurry love . . .*

Brian Wilson and the Beach Boys

Brian Wilson (b. 1942) formed the Beach Boys with his two brothers, a cousin, and a friend in Hawthorne, California, in 1961. The band was achieving national chart hits within a year, and it thrived right through the period of the 'British Invasion' to become not only the best-selling American group of the 1960s, but probably the most nationally and internationally celebrated American rock group ever—and certainly the one with the longest history of chart success (they scored a Number 1 hit as late as 1988, with 'Kokomo'). This said, we should note that the Beach Boys never once topped the charts in Canada, though they did score an impressive 17 Top 10 hits from 1962 to 1967.

As songwriter, arranger, producer, and performer, Brian Wilson was the guiding spirit of the Beach Boys during the first decade of the group's existence—when their artistic and commercial importance and influence were at a peak. Wilson's clear, and stated, model was Phil Spector, and he worked regularly in the Los Angeles recording studios with many of the same musicians who graced Spector's productions. Unlike Spector, however, Wilson was always an essential performing presence on the records he wrote, arranged, and produced for the Beach Boys. Even after he stopped touring with the group in 1964, the sound of Wilson's clear, intense falsetto remained a defining element of the Beach Boys' studio recordings.

Brian Wilson's place in America was, of course, southern California, and that land of sun and surf was celebrated in song after song by the Beach Boys. These songs enshrined Wilson's somewhat mythical, and obviously middle-class, version of California indelibly in the consciousness of boomers—to such an extent that still, for legions of pop music fans, merely the titles are sufficient to summon an entire state of mind: 'Surfin' Safari', 'Surfer Girl', 'The Warmth of the Sun', 'California Girls', and so forth. Wilson's vision was appealingly inclusive, even as it remained place- and class-specific; cars retained their importance to status and young romance in Wilson's California mythology, the models suitably modernized and spruced up to serve the new time and place, as in '409', 'Little Deuce Coupe', 'Little Honda', and other songs.

A few examples may suffice to trace Wilson's journey as a songwriter from imitation, through emulation, to innovation. The Beach Boys' first Top 10 hit, the famous 'Surfin' USA' (Number 2 CHUM, 1963), simply borrows the music of Chuck Berry's 1958 hit 'Sweet Little Sixteen' as a setting for Brian Wilson's paean to California's— and America's—new beach craze. While the words are all new, they also embody an indirect homage to Berry's original lyrics, insofar as Wilson adopts Berry's idea of national celebration while changing its mode of expression from dancing to surfing (we should also note that the line between 'homage' and 'theft' is often razor thin in the rock world, and Berry would successfully sue Wilson over his homage to receive publishing credits on these songs). The many listeners who knew 'Sweet Little Sixteen' encountered in 'Surfin' USA' an unusual hybrid: musically a cover record that shortened and simplified the form of Chuck Berry's original, but lyrically a tribute to the spirit of Berry that reworked and updated his approach to writing rock 'n' roll anthems to suit the requirements of a new time and place. The 'B' side of 'Surfin' USA', 'Shut Down', was a substantial hit as well, reaching Number 2 on the CHUM charts in 1963. In 'Shut Down', Wilson employed an established rock 'n' roll song form, the AABA pattern in which the 'A' sections are 12-bar blues structures (see the discussion of 'Charlie Brown' in Chapter 2), to tell the story of a drag race between two high-powered automobiles. Needless to say, the narrator's car wins!

The Beach Boys' next hit, 'Surfer Girl' (Number 3 CHUM, 1963), reinvigorated the sound and spirit of the doo-wop ballad by infusing it with California beach content. 'Fun, Fun, Fun' (Number 6 CHUM, 1964), the group's first hit of 1964, evoked Chuck Berry again, in an initially overt but ultimately more subtle way. The solo guitar introduction cops its 12-bar blues licks directly from Berry's 'Roll Over Beethoven' and 'Johnny B. Goode'. But after paying its respects (or its dues?) to Berry in this way, the main body of the song pursues an original path. It's a strophic form, with newly composed music and words, whose 16-bar strophes have nothing to do with the structure of the blues—but everything to do with what Brian Wilson learned from Chuck Berry about how to write and perform rock 'n' roll anthems. 'Fun, Fun, Fun' turns imitation into emulation. With its rapid-fire, clearly articulated lyrics that manage to compress a remarkable number of deeply resonant references to youth culture (fancy cars, car radios, fast driving, hamburger stands, schoolwork, parents, the pursuit of romance, and—naturally—fun) into two minutes, and its eminently catchy and danceable music, 'Fun, Fun, Fun' is the kind of song Chuck Berry might have written had he been born into relative affluence 16 years later, in southern California. (In the song 'Do You Remember?'—an album track from the Beach Boys' *All Summer Long* [1964]—Berry is mentioned as 'the greatest' of the early rock 'n' rollers to whom Brian Wilson pays tribute.)

The Beach Boys, with Brian Wilson in the car, leaning back. Capitol Records. Courtesy of EMI Music Canada.

 ## Other Surf Groups

The Beach Boys, of course, were not the only representatives of a distinctive 'California sound' in the early 1960s. The popular duo Jan (Berry) and Dean (Torrence) worked with Brian Wilson and the Beach Boys on a number of mutual projects; Wilson, in fact, co-wrote Jan and Dean's biggest hit, 'Surf City' (Number 1, 1963). In addition, a highly influential style of guitar-dominated instrumental rock 'n' roll was pioneered in southern California, principally by Dick Dale (b. 1937), who performed with his band, the Del-Tones. Dale employed a solid-body guitar, a high-wattage Fender amplifier, and lots of reverb to achieve the 'wet' sound of what came to be known as 'surf guitar'.

A characteristic device was Dale's rapid, descending tremolo—borrowed by a group called the Chantays to open their recording of what became the most famous surf instrumental, 'Pipeline' (the title is a surfing term for the curl of a wave before it breaks). Sustained national recognition eluded Dick Dale in the 1960s, but it finally became his in the 1990s, when his recording of 'Misirlou', from 1962, was used as opening music for the hit film *Pulp Fiction*. The most successful instrumental group associated with surf rock was, paradoxically, a Seattle-based ensemble, the Ventures, who adopted aspects of the style after it became popular in California.

Beatlemania and the British Invasion

We end this chapter with a look at one of the pivotal moments in the development of the rock tradition: Beatlemania and the so-called 'British Invasion'. Beatlemania proved so culturally significant in Canada, and in the United States, that rock historians now typically date the start of 'the Sixties' with the arrival of the Beatles on American soil, in February of 1964. While this obviously overlooks the preceding contributions of free speech and civil rights activists to the decade's anti-authoritarian ethos, the impact of the Beatles on North American popular culture probably cannot be overstated. Indeed, there is reason to situate the group at the precipice of a historical schism that separates all that came before them from everything after.

By 1964, political relations between Canada and Britain had become strained—particularly after Canada refused to back Britain during the Suez Crisis of 1956—and the new Canadian television industry had already begun to reorient Canadian culture along continental lines. However, both Canada and Britain remained close in terms of trade and culture. In fact, the Canadian culture industry was almost as dependent on British, as it was on American, imports in the early 1960s. Under the direction of Paul White, for instance, Capitol Records' Canadian arm established two catalogues specifically for importing releases by EMI Records in Britain and Scotland, and it would not release a single record recorded entirely in Canada until much later in the century: the 6000 series was established for LPs, while the 72000 series was for 12-inch singles. Thus, Capitol Records became, for all intents and purposes, a pipeline for British popular music into Canada, often months before American labels took notice.

Releases on the 6000 and 72000 series included Scottish dance records by Jimmy Shand; symphonic and choral music by the likes of the Glasgow Orpheus Choir; comedy records; documentary records, including an extremely popular study of the investiture of the Prince of Wales; and British folk, pop, and rock records. Capitol also released records by the foremost exponent of British rock 'n' roll in Canada before the Beatles, namely, Cliff Richard and the Shadows. The group would have a tremendous—if often overlooked—impact on Canadian popular music, insofar as both Neil Young and Randy Bachman were strongly influenced as guitarists by their mutual hero, Hank Marvin, who played guitar for the Shadows throughout the 1950s.

It should probably come as no surprise, then, that the Beatles decided to test their mettle in the North American market with releases in Canada. In February of 1963 Capitol released the Beatles 'Love Me Do' on its 72000 label in Canada, and though the record failed to chart it sold well enough to keep the label interested in the group. An American 'indie' label—Vee-Jay Records—released 'Please Please Me' the following month in the US. WLS, a radio station in Chicago, picked up the latter a few days later, while CFGP in Grand Prairie, Alberta, charted the single in its Top 40 in April. Eventually, the record peaked at Number 27 the next week.

Though Beatlemania failed to ignite in the United States until 1964, the groundswell of grassroots support for the band, which was already blossoming in Canada, grew with every record released. Capitol Records continued to release new records by the Beatles in Canada as they were released in Britain, though Paul White insists that none of these records sold in any significant numbers. Nonetheless, by November of 1963, the Beatles' 'She Loves You' (1963) had made it into heavy rotation on 1050 CHUM in Toronto, and it breached the CHUM Top 20 the next month, in December. The band's subsequent LP, *With the Beatles*, was released in Canada— retitled *Beatlemania with the Beatles!*—only three days after its British release, which indicates that the Beatles had achieved a sufficient following in Canada to warrant synchronized releases with Britain. Thus, by the time the Beatles had their first Number 1 record in America, 'I Want To Hold Your Hand', they were already mainstays on the pop charts in Canada. Moreover, the Beatles were already established stars in Great Britain and throughout much of Europe—a fact well known to Canadians, as recent waves of post-war immigration to the country from Britain and Scotland had created a large demand for British newspapers and magazines, and reports on British culture became increasingly prevalent in domestic media.

It was while on vacation in London in 1963 that Ed Sullivan saw Beatlemania first-hand. Sullivan witnessed throngs of screaming adolescent admirers at Heathrow International Airport in London gather to welcome the 'Fab Four' home. In fact, Sullivan's plane was delayed because of it. Immediately, Sullivan decided to book the group on his self-named variety show for CBS.

The Beatles in an open rehearsal for their first television appearance in the United States, February 1964. Left to right: Paul McCartney, George Harrison (both also shown on the monitor), Ringo Starr, John Lennon. Courtesy Library of Congress.

The Beatles' appearance on *The Ed Sullivan Show* in February of 1964 is now legendary, attracting a viewership in the millions, and it encouraged Capitol's American arm to launch a major promotional campaign behind the first Beatles single Capitol chose to release in the United States—'I Want To Hold Your Hand' (1963)—and its accompanying album, *Meet the Beatles* (1964). (Capitol actually had a policy that it would promote records by any group that appeared on the Sullivan show.) 'Beatlemania'—the massive outpouring of collective enthusiasm for the Beatles and their music by adolescent and pre-teen boomers—ensued almost immediately after their appearance. What was once a British, European, and faintly Canadian phenomenon, was now also American.

Unlike in Canada, where it remains common for international superstars—typically from the United States and Great Britain—to achieve popularity verging on mania, Beatlemania represents the first time such adulation was bestowed upon non-native pop musicians in the United States. America had been exporting its popular music to Great Britain, to Europe, and to Canada, and increasingly throughout the industrialized world, with enormous success for a long time by 1964, but the impact of the Beatles in America marked the significant beginning of an aggressively reciprocal process—by the 1970s, as we shall see later in this book, the British Invasion had become an occupation, as British singers regularly appeared on the North American charts. Of course, the reciprocities involved here are deep and complex. After all, North American popular music, especially that of the twentieth century, is built on a complex anagram of influences that may be traced to a variety of world sources. And the most direct, formative influences on the music of the Beatles themselves—and of countless other British bands of the 1960s—were those of 1950s American rock 'n' roll and R&B records.

The close interconnections between North American and British pop music that were established in the wake of the Beatles' stateside success continue to this day. Among the most successful artists on the North American charts in the 1990s were British acts like Eric Clapton, Elton John, Sting, and the rock group Oasis. Even more significantly, the British Invasion was the first of many developments that may be seen as indicative of an accelerating receptivity in North America to overt pop music influences from all over the world. The Beatles themselves modelled such receptivity in their own embrace of influences from Indian classical and folk musics—first heard as a surface element in their employment of an Indian instrument, called the sitar, in 'Norwegian Wood' (a track from the album *Rubber Soul*, 1965), and later heard as a more profound influence on both the sound and structure of 'Within You Without You' from their *Sgt. Pepper's Lonely Hearts Club Band* (1967) LP (see Chapter 4).

This may seem a rather elaborate heritage to trace ultimately to just one group that had a chart run of only seven years in North America. But the remarkable thing about the Beatles is that they proved truly worthy of the early adulation heaped upon them. Up to the end of their career as a group, the so-called 'Fab Four' continued to evolve in new and unexpected directions, and to challenge themselves and their wide audience. They altered the character of pop music profoundly and bequeathed to popular culture a remarkably rich and complicated inheritance.

The Beatles: The Early Years

For all their innovativeness, though, the Beatles started out as a performing band modelled on Buddy Holly's group, the Crickets (see Chapter 2). After some initial shifts in personnel, the Beatles achieved a stable lineup by 1962, consisting of John Lennon and George Harrison (lead and rhythm guitars, and vocals), Paul McCartney (bass and vocals), and Ringo Starr (drums and occasional vocals). During their extended apprenticeship period, the Beatles played at clubs in their home town of Liverpool and elsewhere—most famously in Hamburg, Germany—performing an imitative repertoire that centred on covers of songs by the American rock 'n' roll artists they most admired, such as Chuck Berry, Little Richard, Carl Perkins, and Buddy Holly. (The country/rock 'n' roll duo the Everly Brothers also exercised a significant influence on the Beatles' group singing style.) Several such covers found their way onto early Beatles albums, once their manager, Brian Epstein, succeeded, after much difficulty, to overhaul their image from Teddy Boy rockers to boy-band mods (complete with matching, though overgrown, 'mop-top' haircuts and matching 'Beatle boots'); and, in turn, to wrangle a contract for them with EMI Records in 1962. A few of these 'covers' were also eventually chart hits for the Beatles in North America, among them 'Matchbox', a Carl Perkins tune (Number 17, 1964; Number 6 CHUM, 1964), and probably their best-known 'cover', 'Twist and Shout' (Number 2, 1964; Number 5 CHUM, 1964), a rhythm and blues dance number composed by Phil Medley and Bert Russell that the Beatles doubtless learned from the 1962 hit recording by the Isley Brothers.

'Twist and Shout' was on the Beatles' first album—*Please Please Me*—released in Great Britain in 1963. By the time of this recording the Beatles were entering a period of emulation by writing some of their own songs. *Please Please Me* contains six covers and eight original selections. The Beatles' chief songwriters were John Lennon and Paul McCartney, who, at least at first, worked as a team, but eventually Harrison began to contribute songs as well, and by the end of the Beatles' career even Starr had emerged occasionally as a songwriter. This brings up an important point. Unlike the Beach Boys in the 1960s, whose creative centre was unquestionably found in one member of the group, the Beatles throughout their prime years were a kind of multiple-threat team. The many creative and performing abilities shared among the four Beatles allowed the group to achieve a wonderful collective synergy—a whole both greater than, and different from, the sum of its parts (the after-the-fact proof of this statement may be seen in the four contrasting solo careers the individual members of the group had after the Beatles broke up in 1970). The Beatles were also blessed with a sympathetic and encouraging producer in George Martin. Martin was sometimes called 'the fifth Beatle' in acknowledgement of his increasingly essential role in the recording studio in the later 1960s, as the Beatles came to attempt more and more sophisticated arrangements and electronic engineering effects on their recordings.

Some Canadian Responses to the Beatles

One immediate result of Beatlemania, and of the British Invasion, was the formation and adaptation of North American groups to mimic distinctive aspects of the British

Listening To Four Songs by the Beatles

Four representative songs will serve well to chart the Beatles' career as songwriting performers from 1962 to 1966, the year that they quit touring, gave up live performance, and went on to become the world's first famous studio rock band. These four songs demonstrate their development from emulators to innovators. From very early on, the Beatles' original songs showed considerable individuality and creativity in dealing with the inherited materials of rock 'n' roll. By 1965, with the appropriately titled 'Yesterday', they were revealing an ability to emulate Tin Pan Alley songs as well as American rockers. And with 'Eleanor Rigby' in 1966, the Beatles achieved a song that was—and is—truly 'beyond category', a song that helped certify their new status as not only the most popular band in the history of rock 'n' roll but also the most innovative one.

'Please Please Me'

'Please Please Me' was recorded in late 1962. It was the Beatles' first Top 10 hit in Britain and was one of the songs unsuccessfully released in America by Vee-Jay Records in 1963. But indie label Vee-Jay re-released the single again when 'I Want To Hold Your Hand' began its rapid ascent on the American charts in early 1964, and before long 'Please Please Me' was up in the Top 3 along with 'I Want To Hold Your Hand' and another Beatles hit, 'She Loves You', which had also initially been released in the US in 1963. During a now-famous week in early April 1964 the Beatles achieved the unprecedented and still

unique feat of having all of the top five records on the American charts for the week—an index of the intensity of American Beatlemania at the time; in Canada they occupied four of the Top 5, kept from full chart dominance by the Dave Clark Five's 'Glad All Over', which occupied the Number 3 slot for all four weeks of April that year.

'Please Please Me', a fine example of the early Beatles' songwriting and performing style, is a straightforward up-tempo love song in a typical AABA form. The group sings and plays it crisply, energetically, and efficiently—once through the song, and it's over, in just two minutes. Still, individualistic features in the song already point to the creative energy at work in the group. The lyrics contain some clever internal rhymes, as when *'complainin'* is rhymed with *'rain in* [my heart]' at the beginning of the 'B' section, and the title itself plays with the word 'please', using it both as verb and adverb (effective rhymes and wordplay would become two trademarks of the Beatles' songwriting).

Musically, as shown in the listening chart, the 'A' sections have their own distinctive internal form that proves a source of considerable interest. First, there are two identical phrases ('a', 'a') to set the poetic couplets that open these sections. These 'a' phrases have a basically descending melodic motion over minimal chord changes. In the rather unexpected third phrase, 'b', where the text consists simply of the repeated words *'Come on, come on'*, the music becomes the focus of interest, with continuous chord changes and a steadily ascending melodic line depicting the intensity that underlies the unchanging lyrics. With the final phrase, 'c', a melodic high point is reached as the lyrics arrive at the words of the song's title, 'Please please me', after which the melody descends once again, and the harmony presents a conclusive cadence. The musical form of the 'A' sections, a–a–b–c, also delineates the rhyme scheme in the four-line stanzas of the lyrics.

Listening Chart: 'Please Please Me' (1962)

Written by John Lennon and Paul McCartney; performed by the Beatles

FORM	LYRICS	DESCRIPTIVE COMMENTS
Instrumental intro		As a hook, the lead guitar and harmonica play the melody of the first two phrases of 'A'.
A: a	*Last night . . .*	
a	*I know . . .*	Same melody line, new words.
b	*Come on . . .*	Note steady chord changes, ascending melody.
c	*Please please me . . .*	High point of melody comes on words of the title.
A: a	*You don't . . .*	Same music as before, with new words for the first two lines of the stanza.
a	*Why do I . . .*	
b	*Come on . . .*	
c	*Please please me . . .*	
B: d	*I don't . . .*	Bridge section; new music.
d'	*I do . . .*	Note change and extension at the end of this phrase, leading back to the final 'A'.
A	*Last night . . . (etc.)*	Exact repetition of the opening 'A', with brief extension at the end.

'A Hard Day's Night'

'A Hard Day's Night', a Number 1 hit in 1964, was the title song from the Beatles' first movie. It shares a few surface characteristics with 'Please Please Me'. The name of the song once again demonstrates wordplay, in characterizing the work experience of those who do their 'hard day's work' at night—like members of a rock band. The overall form of the song is once again AABA. But the considerably more subtle and elaborate playing with formal characteristics and expectations clearly demonstrates the increasing sophistication of the Beatles' songwriting. And while the performance of the song is fully as energetic and engaging as that of 'Please Please Me', some novel touches reveal the group's increasing attention to details of sound and arrangement.

In a sense, 'A Hard Day's Night' may be heard as the Beatles' updating of the old Tin Pan Alley classic 'My Blue Heaven': it similarly portrays the delights of returning home to a rewarding domestic relationship. (It is not at all unthinkable that the Beatles knew 'My Blue Heaven', especially since Fats Domino had revived it and made it a hit again, in rock 'n' roll style, in 1956. Domino was very popular in Britain, and the Beatles eventually created an implicit tribute to his New Orleans style by writing and recording 'Lady Madonna' in 1968; Domino appreciated the compliment and returned it by recording the song himself the same year.) Musically, 'A Hard Day's Night' is clearly modelled on those AABA song forms in which the 'A' sections are 12-bar blues stanzas. But while the 'A' sections are indeed 12 bars in length, have three four-bar phrases, and incorporate blue notes, they are not exactly traditional 12-bar blues structures. In the lyrics, the Beatles begin by making a reference to the traditional a–a–b poetic stanza found in many blues, by having the second line begin with the same words as the first (see listening chart). But that second line ends with different words, and the following 'A' stanza features three completely independent lines. In the music of these 'A' sections, the Beatles do not follow the traditional chord structure of 12-bar blues. There are chords used in addition to the traditional three (tonic, subdominant, and dominant—see the discussion of 12-bar blues in Chapter 1), and the traditional chords do not always occur in the expected places. In particular, the usual chord change at the start of the second phrase (the move to the subdominant chord) is postponed to the start of the third and final phrase of the 12-bar sec-

tion. This yields an interesting result: although the lyrics to the 'A' sections do not conform to the a–a–b pattern, the *musical* phrases do.

These musical alterations are not merely technical details, for they serve the meaning of the lyrics. The third line in each of the 'A' stanzas describes the trip home from work and the actual reuniting with the loved one. Thus, it is entirely appropriate that the harmony should wait until this point to make its own anticipated move. (The harmony does return to the tonic at the expected point—in the eleventh bar—as the singer settles down with his lover at home and feels '*all right*', or '*okay*'.)

Lastly, we may mention three aspects of the song's arrangement. The song begins literally with a bang: a loud, isolated guitar chord whose unexpected harsh **dissonance** is permitted to ring in the air before the song actually gets going. This is the most effective and efficient of hooks, and it also perfectly prepares the tense feelings described in the opening words of the song. Notice, also, the unique guitar timbre employed for the instrumental solo in the middle of the record, which allows this solo on the 12-string guitar to stand out from the many other guitar sounds heard elsewhere throughout the performance. The very end brings an unexpected instrumental **coda**, as a solo guitar gently strums a repeating figure that fades out. The abrupt cessation of drums and accompanying chords underlines the relaxed character of this ending, which creates an effective counterbalance to the song's unnerving opening and surely signifies the final lifting of tension after the '*hard day's night*' and the settling in to the delights of being home.

Listening Chart: 'A Hard Day's Night' (1964)

Written by John Lennon and Paul McCartney; performed by the Beatles

FORM	LYRICS	DESCRIPTIVE COMMENTS
Introductory guitar chord		Dissonance followed by open space creates anticipatory tension.
A	*It's been a hard day's night . . .* *It's been a hard day's night . . .* *But when I get home to you . . .*	Music and lyrics of 'A' sections are modelled on 12-bar blues patterns but introduce significant variations.
A	*And you know I work all day . . .* *And it's worth it . . .* *So why on earth should I moan . . .*	Same music, new lyrics.
B	*When I'm home . . .*	Bridge section; new music, consisting of two similar phrases.
A	*It's been a hard day's night . . .*	Exact repetition of the first 'A' section.
A	*[Instrumental interlude]* *So why should I moan . . .*	Guitar solo for the first eight bars, then voices return for the last phrase (four bars) of the section.
B	*When I'm home . . .*	As before.
A	*It's been a hard day's night . . .*	As before.
Instrumental coda		

'Yesterday'

'Yesterday', which reached the Number 1 position on the pop charts in 1965, may be the Beatles song with the most wide-ranging and enduring popularity; certainly, it has been the one most performed by other artists, and its appeal cuts across generational and stylistic divides. The song comes across with a remarkable directness and simplicity, so natural in its verbal and melodic expression that it seems hardly to have been consciously composed. But, as we know from many previous examples of fine popular music, such an effect is difficult to achieve and almost invariably conceals much art.

As a composition, 'Yesterday' obviously evokes Tin Pan Alley models. Musically, it employs a standard AABA form. Its lyrics approach the time-honoured theme of broken romance in a gentle, general, and straightforward manner, such that virtually anyone could understand and empathize, and virtually nobody could take offence. (One aspect of the song's appeal is that the feelings involved are utterly clear, whereas the specific situation remains vague enough to stimulate the imagination of many different listeners: '*Why she had to go I don't know, she wouldn't say.*') But the song may assert its kinship with Tin Pan Alley most tellingly in its emphasis on a distinctive and expressive melodic line, a line that fits the words beautifully. The melody is accompanied by equally expressive harmonies, which explore a wider range of chords than was typical for rock music at this time. The moderate tempo and the general avoidance of any intense rhythmic effects also distance 'Yesterday' from the rock mainstream and edge it closer in spirit to Tin Pan Alley.

The Beatles' recording of 'Yesterday' underlines the song's unexpected character in every way. The use of a solo voice throughout, the similarity of Paul McCartney's lyrical and unaffected style of delivery to Tin Pan Alley-style crooning, the choice of acoustic (rather than electric) guitar, the employment of orchestral string instruments to augment the accompaniment, the lack of any drums or percussion instruments, the prevailingly soft dynamic level—all these elements set the record apart from others of its time, including other records by the Beatles, as if to emphasize that this song is a deliberate venture into new musical territory. While anyone who had been listening carefully to the Beatles knew by 1965 that they were capable of writing beautifully melodic love ballads (such as 'And I Love Her' and 'If I Fell', both from the Beatles' 1964 movie, *A Hard Day's Night*), 'Yesterday' was designed to—and did—make listeners really sit up and take notice. Maybe the Beatles were more than just a good old rock 'n' roll band, or even more than a good new rock band. Maybe they were just something else entirely.

As you listen to 'Yesterday', try to notice some of the artistry involved in its creation and performance. Each of the 'A' sections begins with an isolated, essential word that serves as a decisive hook into the story (see listening chart); these single opening words are set to foreshortened musical phrases (one bar in length, as opposed to the standard two bars) that function equally as focusing hooks. The ascending gestures in the melody always depict the receding past ('*all my troubles seemed so far away*', '*I'm not half the man I used to be*', and so forth), while the immediately following descending gestures always bring us back down to earth in the present ('*Now it looks as though they're here to stay*', '*There's a shadow hanging over me*', etc.). The lyrics to the bridge section reveal again the Beatles' adeptness at internal rhyming: '*I said something wrong, now I long for yesterday*.' And the final word in the bridge, '*yesterday*', links this 'B' section effectively to the final 'A', which begins with the same word. In terms of the arrangement, we can admire how withholding the entrance of the orchestral strings until the second 'A' section makes their arrival a wonderfully rich, intense surprise that goes splendidly with the word 'suddenly'.

'Eleanor Rigby'

'Eleanor Rigby' went to Number 11 in the US in 1966, and reached Number 1 in Canada. Actually, it was issued as the 'B' side of 'Yellow Submarine', a novelty number that went to Number 2 in America and, again, topped the CHUM charts.

'Eleanor Rigby' is a startling song right from the outset. Without any preparation, the voices enter with a high, loud cry of '*Ah*', accompanied by an active string ensemble (violins, violas, and cellos). Orchestral strings are traditionally associated with soothing

Listening Chart: 'Yesterday' (1965)

Written by John Lennon and Paul McCartney; performed by the Beatles (actually Paul McCartney, vocal solo, accompanied by guitar and string ensemble)

FORM	LYRICS	DESCRIPTIVE COMMENTS
Brief intro: acoustic guitar vamp		
A	*Yesterday . . .*	Guitar accompaniment continues.
A	*Suddenly . . .*	String ensemble joins the guitar; fuller sound.
B	*Why she had to go . . .* *I said something wrong . . .*	Bridge section; new music, consisting of two similar phrases.
A	*Yesterday . . .*	Exact repetition of the first 'A' section.
		Repetition of 'B' and 'A' sections, followed by brief coda, in which the voice hums the closing melodic phrase of 'A' accompanied by the strings.

music—an association exemplified by a song like 'Yesterday'—but here they are confined to steady, repeated chords and brief rhythmic figures, assuming functions much like those of the rhythm guitar and drums in a more typical rock configuration. The harmony is equally dislocating. The song opens on a big major chord, but after the initial vocal phrase it settles onto an unexpected minor chord. These two chords alternate throughout the song, and they are, in fact, the only two chords used. The restriction of the chordal vocabulary (which beautifully suits the story of repression told by the song), the oscillation between two chords that do not share a traditional harmonic relationship, and the fact that it is the second, minor chord (rather than the opening major chord) that proves to be the central focus (or tonic) of the song as a whole are all factors contributing strongly to the unique atmosphere of 'Eleanor Rigby'.

The subject matter of the song, loneliness, is not in itself an unusual one in pop music, but 'Eleanor Rigby' looks at loneliness and the lack of human connection from a uniquely philosophical, even spiritual, viewpoint rather than from a romantic viewpoint. Eleanor Rigby and Father McKenzie, introduced in two separate verses of the song, remain isolated from one another—and from other people—in their lives. And even in death. Only Father McKenzie is even aware of Eleanor's passing; they 'meet' in the third and final verse only in a graveyard that finalizes their non-relationship, and the 'good' Father can only wipe dirt from his hands as he walks away from the site of Eleanor's burial. As the lyrics say, so succinctly and eloquently, '*No one was saved.*' This is sombre stuff indeed, and it is to the Beatles' credit that the song conveys its despairing message in an efficient and utterly unsentimental way, which maximizes the effect.

Apart from the striking introduction, the form of the song suggests that of the traditional folk ballad, with verses that tell a developing story alternating with a repeated chorus (see the listening chart). By the mid-1960s the urban folk revival had already been in full swing for years, so it was not surprising to see the Beatles laying claim to the folk ballad form as they continued to expand their musical horizons. It also is not surprising, then, that the following year, in 1967, Joan Baez covered the song on her self-titled *Joan* album. What was, and remains, surprising is the Beatles' unique take on this tradition. The ballad form was conventionally used as a means of telling a large-scale, dramatic, often tragic story. And many of the urban folk performers, such as Bob Dylan, adapted the form in their original songs to serve the same kind of dramatic purpose. In 'Eleanor Rigby', on the other hand, nothing happens in the lives of the protagonists. And that, the Beatles tell us, is the source of this tragedy.

The bowed strings take over the role of a strumming guitar in the 'ballad' of 'Eleanor Rigby', paradoxically giving the song a much harder edge. As you listen, notice the slight variations in the string parts from verse to verse and even in the repetitions of the chorus; they help maintain interest in the emerging story.

A few more musical details deserve mention here. The phrase structure of the verses is distinctive: a long initial phrase (of four bars)—'*Eleanor Rigby picks up the rice in a church where a wedding has been*'—is answered by a very short (one-bar) phrase—'*Lives in a dream.*' The consistent, atypical, extreme asymmetry of these paired phrases gives the song an unquiet quality of continual incompletion—especially since the shorter phrases are left to hang melodically at a relatively high point, without any conventional feeling of resolution. This is a perfect musical illustration of the incompleteness that characterizes the lives being described. (In a sense, this kind of phrase structure is the reverse of that used in 'Yesterday', where the opening phrase of each section is foreshortened while the ensuing phrases blossom out to traditional lengths.) Also, in the chorus, notice how the second phrase goes higher than the first, making the question it asks ('*Where do they all belong?*') even more intense and insistent.

Finally, the Beatles find extremely imaginative uses for their introductory material later on in the song, demonstrating again their originality and mastery of form. Just at the point when two successive verse-chorus sections have us convinced that we are listening to a straightforward strophic form, the introduction is unexpectedly brought back. The renewed cry of '*Ah, look at all the lonely people!*' underlines the song's theme and helps set off the crucial third verse. Then, at the very end, the final chorus is rendered climactic rather than simply repetitive because the introduction's words and melody are sung simultaneously with it in counterpoint. This brings the song full circle; there is nothing left to say, and the strings bring 'Eleanor Rigby' to a quick, brusque conclusion.

Listening Chart: 'Eleanor Rigby' (1966)

Written by John Lennon and Paul McCartney; performed by the Beatles, with accompanying string ensemble

FORM	LYRICS	DESCRIPTIVE COMMENTS
Introduction	*Ah, look at all . . .*	Voices and strings enter at once.
	Ah, look at all . . .	Exact repetition.
Verse 1: a	*Eleanor Rigby . . .*	Solo voice, accompanied by strings marking each beat with a chord; unusual phrasing structure creates a striking effect.
a	*Waits at the window . . .* *Who is it for?*	
Chorus: b	*All the lonely people . . .*	
b'	*All the lonely people*	Second phrase of chorus changes the melody to go higher than the first phrase.
Verse 2: a	*Father McKenzie* *No one comes near . . .*	As before.
a	*Look at him working . . .* *What does he care . . .*	
Chorus: b	*All the lonely people*	
b'	*All the lonely people . . .*	
Introduction recurs	*Ah, look at all . . .*	As before.
Verse 3: a	*Eleanor Rigby . . .* *Nobody came . . .*	As before.
a	*Father McKenzie . . .* *No one was saved . . .*	
Chorus: b	*All the lonely people . . .*	As a conclusion, the melody and lyrics of the introduction are sung in counterpoint against the melody and lyrics of the chorus, then strings bring the song to an abrupt end.
b'	*All the lonely people . . .*	

style, including fashion (particularly Beatles-styled, 'mop-top' haircuts) and pseudo-English accents, along with certain musical characteristics that were supposed to evoke the Beatles and their countrymen. The Walker Brothers offer an extreme example: the group, which was American, actually went to England in 1964 to record, eventually becoming popular there; and they subsequently achieved some North American chart success with 'Make It Easy On Yourself' (Number 16, 1965) and

'The Sun Ain't Gonna Shine (Anymore)' (Number 13, 1966)—as a British Invasion band! Meanwhile, Winnipeg's the Crescendos moved to Liverpool, changed their name to the vaguely British '5 AM Event', and achieved enough popularity to become the first (and only) Canadian rock group to play the Cavern Club (while in England the band's bassist, Stuart McKernan, turned down an offer to join the Bee Gees).

Chad Allan and the Expressions, another rock band from Winnipeg, cashed in on Beatlemania by hiding their identity—under the moniker 'Guess Who?'—and intimating to radio DJs that, rather than a group of adolescent rock musicians from Canada's prairies, they were a secret 'supergroup' of British Invasion stars. Thus, Quality Records, their label, marketed a cover of Johnny Kidd's 'Shakin' All Over' as a record by 'Guess Who?' The ruse seemed to work, as the single shot to Number 1 on the CHUM charts in 1965 and reached Number 22 on the *Billboard* Top 40.

Of course, it didn't hurt the song's popularity that it had a catchy melody and irresistible backbeat, and a quirky attention-grabbing production aesthetic, which conjured a sonic analogue for the state of sexual anticipation described in the song's lyrics. Recorded at CJAY TV studio in December of 1964, Chad Allan's sore throat provided the track's famously raspy vocals, and an engineering mistake blanketed every instrument on the track with a frenetic slapback echo. Rather than encourage greater interest in Chad Allan and the Expressions, however, the marketing of the group created an entirely new group called 'Guess Who?' Disc jockeys continued to call the group 'Guess Who?' well after 'Shakin' All Over' had completed its chart run and, by 1966, the band was ultimately forced to adopt the name as their official moniker (their next two albums would be released as both Chad Allan and the Expressions and Guess Who? records). Soon, however, Allan had left the group and keyboardist Burton Cummings became the lead singer, and in time the Guess Who dropped their question mark (see Chapter 4).

The response in Quebec to the Beatles was equally unique. As we noted in this chapter, when the Beatles first arrived in 1964 Québécois music was characterized by the work of its many *chansonniers* and an emerging nationalism. But the province was also home to a substantial and growing *yé-yé* movement. Musically, *yé-yé* was an admixture of French and American group-harmony pop, sung mostly by males in Quebec (in France, *yé-yé* was much more explicitly linked with American 'girl group' music and, thus, was more often sung by females). While the movement kicked off in 1962 with the release of the Mégatones' *Voici les Mégatones*, which featured the innovative and immensely popular single 'Rideau S.V.P.', the arrival of the Beatles strengthened the grip of *yé-yé* on the provincial psyche. Over 500 *yé-yé* groups emerged after the Beatles toured Canada in 1964, at least 50 of which had substantial careers. Perhaps the best known *yé-yé* groups were the Classels, who performed French versions of hit songs by Paul Anka, the Platters, and Roy Orbison, as well as original songs; and Les Baronets, led by future Céline Dion manager René Angélil, who performed mainly French covers of Beatles songs.

Other British Invasion Groups

Another immediate result of the Beatles' popularity in North America was to unleash a flood of recordings by British bands, an astoundingly large number of which were successful on the CHUM charts. Although the impact of many of these 'British Invasion' bands was short-lived, other groups have retained substantial, long-term importance in shaping North American popular culture; one thinks particularly of the Rolling Stones, the Who, and the Kinks, to name but three examples. Indeed, the other British Invasion acts that did make a long-term impact in America started as the Beatles did: with firm roots in American rhythm and blues and rock 'n' roll. But during their careers, the Rolling Stones, the Animals, the Who, the Kinks, and Eric Clapton, for instance, all remained closer to these roots, on the whole, than did the Beatles. In fact, it was just at the point that the Beatles became a studio band and began producing music that was essentially uncategorizable, like 'Eleanor Rigby' and many of the songs on the album *Sgt. Pepper's Lonely Hearts Club Band*, that the Rolling Stones—who to this day play international live tours—began to call themselves the 'World's Greatest Rock 'n' roll Band'. Regardless of one's feeling about that claim, there is no doubt that, of all the British Invasion acts other than the Beatles, the Rolling Stones have had the greatest cumulative influence in North America.

The Rolling Stones excelled in presenting covers and original songs of an intense, gritty, and often dark character. Thanks largely to the work of their manager, Andrew Loog Oldham, the band cultivated an image as 'bad boys', in deliberate contrast to the friendly public image projected by the Beatles (an ironic twist, given that the Beatles were groomed by their manager, Brian Epstein, to elide their proletarian origins, while the Rolling Stones, a group of mostly bourgeois boys, were groomed to present a 'dangerous' if not working-class image). Perhaps their most famous hit record is '(I Can't Get No) Satisfaction' (Number 1, 1965, composed by band members Mick Jagger and Keith Richards); with its memorable buzzing guitar 'hook', its unrelenting beat, and its unabashedly self-oriented and ultimately sexual lyrics, the song perfectly exemplifies the distinctive low-down, hard-rocking essence both of the Rolling Stones themselves and of their music.

The Rolling Stones experimented occasionally in the later 1960s with unusual instrumentation and unconventional forms, as did virtually every other major British and North American group—one had, after all, to keep up with the Beatles in some sense. But while a record like 'As Tears Go By' (Number 6 on *Billboard*, and Number 1 on CHUM, 1966) is undeniably affecting and effective, its gently sombre atmosphere and employment of orchestral strings render it a highly atypical Stones opus. The ultimate importance of the Rolling Stones lies in the power and longevity with which they kept, and continue to keep, the spirit of basic rock 'n' roll alive. As late as 1986 the group achieved a Top 10 hit with 'Harlem Shuffle', their faithful remake of a neglected American rhythm and blues hit from 1964 by Bob and Earl.

It is impossible to do justice in this book to the Rolling Stones or to many other important British acts of the 1960s and beyond—although we will return to the Stones briefly in Chapter 5. The importance of these artists to the stylistic development of Western popular music may not be extensive, a conclusion that is debatable, but their presence on the Canadian and world pop music landscape has been, and continues to be, a formidable one.

Discussion Questions

1. Many critics describe the period from 1958 to 1964 as a 'fallow time' in the history of rock 'n' roll. Why do you think that is? Is this an accurate assessment? What sort of values and assumptions about rock music does this designation imply?

2. We know that rock 'n' roll was heard by some in the 1950s as the exemplary soundtrack for, and a tool of, Americanization. Do you agree with this assessment? Can you think of any types of music that might be considered 'tools of Americanization' today?

3. *Chansons engagés* were often political songs. Do you have to be aware of the political message behind their lyrics to appreciate *chansons engagés*? Why do you think those interested in sovereignty for Quebec chose popular music as a central medium for transmitting political ideas?

4. What did Stephen Scobie mean when he wrote that, aside from any one song in particular, 'Robert Zimmerman's first and most lasting artistic contribution is Bob Dylan himself'? Is he correct in that assertion? How does knowledge of the Bob Dylan image influence our interpretations of his early 'protest' songs?

5. Why was Yorkville Village considered 'your last stop on the way to somewhere else' as opposed to a destination in its own right?

6. What is the social significance of the twist? How does that social significance register in the sound of Chubby Checker's 'The Twist'?

7. Phil Spector is considered by many historians to be the first auteur producer. How did he encourage that reputation through the sound of his recordings? How would the rock and pop traditions today sound differently had Spector never invented the Wall of Sound?

8. Members of Motown's house band, the Funk Brothers, have claimed to play on more Number 1 records than any other group in history. What degree of the credit for Motown's success should we give the Funk Brothers? How about their songwriters and songwriting teams, such as Holland–Dozier–Holland?

Chapter Four

Rock in/and the Sixties, 1964–1969

The 1960s remain one of the most prosperous decades in Canadian history. Between 1962 and 1972 Canada's economy grew to become the second largest in the world, after only the United States, and the country approached something like full employment for the first (and only) time in its history. Meanwhile, the oldest cohort of baby boomers completed high school—1,760,000 graduated from Canadian high schools in 1965 alone—though fewer attended university than is often remembered. For however much historians describe the baby-boom generation as almost universally university educated, only one in six Canadian boomers actually attended university in the 1960s, and even fewer graduated (roughly one in 10); the rest entered the workforce, primarily in the clerical and related trades, and in construction, sales, and agriculture.

Those boomers who *did* enrol in university nonetheless proved overwhelming for Canada's already established institutions (i.e., Dalhousie, Laval, McGill, Queen's, Toronto, Western Ontario, Manitoba, Saskatchewan, Alberta, and British Columbia). Consequently, a spate of new universities had to be built to keep up with the increased demand, including York, Trent, Brock, Waterloo, Simon Fraser, Regina, Lethbridge, Brandon, Lakehead, and Université du Québec à Montréal. Masses of 'foreign' professors were required to staff these new schools, and most were imported from the United States, further stoking fears of 'Americanization'. Thus, 'Canadianization' made its way back onto the political agenda, that is, a desire on the part of many to place strict legal limits on what, and how many, American resources could be imported into Canada at any given time.

'Canadianization' proved a sticky problem for the minority government of Lester B. Pearson, which found itself publicly torn between the 'continental solidarity' of past Liberal administrations and fears of outright annexation. While Pearson oversaw the introduction of a new post-colonial flag (1965) and national anthem (1966) for Canada during his tenure as Prime Minister—replacing the Red Ensign (or still, sometimes, the Union Jack) and 'God Save The Queen', respectively—both measures proved polarizing. Many saw the adoptions as outright capitulations to Québécois and American interests, not just as betrayals of Canada's British heritage, while others saw them as bold but necessary steps towards true sovereignty. Still others, but especially the country's growing number of so-called 'left-nationalists', complained that Pearson had missed the point entirely—economic sovereignty, they claimed, was necessary for Canada to have anything like cultural sovereignty. As University of Toronto professor George Grant argued in his incendiary essay from 1963, *Lament for a Nation* (1963), a 'branch-plant economy' creates a 'branch-plant culture', and Canada has ever been a 'branch plant'—first of France, then of Britain, and finally, by the early 1960s, of America. Margaret Atwood may have summarized this position best in 1972, in her influential essay on Canadian literature, *Survival*:

> Let us suppose, for the sake of argument, that Canada as a whole is a victim, or an 'oppressed minority', or 'exploited'. Let us suppose in short that Canada is a colony. A partial definition of a colony is that it is a place from which a profit is made, but *not by the people who live there*: the major profit from a colony is made in the centre of the empire. That's what colonies are for, to make money for the 'mother country', and that's what—since the days of Rome and, more recently, of the Thirteen Colonies—they have always been for. Of course there are cultural side effects which are often identified as 'the colonial mentality' . . . but the root cause for them is economic. (Atwood, 1972: 45)

Perhaps out of character for a politician, Pearson seems to have listened in earnest to his critics, and eventually he even agreed that Canada had probably capitulated too much economically to Americans. In 1963 Pearson's Finance Minister, Walter Gordon, delivered a budget that proposed rigid curbs on American investments; critics claimed that Gordon was pandering to economic nationalists with the budget, and the country's business media heckled and mocked Gordon until he was forced to resign. Later that same year, Pearson reversed a campaign promise to refuse nuclear warheads for Bomarc missiles purchased from the US, and the media jeered once more. By 1965, only two years into Pearson's tenure, the country was primed for yet another election—its fourth in only seven years. Suddenly, Canada seemed like a hard place to govern.

Nowhere was this truer than in Quebec. As the optimistic reformism of the Quiet Revolution gave way to a straightforwardly militant nationalism in the province, some activists embraced variously 'soft' and 'hard' forms of terrorism. A number of terrorist organizations formed in Quebec during the early 1960s, each of which was dedicated to some form of sovereignty for the province, often under the banner of a

Cuban-style socialism. The most notorious of these groups, and certainly the most important for understanding Canada's political development into the 1970s, was the Front de Libération du Québec (FLQ). Dedicated wholly to achieving political independence for Quebec through subversion of the democratic process, the FLQ proclaimed three primary grievances as justification for their terrorist activities: first, given that business in Quebec was conducted primarily in English, francophones suffered economic discrimination in their home province; second, the country's constitutional system was corrupt because it did not recognize francophones (let alone the country's Aboriginal population); and, finally, channels to democratic reform were cut off from francophones because Canada was officially anglophone.

Sensing correctly that Quebec would soon set the political agenda in Canada for the foreseeable future, Pearson established the Royal Commission on Bilingualism and Biculturalism in 1963. Its official mission was to ascertain Quebec's place in Confederation once and for all, and it followed three main avenues of inquiry to do so:

- the actual extent of bilingualism in federal government;
- the role of public and private groups in providing better cultural relations between francophone and anglophone Canadians;
- the likelihood that Canada could become bilingual.

The Commission was almost immediately controversial. Francophones, in particular, complained that the Commission was simply a distraction, if not a tool of outright assimilation. And the further west a person went, the more likely it became that the B&B Commission would be described as a means of foisting French language, and Québécois culture, onto the rest of Canada.

As the B&B Commission painstakingly held hearings and broadened its vague mandate through the sixties, between 1963 and 1970 the FLQ carried out over 200 bombings, and a growing number of student activists flocked to the separatist cause, staging sympathy demonstrations to raise awareness about social and economic conditions in the province. The FLQ targeted what they considered to be symbols of anglophone dominance in Quebec, including federal mailboxes, armouries, the Montreal Stock Exchange, stores in Westmount (the wealthy anglophone neighbourhood in Montreal), and even McGill University; at least seven people died, and 27 more were injured, as a result. In October of 1970 the FLQ carried out two terrorist kidnappings—of British Trade Commissioner James Cross and Quebec's Minister of Labour, Pierre Laporte, who was murdered—that precipitated one of the worst crises Canada had yet faced as a country, the 'October Crisis' of 1970 (see Chapter 5).

While the radicalism and turmoil for which the 1960s are now remembered were reflected in many rock records made later in the decade, the presence of experimental or 'radical' music on the pop charts throughout the 1960s is often exaggerated by historians. The rhythm and blues genre not only exerted a tremendous influence on the development of rock music in the 1960s, but continued to develop on its own—as an entirely separate entity. The same is true of country and western, though its influences on the rock tradition are sometimes less obvious. To survey the concurrent progress of these genres throughout the 1960s is, however, beyond our present purpose, which is concerned primarily with providing a Canadian perspective on the historical development of the rock tradition. As such, we begin this chapter with a brief study of the work of Ray Charles, James Brown, and Aretha Franklin—all of whom played pivotal roles in establishing and popularizing the concept of soul music—and the direct, and clear, influence they had on rock musicians and fans well into the 1970s. We then survey two distinctly North American responses to the British Invasion—the surfer rock of Brian Wilson and the Beach Boys, and the folk rock of Bob Dylan and his contemporaries—before turning our attention to the development of acid rock and counterculture rock in the late 1960s. We conclude with a brief study of rock music made in Canada in the later 1960s, and with a look at the rise of so-called 'festival rock'.

Ray Charles and the Dawn of Soul

Ray Charles (born Ray Charles Robinson, 1930–2004) was a constant presence on the R&B charts during the 1950s, but major crossover success eluded him until 1959, when the stunning blues-based and gospel-drenched 'What'd I Say?' topped the R&B charts and hit Number 6 on the pop charts simultaneously. But Charles never consciously addressed his recordings to the 'teen' market—or to any other obviously delimited market, for that matter. As soon as he established himself as a mass-market artist with 'What'd I Say?', Charles immediately changed tack and released a highly individual version of Hank Snow's Canadian country classic 'I'm Movin' On' (1950), which remains to this day one of the biggest country records of all time. Within a year, Charles had achieved his first Number 1 pop hit in America with his version of the old Tin Pan Alley standard 'Georgia on My Mind' (by Stuart Correll and Hoagy Carmichael), which also made it to Number 3 on the R&B chart and Number 28 on the CHUM charts that year. But Charles's most astounding success was with his version of country artist Don Gibson's 'I Can't Stop Loving You', which brought his unique take on country music to top spot on the pop, R&B, and CHUM charts in 1962, earning him the best-selling record of that year in the process.

Ray Charles was certainly not the first artist to assay many different genres, and he was certainly only one of many to achieve remarkable crossover success. What is it, then, that made his career so distinctive, and Charles such a universally admired pop musician—by audiences, critics, and other musicians—that the appellation 'genius' has clung to his name for decades, as if he was born with the title? Part of the answer to this question must surely be the astounding range of talents Charles cultivated: he was a fine songwriter, having written and adapted many of his own early R&B hits, including classics of the genre like 'I've Got a Woman' and 'Hallelujah I Love Her So' (the former was an adaptation of the gospel standard, 'Jesus Is All the World To Me'); he was a highly skilled arranger, as well as an exceptionally fine keyboard player, who was fluent in jazz as well as mainstream pop idioms; and, above all, Charles was an outstanding vocalist, with a timbre so distinctive as to be instantly recognizable, and an expressive intensity that, once heard, is difficult to forget. But this still tells only part of the story. Charles's most characteristic records are not only distinguished and individual but also unique and encompassing statements about popular music style per se. One might even go so far as to call Charles the first, if not the finest, 'meta' musician of the rock tradition.

Although the term 'soul music' would not enter the lexicon until the later 1960s, it is clearly soul music that Ray Charles was pioneering in his gospel-blues synthesis of the 1950s. He is now widely acknowledged as the first important soul artist, and his work proved an incalculable influence on James Brown, Aretha Franklin, Curtis Mayfield, Otis Redding, Sly Stone, and innumerable others. When Charles went on to record Tin Pan Alley and country material in the 1960s, far from leaving his soul stylings behind, he brought them along to help him forge new, wider-ranging, and arguably braver combinations of styles.

When Charles recorded 'Georgia on My Mind', for instance, he did not attempt to turn the Tin Pan Alley standard into a rhythm and blues song the way that Fats Domino did with 'My Blue Heaven'. Neither did Charles remake himself into a crooner the way that Elvis Presley often did when performing mainstream pop-oriented material. Rather than using the jump band group that had backed him on most of his earlier records, and then perhaps adding some strings and a crooning background chorus, Charles wholeheartedly embraced the Tin Pan Alley heritage of the song and presided over a sumptuous arrangement of it, complete with orchestral strings and accompanying chorus, that virtually outdid the Tin Pan Alley version itself in its elaborateness and unrestrained sentiment. But against this smooth and beautifully performed backdrop—Charles always insisted on the highest musical standards from all

Ray Charles in 1960. Courtesy Library of Congress.

personnel involved in his performances—Charles sang 'Georgia on My Mind' as if he were performing a deeply personal blues. While the original words, melody, and phrasing of the song were clearly conveyed, Charles employed an intense and sometimes rough-edged vocal timbre, used constant syncopation, and selectively added shakes, moans, and other improvised touches ('*I said-a, Georgia*') to reflect what was at this point his natural, individual vocal approach, rooted in gospel and blues. And he occasionally provided jazz-based fills on the piano between vocal phrases, to evoke call-and-response within his own performance, while the backing chorus echoed his words at strategic intervals, producing call-and-response between them and Charles himself.

The result of all this was an extraordinary and unprecedented juxtaposition and dialogue of styles within a single recording. And as the description above indicates, this was no haphazard jumble of different elements—the production came across as expressive and utterly purposeful. In effect, Ray Charles did more than reinterpret 'Georgia on My Mind'. Rather, he virtually reinvented the song for a new generation of listeners and, in so doing, left his mark on the song permanently. Indeed, it seems only fitting that, in 1979, Charles's version of the song was legally adopted as 'the official song of the state of Georgia'.

In 1962 Charles cast his stylistic net wider still, producing a concept album—*Modern Sounds in Country and Western Music*—that still stands as a milestone in the history of popular music. When Charles first announced to his record company that he wanted to do an album of country songs, the project was derisively labelled 'Ray's folly'; it was thought that he would lose his audience. Charles is not a man to be crossed, however, and he persevered, with the result that he enlarged his audience even further, and certainly far beyond anyone's expectations. By this point, Charles was aggressively and creatively playing with stylistic mixtures, and the album essentially redrew the map of the rock tradition, both appealing to, and challenging, fans of radically different genres.

Every song on *Modern Sounds in Country and Western Music* was transformed from its origins into something rich and strange. The Everly Brothers' 'Bye, Bye, Love' and Hank Williams's 'Hey, Good Lookin'' became big-band shouts to bookend the album, while other songs received orchestral treatments worthy of the best Tin Pan Alley arrangements (or, of Charles's 'Georgia on My Mind'). It's hard to think of any major aspect of the rock tradition, and North American popular music in general, that isn't represented or at least implied somewhere on this amazingly generous record; the tapestry of stylistic and historical associations it weaves reaches across space, time, and race to build radically new bridges. The enormously popular 'I Can't Stop Loving You', for instance, merges aspects of country, Tin Pan Alley, gospel, blues, and even a hint of jazz piano. Here, Charles engages in stylistic call-and-response with the large background chorus, personalizing the lyrics that they sing in smooth, massed harmony. The deliberateness of this dialogue is clearly revealed towards the end of the record by Charles's seemingly offhand, but illuminating, aside to the chorus: '*Sing the song, children*' (a remark that also confirms, as if there could be any doubt, exactly who's in charge here).

Although Ray Charles's many country-oriented records of the 1960s did extremely well on both pop and R&B charts across North America, they did not register on any country charts until much later (Charles finally cracked the American country charts in the 1980s, with some of his later efforts in the genre). Perhaps Charles's genre-bending approach was a bit too exotic for the typical country music fan. Nonetheless, these records were heard and deeply appreciated by many country musicians. We can take the word of no less an authority than Willie Nelson, who once said that 'with his recording of "I Can't Stop Loving You", Ray Charles did more for country music than any other artist.'

Soul Brother Number One and Lady Soul

Among the many significant artists whose names became linked with the concept of 'soul music' in the 1960s, James Brown and Aretha Franklin are likely most representative. Like Ray Charles, Brown and Franklin are exceptionally popular performers with multi-decade careers; in fact, Brown and Franklin are reportedly the two best-selling rhythm and blues artists of the entire post-war period. Both Brown (known as 'Soul Brother Number One') and Franklin (known as 'Lady Soul') also brought experience with gospel singing to bear upon their performances of secular material. In so doing, they each developed an intense, flamboyant, gritty, and highly individual approach to the singing of pop music.

James Brown

If Charles employed 'soul' as an avenue of approach to the most diverse kinds of material, James Brown (1933–2006) revealed different tendencies virtually from the beginning. His first record, an original called 'Please, Please, Please' (Number 5 R&B, 1956), is indicative: while the song is in the general format of a strophic 1950s R&B ballad, Brown's vocal clings obsessively to repetitions of individual words (the title 'please', or even a simple 'I') so that sometimes the activity of an entire strophe will centre on the syncopated, violently accented reiterations of a single syllable. The result is startling and hypnotic—like a secular version of a transfixed preacher, Brown shows himself willing to leave traditional notions of verbal grammar and meaning far behind in order to convey his heightened emotional condition in song.

Later in his career, Brown would leave the structures of 1950s R&B far behind. In fact, by the late 1960s Brown had abandoned chord changes altogether in many of his songs. Thus, on a characteristic Brown tune from the time like 'There Was a Time' (Number 3 R&B, Number 36 pop, 1968), the focus of musical attention is almost exclusively on the play of rhythm and timbre, in both the instrumental and vocal parts. While the singer does tell a story in this song, the vocal melody is little more than a series of informal reiterations of a small number of brief, formulaic pitch shapes; the harmony is completely static, with the instrumental parts reduced to

James Brown in action, 1964. Courtesy Library of Congress.

repeating **riffs** or held chords. But this description does the song scant justice—when performed by Brown and his band, the song's effect is mesmerizing.

James Brown's fully developed version of soul is a music of exquisitely focused intensity, devoted to demonstrating the truth of the saying 'less is more'. In the politically charged 'Say It Loud—I'm Black and I'm Proud', for instance, which reached Number 1 on the R&B charts and Number 10 on the pop charts in 1968, Brown pares his vocal down to highly rhythmic speech, backed once again by a harmonically static but rhythmically active accompaniment. Although the term would not be in use for at least a decade, 'Say It Loud—I'm Black and I'm Proud' is, for all intents and purposes, a *rap* number—a striking anticipation of important black music to come (both in its musical style and in its emphasis on the black experience as subject matter) and a telling illustration of Brown's pivotal role in the history of pop culture generally.

In the wake of the urban folk movement of the early 1960s, in which white singers sometimes presented themselves as spokespeople for the political and social concerns of their entire generation, regardless of contributions made by the likes of Leon Bibb, Odetta, Miriam Makeba, Harry Belafonte, and numerous other black performers, Brown led black musicians in assuming a significant role for the black community; his contributions were especially significant in the time of enormous unrest and political instability that followed the assassinations of the Reverend Martin Luther King Jr and Robert Kennedy in 1968. Of course, we should note that by the late 1960s francophone–anglophone relations had clearly superseded race divisions in Canada, both in terms of discourse and urgency. Indeed, the takeover and eventual vandalism of the computer centre at Sir George Williams University (now Concordia) in Montreal in a protest against racial intolerance and Canadian 'imperialism' in the Caribbean, which involved black immigrant students from the West Indies and led to nearly 100 arrests, was the exception that proved the rule (see Chapter 5). On the whole, while counterculture activists in Canada continued to stage sympathy demonstrations for the civil rights movement in the United States, as well as focusing on nuclear disarmament and the Vietnam War, once the FLQ kidnapped James Cross and Pierre Laporte the issue of Quebec took on a more pressing character. This partially explains why Brown's more politically explicit songs—such as 'Say It Loud—I'm Black and I'm Proud'—failed to chart in Canada, while his more traditional R&B material, such as 'It's a Man's, Man's World' (1966), topped the charts.

Obviously, Brown was not speaking to Canadian listeners primarily. Thanks largely to Brown's interventions in American politics during the late 1960s, soul musicians in general came to be regarded as essential contributors to what historians now dub the 'black power movement', which emerged to the cultural fore in America during the late 1960s and early 1970s. Based on the public writings and works of Malcolm X, Angela Davies, Stokeley Carmichael (who coined the term 'black power'), and numerous other black nationalists active at the time, black power activists rejected the non-violent protest strategies of previous civil rights groups in favour of an almost militaristic collectivism geared towards achieving self-determination and self-sufficiency for America's black communities (likely the most famous organization to pursue these goals was the Black Panther Party for Self-Defense). Musicians such as James Brown, with songs like 'Say It Loud—I'm Black and I'm Proud', and Aretha Franklin, with 'Think!', both echoed and encouraged these concerns; and those in political power heard their call. For his 'constructive contributions' to 'the politics of his time', Brown, for instance, was publicly honoured by both Vice-President Hubert Humphrey and President Lyndon Johnson.

From the late 1960s through the disco music of the 1970s, from the beginnings of rap on through the flowering of hip-hop in the 1990s, no other single musician has proven to be as influential on the sound and style of black music as James Brown. His repetitive, riff-based instrumental style, which elevated rhythm far above harmony as the primary source of interest, provided the foundation on which most of the dance-oriented music of this entire period was based. His records are **sampled** by hip-hop artists more than those of any other musician—which is not surprising, given his achievement as a pioneer of the rap style.

Brown's focus on rhythm and timbre—and in particular the complex, **interlocking polyrhythms** present in many of his songs—has been cited by many critics and historians as demonstrating his strong conceptual links with West African music styles. Certainly, the minimizing or elimination of chord changes and the consequent de-emphasis on harmony make Brown's music seem, both in conception and in actual sound, a lot less 'Western' in orientation than a good deal of African-American music that preceded it. This quality, more than any other in Brown's work, resonated with African-American culture in the late 1960s and early 1970s, when there was a marked concern with awareness of African 'roots'; and one might also argue that the acceptance and wide influence of the 'non-Western' in Brown's music helped provide a foundation for the recent explosion of interest in world music of many sorts, which was such a significant and distinguishing characteristic of the cultural scene in the 1980s and 1990s.

As influential as his records were, Brown was above all an artist who exulted and excelled in live performance, where his acrobatic physicality and remarkable personal charisma added great excitement to the vocal improvisations he could spin over the ever-tight accompaniment of his band. A typical Brown show ended with the singer on his knees, evoking once again the intensity of the gospel preacher as he exhorts his 'congregation' *'Please, please, please!'* Although he was not the first pop artist to release a live album, Brown's *Live at the Apollo*, recorded in concert at the famed Apollo Theater in Harlem in late 1962, proved an important pop breakthrough both for him and for the idea of the concert album, as it reached Number 2 on the *Billboard* chart of best-selling albums in 1963 and remained on that chart for well over a year. In particular, the album allowed listeners to experience without interruption an example of one of Brown's remarkable extended 'medleys', in which several of his songs were strung together without dropping a single beat to produce a cumulative effect. Many pop artists since have released 'live' albums—in fact, the 'live' album has become virtually an expected event in the recording career of any artist with a significant following—but few have matched the sheer visceral intensity of James Brown's *Live at the Apollo*.

Aretha Franklin

Like Ray Charles and James Brown, Aretha Franklin (b. 1942) underwent a long period of 'apprenticeship' before she achieved her definitive breakthrough as a pop star in 1967. After an unfocused and less than stellar tenure at Columbia Records from 1960 to 1966, during which time she recorded a mixture of Tin Pan Alley standards and unremarkable rhythm and blues songs, Franklin went over to Atlantic Records.

An indie label with a long history of R&B success, Atlantic knew exactly what to do with Franklin. Producers Ahmet Ertegun and Jerry Wexler encouraged her to record strong material well suited to her spectacular voice, and they engaged stellar and empathetic musicians to back her up (usually the Muscle Shoals Sound Rhythm Section, based in Alabama). The rest, as they say, is history. Beginning with 'I Never Loved a Man (The Way I Love You)' (Number 1 R&B, Number 9 pop, Number 15 CHUM, 1967), Franklin produced an extraordinary and virtually

Aretha Franklin performs on
television, 1967. Courtesy
Library of Congress.

uninterrupted stream of hit records over a five-year period that included 13 million-sellers and 13 Top 10 pop hits.

Franklin came by her gospel influences honestly, having literally grown up with gospel music. Her father was the Reverend C.L. Franklin, the pastor of a large Baptist congregation in Detroit and an acclaimed gospel singer himself. Aretha Franklin's first recordings were as a gospel singer, at the age of 14, and she occasionally returned to gospel even in the midst of her career as a pop singer—most spectacularly with the 'live' album *Amazing Grace* (1972), which was actually recorded in a church. *Amazing Grace* built on Franklin's established popularity to introduce legions of pop music fans to the power of gospel music. The album was a Top 10 best-seller, and the best-selling album of Franklin's career, selling over two million copies.

What is arguably most important about Aretha Franklin is the overwhelming power and intensity of her vocal delivery. Into a pop culture that had almost totally identified female singers with gentility, docility, and sentimentality, Franklin belted out huge gusts of revisionist fresh air. When she demanded 'respect' (see the 'Listening To' section), or exhorted her audience to 'think about what you're trying to do to me' (in the hit recording 'Think' of 1968, which she co-wrote), the strength of her interpretations moved her songs beyond the traditional realm of personal intimate relationships and into the larger political and social spheres. Especially in the context of the late 1960s, with the civil rights and black power movements at their heights, and the movement for women's empowerment undergoing the initial stirrings of a powerful post-suffragette resurgence, it was difficult not to hear large-scale ramifications in the records of this extraordinary woman. Although Aretha Franklin did not become an overtly political figure in the way that James Brown did, it may be claimed that she nevertheless made strong political and social statements just through the very character of her performances.

Directly tied to this issue is the fact that Franklin was not only a vocal interpreter on her records, but also—like Charles and Brown—a major player in many aspects of their sound and production. She wrote or co-wrote a significant portion of her repertoire (this involvement goes back to her early days at Columbia). In addition, Franklin is a powerful keyboard player; her piano is heard to great advantage on many of her recordings. And she also provided vocal arrangements, which were coloured by the call-and-response of the gospel tradition in which she was raised. In other words, Franklin not only symbolized female empowerment in the sound of her records but she also actualized female empowerment in the process of making them. By the time she recorded a tune called 'Sisters Are Doin' It for Themselves' (with Annie Lennox of the Eurythmics) in 1985, she was, in effect, telling a story that had been personally true for a long time. But in the 1960s female empowerment was something quite new and important in the history of pop music. And neither its novelty nor its importance was lost on the rising generation of female singer-songwriters—including Laura Nyro, Joni Mitchell, and Carole King, to name but three—whose ascent to prominence began directly in the wake of Aretha Franklin's conquest of the pop charts.

Listening To Two Classics of Soul: 'Papa's Got a Brand New Bag' (1965) and 'Respect' (1967)

'Papa's Got a Brand New Bag', composed by James Brown, performed by James Brown and the Famous Flames (Number 8 pop, Number 1 R&B); 'Respect', composed by Otis Redding, performed by Aretha Franklin (Number 1 pop, Number 1 R&B)

Both James Brown's 'Papa's Got a Brand New Bag' and Aretha Franklin's 'Respect' exemplify the intense vocal performance and use of call-and-response techniques characteristic of soul music. In Brown's case, the call-and-response takes place between his solo vocal and the instrumental accompaniment, while on Franklin's recording a female singing group provides the responses to her lead vocal. Each of the recordings under discussion was career-defining for its respective artist. 'Papa's Got a Brand New Bag' was Brown's first Top 10 pop hit and the

biggest R&B hit of his entire career, while 'Respect' was for Franklin both her first Number 1 pop hit and the biggest R&B hit of her entire career.

'Papa's Got a Brand New Bag' is an excellent representative example for James Brown, for in a sense it looks both forward and back in his career. In terms of its form, the song uses the time-tested 12-bar blues pattern as its basis, breaking up the pattern after two strophes with an eight-bar bridge section (a device we have also seen before; see the discussion of 'Charlie Brown' in Chapter 2) before continuing with further blues-based stanzas. In terms of subject matter, the song's lyrics obviously recall the dance-oriented rock 'n' roll songs of the early 1960s, as the singer praises 'Papa's'—presumably Brown's—ability to do the jerk, the fly, the monkey, the mashed potatoes, the twist, and, even, the 'boomerang'—calling attention to Brown's dancing, which was a legendary aspect of his live shows. However, even if the song itself looks back at the past in its form and its lyrics, Brown's actual recording sounds nothing like a typical blues-based R&B record of its time, nor like a typical teen-oriented dance song. Instead, the record looks forward to the riff-dominated records that would shortly define dance-oriented soul music in the later 1960s and the 1970s.

The critical factor here is the repeating instrumental riff, which embodies a kind of call-and-response pattern, as two strong, short, rhythmic 'stabs' on successive beats are answered by a four-note figure in the horn section of the band, landing on an accented final note (da-da-da-dum). This riff is used for all of the 12-bar blues sections in 'Papa's Got a Brand New Bag'. The pitches change slightly to accommodate the chord change at the fifth bar of these sections (see the discussion of 12-bar blues in Chapter 1), but the really arresting event occurs at the tenth bar, where the instrumental accompaniment stops entirely for a few beats, creating a passage of what jazz musicians call 'stoptime'. This produces enormous tension, and after Brown completes his next vocal phrase, the lead guitar bursts back in with an aggressive pattern of rapidly strummed chords that prepares the return of the riff and of the rhythm section. Thus, the listener's attention is directed away from the harmonic changes in the 12-bar blues pattern and more towards events defined by rhythm: the presence or absence of the riff, and stoptime as opposed to rhythmic continuity. Even the sense of a separate bridge section is downplayed consider-

ably on this recording, as the harmony remains fairly static throughout the bridge (whereas, typically, it would wander, and change, more rapidly than elsewhere), while a slightly different—but nonetheless clearly related—three-note horn riff is heard in every bar.

When listening to 'Papa's Got a Brand New Bag', then, one experiences musical shaping created more emphatically by rhythmic patterns than by chord changes or melodic lines. In terms of the sound and the groove of the record, we are here well on our way towards the minimizing or even elimination of chord changes that would characterize much of Brown's later work. It is this aspect of the record that is so arrestingly novel and that represents such a significant discovery on Brown's part. In fact, 'Papa's Got a Brand New Bag' is worthy of its title and of its enduring popularity. In 1965 it represented an enormous flying leap into the future of soul, a musical analogy to Brown's own daring acrobatic leaps on stage.

Merely by undertaking to record 'Respect', Aretha Franklin took a daring step. The song had already been a significant hit for its composer, Otis Redding, in 1965 (Number 4 R&B, Number 35 pop). By covering the song, Franklin was, in a sense, going head-to-head with one of the most impressive and powerful soul singers of the day—and on his home turf, so to speak, by taking on a song he had written for himself. But the implications of Franklin's cover extend well beyond this, because Redding's song is a demand for 'respect' from one's lover, and by putting the song in a woman's voice Franklin radically shifts the sense of who is in control in the relationship. In her version, it is she—the woman—who has *what you want* and *what you need*', not to mention 'money' as well. And Franklin makes a telling change in the lyrics of the second strophe. In Redding's original, he acknowledges that his woman might do him wrong, yet it's all right with him so long as she only does so '*while I'm gone*'. But Franklin tells her lover that '*I ain't gonna do you wrong while you're gone*' (presumably his doing her wrong is not even in question) but only ''*cause I don't wanna*'. It could not be clearer just who is holding all the cards in Franklin's version.

Of course, none of Franklin's play with the gender issues implicit in 'Respect' would have any effect if it weren't for the overwhelming power and assurance with which she delivers the song and makes it her own. Each strophe of the song builds effectively to the crucial word '*respect*', at which point the backing group joins in call-and-response with Franklin. But Franklin is also careful to structure her entire performance around a steadily building intensity, so that the listener hears something much more than a song with four identical strophes. By the time we reach the third strophe, she is improvising variants on the basic melody, and the call-and-response is varied as well ('*just a, just a, just a, just a, just a, just a, just a, just a little bit*'). After this a brief but completely unexpected instrumental break, with totally unexpected chords new to the song, raises the emotional temperature in preparation for the final strophe. The last time around, Franklin reaches her highest note yet in the song on '*All I want you to do for me*', and the backing group matches her new intensity with its own new response: '*re-re-re-re-re-re-re-spect*'. Then, instead of ending, this final strophe is extended with a stoptime solo for Franklin, after which the group responds with a shot heard 'round the world ('*sock it to me, sock it to me, sock it to me . . .*') and the record fades with Franklin and her backing singers trading shout for shout.

The Beach Boys Better the Beatles: 'Good Vibrations'

By 1965 Brian Wilson had achieved international acclaim as a composer and producer, and the Beach Boys were being touted as the most serious creative and commercial threat to the dominance of the Beatles across North America and in Britain. In 1964 alone the group logged six Top 20 records on both sides of the Atlantic, thanks largely to the increasing novelty of Wilson's studio productions and his maturing compositional style. By mid-1964 Wilson had moved past obvious emulation as a composer, and into a period of aggressive experimentation with inherited styles and forms. 'I Get Around', for instance, which was the Beach Boys' first Number 1 record in the US—the single reached Number 3 on the CHUM charts that year—turns the up-tempo rock 'n' roll anthem into a thoroughly individual kind of expression; the song's adventurous chord changes and quirky phrase structure take it well beyond the boundaries of 1950s rock 'n' roll, without ever sacrificing the immediate appeal and accessibility so essential to the genre. On the other hand, an album track like 'The Warmth of the Sun' (from *Shut Down, Volume 2*, released in 1964), while clearly a descendant of the doo-wop ballad in sound, rhythm, and vocal texture, presents lyrics that probe the dissolution of young romance in a newly poignant and personal way, set to music that so enlarges the melodic and harmonic boundaries of the surf style that one quickly forgets the song's antecedents and focuses instead on its remarkable individuality. While it is questionable whether a song like 'Warmth of the Sun' would have been successful as a single, it is unquestionable that songs like this were heard and appreciated, both by listeners and by those involved in the making of pop music, and thus contributed significantly to the evolution of the rock tradition. We can also see here the beginnings of a significant trend: the increasing importance of album tracks, and eventually of albums themselves, in the development of rock music in the later 1960s.

After 1965, while the Beach Boys were off on tour, Wilson stayed home to prepare his response and challenge to the Beatles, whose late 1965 album *Rubber Soul* had particularly inspired him. His response took the form of an elaborately produced, and strikingly unconventional, album called *Pet Sounds*. Less a work of rock 'n' roll than a nearly symphonic cycle of songs, *Pet Sounds* charts a progression from youthful optimism ('Wouldn't It Be Nice' and 'You Still Believe in Me') to philosophical and emotional disillusionment ('I Just Wasn't Made for These Times' and 'Caroline, No'). Released in mid-1966, *Pet Sounds* was arguably rock's first *concept* album—that is, an album conceived as an integrated whole with interrelated songs arranged in a deliberate sequence (the listening sequence was easier to mandate, obviously, in the days of long-playing records with two numbered sides, played on phonographs without remote controls, than in today's world of single-sided compact discs whose contents listeners may readily program, and edit, for themselves by pushing a few buttons).

Pet Sounds was a modest seller compared to some other Beach Boys albums, but it had an enormous impact on musicians who heard it. With its display of diverse and unusual instrumentation (including orchestral wind instruments as well as strings), its virtuosic vocal arrangements (showcasing the songs' advanced harmonies), and its occasional formal experiments (exemplified by the AA'BCC' form of the remarkable instrumental 'Let's Go Away for Awhile'), the album was state-of-the-art pop music in every sense, designed to push at the boundaries of pop music convention. Its historical importance is certified by Paul McCartney's affirmation that *Pet Sounds* was the single greatest influence on the Beatles' landmark 1967 album, *Sgt. Pepper's Lonely Hearts Club Band*, alongside Frank Zappa and the Mothers of Invention's *Freak Out!* (1965).

Wilson furthered his experimentation with the late 1966 single, 'Good Vibrations', which reached Number 1 on the pop charts across North America and remains probably the Beach Boys' most famous song (see the 'Listening To' section). By this time, Wilson was also at work on an album to be called *Smile*. Eagerly anticipated for many months, *Smile* was abandoned in 1967, and the collapse of what was evidently a strikingly novel and ambitious project—even by Wilson's exceptionally high standards—marked the onset of a decline in his productivity and achievement from which he has only recently recovered. The material from the *Smile* sessions occasionally surfaced on later albums and CD compilations by the Beach Boys, hinting at how unprecedented and stunning the album was intended to be. The promise of *Smile* was finally fulfilled when Wilson returned to and completed the project in 2004.

Listening To the Beach Boys' 'Good Vibrations' (1966)

'Good Vibrations' may well be the most thoroughly innovative rock single from the decade of the 1960s. Virtually every aspect of the record is unusual, from the vocal arrangement to the instrumentation, from the chordal vocabulary to the overall form. Beginning with a gentle unaccompanied sigh in a high solo voice right at the outset—which might be an anticipation of the opening word, '*I*', but could also be just the sighing sound '*ah*'—'Good Vibrations' establishes a unique world of sounds, textures, and feelings.

Probably the only remotely conventional thing about the song is its lyrics, with their admiring references to the beloved's '*colourful clothes*', hair, perfume, smile, and eyes. But there is something otherworldly about the lyrics as well—at least when they claim, '*I don't know where, but she sends me there*', or when they refer to '*a blossom world*', not to mention the '*good vibrations*' themselves. Notice also the extensive periods on the recording where lyrics are of secondary importance, or of no importance at all: the 'C' section; the following instrumental transition; and the concluding 'variations on B' section (see listening chart). These are in no sense secondary or unimportant portions of the record itself; it is just that here sound becomes more significant than sense (literally speaking)—or, better, the sound becomes the sense of the song, that is, the way in which Wilson musically communicates the sensuous experience that is the essential subject matter of 'Good Vibrations'.

Form

There is no name for the form of 'Good Vibrations'; it is as individual and distinctive as everything else about this recording. The best way to follow it is with the listening chart. The formal freedom is that much more effective because Wilson sets the listener up at first to expect a straightforward, predictable verse-chorus form with his initial ABAB pattern—since the lyrics to 'A' change but those to 'B' remain the same—and then goes on to present the unexpected. The 'C' section could seem at first like a bridge, but instead of any return to 'A' we get totally new material in 'D'. In fact, the 'A' music never returns at all, which is probably the second most surprising thing about this formal structure. The most surprising thing is that Wilson somehow manages to make this unconventional form work so effectively.

It works because of subtle interconnections among the different musical sections. The 'C' section has overlapping vocal textures reminiscent of the vocal textures in the song's 'B' sections, even though the specific music and the words are different. In the unexpected 'D' section, the organ and percussion accompaniment maintains a kinship with the 'A' sections, which also prominently feature those instruments. In addition, the clear presence of the words '*good vibrations*' in the 'D' section provides a textual link between it and the preceding 'B' sections, and also ties 'D' to the concluding section, which we are calling 'variations on B'.

This final section—'variations on B'—requires a few comments. Its relationship with the earlier 'B' sections is textually and musically obvious, but it is also clear that this is not a literal repetition, nor is it the kind of slight modification that would mandate a B¹ label. Rather, Wilson is taking verbal, musical, and textural ideas from his 'B' material and arranging them in new ways to create a section that sounds evolutionary rather than stable. We could borrow a term from classical music and call this a kind of 'development' section; 'development' is a term rarely if ever needed to describe formal sections of popular songs, but then, most popular songs do not behave like 'Good Vibrations'. Wilson employs one particularly sophisticated music device here—at the beginning of the 'variations on B' he plays the characteristic chord progression of the earlier 'B' sections, but in reverse order, starting on the final chord and ending on the opening chord; this allows him to proceed by then taking the opening chord again and playing the chords in the original order—but with new, textless vocal parts—such that the material seems to be in constant flux. Remarkably, the song fades out while immersed in this development section, never having returned to its point of origin or to any other stable reference point. In a way, this is a perfect ending for a record so thoroughly liberated from traditional formal constraints.

The Song/The Recording

As a composition, 'Good Vibrations' boasts memorable melodic hooks and a wide and colourful palette of chords. Both the high opening minor-key melody of the 'A' section (which first

ascends, and then descends) and the major-key bass line '*I'm pickin' up good vibrations*' of the 'B' section (which first descends, and then ascends) are instantly memorable tunes—and beautifully contrasting ones. (The lyric line proved to be memorable: Cyndi Lauper, in 1983, used it ironically in her ode to female masturbation, 'She Bop'.) Consequently, these tunes serve as effective landmarks for the listener who is journeying for the first time through this complex musical landscape. The 'D' section offers a new but equally memorable melody. Some details of the harmony are indicated on the listening chart, for those who may wish to follow them.

The instrumentation of 'Good Vibrations' is perhaps the most unusual ever employed on a hit record. Organ, flutes, solo cello, and colourful percussion instruments are all in evidence, clearly differentiating the sound of this recording from anything commonly associated with rock 'n' roll. But the ultimate exotic touch is provided by the *theremin*—the whirring, siren-like, otherworldly instrument that appropriately illustrates the 'good vibrations' in the 'B' sections (there is some question about whether the recording actually employed a theremin or a somewhat different instrument that sounds very much like one; but such questions are not of great significance to many listeners—the exotic effect is sufficient all the same). Notice how Wilson also uses the voices of the Beach Boys as an additional choir of sound colours, pitting solo against group sounds, high voices against low, and so forth. Some prominent details of both the instrumental and vocal parts are indicated in the descriptive comments on the listening chart.

'Good Vibrations' was extremely costly to produce, in terms of time and money. Wilson tried out many different instrumental and vocal arrangements, and a number of different formal schemes, committing literally hours of rehearsal time to tape before he finally settled on the version we hear today on record, which is actually a composite of several tapes made at various times. Thus, 'Good Vibrations', which Brian Wilson called his 'pocket symphony', is an important milestone in the developing history of rock production, as well as a landmark hit record of the 1960s.

Listening Chart: 'Good Vibrations'

Music by Brian Wilson, lyrics by Mike Love, produced by Brian Wilson; as performed by the Beach Boys with instrumental accompaniment

FORM	LYRICS	DESCRIPTIVE COMMENTS
A	*I love the colourful clothes . . .*	High solo voice, with delicate, high-range accompaniment of organ, flutes, and eventually percussion; minor key.
B	*I'm pickin' up good . . .*	Bass voice enters, accompanied by cello, theremin, and percussion, then rest of group comes in with overlapping vocal parts; major key.
A	*Close my eyes, she's somehow closer now . . .*	As before.
	I'm picking up . . .	As before.
C	[soft humming at first, then steadily building tension; no stable key. More vocal activity, then:] *I don't know where, but she sends me there . . .*	
Brief instrumental transition: Organ and percussion		New key established (major).
D	*Gotta keep those lovin' . . .*	Solo voice, then group, with organ accompaniment; the line of text repeats, then fades out while organ finishes the section.
Transition	*Aha! I*	
Variations on B	*I'm pickin' up good . . .*	Full group texture, with overlapping vocal parts; major key; then voices drop out, leaving cello and theremin, which are joined by percussion before fading out; no stable key.

Dylan Goes Electric: The Beginning of Folk Rock

The year 1965 was the pivotal one in Bob Dylan's career. That year Dylan moved from being the most distinctive songwriter among American urban folk artists to become an epochal influence on the entirety of Western popular culture. We may cite four major events that proved decisive in this extraordinary development, involving the release of an album, two hit singles (one by the Byrds and one by Dylan himself), and a live performance.

Early in 1965 Dylan released his fifth album, *Bringing It All Back Home*, in which acoustic numbers demonstrating his now-familiar urban folk style shared disc space with songs using electric guitar and drums. According to Dylan, the inspiration for this move towards electric instrumentation came from two distinct places: (1) a screening of the Beatles film *A Hard Day's Night*, which Dylan greatly admired (the Byrds also cite this movie as their inspiration for 'going electric'); and (2) his attendance while on tour in England at a concert given by the Animals, at which they performed their electric version of 'House of the Rising Sun' (Number 1 CHUM, 1964), which Dylan himself credits as possibly the first folk rock record.

In addition to foreshadowing a radical shift in Dylan's sound, *Bringing It All Back Home* featured several songs that carried the singer-songwriter's flair for intense and unusual poetic imagery into the realm of the surreal. One such song, 'Mr. Tambourine Man', which was not one of those performed by Dylan in a rock-oriented style, though it features both electric guitar and an electric bass (and, curiously, no tambourine), was covered by the fledgling California rock group the Byrds; their truncated version of the song, adapted to fit the customary length for radio play, soared remarkably to Number 1 in June 1965, thus becoming the first landmark folk rock hit in North America (the song reached second spot on the CHUM charts that July). The Byrds' combination of Dylan's lyrics and melody with a musical accompaniment that included tambourine (naturally), drums, and their own trademark electric Rickenbacker 12-string guitar sound was unique, memorable, and—obviously, if unexpectedly—marketable.

The lesson was not lost on Dylan himself. Shortly after hearing the Byrds, Dylan returned to the studio early in the summer of 1965 with a rock band, led by prominent urban blues guitarist Michael Bloomfield and future jazz-rock pioneer Al Kooper on keyboards, to cut his own breakthrough folk rock single, 'Like a Rolling Stone'. This six-minute epic pop single, which made it to Number 2 on the pop charts across North America, certified that a radical shift was taking place in popular culture.

As if to affirm that there would be no turning back, Dylan then appeared at the Newport Folk Festival in late July with an electric band. Many folk purists were appalled by this assault on their home turf, and Dylan was booed off the stage, only to be greeted with applause when he returned to do an acoustic set (famously featuring a sneeringly poignant rendition of 'It's All Over Now Baby Blue'). But Dylan had the last laugh, of course—it was only a short while before many urban folk artists had followed his lead into the electric wonderland of rock music.

From our latter-day vantage point, all the fuss about Dylan's 'going electric' can seem quite silly. We have seen that the rock tradition in its entirety has been a story of influences, interactions, and syntheses among its various streams. The steadily increasing popularity of both urban folk music and rock 'n' roll in the early 1960s made it inevitable that these two supposedly independent styles would eventually interact with one another and even fuse to some extent. But the boost given to this fusion by the fact that the most individual and creative of the young urban folk artists, Bob Dylan, was the first to promote it—and to promote it aggressively and enthusiastically at that—cannot be underestimated.

Bob Dylan as folk rocker (c. 1966). Courtesy Library of Congress.

From Dylan's own point of view, he was probably just following a model already well established by performers in the genres of blues and country music, genres to which his personal performing style had always demonstrated obvious ties; and, as noted, he seemed to be doing nothing different compared to groups like the Animals, who had already topped the pop charts in North America with folk rock productions of their own. Rural blues artists like Muddy Waters and Howlin' Wolf had long ago made their way to the city and developed electric blues, just as country artists like

Hank Williams had developed the honky-tonk style (see Chapter 1). And these newer blues- and country-based styles had themselves played an essential role in the 1950s synthesis that is called rock 'n' roll. Why, then, was there such a shock wave produced by the concept of Bob Dylan as a rock 'n' roll star?

It probably had to do with the differing cultural roles assigned by most people to urban folk music, on the one hand, and to rock 'n' roll, on the other. Urban folk music in the early 1960s was, as we noted in the last chapter, a self-consciously topical, politically and socially conscious music. Even the singing of traditional folksongs often carried a subtext of political identification—with labour, with the poor, with minority groups and other peoples seen as oppressed, and with a movement for international peace and understanding—depending on the nature and origins of the particular songs chosen. Thus the words were of paramount importance in urban folk music, and the acoustic guitar accompaniments enabled the words to be heard clearly. Besides, acoustic guitars were easily portable, readily accessible, and presented no elaborate barrier between performers and audiences. It was a relatively simple matter to bring an acoustic guitar along to a political meeting or demonstration, and to set up and play it there when and if the occasion presented itself, which surely cannot be said of rock 'n' roll band equipment. And, of course, rock 'n' roll was identified—even, perhaps especially, by those who enjoyed it—as a 'fun' music, a music to accompany dancing and other socializing, whose lyric content was by definition light, amusing, sometimes clever, often generic, but virtually never serious. It must surely be one of history's great ironies that historians and critics now take 'Like a Rolling Stone' very seriously indeed, as one of the pivotal singles in rock music history.

Listening To Bob Dylan's 'Like a Rolling Stone' (1965)

Composed and performed by Bob Dylan (with unidentified instrumental accompaniment)

'Like a Rolling Stone' is one of a handful of watershed recordings in the history of rock music. It effectively put an end to previous restrictions on length, subject matter, and poetic diction that had exercised a controlling influence on the creation of pop records. Although surely other records had mounted some challenges to these restrictions before Dylan cut 'Like a Rolling Stone', no other pop record attacked them so comprehensively,

or with such complete success. After the huge success of 'Like a Rolling Stone', literally nothing was the same again.

In discussing the impact of this recording, its sheer sound must not be neglected. 'Like a Rolling Stone' has an overall timbre and a sonic density that were unique for its time, owing to the exceptional prominence of two keyboard instruments—organ and piano—that dominate the texture even more than the electric guitars, bass, and drums. And the distinctive sound of Dylan's vocal cuts aggressively through this thick instrumental texture like a knife. It is difficult to say which was more influential on the future sound of rock: the keyboard-dominated band, or Dylan's in-your-face vocal style, which was positioned on the cutting edge between rhythmic speech and pitched song.

The density of sound and the aggressiveness of the vocal style are clearly suited to this fierce song about a young woman's fall from a state of oblivious privilege into one of desperation. The lyrics range from the bluntest realism:

> *You've gone to the finest school—all*
> *right, Miss Lonely, but you know*
> *You only used to get juiced in it.*
> *Nobody's ever taught you how to live*
> *out on the street, and now*
> *You're gonna have to get used to it.*

to the kind of novel surrealistic imagery that Dylan was pioneering in many of his lyrics at this time:

> *You used to ride on a chrome horse*
> *with your diplomat,*
> *Who carried on his shoulder a*
> *Siamese cat.*

The refrain that concludes each strophe is typical of Dylan insofar as it provides no resolution or answers; instead, it hurls a defiant question at the song's protagonist—and at the listener:

> *How does it feel*
> *To be without a home*
> *Like a complete unknown,*
> *Like a rolling stone?*

Doubtless for many of those in Dylan's audience, reaching adulthood and venturing out on their own for the first time, this question possessed a profound and pointed relevance.

Form

'Like a Rolling Stone' reveals its antecedents in Dylan's acoustic folk style in a number of ways, the most obvious of which relate to form. Like 'Blowin' in the Wind' and many of Dylan's other early compositions, 'Like a Rolling Stone' falls into a strophic verse-refrain pattern (see the 'Listening Outline'). But the strophes in 'Like a Rolling Stone' are extremely long; it is as if every formal aspect present in 'Blowin' in the Wind' has been enlarged to create an effect of great intensity and expansion. In the strophes of 'Blowin' in the Wind' each verse consists of three questions, which are followed by the 'answer' of the chorus. Each of the questions, as well as the 'answer', is eight bars long; the result is a rather typical 32-bar formal unit. In 'Like a Rolling Stone', however, the verse portions alone are 40 bars in length. In the chorus portions, Dylan employs his 'variable strophe' idea on a small scale but to considerable effect: the chorus in the first strophe is 20 bars long (five four-bar phrases), while in succeeding strophes the chorus expands to 24 bars (six four-bar phrases, the result of an additional repetition of a musical phrase, accompanying added words).

This formal expansion is necessary to accommodate the song's poetic content. 'Like a Rolling Stone' feels denser, not looser, than 'Blowin' in the Wind'. Compare, for instance, a typical phrase in the lyrics of the latter:

> *How many roads must a man walk*
> *down before you call him a man?*

with the opening phrase of the former:

> *Once upon a time you dressed so fine, threw the bums a dime in your prime, didn't you?*

Obviously, the lyrics are packed more tightly in an eight-bar phrase of 'Like a Rolling Stone' than they are in a comparable eight-bar phrase of 'Blowin' in the Wind'. The combination of greater verbal density (note the internal rhymes in the line quoted above, which are not atypical of 'Like a Rolling Stone' and add considerably to the effect) with overall formal expansion creates an ongoing, coiled-spring intensity. This is the more marked because Dylan's choruses in 'Like a Rolling Stone' don't even afford the listener the comfort of an ambiguous 'answer'; they only ask questions. Poetically, 'Like a Rolling Stone' takes the question-answer format of 'Blowin' in the Wind' and turns it on its head.

The Song/The Recording

In a strophic form, the lyrics obviously must supply a sense of continuing development. Each succeeding strophe of 'Like a Rolling Stone' widens its focus, as the alienation of the protagonist from her earlier realm of privilege becomes more and more marked and painful. The opening strophe basically describes the protagonist and her behaviour. The second strophe mentions the school she used to attend; the third refers to *'the jugglers and the clowns'* who entertained her and the *'diplomat'* with whom she consorted. With the final strophe we are given a wide-angle picture of *'all the pretty people'* who are *'drinkin', thinkin' that they got it made'*—

a party at which the protagonist is obviously no longer welcome.

Dylan's music serves its purpose of reinforcing the tension embodied in the content of the lyrics. We have already discussed this in terms of the overall sound of the recording. Notice, also, how every phrase in the verse portions ends with a sense of melodic incompletion, keeping the tension alive. This is another structural similarity to 'Blowin' in the Wind'. And, again, as in the earlier song, a cadence is reached only in the chorus portions—although this arguably has an ironic effect in 'Like a Rolling Stone', since the words offer no sense of completion whatsoever at these points; Dylan's recording of 'Like a Rolling Stone' fades out rather than actually concluding—like a typical rock 'n' roll song—while his 'Blowin' in the Wind' comes to a formal ending, like a typical acoustic folksong. One further connection with acoustic folk traditions in the recording of 'Like a Rolling Stone' lies in the fact that this record is, for all intents and purposes, produced to sound like nothing more than an aural document of a live studio performance with minimal, if any, editing or obvious 'studio' effects. Dylan has remained true to this kind of sound ideal—called 'veridic' by critic John Andrew Fisher—throughout his recording career, eschewing the highly produced sound typical of so much 1960s and later rock. While 'veridic' recordings sound as though they were, or could be, achieved by live performance, 'non-veridic' recordings obviously cannot be reproduced via performance; a clear indication of Dylan's preference for 'veridic' production values can be gleaned from the fact that he clearly and publicly disliked the Beatles' *Sgt. Pepper's* LP.

Six minutes long, 'Like a Rolling Stone' was by far the longest 45 rpm pop single ever released up to that time. Dylan's record company knew they were making history; the time '6:00' was emblazoned on the label in huge black numerals, demanding as much attention as the title of the song and the name of the artist. At first, some record stations pared the record down to conventional length by playing only the first two of the song's four strophes. But before long the complete single was being heard widely on national radio, and an important barrier in pop music had been broken. By the end of the 1960s, pop singles lasting over seven minutes had been made—the Beatles' 'Hey Jude' (1968), the biggest chart hit of the entire decade, clocked in at seven minutes and 11 seconds.

Listening Outline: 'Like a Rolling Stone'

FORM	LYRICS
Strophe 1: Verse	*Once upon a time . . .*
CHORUS	*How does it feel . . .*
Strophe 2: Verse	*You've gone to the finest school . . .*
CHORUS [expanded]	*How does it feel . . .*
Strophe 3: Verse	*You never turned around to see the frowns on the jugglers . . .*
CHORUS [expanded]	*How does it feel . . .*
Strophe 4: Verse	*Princess on the steeple and all the pretty people . . .*
CHORUS [expanded]	*How does it feel . . .*

Despite the popularity of 'Like a Rolling Stone' and of a few more folk rock singles that followed, Bob Dylan never really established himself as primarily a singles artist. Rather, he was the first important representative of yet another pop phenomenon: the rock musician whose career was sustained essentially by albums. Among many prominent figures who followed in these particular footsteps of Dylan, we could cite Frank Zappa, Joni Mitchell, Neil Young, Led Zeppelin, and the Grateful Dead. Every single Bob Dylan album except his first has appeared on *Billboard* magazine's 'Top Pop Albums' chart.

By the mid-1960s changes within rock 'n' roll were already in the wind, as we have seen in previous discussions of music by the Beatles and the Beach Boys. But Bob Dylan's electric style and other manifestations of folk rock had the effect of an enormous injection of growth hormones into the pop music scene. Suddenly, it was all right—expected, even—for rock 'n' roll to be as 'adult' as its baby-boomer audience was now becoming itself, and 'rock 'n' roll' abruptly grew up into 'rock'. Pop records on serious subjects, with political and poetic lyrics, sprang up everywhere; before long, this impulse carried over into the making of ambitious concept albums, as we shall see. The later 1960s flowered into a period of intense and remarkable innovation and creativity in pop music; of course, the pressure to be adult and creative also inevitably led to the production of a lot of pretentious music as well.

Dylan was, naturally, the main man to emulate. In the summer and fall of 1965 it seemed that almost everybody was either making cover records of Dylan songs or producing imitations of Dylan's songs and style. For example, both the Byrds and the pop singer Cher were on the charts during the summer with competing versions of Dylan's 'All I Really Want to Do', and the first Number 1 pop hit of the fall was the politically charged, folk rock 'Eve of Destruction'—composed by the Los Angeles songwriter P.F. Sloan in an obviously Dylanesque style, complete with variable strophes, and sung in a gruff Dylanesque voice by Barry McGuire, who had been a member of the acoustic urban folk group the New Christy Minstrels.

Dylan and the Hawks

Bob Dylan has played with literally hundreds of musicians during his almost half-century in the popular music industry, but the musical magic he conjured with the Hawks was truly unique. Credit for bringing the Hawks to Dylan's attention actually belongs to another Canadian, Mary Martin, who worked as a secretary at Albert Grossman's management firm throughout the 1960s. Martin tirelessly advocated for the group, who had only recently left the employ of Rompin' Ronnie Hawkins and struck off on their own as the Canadian Squires in 1963; as we noted in the last chapter, the group quickly shortened their name to only the Squires because they felt the word 'Canadian' lessened their appeal within Canada, before returning to the Hawks in 1964. Thus, at the insistence of Mary Martin, Dylan hired drummer Levon Helm and guitarist Robbie Robertson for an impromptu live audition during two performances at the Hollywood Bowl in the spring of 1965.

By the time of Helm's and Robertson's audition, the pattern that would come to characterize almost every show Dylan subsequently played with the Hawks in the mid-1960s was already well established: Dylan performed an acoustic set to pin-drop silence for the first 45 minutes of the concert, then returned with a rock band to the sound of vociferous booing for the rest of the night (a pause in booing often came during performances of 'Like a Rolling Stone', at which point audiences most often sang along!). Sufficiently impressed with Helm's and Robertson's performances, not to mention their composure as already seasoned veterans, Dylan flew to Toronto to see the Hawks perform at Ronnie Hawkins's nightclub, The Hawk's Nest, above Le Coq D'Or on Yonge Street. To the delight of Hawkins, Dylan decided to hire the group as his official backing band immediately following the show.

The Hawks made their debut as Dylan's backing band one week later in Austin, Texas. For the next nine months, until a crippling motorcycle accident led Dylan to withdraw from live performances altogether, he and the Hawks toured North America and Europe incessantly. The chaos of these shows soon proved overwhelming for Helm, though, who quit after just two months; he was replaced by Mickey Jones for the duration of the tour, but rejoined in the spring of 1967 (a performance by Dylan and the Hawks, minus Helm, from this period can be heard on the 1998 release, *Bob Dylan: Live 1966*).

During Dylan's 'hiatus' from touring, and while he recuperated form his accident, he and the Hawks moved into a house in West Saugerties, New York, which they dubbed 'Big Pink' in honour of a prominent pink barn on the property. At this point the Hawks renamed themselves the Band—on the one hand, the name signalled the back-to-basics and no-nonsense approach they took to performing rock 'n' roll, and on the other hand, the name was an in-joke referencing the fact that, behind Dylan, most people already referred to the group as simply 'the band' anyway. Over the next few months Dylan and the Band recorded more than a double-album's worth of material in a makeshift studio constructed in their basement. This collection of songs was truly remarkable for the time, especially insofar as it explicitly countered the tendency towards baroque 'non-veridic' productions heard on the records of Dylan's acid rock contemporaries, such as the Beach Boys' *Pet Sounds*, the Beatles' *Sgt. Pepper's Lonely Hearts Club Band*, and the Rolling Stones' *Their Satanic Majesties Request*. Dylan apparently felt that these albums sounded exaggerated and pretentious; thus, instead of an epic concept album, Dylan and the Band presented a series of 'live' productions of basic rock 'n' roll songs, each of which lyrically elucidated a historical, if at times surreal, Americana that they felt had been lost amid the more naive and overblown excesses of the psychedelic movement. This collection of songs, appropriately titled *The Basement Tapes*, remained unreleased until 1975.

Oddly, the Band did not back Dylan on his immediate release, the epochal *Blonde On Blonde* (1968). Instead, Dylan opted to work with a group of Nashville studio musicians, having decided to record the album with famed country rock producer Bob Johnson; this collaboration between Dylan and Johnson would reach its logical conclusion in 1969, with the release of *Nashville Skyline*, which was essentially a country music album (for listeners who were still unclear about the musical direction Dylan had decided to take after the preceding year's roots-country classic *John Wesley Harding*, *Nashville Skyline* begins with a vocal duet between Dylan and the country singer and former Sun Records rockabilly, Johnny Cash, on 'Girl from the North Country'). In fact, the Band did not appear on any official Dylan record until *Planet Waves*, released in 1973. They subsequently joined Dylan for his 'comeback tour' in 1974, captured for posterity on the double-live record *After the Flood* (1974). In 1975, however, Dylan and the Band went their separate ways, never to reunite. For their part, the Band had probably outgrown their role as a backing band anyway, having released a spate of seminal 'roots rock' albums by then, including *Music from Big Pink* (1968), *The Band* (1969), *Stage Fright* (1970), *Cahoots* (1971), the live set *Rock of Ages* (1972), and an album of covers, called *Moondog Matinee* (1973) (see Chapter 5).

Buffalo Springfield and the Marketing of Dissent

The success of Buffalo Springfield probably best demonstrates the degree to which 'topicality' and 'protest' had become marketable commodities in the folk rock arena by the mid-1960s. A short-lived though immensely influential folk rock group, comprised of three Canadian expatriates—Neil Young (lead guitar, vocals), Bruce Palmer (bass), and Dewey Martin (drums)—and two Americans —Stephen Stills (lead guitar, vocals) and Ritchie Furay (lead guitar, vocals)—Buffalo Springfield had only one Top 40 single, 'For What It's Worth' (1966), and released only three full-length LPs before they disappeared from the pop charts completely. The group is probably most remembered now as a springboard for the subsequent careers of at least four platinum-selling musicians—Neil Young and Stephen Stills (Crosby, Stills, and Nash; Crosby, Stills, Nash, and Young; Manassas; Crazy Horse), Ritchie Furay (Poco), and Jim Messina (Loggins and Messina)—and for its notorious infighting, which sabotaged any chance the group had at long-term chart success. Neil Young left the band three times, replaced most notably by David Crosby of the Byrds for a performance at the Monterey Pop Festival in 1967 and, the next year, by Jim Messina, before Buffalo Springfield finally disbanded in 1968.

Despite its later tribulations, Buffalo Springfield began auspiciously. Stills and Furay encountered Young and Palmer by chance in a traffic jam on a Los Angeles freeway in April of 1966, and the quartet decided to form a band on the spot; they added drummer Dewey Martin to the lineup a few days later. The timing couldn't have been more propitious: Young and Palmer were jobless after the cancellation of a recording contract with Motown Records, as part of the Mynah Birds (led by future funk star Rick James), and Stills was despondent at being rejected through the auditioning process that created the Monkees for 'bad teeth' and 'thinning hair' just weeks before. Calling themselves Buffalo Springfield after a defunct brand of American tractor, the group quickly established their uniquely laid-back and country-flavoured approach to the folk rock idiom as a mainstay of LA's Sunset Strip, sharing stage time at historic venues such as The Whiskey A-Go-Go and Pandora's Box with the likes of fellow Los Angelians the Doors, the Byrds, and Love.

For however much they now seem entirely the products of their times, Buffalo Springfield never fit the 'hippie' mould exactly. The group's two primary songwriters, Neil Young and Stephen Stills, were notoriously ambivalent towards the political aspirations of most counterculture activists they encountered; moreover, both Young and Furay displayed a clear and sustained interest in country music well before the genre gained currency in the rock and folk rock listening communities. In fact, it was reportedly only at the insistence of band manager Charlie Greene that Stephen Stills wrote 'For What It's Worth', his 'protest' song about the Sunset Strip riots of 1966, which erupted when the city mayor imposed a 10 p.m. curfew for anyone younger than 18. No matter the circumstances of its creation, though, 'For What It's Worth' was received as a searing and epochal generational anthem by many who first heard it. No less an authority on the counterculture than Dennis Hopper called the record 'the most revolutionary' ever made. Yet for all the 'revolutionary' invective surrounding it, 'For What It's Worth' was a fairly standard folk rock production, and it actually sounds quite tame in comparison to a track like Bob Dylan's 'Like a Rolling Stone'. One might even say that 'For What It's Worth' comprises a tidy summary of radio-friendly, pop-oriented folk rock made during the mid-1960s. Like most folk rock records from the time, 'For What It's Worth' features: a medium 'walking' tempo; a clearly delineated verse-chorus form; an interesting introductory hook (comprised in this case of open-string harmonics plucked on the downbeat of each measure); a compelling lead vocal line, clearly foreground in the mix, backed by tight choral harmonizations; a strummed acoustic rhythm guitar; a slightly distorted lead electric guitar; an understated backbeat; and a blues-based electric guitar solo, which paradoxically builds in intensity as the overall volume of the song fades out.

Moreover, 'For What It's Worth' thematically undercuts the political efforts of its primary demographic, depicting members of the so-called 'counterculture', and the Sunset Strip rioters in particular, as a chaotic gathering of unfocused 'children' whose sound and fury ultimately signified nothing. *'There's something happening here'*, Stills explains at the outset of the song, but *'what it is ain't exactly clear.'* Later, Stills describes a massive picket line as *'a thousand people in the street singing songs and carrying signs'*—but their signs are painted with only bland inanities, the most popular being *'hooray for our side!'* And in truly Dylanesque fashion, Stills offers only an ambiguous caution in the song's chorus, leaving listeners to wonder if the riots and protests he describes amount to anything at all: *'I think it's time we stop, children, what's that sound? Everybody look what's going down.'* Regardless of these seemingly contradictory tendencies, 'For What It's Worth' reached the Top 10 in Canada and in the United States in March of 1967.

▌ Simon and Garfunkel

Perhaps nothing illustrates the changes wrought by the phenomenon of folk rock so clearly as the story of Simon and Garfunkel's first hit record, 'The Sounds of Silence'. In early 1965 Paul Simon and Arthur Garfunkel were an urban folk duo with a fine acoustic album to their credit, *Wednesday Morning, 3 A.M.*, that was causing no excitement whatsoever in the marketplace. When folk rock hit the scene in mid-year and Bob Dylan went electric, Simon and Garfunkel's producer, Tom Wilson—who produced Dylan's folk rock classics *Bringing It All Back Home* (1965) and *Highway 61 Revisited* (1965)—had a 'bright idea'. He took one of Simon's original compositions from the *Wednesday Morning* album, a highly poetic song about urban alienation called 'The Sound of Silence', overdubbed a rock band accompaniment of electric guitars, bass, and drums onto the original recording, speeded it up very slightly, changed the title for some reason to 'The Sounds of Silence', and released it as a single—all without Simon's or Garfunkel's prior knowledge or permission! The duo found little to complain about, however, as the track went to Number 1 across North America on New Year's Day 1966. Needless to say, they never looked back; to this

Art Garfunkel (left) and **Paul Simon** in a recording studio, 1966. Courtesy Library of Congress.

day, the duo remains one of the most enduringly popular acts ever to perform in a folk rock style. Although the duo broke up in 1970 (they have occasionally reunited for special occasions), their songs and albums continue to be popular to this day.

We will meet Paul Simon again later on, as he is among the few singer-songwriters to come to prominence in the 1960s who arguably achieved his creative peak considerably later on. To say this is not to denigrate Simon's work with Simon and Garfunkel, which includes such memorable and varied songs as 'A Hazy Shade of Winter', 'America', and 'Bridge over Troubled Water'; it is simply to claim that these earlier compositions would probably not lead one to suspect that Simon would eventually go on to produce such adventurous works of world music as *Graceland* and *The Rhythm of the Saints*.

▌The Rise of a Counterculture

The explosive entrance of folk rock into the wide arena of popular culture coincided with the development of increasingly innovative approaches to rock 'n' roll itself. Both of these phenomena were abetted, of course, by the maturation into early adulthood of the baby-boom generation. This was also a time of intense political restlessness and ferment across North America, though the turmoil was particularly intense in the United States. America's involvement in the Vietnamese civil war had steadily escalated to the point that, by 1965, President Lyndon B. Johnson had begun to dispatch tens of thousands of combat troops to the region, while civil rights activists continued to challenge racial segregation and inequality everywhere. Many boomers sensed a direct relationship between these two volatile political issues, linking what they considered to be external colonialism—an inappropriate involvement with the affairs of a Third World country—with internal colonialism, that is, the systematic oppression of minority peoples and cultures at home.

The youth audience for rock music was directly embroiled in these political battles. Protests and sympathy demonstrations were staged on both sides of the border, but in the US the choice was between life and death for many boomers; all males between the ages of 18 and 26 were eligible to be drafted into the American armed forces, and the number of total inductions grew each year. This proved particularly damaging to diplomatic relations between Canada and the United States, especially since Canada not only refused to officially participate in the American intervention in Vietnam but was often critical of it (despite the facts that over 500 Canadian firms contributed supplies to the American war effort and over 10,000 Canadian citizens volunteered with the American armed forces specifically to serve in Vietnam). Relations between both countries arguably reached their historic low in 1965 when the Canadian Prime Minister, Lester B. Pearson, advocated the immediate cessation of American bombings in North Vietnam during an acceptance speech for a peace award he received at Philadelphia's Temple University. At a private meeting following the ceremony, President Johnson physically assaulted Pearson, lifting the diminutive Prime Minister into the air by his lapels, screaming, '*You pissed on my rug!*'

From 1965 to 1973 over 100,000 draft dodgers fled to Canada. An 'underground railway' of safe houses was established along the Canadian border to aid dodgers in their escape, though they were not typically prosecuted once inside Canada, and most even found it relatively easy to obtain legitimate work visas. The influx of draft dodgers into Canada changed the country's political complexion considerably. Most draft evaders were already committed in their political beliefs, and simply by coming to Canada they demonstrated that they were willing to act on them. Anti-war groups and other 'protest' organizations subsequently formed across Canada with increasing frequency, and they attracted large numbers of boomers (and, by then, a significant number of their parents, too). Besides Vietnam and civil rights—two 'foreign' but nevertheless crucial issues for the development of a distinctly Canadian activism, in that they lent moral legitimacy to those who resisted governmental authority—a number of social issues vied for protestors' attentions: Native peoples' rights, inner-city poverty, the status of women, Quebec sovereignty, student power, and, finally, the 'problem' of Canada's cultural and economic annexation by the United States.

Though most Canadian boomers shared their neighbours' concerns with ending the draft and racial discrimination, there were a few very important differences between youth activism in Canada and in the United States. Canadian activists were clearly concerned about annexation, both cultural and economic, in a way that American activists, of course, were not. Indeed, for all their concern over American imperialism, American youth activists in the 1960s seem to have been almost entirely oblivious to the fact that their Canadian counterparts considered themselves in the midst of a cultural colonization. Canadian officials, many of whom had publicly scoffed at the idea of restricting the flow of culture industry goods into Canada just a few years before, now argued that a daily minimum of 'Canadian content' on the country's television and radio airwaves was probably necessary for the country to survive the 1970s.

Finding support for 'Canadianization' measures became even easier as Canada's Centennial celebrations, scheduled to last for all of 1967, approached. As it completed its first century as a nation, Canada arguably asserted an entirely distinct cultural identity on the world stage for the first time in its history (complete with a new flag and national anthem). Significant amounts of money were devoted by the government to the creation of a cultural infrastructure—towns and cities across Canada built arenas and concert halls in honour of their country's 100th birthday—but popular music was basically passed over (the CBC's commission of Gordon Lightfoot's 'Canadian Railroad Trilogy', for instance, constitutes an exception that proves this rule). There are two possible explanations for this: first, since at least the time of the Massey Commission, there was a tendency on the part of Canadian politicians to conflate not just rock music but mass culture in general with American culture; and, second, popular culture has traditionally been associated with 'low' culture in Canada and is consequently typically considered 'unworthy' of government patronage.

Perhaps no event symbolized Canada's political maturation so fully as Expo 67—the popular shorthand for the World's Fair that took place in Montreal in 1967. Initially scheduled for Moscow, the fair was awarded to Montreal when the Soviets backed out in 1963; the city subsequently earmarked billions of dollars to fund construction of human-made islands in the St Lawrence River designed to serve as futuristic fairgrounds. Though critics initially called it a 'billion dollar boondoggle', by its opening day Expo 67 was an emblem of Canada's new-found modern identity and cultural independence.

Even during the heady days of Expo 67, however, Canada proved unwilling to be pinned to a single identity. During French President Charles de Gaulle's visit to Expo, he consciously and overtly sanctioned the separatist movement in Quebec—and, for some, the terrorist activities of separatist groups such as the FLQ—when, in a televised speech from city hall, he shouted a series of 'vivres', concluding with 'Vive le Québec libre!' De Gaulle was promptly expelled from Canada, to the chagrin of many Québécois in particular, but not before he was reminded by Lester B. Pearson in a nationally televised address that Quebec was indeed 'libre' and, moreover, that over 100,000 Canadians had died in two world wars to keep France 'libre!' His comments elicited a great deal of support in anglophone Canada.

Despite such incidents, the momentum of Expo 67 and the Centennial celebrations carried Canada forward into the 1970s. In 1968 Justice Minister Pierre Elliott Trudeau—a 'swinging' bachelor from Montreal who had come to Parliament at Pearson's request only three years before—reformed the country's Criminal Code, most famously decriminalizing homosexuality ('the state has no place in the bedrooms of a nation', he famously quipped to a reporter when asked about the measure). Within a year Trudeau was swept to power on a wave of popularity, particularly with the nation's oldest contingent of baby boomers, who were just then reaching voting age. So vocal were boomers in their support for Trudeau, in fact, that historians dubbed the phenomenon 'Trudeaumania', consciously echoing the name given to the pandemonium that surrounded the Beatles in North America in 1964. Of course, the election of Trudeau as Prime Minister was far from unanimous, and the country remains divided about his tenure to this day. Typically glossed over in many accounts, for instance, is the fact that Trudeau only barely gained the leadership of the Liberal Party in 1968, significant numbers of delegates considering his three years in office entirely too few for the leader of a political party, let alone of an entire country. Moreover, even as 'Trudeaumania' absorbed the nation's youth into mainstream democratic politics:

> the safe underpinnings of Canadian life obviously came unstuck. Teenagers grew rebellious and sported long hair. Casual sex became the norm as the birth control pill changed social mores. Popular music altered to the point where parents could scarcely bear to listen to it. Quebec grew restive and revolutionary. Governments completed the social welfare state, providing a cradle-to-grave security blanket for Canadians, but there seemed to be no stability in a world and nation come unglued. (Bothwell and Granatstein, 2000: 165)

The meeting of the culture surrounding new rock music with these political and social discontents resulted in a famous, if slippery, phenomenon in the mid- and later 1960s that most historians now call 'the counterculture'. This was never the kind of systematic, highly organized movement that many like to claim it was. Although the mythic typical member of the counterculture was a young rock music fan who supported the civil rights movement and opposed the war in Vietnam, it is important to remember that:

- Many of the older generation opposed the Vietnam War, and many of these probably had no special fondness for the new rock music.
- Many young rock music fans were apolitical, or even were supporters of conservative political agendas.
- Many of the same movements that promulgated utopian visions of a new, more just social order excluded most women and ethnic minorities from leadership positions.

Thus, while it provides a convenient label for the more innovative, rebellious, and radical aspects of the musical, social, and political culture of the 1960s taken in sum, the notion of a 'counterculture' is inevitably a simplification. Unless we are careful, it may involve us in a number of dubious historical fictions. What is most significant, for our purposes, is simply that rock music—the 1960s descendant of rock 'n' roll— was an essential part of the definition of the counterculture, which demonstrates once again the remarkable degree of identification between the baby-boom generation and the music they chose to make and hear.

Along with rock music and radical politics, the counterculture developed its own characteristic jargon, fads, and fashions: long hair for both women and men, signifying in the latter case non-enlistment; beards; beads; 'peasant', 'eastern', and tie-dyed shirts; and blue jeans. The slang terms most often associated with hippies—'groovy', 'far out', 'stoned', and so on—were mainly derived from popular black vernaculars, a continuation of a historical pattern of appropriation with roots in the nineteenth century. In addition, the counterculture's fascination with 'exotic' cultures was heard most explicitly in the appropriation of South Asian instrumentation in rock songs such as the Rolling Stones' 'Paint It Black' and the Beatles' 'Norwegian Wood', 'Tomorrow Never Knows', and 'Within You Without You'; and it was also evident in historic meetings between prominent rock musicians and Eastern spiritual leaders, such as that which occurred between members of the British pop elite and the Maharishi Mahesh Yogi in 1967.

The dilemma of drug use in contemporary North American society, including the abuse of drugs by very young people, makes it hard to provide a simple and unambiguous evaluation of the counterculture's relationship to intoxicants and recreational chemicals. The vulgar catchphrase was 'sex, drugs, and rock 'n' roll'; and instead of (or in addition to) the alcohol of their parents' generation, many young people in the 1960s came to favour hallucinogenic substances, particularly marijuana and LSD (lysergic acid diethylamide, or 'acid'). Unquestionably, there was a lot of drug use by musicians and their audiences in the later 1960s. Many records and concerts were consumed by 'stoned' young people; at least some of those records and concerts were intended to be experienced in that way; and some of the musicians involved made the music while stoned themselves. There is, for example, no possible dispute about the subject matter of a song with a title like 'Don't Bogart That Joint' or 'One Toke Over the Line'. But when questioned about the Beatles' song 'Lucy in the Sky with Diamonds', whose title and psychedelic imagery were widely assumed to be connected to the LSD experience, John Lennon replied that the song was inspired by a picture his four-year-old son drew at school, and that the little boy had himself called the picture 'Lucy in the sky with diamonds'. In fact, Lennon disclaimed any connection between the song and LSD throughout his life (one could choose to be skeptical about Lennon's statement, but the main point is that there is no definitive meaning or 'truth' to the song that can be determined here). Certainly, the flamboyant, colourful visual effects used on rock music posters and record jackets, and in the light shows at rock concerts, were to some degree modelled on the experience of 'tripping'. But it is not easy to determine to what degree the characteristic open-endedness of many rock music performances—including the hours-long musical explorations of bands like Jefferson Airplane and the Grateful Dead—is directly attributable to drug use, nor is it necessary for understanding the connection of songs to the drug culture in Canada and the United States.

An appropriate perspective on drug use in the 1960s would take into account the fact that many participants in the counterculture, including musicians and members of the rock audience, were not involved with drugs. Furthermore, along with the pleasure seekers who sought only to enjoy themselves and follow fashion while repeating the slogans of the time about 'mind expansion' and 'turning on', there were those who quite seriously sought alternatives to the prevailing American bourgeois lifestyle, who may have employed hallucinogens such as peyote, psilocybin mushrooms, and LSD carefully, and sparingly, as an aspect of spiritual exploration in a manner akin to that found in certain non-Western cultures. There was, for example, a good deal of interest in Native American cultures among members of the counterculture, some of it superficial and trendy but some of it assuredly serious. In the end, it appears that the value of psychoactive substances depends on the context and manner of their use; and that the drug culture of the 1960s was, at various times, both an enabler and a destroyer of musical creativity. Indeed, drug use (or experimentation), or heavy drinking, and artistic creativity have often gone hand in glove, from the English Romantic poets of the early nineteenth century, to figures such as poet, essayist, and short story writer Edgar Allan Poe in nineteenth-century America, to such twentieth-century figures as the Beatniks. Most of the time, however, the hand did not fit so well in the glove, and many such creative artists died at a relatively young age without realizing their full talents, as was the case, too, in the history of rock, with such leading lights of the late 1960s as Janis Joplin, Jimi Hendrix, and Jim Morrison dying at an early age as a result of drug and alcohol abuse and misuse. A hard life lesson can certainly be gleaned from the fact that present interviews with rock musicians of the late 1960s are notable for their lack of nostalgia in relation to drug use.

In any event, the legalization of the birth-control pill may well have been the most significant chemical 'breakthrough' of all that occurred in the 1960s. Though the Health Protection Branch of Health and Welfare Canada had approved the birth-control pill for sale already by 1960, it remained officially illegal according to the country's Criminal Code to 'offer to sell, advertise, publish an advertisement or have for sale or disposal any means of preventing contraception' as late as 1969. As such, it remained extremely difficult for unmarried women in Canada to find a doctor who would prescribe them 'the pill' in the 1960s, and even divorcees report having found prescriptions difficult to come by. Given these unsubtle forms of discrimination, it is not surprising that students mobilized on campuses across Canada to advocate for a woman's right to choose birth control and, moreover, for a woman's sovereignty over her own personal biology. Protests at York University, the University of Western Ontario, McGill University, and Simon Fraser University, to name only a few, helped raise awareness about the issue and arguably played a crucial role in changing public attitudes towards contraception across the country.

By 1968 most Canadian universities had made 'the pill' available to their students. A sea change in the sexual behaviour and attitudes of boomers in particular soon followed. With the simple ingestion of a pill, women could now control their reproductive cycles with a precision not previously possible. Thus did they become free, arguably for the first time, to assert themselves sexually without fear of pregnancy. And, indeed, it seems far more than just a historical coincidence that, immediately following the widespread introduction of 'the pill' in Canada, women reported notably longer stays at college and university; and, moreover, that birth rates fell dramatically nationwide. Nowhere did they fall more dramatically than in

Quebec, however, where the birth rate went from highest to lowest in the nation in just under a decade. Furthermore, as the concept of a 'sexual revolution' took hold, many boomers came to view casual sex as a form of protest against the mores of previous generations.

❙ Sgt. Pepper's Lonely Hearts Club Band

The summer of 1967 was known as the Summer of Love, when many young participants in the newly self-aware counterculture followed the advice of a pop hit—Scott McKenzie's 'San Francisco (Be Sure To Wear Flowers in Your Hair)'—that told them to head for San Francisco, where the Haight-Ashbury district was already a legendary centre of countercultural activity, not surprisingly because San Francisco was the 'home' of the legendary Beat poets, writers, and artists of the 1950s, such as Lawrence Ferlinghetti and Jack Kerouac, and was right across San Francisco Bay from Berkeley, where the University of California campus had been the seedbed for much of the civil

The *Sgt. Pepper*-era **Beatles**. Frank Driggs Collection.

rights, anti-war, student, and black power movements of the sixties. But the group celebrations called 'love-ins' were not limited to San Francisco: a sense of participation in the counterculture was readily available that summer to anyone who had a record player and the spending money to purchase the Beatles' new album, *Sgt. Pepper's Lonely Hearts Club Band* (1967), which was as 'revolutionary' a work of pop music art as was ever made.

The countercultural ambience of *Sgt. Pepper* was obvious in a number of ways. The unprecedented and now-famous album cover—a wild collage of faces and figures surrounding the four Beatles dressed in full formal band regalia—pictured a number of people from many different time periods who were associated with various aspects of the counterculture: Karl Marx, Carl Gustav Jung, Sri Chimnoy Lahasy, Maharishi Mahesh Yogi, Oscar Wilde, Marlon Brando, James Dean, Bob Dylan, and even the Beatles themselves, *circa* 1964 (absent, but requested by Lennon, were likenesses of Adolf Hitler and Jesus Christ). The song that opened the second side of the record, 'Within You Without You', was the most thoroughgoing of the Beatles' attempts to evoke the sound and spirit of Indian music; it featured Indian instruments (sitar and tabla in lieu of guitars and Western drums), unusual metres and phrase structures, and deeply meditative, philosophical lyrics. The lyrics to a number of other songs had what could easily be interpreted as drug references, for those so inclined. We have already mentioned 'Lucy in the Sky with Diamonds', but among other examples well noted at the time were 'A Little Help from My Friends', which featured the repeated line '*I get high with a little help from my friends*', and the concluding song, 'A Day in the Life', which ends the album with the famous line '*I'd love to turn you on*' (because of this line, and the narration of having '*a smoke*' and going '*into a dream*', the single was banned from BBC radio).

Arguably more important than any specific counterculture references in *Sgt. Pepper* was the way in which the album was structured to invite its listeners' participation in an implied community. The record is a clearly and cleverly organized performance that reflects an awareness of, and actually addresses, its audience. The opening song, 'Sgt. Pepper's Lonely Hearts Club Band', formally introduces the 'show' to come, and acknowledges listeners with lines like '*We hope you will enjoy the show*' and '*You're such a lovely audience, we'd love to take you home with us.*' This song is reprised, with different words ('*We hope you have enjoyed the show*') as the penultimate selection on the album, after which the 'performance' ends and the performers return to 'reality' with 'A Day in the Life' ('*I read the news today, oh boy*'). Yet even in this final song, the continued presence of the listener is acknowledged, at least implicitly, with the concluding line '*I'd love to turn you on.*'

The Beatles' brilliant conceit of *Sgt. Pepper* as a 'performance' is evident even before the music begins: the opening sounds on the record are those of a restless audience, and of an orchestra tuning. Audience sounds of laughter and applause are heard at schematic points in both the initial presentation and the reprise of the title song. Yet this is clearly not a recording of an actual live performance; that is, the record features obviously non-veridic production values. Virtually every song on the album features a unique instrumental arrangement significantly different from that of the songs that precede and follow it—in other words, the songs are arranged to provide maximum variety and contrast on a record album, not as a practical sequence for a live performance situation. Even more obviously, the album is full of studio-produced effects, the most spectacular of which are the sound collage that actually overlaps the ending of 'Good Morning Good Morning' with the reprise of 'Sgt. Pepper's Lonely Hearts Club Band' and the explosively distorted final chord of 'A Day in the Life', which very gradually fades out over a duration of about 45 seconds. In the employment of these effects, and in many other aspects of the album, the hand of the producer, George Martin, is evident.

There is a profound irony in the fact that the first album made by the Beatles after they decided to abandon live performance is an album that, in effect, mimics and creatively re-imagines the concept of performing before an audience. This irony, of course, would not be lost on Beatles fans, who were well aware of the group's highly publicized decision to retire from performance, and who had to wait longer for this album than for any previous one by the group (more than nine months separated the release of *Sgt. Pepper* from that of the Beatles' immediately preceding album, *Revolver*, which was an eternity in those days; though the double 'A'-side 'single' 'Strawberry Fields Forever'/'Penny Lane' intervened).

Rock 'n' roll had always communicated to its widest audience by means of records. *Sgt. Pepper* turned that established fact into a basis for brilliantly self-conscious artifice. When the Beatles sang 'We'd love to take you home with us' in the opening song of the album, they must have done so with ironic recognition of the fact that it was actually their audience that takes them home, in the form of their records. As we have already attempted to show, everything about *Sgt. Pepper* is inclusionary; it posits the rock album as the creator of an audience community for which that album also serves as a means of communication and identity. And, in fact, the album achieved unprecedented success in reaching a large community, even by the Beatles' standards, selling over eight million copies and charting for more than three years.

The most historically significant fact about *Sgt. Pepper* is the way in which it definitively redirected attention from the single to the album. That *Sgt. Pepper* was conceived as a totality, rather than as a collection of single songs, is apparent in many ways, but most indicative perhaps was the unprecedented marketing decision not to release any of the songs on the album as singles (this 'singles gap' was filled by the release of 'All You Need Is Love' in the summer of 1967, a song later collected on the band's next record, *Magical Mystery Tour*, alongside the likes of 'I Am the Walrus', 'Penny Lane', 'Strawberry Fields Forever', 'Hello Goodbye', and 'Baby You're a Rich Man'). *Sgt. Pepper* may not have been the first concept album, though it is often presented as such, but it was the first album to present itself to the public as a complete and unified marketing package, with a distinctive and interrelated collection of parts, all of which were unavailable in any other form: not just the songs on the record itself, but also the cover art and the inside photograph of the Beatles in their band uniforms; the complete song lyrics printed on the back of the album jacket (a first, and a precedent-setting one); the extra page of 'Sgt. Pepper cutouts' supplied with the album; and even a unique inner sleeve to hold the record that was adorned with 'psychedelic' swirls of pink and red colouring!

Sgt. Pepper ultimately did for the rock album what Bob Dylan's 'Like a Rolling Stone' had done for the rock single two years prior—it rewrote all the rules, and things were never the same again. Countless albums appearing in the wake of *Sgt. Pepper* imitated aspects of the Beatles' tour de force, from its cover art to its printed lyrics to its use of a musical reprise, but few could approach its real substance and achievement. To their credit, the Beatles themselves did not try to imitate the record but went on to other things in subsequent releases, continuing to produce innovative music on albums and singles until they disbanded early in 1970.

San Francisco and the Rise of Acid/Psychedelic Rock

During the late 1960s an 'alternative' rock music scene, inspired in part by the Beatles' experimentalism, established itself in San Francisco. As noted above, the city had already long been a centre for artistic communities and subcultures, including the Beat literary movement, a lively urban folk music scene, and a highly visible and vocal gay community. Psychedelic or acid rock, as the music played by San Francisco rock bands was often called, encompassed a variety of styles and musical influences—including folk rock, blues, hard rock, Latin music, and Indian classical music. In geographical terms, San Francisco's psychedelic music scene was focused on the Haight-Ashbury neighbourhood, which quickly became the de facto capital of the hippie movement in North America, alongside Venice Beach and the Sunset Strip in Los Angeles, New York's Greenwich Village, Toronto's Yorkville Village, and Vancouver's Stanley Park and Kitsilano District.

A number of musical entrepreneurs and institutions supported the growth of the San Francisco rock music scene. Tom Donahue, a local radio DJ, challenged the mainstream Top 40 AM pop music format on San Francisco's KYA, and he later pioneered a new, open-ended, and eclectic broadcasting format on FM station KMPX (Donahue is the spiritual forefather of today's alternative FM formats, including many college stations). The foremost promoter of the new rock bands—and the first to cash in on the music's popularity—was Bill Graham. Graham, a European immigrant who had worked as a taxi driver to support his business studies, began staging rock concerts in San Francisco in 1965. For one of his first rock concerts Graham rented a skating rink, which he later purchased and named the Fillmore. The Fillmore—renamed the Fillmore West when Graham opened the Fillmore East in New York City—was a symbolic centre for the counterculture, and psychedelic posters advertising its concerts are today worth thousands of dollars. Other individuals built professional careers out of the job of creating the psychedelic atmosphere for rock concerts: Chet Helms, for example, was responsible for developing the multimedia aesthetic of light shows at the Fillmore and the Avalon Ballroom.

Jefferson Airplane

Jefferson Airplane was the first internationally successful band to emerge out of the San Francisco acid rock scene. Founded in 1965, the Airplane was originally a semi-acoustic folk rock band, performing blues and songs by Bob Dylan. Eventually, they began to develop a louder, harder-edged style with a greater emphasis on open forms, instrumental improvisations, and visionary lyrics. Along with Quicksilver Messenger Service and the Grateful Dead (see below), Jefferson Airplane was one of the original triumvirate of San Francisco 'acid rock' bands, playing at the Matrix Club (the centre of the San Francisco alternative nightclub scene), larger concert venues such as the Avalon Ballroom and the Fillmore, and at communal outdoor 'happenings' and 'be-ins' in local parks and fields.

In late 1965 the Airplane received an unprecedented $20,000 advance from RCA, one of the largest and most powerful corporations in the world. Despite the anti-commercial rhetoric of the counterculture, this event was responsible for sparking off the formation of dozens of psychedelic bands in the Bay area, eager to cash in on the Airplane's success; and parallels to this seemingly paradoxical link between counter-cultural values and the good old profit motive may sometimes be observed in connection with today's 'alternative' music movements. In any event, the Airplane's 1967 LP *Surrealistic Pillow* sold over one million copies, reaching Number 3 on the pop album charts and spawning two Top 10 singles. Lead vocalist Grace Slick (b. 1939) subsequently became a national celebrity as, alongside Janis Joplin, the most important female musician in San Francisco.

Jefferson Airplane reached a national audience with their recording of 'Somebody to Love', which reached Number 5 on the American pop charts—and Number 4 on the CHUM charts—in 1967. 'Somebody to Love' exemplifies acid rock, including its dense musical textures, its loud volume, and an abundance of electronic distortion and other studio effects (it would seem to be a rule that all acid rock records feature 'non-veridic' production values). The process of making hit singles encouraged the band to trim its normally extended, improvised performances down to a manageable and AM radio-friendly three minutes. And the song itself, written by Grace Slick, her husband, and her brother-in-law, exemplified the tendency of late 1960s rock musicians to compose their own material.

Janis Joplin

Grace Slick's only serious competition as queen of the San Francisco rock music scene came from Janis Joplin (1943–70), the most successful white blues singer of the 1960s. Born in Port Arthur, Texas, Joplin came to San Francisco in the mid-1960s, where she joined a band called Big Brother and the Holding Company. Their appearance at the Monterey Pop Festival in 1967—a three-day pop music festival, the first of its kind, held on the Monterey Fair Grounds in California—led to a contract with Columbia Records, who were eager to cash in on RCA's success with Jefferson Airplane. Big Brother's 1968 album *Cheap Thrills*, graced with a cover design by the underground comics artist Robert Crumb, reached Number 1 on the pop charts in America and included the Top 20 single 'Piece of My Heart', a cover version of a 1960s R&B hit by Erma Franklin. Joplin's only Top 10 charting in Canada was a posthumously released cover of Kris Kristofferson's 'Me and Bobby McGee' (Number 8 CHUM, 1971), which she recorded with the Full Tilt Boogie Band, another group of ex-Hawks, in 1970.

Janis Joplin performs with Big Brother and the Holding Company, 1968.
Courtesy Library of Congress.

Joplin's full-tilt singing style and directness of expression were inspired by blues singers such as Bessie Smith and by the R&B records of Big Mama Thornton (Joplin rediscovered Big Mama in the late 1960s and helped to revive her performing career). She pushed her voice unmercifully, reportedly saying that she would prefer a short, exceptional career to a long career as an unexceptional performer. Although her growling 'blues shouter' singing style made her an icon of blues 'authenticity' for the mainly white audience for rock music, Joplin was not a success with black audiences. In fact, Joplin never once managed to cross over to the R&B charts during her brief career, despite numerous deliberate attempts to do so.

One of Joplin's most moving performances is her rendition of the George Gershwin composition 'Summertime', written in 1935 for the American folk opera *Porgy and Bess*. Although Joplin's recording was criticized for the less-than-polished accompaniment provided by Big Brother and the Holding Company, her vocal performance is riveting. Joplin squeezes every last drop of emotion out of the song, pushing her voice to the limit, and creating not only the rough, rasping tones expected of a blues singer but also multi-pitched sounds called 'multiphonics'. The impression one retains of Janis Joplin, an impression reinforced by listening to any one of her records, is actually that of a sweet and vulnerable young woman whose tough exterior and heavy reliance on drugs and alcohol functioned as defence mechanisms in the face of adult life's inevitable disappointments and compromises. She died of a heroin overdose in October 1970.

The Grateful Dead

No survey of the 1960s San Francisco rock scene would be complete without mention of the Grateful Dead, a thoroughly idiosyncratic band—actually as much an experience or institution as a band in the usual sense—whose career spanned more than three decades. Although it is often stated that the Grateful Dead were not a commercially successful band, eight of their LPs reached the Top 20, including 1987's *In the Dark*, which held the Number 9 position on *Billboard*'s album charts. 'The Dead', as they are known to their passionately devoted followers, grew out of a series of bands involving Jerry Garcia (1942–95), a guitarist, banjoist, and singer who had played in various urban folk groups during the early 1960s. This shifting collective of musicians gradually took firmer shape and, in 1967, was christened the Grateful Dead (a phrase Garcia apparently ran across in an ancient Egyptian prayer book). The Dead helped to pioneer the transition from urban folk music to folk rock to acid rock, adopting electric instruments, living communally in the Haight-Ashbury district, and participating in public LSD parties ('acid tests') before the drug was outlawed (these experiences were chronicled in Tom Wolfe's book, *The Electric Kool-Aid Acid Test*).

It is actually very hard to classify the Grateful Dead's work. For one thing, their records do them scant justice. The Dead were the quintessential 'live' rock band of mid- and late 1960s San Francisco, specializing in long jams that wandered through diverse musical styles and grooves, and typically terminating in unexpected places. The influence of folk music, prominent on some of their early records, was usually just below the surface, and a patient listener may expect to hear a kind of 'sketch-map' of the rock tradition—including folk, folk rock, blues, R&B, and country music, as well as rock 'n' roll—with occasional gestures in the direction of African or Asian music. Their repertoire of songs was, in any event, massive; in any given performance one might have heard diverse songs from different periods in the band's existence. This means that each performance was also a unique musical version of the band's history, at least for those who studied it.

If the Grateful Dead were a unique musical institution, their devoted fans, called 'Deadheads', were a social phenomenon basically unparalleled in the rock tradition. Travelling incessantly in psychedelically decorated buses and vans, setting up camp in every town along the tour, and generally pursuing a peaceful mode of coexistence with local authorities, hardcore Deadheads literally lived for their band. While it has been pointed out that much of the satisfaction of this mobile/communal lifestyle had to do with the creation of a special social ethos, there can be no denying that the core source of appeal for serious Deadheads was the band's music. Fans taped the band's performances—in fact, they were often encouraged to tape the band's performances, a rarity in the popular music business—and then circulated these tapes (called bootlegs), building extensive lists that chronicle every concert the band ever played. There are now entire sites devoted to this purpose on the World Wide Web, with precise descriptions of the repertoires played at particular concerts and statistical breakdowns of the frequency of certain songs and of certain sequences of songs. Although other popular musicians have certainly inspired adoration—Frank Sinatra, Elvis Presley, and the Beatles come immediately to mind—the devotion of Deadheads remains truly unique.

Rock across Canada

While we look closely at Canada's most famous popular music exports from the late 1960s and early 1970s in the next chapter—including the likes of David Clayton-Thomas, Joni Mitchell, Gordon Lightfoot, Neil Young, and Leonard Cohen—for now we simply note that the 1960s was a time of intense growth for rock music in Canada. Without national record charts, however, and with no 'Canadianization' measures in place, the country remained basically an assemblage of regional enclaves and local 'scenes', each with its own unique sound, circuit of venues, and group of star performers. In fact, it was possible for a band to be stars in one Canadian city without anyone ever having even heard of them in another. Though it is obviously impossible to offer a complete survey of every rock band that ever played in Canada in the 1960s, we will now consider a representative sample from the country's major urban centres, beginning in Vancouver and ending in Halifax.

Vancouver

In Vancouver, Little Daddy & the Bachelors—a band that featured future comedy legend Tommy Chong on lead guitar and Tommy Melton on lead vocals—most clearly epitomized the city's R&B-influenced rock sound, especially when their first independently produced single, a cover of Chuck Berry's 'Too Much Monkey Business', began to receive regular airplay on local radio. After a short but ultimately unsuccessful stint in San Francisco, the band changed their name to the rather shocking Four Niggers & a Chink (suggested by Tommy Chong in recognition of their interracial makeup) before deciding to take work back in Vancouver as the official backing band for Bobby Taylor, a known R&B singer on the Tamla/Motown roster. Calling themselves Bobby Taylor & the Vancouvers, the group recorded a series of moderately successful records for Tamla/Motown, the most successful being 'Does Your Mama Know About Me?', which climbed to Number 29 on the pop charts in the US but failed to register in Canada. Aside from any one record in particular, however, the group is probably better known as one of the earliest to feature Jimi Hendrix on lead guitar, albeit for a brief time—Hendrix's father and paternal grandparents lived in Vancouver.

Elsewhere in the city Jayson Hoover & the Epics, whose debut LP *The Trials of Jayson Hoover* to this day remains a 'Vancouver sound' classic, vied for gigs with other Vancouver-based bands such as the Nocturnals, the Stags, Kenneth Steele & the Shentelles, Night Train Review, the Stags, and Soul Unlimited & the

Shockers—all of whom eventually signed with Tom Northcott's New Syndrome Records, a label the folk rock singer started while still in high school. (Northcott himself performed around Vancouver as leader of the Vancouver Playboys and the Tom Northcott Trio, but the folk rock genre failed to amass anything more than a small but devoted following in the city.) At the same time, the Chessmen, a Shadows-inspired group featuring future chart-topper Terry Jacks on lead guitar, caught the ear of local DJ Red Robinson (see Chapter 1), who agreed to produce the group's first three singles for London Records. Jacks left the group in 1966, however, whereupon he formed the internationally successful the Poppy Family with his future wife and lead singer, Susan Jacks.

Alongside guitarist Craig McCaw and drummer Satwan Singh, the Poppy Family presented a clean-cut alternative to the many counterculture rock bands that emerged to the cultural fore in the later 1960s, especially in San Francisco and Los Angeles, but also in Toronto, Winnipeg, and Vancouver. Though the Poppy Family released only two full-length LPs, by far their most successful release was the adult-contemporary classic 'Which Way You Goin' Billy?', which sold over 2.5 million copies and reached Number 1 on the CHUM charts, and Number 2 on the US pop charts, in 1969. By the time of Terry and Susan's—and, thus, the band's—public and somewhat acrimonious split in 1973, after two more Top 10 singles—'That's Where I Went Wrong' (Number 9 CHUM, 1970) and 'Where Evil Grows' (Number 2 CHUM, 1971)—the Poppy Family had become one of the best-loved bands in Canada.

Both Susan and Terry Jacks enjoyed some solo success in the years immediately following their split, but only Terry outsoared the heights they achieved as a team. Susan released two solo LPs, which included the Canadian hits 'Anna Marie', 'All the Tea in China', and 'Tall Dark Stranger', before she receded from the pop world altogether in the late 1970s. In 1974, Terry released his version of the smash hit 'Seasons in the Sun', an anglicized rendition of Jacques Brel's 'Le Moribund'. Though the song was recorded a number of times before Jacks came to it—by the Fortunes, Pearls Before Swine, Bob Shane of the Kingston Trio, and the Beach Boys—Jacks self-consciously 'lightened up' the song, adding a backbeat at strategic moments to emphasize the 'joy' and 'fun' that he and the song's eulogized friend had, over the song's more melodramatic passages (*'goodbye papa, it's hard to die'*, runs one of the song's more dour lines). Amazingly, Jacks nearly did not release the record; it sat on a shelf in his basement for over a year, and it was not until his paperboy heard him auditioning the song in private, and insisted that his friends all hear the song, that Jacks finally decided to release it—a full year after he had recorded it. The record would go on to top the charts around the world, including in Canada, the US, Britain, France, and Germany, and it has sold over 11.5 million copies in the 35 years since its initial release.

A sea change in musical character occurred in Vancouver as the 1960s drew to a close, and American psychedelia drifted north of the border. In fact, of all Canadian cities Vancouver was most receptive to psychedelic culture and music. Acid rock bands such as Papa Bear's Medicine Show, Spring, the Hydro Electric Streetcar, the Collectors (featuring future Chilliwack vocalist and guitarist Howie Vickers and Bill Henderson), the United Empire Loyalists, and Mother Trucker's Yellow Duck soon took over the city. They played the Sound Gallery, Big Mother, the Retinal Cruise, the Afterthought, the Lighthouse, and the many other acid rock nightclubs, modelled on San Francisco's Avalon Ballroom and Fillmore West, that seemed to spring up overnight in the city. By far the most successful of these acid rock bands, at least in terms of international record sales, was Mother Trucker's Yellow Duck, who enjoyed strong support in Vancouver for their debut single, 'One Ring Jane' (1969), and for their first LP, punningly entitled *Home Grown Stuff* (1969); the group's second effort, *Starting a New Day* (1970), was picked up by Capitol Records for American distribution in 1971, but it failed to make any headway on the charts and the band split soon after.

Calgary

East of Vancouver and over the Rocky Mountains, in Calgary, Wes Dakus and the Rebels, Barry Allan & the Lords, and the Stampeders mixed folk rock with country and western to create a uniquely Albertan sound. This 'sound' foreshadowed the hybrid aesthetic of later country rock acts such as the Flying Burrito Brothers, the later Byrds, Poco, and Bob Dylan *circa* 1969, to name a few. But without even one recording studio in the entire province, most Calgary bands were forced to rely on television appearances to document their music, and no surviving footage of their appearances exist today. In fact, most groups from Alberta had no choice but to head east to Toronto or Montreal to record, for these two cities were fast becoming the country's two primary epicentres of rock music. Thus, their country-oriented approach to folk and rock was quickly filtered through the R&B and folk aesthetics that prevailed there.

Toronto

By 1967, Toronto was clearly 'the big time' for most anglophone Canadian rock musicians; and the so-called 'Toronto sound'—an admixture of equal parts rock 'n' roll and R&B, played by mostly white soul musicians—was a national force. As we have already noted, the city's Yorkville Village served as a centre for folk and folk rock in Canada, as was Vancouver's Kitsilano District, but it was Yonge Street and Spadina Avenue that played host to the city's rock and R&B bands.

Perhaps the best-known band to play Toronto in the late 1960s was the Mandala. Managed by Randy 'Dandy' Martin, a former clown on TV, the Mandala was comprised of George Olliver on vocals, founder and ex-Hawk Domenic Troiano on electric guitar, Jozef Chirowsky on keyboards, Don Elliot on bass, and Penti 'Whitey' Glann on drums. The group almost completely dominated the Yonge Street rock circuit between 1967 and 1969. The Mandala's debut album, *Soul Crusade* (1968), proved immensely popular in Canada, though it failed to garner any support in the United States, and all three singles from the album reached the CHUM Top 20: 'Give and Take' (Number 20 CHUM, 1967), 'Opportunity' (Number 3 CHUM, 1968), and 'Love It Is' (Number 9 CHUM, 1968). The group disbanded before they could capitalize on these early successes, however. The Mandala played their final concert on New Year's Day 1969 at the Hawk's Nest.

Like Buffalo Springfield, the Mandala are probably best remembered today for the musicians, rather than for the music they produced (none of the band's music is available on iTunes). Domenic Troiano, the lead guitarist, went on to serve in a number of popular bands after Mandala split, including his own Domenic Troiano Band and the Guess Who. He scored probably the biggest hit of his career with the disco-themed 'We All Need Love' in 1979—'356 Sammon Ave' (1972), a tribute to his former home in East York, and 'My Old Toronto Home' (1973) both had some popular success. Troiano released three influential solo LPs during the later 1970s—*Burning at the Stake* (1977), *The Joke's On Me* (1978) and *Fret Fever* (1979)—and he performed as a studio musician on a number of sessions, most notably with the Pursuit of Happiness singer Moe Berg, James Cotton, Long John Baldry, and Joe Cocker. In 1996 he was honoured with induction into the Canadian Music Hall of Fame; after his untimely death in 2005, the Domenic Troiano Guitar Scholarship was initiated, offering financial aid to talented young Canadian guitarists (the award is panelled by the likes of Alex Lifeson, Rik Emmet, Bernie LaBarge, and Domenic's brother, Frank Troiano).

At the same time as Troiano scored his solo successes, Jozef Chirowsky and 'Whitey' Glann, the Mandala's ex-keyboardist and drummer, joined Canadian producer Bob Ezrin and Jack Richardson at Nimbus Nine Productions in Toronto. Though they did not work with Richardson and Ezra on any of the albums they produced for the Guess Who, Chirowsky and Glann served on a number of Richardson and Ezrin's most famous session dates, including Lou Reed's *Sally Can't Dance* and *Rock and Roll Animal* LPs; Alice Cooper's *Billion Dollar Babies* and *Welcome To My Nightmare*; KISS's *Destroyer* LP; and Peter Gabriel's *Peter Gabriel (I)*. In the mid-1980s Richardson changed career paths entirely, and took a job as a professor in the Music Industry Arts program at Fanshawe College in London, Ontario, where he continues to teach to this day. For his part, Bob Ezrin would go on to become one of the most successful rock record producers ever to emerge from Toronto, putting his stamp on albums by, as noted, Lou Reed, Alice Cooper, KISS, and Peter Gabriel, but also Pink Floyd, David Gilmour, Robert Fripp, Rod Stewart, Julian Lennon, the Jayhawks, Kula Shakur, Jane's Addiction, the Darkness, Nine Inch Nails, the Deftones, Catherine Wheel, and 30 Seconds to Mars, among others, and the Ezrin-produced *The Wall* (1979), by Pink Floyd, was the best-selling record of the 1970s.

Another band that epitomized the 'Toronto sound' in the late 1960s was the Paupers. Comprised of Bill Marion, Chuck Beal, Denny Gerard, and future session stalwart Skip Prokop, the Paupers released a number of popular independently produced records, including 'Never Send You Flowers' for Red Leaf Records, and 'For What I Am' and 'Heart Walking Blues' for Duff Roman's Roman Records. Though the Paupers enjoyed a sizable local following in Toronto throughout the later 1960s, they only managed to breach the CHUM Top 10 once, with 'If I Call You By Some Name' (Number 6 CHUM, 1967). In June of 1969 the Paupers opened for Jefferson Airplane at the Café Au Go Go in New York City. While this show should have been a high point of their career, it was likely their undoing; that night the group's manager, Bernie

Finkelstein, capitalized on their new-found notoriety by selling his management contract with the band to Albert Grossman, who ultimately proved too busy with his
established clients—Bob Dylan and Joan Baez, for instance—to pay the group the
attention it required. Not surprisingly, the Paupers disbanded soon after Grossman
took the helm. Of all the band's musicians, Prokop had the most success finding work
after the split: he played a number of sessions, including Peter, Paul, and Mary's
Number 1 'I Dig Rock and Roll Music' (1967), before starting the 13-piece rock
orchestra Lighthouse with Paul Hoffert in Toronto in 1969.

After the Paupers, Finkelstein turned his attention to Kensington Market. Named
after a trendy area of Toronto, only minutes from Yorkville Village, and featuring Luke
Gibson of the pioneer 'Toronto sound' band Luke & the Apostles, Kensington Market
enjoyed a minor regional hit in 1968 with 'I Would Be the One' (1968), which peaked
at Number 18 on the CHUM charts. Finkelstein wrangled a recording contract for the
group with Warner Brothers in 1968, which resulted in two LPs—*Avenue Road* (1968)
and *Aardvark* (1970)—produced by Felix Pappalardi, who produced all of Cream's
records to great success that decade. The 'major' label attention proved the band's
undoing, however, and they were unable to convert Pappalardi's presence into substantial record sales. Dismayed, Kensington Market disbanded in 1970.

Though their music did not bear the usual R&B influence of a rock group from
Toronto in the 1960s, the Lords of London were indeed from Toronto, and caused a
teen sensation in the summer of 1967 when their 'Cornflakes and Ice Cream' (1967)
shot to Number 1 on pop charts across Canada, and in Boston, Georgia, and
Australia (where the record was licensed by Decca Records). The group performed on
a number of television shows immediately following the success of 'Cornflakes and
Ice Cream', including on CTV's *After Four, It's Happening, In Person,* and *Up Beat.* The
Lords' follow-up release, 'Popcorn Man'/'21,000 Dreams', tanked, however, failing to
reach the Top 40 anywhere in the world. Devoted fans of the Ugly Ducklings, a hard-
rocking 'Toronto sound' group with a residency at Ronnie Hawkins's Hawk's Nest,
the Lords of London set their sights on performing the Nest themselves, which they
did in 1968. By then, however, they had already obviously lost their teen fan base,
and the band's lead singer, Sebastien Angelo, left to pursue solo success.

Ottawa

Though clearly a smaller market than Toronto, Ottawa produced its fair share of rock
and folk rock bands in the late 1960s. Perhaps the best-known group was 3's A
Crowd, which featured during each of its many incarnations a veritable who's who of
future Canadian pop stars, including David Wiffen, Bruce Cockburn, Colleen
Peterson (who was awarded a Juno for Most Promising Female Vocalist in 1967
thanks to her work with the band), and David Wilcox. Cockburn, who worked as a
busker in Paris in the early 1960s and who completed two years of a degree at the
famous Berklee College of Music in Boston, also performed with the Children and
the Esquires in Ottawa, before he set off on his own in 1969 to become the first artist
signed to Bernie Finkelstein's newly minted True North Records label, centred in

Toronto's Yorkville Village (Cockburn's eponymous debut for the label was followed quickly by fellow Yorkville resident Murray McLaughlin's *Song from the Street* in 1971, both records combining to establish Finkelstein's True North Records as probably the pre-eminent folk and folk rock imprint in the nation).

Montreal

By 1970, Montreal had established a rock circuit of its own, notable for the fact that it featured anglophone, francophone, and bilingual acts on a regular basis. J.B. & the Playboys, for instance, quickly established their hard-rocking variant of R&B as a presence in the city, opening for elite rock bands such as the Rolling Stones, the Mamas and the Papas, and the Beach Boys during their appearances in the city. Though they scored some success in Canada with the singles 'I'm a Loner' and 'Poor Anne' in the mid-1960s, J.B. & the Playboys couldn't capitalize on their live successes, and they folded in the early 1970s without once breaching the Top 40.

More successful was Montreal's Mashmakhan, named for Michoacan, a region in Mexico famous in Montreal for its 'high-grade' marijuana. Perhaps more of a jazz-fusion band than anything else, the rock sound heard on Mashmakhan's 'throwaway' single cuts proved most successful. After performing local nightclubs and bars in Montreal, the group caught the attention of record producer Bob Hahn, who orchestrated a recording contract with Columbia Records in Toronto. Their first release for Columbia, 'As the Years Go By' (1970), sold over 100,000 copies in Canada and moved 500,000 units in the United States, where it was licensed by Epic Records; it also surprised the band, and their handlers at Columbia, when the single sold close to 400,000 copies in Japan. The group would eventually participate in the infamous cross-Canada Festival Express tour, with the likes of Janis Joplin, the Flying Burrito Brothers, and the Band, in 1970. Their second record, *The Family* (1971), was their last, however; though it sold moderately well in Japan, the record failed to make any headway in Canada, and the group soon disbanded.

While Mashmakhan soared in Japan, Robert Charlebois was busy sounding the death knell of the *chansonniers* movement in Quebec with his particular brand of francophone rock. A native of Montreal, Charlebois brought the electric guitar, and the rock 'n' roll ethos it represents, to the Québécois francophone pop scene—whether that scene wanted it or not. Always considered something of a rebel, Charlebois has the distinction of being the first *chansonnier* to accompany himself on an electric guitar, a feat he achieved during a live taping of CBC TV's *Jeunesse Oblige*. He was also one of the first Québécois rockers to use '*joual*' in his songs, a Québécois vernacular characterized by its liberal use of English expressions. In 'updating' the *chansonnier*, Charlebois worked to create the musical arm of a distinctly Québécois culture, creating a rock music that was neither obviously French nor clearly English, though it was steeped in the musical traditions of both language groups. Dubbed 'the Dylan of Quebec' by *Rolling Stone* magazine in the late 1960s, Charlebois continued to dominate the pop scene in Quebec well into the 1970s and even scored some minor successes in parts of English-speaking Canada later in the decade.

Halifax

While we return to the rock scene in Quebec next chapter, we should briefly note the presence of 'east coast' musicians both in Montreal and Toronto. Like Calgary, Canada's Maritime region had little in the way of a popular music industry infrastructure. Thus, scores of Maritime musicians travelled west in search of work during the mid- and late 1960s. Probably the best known of this group were Bruce Wheaton, Pam Marsh, and Carson Richards, who established the band Everyday People in the late 1960s in Toronto. They scored two minor chart successes with 'You Make Me Wonder' (1970) and 'Nova Scotia Home Blues' (1970) in 1970, before returning to the Maritimes later in the decade.

Jimi Hendrix

The 1960s saw the rise of a new generation of electric guitarists who functioned as culture heroes for their young fans. Their achievements were built on the shoulders of previous generations of electric guitar virtuosos: Les Paul, whose innovative tinkering with electronic technology inspired a new generation of amplifier tweakers; T-Bone Walker, who introduced the electric guitar to R&B music in the late 1940s; urban blues musicians such as Muddy Waters and B.B. King, whose raw sound and emotional directness inspired rock guitarists; and early masters of rock 'n' roll guitar such as Chuck Berry and Buddy Holly. Beginning in the mid-1960s, the new guitarists—including Jimi Hendrix, Eric Clapton, Jimmy Page, Jeff Beck, the Rolling Stones' Keith Richards, and the Beatles' George Harrison—took these influences and pushed them farther than ever before in terms of technique, sheer volume, and improvisational brilliance.

Jimi Hendrix (1942–70) was the most original, inventive, and influential guitarist of the rock era, and the most prominent black rock musician of the late 1960s. His early experience as a guitarist was gained touring with rhythm and blues bands. In 1966 Hendrix moved to London where, at the suggestion of his producer and manager Chas Chandler (ex-bassist for the Animals), he joined with two English musicians—bassist Noel Redding and drummer Mitch Mitchell—to form the Jimi Hendrix Experience. The Experience was first seen in America in 1967 at the Monterey Pop Festival, where Hendrix stunned the audience with his flamboyant performance style, which involved playing the guitar with his teeth and behind his back, stroking its neck along his microphone stand, pretending to make love to it, and setting it on fire with lighter fluid and praying to it. This sort of guitar-focused showmanship, soon to become commonplace at rock concerts, was not unrelated to the wild stage antics of some rhythm and blues performers. Viewing the Hendrix segment of the documentary film *Monterey Pop*, it is clear that some people in the self-consciously hip and mainly middle-class white audi-

The Jimi Hendrix Experience. Frank Driggs Collection.

ence found themselves shocked by Hendrix's boldness, though most would certainly have been exposed to the wild and often sexually charged performance styles of Al Rappa, bassist with Bill Haley & His Comets, and even Chuck Berry, among many others; and some critics still debate whether Hendrix's performance at the festival was of an 'erotic sacrifice' or a 'violent rape'.

In any event, Hendrix's creative employment of feedback, distortion, and other sound-processing devices such as the wah-wah pedal and fuzz box, coupled with his fondness for aggressive dissonance and incredibly loud volumes, represented important additions to the musical techniques and materials available to rock guitarists. Hendrix was a sound sculptor, who seemed at times to be consciously exploring the borderline between traditional conceptions of music and noise, a pursuit that links him in certain ways to composers exploring electronic sounds and media in the world of art music at around the same time. One of the most famous examples of Hendrix's experimentation with electronically generated sound was his performance of the American national anthem at the Woodstock Festival in 1969. Between each phrase of the melody, Hendrix soared into an elaborate electronic fantasy, imitating 'the rockets' red glare, the bombs bursting in air', and then landed precisely on the beginning of next phrase, like a virtuoso jazz musician.

All of these cited characteristics, along with any number of striking studio effects, may be heard on the first album by the Experience, *Are You Experienced?* (1967), and particularly on its famous opening cut, 'Purple Haze'. In one limited sense, 'Purple

Haze' is a strophic song with clear roots in blues-based melodic figures, harmonies, and chord progressions. But to regard the extraordinary instrumental introduction, the guitar solo between the second and third strophes, and the violently distorted instrumental conclusion all as mere effects added to a strophic tune is really to miss the point. In fact, it could be argued that the strophic tune serves as a mere scaffolding for the instrumental passages; but, at the least, the effects are equal in importance to the elements of the tune itself. The radical character and depth of Hendrix's contribution may be seen in the extent to which he requires us to readjust our thinking and terminology in the effort to describe appropriately what constitutes the real essence of his song. When we add in the impact of the lyrics, with their reference to *'blowin' my mind'* and lines like *"scuse me while I kiss the sky'*, it is easy to see why Hendrix became an iconic figure for the drug culture as well as a role model for rock musicians.

It is emblematic of how far Hendrix had strayed from his rhythm and blues roots in music like 'Purple Haze' that neither this song, nor any other record released by Hendrix, ever made a dent in the R&B charts. Hendrix was not a singles artist in any case—only 'Foxy Lady' and his cover of Dylan's 'All Along the Watchtower' cracked the CHUM charts, earning him Number 25 and Number 5 placements, respectively, in 1969—and his real kinship was with the new rock audience that viewed the record, and not the single, as its essential source of musical communication. In a sense, this made Hendrix a new kind of crossover artist. His audience rewarded him by elevating all of the five LPs he designed for release in his all-too-brief lifetime into the Top 10. Hendrix died in September 1970, only a few weeks before Janis Joplin's death, of an apparent accidental overdose of sleeping pills likely combined with alcohol.

Festivals: Woodstock, Altamont, and the Festival Express

In terms of live performances, the late 1960s came to be increasingly characterized by rock music 'festivals': sprawling multi-day performance events, intended to attract hundreds of thousands of fans, generally held on rural or suburban fairgrounds or fields without prescribed—that is, with 'festival'—seating. Arguably the first rock festival, the Monterey Pop Festival attracted over 50,000 fans in June of 1967. A similar number showed up for a rock festival held in Aldergrove, British Columbia, and at the Toronto Rock Festival that same year (the festival in Aldergrove is notable for the fact that it was marred by violent outbursts from local biker gangs, foreshadowing the debacle at Altamont that would occur only two years later). In 1968 the Newport Folk Festival attracted some 100,000 fans (in 1969, only one year later, the festival attracted 50,000 more, raising the total number to 150,000). And, in 1969, a free concert given by the Rolling Stones in London's Hyde Park, to commemorate the passing of founding guitarist Brian Jones, attracted some 250,000 listeners.

Of course, perhaps no festival occupies so mythic a place in the rock tradition as the Woodstock Music and Art Fair. For three days in August of 1969, rock's elite performed to an audience estimated at 500,000, assembled on Max Yasgur's 600-acre farm in Bethel, New York. Performances at the event have now entered rock legend, and documentarians captured live sets by Joan Baez, Jefferson Airplane, Ritchie Havens, Janis Joplin, the Band, Creedence Clearwater Revival, Joe Cocker, the Who, Santana, Country Joe & the Fish, Jimi Hendrix, Sly and the Family Stone, and the new rock 'supergroup' Crosby, Stills, Nash and Young, among others. Though there were three accidental deaths at the festival, Woodstock was (rather presumptuously) considered by many to demonstrate the viability of the 'peace and love' message of the counterculture to the 'straight' world, who heard about the event almost incessantly as it happened via live updates on mainstream American and Canadian news outlets. As 'hippie' activists such as Abbie Hoffman and Jerry Rubin were quick to note, the 500,000 assembled at Woodstock qualified as a 'nation', if not an 'instant city', and they managed to coexist peacefully, and without incident, even in the face of extreme weather and poor sanitary conditions. And after all, in a city or nation of a half-million people, even young people, one might expect a few deaths over the course of several days.

Yet Woodstock was, according to one critic, 'more of a twilight than a dawn'. Seemingly the second that Woodstock ended, 'breakaway' factions within the counterculture turned towards radicalism and, eventually, to violence—destroying their credibility in the so-called 'straight' world in the process. Members of the Student Nonviolent Coordinating Committee, for instance, broke off into a group of terrorist cells under the banner of the Weather Underground; the group became one of the most notoriously fundamentalist 'radical factions' of the entire counterculture movement. Still, it was only a matter of months after Woodstock that the youth counterculture began to noticeably dissipate, and the idealistic 1960s turned to the materialistic 1970s as the baby-boom generation approached full-time employment.

Perhaps the most damaging 'symbolic nail' in the counterculture's coffin was a massive rock festival held at the Altamont Speedway just outside of San Francisco, in December of 1969. Held only four months after Woodstock, the so-called Altamont Festival was designed to serve a twofold purpose: first, it was to provide a climax for the Rolling Stones' first North American tour since 1966; and, second, it was supposed to introduce North Americans to the band's newest guitarist, slide virtuoso Mick Taylor, who replaced founding member Brian Jones (Jones had been found dead in his pool earlier in the year). Regardless of these good intentions, Altamont had two strikes against it from the outset. The over 300,000 attendees had only a fraction of the area available to them in comparison to the 600 acres used for the Woodstock festival, and the Rolling Stones agreed with the Grateful Dead that they should hire the San Francisco chapter of the Hell's Angels to provide security—in exchange for roughly $500 dollars' worth of beer!

The decision to hire the Hell's Angels as security, and to pay them in beer, seems incredibly naive—and, given what happened at the concert, it almost certainly was. But though it may have been naive, the decision was not malicious, as some critics have intimated. A faction of the Hell's Angels located in Britain had performed security duties at the Rolling Stones' Hyde Park concert the year before, with few incidents of violence; but little did the Rolling Stones know, the British Hell's Angels were more of a 'weekend warrior' club than the brutal criminal gang that prevailed in North America. Moreover, in the late 1960s, the Hell's Angels enjoyed something of an 'image makeover' in counterculture and even in mainstream press outlets. For some, in fact, the gang consisted of 'romantic outlaws' rather than violent urban marauders. Films such as *Easy Rider* portrayed bikers as glamorous victims of 'the system', an opinion encouraged by some of the more facile philosophies of the so-called 'New Left', which cast criminality and deviance as always the products of overly repressive laws and a corrupt social caste system.

Not surprisingly, with the Hell's Angels in charge of security, mayhem reigned at Altamont. In one of the festival's more notorious incidents, Marty Balin, singer and lead guitarist for Jefferson Airplane, was beaten unconscious by members of the Hell's Angels during the group's set, when he tried to stop one of that day's many 'stompings' from happening directly in front of the stage while he performed. Another incident involved Mick Jagger being punched in the face by an obviously intoxicated fan as he made his way from the band's helicopter to their trailer. Performances by the Grateful Dead and the Flying Burrito Brothers were equally marred by violence; during the latter's performance, a naked and obviously inebriated woman was beaten (and, allegedly, later raped) as she tried to make her way onto the stage, and a naked man was likewise beaten a short while later as he tried to do the same. However, the most notorious incident of the festival occurred during the Rolling Stones' set, when members of the Hell's Angels stabbed and then beat an 18-year-old student, Meredith Hunter, to death (Hunter, an African-American male, had brandished a pistol before he was murdered).

According to many critics at the time, the murder of Meredith Hunter clarified to all interested onlookers that the youth counterculture was indiscriminately anti-authoritarian and, as such, dangerously close to establishing a vacuum of authority in Western society. Rock music, they claimed, was that vacuum's exemplary soundtrack. Others argued that, within such a vacuum, only 'might makes right', as the popular saying goes. But perhaps Douglas Owram explains the festival's ultimate significance best:

> Woodstock and Altamont have retained a central place in the imagination of the baby boom. Music, as has been argued earlier, was central to the generation's sense of uniqueness. The journey from utopia to failure symbolized by these two events has since stood as a metaphor for the failure of the counterculture. Woodstock stands for the hopes and dreams of a new age—the summer of love, Haight-Ashbury, the optimism of the LSD trippers and marijuana smokers. Altamont represents the reality that came to pass—the rise of violence in the drug culture, the exploitation of the hippies, the sexual revolution's failure to bring personal happiness, speed, religious cults, and the horror of Charles Manson. People prefer to remember Woodstock, but they cannot forget its immediate aftermath. (Owram, 1996: 285)

In July of 1970 Canadians launched the first cross-country tour in rock history—the so-called 'Trans Continental Pop Festival' or 'the Festival Express', as it is better known today. For this cross-country tour promoted by Ken Walker, Thor Eaton, and Dave Williams, with appearances scheduled in Montreal, Toronto, Winnipeg, Calgary, and Vancouver, the performers included a number of established Canadian and American bands, including the Band, the Buddy Guy Band, the Flying Burrito Brothers, the Grateful Dead, Ian and Sylvia and the Great Speckled Bird, Janis Joplin, Mashmakhan, Mountain, Tom Rush, Traffic, Ten Years After, and Sha Na Na. The tour became the subject of a number of local protests over ticket prices—locals believed that these festival concerts should be free and, indeed, a free concert was held in Calgary in response—and dates in Montreal and Vancouver were eventually cancelled. With the bands riding the rails from city to city on a chartered CN train, a series of legendary impromptu jam sessions were held, the most famous of which involved Rick Danko from the Band, Jerry Garcia, and Janis Joplin.

The Guess Who Breaks Through

Given the various twists and turns the North American record industry has taken since 1970, it is often forgotten that the best-selling band in the entire world that year was Winnipeg's own the Guess Who. While the group is probably best remembered as the first from Canada to score an international Number 1 record without leaving Manitoba, this is a somewhat erroneous claim. In the wake of the Guess Who's first internationally successful hit, the Mersey-beat inspired 'Shakin' All Over', the band's American label, Scepter Records, insisted that they move to New York City—and they did. While there the group recorded a number of songs, the best known being the soft rocker 'Hey Ho (What You Do To Me)'; written by Nickolas Ashford and Valerie Simpson, the same songwriting team responsible for, among other hits, Ray Charles's 'Let's Go Get Stoned', Marvin Gaye and Tammy Terrell's 'Ain't No Mountain High Enough', and Diana Ross's 'Reach Out (And Touch Somebody's Hand)'—the single climbed to Number 33 on the CHUM charts in 1966 but failed to register at all stateside. After a stint backing the Ronnettes, the Crystals, and the Shirelles on one of Dick Clarke's 'Cavalcade of Stars' tours, the band was summarily dismissed from Scepter's roster and had no choice but to return home to Winnipeg. Shortly after, an exhausted and frustrated Chad Allan left the group, replaced by lead vocalist and virtuoso pianist, Burton Cummings. Thus the 'second phase' Guess Who was complete. With Burton Cummings on lead vocal and piano duties, Randy Bachman on lead guitar, Jim Kale on bass, and Gary Peterson on drums, it wasn't long before the group caught the ear of executives at CBC TV, who offered the Guess Who work as the house band for the network's national *Let's Go* teen dance show. After a year of performing covers, the band was eventually encouraged to perform their own original songs by the show's producer, Larry Brown.

By their second year on *Let's Go*, the Guess Who had caught the attention of Canadian record producer Jack Richardson, owner of Nimbus Nine Productions. So convinced of the Guess Who's potential greatness was Richardson that he mortgaged his home to produce a full-length LP by the group at A&R Records recording studio in

New York City, creating the now classic *Wheatfield Soul* LP in the process (the first record Richardson produced for the group was actually shared with a band from Ottawa called the Staccatos, who renamed themselves the Five Man Electrical Band in 1969 and enjoyed international chart success with the classic 'Signs' in 1971). The first single from *Wheatfield Soul*, the Bachman-Cummings original 'These Eyes', peaked at Number 10 on the *Billboard* chart and topped the CHUM chart early in 1969. Later, as the record slid off the charts, DJs flipped the single over to discover Randy Bachman's jazzy anti-drug 'B' side, 'Undun', which again breached the American Top 10, and peaked at Number 3 on the CHUM charts, in November of 1969.

Even as the Guess Who were busy recapturing their former glory, members could not help but feel somewhat typecast as a soft rock band. Thus, it came as a tremendous relief that their subsequent release, the hard rocking 'No Time', charted on both sides of the border. In fact, the single, produced at Richardson's Nimbus Nine Studios, actually did better stateside than its Number 9 placing in Canada, peaking at Number 5 on the American Top 40 in January 1970. A few months later, in May, the band reached its apex, releasing the classic left-nationalist anthem 'American Woman' (1970).

Inspired by an impromptu jam session at a li\ve performance in Mississauga, Ontario, 'American Woman' topped both the CHUM and *Billboard* charts for over three weeks, marking the first and only time in rock history that a Canadian band

The Guess Who became the best-selling rock act worldwide in 1970. Michael Ochs Archives/ Getty Images.

held the Number 1 position across North America. And yet the song was very nearly lost to history. As Burton Cummings remembers:

> 'American Woman' just 'happened' one night on stage. If memory serves me correctly it was at a curling rink in Mississauga called The Broom and Stone. Randy started playing the now-famous guitar riff and I just started singing whatever came into my head. All those lines about 'war machines' and 'ghetto scenes' and 'coloured lights can hypnotize, sparkle someone else's eyes' were just there in one of those 'stream of consciousness' moments. This was the late sixties and cassette machines were a relatively new invention. There was a young guy there bootlegging the show on a portable cassette machine. We confiscated the tape and literally 'learned' 'American Woman' from listening to it. It was a happy accident. (Cummings, 2006, 3–4)

Aided by the over 11.5 million copies of the single that sold in 1970 alone, the Guess Who became the best-selling rock act of that year worldwide (the song was voted Best Canadian Single of All Time in polls for *Chart Magazine* both in 2000 and 2005; and it has been covered by a staggeringly diverse array of rock bands, including Lenny Kravitz, Krokus, and the Butthole Surfers).

Though bassist Jim Kale has publicly countered claims that 'American Woman' is a clear instance of Canadian left-nationalism set to a backbeat—'a lot of people called it anti-American, but it wasn't', he claims—Randy Bachman himself supports the nationalist interpretation, explaining in interviews that the 'American Woman' referred to in the song's lyrics is none other than the Statue of Liberty, and that '*the shadow*' the song's narrator '*don't wanna see no more*' is, indeed, that of an American juggernaut looming ever larger on the Canadian horizon. It is also difficult to interpret the song's penultimate lyric, '*I don't need your war machine/I don't need your ghetto scenes*', as directed towards anything other than the United States, particularly given the issues facing that country in 1970. The song also obviously signals its subject though a minute-long introduction, comprised only of an acoustic blues shuffle performed by Randy Bachman on acoustic guitar, and Cummings's obsessive mantra—'*American woman . . . (she) gonna mess your mind*'—repeated no less than seven times. Finally, we should note that none other than the First Lady of America at the time, Pat Nixon, interpreted the song as having at least some anti-American content, when she requested that the band not perform the song during a performance at the White House for the President's daughter, Tricia (the irony of a band responsible for perhaps the most overtly anti-American rock song in history performing at the White House, at the request of the President's daughter, is almost too grand!).

Despite any assertions to the contrary, nationalism was clearly a key ingredient, if not the key ingredient, of the image the Guess Who presented to the world throughout the later 1960s and early 1970s. Even after Randy Bachman left the group in 1970, his recent conversion to Mormonism considered too 'un-rock 'n' roll' for the tastes of his bandmates, songs such as 'Lightfoot', 'Maple Fudge', 'Runnin' Back To Saskatoon', 'So Long Bannatyne', and 'Grace Bay Blues', among others, openly referenced Canadian cities and towns with the same matter-of-factness as, say, soul singers referencing Detroit. Album titles such as *Wheatfield Soul* and *Canned Wheat* further made a virtue of the band's prairie heritage. Maple-leaf logos and cartoon beavers adorned their stage sets and record covers, and they often wore sweaters advertising local Winnipeg makers of amplifiers and speakers. They set up their headquarters in Winnipeg, and made sure that interviewers knew as much. Moreover, as critic Lester Bangs noted in one of many articles he wrote about the band, published in *Creem* in 1972, the Guess Who's live set often incorporated long anti-American diatribes directly before performances of 'American Woman':

> I saw the Guess Who do 'American Woman' live a year ago, and I have never been more offended by a concert. Burton Cummings indulged himself in a long, extremely cranky rumination on Yankee Yin, in a sort of fallen-out Beat poetic style. . . . Wouldn't you be offended by this Canuck creep coming down here taking all our money while running down our women? Sure you would! Until you realized as I did that the kind of stuff is exactly what makes the Guess Who great! (Cited in Potter, 1996: 109)

Though the Guess Who would go through a number of personnel changes until Cummings called it quits in 1975, and even though they would score many more Top 40 hits both in Canada and in the United States—'Rain Dance', 'Albert Flasher', 'Orly', 'Glamour Boy', 'Dancin' Fool', and 'Clap for the Wolfman', for instance—Cummings himself probably best summarizes the band's most lasting contribution to Canadian culture:

> We had five or six million-selling singles, a couple of million-selling albums—which in those days were great sales—we'd hit number one in *Billboard* with the *American Woman* album and single, and this had happened in every country in the world. Suddenly it was blatant and visible to every Canadian musician that if these four prairie dogs from Winnipeg could make it, they could, too. It was the same thing I'd said five or six years earlier: if a truck driver from Memphis can make it and four working-class guys from Liverpool can make it, we can make it. That's when every little guy from Saskatoon, Estevan, Timmins, Halifax, Dartmouth, wherever, said, 'Hey, if those guys can do it, we can do it. They're not *that* good.' (Potter, 1999: 57)

Discussion Questions

1. How did soul musicians such as James Brown and Aretha Franklin encapsulate the political aspirations of their listeners in the sound of the records they produced during the mid- and late 1960s? In what ways is this also true of folk rock and acid rock musicians?

2. Bob Dylan was booed vociferously at concerts when he first 'went electric' in 1965. The booing became so bad that Levon Helm left his first tour with Dylan. Did Dylan actually betray his urban folk listeners, i.e., did he 'sell out'? What, specifically, about the sound of Dylan's records from the mid-1960s was so provocative to many in his initial fan base?

3. In the 1960s, dissent and protest became marketable commodities, particularly in the rock tradition. How are dissent and protest still woven into the marketing fabric of rock today? How do the different subgenres of rock value dissent and protest differently today? Can you hear these differences in the way songs from these genres are typically composed, performed, and recorded?

4. As the 1960s wore on, productions became increasingly 'non-veridic'. Why? What about 'non-veridic' production values resonated with members of the youth counterculture?

5. What was the designation 'rock' meant to imply in relation to the designation 'rock 'n' roll'? Does 'rock 'n' roll' refer to the rock music made in the mid- and late 1950s, or to an entire genre of popular music? If Elvis is the symbol for rock 'n' roll, who is the symbol for rock?

6. Why did so many rock musicians in the late 1960s begin to experiment with South Asian instruments such as the sitar, tamboura, and tabla? Has something similar happened since?

7. How does the Guess Who's 'American Woman' encapsulate its time? In what ways might the song be considered 'political'? Do the lyrics still have relevance today?

Chapter Five

Rock in the CRTC Era: The 1970s

▌The Late Sixties and Early Seventies in Canada

One of the most pervasive stereotypes about the 1970s—famously captured in novelist Tom Wolfe's epithet, 'The Me Decade'—involves a shift in the values of young adults away from the communitarian, politically engaged ideals of the 1960s counterculture towards more materialistic and conservative attitudes. This shift in values is often called 'the retreat from radicalism' by historians, because it is marked by a large-scale rejection of counterculture experimentalism in youth lifestyles and culture. While this generalization certainly needs to be taken with a large grain of salt, it is undeniable that the 1970s did see a kind of 'turning inward' in North American culture. As the noted rock critic Greil Marcus put it, writing in 1979:

> As happened in the late fifties and early sixties with the disappearance of rock's founders, in the late sixties the music and the audience lost their center, when the Beatles disbanded and Bob Dylan eased up; in any case, the music had lasted far too long to be the possession of any identifiable generation, and the audience had likely grown too big and broad for any center. Rock and roll, as culture, lost much of its shape. The mass movements of the sixties, which for many brought a sense of common endeavor and shared fate to almost every aspect of life, fragmented; people who before took pride identifying themselves as members of a group—no matter how unorganized or spectral—found that they could best identify themselves by their names, and life became more private, more isolated. (Marcus, 1979: xx)

As the 1960s drew to a close, the sense that the entire Western world teetered on the brink of violent revolution was palpable. In 1968 alone, student activists manned barricades with workers in a general strike in Paris, France; Soviet tanks rolled into Prague, Czechoslovakia, brutally quashing calls for 'socialism with a human face' there, that is, the so-called Prague Spring; race riots erupted across the US, and with an alarming frequency, especially after the murders of Martin Luther King Jr and Robert Kennedy that year; separatist groups set off more than 50 bombs across the province of Quebec; and, in Mexico, a massive student movement was brutally suppressed only months before the Olympics were held there. Given that most counterculture activists preferred rock records to other kinds, and that rock musicians typically acted and dressed like counterculture radicals themselves, rock music was linked by proxy with this sort of political radicalism in the popular press.

Canada was by no means exempt from radicalism and student unrest. Rallies and occupations were a mundane fact of life on many Canadian campuses by 1970. Students regularly assembled to 'resist' the Vietnam War, the unequal treatment of women around the world, the status of Canada's Native peoples, the presence of the military–industrial complex on Canadian campuses—Boeing, for instance, was a frequent target for holding job interviews at the University of British Columbia—American cultural and economic encroachment, separatism in Quebec, and so on. Before the 1960s had ended, numerous student disruptions were reported at Carleton University, University of Toronto, University of Western Ontario, University of Waterloo, the Burnaby Mountain campus of Simon Fraser University, University of British Columbia, and University of Alberta, to name only a few campuses.

One of the more notorious student rallies in Canada occurred on 24 October 1968, when Jerry Rubin, the self-professed leader of the 'Yippies' (the Youth International Party), encouraged over 1,000 students at the University of British Columbia to occupy the campus Faculty Club—since it was they, according to Rubin, who actually paid for the club. Though this occupation ended peacefully, only three months later Canadians witnessed the largest, and most destructive, student occupation in national history at Sir George Williams University in Montreal (the university has since been renamed Concordia University). Outraged at what they took to be the administration's intransigence over allegations of racism among faculty members, over 200 students occupied the university's much ballyhooed computer lab on 29 January 1969. The occupation was initially non-violent, the most destructive act involving students dumping computer punch cards out the lab's ninth-floor window. University officials patiently negotiated with protestors, and seemed to take their allegations seriously. But on 11 February, a full two weeks into the occupation, negotiations collapsed and administrators called the police. A fire was subsequently set in the lab, forcing the student occupiers to flee; 97 students were arrested that day, though few were charged, and over $2 million in damage was done.

The 'Sir George Williams Computer Riot', as the occupation came to be known, was basically carefree in comparison to the violence that beset Montreal the next year, in October 1970. As we noted in Chapter 4, the separatist movement in Quebec had gained in both prominence and size throughout the 1960s, but so, too, had a continuing terrorist campaign waged by fringe separatists, which threatened to destroy the movement's mainstream credibility. The passage of the Official Languages Act of 1969, which made Canada an officially bilingual country, did little to appease separatists. In any event, rioters had already made known their feelings about the country's Prime Minister, Pierre Trudeau, when they pelted him and other 'honoured' guests, assembled in the reviewing stand for St Jean de Baptiste Day celebrations in 1968, with garbage and sundry debris (Trudeau famously refused to budge, even as bottles zipped past only inches from his head, and he was elected to his first majority government the next day, taking most of the seats in Quebec with him). Student protestors called for the transformation of McGill University into an entirely francophone school, and members of the FLQ bombed the campus; rioters shattered the windows of department stores in Montreal that conducted business solely in English, and a number of these stores were also bombed; and a bomb injured at least 26 men and women at the Montreal Stock Exchange.

The confrontation between federal and terrorist forces reached a peak in October 1970, when members of the Front de Libération du Québec (FLQ) kidnapped the senior British trade representative in Montreal, James Cross. Trudeau refused to negotiate with the terrorists, who demanded the release of 'political prisoners' and the reading of the FLQ manifesto over the nation's airwaves in exchange for Cross's life. Five days later Quebec's Labour Minister, Pierre Laporte, was kidnapped and, eventually, he was murdered. Support for the kidnappings, and for the FLQ in general, was initially strong in Quebec; massive rallies and sympathy demonstrations were held across the province. But the support was short-lived as the discovery of Pierre Laporte's strangled corpse, unceremoniously stuffed into the trunk of a car, prompted many to reconsider their allegiances early on in the crisis (Cross was found in December, and he was freed in exchange for his captors' safe passage to Cuba). Trudeau declared an 'apprehended insurrection' in Quebec, deployed the federal army, and invoked the War Measures Act to suspend citizens' civil liberties—all at the request of the province's Premier, Robert Bourassa, and with strong support across anglophone Canada. Pro-terrorist demonstrations subsided in the province as the FLQ was declared illegal, and a wave of arrests were carried out, the incarcerated eventually numbering in the thousands.

Though the invocation of the War Measures Act marked the conclusive end of a decade of terrorism in Quebec, and the discovery that terrorists actually comprised only a radical minority in the separatist movement to begin with, this outcome was anything but clear in October of 1970. And it goes without saying that the decision to invoke the War Measures Act, especially by a Prime Minister elected on the promise of making Canada a 'just society', remains controversial. Thus, Canada entered the new decade bitterly—and violently—divided on several fundamental issues. Moreover, it seemed clear to the vast majority of Canadians that their country was actually disappearing, caught in the midst of a cultural annexation by the United States. In fact, by 1970 the very notion of a Canadian culture had become inherently questionable, so much so that Trudeau passed so-called '**CanCon**' regulations to mandate a daily minimum of Canadian programming on the country's broadcast media. However the rest of the world interpreted the measures, there could be no question that the Canadian government was now watching its southern border with an extreme degree of caution.

To make matters worse, for the first time in many years Canada faltered economically in the 1970s. In 1971 American President Richard Nixon introduced a series of tax credits and incentives designed to repatriate American foreign investments and to discourage further 'capital exports' (including to Canada). This was a particularly difficult pill to swallow for the Liberal Party of Canada, which had spent much of the postwar era convincing Canadians that integrating their economy with American interests was the only viable option. In a few years Trudeau would openly defy the American hegemony, symbolized loudly in his decision to brazenly ignore the American embargo on Cuba and to establish a now famous friendship with the country's leader, Fidel Castro. But Trudeau was slow in responding to Nixon at first. And his symbolic resistance meant little to a country faltering economically. In fact, Trudeau's later actions were interpreted by many Canadians as widening rather than repairing the growing rift between Canada and the United States, which did little to endear Trudeau with those bearing the brunt of 'stagflation' (i.e., escalating inflation conjoined with stagnant wages). Not surprisingly, then, Canada prepared for yet another election in 1972.

Prosperity and cultural sovereignty meant little in the face of a sizable youth population evidently on the brink of 'coming unglued', as historians Robert Bothwell and Jack Granatstein (2000: 165) put it, and seemingly unconflicted about taking down the entire democratic way of life with them. Indeed, if readers retain just one image of Canada in the early 1970s it should probably be of a country divided, and apparently in decline. The economy had scaled unprecedented heights only a few years before, but now slipped and began to stumble, and the country was mired in radicalism and violence: in one month alone the Premier of Quebec was moved into a guarded suite in Montreal; troops were posted outside the homes of federal cabinet ministers in the nation's capital; a British trade commissioner was held for ransom; a provincial Labour Minister was kidnapped and murdered; citizens were stripped of their basic constitutional rights, and thousands were arrested without due process; and, when asked by a reporter how far he would be willing to go in pursuit of terrorists, the country's Prime Minister only shrugged and said, 'Just watch me.'

Just as Canada seemed increasingly fragmented as the 1970s dawned, so the fragmentation of rock into a number of 'roots', 'soft', and 'pop' subgenres in the early 1970s signalled a general retreat from—if not an outright repudiation of—experimentalism in popular culture and music. Many of rock music's makers and fans began to seriously reconsider basic assumptions about the nature of power that underpinned much counterculture thought and expression in the late 1960s; and many simply outgrew the idea of revolution, coming to see value in democratic capitalism and nobility in working to effect 'change from within'. On both sides of the border, a level of exhaustion beset the ranks of youth counterculture activists as violence, murder, and mass incarcerations took the romance out of radicalism and revolution for the better part of an entire generation. And, by 1971, rock music had begun to reflect these changes—somehow managing to become a multi-billion dollar industry in the process.

The Rock Industry in the 1970s

During the 1970s the rock industry reached new heights of consolidation in North America. While most major record labels in Canada remained wholly subsidiary units of corporations situated either in the United States or in Britain, six large corporations—Columbia/CBS, Warner Communications, RCA Victor, Capitol-EMI, MCA, and United Artists-MGM—were responsible for an estimated 80 per cent of all records sold in North America. Moreover, total profits from the sale of recorded music achieved new heights, reaching an estimated $2 billion by 1973 and $4 billion by 1978, in part owing to the increasing popularity of pre-recorded tapes. The eight-track cartridge and cassette tape formats had initially been introduced during the mid-1960s, but their popularity expanded exponentially during the early 1970s—by 1975, sales of pre-recorded tapes accounted for almost one-third of all music sold in the US.

However, the music industry had also become increasingly risky. During the 1970s the industry came to depend on a relatively small number of million-selling ('platinum') LPs to turn a profit. A small number of 'multi-platinum' superstars—including Paul McCartney, Elton John, and Stevie Wonder—were able to negotiate multi-million dollar contracts with major record companies. Unable to compete in this high-end market, small independent labels—of the sort that had pioneered rock 'n' roll in the 1950s—accounted for only about one out of every 10 records sold in the early 1970s. Only making matters worse for these indies, the energy crisis of 1973 created a shortage of polyvinyl chloride, the petroleum-based substance from which tapes and discs were made, and this also helped to drive many small record companies out of business. Yet, as we shall see in Chapter 6, the indies came back to exert a tremendous musical influence in the second half of the decade, introducing new genres such as disco, punk rock, funk, reggae, and rap.

Like other big businesses, the record industry was increasingly impelled to present more choices—or, at least, to create the impression of more choice—for its customers. This led to the emergence of dozens of specialized types of popular music— middle of the road (MOR), easy listening, adult contemporary, singer-songwriters, country pop, soft soul, urban contemporary, funk, disco, reggae, oldies, and lots of subgenres of rock music, including country rock, folk rock, soft rock, hard rock, pop rock, heavy metal, southern rock, jazz rock, blues rock, Latin rock, art rock, glam rock, punk rock, and so on—each with its own constellation of stars and target audience. Record stores were organized in more complex patterns, with dozens of distinct categories listed on the labels of record bins.

Even as record labels increased the choices available to customers, the Top 40 playlist format—based on nationally distributed, pre-taped sequences of hit songs—increasingly dominated the AM radio airwaves, resulting in a diminished range of choices for AM radio listeners. By the mid-1970s most AM radio stations relied heavily on professional programming consultants, who provided lists of records that had done well in various regions. Throughout the decade, these playlists grew more and more restricted, making it difficult for bands without the backing of a major label to break into the Top 40.

While some hard rock or progressive rock bands were able to get singles onto Top 40 radio, the primary medium for broadcasting rock music was FM radio. During the 1970s the number of FM radio stations in North America increased by almost a thousand, and the popularity of FM—with its capacity for high-fidelity stereo broadcasting—surpassed that of AM radio. The eclectic free-form FM programming of the late 1960s, in which a DJ might follow a psychedelic rock record with a jazz or folk record, became restricted mainly to community- or college-based stations situated at the left end of the dial, where many such stations remain today.

The CRTC Era

Established by the Broadcasting Act of 1968 to replace the earlier Board of Broadcast Governors, the Canadian Radio-Television Commission (CRTC, renamed the Canadian Radio-television and Telecommunications Commission in 1976) is an independent agency that regulates and supervises the Canadian broadcasting system, including AM and FM radio, television, cable television, and pay-per-view TV. In 1970 the agency implemented radio broadcast regulations mandating that AM radio programming include at least 30 per cent 'demonstrably' Canadian content, and that FM radio programming include from 10 to 30 per cent 'demonstrably' Canadian content. Most agree that these regulations basically created a viable rock music industry in Canada practically overnight. Before the implementation of these Canadian content ('CanCon') regulations in 1970, the few major labels with offices in Canada—RCA, Warner Brothers, CBS, and Capitol—were all American- or British-owned, and they were simply uninterested in developing Canadian talent; and for the most part, Canada's indie labels were only equipped to service small, basically regional markets.

In the wake of the CanCon ruling, Canadian musicians no longer had to move to the United States to make a living in rock. In fact, the Guess Who made a point of telling interviewers throughout the 1970s that Winnipeg was their home, that they recorded primarily in Canada—at Jack Richardson's Nimbus Nine Studios in Toronto—and that they simply would not budge. As a result of this new-found support structure at home, a number of Canadian singers and bands found extended levels of success both in Canada and abroad. So-called CanCon groups such as the Stampeders, Copperpenny, Fludd, Chilliwack, Prism, April Wine, Crowbar, BTO, Lighthouse, Five Man Electrical Band, Triumph, Trooper, Beau Dommage, and Harmonium, to name only a few, enjoyed heightened—though certainly not undeserved—levels of success in Canada, often aided in no small part by the fact that most Canadian radio stations initially had only a limited pool of Canadian content records to choose from.

While CanCon regulations are still lauded by most culture industry workers in Canada, critics complain that the regulations were based on too vague or narrow a definition of 'Canadian', and they typically point to certain records by international superstars such as Bryan Adams and Shania Twain that famously failed to qualify as 'Canadian' (both, coincidentally, due to the input of producer and co-composer Robert 'Mutt' Lange). According to CRTC radio regulations, a 'Canadian' record is any for which a Canadian citizen fulfills at least two points of the so-called 'MAPL code': (1) music, (2) artist, (3) production, or (4) lyrics. More specifically, section 2.2 of the CRTC Radio Regulations, entitled 'Canadian Content', defines a 'demonstrably Canadian musical selection' as:

> a selection that: (a) meets at least two of the following conditions, namely, (i) the music or lyrics are performed principally by a Canadian, (ii) the music is composed by a Canadian, (iii) the lyrics are written by a Canadian, and (iv) the musical selection consists of a live performance that is (A) recorded wholly in Canada or (B) performed wholly in and broadcast live in Canada; (b) is an instrumental performance of a musical composition that meets the conditions of subparagraph (a) (ii) or (iii); or (c) is a performance of a musical composition that a Canadian has composed for instruments only. . . . (3) For the purpose of the Regulations, 'Canadian' means: (a) a Canadian citizen, (b) a permanent resident, as defined in the Immigration Act, 1976, (c) a person whose ordinary place of residence was in Canada throughout the six months immediately preceding that person's contribution to a musical contribution, performance or concert or to the production of a foreground segment . . . or (d) a licensee.

National Pop Charts in Canada

Despite the controversies that dogged it, evidence of the CRTC's almost immediate success in fostering a viable support structure for rock music in Canada was seen in the first 'Steede Report Top 20', published in June 1975, on which Canadians had a significantly greater presence than had been the case on the earlier CHUM charts. That report tallied broadcasts for songs on radio stations across Canada and thus became Canada's first national singles chart. Later that same year, in August, the Steede Report expanded to a Top 30 listing, and in March 1976 the Report began listing the national Top 40. The next year, in May 1977, the Steede Report Top 40 was published on a biweekly basis.

To rectify the absence of sales as a chart indicator, Canadian Recording Industry Association (CRIA) 'National Best-Selling Record Charts' were published, beginning in August 1977. These so-called 'CRIA Charts' soon replaced the Steede Report listings. By August 1980, however, the charts had to be discontinued due to budget constraints. Thus, from September 1980 to April 1981 the nationally popular CBC radio show *90 Minutes with a Bullet* counted down the Canadian Top 40, after which point the network established a 'Beaver Bin' of top-charting singles and, in January of 1983, a CBC Top 30. Both of these charts were short-lived. They were replaced in 1984 when *The Record*, a weekly trade publication founded in 1981 by David Farrell, who was editor for *Record Week* from 1975 to 1977, began to publish multiple charts based on record sales at various retailers across Canada and on performance on national Top 40, adult-contemporary, and rock radio stations.

The Record survived for 12 years as Canada's foremost national chart listing. But in October 1996 the SoundScan Singles Chart replaced the listing. SoundScan is based on record sales and radio play on 'reporting stations' across Canada; sales data are compiled through bar-code scans at over 800 record stores across Canada, while radio play is tabulated via computerized programming reports. The SoundScan charts were published weekly, and were reprinted in both *CANOE*, an on-line journal of Canadian popular culture, and *Billboard* magazine, throughout the later 1990s.

The accuracy of the SoundScan method has recently come into question. This is in large part due to a series of so-called 'pay-per-play' scandals that have rocked the pop music world since the year 2000, when the New York attorney general, Eliot Spitzer, began investigations into ongoing payola practices on national radio. Besides simple cases of bribery—CBS radio and Epic Records, for instance, allegedly worked out a 'listener contest' that sent winners to Las Vegas to see Canadian chanteuse Céline Dion perform in exchange for adding her most recent single, 'Goodbye', to station playlists—it was discovered that SoundScan does not distinguish between regular broadcasts and purchased broadcasts on late-night 'pay-per-play' radio, in which case labels could purchase multiple late-night spins for a record that SoundScan would then tabulate and translate into an exaggerated chart listing. Likewise, indie promoters, working on behalf of major labels, began to pay upward of $400,000 to stations for the right to exclusively 'represent' them, meaning that radio stations would only consider broadcasting recordings that they, in their capacity as 'exclusive promoters', passed along to the stations; Clear Channel Communications, CBS, Entercom, and Citadel Broadcasting have all been implicated in the scandal, as have records by Avril Lavigne, Nick Lachey, Nine Inch Nails, and Céline Dion, among others.

In any event, radio spins and record sales are likely outdated markers of a single's success in Canada. At the very least, they are no longer an accurate gauge of national listening preferences, particularly among Canadian youth. To reflect these changes, and in a continuing bid for relevance, SoundScan has begun to tabulate digital downloads of songs, though this, too, is rife with peril as a gauge.

CanCon Singers and Groups

Anne Murray is generally agreed to be the first pop star of the CRTC era. Not surprisingly, given the province's long tradition of producing extremely talented country musicians, Murray was born in Nova Scotia, and her distinctive alto voice was first heard nationally on Don Messer's local *Singalong Jubilee* television program for CBC-TV. From there, Murray went on to become the first female solo singer in Canadian history to hit Number 1 on the American pop charts and to earn a gold record—both for her signature song, 'Snowbird' (1970), which she co-wrote with fellow *Singalong Jubilee* cast member Gene MacLellan. Typical of most Canadian country songs, 'Snowbird' was not easily categorizable; the track charted on American and Canadian country, pop, and adult-contemporary charts simultaneously. Sensing massive crossover appeal, the savvy Murray continued to merge country and pop sensibilities throughout her career (which has lasted for more than four decades now), selling over 54 million records in the process and paving the way for the likes of future global pop stars such as Céline Dion, Sarah McLaughlin, and, perhaps most like Murray, Shania

Anne Murray: The first pop star of the CRTC era. Getty Images.

Twain. A small sample of Murray's crossover hits from the 1970s would have to include the Number 1 adult-contemporary hit 'Danny's Song' (1972); the pop chart topping 'He Thinks I Still Care' (1974) and 'You Needed Me' (1978); and 'Shadows in the Moonlight' and 'Broken Hearted Me', which topped the country and adult-contemporary charts in the US, and reached the CHUM Top 20 in Canada, in 1979.

Though he never enjoyed the same level of success as Murray, Canadian singer-songwriter Dan Hill is generally considered Murray's male equivalent, particularly during the late 1970s. Born and raised in Toronto, Hill's emotional—if at times maudlin—singing, applied to a series of mostly sentimental ballads, earned the singer-songwriter a significant share of the Canadian pop market from the time of his first Juno award—won in 1976 for Most Promising Male Singer—to the present, though Hill remains best known for his work in the late 1970s and early 1980s. Leaving high school at 17 years of age to work as a songwriter for RCA, Dan Hill started his performing career at the Riverboat in Toronto's Yorkville Village. 'You Make Me Want To Be', from Hill's eponymous debut LP, sold well in Canada, but it was Hill's third LP release, *Longer Fuse* (1978), that spawned the international hit 'Sometimes When We Touch'. Selling over 200,000 copies in Canada, more than 500,000 in the US, and going on to sell over a million copies worldwide, 'Sometimes When We Touch' has been covered by Oscar Peterson, Marty Robbins, Tina Turner, Rod Stewart, and Cleo Laine, among others.

The rock field also blossomed during the CRTC era. Randy Bachman's first band after leaving the Guess Who, the 'classic' rock group Bachman-Turner Overdrive

(BTO), scored two international Number 1 pop hits in 1974 with 'Takin' Care of Business' and 'You Ain't Seen Nothin' Yet' and another Number 1 on the CHUM charts with 'Hey You' (1975) the next year; and the band reached the CHUM Top 5 three more times the next year with 'Let It Ride', 'Quick Change Artist', and 'Roll On Down the Highway'. The jazz-rock orchestra Lighthouse—featuring Skip Prokop on drums, Paul Hoffert on keyboards, and Ralph Cole on guitar—received considerable airplay for tracks such as 'One Fine Morning', 'Pretty Lady', 'Hats Off To the Stranger', and 'Sunny Days' without breaching the Top 20 pop charts anywhere in the US, while the Five Man Electrical Band (formerly the Staccatos) scored a major international hit with the song 'Signs' in 1971. Finally, Crowbar hit the CHUM Top 20 with 'Oh, What a Feeling' in 1971, becoming the third group of ex-Hawks, after the Band and Janis Joplin's Full-Tilt Boogie Band, to go on to major pop chart success after leaving Ronnie Hawkins's employ.

Soft Rock from Montreal

Canadian record buyers demonstrated a clear preference for the 'softer side' of the rock tradition throughout the 1970s. The Number 1 single in Canada during January of 1976, for instance, was the Bay City Rollers' bubblegum classic 'Saturday Night'. The track was replaced next month atop the pop charts by Barry Manilow's adult-contemporary hit, 'I Write the Songs', and then, later in the year, by Chicago's soft rocker 'If You Leave Me Now'. In fact, a brief study of Canada's singles charts, published since 1975, demonstrates the country's clear preference for songs from the 'softer side' of the rock tradition. The two best-selling pop singers in Canadian history—Elton John and Madonna—obviously approach the charts from a decidedly soft rock, adult-contemporary, and basic Top 40 pop perspective, and, especially in Elton John's case, they have a talent for transitioning seamlessly between Top 40 and adult-contemporary fare. That Canadians approve is easy to see—Madonna and John have spent a combined 124 weeks at Number 1, and 1,306 weeks in the Top 40, in Canada; they have scored no less than 22 Number 1 hits and 88 Top 40 placements between them.

Perhaps the most prominent Canadian acts to mine the 'soft side' of the rock tradition in the early 1970s were the Bells and Andy Kim, both from Montreal. With a sound that still often elicits comparisons to the Carpenters by both critics and fans, the Bells first performed publicly in 1965. Formed as the Five Bells in Montreal—with sisters Ann and Jackie Ralph, Cliff Edwards, Doug Gravelle, and Gordie McLeod—the band's 'rock-of-all-ages appeal', as *CANOE* magazine described it, saw them quickly ascend to national renown. In 1969 the group recorded their first single—'Moody Manitoba Morning'—and then a full-length LP, called *Dimensions*, for Polydor Records. That same year, though, Ann Ralph, who was married to bandmate Cliff Edwards at the time, left the group to become a stay-at-home mom.

After Ann's departure, the Five Bells became simply the Bells and set about to recording a follow-up to their debut LP. The Bells hit the CHUM Top 10 for the first time in December 1970 with the title cut from their second album, *Fly, Little White Dove, Fly*. Their next release from the same album, 'Stay Awhile' (1971), established the Bells as a global pop phenomenon. A vocal duet between Jackie Ralph and Cliff Edwards, composed by Newfoundlander and ex-*Singalong Jubilee* cast member Ken Tobias, 'Stay Awhile' topped the CHUM charts in Canada, went to Number 7 in the United States, and sold over four million copies worldwide by the end of 1972. Given the highly sexual nature of the lyrics—and the fact that the lovers depicted in the song clearly intend to stay with each other only for 'a while'—'Stay Awhile' was banned by some North American radio stations:

Jackie Ralph: *Into my room he creeps without making a sound*
Into my dreams he peeps with his hair all long and hanging down
How he makes me quiver
How he makes me smile
With all this love I have to give him
I guess I'm gonna stay with him awhile

Cliff Edwards: *She brushes the curls from her eyes*
She drops her robe on the floor
And she reaches for the light on the bureau
And the darkness is her pillow once more
How she makes me quiver
How she makes me smile
With all this love I have to give her
I guess I'm gonna stay awhile

Born in Montreal in 1952, Andy Kim (b. Andrew Youakim) remains the best-selling bubblegum, soft rock, and pop songwriter in Canadian history. Kim's career as a songwriter began in New York City in 1968, when he was only 16 years old. He signed a contract with ex-Brill Building songwriter Jeff Barry's Steed Records in New York City, and Kim and Barry had their first Top 20 hit in the US with Kim's 'How'd We Ever Get This Way?' That same year, Kim's 'Shoot 'Em Up Baby' was banned from Canadian and American airwaves when officials mistook the song's chorus for advocacy of the escalating political violence in North America and abroad; a Number 1 hit nonetheless, the CHUM chart for the week of 19 October 1968 featured only a blank entry at Number 1 to indicate the censored single's chart position. Kim made the Top 20 twice more the next year with 'Rainbow Ride' and 'Baby, I Love You', the latter peaking at Number 5 in the US and Number 7 on the CHUM charts, and earning Kim a Juno award for Top Male Vocalist. Kim and Barry next co-wrote the Number 1 bubblegum hit 'Sugar, Sugar' for the Archies—an animated television show featuring the popular comic book character Archie Andrews and the rest of 'the gang' from Riverdale—which was eventually certified as the RIAA's Record the Year for 1969 and has since sold over 10 million copies.

Barry and Kim continued to write for the Archies, and contributed songs to the Monkees final album, *Changes*, from 1970 to 1972. By 1974, though, Kim had transformed completely from a bubblegum soft-rocker into a singer-songwriter in the vein of Carole King and Leonard Cohen, scoring another Number 1 hit in 1974 with the soft rocker 'Rock Me Gently'. During the mid-1970s, however, Kim slowly withdrew from public life. A solo LP released under the inexplicable pseudonym Baron Longfellow came in 1980, and another record entitled *Prisoner By Design* was released in 1984, but Kim basically remained retired. In 1995, Ed Robertson of the Barenaked Ladies coaxed Kim out of retirement to co-write 'I Forgot To Mention', and he has since written songs with Ron Sexsmith.

Roots Rock and the Retreat from Radicalism

A look at the pop charts any time between 1969 and 1971 demonstrates that the so-called 'retreat from radicalism' manifested itself in the predominant record-buying patterns of North American rock fans. By 1969, themes of social and cultural revolution, musical experimentalism, and overtly non-veridic production values had given way to more 'traditional' rock 'n' roll subject matter and sounds. Rock traditionalists such as Creedence Clearwater Revival, the Band, and Blood, Sweat & Tears (BS&T) took up residency atop the pop charts, scoring no less than 15 Top 5 singles between them in the 18 months from February 1969 to August 1970. In the process they created the so-called 'roots rock' genre, demonstrating that rock 'n' roll had grown old enough by 1970 to spawn traditionalists.

It is interesting to note that, precisely as the pop charts took this conservative turn, counterculture dress and slang, psychedelic imagery, and acid rock music entered the cultural mainstream of AM radio, network television, and Hollywood movies. In the early 1970s the market for popular music became focused on two main categories of consumers: a new generation of teenagers, born in the late 1950s and early 1960s; and adults aged 25 to 40, who had grown up with rock 'n' roll and were looking for more mature (i.e., more conservative) material. Nostalgic fare such as the film *American Graffiti* (1973), the Broadway musical and film *Grease* (1972 and 1978, respectively), and the popular television series *Happy Days* used early rock 'n' roll—now nearly 20 years old—to evoke the so-called Golden Age of the 1950s, before the escalating social conflicts of the late 1960s supposedly 'hijacked' the culture.

If many wished that the 1960s would just go away, others mourned the decade's passing. For rock fans, the end of the counterculture was poignantly symbolized by the deaths of Jimi Hendrix (1970), Janis Joplin (1970), and Jim Morrison of the Doors (1971), and by the breakup of the Beatles, who, more than any other group, inspired the triumphs—and excesses—of rock music. On 31 December 1970, Paul McCartney filed the legal brief that was to formally dissolve the business partnership of the Beatles. For many rock fans, the demise of the 'Fab Four' was incontrovertible proof that the 1960s were dead and gone. But this certainly didn't mean that rock music itself was moribund. If in the late 1960s rock music was the music of the counterculture, defined by its opposition to the mainstream of popular music, by the 1970s it had helped to redefine the popular mainstream, becoming the primary source of profit for an expanding and ever more centralized entertainment industry.

Creedence Clearwater Revival

Creedence Clearwater Revival was a deliberately 'old-fashioned' rock 'n' roll band, consisting of two guitarists, a bass player, and a drummer. The group performed both original material and rock 'n' roll 'standards' in an essentially 'veridic' style, with no exotic instruments, no unusual or extended guitar solos, no studio effects (unless they contributed to a record's general 'liveness'), and no self-conscious experimentation with novel harmonies, rhythms, or song forms. CCR also rejected the new-found primacy of the album in the rock genre, though all their LPs sold very well; one of the great singles bands of the era, the group turned out a spate of incredibly catchy up-tempo two- and three-minute pop records. In 1969 and 1970 alone, CCR scored 11 Top 5 placements on the CHUM charts, more than half of which went to Number 1. A sample of their hits from this time would have to include 'Bad Moon Rising' (Number 1 CHUM, 1969), 'Down on the Corner' (Number 1 CHUM, 1969), 'Fortunate Son' (Number 1 CHUM, 1969), 'Proud Mary' (Number 2 CHUM, 1969), 'Lookin' Out My Back Door' (Number 1 CHUM, 1970), 'Run Through the Jungle' (Number 4 CHUM, 1970), 'Travelin' Band' (Number 1 CHUM, 1970), 'Up Around the Bend' (Number 1 CHUM, 1970), and 'Who'll Stop the Rain' (Number 1 CHUM, 1970). Given the complete lack of pretension evident in both the composition and production of these songs, most of which lead vocalist John Fogerty oversaw himself, they were equally effective live performance vehicles as they were pop records.

CCR restored to the rock genre a sense of 'roots' precisely when the majority of important rock musicians seemed intent on pushing the envelope of novel musical possibilities as far, and as rapidly, as humanly possible. But CCR was in no sense a reactionary phenomenon; the group's choice of the word 'revival' was an astute one. The many original songs in their repertoire possessed solid musical virtues, and several of them also reflected a decidedly up-to-date political awareness (such as 'Bad Moon Rising' and 'Fortunate Son') that nevertheless remained free of any specific political agenda, much like the kind of awareness found in Bob Dylan's songs from the time.

The Band

CCR is often credited with being the first widely successful 'roots rock' band. They were certainly the most successful at selling records and scoring chart hits with the formula. Owing to their extraordinary popularity, many other roots artists have appeared as rock has continued to evolve. But CCR arguably owed much of their popularity to path-breaking work in the genre already done by the Band, both backing Bob Dylan and alone. In the last two chapters, we have charted the development of the Band from their beginnings with Rompin' Ronnie Hawkins to later work with Bob Dylan. But during the late 1960s and early 1970s, the Band began to capture a significant number of fans themselves, as avatars of the emerging roots rock genre. Of course, by the sound of the Band's debut album, *Music From Big Pink* (1968), it was apparent that the group's two main songwriters—Richard Manuel and Robbie

Robertson—had learned much about the craft from their previous employer. Like Dylan's songs from the same time, Manuel's and Robertson's unadorned rock songs 'came across as a calming and restrained voice in a world of feedback-drenched guitar solos', as one critic put it; and though the record failed to produce a single Top 40 hit, *Music From Big Pink* (1968) nonetheless remains one of the most instantly recognizable and influential rock records in the repertoire.

The Band traded on a notion of roots that delved even further back in time than CCR's 'revival'. Robertson's songs in particular—'The Weight', 'The Night They Drove Old Dixie Down', 'King Harvest (Has Surely Come)', and 'No More Cain on the Bayzor', to name only a few—obviously have as their subject an intentionally arcane America, most often set in either the Wild West or the Civil War era. The group's backing on these tracks conveys a deep sense of unmediated community that was all but unknown elsewhere in the rock world at the time. Most apparent in this respect was the fact that all four of the Band's primary singers—Robbie Robertson, Levon Helm, Richard Manuel, and Rick Danko—traded call-and-response vocals on many songs, most of which told simple and unembellished stories about life in historical times. Moreover, each band member was free to switch instruments with any other members as he saw fit, according to a song's individual needs. And their arrangements were 'stripped' to practically nothing, leaving each song to recommend itself to listeners purely on its own merits.

There is a powerful irony in the fact that the Band—a group of five Canadians and one American, who began playing together behind an American rockabilly singer expatriated in Canada—traded so overtly on themes of historical Americana in their records. The apparently American image that the group consciously cultivated can seem incongruous given their nationality, especially to Canadian observers, and especially in relation to the overt nationalism of contemporary rock bands like the Guess Who. But we should remember when interpreting this image that the five Canadian members of the Band were not raised in any major Canadian metropolis such as Vancouver, Winnipeg, Montreal, or Toronto; each member initially hailed from 'small-town' Ontario, where pioneer culture has a tendency to resonate regardless of nationality. Regardless, by far the vast majority of rock historians and critics active at the time noted that the Band's albums sounded like a folk history of rural America, and the uncomplicated 'small-town' ethos of their image and sound cut through the baroque trappings of the late 1960s acid rock world with remarkable ease.

Within a few years of their breakthrough, however, the Band collapsed under the weight of their own success. Richard Manuel, in particular, seems to have found it exceedingly difficult to compose new material, and he struggled with alcohol abuse until his unfortunate suicide in 1986. Robertson, who himself suffered from debilitating stage fright—the guitarist was famously hypnotized backstage before the group's first show as the Band—was forced to pick up the slack, and he soon became the Band's de facto leader. By 1976, however, even Robertson had had enough, and he announced his departure from the group. A final concert, called 'The Last Waltz', was scheduled for Thanksgiving Day at the Winterland Ballroom in San Francisco that same year. The concert included guest appearances by Muddy Waters, Van Morrison, Bob Dylan, Neil Young, and Joni Mitchell—a strong testament to the group's popularity among rock musicians as well as listeners. And Martin Scorsese's accompanying film of the concert is generally considered one of the finest moments in rockumentary history.

Blood, Sweat & Tears

Blood, Sweat & Tears (BS&T) was another rock band to enjoy massive chart success in the late 1960s with their welding of the rock genre to yet another 'roots' music, American jazz. Formed in 1967 by former Blues Project members Al Kooper—who played organ on Bob Dylan's 'Like a Rolling Stone' (1965)—guitarist Steve Katz, and drummer Bobby Colomby, BS&T's first album, *Child Is Father to the Man* (1968), featured a heavily orchestrated Beatles-inspired pop sound, unlike the fusion of rock and jazz that the band would pioneer beginning the next year. Kooper left in late 1968 to participate in so-called 'Super Sessions' with fellow Dylan alumnus Mike Bloomfield and Stephen Stills.

David Clayton-Thomas, an R&B singer from Ontario who, after a brief stint in jail, had already hit the Top 5 in Canada with the Bossmen and the Shays, was hired to replace Kooper. BS&T's second album, *Blood, Sweat & Tears* (1969), became their first (and only) million-selling record, taking top honours as Album of the Year at the 1969 Grammy Awards, and spawning three million-selling singles—covers of Laura Nyro's 'And When I Die' (Number 3 CHUM, 1969) and Brenda Holloway's 'You've Made Me So Very Happy' (Number 3 CHUM, 1969), and the Clayton-Thomas original 'Spinning Wheel' (Number 1 CHUM, 1969). Also on the album were two separate variations on Erik Satie's 'Trois Gymnopedie' and a cover of the Billie Holiday torch-song, 'God Bless the Child', both of which clearly presaged the emergence of the progressive rock genre a few years later.

Having hit on the sound they would become famous for—straightforward rock songs embellished with largely ornamental horn stabs, taken almost directly from the big-band swing genre—BS&T struggled to maintain their counterculture cachet, if they ever really established one. Unlike, say, 'free jazz' or the 'jazz–rock fusion' being pioneered at the same time by Miles Davis on remarkable records such as *In a Silent Way* (1968) and *Bitches Brew* (1969/1970), big-band swing was seen by many boomers as a 'conservative' genre; it was even popular with their grandparents! The fact that BS&T participated in a state-sponsored tour of Eastern Europe in 1970 only further complicated matters, as did the group's decision to play the decidedly unhip Las Vegas–Lake Tahoe circuit, though it is now clear that BS&T only accepted the tour as a 'good-faith gesture' in exchange for better terms on Clayton-Thomas's work visa. Not surprisingly, then, BS&T's third album, *Blood Sweat & Tears 3* (1970), yielded the Top 20 Clayton-Thomas original 'Lucretia McEvil' (Number 11 CHUM, 1970) but otherwise failed to chart; the record also featured a cover of Carole King's 'Hi-De Ho' (1970), which charted briefly stateside. Clayton-Thomas left the group in 1972 to pursue a solo career, and BS&T disbanded a few days later.

Pop Singer-Songwriters

As roots rock ruled the musical roost during the late 1960s, another alternative to acid rock radicalism emerged in the form of the singer-songwriter genre. A cross between the urban folk music of Peter, Paul, and Mary and Bob Dylan and the commercial pop style of Brill Building tunesmiths, the singer-songwriter genre seemed to provide a perfect soundtrack for the 'turning inward' that marked the broader culture in the 1970s. Quiet and introspective, autobiographical if not confessional, and basically acoustic, the singer-songwriter genre was perfectly suited to accompany boomers into early adulthood.

Carole King

Carole King's career in the early 1970s epitomizes the emergence of the singer-songwriter genre. By 1970 Carole King had already been an important songwriter for more than a decade, having penned a number of hit songs during the 1960s with Gerry Goffin, her husband at the time (see Chapter 3). But King remained virtually unknown as a performer until she released her debut album, *Tapestry*, in 1971. It was from this album that the chart-topping single 'It's Too Late' was drawn. The astounding popularity of both the single and the album established Carole King as a major recording star, and it secured her position atop the emerging singer-songwriter field. It also positioned her as a musical innovator: in the aftermath of *Tapestry* relatively few songwriters were content to remain behind the scenes, and it came to be expected that pop songwriters would perform their own material and, conversely, that pop singers would record material that they themselves had written. Just the same, few singer-songwriters were able to match King's success. 'It's Too Late', for instance, held the Number 1 spot in America for five weeks in 1971, and it peaked at Number 5 on the CHUM charts. Even the song's flip side, 'I Feel the Earth Move'—another cut from *Tapestry*—proved popular and was frequently played on the radio as well, and both 'So Far Away' and 'Smackwater Jack' reached Number 12 on the CHUM charts in Canada.

As an LP, *Tapestry* was an unprecedented hit. It was the Number 1 album for no less than 15 weeks in America, remaining on the charts for nearly six years and selling in excess of 10 million copies—more than any one album by the Beatles at the time. And yet Carole King was approaching the age of 30 when she recorded 'It's Too Late'. Clearly, she was far from being the teenager who had written such songs as 'Will You Love Me Tomorrow?' and 'Take Good Care of My Baby' for a market consisting principally of other teenagers. King had obviously matured since then, and her audience had obviously matured along with her. 'It's Too Late' is an adult relationship song, written from the point of view of someone who has long left behind teenage crushes, insecurities, and desperate heartbreak; the singer describes the ending of a significant relationship with a feeling of sadness, but also with a mature philosophical acceptance that people can change and grow apart and an understanding that this does not represent the end of the world for either of them.

The music of 'It's Too Late' also reflects King's maturity. Her acoustic piano is the song's backbone, and it leads us through a sophisticated progression of relatively complex chords that portray a musical world far removed from the harmonic simplicity of early rock 'n' roll. Towards the end of the substantial instrumental interlude preceding the final verse of the song, when the saxophone enters to play a melody, the context evokes a kind of light jazz rather than rock 'n' roll. (The recording as a whole epitomizes the kind of sound that came to be known—fortunately or otherwise—as 'soft rock'.) Like the words of the song, the sound of its music was clearly geared towards an audience of maturing young adults. It is equally clear that the audience was out there, and more than ready to appreciate a record like this one.

Elton John

Another successful singer-songwriter in the early 1970s was Reginald Kenneth Dwight, a.k.a. Elton John. Though John would go on to adopt a clearly glam rock aesthetic in the mid- and late 1970s, and though his songwriting practice was basically restricted to composing musical settings for Bernie Taupin's lyrics, John's earliest recordings—*Empty Sky* (1969), *Elton John* (1970), and *Tumbleweed Connection* (1970)—were clearly produced in the singer-songwriter mould; his 'live' performances from the time were even more explicitly situated within that genre, John often performing alone at a piano. If anything, John's career in the early 1970s demonstrates that the so-called 'British Invasion' of the 1960s had become a long-running 'British occupation' of the North American pop charts by the 1970s. Named in Joel Whitburn's *Top Pop* book as 'the #1 Pop artist of the 70s' in America and the third best-selling pop singer in Canadian history (after Madonna and Shania Twain), John's career on the pop charts began in January 1973 when 'Crocodile Rock' became the first of six Number 1 hits for John that decade. It was a featured single on John's album *Don't Shoot Me I'm Only The Piano Player*, the second of seven consecutive million-selling Number 1 albums for John during this same period. Finally, no tally of John's successes in the 1970s would be complete without also mentioning that, after 'Crocodile Rock', John went on to score nine more Top 10 singles, two Top 20s, and one more Top 40 on the CHUM charts before the decade was through.

Like Carole King, Elton John was a virtuoso piano player, as well as a spectacular singer and a songwriter. The sound of John's piano is essential to the character of 'Crocodile Rock' and to many of his other hits. Lyricist Bernie Taupin was John's songwriting partner not only for 'Crocodile Rock' but for all of John's major hits of the 1970s. Thus, 'Crocodile Rock' also occupies an important position in John's pop repertoire because it essentially encapsulates his performance and compositional style.

'Crocodile Rock' reveals how thoroughly Elton John had assimilated the basic sounds and feelings of American rock 'n' roll while still being able to add his personal touch. The song capitalizes in a savvy way on the wave of nostalgia we noted in the introduction to this chapter, which seemed to sweep the pop music landscape in the early 1970s. By late 1972 Chuck Berry and Rick Nelson (who, as 'Ricky', had been the younger son on the *Ozzie and Harriet* TV sitcom of the fifties and had early

Elton John receives an obviously unexpected hug from a grinning **Barry White** in California, c. 1975. James Fortune/ Hulton Archive.

recording success covering such artists as Fats Domino) were both back in the Top 10 for the first time in many years, and Elvis Presley was enjoying one of the biggest hits of his career, and his last Top 10 hit, with 'Burning Love' (Number 4 CHUM, 1972). This was also a time when aging baby boomers began to flock to rock 'n' roll revival shows, in which artists from the 1950s and early 1960s (frequently including vocal groups with old names but lots of new faces) appeared to play their original, now 'classic', hits. (Note the sly reference to the old Bill Haley hit 'Rock Around the Clock' in the opening verse of 'Crocodile Rock'.) Not insignificantly, just a year before 'Crocodile Rock' hit Number 1, the singer-songwriter Don McLean made an enormous impact with his own Number 1 hit, 'American Pie'—a record whose subject matter was nostalgia for the early years of rock 'n' roll and the conviction that something of great innocence and promise had been lost amid the tumult and violence that marked the end of the 1960s.

Like 'American Pie', 'Crocodile Rock' deals with nostalgia and the sense of loss, but in a much more lighthearted fashion. It seems to emphasize the happy memories ('*I remember when rock was young, me and Susie had so much fun*') over the unhappy present ('*But the years went by and rock just died*'); in fact, the second verse ends up affirming the persistence of remembered joy ('*But they'll never kill the thrills we've got*'), and the final verse is simply a return back to the first, '*when rock was young*'. Musically, the flavour is clearly that of an upbeat teenage dance song, and even though there never actually was a famous rock 'n' roll dance called the 'crocodile', the song may be deliberately evoking the memory of other 'animal' dances, like the monkey, as well as Haley's 'See Ya Later, Alligator' (1956). The chord progressions of 'Crocodile Rock' obviously recall those of early rock 'n' roll songs without duplicating them exactly, and an element of novelty is added in the wordless part of the chorus with the kazoo-like sound of John's Farfisa organ.

Canadian Singer-Songwriters

Despite the heights that Carole King, Elton John, and their contemporaries achieved in the early 1970s, according to Ritchie Unterberger (2003: 117), 'the most startling injection of new blood into the folk rock singer-songwriter mainstream in the late 1960s came not from New York or California but from Canada, even if the performers recorded and often lived in the US.' Unterberger is, of course, talking about the likes of Gordon Lightfoot, Joni Mitchell, Leonard Cohen, and Neil Young. And while it is difficult to pinpoint anything distinctly 'Canadian' in their records, all four agree that their Canadian upbringing somehow played a crucial role in shaping their performance and songwriting styles.

In fact, if Joni Mitchell is to be believed, records made by Canadian singer-songwriters during the late 1960s and early 1970s all share at least three general characteristics. First, most if not all were made in the US, it 'being very difficult to make a living in Canada, let alone be a star', as Mitchell told KRLA in Los Angeles in 1968. Second, they feature notably conservative—or, to borrow Mitchell's term, 'nosegay'—themes in comparison to those written at the same time by American singer-songwriters. And, finally, they capture a rural or small-town Canadian ethos through a heavy preponderance of space and silence in arrangements. As Mitchell herself put it in a 1969 interview with the *New York Times*, Canadian singer-songwriters:

> are a bit more nosegay, more Old-Fashioned Bouquet than Americans. We're poets because we're such reminiscent kind of people. My poetry is urbanized and Americanized, but my music is influenced by the prairies. When I was a kid, my mother used to take me out to the fields to teach me bird calls. There was a lot of space behind individual sounds. People in the city are so accustomed to hearing a jumble of different sounds that when they come to making music, they fill it up with all sorts of things.

While we will come across Joni Mitchell later in this chapter, in our discussion of the album-oriented rock genre, for now we turn our attention to Gordon Lightfoot, Leonard Cohen, and Neil Young—arguably the three most distinctive male singer-songwriters from Canada to chart in the late 1960s and early 1970s.

Gordon Lightfoot

Gordon Lightfoot's records consistently present listeners with a sense of deliberate reserve. Indeed, aside from a few folk rock records made in the mid-1960s, the most successful being a cover of Bob Dylan's 'Just Like Tom Thumb's Blues' (Number 8 CHUM, 1965), Lightfoot's musical output has remained remarkably consistent over the past four decades. Like Dylan, Lightfoot's initial successes came as a songwriter rather than as a performer. In 1965 alone, his songs were recorded by a number of top pop and urban folk performers, including the likes of Peter, Paul, and Mary; Ian and Sylvia; and Nico, who recorded 'I'm Not Sayin'' just months before she joined the Velvet Underground. Since then, Lightfoot's songs have been covered by the likes of Bob Dylan, Ronnie Hawkins, Johnny Cash, Anne Murray, the Carter Family, Waylon Jennings, and Judy Collins, to name only a few.

Gordon Lightfoot: Canada's legend of folk. © Michael Ochs Archives/Corbis.

A star of the early 1960s Yorkville scene in Toronto, Lightfoot didn't release his first full-length album in the United States until 1966. Entitled simply *Lightfoot* (1966), the singer-songwriter's debut included at least five songs that have by now entered the folk repertoire as standards: 'Early Mornin' Rain', 'I'm Not Sayin'', 'The Way I Feel', 'For Lovin' Me', and 'Ribbon of Darkness'. Evident throughout the album was Lightfoot's controlled yet clipped singing style, his lyrical fingerpicking on the acoustic guitar, and the straightforward 'no-muss no-fuss' approach to record production he preferred—all of which won the quiet Canadian a small, but extremely loyal, following across North America.

Lightfoot was perhaps the least politically motivated of all the singer-songwriters of his generation. A Lightfoot song from the 1960s or 1970s was generally either a lyrical ballad about love lost or found (i.e., 'Early Morning Rain' and 'Go Go Round') or, more interestingly, a historical broadside (i.e., 'Canadian Railroad

Trilogy', commissioned by the CBC for the Canadian Centennial in 1967, and 'The Wreck of the *Edmund Fitzgerald*', which he recorded in 1976). As Canadian pop music historian Martin Melhuish explains, while Bob Dylan, Joan Baez, Pete Seeger, and others in the urban folk community were busy documenting the brute realities of Western capitalist modernity in the 1960s, Lightfoot incongruously wrote 'odes to the "verdant country" whose "wild majestic mountains", "green dark forests", and "wide prairies" were a source of constant awe and inspiration to him.'

A rare exception was Lightfoot's 'Black Day in July' (Number 17 CHUM, 1968), which he penned in reaction to race riots in Detroit during the summer of 1967. Even here, though, Lightfoot remains somewhat unclear as to who, if anyone, should bear the brunt of responsibility for the bloodshed and violence:

> *Black day in July*
> *In the streets of motor city*
> *Is a deadly silent sound*
> *And the body of a dead youth*
> *Lies stretched upon the ground*
> *Upon the filthy pavement*
> *No reason can be found*

In a rare twist, 'Black Day in July' was banned for a short while from American radio in 1968, after the assassination of the Reverend Martin Luther King.

By 1970, Lightfoot had basically resigned from writing overtly political songs almost entirely. This move away from topicality served Lightfoot well, as his first album of the new decade, *If You Could Read My Mind* (1970), produced the biggest hit of his career up to that point; the album's eponymous title-cut, a ballad about a futile but undying love, went to Number 4 on the CHUM charts and broke the American Top 40, peaking at Number 5 later the same year. Lightfoot's follow-up, *Summer Side of Life* (1971), topped the *Billboard* and CHUM charts simultaneously in 1971, securing Lightfoot's position alongside the likes of Carole King atop the emerging singer-songwriter field. The folksinger would go on to score three more Number 1 adult-contemporary hits—'Sundown' (1974), 'Carefree Highway' (1974), and 'Rainy Day People' (1975)—and a Number 2 placement on the pop charts with 'The Wreck of the *Edmund Fitzgerald*' (1976), written about the sinking of the SS *Edmund Fitzgerald* on Lake Superior in November of 1975, before withdrawing from the charts almost completely beginning in 1980.

Leonard Cohen

In stark contrast to Gordon Lightfoot's career as a folksinger, which began when he was still a teen, Leonard Cohen did not begin singing and writing songs in earnest until he was already 30 years old. A native of Montreal, Cohen had earned enough national accolades for his poetry and prose in Canada that, in 1966, he was made the subject of a film documentary by the National Film Board of Canada, *Ladies and*

Gentlemen . . . Mr. Leonard Cohen. Cohen was something of a prodigy in the field of literature, a fact that is often overlooked given the heights he reached with his later singing career. In 1956, while still an undergraduate at McGill University, Cohen published his first book of poems, *Let Us Compare Mythologies.* His follow-up collection, *The Spice-Box of Earth* (1961), established Cohen as a leading Canadian poet, though he moved to the Greek island of Hydra shortly after publishing the collection. The title of a collection of poems he wrote while on Hydra, *Flowers for Hitler* (1964), is typical of Cohen's propensity for shock and taboo during this time.

Leonard Cohen: Canadian rock's 'poet laureate of the sex act' during the late 1960s and early 1970s. © Alain Denize/ Kipa/Corbis.

Cohen's mature literary work explores themes of religion, sexuality, isolation, monogamy and polyamory, and the vagaries of romantic love in general—all of which recur continuously throughout the repertoire of songs he started writing in the mid-1960s. Before becoming rock's 'poet laureate of the sex act' during the late 1960s and early 1970s, a reputation that Cohen himself describes as fundamentally misguided since he supposedly struggled for companionship despite his reputation as popular music's most successful Don Juan at the time, Cohen was already known for his frank and explicit approach to sexuality as an author. His novel, *Beautiful Losers* (1966), now respected as a classic in the field of Canadian literature, seriously shocked reviewers at the time of its publication: reflecting Cohen's Quebec roots and his conflicted relationship with Montreal's prominent Jewish community, a recurring motif in the novel involves a young Jewish male—an obvious stand-in for Cohen himself—fantasizing about Kateri Tekakwitha, a Roman Catholic Iroquois mystic of the 1600s. As noted, this 'explicit' approach to dealing with sexuality would come to characterize Cohen's later musical output, most evident in song titles such as 'Don't Go Home With Your Hard-On', produced by Phil Spector for Cohen's *Death of a Ladies Man* (1977) LP, and in lyrics such as the opening verse to 'The Future':

Lie beside me baby—
That's an order!
Give me crack and anal sex
Take the only tree that's left
And shove it up the hole in your culture.

For all his successes as an author, Cohen claims that he still had trouble mustering enough money for a cup of coffee most mornings. Thus, just as Ed Sanders joined the Fugs with the explicit intention of making more money as a folk rock singer than he had as a poet, so, too, did Leonard Cohen pursue folk music as a gateway to profit. 'A lot had to do with poverty', Cohen later explained to *Rolling Stone*. 'I was writing books—two novels and four volumes of poetry—and they were being very well received . . . but I found it very difficult to pay my grocery bill, so then I started bringing some songs together.' Cohen moved into New York's notorious Chelsea Hotel at the start of his career, a period of his life frankly eulogized in a song about a brief sexual affair Cohen had with Janis Joplin, called 'Chelsea Hotel No. 2':

I remember you well in the Chelsea Hotel
You were talking so brave and so sweet
Giving me head on the unmade bed
While the limousine waited in the street. . . .
I remember you well in the Chelsea Hotel
You were famous, your heart was a legend
Told me again you preferred handsome men
But for me you would make an exception

In 1974, on tour in support of *New Skin for the Old Ceremony* (1974), Cohen described the genesis of 'Chelsea Hotel No. 2':

Once upon a time, there was a hotel in New York City. There was an elevator in that hotel. One evening, about three in the morning, I met a young woman in the hotel. I didn't know who she was. Turned out she was a very great singer. It was a very dismal evening in New York City. I'd been to the Bronco Burger; I had a cheeseburger; it didn't help at all. Went to the White Horse Tavern, looking for Dylan Thomas, but Dylan Thomas was dead. Dylan Thomas was dead. I got back in the elevator, and there she was. She wasn't looking for me either. She was looking for Kris Kristofferson. . . . I later found out she was Janis Joplin and we fell into each other's arms through some divine process of elimination which makes a compassion out of indifference, and after she died, I wrote this song for her. It's called 'Chelsea Hotel'. (Cited in Nadel, 1996: 144)

Cohen did not have to wait long to be 'discovered'. Soon after arriving in New York City, he caught the ear of one of the urban folk community's soon-to-be pop successes: Judy Collins. Though Collins would score her biggest hit with a song by another Canadian singer-songwriter—Joni Mitchell's 'Both Sides Now' (1967)—the folk chanteuse recorded Cohen's 'Suzanne' and 'Dress Rehearsal Rag' for her debut *In My Life* (1966) LP; and she recorded three more Cohen compositions—'Sisters of Mercy', 'Priests', and 'Hey That's No Way To Say Goodbye'—for her *Wildflowers* (1967) LP, released the next year. Always fond of writing 'answer songs', Joni Mitchell then 'answered' Cohen's 'Suzanne' with a song of her own called 'Marcie', which appeared on her *Song to a Seagull* (1968) LP—Mitchell had already 'answered' Neil Young's 'Sugar Mountain' with 'The Circle Game' while she was still a resident of Toronto's Yorkville Village—thus placing her stamp of approval on the newcomer's compositions.

Though he has composed a great many songs in his career, and though a recent cover of 'Hallelujah' by Jeff Buckley has garnered massive interest in that song, Cohen remains best known for 'Suzanne'. Ostensibly about Susan Vaillancourt, the wife of a prominent Montreal socialite in the early 1960s, Cohen claims that 'Suzanne' (1966) is actually about the city of Montreal. As he noted in an interview with the BBC:

The song was begun, and the chord pattern was developed, before a woman's name entered the song. And I knew it was a song about Montreal. It seemed to come out of that landscape that I loved very much in Montreal, which was the harbour and the waterfront, and the sailors' church there, called Notre Dame de Bon Secour, which stood out over the river. I knew that there're ships going by, I knew that there was a harbour, I knew that there was Our Lady of the Harbour, which was the virgin on the church which stretched out her arms towards the seamen. You can climb up to the tower and look out over the river, so the song came from that vision, from that view of the river. At a certain point I bumped into Suzanne Vaillancourt, who was the wife of a friend of mine . . . and she invited me down to her place near the river. She had a space in a warehouse down there, and she invited me down, and I went with her, and she served me Constant Comment tea, which has little bits of oranges in it. And the boats were going by, and I touched her perfect body with my mind, because there was no other opportunity. (Cited in Unterberger, 2003: 120)

Aside from its richly detailed lyrical content, which reads as well as it sounds, 'Suzanne' also contains all the musical hallmarks of a Cohen record from this time. Cohen's 'droning sing-speak', as critic Ritchie Unterberger aptly describes it, dominates the mix; an arpeggiated nylon-string or 'classical' guitar accompaniment fills in the empty spaces behind; there is a notable lack of percussion instruments; female backup vocals appear sporadically throughout, treated with so much reverb that they sound basically spectral; and a minimal orchestral arrangement fills out the arrangement at strategic moments, particularly during the song's transitions and choruses.

'Suzanne' would appear on Cohen's debut album for Columbia Records, *Songs of Leonard Cohen* (1967). The record was supposed to be produced by John Hammond, the venerable producer credited with 'discovering' Bob Dylan, Billie Holiday, and Bruce Springsteen; and two Hammond-produced tracks, 'Store Room' and 'Blessed Is the Memory', survive. When Hammond fell ill, however, production duties fell to John Simon, with whom Cohen fought bitterly about the direction his album subsequently took. To Simon's mind, Cohen's minimal aesthetic was entirely too stark to capture a sizable pop listenership, and the embellishments Simon added, against Cohen's often bitter protestations, remain divisive for listeners. In any event, it is a testament to Cohen's dissatisfaction with his debut that his next two releases, *Songs from a Room* and *Songs of Love and Hate*, were produced by famed country rock producer Bob Johnson. Though *Songs of Leonard Cohen* failed to chart in the United States, it landed in the Top 40 on Canada's new RPM album charts for 13 weeks and charted in England for over a year. Cohen's next four albums for the label—*Songs from a Room* (1969), *Songs of Love and Hate* (1971), *Live Songs* (1973), and *New Skin for the Old Ceremony* (1974)—all earned the songwriter a dedicated and rabidly loyal following on both sides of the Atlantic, but generally little in the way of fan support in the United States.

Not surprisingly, Cohen is typically credited with playing a key role in establishing the author as a viable figure in the pop music field. By late 1968, in fact, only one year after the release of *Songs of Leonard Cohen*, panel discussions were organized at the New School for Social Research in New York City on the topic of rock lyrics as 'the poetry of the age', and some labels had begun to advertise new releases by publishing complete sets of lyrics in newspapers and magazines. As Cohen explained to an interviewer at the *New Musical Express* in 1970, 'every time I pick up a pen to write something, I don't know if it is going to be a poem, a song or a novel.' Since then, Cohen has obviously taken his place alongside some of pop music's most serious lyricists: Jim Morrison of the Doors, Tuli Kupferberg and Ed Sanders of the Fugs, Larry Beckett with Tim Buckley, Tim Rice with a young Andrew Lloyd Webber, Robert Hunter with the Grateful Dead, Keith Reid with Procol Harum, Peter Singield with King Crimson, Pete Brown with Cream, Bernie Taupin with Elton John, and so on.

Neil Young

The late 1960s and early 1970s were a time of extreme transitions for Neil Young. After the acrimonious split of Buffalo Springfield in May 1968, Young signed a solo contract with Reprise Records (the label was also home to Young's friend from Yorkville Village, Joni Mitchell, with whom he shared a manager, Elliot Roberts). Young's first album for Reprise—a bombastic and heavily orchestrated collaboration with ex-Wrecking Crew arranger Jack Nitzsche—entitled simply *Neil Young*, was released to mixed reviews in 1968. For his next album, the critically lauded *Everybody*

Knows This Is Nowhere (1969), Young pilfered three musicians from a Los Angeles area garage band called the Rockets—Danny Whitten on guitar, Billy Talbot on bass, and Ralph Molina on drums. Calling themselves Crazy Horse, the band's 'garage rock' ethos helped propel 'Cinnamon Girl' to Number 7 on the CHUM charts in 1969, marking Young's first official appearance there as a solo singer-songwriter.

Almost immediately after 'Cinnamon Girl', though, Young was recruited by Atlantic Records owner Ahmet Ertegun to join the new American 'supergroup' CSNY (Crosby, Stills, Nash, and Young), featuring ex-Byrd David Crosby, ex-Holly Graham Nash, and fellow Buffalo Springfield alumnus Stephen Stills. CSNY debuted in Chicago, in August of 1969, and, later that same year they performed a now canonic set at the Woodstock Music and Art Fair. Their only album, *Deja Vu* (1970), featured two notable Young compositions—'Helpless' and 'Ohio', the latter about the killing of four students at Kent State University by National Guard soldiers during an anti-war demonstration—both of which continue to occupy pride of place in Young's oeuvre.

When CSNY became yet another of Young's bands to dissolve into acrimony and inflated egos, he left the group. Young next recorded another solo album, *After the Gold Rush* (1970), which featured his first US Top 40 single, 'Only Love Can Break Your Heart' (Number 33 *Billboard* and Number 4 CHUM, 1970). *After the Gold Rush* was initially supposed to feature Crazy Horse on electric tracks, but Young cut the

Despite **Neil Young's** success in Canada, he felt that 'the great Canadian dream is to get out.' © Neal Preston/Corbis.

group after only a few sessions, feeling that the new material was simply too advanced for them; instead, Young opted for the likes of Nils Lofgren, Stephen Stills, and CSNY bassist Greg Reeves, among others. Though the decision to feature mostly acoustic tracks on the album was intentional, there was another reason for the obvious shift in emphasis—suffering from debilitating back pain, Young simply could not hold an electric guitar for extended periods of time.

Aside from his obviously maturing compositional style, *After the Gold Rush* also marked a crucial turning point in Neil Young's practice inside the recording studio. Whereas he had once laboured obsessively over meticulous productions of basic folk-songs, producing epic tracks such as 'Expecting To Fly' and 'Broken Arrow', Young now turned towards a more spontaneous aesthetic, his new goal being to capture finalized tracks in a single unedited take. An indication of this new approach to record production can be gleaned from the fact that, in a move reminiscent of Miles Davis, Young had the accomplished rock guitarist Nils Lofgren play piano on a number of takes, and in the fact that even CD transfers of the album generally feature a high degree of analog tape hiss. In interviews about the album, Young rather famously encapsulated his new approach to record production by explaining that, in his opinion, when recording 'the more you think the more you stink.'

With the split of CSNY in 1971, and with Crazy Horse off performing and record-ing on their own, Young toured a solo acoustic 'greatest hits' package across North America, spanning his work with Buffalo Springfield, CSNY, Crazy Horse, and alone (the show was captured on the recently released *Live at Massey Hall (1971)*). Young's intention, at first, was to record a 'live' record of the tour as a follow-up to *After the Gold Rush*. The next year, however, while in Nashville to tape an episode of *The Johnny Cash Show*, Young met producer Elliot Mazer at a dinner party thrown in his honour. At Young's request, Mazer assembled a team of accomplished Nashville stu-dio musicians for a three-hour session the next day. The band that Mazer assembled, eventually dubbed 'the Stray Gators' by Young, was comprised of Ben Keith on pedal steel guitar, Kenny Buttrey on drums, Troy Seals on electric bass, session guitarist Teddy Irwin, and fellow *Johnny Cash Show* stars Linda Rondstadt and James Taylor on backup vocals—and, amazingly, in their first three hours playing together the group managed to record the versions of 'Old Man' and 'Heart of Gold' that are still heard on Top 40 radio. Despite this professionalism, evidence of Young's new 'you think you stink' approach to record productions is everywhere apparent on these tracks, but perhaps nowhere more so than in the banjo part on 'Old Man', which is an unedited recording of James Taylor's very first time playing the instrument.

The Mazer-led sessions comprised the first for Young's follow-up to *After the Gold Rush*, the massively successful *Harvest* (1972) LP. The album's opening cut, 'Are You Ready for the Country?' (1972), decisively announced the new country rock direction Young had decided to take, and also managed to encapsulate the laid-back and almost stubbornly acoustic sound of the record as a whole in its first five minutes. That said, Young did not entirely abandon large-scale productions on the album; two standout cuts feature Young backed by the London Symphony Orchestra, the most famous being 'A Man Needs a Maid'. Featuring the only Number 1 single of Young's career, 'Heart of Gold' (Number 1 *Billboard* and CHUM, 1972) and the Top 20 'Old Man' (Number 11

CHUM, 1972), *Harvest* quickly became the best-selling record of 1972. But the record also occupies pride of place in Young's oeuvre because it marks the first collaboration between him and pedal steel guitarist Ben Keith. As critic Sam Inglis explains:

> Young's bare-bones arrangements on songs like 'Out on the Weekend' boldly left acres of open space, and Ben Keith's playing did not so much fill these open spaces as emphasize their presence. His thin chords skirted around the edges of the songs, pointing up the sparseness of the music rather than padding it out. Keith would become one of Young's most constant musical collaborators in the years to come, and it's easy to see why. (Inglis, 2006: 41)

Young claims that the success of *Harvest* deeply troubled him. In his liner notes for *Decade*, a greatest-hits package he oversaw production of for Reprise, the singer-song-writer wrote that *Harvest* 'put me in the middle of the road; traveling there soon became a bore, so I headed for the ditch.' Only making matters worse, Young was forced to fire Crazy Horse guitarist Danny Whitten almost as soon as he reunited with the band in 1972 because his behaviour had grown erratic due to a prolonged heroin addiction—and Whitten died of an overdose later that same day. Thus began Young's so-called 'Ditch Trilogy', which, true to his fondness for extremes, is comprised of what many consider to be the least commercial records of his career: *Time Fades Away* (1973), which remains the only out-of-print record on Young's roster; *On the Beach* (1974), which features the cynical fan favourite 'For the Turnstiles' (1974) but otherwise remains a difficult record; and *Tonight's the Night* (1975), recorded in one drug-fuelled night in 1973 but not released until 1975.

Perhaps the standout track of the trilogy is 'Borrowed Tune' (1975). An acoustic piano ballad from *Tonight's the Night*, which Reprise initially refused to release because it was 'too different' from Young's work with CSNY, 'Borrowed Tune' constitutes an extended meditation on the heroin overdoses of guitarist Danny Whitten and roadie Bruce Berry, and on the demise of the counterculture in general, which was apparent to Young by 1973. Sparsely arranged, and featuring ragged vocals from Young that sound as emotionally numb as the river symbolically *'frozen six-feet deep'* in the song's lyrics, the melody and harmony of 'Borrowed Tune' are admittedly plagiarized from the Rolling Stones' 'Lady Jane' (1967), the singer claiming to be 'too wasted to write my own'. While some have described this admitted act of plagiarism as an overly 'gimmicky' way to go about writing songs, others consider the rhetorical ploy an excellent, if somewhat heavy-handed, commentary on the toll that drug addiction had obviously exacted on the creative life of many rock musicians by 1973—including the Rolling Stones themselves, who had already become symbolic of the rock lifestyle's many excesses in the popular press. 'A suicide note without the suicide' according to Young, 'Borrowed Tune' is perhaps the most emotionally harrowing of Young's 'Ditch Trilogy' songs, if not the darkest in his entire oeuvre.

In recent years *Tonight's the Night* has enjoyed a resurgence of interest from critics and fans. In the early 1990s, in fact, Young was dubbed the 'Godfather of Grunge' by music groups such as Nirvana and Pearl Jam, based largely on work such as *Tonight's the Night* (we should also note that 'For the Turnstiles', perhaps the most cynical song from Young's deeply cynical *On the Beach* LP, was recently covered to great effect by Canadian roots rockers the Be Good Tanyas). In any event, as is apparent from Dave Marsh's review of the album for *Rolling Stone* magazine in 1975, Young had already captured the 'artful artlessness' of punk and grunge by 1973:

> The music has a feeling of offhand, first-take crudity matched recently only by [Bob Dylan's] *Blood on the Tracks*, almost as though Young wanted us to miss its ultimate majesty in order to emphasize its ragged edge of desolation. More than any of Young's earlier songs and albums—even the despondent *On the Beach* and the mordant, rancorous *Time Fades Away*—*Tonight's the Night* is preoccupied with death and disaster. There is no sense of retreat, no apology, no excuses offered and no quarter given. If anything, these are the old ideas with a new sense of aggressiveness. The jitteriness of the music, its sloppy, unarranged (but decidedly structured) feeling is clearly calculated.

Canadian Country in the 1970s

Before moving on to examine the rise of album-oriented rock, we should briefly note the careers of two Canadian country musicians active during the 1970s: Rita MacNeil and Stompin' Tom Connors. Born in Big Pond, Nova Scotia, Rita MacNeil came to national prominence in Canada with her first LP, *Born a Woman* (1974), which is now generally considered one of the earliest explicitly 'feminist' records in Canadian popular music history. MacNeil penned the album's eponymous title track in protest over a beauty pageant; and another song on the album, 'Need for Restoration', the first song MacNeil wrote, was a call for women around the world to find their collective voice and to assert themselves. Though *Born a Woman* did not cross over onto the pop charts—it has since gone out of print—and though MacNeil would not record another LP until 1981, by the early 1990s the silky-voiced country crooner had become the best-selling country singer in all of Canada, regularly outselling the likes of Anne Murray, Garth Brooks, and Clint Black across the country in 1990 and 1991. Between 1994 and 1997 MacNeil hosted her own musical variety show on CBC-TV, *Rita and Friends*, and she has since periodically hosted a number of specials for the network. As a songwriter, MacNeil has kept as her subject matter the everyday and ordinary, resonating with the country genre's traditional working-class ethos. According to playwright Charlie Rhindress, writing on MacNeil's official website, 'MacNeil's songs are about conversations, friends getting together, community roots, believing in dreams, both good and bad times, working people, taking risks, home and paying tribute to a loving family—things that ring true for everybody.'

Born in Saint John, New Brunswick, but raised on Prince Edward Island, Tom Connors left home at 15 years of age to hitchhike across Canada—with only a duffel bag of clothes and an acoustic guitar strapped across his back. Known for his peculiar habit of stomping the stage while he sang his mostly acoustic country songs, Tom Connors was soon given the nickname 'Stompin' Tom Connors' by his fans. In the mid-1970s Connors came to national attention when CBC-TV's *The Marketplace* adopted his song 'The Consumer' as its theme.

As a songwriter, Connors distinguished himself from his contemporaries with the almost single-minded focus he put on Canadian stories, national mythologies, historical narratives, and basic national concerns in his songs. Songs such as 'Bud the Spud', 'The Black Donnelys', 'Sudbury Saturday Night', and 'The Hockey Song', among many others, tell stories that only a Canadian could fully appreciate, prompting voters to make Connors a serious contender for the crown of 'The Greatest Canadian' on CBC-TV's recent show of the same name. Given his iconic status in Canadian culture, it is often overlooked that Connors has been a vocal activist for Canadian popular musicians throughout his career. In the later 1970s, for instance, Connors retired from performance to his farm in Norval, Ontario, in protest over the fact that CRTC regulations gave no special consideration to Canadian stories or national myths; Connors also publicly opposed Juno awards going to Canadian musicians who work primarily in the US. Indeed, according to many listeners, no more Canadian a country singer ever existed than Stompin' Tom Connors; and possibly no more Canadian a set of lyrics were penned than those Connors composed for 'The Hockey Song', from his 1973 LP, *Stompin' Tom Connors and the Hockey Song* (an indication of the song's iconic status in Canadian culture can be gleaned from the fact that pop-punk princess Avril Lavigne recently recorded a cover of the song):

Hello out there we're on the air it's hockey night tonite
Tension grows the whistle blows-& the puck goes down the ice.
The goalie jumps and the players bump and the fans all go insane
Someone roars 'Bobby scores!' at the good ole hockey game
Oh the good ole hockey game is the best game you can name
And the best game you can name is the good ole hockey game

2nd Period:
Where players dash with skates aflash the home team trails behind
But they grab the puck and go bursting up
And they're down across the line
They storm the crease like bumble bees
They travel like a burning flame
We see them slide the puck inside
It's a '1–1' hockey game!

3rd Period:
Last game in the playoffs, too . . .
Oh take me where the hockey players face off down the rink—
And the Stanley Cup is all filled up for
The chaps who win the drink—
Now the final flick of the hockey stick and a one gigantic scream—
The puck is in! The home team wins! The good ole hockey game!

Rock Comes of Age

During the 1970s rock music, the brash child of rock 'n' roll, diffused into every corner of the music industry. Influenced by the Beatles, Bob Dylan, Brian Wilson, and Jimi Hendrix, many progressive rock musicians came to view themselves as Artists and their records as works of Art. While this occasionally led to the production of what some critics considered to be self-indulgent dross, some musicians used the medium of the long-playing record album to create innovative and challenging work in the 1970s. At the same time, the music industry moved to co-opt the appeal of rock music, creating genres like 'pop rock' and 'soft rock' designed to appeal to the widest possible demographic and promoted on Top 40 radio and television. Musicians as diverse as Led Zeppelin; Stevie Wonder; Elton John; Carole King; Pink Floyd; Paul Simon; Neil Diamond; Crosby, Stills, and Nash; the Rolling Stones; Frank Zappa and the Mothers of Invention; and Santana were promoted by record companies under the general heading of rock music. Even Frank Sinatra, scarcely a rock musician, tried his hand at a Beatles song or two. This industrial imperative led to a remarkable fragmentation of the rock repertoire.

A survey of Canadian and American pop charts from the 1970s reveals a complex picture in which the various traditions discussed throughout this book—folk, pop, 'soul', and country music, for instance—continued to intermingle with one another, as well as with rock music in general. The commercial mainstream across North America, as defined mostly by AM radio, featured a variety of styles, each designed to reach a mass audience:

- *Pop rock* was an upbeat variety of rock music (represented by artists such as Andy Kim, the Bells, Paul McCartney, Lighthouse, Peter Frampton).
- *Adult contemporary* extended the old crooner tradition, with varying degrees of rock influence (Anne Murray, Barbra Streisand, Neil Diamond, the Carpenters).
- *Singer-songwriters* reflected a cross between the urban folk music of Peter, Paul, and Mary and Bob Dylan and the commercial pop style of the Brill Building tunesmiths (Leonard Cohen, Gordon Lightfoot, Joni Mitchell, Neil Young, Cat Stevens, Jim Croce).
- *Soft soul*, a slick variety of rhythm and blues, often included lush orchestral accompaniment (the O'Jays, the Spinners, Al Green, Barry White).
- *Country pop*, a style of soft rock, was lightly tinged with country music influences (Anne Murray, John Denver, Rita MacNeil, Olivia Newton-John).
- *Bubble gum* music consisted of cheerful songs aimed mainly at a pre-teen audience (the Archies, the Jackson Five, the Osmonds).
- *Disco*, a new form of dance music in the late 1970s, was characterized by elaborate studio production and an insistent beat (Patsy Gallant, Donna Summer, the Village People).

The 1970s also saw the beginnings of 'oldies radio', which played hits of the 1950s and early 1960s. This is a further instance of the nostalgic tendencies that characterized the period—tendencies also symbolized by the renewed popularity of Elvis Presley, who scored more than 20 Top 40 hits during the 1970s, and of Chuck Berry, who charted his first Number 1 pop record in 1972, the double-entendre song 'My Ding-a-Ling'.

It is worth taking a moment to consider what these changes meant for black musicians, who had, after all, provided much of the inspiration for new forms of popular music. By the mid-1970s older soul and R&B stars such as Aretha Franklin and James Brown found it obviously more difficult to penetrate the pop- and rock-dominated Top 40 charts than before; it would not be until the 1980s that Franklin and Brown staged their 'comebacks'. Atlantic Records, a pioneer in the field of R&B and soul music, increasingly turned its attention to grooming and promoting white rock acts such as Led Zeppelin. Motown Records continued to score successes on Top 40 radio and the pop singles charts with artists such as Diana Ross (who left the Supremes to become a solo act in 1970), the 'bubblegum' pop group Jackson Five, the Spinners, and Marvin Gaye. But Motown no longer enjoyed its former dominance of the crossover market, possibly due to the fact that the move to LA led to the dissolution of the legendary Funk Brothers.

Many of the black performers who did make it into the AM radio airwaves and Top 40 charts in the 1970s specialized in a smooth, romantic style called 'soft soul', clearly indebted to the Motown sound of the early to mid-1960s. One of the most commercially successful forms of soul music during the 1970s was the so-called 'Philadelphia sound', produced by the team of Kenny Gamble and Leon Huff, and performed by groups such as the O'Jays ('Love Train') and Harold Melvin and the Blue Notes ('If You Don't Know Me by Now'). These groups had a great deal of crossover success in the 1970s, regularly scoring Top 10 hits on the pop and soul charts. In retrospect, it does seem that much 1970s soul music was less assertive in its lyrics and its rhythms than its 1960s counterpart, and some observers have suggested that this was a strategic counter-reaction on the part of radio stations and record companies to the racial violence that had erupted on the streets of inner-city black neighbourhoods in such places as the Watts district of Los Angeles, Detroit, and Newark during the late 1960s.

Watching today's cable television advertisements for collections of 'classic seventies hits', one could come to the conclusion that rock music had, by 1970, pushed the old Tin Pan Alley songwriting tradition off the map entirely. That would be inaccurate, however, for the first Number 1 single of the 1970s was a throwback to the Brill Building era of the early 1960s, a sprightly and thoroughly escapist pop song entitled 'Raindrops Keep Fallin' on My Head' performed by former country singer B.J. Thomas. This record—which stayed on the charts for nearly six months, in no small part owing to its being featured in the soundtrack of a popular film, *Butch Cassidy and the Sundance Kid*—was composed by Hal David and Burt Bacharach, third-generation Tin Pan Alley songwriters, and the song was shopped around to various other singers (including Bob Dylan!) before Thomas was chosen to record it. Interestingly, the song was a crossover hit, reaching Number 38 on the R&B charts in 1970 in a cover version by the black soul singer Barbara Mason. Several Number 1 singles of the 1970s—such as Roberta Flack's 'Killing Me Softly with His Song' (1973), Debby Boone's 'You Light Up My Life' (1977), Barbra Streisand's film theme, 'The Way We Were' (1973), and her romantic duet with Neil Diamond, 'You Don't Bring Me Flowers' (1978)—attest to the continuing popularity of an approach to composing and performing songs directly derived from the Tin Pan Alley tradition. While rock critics tend to regard most 'soft rock' and 'adult contemporary' records as the musical equivalent of pond scum, there is no denying their mass popularity throughout the 1970s.

In fact, there were some important exceptions to the general popular appeal of rock music in the 1970s. Record sales in black communities, as reflected in the *Billboard* soul and RPM charts during the 1970s, do not suggest much interest in rock music. The Rolling Stones managed to get only one of their singles into *Billboard*'s soul Top 40 chart during the decade, and multi-platinum rock acts such as Led Zeppelin, the Guess Who, and Pink Floyd made no dent whatsoever. While the Monterey and Woodstock festivals had featured performances by black artists, the promise of rock music as a zone of interracial interaction seemed to have largely vanished by the early 1970s. Many of the white rock stars who had formed their styles through exposure to earlier styles of blues and R&B seemed to have little interest in contemporary black popular music in the 1970s. As one critic put it in 1971, 'black musicians are now implicitly regarded as precursors who, having taught the white men all they know, must gradually recede into the distance' (Morse, 1971: 108).

While there was no clear successor to Jimi Hendrix in the decade following Woodstock—that is, no single artist who could champion the presence of black musicians in rock music—we can point to a number of interestingly diverse interactions between soul music and rock. Several prominent black musicians—Sly Stone, Stevie Wonder, Marvin Gaye, and George Clinton—were able to connect long-standing aspects of blues-based musical traditions with elements from rock, including the notions of the musician as an artistic mastermind and of the LP as a work of art. In addition to their intrinsic importance, the varied work of these musicians paved the way for later artists such as Prince and Michael Jackson.

Listening To Stevie Wonder's 'Superstition' (1973)

Stevie Wonder was a highly successful singer and songwriter during his teenage years with Motown in the 1960s, though he certainly did not fit the singer-songwriter mould established by the likes of Carole King and, to a lesser extent, Elton John in the early and mid-1970s. Nonetheless, Wonder established a new benchmark of achievement for a pop music figure in 1971 when, at the age of 21, he negotiated a new contract with the Motown organization that guaranteed him full artistic control over all aspects of his music. As a master of all trades—singer, songwriter, multi-instrumentalist, arranger, and producer—Wonder was able to use this control to his utmost advantage, and he made all his subsequent recordings his own to a degree that has rarely been approached by other artists in the field. We can hear the results of this on an incredibly tight cut like 'Superstition', on which Wonder plays most of the instruments himself, synchronizing the performance by *over-dubbing* several tracks on the recording tape, to accompany his own singing of his own composition. 'Superstition' was the first featured single from the album *Talking Book*, which also achieved tremendous popularity; the single reached Number 3 on the CHUM charts in 1973, and was one of no less than eight Top 5 placements for Wonder throughout the decade. 'Superstition' blends elements borrowed from different aspects of African-American musical traditions and adds its own distinctive flavourings to the mix. The use of a repeated riff over an unchanging chord as the song's hook—a riff heard right from the outset, and which persists throughout all three verse sections of the song—obviously reflects the influence of James Brown's brand of late 1960s soul music (see Chapter 4). But Wonder gives this music his own inflection through his employment of the electric keyboard instrument called the clavinet—a novelty at the time—to play the riff (throughout the early 1970s, Wonder was a pioneer in the use of new electronic instruments, including synthesizers, in pop music). The chorus section ('*When you believe . . .*') introduces chord changes that are suggestive of blues influence; taken as a whole, the large verse-chorus unit of the song may be heard as an expanded variant of the 12-bar blues in terms of both phrase structure and harmonic vocabulary. The persistence and flexibility of blues traditions in American popular music remain a source of wonder. The lyrics, however, take a thoroughly modern, sophisticated stand ('*Superstition ain't the way*'). Thus, in 'Superstition', Stevie Wonder fused something old and something blue with the borrowed and the new to create an irresistible pop hit.

Early rock festivals such as Monterey (1967) and Woodstock (1969), regarded by many as the ultimate climax of the 1960s counterculture, had mutated by the early 1970s into highly profitable mass-audience concerts, held in civic centres and sports arenas. In 1973 the British hard rock group Led Zeppelin (see below) toured the United States, breaking the world record for live concert attendance set by the Beatles during their tours of the mid-1960s. A whole series of bands that sprang up in the early 1970s—Styx, Journey, Kansas, REO Speedwagon, ZZ Top, Rush, and others—tailored their performances to the concert context, touring the country with elaborate light shows, spectacular sets, and powerful amplification systems transported in caravans of semi trucks.

For most rock fans, the live concert was the peak of musical experience—you hadn't really heard Led Zeppelin, it was said, until you'd heard and seen them live (and spent a little money on a poster or T-shirt, imprinted with the band's image). Of course, the relationship between rock stars and their devotees at these concerts was anything but intimate. Nonetheless, the sheer enormity, and the sound and spectacle of a rock concert, helped to create a visceral sensation of belonging to a larger community—a temporary city formed by fans, as Jerry Rubin had suggested when he spoke of 'Woodstock Nation'.

▌Album-Oriented Rock

In the 1960s, recordings such as the Beach Boys' *Pet Sounds* (1966), the Beatles' *Sgt. Pepper's Lonely Hearts Club Band* (1967), and the Who's rock opera *Tommy* (1969) established the idea of the record album as a thematically and aesthetically unified work, and not simply a collection of otherwise unrelated cuts. By the early 1970s, the 12-inch high-fidelity LP had become established as the primary medium for rock music.

Seeking to boost their advertising revenues, many FM stations moved to a format called 'AOR' (album-oriented rock), aimed at young white males aged 13 to 25. The AOR format featured hard rock bands, such as Led Zeppelin and Deep Purple, and art rock bands like King Crimson; Emerson, Lake, and Palmer; and Pink Floyd. AOR generally excluded black artists, who were featured on a radio format called 'urban contemporary' (the only exceptions to this rule seem to have been Marvin Gaye, Stevie Wonder, and Sly and the Family Stone, whose music transcended the boundary between soul and rock). While these changes led to greater economic efficiency, the definition of rock as white music, and the increasingly strict split between black and white popular music formats, reflected the general conservatism of the radio business and of the music industry as a whole in the 1970s.

What makes a rock album more than a mere collection of singles? Let's start with a basic fact about the medium, its capacity: a 12-inch disc, played at $33^1/3$ rpm, could accommodate more than 40 minutes of music, over 20 minutes per side. In the 1950s and early 1960s little creative use was made of this additional real estate—most rock 'n' roll-era LPs consist of a few hit singles interspersed with a lot of less carefully produced filler. During the second half of the 1960s rock musicians and producers began to treat the time span of the LP as a total entity, a field of potentiality akin to a painter's canvas. They also began to put more effort into all of the songs on an album and to think of creative ways to link songs together—creating an overall progression of peaks and valleys over the course of an entire LP. That said, old habits die hard, and most progressive rock albums still used songs, each approximately three to six minutes in length, as basic building blocks.

The development of studio technology also encouraged musicians to experiment with novel techniques. High-fidelity stereo sound, heard over good speakers or headphones, placed the listener in the middle of the music (and the music in the middle of the listener!) and allowed sound sources to be 'moved around'. The advent of 16-, 24-, and 32-track recording consoles and electronic sound devices allowed musicians—and the record producers and studio engineers with whom they worked—to create complex aural textures and to construct a given track on an LP over a period of time, adding and subtracting (or 'punching in' and 'punching out') individual instruments and voices. Innovations in the electronic synthesis of sound led to instruments like the mellotron, which could imitate the sound of a string orchestra in the studio and at live performances.

The musical response to the opportunities provided by these technological changes varied widely. Some rock bands became famous for spending many months (and tons of money) in the studio to create a single rock 'masterpiece'. A few multi-talented musicians, such as Stevie Wonder and Edgar Winter, took advantage of multi-tracking to play all of the instruments on a given track. Other musicians reacted against the dependence on studio technology, recording their albums the old-fashioned way, with little overdubbing (as we shall see, when punk rock arose in the late 1970s as a reaction against the pretentiousness of studio-bound progressive rock, musicians insisted on doing recordings in one take to create the sense of a live performance experience). Studio technology could even be used to create the impression that studio technology was not being used, as in many folk rock albums.

Although the ideas of creating some sort of continuity between the individual tracks and of creating an inclusive structure that could provide the listener with a sense of progression were shared widely, rock musicians took a range of approaches to this problem. One way to get a sense of this range is to listen to a handful of classic rock LPs from the early 1970s. Some rock albums are centred on a fictitious character whose identity is analogous to that of one or more musicians in the band. Perhaps the best-known example of this strategy is *The Rise and Fall of Ziggy Stardust and the Spiders from Mars* (1972), the creation of 'glam rock' pioneer David Bowie. (Glam—short for glamour—rock emphasized the elaborate, showy personal appearance and costuming of its practitioners.) In this case, the coherence of the album derives more from the imaginative and magnetic persona of the singer and his character than from the music itself. As Bowie put it, 'I packaged a totally credible plastic rock star', a bisexual alien who comes to visit Earth and becomes first a superstar and finally a 'Rock 'n' roll Suicide', perishing under the weight of his own fame. Much of the LP's effect was connected with the striking image of Bowie playing the role of Ziggy, decked out in futuristic clothing and heavy facial makeup, a sensitive rocker, and sexy in an androgynous, cosmic way. The *Ziggy Stardust* concert tour was a theatrical tour de force, with special lighting effects and spectacular costumes, and set the standard for later rock acts, ranging from 'new wave' bands like the Talking Heads (see Chapter 6) to hard rockers like KISS.

Other successful rock albums were held together not by a central character or coherent plot line, but by an emotional, philosophical, or political theme. The album *Blue* (1971), composed and performed by Canadian singer-songwriter Joni Mitchell, consists of a cycle of songs about the complexities of love. The album is carefully designed to create a strong emotional focus, which is in turn clearly related to the autobiography of the singer herself. In some ways *Blue* is a culmination of the tendency inherent in the folk rock and singer-songwriter genres towards self-revelation. Even the most optimistic songs on the album—'All I Want', 'My Old Man', and 'Carey'—have a bittersweet flavour. Some, such as 'Little Green', about a child given up for adoption, and the concluding track, 'The Last Time I Saw Richard', are delicate yet powerful testimonials to the shared human experience of emotional loss. The sound of the LP is spare and beautiful, focusing on Mitchell's voice and acoustic guitar. This is a case where studio technology is used to create a feeling of simplicity and immediacy, which is to say, the album clearly features 'veridic' or 'true-to-performance' production values.

Dark Side of the Moon (1973), an album by the British rock band Pink Floyd, is based on the theme of madness and the things that drive us to it—time, work, money, war, and fear of death. The LP opens with the sound of a beating heart, then a ticking clock, a typewriter, a cash register, gunfire, and the voices of members of Pink Floyd's stage crew, discussing their own experiences with insanity. The album's feeling of unity has something to do with its languid, carefully measured pace—most of the songs are slow to mid-tempo—as well as its musical texture and mood. In terms of style, the progression moves from spacey, neo-psychedelic sound textures to jazz- and blues-influenced songs, and then back to psychedelic. The sound of the record, produced by Alan Parsons, is complex but clear, and interesting use is made of sound effects, as in the song 'Money', with its sampled sounds of clinking coins and cash registers, treated as rhythmic accompaniment. (This achievement is particularly impressive when we recall that 1973 was before the advent of digital recording techniques.)

If there was ever an antidote to the notion that popular music must be cheerful and upbeat to be successful, *Dark Side of the Moon* is it. This meditation on insanity stayed on the *Billboard* Top LPs charts for over 14 years, longer than any other LP in history, and sold 25 million copies worldwide. In recent years, various mythologies have grown up around *Dark Side of the Moon*. For example, it is claimed that the album can be synchronized with the 1939 film *The Wizard of Oz*. Many people maintain that if you start the album up after the MGM Lion's third roar, there are some amazing synchronicities. For example, the song 'Brain Damage' begins playing just as the Scarecrow starts to sing 'If I Only Had a Brain', and a heartbeat becomes audible precisely as Dorothy presses her ear to the Tin Man's chest when they first meet. Whatever the merit of these claims, it is clear that Pink Floyd's *Dark Side of the Moon* continues to exert a powerful, if somewhat dark, fascination upon millions of rock fans.

Listening To a Classic Album of the AOR Genre: Meat Loaf's *Bat Out Of Hell* (1977)

Composed by Jim Steinman and sung by Meat Loaf (a.k.a. Marvin Lee Aday), *Bat Out Of Hell* was one of the best-selling albums of the AOR era. Developed out of sketches for a musical play composed by Steinman titled *Neverland*, which was to be a loose retelling of *Peter Pan* set in the future, *Bat Out Of Hell* features only seven tracks, three of which clock in at over eight minutes in length. The album was consciously developed by Steinman and Meat Loaf, and eventually by album producer and guitarist Todd Rundgren, as a 'rock 'n' roll musical'. The title track, 'Bat Out Of Hell', was taken directly from *Neverland*, and represents the product of Steinman's desire to write what he calls 'the most extreme crash song of all time' (Jim Steinman in the DVD *Classic Albums: Meat Loaf Bat Out Of Hell*, Image Entertainment, 1999). The opening dialogue heard on the album's second track, 'You Took the Words Right Out Of My Mouth', performed by Steinman and Marcia McClain, was also taken directly from *Neverland*, as were the next two tracks, 'Heaven Can Wait' and 'All Revved Up with No Place To Go'. The latter song provides a good example of the frank and uncompromising approach to young lust that Steinman took in composing the album's lyrics, casting the loss of virginity in almost purely biological terms:

You and me 'round about midnight
Someone's got to draw first
Draw first
Someone's got to draw first blood . . .
Oooh I got to draw first blood

The remaining three tracks on *Bat Out Of Hell*, all on Side Two of the original LP release, were written specifically for the album. 'Two Out of Three Ain't Bad' was a million-seller as a single, but it was the next track, 'Paradise by the Dashboard Light', that earned *Bat Out Of Hell* its notoriety. Providing a perfect counterpoint to 'the most extreme crash song' motif of the album's opening song, the eight-minute epic 'Paradise by the Dashboard Light' was conceived by Steinman as 'the ultimate car sex song'

(Jim Steinman in the DVD *Classic Albums: Meat Loaf Bat Out Of Hell*, Image Entertainment, 1999). A duet between Ellen Foley and Meat Loaf, the song features a classic 'make out' section in the middle: a metaphorical play-by-play commentary, provided by New York Yankees announcer Phil Rizzuto, casts the adolescent mating ritual in terms of a baseball game, borrowing common adolescent colloquialisms for basic acts of physical intimacy (i.e., 'first base' as hand holding, 'second base' as kissing, 'third base' as heavy petting, and 'home run' or 'scoring' as intercourse). This extended middle section epitomizes what Ellen Foley has described as the album's 'pre-pubescent sexual mentality', Foley's character insisting that Meat Loaf profess his love for her, and Meat Loaf humorously dodging the demand (Ellen Foley in the DVD *Classic Albums: Meat Loaf Bat Out Of Hell*, Image Entertainment, 1999).

Radio Broadcaster:
Ok, here we go, we got a real pressure cooker
going here, two down, nobody on, no score,
bottom of the ninth, there's the wind-up, and
there it is, a line shot up the middle, look
at him go. This boy can really fly!
He's rounding first and really turning it on
now, he's not letting up at all, he's gonna
try for second; the ball is bobbled out in center,
and here comes the throw, and what a throw!

*He's gonna slide in head first, here he
comes, he's out!
No, wait, safe—safe at second base,
this kid really
makes things happen out there.
Batter steps up to the plate, here's the
pitch—
He's going, and what a jump he's got,
he's trying
for third, here's the throw, it's in the
dirt—
safe at third! Holy cow, stolen base!
He's taking a pretty big lead out
there, almost
daring him to try and pick him off.
The pitcher
glances over, winds up, and it's
bunted, bunted
down the third base line, the suicide
squeeze is on!
Here he comes, squeeze play, it's
gonna be close,
Here's the throw, there's the play at
the plate,
holy cow, I think he's gonna make it!*

Ellen:
*Stop right there!
I gotta know right now!
Before we go any further—
Do you love me?
Will you love me forever?
Do you need me?
Will you never leave me?
Will you make me so happy for the
rest of my life?
Will you take me away and will you
make me your wife?
. . .*

Meat Loaf:
*Let me sleep on it
Baby, baby let me sleep on it*

*Let me sleep on it
And I'll give you my answer in the
morning
. . .*

Ellen:
*I gotta know right now!
Do you love me?
Will you love me forever?
Do you need me?
. . .*

Meat Loaf:
*Let me sleep on it
Baby, baby let me sleep on it
Let me sleep on it
And I'll give you my answer in the
morning
. . .*

Ellen:
Will you love me forever?

Meat Loaf:
Let me sleep on it!!!

Ellen:
Will you love me forever!!!

For his part, Meat Loaf was more than comfortable to perform in the theatrical style prescribed by Steinman's compositions, flourishing a red silk scarf much in the manner of an operatic tenor. The singer's professional background was as a cast member in various musicals, including *Hair* and *The Rocky Horror Picture Show*. In fact, Meat Loaf began his professional career in the Detroit production of the musical *Hair*. The album *Stoney and Meatloaf* (1971), a collaboration with fellow *Hair* cast mate Shaun Murphy, was released in 1971, but it failed to generate any momentum for either singer. After a fairly uneventful tour in support of the album, Meat Loaf rejoined the cast of *Hair*, this time on Broadway.

Meat Loaf met Jim Steinman at an audition for the Public Theater. Although *Stoney and Meatloaf* had failed to chart, Steinman was a fan of one track off the album, 'I'd Love To Be as Heavy as Jesus', and the two hit it off immediately. Though Meat Loaf and Steinman would not forge a working partnership at the time, they kept in touch. In 1973, Meat Loaf joined the cast of *The Rocky Horror Picture Show*, playing the parts of Eddie and Doctor Scott, after which point he appeared in the musical's film version as Eddie.

Meat Loaf and Steinman began working on *Bat Out Of Hell* in 1972. The concept album was rejected by a number of potential producers before Todd Rundgren finally agreed to produce and finance the record; it took four years for Steinman and Meat Loaf to find a record label—Cleveland Records International—willing to release the unconventional record. A musician himself, Rundgren's (and Steinman's) admiration for Phil Spector's production work in the early 1960s is apparent in the accompaniments he devised for Steinman's anthemic songs. In fact, *Bat Out Of Hell* is often compared with Bruce Springsteen's *Born To Run* (1975), and Springsteen's admiration of Spector is apparent in the epic arrangements heard on *Born To Run*. While Steinman has stated that he finds any comparison between *Bat Out Of Hell* and *Born To Run* 'puzzling, musically', in an interview with *Gallery Magazine* in May

1978 Steinman acknowledged that 'Springsteen was . . . an inspiration' (jimsteinman.com/gallery1.htm). Only furthering the cause of those who would associate the albums, Max Weinberg and Roy Bittan—the drummer and keyboardist for Springsteen's E Street Band in the mid-1970s—provided drum and keyboard parts for *Bat Out Of Hell*.

Aside from his production work, Rundgren also added his unique guitar playing to the album, a fact often overshadowed in critical accounts given his work as a producer. Rundgren would go on to produce the likes of Badfinger, the New York Dolls, Grand Funk Railroad, Hall & Oats, Patti Smith, XTC, Cheap Trick, the Pursuit of Happiness, the Band, and the Psychedelic Furs.

Though it only ranked ninth in record sales during the 1970s, *Bat Out Of Hell* has sold an estimated 34 million copies worldwide, at a rate of 200,000 copies per year, since its release in October 1977. Steinman and Meat Loaf released a sequel in 1993—*Bat Out Of Hell II: Back Into Hell*—featuring the hit single 'I'd Do Anything For Love (But I Won't Do That)', and another sequel album, *Bat Out Of Hell III: The Monster Is Loose*, was released in October 2006, but none of the three major players in the original *Bat Out Of Hell* production has repeated the full success of that album, though Meat Loaf would later perform with the Italian opera star, Luciano Pavarotti (1935–2007), and Steinman wrote and produced a number of hits for, among others, the British singer Bonnie Tyler, notably 'Total Eclipse of the Heart' (1983) and 'Making Love out of Nothing At All' (1983), the latter also a hit for Air Supply.

A final example of the 'theme album' is Marvin Gaye's best-selling LP, *What's Going On* (1971), which fused soul music and gospel influence with the political impetus of counterculture rock. The basic unifying theme of this album is social justice. The title track, inspired by the return of Gaye's brother from Vietnam, is a plea for non-violence, released during the peak of anti-war protests in the United States. Other songs focus on ecology, the welfare of children, and the suffering of poor people in America's urban centres. Gaye co-wrote the songs and produced the album himself, supporting his voice—overdubbed to sound like an entire vocal group—with layers of percussion, strings, and horns. Once again, the producer's consideration of the overall sound texture of the album had a great deal to do with its aesthetic effect and commercial success.

Motown owner Berry Gordy initially didn't want to release *What's Going On*, thinking it had no commercial potential. This was a rare case of misjudgement on Gordy's part; the album reached Number 2 on the LP charts and generated three Number 1 singles on the soul charts, all of which crossed over to the pop Top 10: the title song, 'Mercy Mercy Me (The Ecology)', and 'Inner City Blues (Make Me Wanna Holler)'. Two other tracks, 'Wholly Holy' and 'Save the Children', inspired hit cover versions by Aretha Franklin and Diana Ross. But the significance of this album, and of Marvin Gaye's commitment to a socially responsible aesthetic vision, surpasses any measure of commercial success. Along with Stevie Wonder and Sly Stone, Marvin Gaye showed that soul and R&B albums could provide artistic coherence that transcended the three-minute single; managed to bridge the divide between AM Top 40, FM album-oriented radio, and the soul music market; and held open the possibility that popular music might still have something to do with social change, as well as money-making and artistic self-expression.

Listening To a Classic Single from the AOR Genre: The Eagles' 'Hotel California' (1976)

California in the 1970s retained the central position in American popular culture that it had attained during the 1960s, and if the Beach Boys epitomized the culture of southern California in the earlier decade, then the Eagles were the group that most obviously inherited that distinction. Indeed, the close association of this Los Angeles-based group with the Golden State was so well established at the time of their peak popularity (1975–80) that it lent particular author-

ity to their ambitious saga of 'Hotel California'—the million-selling single from the extraordinarily successful album of the same name (which has sold in excess of 14 million copies).

The Eagles serve as an excellent case in point to illustrate the accelerating ascendancy in importance of albums over singles during the 1970s. When the Eagles issued their first compilation of singles in album form—*Eagles: Their Greatest Hits, 1971–1975*—the album achieved sales far beyond those of all its hit singles taken together; it was, in fact, the first record to be certified by the Recording Industry Association of America (RIAA) as a million-selling ('platinum') album, and it went on to sell more than 26 million copies.

Starting out in 1971 with feet firmly planted in what was called 'country rock', the Eagles had moved from laid-back tunes like 'Take It Easy' and 'Peaceful Easy Feeling', and songs that evoked traditional Western imagery like 'Desperado' and 'Tequila Sunrise', to harder-hitting material like 'One of These Nights' by 1975. 'Hotel California' was the fourth of their five Number 1 singles, and it introduced a new, complex, poetic tone into the Eagles' work. In fact, 'Hotel California' almost sounds like an ambitious late 1960s record rather than a song recorded in the mid-1970s. This is due to several factors: its length, its minor-key harmonies, and its rather unusual overall shape (with extended guitar solos at the end of the record) all contribute to the effect, but surely it is the highly metaphoric lyrics that establish the most obvious kinship with the songwriting trends of the 1960s.

The tone of 'Hotel California', however, is pure 1970s. The sense of loss and disillusionment treated so casually in 'Crocodile Rock' here assumes a desperate, almost apocalyptic character:

Her mind is Tiffany twisted. She got the Mercedes bends.
She got a lot of pretty, pretty boys that she calls friends.
How they dance in the courtyard; sweet summer sweat.
Some dance to remember; some dance to forget.

When the visitor asks the hotel captain to bring up some wine, he is told, '*We haven't had that spirit here since nineteen-sixty-nine.*' Finally, as the last verse ends, the fleeing visitor is told by the 'night man' at the door that '*you can check out any time you like, but you can never leave.*' As if to illustrate all the implications of this memorable line, the song neither proceeds to the now-expected chorus ('*Welcome to the Hotel California*', whose pop-friendly major-key music assumes an increasingly ironic edge as the record progresses) nor fades out quickly. Instead, those words become the final words we hear, and the Eagles launch into lengthy guitar solos—over the chords of the verses, not those of the chorus—as if to underline our 'stuck' situation and to eliminate anything that remotely suggests 'welcoming'. California, that sun-blessed beacon to the generation of 'peace and love' in the 1960s, has here become a sinister trap for those who have no place left to go.

▌Appropriating the Classical Tradition: Progressive Rock

A strategy that was fairly unusual in rock music was the adoption of elements of large-scale structure from European classical music. Some rock bands even went so far as to record with symphony orchestras—two pioneering efforts in this respect being the Moody Blues' *Days of Future Passed*, which they recorded with the London Symphony in the late 1960s, and Procul Harum's *Procol Harum Live in Concert*, which they recorded with the Edmonton Symphony Orchestra (the ESO had already collaborated with the Canadian rock orchestra Lighthouse for an extremely successful 'live' show by this point).

The live album *Pictures at an Exhibition* (1971), another example of early 'progressive rock' recorded by the art rock band Emerson, Lake, and Palmer, adopts its main themes and some of its structural elements from a suite of piano pieces by the Russian composer Modest Mussorgsky (1839–81), which the French composer Maurice Ravel orchestrated in the early twentieth century. This was a canny choice, since Musorgsky's composition—inspired by a walk through an art gallery of paintings made by a recently deceased friend—consists of a sequence of accessible, reasonably short, easily digestible 'paintings', a parallel with the song format of much popular music. Some sections of the LP are re-orchestrations of the original score (making prominent use of Keith Emerson's virtuosity on organ and synthesizer), while others are improvisations on the borrowed materials, and still others are new songs by the band, musing on ideas in the music. The album concludes with 'Nutrocker', a rock 'n' roll version of Tchaikovsky's *Nutcracker Suite*.

Other groups, such as Canada's Rush, adopted musical techniques from the classical tradition without openly referencing the repertoire. A rock trio formed in 1968 by guitarist Alex Lifeson and bassist, keyboardist, and vocalist Geddy Lee—with Neil Peart added on drums in 1974—Rush came to be highly regarded among musicians for their technical virtuosity and for the obvious complexity of many of their instrumental arrangements, even if they received mixed reviews from the critical community. Rush made most overt use of the compositional device of the song-suite from the classical tradition (e.g., 'By-Tor & the Snow Dog', 'The Fountain of Lamneth', '2112', 'Cygnus X-1', and 'Cygnus X-1 Book II, Hemispheres'), though this did not deter the group from writing a number of Top 20 CHUM hits at the same time, most notably 'Closer to the Heart' (Number 13 CHUM, 1977), 'The Spirit of Radio' (Number 7 CHUM, 1980), 'Limelight' (Number 7 CHUM, 1981), and 'Tom Sawyer' (Number 14 CHUM, 1981). Interestingly, a few francophone rock groups were able to crossover into the English-Canadian and American markets in the 1970s with a similar admixture of progressive rock and pop sensibilities. Groups such as Harmonium, for instance, and Beau Dommage enjoyed a cult-like following in Quebec, complemented by steady sales outside of the province, as did the more straightforwardly blues-rock band Offenbach, who enjoyed considerable chart success in France as well. Comprised of multi-instrumentalists Pierre Bertrand, Marie-Michele Derosiers, Real Derosiers, Robert Léger, and Michel Rivard, Beau Dommage remains one of the most successful francophone rock groups of all time. 'La Complainte du Phoque en Alaska' (1974), from their eponymous release for Capitol Records Canada in 1974 (which was the best-selling release in Quebec history at the time), enjoyed consistent play on anglophone radio across Canada throughout the decade.

Listening To Rush's 'Closer to the Heart' (1977)

Though any album released by Rush during the 1970s easily encapsulates the progressive rock genre's two main songwriting tendencies—i.e., 'art rock' epics and mid-tempo pop songs—we will consider the band's fifth studio release, *A Farewell to Kings* (1977). The album clearly demonstrates the central position Neil Peart came to occupy in Rush's songwriting practice after his arrival in 1974. A devoted Ayn Rand acolyte who often referenced the objectivist philosopher's writings in songs, Peart penned words for all but 'Cinderella Man' on the album, which was written by Geddy Lee, and for 'Closer to the Heart', which Peart co-wrote with Peter Talbot. Recorded at Rockfield Studios in Wales, mixed at Advision Studios in London, and released by Anthem Records in Canada and Mercury Records in the United States, the six songs that together comprise *A Farewell to Kings* clock in at a combined 37 minutes and 13 seconds, making the album the shortest in the entire Rush ouevre. Featuring the band's trademark instrumental song suites—the 11-minute 'Xanadu' and the 10-minute 'Cygnus X-1'—it is nonetheless the shorter pop fare on *A Farewell to Kings*, but especially 'Closer

Rush—from left, Neil Peart, Geddy Lee, Alex Lifeson—were praised in the musical community for their technical virtuosity and complex instrumental arrangements.

to the Heart', that earned the trio their first gold and, eventually, platinum certifications. In fact, 'Closer to the Heart' represents the first time that Rush hit the Top 20; the song peaked at Number 13 in Canada in November 1977.

The lyrics of Peart, Talbot, and Lee for *A Farewell to Kings* illustrate another aspect of the progressive rock genre—the literary ambitions of its lyricists. *A Farewell to Kings* is clearly a 'concept album', thematically charting humanity's evolution from medieval feudalism and absolute monarchism to a future of space travel and black holes. Thus, track titles such as 'Madrigal' and 'Xanadu' clash with more futuristic fare, such as the concluding 'Cygnus X-1', a 10-minute multi-movement epic 'rock suite' featuring avant-garde electronic soundscapes coupled with more straightforward rock 'n' roll fare. A reference to somewhat obscure Canadiana—the title, 'Cygnus X-1', was actually borrowed from Tom Bolton, the Canadian scientist who discovered a black hole candidate called 'Cygnus X-1' while working at the David Dunlap Observatory at the University of Toronto—Rush would continue the story in 'Cygnus X-1 Book II: Hemispheres', which appears on their next LP, *Hemispheres*. A progression from feudalism to space exploration can be heard in miniature on the album's opening cut—'A Farewell to Kings', which progresses from a trio between classical guitar, glockenspiel, and synthesizer to a fully electric up-tempo rocker. 'Xanadu', the album's first multi-movement 'rock suite', features lyrics based on Samuel Taylor Coleridge's 'Kubla Khan', and also represents one of the few Rush recordings to feature Geddy Lee on rhythm guitar; and

here, too, the epic progresses from a quiet, almost ambient electronic introduction to a heavy rocker, before it reaches its quieter, decidedly orchestral conclusion.

As noted, though, it was 'Closer to the Heart', the album's catchiest number, that captured a pop listenership for the progressive rock trio. Set in ABA ('ternary') form, with strophic 'A' sections—each strophe concluding with the refrain 'closer to the heart'—juxtaposed with a 'B' section comprised entirely of Alex Lifeson's virtuosic electric guitar solo, the acoustic-to-electric metaphor of the album's opening cut—and of the album in general—is repeated once more on this track. The 'A' section begins with an acoustic guitar solo, composed by Geddy Lee but performed by Alex Lifeson on a 12-string acoustic guitar, which is quickly joined by an electric bass—performed on a slightly distorted synthesizer, and panned to the right side of the stereo spectrum—and a glockenspiel panned to the left side of the stereo spectrum. Lee's high-pitched vocals are then 'layered-in', followed quickly by Peart's drum kit track and Lee's electric bass. The group then progresses through two more strophes that build in dynamic intensity into Lifeson's guitar solo in the 'B' section of the song. The group returns to the 'A' section once more, with an ensemble iteration of Lee's melody from the introductory section of the track—ensemble virtuosity of this sort would become crucial to the hardcore and heavy metal genre throughout the early and mid-1980s—before a final strophe set to a fully electric backing leads the song to its abrupt conclusion.

Led Zeppelin and Heavy Metal

By the early 1970s the British hard rock band Led Zeppelin, formed in London in 1968, was well on its way to becoming one of the most profitable and influential acts in rock music history. 'Zep', as fans called the band, was comprised of Jimmy Page, a brilliant guitarist who had honed his skills as Eric Clapton's successor in a pioneering British band called the Yardbirds; John Bonham, who established the thunderous sound of heavy metal drumming; John Paul Jones, who provided the band's solid 'bottom', doubling on electric bass and organ; and Robert Plant, whose agile high tenor voice established the norm for subsequent heavy metal singers, alongside similar vocalists such as Ozzy Osborne and Geddy Lee. Zeppelin's sledgehammer style of guitar-focused rock music drew on various influences, including urban blues, San Francisco psychedelic rock, and the guitar playing of Jimi Hendrix. Although Led Zeppelin is usually associated with the heavy textures and extremely loud volume of their hard rock repertoire, their recordings also included another important stream— an interest in folk music, particularly the traditions of the British Isles.

'Stairway to Heaven' is Led Zeppelin's most famous recording, and it reflects certain unique features of the band's musical approach, as well as its position vis-à-vis the commercial mainstream of pop music. To begin with, the song presents us with a fascinating marketing strategy—at first glance perverse, but actually quite brilliant. Although 'Stairway to Heaven' was the most frequently requested song on FM radio during the 1970s, the eight-minute track was never released as a single. In other words, to own a copy of 'Stairway to Heaven' you had to buy the album. Of course, that could prove difficult for the uninitiated consumer, since the band insisted on an album cover that bore neither the name of the album, nor the name of the band, nor the name of the record company. Atlantic Records was horrified by this design, but the band held the master tapes for the album hostage, and the record company had no choice but to go along. Driven in part by the popularity of 'Stairway to Heaven', the LP *Led Zeppelin IV* reached the Number 2 position on the *Billboard* Top LP charts and stayed on the charts for five years, eventually selling 14 million copies.

'Stairway to Heaven' has been called the 'anthem' of heavy metal music—a genre that developed out of hard rock in the 1970s and achieved mainstream success in the 1980s. Generally characterized by 'power chords' (chords strummed with only the first and fifth scale degree on a heavily distorted electric guitar); riffs performed in unison by electric guitar and bass; copious amounts of distortion and overdrive; high tenor vocals and frequent, practically gymnastic displays of technical virtuosity; and extreme volumes, the label 'heavy metal' has nonetheless proven extremely slippery, and seems to have been practically interchangeable with 'hard rock' throughout the 1970s (Canadian John Kay, of Steppenwolf, is often credited with coining the musical meaning of the term 'heavy metal' in the song 'Born To Be Wild'—*I like smoking lightning, heavy metal thunder*'). In Canada, for instance, bands such as Rush, April Wine, BTO, Haywire, Headpins, Max Webster, Loverboy, Prism, Triumph,

Trooper, Thundermug, FM, Saga, and Mahogany Rush were all classified at some point or another by critics as 'heavy metal' bands in the 1970s, though most are now clearly considered either progressive or hard rock groups.

Listening To Led Zeppelin's 'Stairway to Heaven' (1971)

Regardless of whether we call it 'hard rock' or 'heavy metal', Led Zeppelin's 'Stairway to Heaven' remains one of the most popular songs in rock music history. In fact, 'Stairway to Heaven' is reportedly the most requested song in rock radio history. What accounts for its tremendous commercial success, and its ability to ignite the imaginations and inspire the loyalty of millions of fans? To begin with, 'Stairway' skilfully juxtaposes two dimensions of Led Zeppelin's musical persona—the bone-crushing rock band, known for inspiring riots and dismantling hotel rooms, and the folk music aficionados, steeped in a reverence for ancient English and Celtic mythology. While these two sensibilities might seem diametrically opposed, the twin musical threads of sonic aggression and acoustic intimacy run throughout the entire history of heavy metal. In fact, most heavy metal albums include at least one so-called 'power ballad', a term that in this context usually implies the use of acoustic guitar.

For many fans in Zeppelin's audience, the combination of rock physicality and folk mysticism in 'Stairway to Heaven' created something akin to a sacred experience. The somewhat inscrutable song text, composed by singer Robert Plant during a rehearsal, was also an important source of the recording's attraction.

Both Plant and Jimmy Page were at the time exploring the writings of the noted English mystic and founder of the First Church of Satan, Aleister Crowley—into whose house Page eventually moved—and reading scholarly tomes like *Magic Arts in Celtic Britain*, which Plant later said influenced the lyrics for 'Stairway'. The references to mythological beings (the May Queen and the Piper) and rural images (paths and roads, rings of smoke through the forest, a songbird by a brook, the whispering wind) helped to create a cumulative mood of mystery and enchantment.

Form

Although the basic building blocks of 'Stairway to Heaven' are straightforward four- and eight-bar phrases, the overall arrangement is quite complex in formal terms (see the listening chart). There are three main sections. Section One alternates two eight-measure phrases, which we are calling 'A' and 'B'. The basic form of Section One is ABABAA¹ (the last section being an abridged version of 'A'). Section Two reverses the order of the phrases and inserts a brief one-measure linking phrase (which we are calling 'X'). The form of Section Two is BAXBAXB. Section Three, which takes up almost half of the total eight minutes of recording time, introduces a new (though closely related) chord progression and melody, which we are calling 'C'. The first part of Section Three has the form CXBCX. After a one-measure pause, this is followed by an instrumental fanfare that propels us into Jimmy Page's guitar solo. Robert Plant's voice then re-enters, and there is an extended vocal section, using the harmonies from phrase 'C'. The arrangement concludes with an instrumental phrase, slowing down and becoming much quieter in the last two measures. The track concludes quietly, with Robert Plant repeating the key line of the text: *'And she's buying a stairway to heaven.'* Thus, the arrangement of 'Stairway to Heaven' is constructed to create a continual escalation in density, volume, and speed. The tempo increases from around 72 beats per minute at the opening of the recording to 84 beats per minute at the beginning of Section Three, and peaking at around 98 beats per minute during the guitar solo. This substantial, though gradual, increase in speed is crucial to the overall impact of the recording.

If 'Stairway' seems complex in purely structural terms, this may be because the logic of its organization is fundamentally emotional and metaphoric. The recording can itself be seen as an analogue of the heavenly stairway, springing from the rural, mythological past (symbolized by acoustic instruments), soaring on jet-powered wings of metal, and finally coming to rest on a high, peaceful plateau. Similarly, the outer cover of the original album juxtaposes the sepia image of a peasant with that of a modern skyscraper rising over the formerly rustic landscape. The inner jacket portrays a mysterious hooded figure standing atop an icy peak with a staff and a lantern, looking down at a bell-bottomed seeker of knowledge who struggles to reach the top. Also included inside the album dust jacket are the lyrics to 'Stairway to Heaven' and a set of mystical symbols, or runes, one of which inspired the informal name for the album, 'Zoso'. In seeking to understand what a recording like 'Stairway' meant to its fans, the analysis of musical form must be coupled with a consideration of its other expressive dimensions, including the song text and the graphic design of the album on which it appeared.

Listening Chart: 'Stairway to Heaven'

Music and lyrics by Jimmy Page and Robert Plant; performed by Led Zeppelin

FORM	DESCRIPTIVE COMMENTS
Section One (0:00):	
A (8 measures)	Instrumental: 6-string acoustic guitar; double-tracked recorder (flute) duet enters in measure 5; slow tempo (72 beats per minute).
B (8)	Guitar and recorders continue.
A (8)	Vocal enters.

B (4)

A (8)

A[|] (4)   Instrumental: 6-string guitar and recorders continue.

Section Two (2:14):

                                   12-string guitar, soft electric guitar, electric piano; intensity
                                   increases, tempo slightly faster (80 bpm).

B (8)

A (8)

X (1)   Instrumental: One-measure linking section;guitar becomes
                                   more dominant.

B (8)   Texture thickens, volume and tempo increase slightly.

A (8)

X (1)   Instrumental: Linking section.

B (8)   Slight crescendo, slight tempo increase. Drums enter at end,
                                   leading us into next section.

Section Three (4:19):

C (8)   New minor chord progression; electric guitar, 12-string
                                   acoustic guitar, plus electric bass and drum set; tempo
                                   increases (84 bpm).

X (1)   Instrumental: Linking section.

B (8)

C (8)

X (2)   Instrumental: Linking section, plus one measure pause.

D (8)   Instrumental fanfare using chords from 'C'; tempo speeds up,
                                   leading us into next section.

Guitar solo (20)   Chord pattern continues; tempo increases (*c.* 98 bpm);
                                   multi-tracked guitar plays supporting pattern under solo
                                   (last eight measures).

C (18)

C (8)   Instrumental: Tempo slows down, intensity decreases.

B (3)   Solo voice (rubato).

▌Santana: The Roots of Rock Multiculturalism

If rock was quintessentially defined for many listeners by white bands like Led Zeppelin, Pink Floyd, and the Rolling Stones, the San Francisco-based group Santana reveals a nascent trend within rock music towards multicultural engagement. The band was led by guitarist Carlos Santana (b. 1947, in Mexico), who began his musical career playing guitar in the nightspots of Tijuana. As a child he was exposed to the sounds of rock 'n' roll, including the music of Mexican-American musicians such as Ritchie Valens, whose version of 'La Bamba' had broken into the *Billboard* Top 40 in early 1959. Santana moved to San Francisco at age 15, where he was exposed to other forms of music that were to play a profound part in shaping the style and sensibility of his music: jazz, particularly the experimental music of John Coltrane and Miles Davis; salsa, a New York-based style of Latin dance music strongly rooted in Afro-Cuban traditions; and in the late 1960s, San Francisco rock, including artists as diverse as Janis Joplin, Jimi Hendrix, and Sly and the Family Stone (see Chapter 4). Around 1968, Santana put together a group of middle- and working-class Latino, black, and white musicians from varied cultural backgrounds. The band's eponymous first album, *Santana*, released in 1969, reached Number 4 on the Top LPs chart, in large part due to the band's spectacular performance in the film and soundtrack LP of *Woodstock*.

In 1970 Columbia Records released Santana's second LP, which firmly established both the band itself and a strong Latin American substream within rock music.

Carlos Santana. Frank Driggs Collection.

Abraxas held the Number 1 position on the LP charts for six weeks, spent a total of 88 weeks on the charts, and sold over four million copies in the United States alone. The album also produced two Top 40 singles: 'Black Magic Woman' (Number 4 pop in 1970), originally recorded by the English blues rock band Fleetwood Mac; and the infectious 'Oye Como Va' (Number 13 pop, Number 32 R&B in 1971), composed by New York Latin percussionist and dance music king Tito Puente. These two singles, which had a great deal to do with the success of the album, were shorter versions of the tracks found on the LP. (This was a typical strategy, given the duration of tracks on many rock LPs in the 1970s.) Tying blues, rock, and salsa together in one multicultural package, *Abraxas* also featured less commercial tracks such as 'Gypsy Queen' (composed by the jazz guitarist Gabor Szabo) and the impressionistic 'Singing Winds, Crying Beasts'.

We will take a closer look at the LP version of 'Oye Como Va' (see box), since it allows the band to stretch out a bit and best illustrates certain features of Santana's style. To appreciate what goes into a recording like 'Oye Como Va', we must consider not only the instrumentation—essentially a guitar–bass–keyboards–drums rock band plus Latin percussion—but also the recording's 'mix', that is, the precise tonal quality, balancing, and positioning of sounds recorded on various tracks in the studio. (*Abraxas* was co-produced by the band and Fred Catero, whose straightforward approach to studio production can also be heard on early LPs of the jazz rock band Chicago.) Santana's instantly recognizable sound focused on the fluid lead guitar style of Carlos Santana and the churning grooves created by the drummer (Mike Shrieve), the bass player (Dave Brown), and two Latin percussionists (Jose Areas and Mike Carabello).

 ### Listening To Santana's 'Oye Como Va' (1971)

The rhythmic complexity of 'Oye Como Va'—essentially an electrified version of an Afro-Cuban dance rhythm—required that the recording be mixed to create a 'clean' stereo image, so that the various instruments and interlocking rhythm patterns could be clearly heard. Listening over headphones or good speakers, you should be able to hear where the various instruments are positioned in the mix. The electric bass is in the middle, acting as the band's rhythmic anchor; the guitar and keyboards are placed slightly to the left and right of centre, respectively, and thus kept out of each other's way; and the percussion instruments (including guiro, a ridged gourd scraped with a small stick; timbales, a set of two drums played with flexible sticks; agogo, a metal bell; and congas, hand-played drums) are positioned even farther out to the left and right.

The track opens with the electric bass and Hammond B-3 organ—one of the most characteristic sounds of 1970s rock music—playing the interlocking pattern that functions as the core of the groove throughout the recording. (In a salsa band, this two-measure pattern would be called the *tumbao*.) In the background we hear someone say 'Sabor!' ('Flavour!') and at the end of the fourth measure the timbales and agogo enter, bringing in the rest of the instruments at the beginning of the fifth measure. At this point all of the interlocking repeated patterns—bass, organ, bell, scraper, and congas—have been established. The signature sound of Carlos Santana's guitar enters in the ninth measure, as he plays a two-measure melodic theme four times. This is followed by the first of four sections in which the whole band plays a single rhythmic and melodic pattern in unison (in the listening chart we call these sections 'B' and 'B¹', respectively). Throughout the track, the rhythm functions as the heart of the music. As if to remind us of the importance of this deep connection with Afro-Latin tradition, all of the other layers are periodically stripped away, laying bare the pulsing heart of the music.

At the most general level, we can make a few observations about how the four minutes and 17 seconds of 'Oye Como Va' are organized. The whole arrangement is 136 measures in length; out of that total only 16 measures (about 12 per cent of the total) are devoted to singing, which in this context seems almost a pretext for the instrumental music. In general, song lyrics are less important than the musical groove and texture in most of Santana's early recordings (the lyric for this song consists of a short phrase in Spanish, repeated over and over, in which the singer boasts about the potency of his 'groove' to a brown-skinned female dancer).

Taking away the other obviously pre-composed elements—the guitar melody (phrase 'A'), unison figures played by the whole band ('B', 'B¹'), and the call-and-response figure after the first guitar solo and the other interlude sections—we find that nearly half of the recording (66 measures) is devoted to improvised solos by the guitar and organ. The other elements of the arrangement, including the dramatic group crescendos that lead into the last two solos, seem designed to support improvisation. In essence, then, 'Oye Como Va' is a vehicle for instrumental soloing, more like a jazz performance than a Top 40 pop song. Not surprisingly, in fact, it was precisely the solos that Columbia Records chose to cut when they edited the track for AM radio airplay. In particular, Carlos Santana's solos on 'Oye Como Va' provide us with a good example of the work of a talented rock improviser. Rather than playing torrents of fast notes to show off his guitar technique (which was and remains considerable), Santana uses the electric guitar's ability to sustain notes for long periods of time to create long, flowing melodic lines that gradually rise in intensity, lifting the whole band with him. In live performance, of course, Santana and other instrumental soloists could stretch out for much more than four and a half minutes. If the soft side of rock often worked within the restricted time format imposed by Top 40 radio, progressive rock bands such as Santana, the Allman Brothers, and the Grateful Dead kept alive the notion of extended, open-ended performance, an important part of the legacy of the San Francisco rock scene of the late 1960s (see Chapter 4).

Listening Chart: 'Oye Como Va'

Music and lyrics by Tito Puente; performed by Santana

FORM	LYRICS	DESCRIPTIVE COMMENTS
Groove (8)		Instrumental: The basic cha-cha rhythm is established on organ, electric bass, and (from the fifth measure) percussion.
A (8)		The guitar states a 2-measure melodic phrase four times (with minor embellishments).
B (4)		A unison figure, played by the whole band.
C (8)	Oye como va . . .	Vocals (two 4-measure phrases).
Bⁱ (2)		Instrumental: The unison figure again (first half only).
Guitar solo (20)		Extended solo by Carlos Santana.
Interlude (6)		Call-and-response exchange between guitar and band.
Groove (4)		Stripped down to the basics again.
Interlude (8)		Suddenly quieter; organ and guitar play chord pattern; gradual crescendo.
Organ solo (22)		
Groove (4)		One more time!
B' (2)		The unison figure again (first half only).
C (8)	Oye como va . . .	Vocals (two 4-measure phrases).
Interlude (4)		Instrumental: Suddenly quieter, then crescendo.
Guitar solo (24)		Another solo by Carlos Santana.
B (4)		The unison figure again, functioning as a tag.

Canada and Its Discontents: Closing Out the 1970s

The mid-1970s may well have been the most fractious period in Canadian history. After running a lacklustre campaign in 1972 that narrowly returned them to office with a minority government, the Trudeau Liberals were forced to curry favour with the 'left-nationalist'—some might still have said 'prairie socialist'—New Democratic Party (NDP) to maintain power. Thus, in the 1972–4 years the Trudeau government enacted a series of economic reforms that left many Canadians wondering whether their Prime Minister was actually a left-nationalist (if not an outright socialist), even though he expressed obvious disdain for Québécois nationalism.

Between 1970 and 1974 world oil prices rose by roughly 400 per cent. American support for Israel during the so-called 'Yom Kippur War' (or 'October War') in 1973 waged between Israel and certain Arab states prompted the Organization of Petroleum

Exporting Countries (OPEC) to enact a series of embargoes and reductions in oil pro-duction, which artificially inflated oil prices worldwide. In an effort to control the price of oil in Canada, Trudeau created Petro-Canada, a Crown corporation, in 1975, which, alongside the National Energy Program (established in 1980), worked to basi-cally nationalize western oil from the mostly American interests controlling it and dictate prices well below global averages. In the early 1970s, too, the Liberal govern-ment created the Foreign Investment Review Agency (FIRA), to scrutinize foreign takeovers of Canadian businesses, and the Canadian Development Corporation (CDC), to oversee domestic industrial policy.

Having ridiculed his opponents for suggesting price and wage controls during the next election campaign in 1974—world oil prices had continued to rise, and inflation finally hit 10 per cent, but Trudeau only pointed his finger and said 'Zap, you're frozen!' when asked by reporters about controls—Trudeau did precisely what he said he would not do, enacting price and wage controls when stagflation continued to persist. Soon after, he struck up a public friendship with Fidel Castro, and he mused on national television that democratic capitalism might be 'a failed system'. Thus, the notion that Trudeau was a socialist came into vogue; that he was at least 'untrustwor-thy' became a common concern; and some went so far as to accuse his government of basic incompetence, alleging that it was incapable of managing the Canadian economy.

Moreover, after selling their oil to Canadians at artificially deflated prices for almost half a decade under the auspices of Petro-Canada and, later, the NEP, Canada's western provinces—especially Alberta—began publicly venting their frus-trations, giving notice that western alienation was something to be taken seriously by politicians. At one point bumper stickers with the phrase '*Let Those Eastern Bastards Freeze!*' came into vogue in Alberta; and Trudeau famously raised his mid-dle finger to some of his more vocal critics during a tour of the province. The phe-nomenon has only grown since then: in 2004 the Separation Party of Alberta nominated candidates for election to the provincial assembly, while a poll conducted by the *Western Standard* in 2005 found that over 39 per cent of citizens living in Manitoba, Saskatchewan, and Alberta agreed that they should 'begin to explore the idea of forming their own country'.

The issue of separatism had reshaped provincial politics in Quebec radically since the Quiet Revolution. In 1967, René Lévesque bolted the provincial Liberal Party, in which he had been the architect of major Quiet Revolution reforms, and managed to weld a highly fractious coalition of separatist interests into a viable political party: the Parti Québécois (PQ). Soon after the October Crisis of 1970 the PQ became a force to be reckoned with in provincial politics. Obviously, the PQ was in favour of Quebec's secession from the rest of Canada, but it was also dedicated to a social dem-ocratic form of governance. Robert Bourassa's provincial Liberals managed to win two elections in 1970 and 1972, calling for a 'profitable confederation', and in 1970 the PQ won only a fifth of the popular vote, even though 80 per cent of voters self-identified as francophones. Journalists writing at the time did not seem so far off the mark, then, when they eulogized Quebec separatism.

The issue of Quebec's separation also seemed trivial given the rapid change occurring in Canadian demographics; in 1960, over 83 per cent of Canadians self-identified as English-, Irish-, Scottish- or French-Canadian, but by the late 1970s a number of immigration policy reforms had brought a massive influx of so-called 'visible minorities'—mostly from Asia, Africa, and Latin America—who comprised over one-third of the entire Canadian population by 1979. Thus, Canada seemed to be transforming from a nation of 'two solitudes', as Hugh MacLennan famously called it, to multicultural modernity—and quickly, too.

The year 1976, however, proved pivotal in the re-emergence of separatism. That year a seemingly innocuous regulation allowing bilingual air traffic control in Quebec prompted francophone pilots and controllers to strike. Robert Bourassa then introduced 'language laws' in Quebec making French the official language of the province, which in turn made French the sole language of education, thus commencing an exodus of businesses, chiefly to Toronto. Bourassa's decision split his own party, and the provincial economy stumbled alongside the federal economy. Nonetheless, the Premier called another election in 1976, believing that the Liberal Party would still easily win because it was the only federalist party on the slate. Lévesque smartly waged his campaign based not on the issue of separatism but, more simply, on 'good government', and on 15 November 1976 the PQ became the first separatist government elected to power in Quebec. Though the party did not run on the issue of independence—or, as they now called it, 'sovereignty-association'—the PQ promised a referendum on the issue before their term in office was over. They would lose the referendum by a margin of 60 per cent to 40 per cent in 1980.

The relative conservatism and greater commercialism that seemed to take hold of much of the rock world in the 1970s south of the border, and Joni Mitchell's characterization of Canadian arts and artists as an 'Old-Fashioned Bouquet', did not always hold true in the larger Canadian world of this period. Indeed, where Trudeau was seen by many as a 'rock star' Prime Minister—flipping the bird to protestors, making caustic off-the-cuff remarks to reporters and parliamentarians, courting glamorous celebrities before his marriage to Margaret Sinclair in 1971, and befriending the Cuban 'pariah', Fidel Castro, much to the consternation of the American ally—his much younger 'flower child' wife of a few short years dashed off to Toronto to see the Rolling Stones and then went straight to New York City, where she hung out at the notorious Studio 54. As Richard Gwyn wrote in *The Northern Magus*, his 1980 biography of Trudeau:

> she spent her sixth wedding anniversary in Toronto at a Rolling Stones' concert, to be spotted wandering the corridors of their hotel in a white bathrobe. From there to New York, where *People* published the famous interview . . . in praise of Trudeau's body—'It's like that of a twenty-five-year-old'—and in praise of garter-belts as a 'turn-on'. She also discussed the effect of her nipples, as outlined through her dress, upon state visitors. (Gwyn, 1980: 213)

One would be hard-pressed to determine whether life and politics imitated rock, or rock imitated life and politics. But the Canadian state would remain in turmoil for years to come, and some segments of popular music, by the late 1970s and early 1980s, would swim into more dangerous waters.

Discussion Questions

1. How do records by roots rock bands such as the Band and Blood, Sweat & Tears musically encapsulate the so-called 'retreat from radicalism' that clearly came to characterize North American popular culture during the early 1970s? Has anything similar happened more recently? Can you think of some examples of bands active today whose music might be considered 'roots rock'?

2. How would you describe the importance of the introduction of Canadian content regulations during the early 1970s to the development of a rock industry in Canada? Do you agree with the so-called 'MAPL system'? Are Canadian content regulations still necessary?

3. In your opinion, is there something distinctly Canadian in the records made by Gordon Lightfoot, Joni Mitchell, and Leonard Cohen during the late 1960s and early 1970s? Why do you think Canadian singer-songwriters came to dominate the troubadour tradition?

4. The AOR tradition was the first to be tied directly to a particular medium by its title (*album*-oriented rock). Given Internet downloading, many would claim that the single is now the pre-eminent form of rock. Is this true? If so, can AOR survive the iPod? What would have to happen for AOR to thrive again?

5. Why did progressive rock musicians typically look to the Western art tradition for inspiration rather than, say, the blues or country traditions?

Chapter Six

Outsiders' Music: Progressive Country, Reggae, Punk, Funk, and Disco

A lthough the 1970s are often described as a period of stylistic conservatism and corporate consolidation in popular music, the decade also fostered music that did not fit neatly into any mainstream frameworks. The genres we consider in this chapter arose, for the most part, as a response to the conservatism of the music industry; the exception is reggae music, which came from completely outside the commercial mainstream of the North American music industry. Moreover, most clearly emerged from, and enjoyed their clearest support in, contexts outside of Canada, though they bore a direct influence on the rock tradition in general and thus warrant our consideration. Each of these genres embodied in its own way the contradictions built into the popular music industry, and they reflect the complex processes by which the mainstream and the margins of popular music are continually redefined.

▌The Outlaws: Progressive Country

During the late 1960s and early 1970s, mainstream country music was dominated by the slick Nashville sound, by the hardcore country of artists like Merle Haggard, and by various blends of country and pop promoted on AM Top 40 radio and sung by such performers as Glen Campbell. But a new generation of country musicians at this time began to embrace the music and attitudes that had grown out of the 1960s counterculture. *Progressive country*, as this movement came to be known, was inspired by the honky-tonk and rockabilly amalgam of Bakersfield country music, the singer-songwriter genre (especially the work of Bob Dylan), and the country rock style of musicians like Gram Parsons, who was a member of the Byrds for a brief time in the late 1960s before he founded the Flying Burrito Brothers with fellow ex-Byrd Chris Hillman. In general, progressive country performers wrote songs that were more intellectual and liberal in outlook than were those of their contemporaries; and they seem to have been more concerned with testing the limits of the country music tradition than with scoring hits. Many of the movement's key artists—including Willie Nelson, Kris Kristofferson, Tom T. Hall, and Townes Van Zandt—were not polished singers by conventional standards, yet they wrote distinctive, individualistic songs and had compelling voices. Such artists developed a sizable cult following, and progressive country began to inch its way into the mainstream, usually in the form of cover versions. Tom T. Hall's 'Harper Valley PTA' was a Number 1 pop and country hit for Jeannie C. Riley in 1968 both in Canada and in the United States, while Sammi Smith took Kris Kristofferson's 'Help Me Make It through the Night' to the top of the country charts and into the pop Top 10 in 1971; also important was Bobbie Gentry's 'Ode To Billie Joe', which in 1967 simultaneously topped the *Billboard* Pop LP and singles charts and the CHUM charts.

One of the most influential figures in the progressive country movement was Willie Nelson (born in Texas in 1933). Nelson had already developed a successful career as a professional songwriter when he left Nashville to return to Texas in 1971; his song 'Crazy' was a Top 10 country and pop hit for Patsy Cline in 1961. He settled in Austin, a university town and home to one of the most energetic and eclectic live music scenes in the country. At 'cosmic cowboy' venues such as the Armadillo World Headquarters, and on Austin radio station KOKE-FM, a fusion of country music and countercultural sensibilities was already well underway. Nelson fit right into the Austin scene, letting his hair and beard grow long, and donning a headband, an earring, jogging shoes, and blue jeans (one of the few markers of cultural identity shared by rednecks, cowboys, and hippies!). Singing in an unpolished, almost conversational voice—an approach that had frustrated his attempts to gain success as a recording artist in Nashville—Willie Nelson bridged the gap between rock and country without losing touch with his honky-tonk roots. In the summer of 1971 he organized the first of a series of outdoor festivals that included older country musicians (e.g., Roy Acuff and Earl Scruggs) as well as younger musicians who were experimenting with a blend of country and rock music. These 'picnics', closer in ethos to Woodstock than to the Grand Ole Opry, brought thousands of rock fans into the fold of country music, and prepared the way for Nelson's ascendance as the pre-eminent male country music star of the 1980s.

Willie Nelson's initial rise to national fame came in the mid-1970s, through his association with a group of musicians collectively known as 'the Outlaws'. The centrepiece of the Outlaws was another Texas-born musician, Waylon Jennings (1937–2002). Jennings began his career as a musician and disc jockey, and in 1958 he joined Buddy Holly's rock 'n' roll group, the Crickets. In the early 1960s he set up shop at

Willie Nelson, looking very much the country outlaw. Frank Driggs Collection.

a nightclub in Phoenix, Arizona, where the clientele included businessmen, college students, and cowboys—a diverse audience that encouraged him to develop a broad repertoire. In 1965 he was signed by RCA-Victor and relocated to Nashville. Although RCA producer Chet Atkins—who had remoulded Elvis into a pop star in 1956—attempted to push him in the direction of the 'countrypolitan' sound popular at the time, Jennings resisted these efforts, eventually winning substantial leeway in his choice of material. Thus, Jennings's 1970s LPs included country covers of classic Beatles songs such as 'Norwegian Wood' and 'You've Got to Hide Your Love Away'.

While he chose to remain close to the music industry in Nashville rather than return to Texas, Jennings cultivated an image as a rebel, and in 1972 he recorded an album called *Ladies Love Outlaws*. On the cover he appeared in 'bad guy' costume, complete

A Country Concept Album:
Willie Nelson's *Red-Headed Stranger* (1975)

One of the ideas that progressive country musicians adopted from rock music during the 1970s was that of the concept album. The central medium for the transmission of country music during the 1970s was still the individual song: some country LPs sold well, but 45 rpm singles remained the bread-and-butter of the industry. During the mid-1970s, however, progressive country musicians began to create albums unified around a single theme or dramatic character. Perhaps the best example of this trend is Willie Nelson's *Red-Headed Stranger* (1975), which sold over two million copies and reached number 28 on *Billboard*'s Top LPs chart (*Billboard* had no separate LP charts for country or soul music, since these genres were assumed by definition to be singles-oriented). *Red-Headed Stranger* included Nelson's first big crossover hit as a singer, rather than as a songwriter—'Blue Eyes Crying in the Rain', Number 21 pop and Number 1 country in the US—and established the notion of the country concept album (Nelson's only Number 1 pop hit in Canada was a duet with Julio Iglesias, 'To All the Girls I've Loved Before', released in 1984).

Of course, the technique of telling stories through song had long been part of the Anglo-American ballad tradition, one of the main taproots of country music. In putting together *Red-Headed Stranger*, a meticulously crafted song cycle outlining the saga of a brokenhearted cowboy, Nelson stuck close to the traditional time limit of three minutes per song, alternating songs with shorter bits of material that established the narrative context (for example, dance music to give us the feeling of a turn-of-the-century saloon in Denver). The musical accompaniment—acoustic guitar, electric guitar, mandolin, piano, harmonica, electric bass, and drums—is strikingly spare and restrained, and some tracks use only acoustic guitar and piano (played by Nelson's sister). The jacket sleeve featured excerpts from the lyrics, accompanied by paintings of the red-headed stranger in the various scenarios portrayed by the songs.

The album opens with the song 'Time of the Preacher':

It was a time of the preacher, when the story began
Of a choice of a lady, and the love of a man
How he loved her so dearly, he went out of his mind
When she left him for someone that she'd left behind
He cried like a baby, and he screamed like a panther in the middle of the night
And he saddled his pony, and he went for a ride
It was a time of the preacher, in the year of '01
Now the preaching is over, and the lesson's begun.

In the next song, only a minute and a half in length, Nelson adopts the first-person voice of the jilted cowboy, who discovers his wife's infidelity—'*I couldn't believe it was true*'. This is followed by a reappearance of the 'Time of the Preacher' song, which functions throughout the album as a thematic refrain, connecting the various songs. As the story unfolds, we observe the red-headed stranger tracking down his wife and her lover, shooting them dead in a tavern, and riding off on his black stallion. As in rock concept albums based on a dramatic character—say, *The Rise and Fall of Ziggy Stardust and the Spiders from Mars*—the line dividing the fictional persona in the song and the musician who sings the song is thin indeed. The album cover of *Red-Headed Stranger* portrays Nelson in cowboy outfit, with a beard and long, ragged red-tinted hair, an image clearly intended to reinforce the long-time Nashville songwriter's public image as an outlaw musician.

with a black cowboy hat and a six-shooter. The commercial potential of the outlaw image was soon recognized by music publicists in Nashville, who lost no time turning it into a commercial term. The Outlaws were never a cohesive performing group; the label 'outlaw country' was basically a product of the record industry's search for a way to capitalize on the overlap between audiences for rock and country music.

In 1976, after musicians such as Willie Nelson and Waylon Jennings had begun to receive substantial radio airplay, RCA-Victor released a compilation of their early 1970s recordings entitled *Wanted: The Outlaws*. This LP included a mix of material, ranging from a version of the country music classic 'T for Texas', first recorded under the title 'Blue Yodel' by Jimmie Rodgers in 1927, to a cover of an Elvis Presley hit ('Suspicious Minds') and to Willie Nelson's humorous song 'Me and Paul', in which the country singer compares his problems on the road to those of rock star Paul

Listening To Townes Van Zandt's 'Pancho and Lefty' (1972)

The song 'Pancho and Lefty', performed by its composer, Townes Van Zandt (born 1944 in Fort Worth, Texas, died 1997), is an instructive example of the idiosyncratic sensibility of much progressive country. Van Zandt was a singer-songwriter who became a cult hero of the progressive country movement. Though Van Zandt never placed a record on the country Top 40 charts, his 15 LPs became underground classics, and his songs were covered by prominent country musicians. Willie Nelson and Merle Haggard, for instance, took a version of 'Pancho and Lefty' to the top of the country charts in 1983.

Van Zandt's performance of 'Pancho and Lefty', from his 1972 LP *The Late, Great Townes Van Zandt*, is typical of his work: a spare, unpolished vocal style, with guitar accompaniment that often uses more complex harmonies than are typical in country music. The use of Mexican mariachi-style trumpets at some points in the arrangement evokes the story's location, near the Rio Grande River. In structural terms, this song fits within the European-derived ballad tradition that was such an important influence on early country music. More specifically, 'Pancho and Lefty' evokes an old Spanish ballad tradition that took root in Mexico, where it developed into a genre known as the *corrido*. Typical *corridos* exhibit the familiar ballad form, a series of four-line stanzas that tell a story about famous heroes and villains, historical events or tragic romances, sung to a repeated melody and interrupted at regular intervals by a chorus.

Since the very beginnings of recorded country music, songwriters have drawn on the themes and images of the American cowboy ballad, and the Mexican *corrido*, in creating their stories of the exploits of heroes and outlaws along the Rio Grande. In a manner typical of progressive country songwriters, however, Van Zandt manages to put some new twists into an old form. The tale of Pancho and Lefty begins with a four-line stanza that functions as a framing device, in which the singer seems to be addressing one of the characters in the story in a direct, second-person voice:

> *Livin' on the road my friend, was*
> *gonna keep you free and clean*
> *Now you wear your skin like iron,*
> *and your breath's as hard as kerosene.*
> *You weren't your mama's only boy,*
> *but her favorite one it seems*
> *She began to cry when you said*
> *good-bye, and sank into your*
> *dreams.*

Van Zandt then sinks into the typical third-person voice of the ballad singer, becoming an observer recounting a sequence of events. In a series of carefully constructed stanzas he describes the outlaw team of Pancho and Lefty, the former a young Mexican bandit who dies at the beginning of the story, the latter his Anglo accomplice. Through a series of misfortunes, Lefty ends up in a flophouse in Cleveland, Ohio, wasting away as an old man.

> *Well the poets tell how Pancho fell,*
> *and Lefty's living in a cheap hotel*
> *The desert's quiet and Cleveland's*
> *cold, so the story ends we're told*
> *Pancho needs your prayers it's true,*
> *but save a few for Lefty, too*
> *He just did what he had to do, and*
> *now he's growing old.*

This is not the usual fate of outlaw heroes in the ballad tradition, who typically either meet their end in a hail of bullets or, through sheer wits, manage to

escape to fight another day. As Van Zandt moves through the song, it becomes increasingly apparent that Lefty isn't such a hero after all, a point driven home by the chorus, which describes the 'kindness' shown Lefty by the federal marshals (*Federales*), who were his natural enemies:

> *And all the Federales say they could*
> *have had him any day*
> *They only let him hang around out*
> *of kindness, I suppose.*

The chorus becomes the object of a subtle manipulation, in which just a few words are altered each time through. After we find out that Lefty has fled to Ohio, the chorus informs us that the *Federales* claim to have purposefully allowed the pitiful sap to escape with his life, out of kindness. By the end of the song, the federal marshals, too, have aged, and the chorus takes on an ironic tone:

> *A few grey Federales say they could*
> *have had him any day*
> *They only let him go so wrong out of*
> *kindness, I suppose.*

In the end, the listener is left uncertain—did Lefty betray his Mexican partner, leaving him at the mercy of the federal marshals, or is the whole story simply the dream-like fantasy of a lonely old man, as the first stanza suggests?

Townes Van Zandt died prematurely at the age of 52. However, his songs—which combine the straightforwardness of traditional country music with the poetic subtlety of singer-songwriters such as Bob Dylan—have inspired country and rock musicians ranging from Lyle Lovett to Neil Young.

McCartney. The album was a huge success—it reached the Top 10 on *Billboard*'s Top LPs chart, sold well in Canada (though it didn't chart), soon became the first platinum country music LP, and eventually sold over two million copies. Though the Outlaws—like most 'alternative' music movements—had a commercial dimension, they did represent a heartfelt rebellion against the conservatism of the country music establishment. Their approach found common ground in the past and the future of country music, managed to challenge—however briefly—country pop's hold on the charts in the mid-1970s, and paved the way for later alternative country artists such as k.d. lang, Dwight Yoakam, and Lyle Lovett.

▌'I Shot the Sheriff': The Rise of Reggae

Reggae, a potent mixture of Caribbean folk music and North American rhythm and blues, was the first style of the rock era to originate in the so-called Third World. The popularity of reggae in North America may be related both to earlier 'exotic' music crazes—the Argentine tango and the Cuban rumba, for instance—and to the coming world beat movement of the 1980s and 1990s.

Born in the impoverished shantytowns of Kingston, Jamaica, reggae first became popular in North America in 1973, after the release of the Jamaican film *The Harder They Come* and its soundtrack album. During the 1970s a handful of Jamaican musicians—notably Bob Marley and Jimmy Cliff—achieved a measure of commercial success in North America and in England, while numerous American, Canadian, and British rock musicians—including Eric Clapton, Bruce Cockburn, Nana McLean, Paul Simon, the Police, Elvis Costello, and, more recently, Sinead O'Connor—found inspiration (and profit) in the style. In addition, as we shall see later in this chapter, rap music of the 1980s was strongly influenced by Jamaican 'dub', a branch of the reggae tradition in which verbal performances are improvised over pre-recorded musical accompaniments.

Reggae music was itself a complex composite of influences, only some of them from the rock tradition. The history of reggae thus gives us an opportunity to examine not only the burgeoning interest of North American popular musicians in 'world music', but also the influence of rock forms on local music elsewhere—a fascinating story that, for better or worse, mainly lies outside the scope of this book.

The roots of reggae lie in the Jamaican equivalent of country music, a genre called mento. Mento, a mixture of Jamaican folksongs, church hymns, sailors' shanties, and Cuban influences, arose in rural Jamaica during the late nineteenth century. By World War II, mento had lost its popularity among the thousands of young Jamaicans who were migrating to the capital city of Kingston. In fact, today's tourist resorts on Jamaica's north coast are among the last places where mento may still be heard. During the 1940s and early 1950s dance bands, mainly from the United States—including those of Benny Goodman, Count Basie, and Glenn Miller—became popular in the dance halls of Kingston. Jamaican musicians formed what they called 'road bands', local bands that toured from town to town, playing public dances.

Starting in the 1950s, rhythm and blues—broadcast by powerful radio stations in Miami and New Orleans—became popular among youth in Kingston. Migrant Jamaican workers in Costa Rica, Panama, Cuba, Canada, and the United States brought back the hit records of R&B artists such as Louis Jordan and Fats Domino, and local entrepreneurs set up portable **sound systems** to play R&B records for dances and parties, driving the road bands out of business. In the 1960s a shortage of records from Canada and the US encouraged some sound system operators to set up their own recording studios in Kingston. Some of these men—including Sir Coxsone Dodd, Lee 'Scratch' Perry, and Leslie Kong—became leading producers in the Jamaican popular music business and extremely significant 'dub plate' producers in their own right.

During the 1960s a succession of new popular genres emerged out of the intersection of Jamaican folk music and rhythm and blues. The first of these was ska—an onomatopoeic term derived from the style's typical sharp offbeat accents. The instrumentation of ska bands was derived from R&B, if not the jump blues style per se, with a rhythm section of piano, bass, guitar, and drums and a horn section including some combination of brass instruments and saxophones. Ska music was usually played at fast tempos, with the bass playing a steady four-beat pattern and the piano, guitar, and drums emphasizing beats two and four. The singing on ska records was strongly influenced by R&B, ranging from rougher blues-influenced styles to romantic crooning. The biggest star of Jamaican ska was Don Drummond, a trombonist and leader of a band called the Skatalites. The Skatalites also worked as a studio band, backing many of the most popular singers of the time and exerting a substantial influence on the youth culture of Kingston, particularly when several members of the band joined the Rastafarian religious movement.

It is worth taking a moment here to discuss the Rastafarian movement, since it is such a prominent theme in reggae music. Rastafarianism was founded by Josiah Marcus Garvey (1887–1940), a Jamaican writer and political leader who inspired a 'Back to Africa' repatriation movement among black Americans in the 1920s. Before leaving Jamaica for the United States in 1916, Garvey wrote, 'Look to Africa for the crowning of a black king; he shall be the redeemer'—a phrase that was taken quite literally as prophecy by Garvey's followers. In 1930, when Haile Selassie ('Power of the Trinity') was crowned king of the African nation of Ethiopia, preachers in Kingston saw this as confirmation of Garvey's prediction and proceeded to scrutinize the Old Testament in search of passages that supported the authenticity of Selassie's divinity. The Rastafarians' reinterpretation of the Bible focused on passages that dealt with slavery, salvation, and the apocalyptic consequences that would eventually be visited upon oppressors (collectively referred to in the religion as 'Babylon'). Rastafarianism became associated with a unique set of cultural practices, including special terminology (for example, 'I-and-I' is substituted for 'we'), the use of marijuana (*ganja*) as a sacramental herb, and the wearing of a distinctive hairstyle called 'dreadlocks'.

The Rastafarian movement spread rapidly through an extensive network of neighbourhood churches and informal prayer meetings, where music and dance were used to 'give praise and thanks' (*satta amassanga*) and to 'chant down Babylon'. In the mountainous interior of Jamaica, where communities of escaped slaves called 'maroons' had been living since the nineteenth century, Rastafarian songs and chants were mixed with an African-derived style of drumming called *burru*, creating a heavier, slower sound. This style in turn fed back into urban popular music, resulting around 1966 in an updated version of ska called *rock steady*. Rock steady was considerably slower in tempo than ska, reflecting the aforementioned influence of *burru* drumming, and some of its leading exponents—notably Alton Ellis, who had the first big rock steady hit in 1966—began to record songs with social and political content.

The main patrons of rock steady were the Rude Boys, a social category that included anyone against 'the system'—a category that included urban Rastas, thugs hired by competing political parties, and lower-class youth generally. An informal and unruly Jamaican youth movement—halfway between the Black Panthers and urban street gangs in the United States—Rude Boys increasingly came into conflict with the Jamaican police, and media coverage of their exploits helped to create the image of romantic outlaw heroes. The film that helped initiate reggae music's popularity in the North America, *The Harder They Come* (1972), was in fact a thinly disguised biography of one such 'ghetto hero': Vincent Martin, a.k.a. Rhygin', a Jamaican outlaw of the early 1960s. Bob Marley's song 'I Shot the Sheriff' (see box) is about a young man who is persecuted by the local sheriff and then accused of murdering both the sheriff and his deputy in cold blood.

Under the influence of Rastafarian religiosity and Rude Boy street politics, a new genre called reggae took shape in Kingston during the late 1960s. The word 'reggae' was derived from 'raggay', a Kingston slang term meaning 'raggedy, everyday stuff'. In musical terms reggae was a further extension of the evolution from ska to rock steady. In reggae music the tempo was slowed down even further, creating wide spaces between notes, allowing the music to breathe and emphasizing the polyrhythmic heritage of Afro-Jamaican traditions. Each instrument in a reggae band has its own carefully defined role to play. The heart of reggae music consists of 'riddims', interlocking rhythmic patterns played by the guitar, bass, and drums. The guitar often plays short, choppy chords on the second and fourth beat of each measure, giving the music a bouncy, up-and-down feeling. The bass–drum combination is the irreducible core of a reggae band, sometimes called the 'riddim pair'; the most famous 'riddim pairs' in all reggae remain the brothers Aston and Carlton Barrett, who played in Bob Marley's band, and Sly Dunbar and Robbie Shakespeare, who have appeared on literally hundreds of reggae recordings and on the LPs of rock artists such as Bob Dylan, Mick Jagger, and Peter Gabriel. This musical mixture was further enlivened by the influence of contemporary black popular music primarily from the US, especially the soul recordings of James Brown and Aretha Franklin, whose messages of 'black power' and personal empowerment undoubtedly resonated with listeners in Jamaica. Political messages were central to reggae music—while ska musicians of the early 1960s, like their American R&B counterparts, sang mainly about love and heartbreak, the most popular reggae artists focused their attention on issues such as social injustice and racism.

The film *The Harder They Come* featured reggae songs by a number of the most popular Jamaican musicians. The star of the film, and the vocalist on the title track of the soundtrack LP, was Jimmy Cliff (b. 1948). Like Ivan, the outlaw character he portrayed in the film, Cliff was only a teenager when he left the rural Jamaican town of St James for the city of Kingston. Cliff arrived in Kingston in 1962 and made his first record within a year. Working with the producer Leslie Kong, he recorded a series of Jamaican Top 10 hits during the mid-1960s. While performing at the 1964 World's Fair in New York City, Cliff met Chris Blackwell of the English independent label Island Records, who convinced him to move to London. After working as a backup singer and scoring a few hits on the European charts, Cliff returned to Jamaica in 1969 and recorded the song 'Many Rivers to Cross', which inspired the director Perry Henzel to offer him the lead role in *The Harder They Come*. Although the film did not reach the mass audience commanded by many Hollywood movies, it did create a devoted audience for reggae music in the United States, particularly among young, college-educated adults, who were attracted by the rebellious spirit of the music and its associations with Rastafarianism and *ganja* smoking. The film played for seven years at a movie theatre in Boston, Massachusetts, sustained mainly by the enthusiasm of that city's large student population.

Jimmy Cliff's 1972 recording of 'The Harder They Come' exemplifies the reggae style of the early 1970s. It features a moderate tempo, strong guitar chords on the second and fourth beats of each measure, R&B-influenced singing, and a gritty lyric about the individual's struggle against oppression:

I keep on fighting for the things I want
Though I know that when you're dead you can't
But I'd rather be a free man in my grave
Than living as a puppet or a slave
So as sure as the sun will shine
I'm gonna get my share now what is mine
And then the harder they come, the harder they fall
One and all

Although Cliff was the first Jamaican musician to gain recognition in North America—and though he actually hit the CHUM Top 10 two years before *The Harder They Come* was released stateside, with 'Wonderful World, Beautiful People' (Number 8 CHUM, 1970)—Cliff's contemporary Bob Marley (1945–81), leader of the Wailers, quickly surpassed every other reggae artist, including Cliff, in popularity. A national hero in his native Jamaica, Marley was reggae's most effective international ambassador. His songs of determination, rebellion, and faith, rooted in the Rastafarian belief system, found a worldwide audience that reached from America to Japan and from Europe to Africa. Through many of his songs, Marley proselytized the Rastafarian faith—in fact, a number of his songs denounce Christianity as deluded and damaging—and his records occupy a grey area somewhere between pop and liturgical. Consider the lyrics Marley penned to his now classic 'Get Up Stand Up':

Preacherman, don't tell me,
Heaven is over the earth.
I know you don't know
What life is really worth.
It's not all that glitters is gold;
Half the story has never been told:
So now you see the light—
Stand up for your rights . . .
Most people think
Great God will come from the skies,
Take away everything
And make everybody feel high.
But if you know what life is worth,
You will look for yours on earth!
And now you see the light,
You stand up for your rights!

The son of a British naval officer who deserted his family when Bob was six years old, Marley migrated to Kingston from the rural parish of St Ann at the age of 14. His early career reflects the economic precariousness of the music industry in a Third World country. After making a few singles for the Chinese-Jamaican producer Leslie Kong, Marley formed the Wailers in 1963 and signed with Sir Coxsone Dodd's studios. Following a long period with little financial success (including a year of factory work for Marley in Wilmington, Delaware), the Wailers signed with the producer Lee 'Scratch' Perry, a crucial dub pioneer, who added Aston and Carlton Barrett to the mix—a masterful bassist-and-drummer 'riddim pair'.

In 1972 Chris Blackwell, who had launched Jimmy Cliff's international career, signed Bob Marley and the Wailers to Island Records and advanced them the money to record at their independent Tuff Gong Studio in Jamaica. Marley's recognition abroad was boosted by the success of Eric Clapton's cover of 'I Shot the Sheriff', from the Wailers' second LP for Island Records (see below). The Wailers' first major concert in the United States took place in 1974 in Boston, where *The Harder They Come* enjoyed a high degree of popularity, especially with the city's sizable student population. Between 1975 and 1980 Marley recorded six gold LPs for Island Records, including *Rastaman Vibration*, which reached Number 8 on the *Billboard* Top LPs charts in 1976; Marley's only chart placement in Canada would not come until the posthumous 'Iron Lion Zion' peaked at Number 22 in 1992. Wounded in a politically motivated assassination attempt in 1976, Marley died of cancer in 1981, at the age of 36. His appeal and popularity, both in America and worldwide, has only grown in the years since his death: the 1984 LP compilation *Legend* has sold over eight million copies in the United States alone.

Bob Marley. © Michael Ochs
Archives/Corbis

Reggae in Canada and the Canadian Style

Although the majority of North American listeners became conscious of reggae as a distinctive musical style only in the mid- to late 1970s, with the steadily increasing popularity of Bob Marley and the Wailers, there are individual instances long before this of Jamaican music appearing on the CHUM charts. In fact, among the many imported hits during the British Invasion year of 1964 was a ska-flavoured recording by the Jamaican teenager Millie Small called 'My Boy Lollipop', which topped the CHUM charts in 1964. In 1968 Johnny Nash, an African-American pop singer who established a recording studio in Jamaica, had a Top 5 hit in Canada with the reggae-influenced 'Hold Me Tight'—though he likely remains best known for his recording of 'I Can See Clearly Now', which topped the CHUM charts in 1972—and 1969 and 1970 saw the North American success of two reggae records by Jamaican artists: 'Israelites' by Desmond Dekker and the Aces (Number 1 CHUM, 1969) and, as noted, 'Wonderful World, Beautiful People' by Jimmy Cliff (Number 8 CHUM, 1970).

Both Johnny Nash and Jimmy Cliff went on to bigger things in the early 1970s. Nash hit the Number 1 spot for four weeks in 1972 with his reggae-flavoured 'I Can See Clearly Now', which he wrote—as was also the case with 'Hold Me Tight'—but he assured a sense of Jamaican authenticity by arranging for members of the Wailers to provide his instrumental support on the track. He then followed this up with a

Top 10 cover version of Bob Marley's 'Stir It Up' (Number 8 CHUM, 1973). As for Jimmy Cliff, his starring role in the 1972 movie *The Harder They Come* introduced both him and the Jamaican music scene to a significant audience previously unaware of both. In a fine illustration of the reciprocal relationships that tend to characterize so much of pop music history, Cliff returned to the CHUM charts for the first time in many years, and hit the Top 20 for the first time, in the early 1990s with nothing other than his own cover of Nash's 'I Can See Clearly Now' (Number 18 pop, 1994), which was featured in *Cool Runnings*, the John Candy film about the Jamaican Olympic bobsled team.

We should also note the existence of a vibrant soul and reggae scene in Toronto during the late 1960s and early 1970s, which undoubtedly paved the way for the genre's widespread acceptance in Canada later in the decade. In fact, so cohesive was the Toronto reggae scene that critics coined the term 'Canadian Style' to describe the reggae music made there, which was generally marked by a pronounced melodicism and the conspicuous absence of confrontational lyrics, and was often made by racially integrated bands. Ska and rock steady groups such as the Rivals, the Sheiks, the Cougars, and the Cavaliers played nightclubs in Toronto that catered to the city's growing West Indian and Jamaican communities throughout the 1960s, including the WIF (West Indian Federation) Club, Club Jamaica, Tiger's Den, Blue Angel, and Club Blue Note's 'midnight floor show' on Yonge Street, where Eddie Spencer came to prominence performing songs such as 'If This Is Love (I'd Rather Be Lonely)' and 'You're So Good To Me Baby' (Spencer would eventually join the Skip Prokop-led jazz-rock combo Lighthouse later in the decade).

A number of reggae bands formed in Toronto in the early 1970s, and they began to make records for local imprints. Musicians such as Jackie Mittoo, Stranger Cole, Tony Eden, the Webber Sisters, and Joe Isaacs made records for labels such as Jerry Brown's Malton-based Summer Records, which debuted with the release of Johnnie Osbourne's 'Sun Rise' and 'Love Makes the World Go Round' (Osbourne would join Ishan People later in the decade). Based largely on the successes of these early bands and singers, a few reggae musicians began to record for 'major' labels in Canada later in the 1970s, including Toronto's Ishan People, who recorded for GRT in 1976 (the London, Ontario, label responsible for records by the likes of Lighthouse, Prism, Moe Berg, Klaatu, Ian Thomas, Dan Hill, Crowbar, and Thundermug during the late 1970s), Messenjah, the Sattalites, and Leroy Brown. At the same time, Leroy Sibbles—who had achieved stardom in Jamaica as lead singer of the Heptones in the late 1960s—moved to Toronto in 1971, where he pioneered a unique reggae–rock fusion on records for the Micron, Boots, A&M, and Attic labels. By the end of the decade, once the existence of a North American record-buying market for reggae music had been established without question (thanks largely to Bob Marley's global popularity), Canadian 'major' labels initiated regular releases of records by Canadian reggae musicians such as Nana McLean, Ital Groove, Winston Hewitt, and One Love.

The vibrancy of this music, and its importance to the development of the rock tradition in Canada (and to Canadian popular music in general), probably cannot be overestimated. Sadly, though, the movement's earliest moments were seldom documented. A recent compilation CD, entitled *Jamaica To Toronto: Soul Funk & Reggae 1967–1974*, has done much to rectify this situation, collecting together tracks by such Canadian Style pioneers as Jo-Jo and the Fugitives, Eddie Spencer, Jackie Mittoo, Lloyd Delpratt, Johnnie Osbourne, the Sheiks, the Cougars, Wayne McGhie and the Sounds of Joy, and others.

Listening To Bob Marley's and Eric Clapton's 'I Shot the Sheriff' (1973)

Surely the best-known cover version of any reggae number is Eric Clapton's million-selling version of Bob Marley's 'I Shot the Sheriff'—a Number 1 hit on both sides of the border in 1974, which appears on Clapton's Number 1 album from the same year, *461 Ocean Boulevard*. Clapton's name on the label, along with his easy-going vocal delivery, doubtless helped to propel the single to the top of the charts. Indeed, considered in terms of the song's lyrics and music, 'I Shot the Sheriff' seems an unlikely 1970s hit. It is clearly a political song, but for anyone not thoroughly versed in contemporary Jamaican politics, its precise significance is difficult to grasp. This is an example of a 'coded' lyric—a phenomenon also found in **blues** lyrics—that communicates something extra to members of a specific group who are attuned to its message. Furthermore, the music of the song is appropriately dark in colour, with a predominance of minor chords.

It is instructive to compare Clapton's version with Bob Marley's own recording of 'I Shot the Sheriff', which may be found on the 1973 album *Burnin'* and on the numerous compilations issued since Marley's death in 1981. Marley's version

sounds much more insistently rhythmic and intense than Clapton's. Actually, Marley's tempo is only a hairbreadth faster than Clapton's, but the greater prominence of both bass and percussion in Marley's recording emphasizes the distinctive 'riddims' of Jamaican reggae and creates the illusion of a considerably faster performance, and the record closes with just the bass guitar and drums—the heartbeat of reggae—played by the riddim pair of Aston and Carlton Barrett. In addition, the high range of the Wailers' voices creates a strong element of urgency that is lacking in the Clapton recording. Marley and the Wailers add small but effective and apparently spontaneous variations in the vocal lines of the successive verses of the song, giving a sense of familiarity and freedom with the material that also has no real counterpart in the cover version. And there is, of course, no substitute for the Jamaican patois—a dialect of English with strong African influence—in Marley's original: '*Ev'ry day the bucket a-go-a well; one day the bottom a-go drop out.*' It is to Clapton's credit, however, that he doesn't even try to mimic Marley's rendition of a Jamaican proverb about the eventual triumph of the oppressed. Instead, Clapton sings '*every day the bucket goes to the well, but one day the bottom will drop out.*'

In sum, Clapton made an effective 1970s pop single out of Marley's 'I Shot the Sheriff' by smoothing out its sound. The traditional rock backbeat (emphasizing with the drums the second and fourth beats of the four-beat measures), clearly heard on Clapton's recording, ties it to the rock mainstream, while the basic rhythmic character of Marley's version is decidedly outside that mainstream (with all the beats much more evenly emphasized, and the **syncopated** patterns imposed over them brought strongly forward). It may seem ironic to find a hero of the 1960s counterculture like Eric Clapton cast in the role of mainstream popularizer for a new marginal music in the 1970s, but the rock tradition is full of such ironies, as one decade's rebels become the next decade's establishment.

▌'Psycho Killer': The Dawn of Punk and New Wave

During the 1970s the first 'alternative' movements emerged within rock music. While rock—as opposed to the earlier rock 'n' roll—had begun as a vital part of the 1960s counterculture, by 1975 it had come perilously close to occupying the centre of popular taste—a development that left some young musicians feeling that the genre's rebellious, innovative potential had been squandered by pampered, pretentious rock stars and the major record companies that promoted them. The golden age of punk rock—a 'back-to-basics' rebellion against the perceived artifice and pretension of corporate rock music—lasted from around 1975 to 1978, but both the musical genre and the sensibility with which it was associated continue to exert a strong influence today on alternative rock musicians. New wave music, which developed alongside punk rock, approached the critique of corporate rock in a more self-consciously artistic and experimental manner (the term 'new wave' was soon picked up by record companies, which began using it in the late 1970s to refer to pop-influenced performers such as Blondie, the Cars, and, eventually, Platinum Blonde). Although the initial energy of the punk and new wave scene was largely expended by the start of the 1980s, young musicians inspired by the raw energy and minimalism of this movement went on to create distinctive regional punk and hardcore punk 'scenes' in Los Angeles, Minneapolis, Seattle, Vancouver, Montreal, and elsewhere.

Punk was as much a cultural style—an attitude defined by a rebellion against authority and a deliberate rejection of middle-class values—as it was a musical genre. The contrarian impulse of punk culture is evoked (and parodied) in the song 'I'm Against It', recorded by the Ramones in 1978:

I don't like sex and drugs
I don't like waterbugs
I don't care about poverty
All I care about is me

I don't like playing Ping-Pong
I don't like the Viet Cong
I don't like Burger King
I don't like anything

Well I'm against it, I'm against it

In its automatic gainsaying of everything from sex and drugs to the Viet Cong and Burger King, this song evokes the motorcycle gang leader played by Marlon Brando in the archetypal teen rebellion film *The Wild One* (1954). When asked by a young woman, 'What are you rebelling against?', the Brando character responds, 'Whaddaya got?'

Punk was, in fact, both the apotheosis and the ultimate exploitation of rock 'n' roll as a symbol of rebellion—a tradition that began in the 1950s with white teenagers gleefully co-opting the energy and overt sexuality of black rhythm and blues to annoy their parents, and that continued through the 1960s with songs like the Who's 1966 youth anthem 'My Generation' (*'Why don't you all just f-f-fade away?'*). To many of its fans, punk rock represented a turn towards the 'authentic' risk-taking spirit of early rock 'n' roll, and away from the perceived pomposity and self-conscious artistry of album-oriented rock. It is ironic, and it speaks to the contingency of the concept of 'authenticity' in popular music, that punk musicians chose early rock 'n' roll as their model of sincere musical expression, especially when just over a decade before, during the early 1960s, urban folk musicians clearly held rock 'n' roll in disdain and denounced the genre as the apotheosis of crass and manipulative commercialism.

Like all alternative styles of popular music, punk rock was full of contradictions. To begin with, if punk was explicitly against the standards of traditional commercial fashion, it was also a fashion system in its own right, with a very particular look: torn blue jeans, ripped stockings, outfits patched with ragged bits of contrasting materials, and, perhaps, a safety pin through the cheek. If some punk musicians framed their challenge to established authority in terms of progressive social values, others flirted with fascist imagery, attaching Nazi swastikas to their clothing and associating with the racist 'skinhead' movement. Many punk fans saw punk as a progressive response to the conservatism of the record industry. Yet the nihilism of much punk rock—the music's basic 'I don't give a fuck' posture—posed a crucial question that still resonates in today's alternative rock music: is it possible to make music that is 'authentic' or 'real' and at the same time loudly proclaim that you don't care about anything, including whether or not things are 'authentic' or 'real'?

In musical terms, punk rock turned progressive rock—with its artistic aspirations and corporate backing—on its head. As the drummer for the Ramones, widely regarded as the first punk rock band, put it:

We took the rock sound into a psychotic world and narrowed it down into a straight line of energy. In an era of progressive rock, with its complexities and counterpoints, we had a perspective of non-musicality and intelligence that took over from musicianship. (Laing, 1985: 23)

Punk was ultimately a stripped-down and often purposefully 'non-musical' version of rock music, in some sense a return to the wildness of early rock 'n' roll stars like Jerry Lee Lewis and Little Richard, but with lyrics that stressed the ironic or dark dimensions of human existence—drug addiction, despair, suicide, lust, and violence. As David Byrne, the leader of the new wave band Talking Heads, put it on the PBS television series *Rock & Roll*:

> Punk . . . was more a kind of do-it-yourself, anyone-can-do-it attitude. If you only played two notes on the guitar, you could figure out a way to make a song out of that, and that's what it was all about.

Garage Bands: The Velvets, the Stooges, and the New York Dolls

Punk rock and its more commercial cousin, new wave, took shape in New York City during the mid-1970s. One of the predecessors of punk rock was an American musical institution called the garage band—typically a neighbourhood operation, made up of young men who played mainly for themselves, their friends, and the occasional high school dance. A few of these local groups went on to enjoy some commercial success, including the Los Angeles-based Standells (whose 'Dirty Water' was a Number 11 pop hit in 1966); the Mysterians, from the industrial town of Flint, Michigan (who took '96 Tears' to the top of the charts in the same year); and Portland's Kingsmen, best known for their cover version of the 1950s R&B song, 'Louie, Louie' (Number 2 pop in 1963). The rough-and-ready, do-it-yourself attitude of the garage bands—something akin to a rock 'n' roll-based folk music movement—paved the way for punk rock.

Three groups, none of them very successful in commercial terms, are frequently cited as ancestors of 1970s punk music, and of later genres such as new wave, hardcore, industrial, and alternative rock: the Velvet Underground, the Stooges, and the New York Dolls. The Velvet Underground, a New York group, was promoted by the pop art superstar Andy Warhol, who painted the famous cartoon-like image of a banana on the cover of their first LP. Their music was rough-edged and chaotic, extremely loud and deliberately anti-commercial, and the lyrics of their songs focused on topics such as sexual deviancy, drug addiction, violence, and social alienation. The leaders of the Velvet Underground were singer and guitarist Lou Reed—who had worked previously as a pop songwriter in a Brill Building-style 'music factory' for Pickwick Records—and John Cale, a viola player active in the avant-garde art music scene in New York, who introduced experimental musical elements into the mix, including electronic noise and recorded industrial sounds.

If the Velvet Underground represented the self-consciously experimentalist roots of 1970s new wave music, the Stooges, formed in Ann Arbor, Michigan, in 1967, were the working-class, motorcycle-riding, leather-jacketed ancestors of punk rock. The lead singer of the Stooges, Iggy Stooge (a.k.a. Iggy Pop, James Osterburg), was famous for his outrageous stage performances, which included flinging himself into the crowd, cutting himself with beer bottles, and rubbing himself with raw meat and peanut butter. Guitarist Ron Asheton has described the Stooges' approach:

> Usually we got up there and jammed one riff and built into an energy freak-out, until finally we'd broken a guitar, or one of my hands would be twice as big as the other and my guitar would be covered in blood. (Palmer, 1995: 263)

The Stooges' eponymous first album (1969), produced by the Velvet Underground's John Cale, created a devoted if small national audience for the Stooges' demented garage band sound. A good example of the sensibility that underlay much of the Stooges' work—the depression of unemployed Michigan youth caught in the middle of a severe economic recession—is the song '1969', which evokes a world light years distant from the utopianism of the hippie movement and the Woodstock festival, held that same summer:

> *Well it's 1969 OK all across the USA*
> *It's another year for me and you*
> *Another year with nothing to do*
> *Last year I was 21 I didn't have a lot of fun*
> *And now I'm gonna be 22 I say oh my and a boo-hoo*
> *Another year with nothing to do*
> *It's 1969, 1969, 1969, 1969, 1969, baby*

Another band that exerted a major influence on the musical and visual style of the punk rock movement was the New York Dolls, formed in New York City in 1971. Dressed in fishnet stockings, bright red lipstick, cellophane tutus, ostrich feathers, and army boots, the all-male Dolls were an American response to the English glam rock movement, typified by the reigning master of rock gender bending, David Bowie (see Chapter 5). Their professional career began inauspiciously—at a Christmas party in a seedy welfare hotel in Manhattan—but by late 1972 they had built a small and devoted following. Although the New York Dolls soon succumbed to drug and alcohol abuse, they did establish certain core features of punk 'anti-fashion' and helped to create a new underground rock music scene in New York City.

CBGB & OMFUG

The amateur energy of garage band rock 'n' roll, the artsy nihilism of the Velvet Underground, the raw energy and abandon of the Stooges, and the 'anti-fashion' of the New York Dolls converged in the mid-1970s in New York City's burgeoning club scene. The locus of this activity was a converted folk music club called CBGB & OMFUG—that is, 'Country, Bluegrass, Blues & Other Music for Urban Gourmandizers'—located in the run-down Bowery area of Manhattan. The first rock musician to perform regularly at CBGB was Patti Smith (b. 1946), a New York-based poet, journalist, and singer who had been experimenting with combining the spoken word and rock accompaniment. In 1975 Smith began a stint at CBGB, establishing a beachhead for punk and new wave bands, and signed a contract with Arista, a new label headed by Clive Davis, the former head of Columbia Records. Her critically acclaimed album *Horses* reached Number 47 on the *Billboard* charts in 1976. Other influential groups who played at CBGB during the mid-1970s included Television—whose lengthy instrumental improvisations were inspired by the Velvet Underground and avant-garde jazz saxophonist Albert Ayler—Blondie, and the Voidoids, featuring the alienated lyrics and howling voice of lead singer Richard Hell, one of the original members of Television.

The Ramones

The first bonafide punk rock band was the Ramones, formed in 1974 in New York City. The Ramones' high-speed, energetic, and extremely loud sound influenced English punk groups such as the Sex Pistols and the Clash, and also became a blue-

The Ramones: Johnny, Dee Dee, Tommy, and Joey. Frank Driggs Collection.

print for hardcore punk bands in the later 1970s and early 1980s. Although they projected a street-tough image, all of the band's members were from middle-class families in the New York City borough of Queens. The band—not a family enterprise, despite their stage names—consisted of Jeffrey Hyman (a.k.a. Joey Ramone) on vocals, John Cummings (Johnny Ramone) on guitar, Douglas Colvin (Dee Dee Ramone) on bass, and Tom Erdelyi (Tommy Ramone) on drums. The band's first manager, Danny Fields, had previously worked with the Stooges and Lou Reed, and, thus, had a good sense of the Ramones' potential audience.

Taking the stage in blue jeans and black leather jackets—a look calculated to evoke the sneering, rebellious ethos of 1950s rock 'n' rollers—the Ramones began playing regularly at CBGB in 1975. By the end of the year they had secured a recording contract with Sire Records, an independent label that signed a number of early punk groups. Their eponymous debut album was recorded in 1976 for just over $6,000, an incredibly small amount of money in an era of expensive and time-consuming studio sessions. The album gained some critical attention and managed to reach Number 111 on the *Billboard* album charts.

Later that year the Ramones staged a British Invasion in reverse. Their concerts in English cities, where their records had already created an underground sensation, were attended by future members of almost every important British punk band, including the Sex Pistols (see box), the Clash, Siouxsie Sioux and the Banshees, and the Damned. In 1977 the Ramones scored a UK Top 40 hit with the song 'Sheena Is a Punk Rocker' (Number 81 in the US; failed to chart in Canada), which announced that the centre of the rock 'n' roll universe had shifted from the beaches of southern California to the lower east side of Manhattan:

Well the kids are all hopped up and ready to go
They're ready to go now
They've got their surfboards
And they're going to the discotheque au go go
But she just couldn't stay
She had to break away
Well New York City really has it all
Oh yeah, oh yeah!

Sheena is a punk rocker, Sheena is a punk rocker, Sheena is a punk rocker now!

The Ramones' music reflected their origins as a garage band made up of neighbourhood friends. As the guitarist, Johnny Ramone, phrased it in an interview with the popular music scholar Robert Palmer:

I had bought my first guitar just prior to starting the Ramones. . . . It was all very new; we put records on, but we couldn't figure out how to play the songs, so we decided to start writing songs that were within our capabilities. (Palmer, 1995: 274)

These songs had catchy, pop-inspired melodies, were played at extremely fast tempos, and generally lasted no more than two and a half minutes. In live performances, the Ramones managed to squeeze 12 or 13 songs into a half-hour set. The band's raw, hard-edged sound was anchored by a steady barrage of notes, played on drums, bass, and guitar. Johnny Ramone rarely, if ever, took a guitar solo, but this makes sense when you consider the band's technical limitations (an inability to perform such solos anyway) and the aesthetic goal of the music (a rejection of the flashy virtuosity of progressive rock music, with its extended and sometimes self-indulgent solos).

The song 'I Wanna Be Sedated', from the band's fourth album, *Road to Ruin* (1978), is a good example of the Ramones' style, and of their mordant—one is tempted to say twisted—sense of humour:

> *Twenty-twenty-twenty-four hours to go, I wanna be sedated*
> *Nothin' to do and nowhere to go-o-o, I wanna be sedated*
> *Just put me in a wheelchair, get me to the show*
> *Hurry hurry hurry, before I gotta go*
> *I can't control my fingers, I can't control my toes*
> *Oh no no no no no*
>
> *Ba-ba-bamp-ba ba-ba-ba-bamp-ba, I wanna be sedated*
> *Ba-ba-bamp-ba ba-ba-ba-bamp-ba, I wanna be sedated*

The song text's images of drug-induced insanity—and its putative antidote, drug-induced paralysis—are juxtaposed with a catchy pop melody and Beach Boys-like chorus, a combination that affirms Joey Ramone's early description of the band's style as 'sick bubblegum music'.

It is, in fact, hard to know how seriously to take the Ramones. Although they played alongside self-consciously 'cutting-edge' bands like the Patti Smith Group and Television, recorded with such pop luminaries as Phil Spector, and scored a number of Top 40 singles both in North America and in England, the Ramones identified themselves as no more than a band that was 'able to just play and be song-oriented and sound great, people who play real rock 'n' roll.' Nonetheless, some of their recordings did provide grim 'news flashes' on the facts of life in many working-class and middle-class homes during a period of severe economic recession. The song 'I Wanted Everything' (1978) is a kind of punk counterpart to Merle Haggard's hardcore country song, 'If We Make It through December' (1973), sung, however, by a dispossessed son rather than a struggling father. The stark realism of this tale of a good boy gone wrong is reminiscent of the work of Bruce Springsteen throughout the decade, who is often regarded as a working-class rock 'n' roll hero of the 1980s (see Chapter 7). In any event, this social realism suggests that New York City punk rock was not a totally nihilistic movement, despite its makers' loud claims to the contrary.

'The Death of Rock 'n' Roll': The Sex Pistols

We have already mentioned the impression made by the Ramones on musicians in the United Kingdom—an 'American Invasion' that began some 12 years after the Beatles stormed New York City. The English stream of punk rock bubbled up during the summer of 1976, which was an unusually hot summer and a high point of unemployment, inflation, and racial tension in cities like London, Birmingham, Manchester, and Liverpool. In England, more than in North America, punk rock was associated with a mainly white working-class youth subculture. More explicitly political and less artsy than some of the New York City bands, groups like the Sex Pistols, the Clash, and the Damned succeeded in outraging the British political establishment and the mainstream media while achieving commercial success in the late 1970s.

The most outrageous—and therefore most famous—punk band was the Sex Pistols, formed in 1975 in London. They were the creation of Malcolm McLaren, co-owner, with Vivanne Westwood, of a London 'anti-fashion' boutique called Sex, which specialized in leather and rubber clothing. McLaren had begun his career in the music business in 1974, when he managed unsuccessfully the short-lived New York Dolls. Upon his return to London, McLaren conceived the idea of a rock 'n' roll band that would subvert the pop music industry and horrify England's staid middle class, while simultaneously advertising his and Westwood's designer clothes (the name 'Sex Pistols' was, in fact, consciously chosen to echo the name of McLaren's store). Glen Matlock (bass), Paul Cook (drums), and Steve Jones (guitar) were regu-

The Sex Pistols. Frank Driggs Collection.

lar customers at the shop, and they were looking for a singer. McLaren introduced them to John Lydon, a young man who hung around listening to the jukebox at Sex and who had never sung in public before. (Lydon's inconsistent approach to personal hygiene led Steve Jones to christen him Johnny Rotten, a stage name that stuck.) The Sex Pistols got their first gigs by showing up and posing as the opening band. Given the nature of Johnny Rotten's stage act—sneering and screaming obscenities at the audience, commanding them to applaud and throwing beer on them when they didn't—it is perhaps not surprising that they were banned from many nightclubs.

The trajectory of this band's rapid ascent and implosion is complex, and we can present only a summary here. EMI Records, England's biggest and most conservative label, signed the Sex Pistols for around $60,000 in 1976, releasing their first single, 'Anarchy in the UK', in December. The single—a straightforward bubblegum pop song produced by ex-Beatles engineer Chris Thomas—was a Top 40 hit in the UK, but it was withdrawn from record shops after Rotten uttered an obscenity during a television interview. At an annual meeting of shareholders in December 1976, the chairman of EMI, Sir John Read, made the following statement (as recorded in the Report of the EMI General Meeting, 7 Dec. 1976):

> Sex Pistols is the only 'punk rock' group that EMI Records currently has under direct recording contract and whether EMI does in fact release any more of their records will have to be very carefully considered. I need hardly add that we shall do everything we can to restrain their public behaviour, although this is a matter over which we have no real control.

The resulting uproar caused EMI to terminate the Sex Pistols' contract in January 1977, and all but five of 21 dates on a planned concert tour of the UK were promptly cancelled. In March, bassist Glen Matlock was replaced by John Ritchie, a non-musician friend of John Lydon who went by the stage name Sid Vicious, and he learned to play the bass during live performances. The American label A&M Records then signed the Pistols for over $200,000, only to fire them the very next week! In May 1977, Virgin Records signed the band and released their second single, 'God Save the Queen (It's a Fascist Regime)'—just in time for the Queen's Silver Jubilee celebrations in England. Despite being banned from airplay, the song went to Number 2 (cited as a blank on the UK charts). The band was featured in a 1978 film called *The Great Rock 'n' Roll Swindle*, a title that some critics thought captured perfectly the essence of the band's exercise in manipulation. The Sex Pistols broke up that same year, during their only US tour—a tour undertaken to support the release of their only studio album, *Never Mind the Bollocks, Here's the Sex Pistols* (1977). In 1979 Sid Vicious was imprisoned in New York on charges of stabbing his girlfriend to death—notorious rock groupie Nancy Spungen—and he died of a heroin overdose while out on bail. In 1986, the surviving members of the group sued Malcolm McLaren for cheating them out of royalties and were awarded around $1.5 million. Though they did not represent 'the death of rock 'n' roll', the Sex Pistols did manage to do away with themselves quite efficiently.

New Wave: The Talking Heads

If the Ramones and the Sex Pistols epitomized punk rock's connections to the rebellious energy of early rock 'n' roll, another band, the Talking Heads, represented the more self-consciously artistic and exploratory side of the alternative rock scene of the mid-1970s. The Talking Heads was formed in 1974 by David Byrne (born in Scotland in 1952), Chris Frantz, and Tina Weymouth, who met as art students at the Rhode Island School of Design. They first appeared at CBGB in 1975 as the opening act for the Ramones, though they attracted a somewhat different audience, made up of college students, artists, and music critics. In 1976 they signed a recording contract with Sire Records, and their first album, *Talking Heads: 77*, achieved critical acclaim and broke into the Top 100 on the *Billboard* and *RPM* album charts.

The band's style reflected their interest in an aesthetic called minimalism, which stresses the use of combinations of a limited number of basic elements—colours, shapes, sounds, or words. This approach was popular in the New York art music scene of the 1960s and 1970s, as represented in the work of composers such as Steve Reich, Terry Riley, La Monte Young, and Philip Glass, who made use of simple musical patterns, repeated and combined in various ways. The Talking Heads' instrumental arrangements fused this approach with the interlocking, riff-based rhythms pioneered by African-American popular musicians, particularly James Brown (see the discussion of funk music below). Clarity is another important aspect of the minimalist aesthetic, and the Talking Heads' songs were generally quite simple in structural terms, with strong pop hooks and contrasting sections marked off by carefully arranged changes in instrumental texture.

In their visual presentation and stage demeanour, the Talking Heads were from another universe than the other CBGB bands. They dressed in slacks, sweaters, and vests, projecting the image of cerebral but nerdy college students. David Byrne's stage presence was described by reviewer Michael Aron for *Rolling Stone* magazine (17 Nov. 1977):

Listening To the Talking Heads' 'Psycho Killer' (1977)

The centre of attention on most Talking Heads recordings was David Byrne's trembling, high-pitched voice and his eclectic songwriting. Byrne often delivered his lyrics in a nervous, almost schizophrenic stream-of-consciousness voice, creating something like overheard fragments from a psychiatrist's office. A good example of this approach—as well as the only single from the Heads' first LP to appear on the singles charts (peaking at Number 92)—was the song 'Psycho Killer', inspired by Norman Bates, the psychotic murderer in Alfred Hitchcock's film *Psycho*. Although it now seems like an ironic commentary on mass-media portrayals of 'the serial killer', this song had a darker, more immediate resonance when it was released in 1977 during the Son of Sam killing spree, when a deranged man shot 13 people in New York City.

The recording opens with Tina Weymouth's electric bass, playing a simple riff reminiscent of mid-1970s funk or disco music (see below). She is soon joined by two guitars, playing crisply articulated, interlocking chord patterns. David Byrne's voice enters in the thirteenth bar, enunciating the lyrics in a half-spoken, half-sung style, over a simple melody that uses only a few pitches and stays mainly on the tonic note. The first verse ('A^1') gives us a glimpse into the psychosis of the narrator:

> *I can't seem to face up to the facts*
> *I'm tense and nervous and I can't relax*
> *I can't sleep 'cause my bed's on fire*
> *Don't touch me I'm a real live wire*

This verse is followed by two statements of the chorus ('B'), which references the title of the song, dips abruptly and somewhat schizophrenically into a second language (French), and ends with a stuttered warning to the listener:

> *Psycho Killer, Quest-ce que c'est*
> *[What is it?]*
> *Fa fa fa fa fa fa fa fa fa far better*
> *Run run run run run run run away*

The chorus blends into a four-bar vocal interlude, with Byrne's voice leaping up an octave and emitting a distressed 'Ay yai yai yai', and a two-bar instrumental section that re-establishes the basic groove. In the second verse ('A^2'), Byrne shifts from singing to speech, becoming more agitated as he expresses his anger at people who talk a lot,

despite having nothing to say, and at his own inability to communicate with others:

> *You start a conversation, you can't even finish it.*
> *You're talking a lot, but you're not saying anything.*
> *When I have nothing to say, my lips are sealed.*
> *Say something once, why say it again?*

The chorus ('B') is heard two more times, followed by the interlude, and then by a new section ('C'), in which Byrne's character struggles to confess his crime in an awkward, strangled variant of French:

> *Ce que jai fais, ce soir la [The things I did on that night]*
> *Ce qu'elle a dit, ce soir la [The things she said on that night]*
> *Realisant mon espoir [Realizing my hope]*
> *Je me lance vers la gloire ... Okay [I throw myself towards glory . . . Okay]*

Eventually Byrne switches back into English, focusing obsessively on a single pitch and revealing more of his character's motivation for committing an unspecified though presumably horrific act:

> *We are vain and we are blind*
> *I hate people when they're not polite*

After final repetitions of the 'Psycho Killer' chorus ('B') and interlude, the band moves into a concluding 24-bar instrumental section (or coda), in which the basic groove is elaborated with distorted textures, wavering pitches on the guitars, strange vocal sounds from Byrne, and the panning of one guitar back and forth from left to right across the stereo spectrum, like the unanchored movement of a madman's thoughts. The last sound we hear is the squeal of feedback from one of the microphones, fading into silence and darkness.

Rather like David Bowie's Ziggy Stardust, the persona projected in 'Psycho Killer'—tongue-tied, nervous, emotionally distant, and obsessively intellectual—provided David Byrne with a durable, if sometimes unmalleable, stage persona. In a review of the 1984 Talking Heads concert film *Stop Making Sense*, one critic remarked on Byrne's ability to project 'a variant on his basic "Psycho Killer" self for each song; he demonstrates over and over that a public self is a Frankenstein self, a monster put together from bits and pieces of image tissue.' Throughout the late 1970s and 1980s Talking Heads recorded a series of critically acclaimed albums, most of which reached the Top 40 in Canada and the US, and achieved either gold or platinum status. The commercial success was linked to the accessibility of Talking Heads' music, which mixed in influences from rhythm and blues and funk music, and from West African music, with its complexly interlocking but catchy polyrhythmic patterns. David Byrne went on to become a major figure in the world beat movement of the 1980s and 1990s, introducing American audiences to recording artists from Africa, Brazil, and the Caribbean, among other places.

Listening Chart: 'Psycho Killer'

Music and lyrics by David Byrne, Chris Frantz, Tina Weymouth; performed by Talking Heads

FORM	LYRICS	DESCRIPTIVE COMMENTS
Intro (12) Instrumental		Bars 1–4: The electric bass plays a simple 2-bar pattern two times. Bars 5–8: The bass drum enters with a steady pulse, and electric guitar plays sustained chords. Bars 9–12: The second electric guitar enters, completing the basic groove—the two guitars play choppy, rhythmically interlocking chords (à la James Brown).
A¹ (8)	*I can't seem to . . .* *I'm tense and . . .* *I can't sleep . . .* *Don't touch me . . .*	Vocal enters; simple melody, centred on tonic pitch; instrumental accompaniment is based on interlocking riffs.

FORM	LYRICS	DESCRIPTIVE COMMENTS
(8)	*Psycho killer . . .* *Fa fa fa fa fa . . .* *Run run . . .* *Oh-oh-oh-oh . . .*	New harmonies, sustained chords on guitar mark beginning of chorus; bass and drums continue pulse.
(8)	*Lyrics repeat*	
Interlude (6)	*Oh . . . Ai yai yai yai yai (4)*	Byrne sings nonsense syllables, makes muffled vocal sounds in background.
Instrumental (2)		Bass, drums, and guitars play basic groove for last two bars.
A² (8)	*You start a conversation . . .* *You're talking a lot . . .* *When I have nothing to say . . .* *Say something once . . .*	Byrne moves from singing into speech mode; uses vocal quality to evoke psychotic persona.
(8)	*Psycho killer, Quest-ce que c'est?* *Fa fa fa fa fa fa fa fa fa fa far better* *Run run run run run run run away* *Oh-oh-oh-oh . . .*	
(8)	*Lyric repeats*	
Interlude (2)	*Oh . . .Ai yai yai yai yai*	First part only.
C (20)	*Ce que jai fais, ce soir la . . .* *Ce que jai fais, ce soir la . . .*	Rhythm section plays march-like pulse in unison for first 8 bars, while Byrne speaks the lyrics.
	Realisant mon espoir	Guitar plays sustained chords (4 bars).
	Je me lance, vers la glorie . . .Okay . . . *Ya ya ya ya ya ya ya . . .*	Rhythm section re-establishes basic groove (4 bars).
	We are vain and we are blind . . . *I hate people when they're not polite . . .*	Groove continues (4 bars).
(8)	*Psycho killer, Quest-ce que c'est?* *Fa fa fa fa fa fa fa fa fa fa far better* *Run run run run run run run away* *Oh-oh-oh-oh . . .*	
(8)	*Lyric repeats*	
Interlude (4)	*Oh . . .* *Ai yai yai yai yai*	Byrne sings nonsense syllables, makes vocal sounds in background.
Coda instrumental (3 x 8 = 24)		Bass, drums, and guitars elaborate on basic groove for last 24 bars, building in intensity. Last 8 bars feature stereo effect, guitar moving back and forth from left to right speaker.

Everything about him is uncool: his socks and shoes, his body language, his self-conscious announcements of song titles, the way he wiggles his hips when he's carried away onstage (imagine an out-of-it kid practicing Buddy Holly moves in front of a mirror).

Just as the punk rockers' anti-fashion became a new kind of fashion, so David Byrne's studied awkwardness established a new kind of cool, one still much in evidence on college campuses today, and on the pop charts with bands such as Weezer and the emerging subgenre of rap called 'Nerdcore'.

D.O.A.: Hardcore Punk in Canada

Though punk rock did not enjoy the same level of support in Canada as it did in parts of the American Northeast and in London, a number of extremely influential hardcore punk groups emerged in Canada during the later 1970s, particularly in Vancouver and Victoria. While Canadian post-punk and new wave bands—including Martha & the Muffins, Rough Trade (see Chapter 7), the Payola$, the Spoons, Rational Youth, Images in Vogue—consciously toed the generic line between pop and punk after punk's 'first wave' of success (c. 1975–8), west coast punk bands like D.O.A. and the Young Canadians created an intense, often abrasive, and always extremely fast variant of the genre. It was D.O.A., in fact, who dubbed the music they played 'hardcore' punk with the title of their second LP release, *Hardcore 81* (1981)—the title meant to signify, among other things, that the music generally featured faster tempos than preceding generations of punk music; an even more aggressive vocal delivery style, which verged on straightforward shouting; and a commitment to a life of poverty and squalor if that was all the material profit one's musical practice afforded—and the term was soon adopted across the continent. Elsewhere in the country, but particularly in the Toronto, Hamilton, and London areas, a number of hardcore-influenced punk and post-punk bands emerged at roughly the same time, including Teenage Head, the Viletones, the Diodes, the Forgotten Rebels, and the Demics. In the late 1970s and early 1980s, and back in Vancouver, Skinny Puppy and the Dayglo Abortions took the influence of hardcore with them into the industrial and alternative rock realms.

Established in 1978 by singer, guitarist, and songwriter Joey 'Shithead' Keighley, D.O.A. (Dead On Arrival) is likely the most influential hardcore punk band to emerge in Canada. The original lineup of D.O.A., which lasted until 1985, included Keighley alongside Randy Rampage on bass and Chuck Biscuits on drums. Biscuits, who left the group in 1985 and was replaced by Ken 'Dimwit' Montgomery and, later, Jon Card, is considered by many to be the pre-eminent percussion stylist of hardcore punk, having gone on from D.O.A. to work with the likes of the Circle Jerks, Social Distortion, Black Flag, and Danzig. (Biscuits also drummed for the Red Hot Chili Peppers in 1986, and was a sampled artist on Run D.M.C.'s 1988 release, 'Tough As Leather'.)

As noted, Keighley is often credited with having coined the title 'hardcore punk'. He is also credited with having made hardcore punk a viable arena for the negotiation of (obviously leftist) political values. Creating his own unique subgenre of songwriting, which he called 'instant singles' (a striking inversion of Phil Spector's 'teenage symphony' concept), Keighley released a number of songs about very specific events in Vancouver and abroad, almost as soon as they happened. The best known of these 'instant singles' include 'Right To Be Wild', 'Expo Hurts Everyone', 'Rich Bitch', 'War on 45', and, most famously, 'General Strike', which the band wrote as a direct missive against the Premier of BC in the early 1980s, Bill 'Mr Tough Guy' Bennett, who repealed a number of welfare policies and, in so doing, inspired the creation of Solidarity, a protest movement dedicated to, among other things, shutting the province down with a general strike ('God Giveth—Bill Tooketh' read a particularly popular picket sign at the time):

Shut it down!
We're tired, yeah, tired of workin'.
Yeah, workin' for nothin'.
We all want what we got comin'.
All we need is a break, come on take a break.
Everything is not all right
And there's no end in sight.
You can call it, what you like.
Come on, stand up for your rights.

Stand up, stand and unite.
It's time for a general strike.

We been out, breakin' our backs.
Been out workin' gettin' no slack.
All week long, payin' those bills.
That's just the people, that still got a job.
What about the rest of us, on the soupline.
Stand up, stand, stand and unite.
It's time for a general strike.
. . .
Stand up, stand and unite.
It's time for a general strike.
It's time!!!

Keighley also explicitly countered the emergence of fascist paraphernalia in the punk genre during the late 1970s in songs such as 'Nazi Training Camp':

You're at the cattle trough
Electric prod up your ass
But you seem to enjoy it
Swastikas are in your brain
Don't you see it?
Don't you see it?
Don't you see it?
This is a Nazi training camp!

I'm talking about the greedy sluts!
I'm talking about the nifty pricks!
It's your world I'm yellin' about!
Swastikas are in your brain!

Finally, revealing that annexation remained a strong source of anxiety for Canadian bands even in the later 1970s—well after the CanCon rules established a Canadian rock music industry—D.O.A. released '51st State' and, more recently, 'I Am Canadian'.

From their centre of operations during the late 1970s, the so-called Smilin' Buddha in Vancouver, D.O.A. adopted the hard-working, almost ascetic 'straight-edge' lifestyle popular with many hardcore bands, and they began excruciatingly long tours of Canada, the United States, and, starting in 1981, parts of Western Europe. ('Straight-edge' refers to a movement within the hardcore community in which adherents not only abstained from drinking, smoking, and ingesting other substances themselves, but often expected others to do the same.) A testament to their work ethic, the band reportedly performed in 105 cities within an eight-month period in 1985. A surprising move for some, D.O.A.'s decision to release covers of BTO's 'Takin' Care of Business' and the Poppy Family's 'Where Evil Grows' in the later 1980s brought the band increasing mainstream success, until their final 'farewell' concert at Vancouver's the Commodore in 1990. Since then, the band has periodically reformed to record and tour.

▌'Tear the Roof off the Sucker': Funk Music

If punk rock was a reaction against the pretentiousness of progressive rock and its multi-millionaire superstars hidden behind designer sunglasses, limousine windows, and mansion walls, *funk music* represented yet another back-to-basics impetus, specifically, the impulse to dance. Most album-oriented rock music was aimed at a predominantly white male audience and was designed for listening rather than dancing. While rock fans certainly engaged in free-form movement, the idea of organized social dancing was anathema to the 'do your own thing' ethos of the counterculture and to the 'high art' aspirations of some rock musicians. In urban black communities across North America, however, dance remained a backbone of social life, a primary means for transmitting traditional values and for generating a sense of novelty and excitement. And for the first time since the twist craze of the early 1960s, funk music—and its commercial offspring, disco—brought this intensive focus on dancing back into the pop mainstream.

The word 'funky'—probably derived from the (central African) BaKongo term *funki*, meaning 'healthy sweat'—was already in wide use by New Orleans jazz musicians during the first decade of the twentieth century. Today, 'funky' carries the same ambivalent meaning that it did a century ago: strong body odours (particularly those related to sex) and a quality of earthiness and authenticity quintessentially expressed in music. If the concept of soul symbolized the spiritual, uplifting side of black consciousness, then funk was its profane and decidedly down-to-earth counterpart.

By the early 1970s the term 'funk' was being used as a label for a genre of popular music characterized by emphatic, dance-oriented rhythms, catchy melodies, call-and-response exchanges between voices and instruments, and a heavy reliance on repeated, rhythmically interlocking patterns or 'grooves'. Most funk bands, echoing the instrumentation of James Brown's hits of the late 1960s, consisted of a rhythm section—i.e., guitar, keyboards, electric bass, and drums—and a horn section, which effectively functioned as part of the rhythm section and occasionally supplied jazz-influenced solos (this instrumentation once again demonstrates the centrality of the jump combo to R&B-derived dance music after World War II). Although funk music was initially targeted mostly at the predominantly urban black audience for soul music, funk groups such as Kool and the Gang, the Ohio Players, and Chic, for instance, were able to score several Number 1 pop hits in America and Top 20 chart placements in Canada during the 1970s. Funk represented a vigorous reassertion of 'functional' dance-oriented musical values in the face of soft soul's dominance of the R&B/pop crossover market, and it paved the way for the more commercialized sounds of disco music in the mid-1970s (see next section).

As we have suggested, James Brown was one of the prime inspirations for funk musicians. Even as he became an important funk musician himself in the 1970s, Brown continued to score successes with dance-oriented hits, including 'Super Bad' (Number 13 pop, Number 1 R&B in 1970), 'Hot Pants (She Got to Use What She Got to Get What She Wants)' (Number 15 pop, Number 1 R&B, 1971), 'Get on the Good Foot' (Number 18 pop, Number 1 R&B, 1972), and 'The Payback' (Number 26 pop, Number 1 R&B, 1974). Brown's ranking on the pop charts declined gradually throughout this period, however, in large part owing to competition from a new generation of musicians who played variations on the basic style he had established the decade before. This approach—the core of funk music—centred on the creation of a strong rhythmic momentum or groove, with the electric bass and bass drum often playing on all four main beats of the measure, the snare drum and other instruments playing equally strongly on the second and fourth beats (the backbeats), and interlocking ostinato patterns distributed among other instruments, including guitar, keyboards, and horns.

Another important influence on 1970s funk music was the group Sly and the Family Stone, an interracial and mixed gender 'psychedelic soul' band whose recordings bridged the gap between rock music and soul music. Sly Stone (Sylvester Stewart) was born in Dallas, Texas, in 1944 and moved to San Francisco with his family in the 1950s. He began his musical career at the age of four as a gospel singer, went on to study trumpet, music theory, and composition in college, and later worked as a disc jockey at both R&B and rock-oriented radio stations in the San Francisco Bay area. Sly formed his first band (the Stoners) in 1966 and gradually developed a style that reflected his own diverse musical experience: a blend of jazz, soul music, San Francisco psychedelic, and the socially engaged lyrics of urban folk and folk rock. The Family Stone's national popularity was boosted by their fiery performance at the Woodstock festival in 1969, which appeared in the film and soundtrack album *Woodstock*.

Between 1968 and 1971 Sly and the Family Stone recorded a series of albums and singles that reached the top of both the pop and soul charts. Recordings like 'Dance to the Music' (Number 8 pop and Number 9 R&B in 1968), the double-sided hit sin-gles 'Everyday People'/'Sing a Simple Song' (Number 1 pop and R&B, and Number 4 CHUM, in 1969) and 'Thank You (Falletinme Be Mice Elf Again)'/'Everybody is a Star' (Number 1 pop and R&B in 1970), and their last big crossover hit, 'Family Affair' (Number 1 pop and R&B, and Number 6 CHUM, 1971) exerted a big influ-ence on funk music. The sound of the Family Stone was anchored by the electric 'slap' bass of Larry Graham—positioned prominently in the studio mix—and by an approach to arranging that made the whole band, including the horn section, into a collective rhythm section.

By 1973 funk music had burst onto the pop music scene, pushed to the top of the charts by a large and heterogeneous audience united by their thirst for rhythmically propulsive dance music. Crossover gold records such as Kool and the Gang's 'Jungle Boogie' (Number 4 pop and Number 2 R&B in 1973) and 'Hollywood Swinging' (Number 6 pop and Number 1 R&B in 1974); the Ohio Players' 'Fire' (Number 1 pop and R&B, Number 6 CHUM, 1974) and 'Love Rollercoaster' (Number 1 pop, R&B, and CHUM in 1975); and the multimillion-selling 'Play That Funky Music' (Number 1 pop, R&B, and CHUM in 1976) by the band Wild Cherry, were played constantly on AM radio and in nightclubs and discotheques. These bands kept the spirit and style of James Brown and Sly Stone alive, albeit in a commercialized and decidedly non-polit-ical manner. The image of black 'funkmasters' dancing in Afro hairdos, sunglasses, and brightly coloured clothing on television shows like *American Bandstand* and *Soul Train* occasionally came uncomfortably close to racial stereotyping. Certainly, the record industry's packaging of black 'authenticity'—as symbolized by strongly rhythmic, body-oriented music—had a great deal to do with the sudden crossover success enjoyed by bands such as Kool and the Gang and the Ohio Players (who had strug-gled for success as an R&B band since 1959). However, if the success of funk music in the mainstream pop market capitalized to some degree on long-standing white American fantasies about black culture, white funk bands such as Wild Cherry and the Average White Band were also able to place records in the R&B Top 10.

Although they did not share the huge commercial success of the groups just men-tioned, the apotheosis of 1970s funk music may well have been a loose aggregate of around 40 musicians, variously called Parliament or Funkadelic, led by George Clinton (a.k.a. Dr Funkenstein). Clinton (b. 1940), an ex-R&B vocal group leader and songwriter, hung out with Detroit hippies, listened to the Stooges, and altered his style (as well as his consciousness) during the late 1960s. Enlisting some former members of James Brown's band—i.e., bassist William 'Bootsy' Collins and saxophone players Maceo Parker and Fred Wesley—Clinton developed a mixture of compelling polyrhythms, psychedelic guitar solos, jazz-influenced horn arrangements, and R&B vocal harmonies. Recording for the independent record company Casablanca—also a major player in the field of disco music—Parliament/Funkadelic placed five LPs in the *Billboard* Top 40 between 1976 and 1978, two of which went platinum.

The band's reputation was in substantial measure based on their spectacular concert shows, which featured wild costumes and elaborate sets (including a huge flying saucer called 'the Mothership'), and their innovative concept albums, which expressed an alternative black sensibility, embodied in a patois of street talk, psychedelic imagery, and images of intergalactic travel derived from science fiction. George Clinton took racial and musical stereotypes and played with them, reconfiguring black popular music as a positive moral force. On his albums, Clinton wove mythological narratives of a primordial conflict between the 'Cro-Nasal Sapiens', who 'slicked their hair and lost all sense of the groove', and the 'Thumpasorus People', who buried the secret of funk in the Egyptian pyramids and left Earth for the Chocolate Milky Way, under the wise leadership of 'Dr Funkenstein'. Parliament concerts featured a cast of characters such as 'Star Child' (a.k.a. 'Sir Lollipop Man'), the cosmic defender of funk, and 'Sir Nose D'VoidOfFunk', a spoof of commercialized, soulless, rhythmically challenged pop music and its fans. Clinton's blend of social criticism, wacky humour, and psychedelic imagination is perhaps best captured in his revolutionary manifesto for the funk movement: 'Free Your Mind, and Your Ass Will Follow.'

'Give Up the Funk (Tear the Roof off the Sucker)', from the million-selling LP *Mothership Connection*, was Parliament's biggest crossover single (Number 5 R&B, Number 15 pop in 1976). It exemplifies the band's approach to ensemble style, known to fans as 'P-Funk': heavy, syncopated electric bass lines; interlocking rhythms underlain by a strong pulse on each beat of each measure; long, multi-sectioned arrangements featuring call-and-response patterns between the horn sections and keyboard synthesizer; R&B-styled vocal harmonies; and verbal mottoes designed to be chanted by fans ('We want the funk, give up the funk; We need the funk, we gotta have the funk'). Arranged by Clinton, bass player Bootsy Collins, and keyboardist Bernie Worrell, the recording is constructed out of these basic elements, alternated and layered on top of one another to create a series of shifting sound textures, anchored in the strong pulse of bass and drums.

Clinton and other former Parliament/Funkadelic musicians continued to tour and record throughout the 1980s, but public and critical disdain for 1970s popular culture—especially disco and the dance-oriented music that preceded and inspired it—had a negative impact on the band's fortunes. During the early 1990s the rise of funk-inspired rap (e.g., Dr Dre) and rock music (e.g., Red Hot Chili Peppers) established the status of George Clinton and his colleagues as one of the most important—and most frequently sampled—forces in the recent history of pop. Discovered by a new generation of listeners, Clinton is still performing as of this writing, having appeared to great acclaim at the 1999 reincarnation of the Woodstock festival, as is Bootsy Collins, who was one of several featured performers in the critically acclaimed 2002 documentary on Motown's often forgotten Funk Brothers, *Standing in the Shadows of Motown*.

▌ 'Night Fever': The Rise and Fall of Disco

If funk music heralded the return of black social dance music to the mainstream of popular music, the era of disco—roughly 1975 to 1980—represents the commercial apotheosis (and sudden though temporary decline) of this trend. Like punk rock, disco music represented a reaction against two of the central ideas of album-oriented rock: the LP as Art and the rock group as Artists. Unlike punk, disco de-emphasized the importance of the band—which, in disco music, was usually a concatenation of professional session musicians—and focused attention on the producers who oversaw the making of recordings, the DJs who played them in nightclubs, and a handful of glamorous stars, who sang with the backing of anonymous studio musicians and often had quite short-lived careers. Disco also rejected the idea of the rock album as an architecturally designed collection of individual pieces. Working night after night for audiences who demanded music that would keep them dancing for hours at a stretch, DJs rediscovered the single, expanded it to fill the time frame offered by the 12-inch long-playing vinyl disc, and developed techniques for blending one record into the next without interruption. These turntable techniques paved the way for the use of recordings in popular genres of the 1980s and 1990s, such as hip-hop, house, acid jazz, and techno.

The term 'disco' was derived from 'discotheque', a term first used in Europe during the 1960s to refer to nightclubs devoted to the playing of recorded music for dancing. By the mid-1970s clubs featuring an uninterrupted stream of dance music were increasingly common in the United States and parts of Canada, particularly in urban black and Latino communities, where going out to dance on a weekend night was a well-established tradition, and in the increasingly visible gay communities of cities such as New York, Toronto, and San Francisco. The rise of disco and its invasion of the Top 40 pop music mainstream were driven by several factors: the inspiration of black popular music, particularly Motown, soul, and funk; the rise in popularity of social dancing among middle-class Americans; new technologies, including synthesizers, drum machines, and synchronized turntables; the role of the Hollywood film industry in promoting musical trends; and the economic recession of the late 1970s, which encouraged many nightclub owners to hire disc jockeys rather than live musicians.

The archetypal early disco hit is Donna Summer's 'Love to Love You Baby' (Number 2 pop, Number 2 R&B, 1975), recorded in Germany and released in the United States by Casablanca Records, the independent label that also released LPs by Parliament/Funkadelic. 'Love to Love You Baby' reflects the genre's strong reliance on musical technologies of the mid-1970s and the central importance of the record producer in shaping the sound texture of disco recordings. Producer Giorgio Moroder's careful mix takes full advantage of multi-track recording technology (which allows Summer's voice to appear in several places at the same time), clear stereo separation of instruments, keyboard synthesizers with the ability to play more than one note at a time and to imitate other musical instruments, and electronic reverb, which plays a crucial role in establishing the spatial qualities of a recording. The original recording is much longer than the usual pop single—almost 17 minutes long—and was produced specifically for use in discotheques, where customers demanded unbroken sequences of dance music. The version that made the *Billboard* singles charts was edited down to under five minutes in length to fit the framework of Top 40 radio. The performance is clearly seductive in intent, an impression created not only by the lyrics themselves but also by Summer's languorous and sexy whispers, orgasmic moans, and growls. And this impression was only further reinforced by the nicknames bestowed on Donna Summer at the time by the popular music press, including 'First Lady of Lust' and 'Disco's Aphrodite'.

The recording opens with an intake of breath and Summer's voice singing the hook of the song ('*Ahhhh, love to love you baby*') in an intimate, almost whispering voice, accompanied by the gentle sound of a closed hi-hat cymbal (a pair of cymbals opened and closed by the drummer's left foot). The next sounds to appear are the electric guitar, played with a wah-wah pedal (a foot-operated device that allows the guitarist to change the timbre of his instrument), and the bass drum, playing a solid four-to-the-bar beat. The core elements of early disco music are thus presented within the first few measures of the recording: a sexy, studio-enhanced female voice, and a rhythm track that is borrowed in large part from funk music and anchored by a hypnotic steady pulse. The overall arrangement is made up of two basic phrases, which are alternated, always returning to the hook. Working with his then state-of-the-art multi-track mixing board, Giorgio Moroder gradually builds up layers of sound texture and then strips them away to reveal the basic pulse of the music.

The Mainstreaming of Disco

By the late 1970s disco had taken over the popular mainstream, owing in large part to the success of the film *Saturday Night Fever* (1977)—the story of a working-class

Listening To an Early Disco/Soft Soul Classic: The Love Unlimited Orchestra's 'Love's Theme' (1973)

A dizzying upward sweep in the strings; the pulse kicks in, subtly at first, but becoming progressively stronger; and a downward lunge on the keyboard ushers in 'Love's Theme'—one of the biggest instrumental hits of the 1970s. The Love Unlimited Orchestra, a 40-piece studio ensemble, was the brainchild of Barry White, a multi-talented American singer, songwriter, arranger, conductor, and producer who had already begun to have a string of solo vocal hits by the time that 'Love's Theme' hit the Number 1 spot on the pop charts in February 1974. Originally formed to back the female trio Love Unlimited, which was yet another one of White's projects as a writer and producer, the Love Unlimited Orchestra also played on some of White's solo recordings, in addition to having hit instrumental records under its own name. 'Love's Theme' was featured on *Rhapsody in White*, the cleverly titled Top 10 album by the Love Unlimited Orchestra.

The instrumental pop hit, which reached its pinnacle as a genre during the big band years (1935–45), never totally died out during the early years of rock 'n' roll or during the emergence of rock in the 1960s. In fact, as we have seen, instrumental virtuosity on the electric guitar became one of the defining elements of late 1960s and 1970s rock. Still, 'Love's Theme' represented a different kind of instrumental for the 1970s; guitar pyrotechnics play no part in the arrangement, although the use of the 'scratch' guitar sound as a recurring percussive element throughout the recording does constitute a nod to the more advanced guitar styles of the period cultivated by artists such as Jimi Hendrix. Instead, the emphasis in 'Love's Theme' is on two things: danceability and the sweet sound of a string-dominated melody. Its successful synthesis of these two elements, which might seem at first to be unlikely bedfellows, is one of the strikingly original—and, eventually, very influential—aspects of this record.

The danceability of 'Love's Theme' made it one of the earliest disco-styled hits, as it quickly became a favourite in dance clubs. This recording was the first in a long line of instrumental, or largely instrumental, disco records. These records followed the lead of 'Love's Theme' insofar as they typically presented a similar combination of a strong beat with an elaborate arrangement featuring bowed string instruments; examples include the Number 1 hits 'TSOP (The Sound of Philadelphia)' by MFSB (which topped the charts later in 1974), 'The Hustle' by Van McCoy and the Soul City Symphony (1975), and 'Fly, Robin, Fly' by Silver Convention (also 1975). In addition, the lush arrangement of 'Love's Theme'—featuring a melody designed to take full advantage of the way orchestral string instruments can hold long notes—

links this instrumental in a general way to the sound of 'soft soul', a popular genre in the later 1960s and throughout the 1970s, exemplified by languid or mid-tempo love songs with similarly 'romantic' arrangements. (Examples include recordings by the Delfonics, the Spinners, the Stylistics, and by Barry White himself as a solo vocalist.) In a sense, 'Love's Theme' has it both ways; it's like a love ballad for instruments, but with a double-time dance beat. The steady, syncopated dance groove keeps the string sounds from spilling over into sentimentality, while the smooth string melody prevents the dance pulse from seeming overly mechanical or depersonalized. While listening to 'Love's Theme', it is a relatively simple matter to pick out the tune's basic AABA structure—yet another testament to the remarkable durability of this formal arrangement. Note how the bridge section ('B') is slightly longer than the others, and how effective this extension of the bridge is as we wait for the return of 'A'.

Barry White was best known for his full, deep voice, which he could employ to great and seductive effect, not only in actually singing his love songs, but also in the spoken introductions he sometimes provided for them (as in his 1974 Number 1 solo hit, 'Can't Get Enough of Your Love, Babe'). Still, the single biggest hit record with which White was associated remains 'Love's Theme', and in terms of the long-range impact of its sound on the pop music market, it may also be his most influential recording. It is no accident that the lead-off cut on *The Disco Box*, a four-CD compilation of the dance-oriented music of the 1970s and early 1980s (issued by Rhino in 1999), is 'Love's Theme'.

Italian kid from New York who becomes a championship dancer. *Saturday Night Fever*—shot on location at a Brooklyn discotheque—strengthened interest in disco stars like Donna Summer and Gloria Gaynor. The film also launched the second career of the Bee Gees, an Australian group known theretofore mainly for sentimental pop songs like 'Lonely Days' (Number 2 CHUM, 1971) and 'How Can You Mend a Broken Heart' (Number 1 CHUM, 1971). The Bee Gees reinvented themselves by combining their polished Beatle-derived vocal harmonies with funk-influenced rhythms, played by Miami studio musicians, and created a mix that appealed both to committed disco fans and a broader pop audience. Their songs from the *Saturday Night Fever* soundtrack, such as 'Stayin' Alive' and 'Night Fever', were among the most popular singles of the late 1970s. At a more general level, *Saturday Night Fever* also helped to link disco music and dancing to traditional values in American culture: upward mobility and heterosexual romance. Spreading from the urban and often gay communities where it first bloomed, disco dancing offered millions of working-class and middle-class Americans, from the most varied of cultural and economic backgrounds, access to a kind of glamour that hadn't been experienced widely since the days of the grand ballrooms.

The strict dress codes employed by the most famous discotheques implied a rejection of the torn T-shirt and jeans regalia of rock music and the reinstatement of notions of hierarchy and classiness—if you (and your clothes) could pass muster at the velvet rope, you were allowed access to the inner sanctum. Walking through the front door of a disco in full swing was like entering a sensory maelstrom, with thundering music driven by an incessant bass pulse, flashing lights and mirrors on the ceiling, walls, and floor, and—most important—a mass of sweaty and beautifully adorned bodies packed onto the always limited space of a dance floor. For those committed to this cultural phenomenon, the discotheque was a shrine to hedonism, an escape from the drudgery of everyday life, and a fountain of youth (the death throes of this scene are evocatively rendered in the 1998 film, *The Last Days of Disco*).

A few examples must suffice here to give a sense of how thoroughly disco had penetrated popular musical taste by the late 1970s. One important stream of influence involved a continuation of the old category of novelty records, done up in disco style. A band called Rick Dees and his Gang of Idiots came out of nowhere to score a Number 1 hit with the goofy 'Disco Duck' (1976), followed by the less successful zoo-disco song 'Dis-Gorilla' (1977). The Village People—a group built from scratch by the French record producer Jacques Morah and promoted by Casablanca Records—specialized in over-the-top burlesques of gay life and a style of fashion once described as 'same-sex drag', and scored Top 5 hits in Canada with songs like 'Macho Man' (Number 4, 1978), 'YMCA' (Number 2, 1978), and 'In the Navy' (Number 1, 1979). For those who caught the inside references to gay culture, the Village People's recordings were charming, if simple-minded parodies; for many in disco's new mass audience, they were simply novelty records with a disco beat. And the group's appeal was obviously not restricted to Canada. Morah's double-entendre strategy paid off— for a short while in the late 1970s, the Village People were the best-selling pop group across North America.

For a few years everyone seemed to be jumping on the disco bandwagon. Barbra Streisand teamed up with disco artists, including the Bee Gees' Barry Gibb, who produced her multi-platinum 1980 album *Guilty*; and she also teamed up with Donna Summer for the single 'No More Tears' (Number 1 across North America in 1979). Disco met the surf sound when Bruce Johnston of the Beach Boys produced a disco arrangement of 'Pipeline', which had been a Number 4 instrumental hit for the Chantays back in 1963. Even hard rock musicians like the Rolling Stones released disco singles (such as 'Miss You', Number 1 in 1978). On the other side of the Atlantic a genre called Eurodisco developed, featuring prominent use of electronic synthesizers and long compositions with repetitive rhythm tracks, designed to fill the entire side of an LP. (This sound, as developed by bands like Germany's Kraftwerk, was to become one important root of techno.) Meanwhile, in America, Motown diva Diana Ross scored several disco-influenced hits (e.g., 'Love Hangover', Number 1 in 1976, and 'Upside Down', Number 1 in 1980); and James Brown—who was knocked off the pop charts by disco music—responded in the late 1970s by promoting himself as the 'Original Disco Man', prompting more than one critic to openly wonder whether there was a genre of dance music James Brown would not take credit for inventing.

Listening To Donna Summer's 'Bad Girls' (1979) and Le Chic's 'Good Times' (1979)

Dance-oriented music dominated the American pop charts in the late 1970s. The titles of the Number 1 pop records from the end of 1977 through the summer of 1979 would read, with few exceptions, like a track listing for a 'Disco's Greatest Hits' album. Disco's spectacular hold on the Number 1 spot ended with two splendid examples of the genre: 'Bad Girls', performed by Donna Summer, and Le Chic's 'Good Times'. A brief consideration of the similarities shared by these records, and of the differences between them, will offer us a useful look at the essential characteristics, as well as the diversity, of disco music.

What Makes These Records 'Disco'?
1. The BEAT! This is dance music, of course, and the pounding beat defines the music as disco. Indeed, the beat is established immediately on both 'Bad Girls' and 'Good Times', and it never lets up, persisting right through the fade-outs that end these records. The beat constitutes the essential hook on all disco records. It is characteristic of disco that every pulse is rhythmically articulated by the bass and/or the drums. There is no such thing as stoptime in this music, and the signature *thump!—thump!—thump!—thump!* of disco creates and maintains an irresistible dance groove; disco dancers literally never have to skip a beat. Consequently, although there are many changes in the musical texture during 'Bad Girls', the rhythm continues ceaselessly, regardless of whatever other instruments or vocal parts enter or leave the mix. On the other

hand, the fact that there are only slight alterations in texture throughout 'Good Times' helps assure that attention remains focused on the rhythm itself, and the minimal feel of this particular recording offers an excellent example of how hypnotic a basic rhythm-propelled track can be.

2. A steady, medium-fast tempo. Like most social dance music, disco recordings maintain an unvarying tempo throughout. Above and beyond this obvious characteristic, however, the tempos of most disco records tend also to be fairly similar to one another, to accord with the active dance styles preferred by the patrons of discotheques. The tempo of 'Bad Girls' is slightly faster than that of 'Good Times', but obviously the same kinds of steps and body movements would fit both records equally well. Recordings intended for use in discotheques often bore indications of their tempos in the form of beats per minute (bpm), to assist the club disc jockeys in arranging relatively seamless sequences of dance numbers,

and if the DJ had an adjustable-speed turntable, it was possible to adjust the tempos of individual records slightly so that the dance beat wouldn't vary at all from one to the next—then, even when the song changed, the dancers still would never have to skip a beat.

3. Straightforward, repetitive song forms. With the emphasis on dancing, it would obviously be pointless for disco records to employ complex, intricate song forms, such as those developed by some artists in the late 1960s and 1970s. Such niceties suggest an entirely different kind of listening environment and, if they weren't just missed entirely by disco fans, might prove distracting and even annoying on the dance floor. Both 'Bad Girls' and 'Good Times' are based clearly on a verse-chorus kind of form. Furthermore, in both, the chorus is heard first, and this serves a number of purposes. Each song's chorus begins with the title words (*'Bad girls', 'Good times'*), identifying the song immediately and functioning as a concise, and extremely effective, verbal and musical hook.

Le Chic and **Donna Summer:** kings and queens of disco. Frank Driggs Collection

Counting the initial statement, the chorus in each of these recordings is heard a total of three times, which results in a readily accessible, repetitive kind of structure that assures memorability.

4. Straightforward subject matter and lyrics. No Dylanesque imagery or poetic obscurities, please—again, for obvious reasons. There is no doubt what either 'Bad Girls' or 'Good Times' is about. This is not to say that the lyrics to disco songs are without interest, however; see the further discussion, especially in reference to 'Bad Girls', below.

5. Limited harmonic vocabulary. In essence, the harmony of 'Good Times' simply oscillates between two chords, with the change occurring on the downbeat of every other measure. 'Bad Girls' has only a slightly wider harmonic vocabulary, but it, too, gives the sense of being built around two basic, alternating chords much of the time; these two chords underlie the entire chorus and do not shift when the choruses give way to the verses. Both records thus achieve a highly focused, almost hypnotic, effect in the harmonic realm that is analogous to—and abets—their virtually obsessive rhythmic character. (The conceptual debt that recordings of this type owe to the late 1960s music of James Brown should be obvious; see Chapter 4.)

The five characteristics listed above—emphasis on the beat; steady, relatively fast, tempo; avoidance of formal complexity; direct lyrics; and a limited chord vocabulary—clearly do not apply only to typical disco music. They also would serve well in a general way, for example, in describing much typical early rock 'n' roll. The point to be made here is that, in the context of album-oriented rock, the output of singer-songwriters, and several other manifestations of 1970s pop music, the 'return to basics' (that is, the return to danceable music)—with a new twist—that disco represented came across, to many, as both novel and refreshing. It is also important to emphasize here that disco music proved, in certain ways, to be forward-looking. The most immediate example of this is the fact that the chords and rhythmic patterns of 'Good Times' were borrowed wholesale to constitute the instrumental backing for the single that broke rap music into the commercial mainstream for the first time: 'Rapper's Delight' by the Sugarhill Gang (see later in this chapter).

Some Distinguishing Characteristics of 'Bad Girls' and 'Good Times'

We have already noted the greater textural variety of 'Bad Girls'. Donna Summer's lead vocal, responding voices, brass instruments, and even a police whistle appear, disappear, and reappear—sometimes expectedly, sometimes not—over the course of the recording, creating a feeling evocative of the action, excitement, and occasional unpredictability of a busy street scene. It also seems appropriate that 'Bad Girls' is more elaborate from a formal point of view than 'Good Times'. The verse sections of 'Bad Girls' fall into two distinct parts, the second part marked by a pause in the vocals and the interjection of short, accented chords on the brass instruments. (This part has a formal effect somewhat similar to that of a bridge section in other song structures.) In addition, after the third and final verse, there is a coda in place of the expected concluding chorus. In this coda, the lead vocalist abandons at last her position as observer of the scene and actually joins the 'bad girls' with a shout of *'Hey, mister, have you got a dime?'*—acting, in effect, upon her earlier realization (in the third verse) that she and the 'bad girls' are 'both the same', even though the others are called 'a different name'.

The vocal styles used in the two recordings are decidedly different. Donna Summer's emphatic, expansive style clearly derives from roots in R&B and gospel; her background, like that of so many African-American pop stars, included church singing. Summer's personal intensity solicits our involvement in, and concern with, the story of the 'bad girls'. In short, 'Bad Girls' is a brilliantly performed pop record that is enhanced by an elaborate and clever production. Yet the question suggests itself: can any recording so irresistibly danceable, with such an upbeat rhythmic feeling, really convey a downbeat social 'message'—especially about an issue as thorny and complex as prostitution? Won't people be too busy dancing to notice? And doesn't it sound as if these 'bad girls' are really just out for, and having, 'good times'?

In a way, the inverse situation applies to 'Good Times'. This apparently carefree anthem is intoned by a small group of voices singing in unison in a clipped, unornamented, basically uninflected style that comes across as intentionally depersonalized. Is there ultimately something just a little too mechanistic about the voices, and the obsessive chords and rhythms, in these 'good times'? Some rock critics have suggested that the song has an ironic edge to it, and they could certainly support this idea by pointing to those occasional darker phrases that pop up in the lyrics like momentary flickering shadows: '*A rumor has it that it's getting late*' and '*You silly fool, you can't change your fate.*' On the other hand, it might be claimed that those looking for hidden depths in a song like 'Good Times' are those who have simply lost the ability to enjoy a superb party record.

Disco in Canada

In 1979, according to *Billboard* magazine, Montreal became the second most important market for disco records in North America, after only New York City. Montreal was already home to one of the continent's most prominent 'DJ pools', called the 'Canadian Record Pool' (CRP)—a loose organization of disco DJs devoted to promoting the disco genre—which established the Canadian Disco Awards in 1977, began publishing a newsletter that same year, and oversaw distribution of new records to DJs nationwide. Montreal was also home to no less than 50 dance clubs, most notably Kébek Elektric, named after Canadian 'Eurodisco' star Gino Soccio's first band, as well as the Limelight and Régines; and Inter-Global and Les Disque Parpluies, two important indie disco labels in Canada, were centred in the city.

Of course, Canadian disco was not confined to Montreal. Toronto was another important centre for the genre. Both Direction and Rio Records, for instance, two important 'indie' disco labels, had Toronto as their base of operations. The city was also home to CHIC-AM, which broadcast disco music 'all day every day'.

In fact, an estimated 90 radio stations across Canada regularly programmed disco records by the end of the decade. And Canadian disco singers and producers comprised a significant portion of their programming—including THP (Three Hats Productions) Orchestra's 'Theme from S.W.A.T.', Cherrill and Robbie Rae's 'A Little Lovin'', Laurie Marshall's 'Disco Spaceship', Denice McCann's 'Tattooed Man', Wayne St John's 'Something's Up', Claudja Barry's 'Boogie Woogie Dancin' Shoes', Patsy Gallant's 'From New York to LA' (1976) and 'Are You Ready For Love' (1977), and Gino Soccio's 'Dancer' (1979), which topped the American *Billboard* charts and reached Number 22 in Canada in 1979.

Perhaps the most successful disco singer in Canada was Patsy Gallant, who became the country's reigning 'Queen of Disco' during the mid- and late 1970s. One of 10 children, Patsy Gallant's first commercial work as a singer was with her older siblings Angeline, Ghislaine, and Florine, who performed together as the Gallant Sisters; a string of performances in Canada's Maritime region, particularly around New Brunswick, led to a residency at Montreal's numerous nightclubs. In 1967, Patsy left her sisters for a solo career and quickly earned a spot on CBC-TV's francophone musical variety show, *Discotheque*, and its anglophone equivalent, *Music Hop*.

In 1970, Gallant signed a recording contract with Columbia Records. In so doing, she became yet another pop singer from Quebec to release albums in both English and French, including: *Toi l'enfant* (1971), *Tout va trop vite* (1972), *Upon My Own* (1972), and *Power* (1973). In 1973, Columbia rather cynically pushed Gallant to record a country-flavoured album, to capitalize on the growing popularity of the country rock genre. Thus, Gallant recorded her fourth LP, *Power*, in Nashville, employing a number of the city's famed studio musicians on sessions for the album. However, the three singles Columbia released from the album—'Save the Last Dance for Me', 'Make My Living', and 'Doctors Orders'—failed to chart in the United States, and the fact that they all received considerable radio play in Canada did little to impress the label.

A short while later, when it became clear that her career with Columbia had stalled, Gallant stoked the flames of Quebec nationalism and recorded an up-tempo version of Gilles Vigneault's 'Mon Pays' for Kébec-Disc in Montreal. The recording attracted the attention of Attic Records, based in Toronto. Executives at Attic had Gallant perform an updated and significantly altered English-language version of the track in 1976, the newer version retaining only the refrain from 'Mon Pays' as a melodic and harmonic basis for it chorus; the resulting track, the proto-disco 'From New York to LA' (Number 9 Canada, 1976), earned Gallant her first Top 10 placing in Canada. Her next two releases—'Are You Ready For Love' and 'Sugar Daddy'—reached the Top 10 in Canada the next year, the latter all the more remarkable for the fact that it appeared on one of Gallant's French-language albums, *Besoin D'amour* (1977).

We should also briefly note the work of Gino Soccio during the late 1970s, perhaps Canada's most important disco producer and an often overlooked pioneer of the techno aesthetic. Born and raised in Montreal, Soccio first came to prominence as a member of the Québécois dance outfit Kébek Elektric (pronounced 'Québec

Electric'), who enjoyed chart success with the techno-sounding Eurodisco hits 'Magic Fly' and 'War Dance', both released in 1977. Soccio left the group the next year to take up a position as a producer at the famed Muscle Shoals Sound Studios in Alabama. Using the house band there, Soccio produced and assembled the group Witch Queen, perhaps their best-known release being a disco cover of T. Rex's 'Bang a Gong' (1979), which entered the American Top 10 Dance charts even as it failed to chart in Canada. Soccio topped the US Hot Dance Music/Club Play charts later that same year with the solo 'Dancer'/'Dance to Dance' (1979), and then again in 1981, with the decidedly 'down-tempo' tracks 'Try It Out' and 'Hold Tight' (1981). Beginning in the early 1980s, Soccio began a successful collaboration with Canadian post-disco diva Karen Silver, their most notable records being 'Fake' (1980), 'Nobody Else' (1981), 'Set Me Free'(1981), and 'Clean Up Woman' (1982).

Though Gino Soccio would score a few more solo hits during the early 1980s, including 1982's 'Face to Face' and 1984's 'Turn It Around', the disco genre was all but spent as a national force by 1980. Indeed, by 1984 most Canadians were jumping to the sound of a new kind of dance music, and soon they would be tuning in on their television sets to hear the latest hits. The record industry in general would face its first real slump, and pop music, both in Canada and in the United States, would take a decidedly conservative turn once more.

Disco Sucks!

Few styles of popular music have inspired such passionate loyalty, or such utter revulsion, as disco music. And it is worth taking a few moments to consider the negative side of this equation. If you were a loyal fan of Led Zeppelin, Pink Floyd, and other album-oriented rock groups of the 1970s, disco was likely to represent a self-indulgent, pretentious, and vaguely suspect musical orientation. The rejection of disco by rock fans reached its peak at a 1979 baseball game in Chicago, when, in a light-hearted but ill-conceived promotion by the White Sox baseball organization, several hundred disco records were blown up and a riot ensued.

Canada never displayed the same violent anti-disco sentiment as was seen at the 'Death to Disco' rally (and eventual riot) in Chicago's Comiskey Park, but a disco backlash did emerge across the nation as radio stations devoted to a pop audience decreased the amount of disco in their programming until, eventually, phasing the genre out almost entirely. Vancouver's D.O.A. even went so far as to release a single called 'Disco Sucks' (1979):

Disco Sucks!
I was walkin', walkin' around
Walkin' round, round downtown
Saw some people stompin' around
Sayin' 'Disco sucks Like Shit!'
. . .

Lots of plastic people, building a plastic steeple
Lots of plastic people, building a plastic steeple

Disco sucks!
Disco sucks!
Disco sucks like shit!
Disco sucks!
Disco sucks!
Disco sucks like shit!
. . .

Some critics connect the anti-disco reaction of the 1970s with the genre's links to gay culture. The disco movement initially emerged in Manhattan nightclubs such as the Loft and the Tenth Floor, which served as social gathering spots for homosexual men. According to this interpretation, gays found it difficult to get live acts to perform for them. The disc jockeys who worked these clubs responded to the demands of customers by rummaging through the bins of record stores for good dance records, often coming up with singles that had been successful some years earlier in the black and Puerto Rican communities of New York City.

That disco was to some degree associated in the public imagination with homosexuality has suggested to some observers that the phrase 'Disco Sucks!'—the rallying cry of the anti-disco movement—evinces a strain of homophobia among the core audience for album-oriented rock: young, middle- and working-class, and presumably heterosexual white men. Certainly, the associations of disco with a contemporary version of ballroom dancing did not conform to contemporary models of masculine behaviour—the tradition of dancing to prefigured steps, and to music specifically designed to support such dancing, which had found its last expression in the early 1960s with dance crazes like the twist, had fallen out of favour during the rock era. It may therefore have seemed to many rock fans that there was something suspect, even effeminate, about men who engaged in ballroom dancing.

Still, it can safely be assumed that: (1) the audience for album-oriented rock wasn't entirely straight; (2) not every homosexual was a fan of disco; and (3) heterosexuals did patronize discos with large homosexual clienteles, at least in the big cities. The initial rejection of disco by many rock fans may have had as much to do with racism as with homophobia, since the genre's roots lay predominantly in black dance music. And, of course, the majority simply did not like the music and became increasingly frustrated as the genre all but consumed the culture for a few years in the late 1970s. Indeed, for such interpretations of the 'disco sucks' movement to be true, one would have to consider it a real possibility that black record producer Quincy Jones, for instance, was a racist and a homophobe because he often decried disco's popularity during the 1970s.

The musical values predominant among rock fans—including an appreciation of instrumental virtuosity, as represented in the guitar playing of Jimi Hendrix, Eric

Clapton, or Jimmy Page—would not have inclined them towards a positive regard of disco, which relied heavily on studio overdubbing and consisted mainly of fairly predictable patterns designed for dancing. Although disco cannot simply be identified as 'gay music', there is no doubt that the genre's mixed reception during the late 1970s provides additional evidence of the transformative effect of marginalized musical styles and communities on the commercial mainstream of popular music.

▌'Droppin' Science': Hip-Hop and Rap Music

Of all the genres of popular music surveyed in this book, none—not even disco—spurred more vigorous public debate than rap music. Rap has been characterized as a vital link in the centuries-old chain of cultural and musical connections between Africa and the Americas, as the authentic voice of an oppressed urban underclass, and as a form that exploits long-standing stereotypes of black people. In fact, each of these perspectives has something to tell us about the history and significance of rap music.

Rap is indeed based on principles ultimately derived from African musical and verbal traditions, as well as from the rock tradition. Evidence of these deep continuities may be found in features familiar throughout the history of African-American music: an emphasis on rhythmic momentum and creativity; a preference for complex tone colours and dense textures; a keen appreciation of improvisational skill (in words and music); and an incorporative, innovative approach to musical technologies. Moreover, much rap music does constitute a cultural response to oppression and racism, a system for communication among black communities throughout North America ('black America's CNN', as rapper Chuck D once put it), and a source of insight into the values, perceptions, and conditions of people living in beleaguered urban communities across North America. And finally, although rap music's origins and inspirations flow from black culture, the genre's audience has become decidedly multi-racial, multicultural, and transnational. As rap has been transformed from a local phenomenon, located in a few neighbourhoods in eastern US urban areas, to a multimillion-dollar industry and a global cultural phenomenon, it has grown ever more complex and multi-faceted.

The Origins of Hip-Hop, 1975–1979

Rap initially emerged during the 1970s as one part of a cultural complex called *hip-hop*. Hip-hop culture, forged by African-American and Caribbean-American youth in New York City, included distinctive styles of visual art (graffiti), dance (an acrobatic solo style called breakdancing and an energetic couple dance called 'the freak'), music, dress, and speech. Hip-hop was at first a local phenomenon, centred in certain neighbourhoods in the Bronx, the most economically devastated area of New York City. Federal budget cuts caused a severe decline in low-income housing and social services for the residents of America's inner cities during the mid-1970s. By

1977, when President Carter conducted a highly publicized motorcade tour through New York's most devastated neighbourhoods, the South Bronx had become, as the *New York Times* put it, 'a symbol of America's woes'.

The youth culture that spawned hip-hop can be interpreted on one level as a response to the destruction of traditional family- and neighbourhood-based institutions and the cutting of funding for public institutions such as community centres, and as an attempt to lay claim to—and, in a way, to 'civilize'—an alienating and hostile urban environment. The young adults who pioneered hip-hop styles such as breakdancing, graffiti art, and rap music at nightclubs, block parties, and in city parks often belonged to informal social groups called 'crews' or 'posses', each associated with a particular neighbourhood or block. It is important to understand that hip-hop culture began as an expression of local identities. Even today's multi-platinum rap recordings, marketed worldwide, are filled with inside references to particular neighbourhoods, features of the urban landscape, and social groups and networks.

Enter the DJ

If hip-hop music was a rejection of mainstream dance music by young black and Puerto Rican listeners, it was also profoundly shaped by the techniques of disco DJs. The first celebrities of hip-hop music—Kool Herc (Clive Campbell, born in Jamaica, 1955), Grandmaster Flash (Joseph Saddler, born in Barbados, 1958), and Afrika Bambaata (Kevin Donovan, born in the Bronx, 1960)—were DJs who began their careers in the mid-1970s, spinning records at neighbourhood block parties, gym dances, and dance clubs and in public spaces such as community centres and parks. These three young men—and dozens of lesser-known DJs scattered throughout the Bronx, Harlem, and other areas of New York City and New Jersey—developed their personal styles within a grid of fierce competition for celebrity and neighbourhood pride. As Fab Five Freddie, an early graffiti artist and rapper, put it:

> You make a new style. That's what life on the street is all about. What's at stake is honor and position on the street. That's what makes it so important, that's what makes it feel so good—the pressure on you to be the best . . . to develop a new style nobody can deal with. (George et al., 1985: 111)

The disco DJ's technique of 'mixing' between two turntables to create smooth transitions between records was first adapted to the hip-hop aesthetic by Kool Herc, who had migrated from Kingston, Jamaica, to New York City at the age of 12. Herc noticed that the young dancers in his audiences responded most energetically during the so-called '**breaks**' on funk and salsa records—brief sections where the melody was stripped away to feature the rhythm section. Herc responded by isolating the breaks of certain popular records, such as James Brown's 'Get on the Good Foot', and mixing them into the middle of other dance records. These rhythmic sound collages came to be known as 'breakbeat' music, a term subsequently transferred to 'breakdancing': acrobatic solo performances improvised by the young 'B-boys' who attended hip-hop dances.

Another innovation helped to shape the sound and sensibility of early hip-hop: the transformation of the turntable from a medium for playing back recorded sound into a playable musical instrument, that is, from a tool of consumption to one of production. Sometime in the mid-1970s Kool Herc began to put two copies of the same record on his turntables. Switching back and forth between the turntables, Herc found that he could 'backspin' one disc (i.e., turn it backwards, or counterclockwise, with his hand) while the other continued to play over the loudspeakers. This allowed him to repeat a given break over and over, by switching back and forth between the two discs and backspinning to the beginning of the break. This technique was refined by Grandmaster Flash, who adopted the mixing techniques of disco DJs, particularly their use of headphones to synchronize the tempos of recordings and to create smooth transitions from one dance groove to the next. Using headphones, Flash could more precisely pinpoint the beginning of a break by listening to the sound of the disc being turned backward on the turntable; he called this the 'peek-a-boo system'. Flash spent many hours practising this 'peek-a-boo' technique and gained local fame for his ability to 'punch in' brief, machine gun-like segments of sound.

A new technique called 'scratching' was developed by Flash's young protege, Theodore, who broke away and formed his own hip-hop crew at the tender age of 13. In 1978 Theodore debuted a new technique that quickly spread through the community of DJs. While practising backspinning in his room, Theodore began to pay closer attention to the sounds created in his headphones as he turned the disc counterclockwise. He soon discovered that this technique yielded scratchy, percussive sound effects that could be punched in to the dance groove. At first Theodore wasn't sure how people would react:

> The Third Avenue Ballroom was packed, and I figured I might as well give it a try. So, I put on two copies of [James Brown's] 'Sex Machine' and started scratching up one. The crowd loved it . . . they went wild. (Hager, 1984: 38)

The distinctive sound of scratching became an important part of the sonic palette of hip-hop music. Even in the 1990s, after digital sampling had largely displaced turntables as a means of creating the musical textures and grooves on rap records, producers frequently used these sounds as a way of signalling a connection to the 'old school' origins of hip-hop.

Enter the Rapper

Although all DJs used microphones to make announcements, Kool Herc was also one of the first DJs to recite rhyming phrases over the 'breakbeats' produced on his turntables. Some of Herc's 'raps' were based on a tradition of verbal performance called 'toasting', a form of poetic storytelling with roots in the trickster tales of West Africa.

The trickster—a sly character whose main goal in life is to defy authority and upset the normal order of things—became a common figure in the storytelling traditions of black slaves in the United States, where he took on additional significance as a symbol of cultural survival and covert resistance. After the Civil War the figure of the trickster was in part supplanted by more aggressive male figures, the focus of long, semi-improvised poetic stories called 'toasts'. The toasting tradition frequently focused on 'bad men'—hard, merciless bandits and spurned lovers who vanquished their enemies, sometimes by virtue of their wits, but more often through physical power.

Although the toasting tradition had largely disappeared from black communities by the 1970s, it took root in prisons, where black inmates found that the old narrative form suited their life experiences and present circumstances. One of the main sources for the rhymes composed by early hip-hop DJs in the Bronx was the album *Hustler's Convention* (1973), by Jala Uridin, leader of a group of militant ex-convicts known as the Last Poets. *Hustler's Convention* was a compelling portrait of 'the life'—the urban underworld of gamblers, pimps, and hustlers—comprising prison toasts with titles like 'Four Bitches Is What I Got' and 'Sentenced to the Chair'. The record, featuring musical accompaniment by an all-star lineup of funk, soul, and jazz musicians, became enormously popular in the Bronx and inspired Kool Herc and other DJs to compose their own rhymes. Soon DJs were recruiting members of their posses to serve as verbal performers, or 'MCs' (an abbreviation of the term 'master of ceremonies'). MCs played an important role in controlling crowd behaviour at the increasingly large dances where DJs performed, and soon became more important celebrities than the DJs themselves. If DJs are the predecessors of today's rap producers—responsible for shaping musical texture and groove—MCs are the ancestors of contemporary rappers.

We should also mention the crucial influence the dub genre exerted on these pioneers of the rap genre, many of whom, like Kool Herc and Grandmaster Flash, spent their formative years in the West Indies, where dub was extremely popular. In an effort to distinguish a sound system from its competition—and, thus, to attract more listeners—many 'record selectors' (i.e., DJs) in Jamaica played exclusive 'dub versions' of songs—i.e., beat-heavy, echo-laden, mostly instrumental remixes of popular songs created by producers such as King Tubby (who is generally recognized as the single most important pioneer of the genre), Bunny Lee, Lee 'Scratch' Perry, and Leslie Kong, to name only a few. At the same time, as competition between 'sound systems' intensified, record selectors began to 'toast' the superiority of their sound systems using mostly rhyming couplets. Eventually these rhyming toasts became an expected part of sound system practice, and selectors hired skilled MCs (rappers) to provide increasingly longer rhymes as a matter of course; U-Roy, for instance, became identified with the practice in the later 1960s, distinguishing himself as one of the pre-eminent MCs in the country.

As noted, one person who would have seen such sound system performances as a child was Clive Campbell, a.k.a. DJ Kool Herc. In fact, according to Kool Herc, rap in its earliest stages was basically dub set to a rhythm and blues and funk, rather than a reggae, beat. Campbell grew up in Jamaica, and did not move to the United States until 1967, when he was 12 years old. By age 18, he had set up what was, to his mind, an Americanized sound system, and he often 'toasted' rhymes in the Jamaican style over hit funk and R&B records. To focus exclusively on his mixing, Campbell soon left the rhyming to MCs such as Coke La Rock and Clark Kent, the trio eventually forming Kool Herc & the Herculoids—for all intents and purposes a sound system unit in the Jamaican style, set to American dance and funk records, and one of the first modern rap units.

Hip-Hop Breaks Out, 1979–1988

Until 1979 hip-hop music remained primarily a local phenomenon. The first indication of the genre's broader commercial potential was the 12-inch dance single 'Rapper's Delight', recorded by the Sugarhill Gang, a crew based in Harlem. This record, which popularized the use of the term 'rapper' as an equivalent for MC, established Sugar Hill Records—a black-owned independent label based in New Jersey— as the predominant institutional force in rap music during the early 1980s. The recording recycled the rhythm section track from Le Chic's 'Good Times', played in the studio by session musicians usually hired by Sugar Hill to back R&B singers. The three rappers—Michael 'Wonder Mike' Wright, Guy 'Master Gee' O'Brien, and Henry 'Big Bank Hank' Jackson—recited a rapid-fire succession of rhymes, typical of the performances of MCs at hip-hop dances.

Well it's on-n-on-n-on-on-n-on
The beat don't stop until the break of dawn

I said M-A-S, T-E-R, a G with a double E
I said I go by the unforgettable name
Of the man they call the Master Gee

Well, my name is known all over the world
By all the foxy ladies and the pretty girls

I'm goin' down in history
As the baddest rapper there could ever be

The text of 'Rapper's Delight' alternates the braggadocio of the three MCs with descriptions of dance movements, exhortations to the audience, and humorous stories and references. One particularly memorable segment describes the consternation of a guest who is served rotting food by his friend's mother, seeks a polite way to refuse it, and finally escapes by crashing through the apartment door. The record reached Number 4 on the R&B chart and Number 36 on the pop chart in America— and it topped the pop charts in Canada for eight weeks—introducing hip-hop to millions of people throughout North America in the process. The unexpected success of 'Rapper's Delight' ushered in a series of million-selling 12-inch singles by New York rappers, including Kurtis Blow's 'The Breaks' (Number 4 R&B, Number 87 pop in

1980), 'Planet Rock' by Afrika Bambaata and the Soul Sonic Force (Number 4 R&B, Number 48 pop in 1982), and 'The Message' by Grandmaster Flash and the Furious Five (Number 4 R&B, Number 62 pop in 1982).

While most of the early hip-hop crossover hits featured relatively predictable party-oriented raps, 'The Message' established a new—and, in the end, profoundly influential—trend in rap music: social realism. In a recording that links the rhythmic intensity of funk music with the toast-derived images of ghetto life in *Hustler's Convention*, 'The Message' is a grim, almost cinematic portrait of life in the South Bronx. The rap on the first half of the recording was co-written by Sylvia Robinson, a former R&B singer and co-owner of Sugar Hill Records, and Duke Bootee, a sometime member of the Furious Five (resident Sugar Hill percussionist Ed Fletcher composed the musical track, using a Roland 808 digital drum machine and keyboard synthesizer, embellished with various studio effects). On top of the stark, cold electronic groove Grandmaster Flash intones the song's grim opening hook:

It's like a jungle sometimes, makes me wonder how I keep from goin' under

The sudden sound of glass shattering (produced on the drum machine) introduces a rhythmically complex, and carefully articulated, performance that alternates the smooth, slyly humorous style of Grandmaster Flash with the edgy, frustrated tone of MC Melle Mel:

Don't push me 'cause I'm close to the edge
I'm tryin' not to lose my head
Ah huh huh huh huh

The two MCs, but especially Melle Mel, time their performances with great precision, speeding up and slowing down, compressing and stretching the spaces between words, and creating polyrhythms against the steady musical pulse. The lyric alternates between the humorous wordplay typical of hip-hop MC performances and various images of desperation: threatening bill collectors, a homeless woman 'living in a bag', violent encounters in Central Park, a young child alienated by deteriorating public schools. The relationship between the grim reality of ghetto life and the tough-minded humour that is its essential antidote is summed up by Melle Mel's humourless quasi-laugh: 'Ah huh huh huh huh'.

The second half of 'The Message'—a *Hustler's Convention*-style toast written and performed by Melle Mel—paints an even more chilling picture, as listeners are confronted with an account of the life and death of a child born into poverty in the South Bronx:

A child is born with no state of mind
Blind unto the ways of Mankind
God is smiling on you, but he's frowning too
Because only God knows what you'll go through . . .

You'll admire all the number-book takers,
Thugs, pimps and pushers, and the big money makers
Driving big cars, spendin' 20s and 10s
And you want to grow up to be just like them, huh-huh . . .

Now you're unemployed, all null and void
Walkin' round like you're Pretty Boy Floyd
Turned stick-up kid, but look what you done did
Got sent up for a eight year bid . . .

It was plain to see that your life was lost
You was cold and your body swung back and forth
But now your eyes sing the sad, sad song
Of how you lived so fast and died so young.

This recitation is followed by the sound of the Furious Five—MCs Cowboy, Kidd Creole, Rahiem, Scorpio, and Mel—meeting and greeting on a street corner and discussing the evening's plans. Suddenly a police car screeches up and officers emerge, barking orders at the young black men. 'What are you, a gang?', one of the policemen shouts. 'Nah, man, we're with Grandmaster Flash and the Furious Five.' Flash enters from one side to defend his friends: 'Officer, officer, what's the problem?' 'You're the problem', the cop shouts back, 'get in the car!' We hear the car driving away with the Furious Five in custody, arrested evidently for the crime of assembling on a street corner, and the track quickly 'fades to black'.

A whole stream within the subsequent history of rap music can be traced from this gritty record, ranging from the explicitly political raps of KRS-One and Public Enemy to the 'gangsta' style of Los Angeles rappers like N.W.A., Snoop Doggy Dogg, and Tupac (a.k.a. '2Pac') Shakur. As the first realist description of life on the streets of the nation's urban ghettos in the 1980s to achieve wide commercial circulation, 'The Message' helped to establish canons of reality and street credibility that are still vitally important to rap musicians and audiences.

Gold records like 'Rapper's Delight' and 'The Message' created opportunities for New York rappers to perform at venues outside their own neighbourhoods and thereby widen their audience. They also alerted the major record companies to the commercial potential of hip-hop, eventually leading to the transition from the 12-inch dance single as the primary medium for recorded rap (an inheritance from disco) to the rap album. The mid-1980s saw a rapid acceleration of rap's movement into the popular mainstream. In 1983 the jazz fusion musician Herbie Hancock collaborated with DJ Grandmixer DST on 'Rockit', which made the R&B Top 10 and was played frequently on the still-young MTV channel. The following year, the popular soul singer Chaka Khan invited Melle Mel to provide a rap introduction for her hit single, 'I Feel for You', an adaptation of a Prince song that went to Number 1 R&B and Number 3 pop in the US but failed to chart in Canada.

Discussion Questions

1. Why do historians typically designate progressive country, reggae, punk, funk, and disco as 'outsiders' music'? What do these genres all share that ensure their 'outsider' status? Are these genres still examples of 'outsiders' music' or have they become 'mainstream'? For those that have become 'mainstream', are there any residual elements from their 'outsider' days?

2. Given the development of certain genres studied in this chapter, why might immigration be considered a powerful and musically productive force?

3. Consider the notion that 'punk was as much a cultural *style* . . . as it was a musical genre.' Do you agree or disagree with this statement?

4. George Clinton claims to have been influenced by Iggy Pop and acid rock in equal measure. How are these influences apparent in the records he produced during the mid- and late 1970s?

5. Disco elicited a violent reaction from many rock fans. Why? Do you think that disco and rock, and subgenres clearly influenced by both genres, are still so violently at odds today? Why? Can you think of other genres that tend to elicit similarly violent responses? What do fans have invested in their music that they should react so violently to another tradition?

6. Rap was not initially considered 'music' by many critics. Why do you think that is the case? How does rap resemble the soul music of James Brown?

Chapter Seven

MuchMusic, Mega-Stars, and Mega-Events: Rock in the 1980s

▌ Canada Enters the Eighties

The 1980s began in earnest in Canada with the election of Joe Clark to the office of Prime Minister in June of 1979, marking the first time in over a decade that someone had managed to wrest political power from Pierre Trudeau. In winning the election, Clark, an often straightforwardly partisan politician from Alberta who twice flunked out of law school before entering politics, became the youngest Prime Minister in Canadian history, taking office on the eve of his fortieth birthday. Beaten by a relative lightweight—newspapers ran the headline 'Joe Who?' when Clark bettered Brian Mulroney in the 1976 Progressive Conservative leadership convention—Trudeau promptly resigned from public office. Having spent more than a decade stewarding Canada through some of the most dramatic social and political upheavals in its relatively short history, Trudeau's sudden departure seemed to mark a conclusive, and appropriately abrupt, ending to what had turned out to be a tense and difficult political tenure.

Trudeau's retirement was remarkably short-lived, however. Within just months of taking office, Clark's minority government fell with its first budget (seemingly unaware that he trailed a basically leaderless Liberal Party by 20 points in opinion polls, Clark brazenly created a massive four-cents-per-gallon gasoline tax, which many saw as a blatantly self-interested move for a politician from Alberta to make). Clark was soundly squashed in the ensuing election, after Liberal Party insiders prevailed upon Trudeau to return to the party helm for one last run on Parliament. If it seemed to some that, with Trudeau back, Canada could look forward to a period of relative peace and prosperity, the election results clarified to others that, during the first half of the 1980s, Trudeau would have to govern a rudderless country with no national party and, thus, no real national mandate—the Liberals took only one seat west of the Great Lakes, in Winnipeg, while Clark took only one seat east of Toronto, a product of the East–West tensions over the distribution of oil revenues from Alberta and of other historical grievances that those in the West would not let go.

Before he stepped down in February 1984 after a famous 'walk in the snow', Trudeau completely reshaped the Canadian social and political landscape one last time, and practically through sheer force of will. Considering it a humiliating and demeaning vestige of colonial subordination that constitutional amendments still had to be approved in the British Parliament, largely because the country's provincial leaders could not agree on an amendment formula, Trudeau sought to patriate the British North America Act before his tenure ran out, after first prevailing one last time over René Lévesque in a Quebec referendum held on the issue of 'sovereignty-association' in May 1980 (the federalist 'Non' side scored a crushing 60 per cent majority). Trudeau also sought to entrench a new Charter of Rights and Freedoms in the newly patriated constitution, which would make the Supreme Court, rather than Parliament, the final arbiter of constitutional rights for Canadians.

With these goals in mind, Trudeau convened a lengthy and often vicious round of constitutional negotiations. Countered at first by a 'gang of eight' provincial leaders, who balked at what they took to be an overly centralist vision of government, Trudeau prevailed after forcing the premiers back to the table in November 1981. Only Lévesque, backed by a unanimous vote in the Quebec National Assembly, refused to sign the Constitution Act that the leaders eventually hammered out. Thus on the 17 April 1982, Canada finally achieved constitutional sovereignty, when Queen Elizabeth II appended her name to the Constitution Act on Parliament Hill. At the same time, the country received a Charter of Rights and Freedoms that reshaped the concept of citizens' rights entirely. Though far from perfect, as historians Robert Bothwell and J.L. Granatstein explain:

> Pressure groups, ethnic and First Nations lobbies, and ordinary citizens now had the chance to change the law. And they seized the opportunity with a will. Within a very short time Canada was well on the way to becoming as litigious as the United States, though, in that special Canadian way, the federal government funded many of those Charter challenges. The Charter of Rights and Freedoms became an icon in the Canadian pantheon, a defining force in Canadian nationalism every bit as strong as medicare. (Bothwell and Granatstein, 2000: 211–12)

The Early 1980s: Record Recession

If the 1980s began with political intrigue in Canada, they began on an unambiguously sour note from the perspective of the pop music industry. Following a period of rapid expansion in the mid-1970s, 1979 saw an 11 per cent drop in annual record sales across North America—the first major recession in the industry in 30 years. Profits from the sale of recorded music in North America hit rock bottom in 1982 ($4.6 billion), down half a billion dollars from the peak year of 1978 ($5.1 billion). The major record companies—now subdivisions of huge transnational conglomerates—trimmed their staffs, cut back expenses, signed fewer new acts, raised the prices of LPs and cassette tapes, and searched for new promotional and audience-targeting techniques. The pattern of relying on a small number of multi-platinum artists to create profits became more pronounced in the 1980s. By the mid-1980s, when the industry began to climb out of its hole, it was clear that the recovery was due more to the mega-success of a few recordings by superstar musicians—Michael Jackson, Madonna, Bryan Adams, Prince, Bruce Springsteen, Whitney Houston, Phil Collins, Janet Jackson, and others—than to any across-the-board improvement in record sales.

A number of reasons have been cited for the crash of the early 1980s—the run-up to and onset of a worldwide recession in 1982, which lasted for roughly two years, that sent unemployment rates rocketing upward and tax revenues plummeting, forcing the governments of most industrialized countries to divert more than 25 per cent of their spending to paying down interest on national debt; competition from new forms of entertainment, including home video, cable television, and video games; the decline of disco, which had driven the rapid expansion of the record business in the late 1970s; and an increase in illegal copying ('pirating') of commercial recordings by consumers with cassette tape decks. In 1984, sales of pre-recorded cassettes, boosted by the popularity of the Sony Walkman personal tape player and larger portable tape players called 'boom boxes', surpassed those of vinyl discs for the first time in history. (The introduction of digital audio tape, or DAT, in the early 1990s, and of writeable compact discs, or CD-Rs, at the turn of the century, provided consumers with the ability to make near-perfect copies of commercial recordings, a development that prompted the music industry to respond with new anti-copying technologies.)

The 1980s also saw the rise of technologies that would revolutionize the production of popular music. The development of *digital sound recording* led to the introduction of the five-inch *compact disc* (CD) and the rapid decline of the vinyl disc. The sounds encoded on a compact disc are read by a laser beam and not by a diamond needle, meaning that CDs are not subject to the same wear and tear as vinyl discs. The first compact discs went on sale in 1983, and by 1988 sales of CDs surpassed those of vinyl discs for the first time. Although CDs cost about the same as vinyl LPs to manufacture, the demand for the new medium allowed record companies to generate higher profits by pricing them at $13 or more, rather than the $8 or $9 charged for LPs. Digital technology also spawned new and more affordable devices for producing and manipulating sound, such as *drum machines* and *sequencers, samplers* for digital sampling, and the *musical instrument digital interface* (MIDI) specification, which standardized these technologies, allowing devices produced by different manufacturers to 'communicate' with one another. Digital technology—portable and relatively cheap—and the rapid expansion of the personal computer (PC) market in the early 1990s allowed musicians to set up their own home studios, stimulating the growth of genres like hip-hop and techno, both of which rely heavily on digitally constructed sound *samples*, *loops*, and *grooves*. For the first time, satellite technology allowed the worldwide simultaneous broadcast of live concerts, and the development of fibre optics allowed musicians in recording studios thousands of miles apart to work together in real time.

The Sudden Rise of Music Videos

Music Television in the United States: MTV

Deregulation of the entertainment industry led to an explosion in the growth of cable television, one by-product of which was the launching of Music Television (MTV) in the US in 1981. MTV changed the way the industry operated, rapidly becoming the preferred method for launching a new act or promoting the latest release of a major superstar. The advent of videos designed to promote rock recordings is sometimes traced to the band Queen's mock-operatic hard rock extravaganza 'Bohemian Rhapsody' (1975) and, before that, to promotional videos made by the Beatles during the late 1960s for tracks like 'Strawberry Fields Forever', 'Penny Lane', and 'Revolution'. However, such early music videos were essentially advertisements for the sound recordings and not viewed as products that might be sold on their own merits. Although the first song broadcast on MTV bore the title 'Video Killed the Radio Star', it is more accurate to say that music television worked synergistically with radio and other media to boost record sales and create a new generation of rock superstars. It also strongly influenced the direction of popular music in the early 1980s, sparking what has been called a second British Invasion, by promoting British artists such as the Eurythmics, Flock of Seagulls, Adam Ant, Billy Idol, and Thomas Dolby. In July 1983, 18 of the singles in *Billboard*'s Top 40 chart were by English artists, topping the previous record of 14, set in 1965 during the height of the first British Invasion (slightly less pronounced than in the United States, the CHUM charts for July 1983 reveal a similar pattern, with 15 of the Top 40 being releases from British artists).

MTV's relentless focus on white rock artists reminded many critics of the exclusionary practices of album-oriented rock radio in the 1970s. Out of more than 750 videos shown on MTV during the channel's first 18 months, only about 20 featured black musicians (a figure that includes racially mixed bands). At a time when black artists such as Michael Jackson and Rick James were making multi-platinum LPs, they could not break into MTV, which put Phil Collins's cover version of the Supremes' 'You Can't Hurry Love' into heavy rotation while videos by Motown artists themselves remained conspicuously absent. Executives at MTV responded to widespread criticism of their policy with the argument that their format focused on rock, a style played by few black artists. Of course, this was a tautological argument—the restrictive format of MTV was the cause, and not merely a by-product, of the problem.

The mammoth success of Michael Jackson's *Thriller*, released by Columbia Records in 1982, forced a change in MTV's essentially all-white rock music format. The three videos made to promote the *Thriller* LP—'Billie Jean', 'Beat It', and 'Thriller'—set new standards for production quality, creativity, and cost, and established the medium as the primary means of promoting popular music. 'Thriller'—a horror movie cum musical directed by John Landis, who had previously made the feature film *An American Werewolf in London*—metamorphosed into a 60-minute home video entitled *The Making of Michael Jackson's Thriller*, with the original 15-minute video and lots of filler material, including interviews with the star. *The Making of Michael Jackson's Thriller* sold 350,000 copies in the first six months, yet MTV still refused to air Jackson's videos. Finally, after Columbia Records threatened to ban its white rock groups from performing on MTV, the channel relented, putting Jackson's videos into heavy rotation. (*Thriller* will be discussed in more detail later; for now we will simply note that Jackson did not share the segregationist sentiments of MTV executives, going out of his way to include white rock stars such as Paul McCartney and Eddie Van Halen on the LP.)

Music Television in Canada: MuchMusic

MuchMusic, 'the nation's music station', first took to the Canadian airwaves on 31 August 1984. Established by Moses Znaimer, an executive at City-TV (a Toronto-based television station eventually purchased by CHUM Ltd), MuchMusic followed MTV's lead, beginning life as a discretionary pay-TV channel before becoming a part of basic Canadian cable service in 1989. (Znaimer established MusiquePlus, a francophone version of MuchMusic aimed specifically at Québécois

Erica Ehm: MuchMusic VJ from 1985 until 1994.

viewers, on 2 September 1986; the network became part of basic cable services in the province in 1988, thanks largely to a partnership deal struck with Radio Mutuel.) At its peak in the mid-1990s, MuchMusic is estimated to have reached some 5 million Canadian viewers on a daily basis

MuchMusic adopted a Top 40 format at first, differing only slightly from its counterpart to the south in terms of programming. Like MTV, MuchMusic featured a number of VJs (video jockeys) such as Jeanne Beker, Steve Anthony, Erica Ehm, J.D. Roberts (now an anchor on CNN), Kim Clark Champniss, Bill Welychka, Terry David Mulligan, Sook-Yin Lee, and Master T, who introduced videos slated into 'heavy', 'medium', and 'light' rotation. 'Light' rotation videos changed from week to week, while 'medium' and 'heavy' rotation videos changed on a monthly basis. Added to this were weekly 'discrete programming' shows devoted to airing videos from particular genres, including francophone (*French Kiss*), novelty (*Fromage*), indie (*The Wedge*), regional (*Going Coastal*), rap (*Rap City*), and world (*Clip Trip*). Live performances were added to the mix, alongside artist interviews and news coverage of primarily cultural affairs. The highest-rated show in the network's history remains *Video On Trial*, a half-hour weekly program that first aired in 2001 involving a panel of young Canadian comedians—Trevor Boris, Nicole Arbour, Debra DiGiovanni, Dini Dimakos, Sabrina Jalees, Ron Josol, David Kerr, Nikki Payne, Alex Nussbaum, Ron Sparks, and Fraser Young, to name only a few—providing generally hilarious commentary on popular videos while they play.

MuchMusic quickly became a tastemaker—some might say a cultural gatekeeper—for Canadian audiences. Recognizing the new-found significance of the music video and eager to support homegrown talent, the station established VideoFACT (Foundation to Assist Canadian Talent) in 1984, which was devoted to funding the production of music videos by Canadian artists; by 1991 the institution had helped finance the creation of more than 450 music videos, including an estimated 127 videos financed in 1990 alone. An early indication of MuchMusic's immense popularity came in 1987 when, in conjunction with Sky Channel London (UK), the station transmitted the first *World Music Video Awards* program, which reached an estimated audience of 750 million viewers in more than 45 countries. This success undoubtedly influenced the station's decision to create its own annual *Canadian Music Video Awards* program in 1990.

As the influence of MuchMusic grew, some critics have argued that Canadian popular music styles became increasingly integrated with American styles (whether they were ever all that divergent is, of course, debatable). In fact, critics point to the launch of MuchMusic as the precise moment when the possibility of anything like a 'distinctly Canadian' style of popular music making disappeared completely, as the country's Top 40 chart listings became increasingly international in scope after MuchMusic aired. To foster and recognize Canadian video makers, a Juno award for best video by a Canadian artist was established in 1984. The first seven awards went to, in order, Corey Hart ('Sunglasses at Night', 1984), Gowan ('Criminal Mind', 1985), Luba ('How Many Rivers To Cross', 1986), the Parachute Club ('Love Is Fir', 1987), Blue Rodeo ('Try', 1988), Andrew Cash ('Boom Town', 1989), and Maestro Fresh-Wes

('Drop the Needle', 1990). Félix awards, for French-language videos, were awarded from 1985 to 1990 to Michel Rivard ('Rumerus sur la ville', 1985), Rivard ('Rock et belles oreilles' and 'Le feu sauvage de l'amour', 1986), the Box ('Closer Together', 1987), Nathalie and René Simard ('Tourne la page', 1988), Luc de Larochelliere ('Amere America', 1989), and Laurence Jalbert ('Tomber Tomber', 1990).

Despite the reservations of a few critics, most celebrated MuchMusic for ushering in what some have called a 'second golden age' for Canadian popular music, the first having immediately followed the introduction of CanCon regulations by the CRTC in the early 1970s (see Chapter 5). Throughout the 1980s it sometimes seemed that heavy rotation on MuchMusic was all it took for an anglophone pop group to make the national Top 40. Just as CRTC regulations spawned a number of so-called 'CRTC bands' in the 1970s—bands who critics claim enjoyed an exaggerated level of success due to overexposure in an age of strict CanCon regulations—so did the 1980s see the rise of the so-called 'MuchMusic group', whose popularity critics attribute to frequent video play on the station. The moniker generally refers to bands such as Loverboy, Platinum Blonde, Rough Trade, the Pursuit of Happiness, the Box, and numerous other anglophone (and, in the case of the Box, bilingual) rock groups that enjoyed

A rare Canadian success story: **Glass Tiger** found more fame and popularity in the United States than in their home country. Photo Bill Kanerva.

chart success in Canada throughout the 1980s thanks to placing videos in heavy rotation on MuchMusic, but never scored another hit once their videos were pulled.

In fact, for many bands heavy rotation was entirely unnecessary for success. The
Newmarket pop group Glass Tiger, for instance, fronted by Alan Frew, was certainly
helped by MuchMusic when they sold over 400,000 copies of their debut LP, *The Thin
Red Line*, in Canada in 1986, backed by two hit videos. But the group actually did better in the United States, selling more than 500,000 copies of the LP there, where their
two biggest hits—'Don't Forget Me (When I'm Gone)' and 'Someday'—failed to garner much play on MTV at all. Similarly, Corey Hart, a pop singer-songwriter, pianist,
and producer from Montreal, enjoyed massive success both within Canada and abroad,
despite failing to produce a heavy rotation placement on MTV. Hart's first album, *First
Offense* (1983), earned him a Grammy nomination for best new male vocalist in 1984
and spawned the million-selling singles 'Sunglasses at Night' and 'It Ain't Enough'.

Finally, there was Vancouverite Bryan Adams. After an early disco hit ('Let Me Take
You Dancing') and a songwriting partnership with Jim Vallance (some of their songs
were recorded by the Canadian bands Prism and Loverboy), Adams signed a management contract with Bruce Allan in 1979. Allan took Adams's brand of 'classic rock'—
reminiscent of that created later in the decade by Tom Cochran ('Big League'), Kim
Mitchell ('Patio Lanterns'), David Wilcox ('Riverboat Fantasy'), and, even, the
Tragically Hip ('Blow at High Dough')—to the top of the global pop charts throughout the 1980s. Adams's albums from 1983 and 1984, *Cuts Like a Knife* and *Into the
Fire*, produced a number of international hits, including 'Cuts Like a Knife', 'Run To
You', 'Summer of 69', and 'It's Only Love' (a duet with Tina Turner), even if the singer
failed to receive an equal amount of video play in the US to what he had in Canada.
At the same time, Adams's songwriting partnership with Vallance continued to produce results, with songs by the duo recorded by BTO, Joe Cocker, Roger Daultry, Neil
Diamond, Paul Hyde and the Payolas, KISS, Bonnie Raitt, Carly Simon, Rod Stewart,
Tina Turner, Bonnie Tyler, and Uriah Heap, to name only a few. Perhaps Adams's
highest—and lowest—point would come in 1991, however, when his '(Everything I
Do) I Do It For You' stayed at Number 1 for 12 weeks in Canada, for seven weeks in
the US, and for a staggering four months in the United Kingdom, even though it
failed to qualify as 'Canadian content', according to CRTC regulations, because of the
prominent work of Zambian-British producer Robert 'Mutt' Lange. Adams questioned the validity of the regulations afterwards, but soon fell silent on the matter.

This said, a number of bands obviously benefited from the attention of producers
at MuchMusic, establishing themselves as superstars within Canada even as they
struggled to gain any kind of recognition abroad. Bruce Cockburn, though a popular singer-songwriter around the world, achieved practically iconic status in Canada
after placing a number videos into heavy rotation on MuchMusic during the mid-
1980s, including 'If I Had a Rocket Launcher', 'If a Tree Falls in the Forest', and
'Lovers in a Dangerous Time'. So, too, bands such as the Cowboy Junkies (*Trinity
Sessions*), the Crash Test Dummies ('Superman Song'), the Grapes of Wrath ('You
May Be Right'), and the Pursuit of Happiness ('I'm an Adult Now') benefited from
frequent MuchMusic airplay.

But likely the best-known example of a rock band achieving 'national icon' status within Canada, while barely registering in the United States, is Kingston's the Tragically Hip, formed in 1983 by vocalist Gord Downie, guitarists Bobby Baker and Paul Langlois, bassist Gord Sinclair, and drummer Johnny Fay. Catching the ear of the president of MCA Records, Bruce Dickinson, during a performance at the Horseshoe Tavern in Toronto in 1986, the group recorded their first full-length album for the label in 1989, the triple platinum CanCon classic, *Up To Here*, which included the hit singles 'Blow at High Dough' and 'New Orleans Is Sinking'. Their next release, *Road Apples* (1990), cemented the Hip's reputation as a heavy-hitting 'trad rock' combo with a literary bent, as videos for 'Little Bones' and 'Twist My Arm' made it into heavy rotation on MuchMusic that year and garnered breathless accolades from numerous Canadian critics. A concerted effort in the mid-1990s, including an appearance on *Saturday Night Live* in 1995, failed to produce a breakthrough on the American charts, after which point references to Canadian places and cultural myths seemed to become increasingly prominent in the band's songwriting. By the time of *Phantom Power* (1998), songs about sinking American cities had been almost entirely replaced with references to riots in Toronto, constellations revealing themselves 'one cloud at a time' in a provincial park near Bobcaygeon, Ontario, first girlfriends who shockingly 'didn't give a fuck about hockey' or Bobbie Orr, and women drawn from paintings by the iconic Canadian Tom Thomson.

The Global Record Industry: Horizontal Integration

The process of corporate consolidation (sometimes called 'horizontal integration'), which has emerged at intervals throughout rock's historical development, once again reared its head during the late 1980s and early 1990s. To a greater extent than ever before, record labels could no longer be considered stand-alone institutions but rather sub-departments of huge transnational corporations. By 1990 six corporations collectively controlled over two-thirds of global sales of recorded music:

- the Dutch Polygram conglomerate (owner of Mercury, Polydor, Island, A&M, and other labels);
- the Japanese corporations Sony (Columbia Records) and Matsushita (MCA and Geffen Records);
- the British firm Thorn (EMI, Virgin, Capitol);
- the German Bertelsmann conglomerate (BMG and RCA Records); and
- Time Warner, the only American-based corporation in this list (Warner, Elektra, and Atlantic Records).

Similarly, the North American market for recorded music now had to be seen as part of a wider global market that transcended national borders. In 1990 the largest market for recorded music in the world remained the United States, which, at $7.5 billion, accounted for approximately 31 per cent of world trade, followed at some distance by Japan (12 per cent), the United Kingdom and Germany (9 per cent each), and France (7 per cent). Even in the US, however, record company executives concerned themselves to an unprecedented degree with global sales and promotion.

This move towards global corporate consolidation of the music business was accompanied by a further fragmentation of the marketplace for popular music and the creation of dozens of new musical genres, marketing categories, and radio formats. Some of these were more novel than others, but all bore some relationship to musical forms of the past. Country music continued its six-decade journey from the margins to the centre of popular taste, becoming the best-selling genre of music in the US with rock- and pop-influenced country superstars such as Garth Brooks, Clint Black, and Reba McEntire. Rock music, which had undergone a process of fragmentation in the early 1970s, shattered into a hundred specialized genres and subgenres, some with huge audiences (adult contemporary and heavy metal) and others supported by smaller but devoted groups of fans (hardcore, thrash, and techno, the respective children of punk rock, heavy metal, and Eurodisco). Rap music, which had emerged during the mid-1970s from the hip-hop culture of black, Latino, and Caribbean American youth in New York City, had grown by the late 1980s into a multi-million dollar business. Indeed, during the 1990s the relationship between the centre and periphery of the music business, and between mainstream and marginalized types of music, became even more complicated, with self-consciously anti-commercial genres like gangsta rap, speed metal, and grunge reaching the top of the pop charts and generating huge profits for the music industry; and with musicians from Latin America (Ricky Martin), Ontario (Shania Twain and Alanis Morissette), and French Canada (Céline Dion) ranking among the most profitable superstars on the planet at the end of the second millennium.

▌Digital Technology and Popular Music

During the 1980s, new technologies—digital tape recorders, compact discs, synthesizers, samplers, and sequencers—became central to the production, promotion, and consumption of popular music. These devices were the fruit of a long history of interactions between the electronics and music industries, and between individual inventors and musicians. *Analog recording*—the norm since the introduction of recording in the nineteenth century—transforms the energy of sound waves into physical imprints (as in pre-1925 acoustic recordings) or into electronic waveforms that closely follow, and can be used to reproduce, the shape of the sound waves themselves. *Digital recording*, on the other hand, samples the sound waves and breaks them down into a stream of numbers (0s and 1s). A device called an analog-to-digital converter does the conversion; to play back the music, the stream of numbers is converted back to an analog wave by a *digital-to-analog converter* (DAC). The analog wave produced by the DAC is amplified and fed to speakers to produce the sound. There have been many arguments among musicians and audiophiles over the relative quality of the two technologies—many musicians initially found digital recording too 'cold' (perhaps a metaphor for the process itself, which disassembles a sound into millions of constituent bits). Today, however, almost all popular recordings are digitally recorded.

Synthesizers—devices that allow musicians to create or 'synthesize' musical sounds—began to appear on rock records during the early 1970s, but their history begins much earlier. One important predecessor of the synthesizer was the theremin, a sound generator named after the Russian inventor who developed it in 1919. This instrument used electronic oscillators to produce sound, and its pitch was controlled by the player waving his or her hands in front of two antennae. The theremin was never used much in popular music, although its familiar sound can be heard in the soundtracks of 1950s science fiction films such as *The Day the Earth Stood Still* and on the Beach Boys' 1966 hit 'Good Vibrations'.

Another important stage in the interaction between scientific invention and musical technology was the *Hammond organ*, introduced in 1935 by the inventor Laurens Hammond. The sound of the Hammond B-3 organ was common on jazz, R&B, and rock records (e.g., Santana's 'Oye Como Va'), and its rich, fat sound is frequently sampled in contemporary popular music. The player could alter the timbre of the organ through control devices called 'tone bars', and a variety of rhythm patterns and percussive effects were added later. Although the Hammond organ was not a true synthesizer, it is certainly a close ancestor.

In the early 1970s the first synthesizers aimed at a mass consumer market were introduced. These devices, which used electronic oscillators to produce musical tones, were clumsy and limited by today's standards, yet their characteristic sounds are viewed with some nostalgia and are often sampled in contemporary recordings. The first synthesizers to be sold in music stores alongside guitars and pianos were the *Minimoog*, which had the limitation of being able to play only one pitch at a time, and the *Arp synthesizer*, which could play simple chords. The *synclavier*, a high-end (and expensive) digital synthesizer, was introduced to the market in 1976. The more affordable *Prophet-5*, introduced in 1978, was an analog synthesizer that incorporated aspects of digital technology, including the ability to store a limited number of sampled sounds.

The 1980s saw the introduction of the first completely digital synthesizers—including the widely popular Yamaha DX-7—capable of playing dozens of 'voices' at the same time. The MIDI (musical instrument digital interface) specification, introduced in 1983, allowed synthesizers built by different manufacturers to be connected and to communicate with one another, introducing compatibility into a highly competitive marketplace. Digital samplers—for example, the Mirage keyboard sampler, introduced by Ensoniq in 1984—were capable of storing both pre-recorded and synthesized sounds, the latter often called 'patches', a nostalgic reference to the wires or 'patch cords' that were used to connect the various components of early synthesizers. *Digital sequencers*, introduced to the marketplace at around the same time, are devices that record musical data rather than musical sound, and allow the creation of repeated sound sequences (loops), the manipulation of rhythmic grooves, and the transmission of recorded data from one program or device to another. *Drum machines* such as the Roland TR 808 and the Linn LM1—almost ubiquitous on 1980s dance music and rap records—rely on 'drum pads' that can be struck and activated by the performer, and which act as a trigger for the production of sampled sounds (including not only conventional percussion instruments but also glass smashing, cars screeching, and guns firing).

Digital technology has given musicians the ability to create complex 128-voice textures, to create sophisticated synthesized sounds that exist nowhere in nature, and to sample and manipulate any sound source, creating sound loops that can be controlled with great precision. With compact, highly portable, and increasingly affordable music equipment and software, a recording studio can be set up literally anywhere. As the individual musician gains more and more control over the production of a complete musical recording, distinctions between the composer, the performer, and the producer sometimes melt down entirely.

Certain contemporary genres make particularly frequent and effective use of digital technologies, particularly rap/hip-hop, ambient electronica, and various genres of electronic dance music. The technology of digital sampling allows musicians to assemble pre-existing sound sources and to cite performers and music from various styles and historical eras in their songs. During the 1980s musicians began to reach back into their record collections for sounds from the 1960s and 1970s. It has been suggested that this reflects a more general cultural shift towards a 'cut-and-paste' approach to history, in which pop music cannibalizes its own past. However, it is worth remembering that, while the technology is new, the idea of recycling old materials—and thereby selectively reinventing the past—is probably as old as music itself.

Some interesting legal dilemmas are connected with the widespread use of digital sampling. American intellectual property law has always made it difficult to claim ownership of a groove, style, or sound—precisely those things that are most distinctive about popular music, like the timbre of James Brown's voice, the electric bass sound of Parliament/Funkadelic's Bootsy Collins, or the distinctive snare drum sound used on many of Phil Collins's hit recordings (a sound constructed in the studio out of a combination of sampled and synthesized sources and expert signal processing). In recent years many lawsuits have centred on these issues, in which musicians and producers claim that their sound has been stolen by means of digital sampling. George Clinton has responded to the wholesale sampling of his albums by rap musicians by releasing a collection of sounds and previously unreleased recordings called *Sample Some of Disc, Sample Some of D.A.T.* The collection comes with a copyright clearance guide and a guarantee that users will only be 'charged per record sold, so if your single flops, you won't be in the red.'

Of course, no technology is inherently good or evil—it's what humans do with their tools that counts. On the one hand, many musicians mourn the replacement of acoustic musical instruments—and the physical discipline and craft involved in mastering them—by machines. Others tout the democratization of popular music made possible with the introduction of successively cheaper digital technologies. And still others point out that, no matter how good the technology, only a small percentage of musicians are able to gain access to the powerful corporations that control the music industry. The odds that a musician will succeed have not changed much, precisely because almost everyone now has access to the new technology. While high-quality demonstration tapes ('demos') used to be a luxury available to only those musicians who could afford to rent a professional recording studio, now it can sometimes seem like everyone on the block has a demo.

Now Playing on MuchMusic

MuchMusic did more to revitalize the rock tradition in Canada than any other institution during the 1980s. As we have already noted, at the peak of its popularity in the mid-1990s the station reached more than 5 million viewers per day. Though this may seem like a small cohort compared to the tens of millions of viewers MTV attracted at the same time, it is actually a far more significant number when we take into consideration Canada's relatively small national population. In 1991, for instance, when the population of Canada was estimated at roughly 27 million people, more than 15 per cent of the nation tuned in daily. Not surprisingly, then, MuchMusic began to wield a significant influence over national tastes and preferences. In fact, the most successful pop singer in Canadian history—Madonna—worked primarily in the medium of music television, using radio and live performance as ancillary tools for selling records.

For the first time in the 1980s, videos rather than records by Canadian artists competed for airtime and attention, and they did so against videos from stars based in the US, England, and, sometimes, even further abroad. A video for the Cold War-era protest song '99 Luftballons' by the German rock band Nena, for instance, renamed '99 Red Balloons' and translated into English, made it into heavy rotation on MuchMusic in 1984, eventually topping the Canadian Top 40 in March of that year. As noted, this circumstance forced what some critics consider to have been a widespread homogenization of Canadian rock music, as many local bands felt increasingly compelled to adopt the musical and visual aesthetic and ethos of their internationally successful peers in order to compete.

Platinum Blonde, a new wave rock outfit from Toronto, springs immediately to mind. The band appeared in its immensely popular videos attired in the androgynous glam rock outfits favoured by their new romantic and new wave contemporaries from 'across the pond' in England—a uniform comprised of often fluorescent pink, red, green, and yellow suits (complete with shoulder pads, of course); lipstick and dangling earrings; long teased and feathered hair, with stark platinum-blonde highlights; and oversized, brightly coloured plastic sunglasses, worn even in the dark. Dubbed 'Canada's Duran Duran' by the national press, the group rocketed up the charts in 1983 after releasing videos for 'Standing in the Dark' and 'It Doesn't Really Matter', both from their double platinum debut LP, *Standing in the Dark* (1983). Platinum Blonde's follow up LP, 1985's *Alien Shores*, was even more successful, achieving quintuple platinum certification based on sales in Canada alone.

But while many Canadian bands adopted an obviously international aesthetic, just as many, if not more, pursued a staunchly—some might say stubbornly—local one. Videos produced by Canadians in the 1980s often emphasize the musicians'

Canadian roots, many clearly revelling in certain esoteric aspects of the national culture. The video for The Rheostatics' 'The Ballad of Wendel Clark, Part 1&2' (1986)—directed by Scott Dobson as an homage to the much-loved Toronto Maple Leafs' All-Star forward—with its many images of betoqued 'hoser' teens in lumberjack jackets wandering around small-town Ontario with road hockey sticks dutifully strapped to their backs, serves as a good example. More than just homage to a particularly popular and gifted hockey player, the video is actually about the central position hockey occupies in Canadian culture, that is, it explores what it means to live in a culture where hockey players serve as first role models for much of the nation's youth—a point reinforced by the fact that, even as the singer runs down a veritable laundry list of reasons to admire the Leafs forward, we are never once confronted with an image of any professional hockey player, let alone Wendell Clark himself.

As more bands adopted this 'proudly Canadian' ethos, a distinctly Canadian approach to rock songwriting, performance, and video making eventually emerged—one that often, and often humorously, emphasized musicians' awareness that they lacked the requisite funds to create slickly produced videos like their American and British peers. (This is, in fact, a basis of one particular brand of Canadian humour, which involves a kind of self-deprecating willingness to revel in the 'amateurishness' of one's productions compared with lavish, and obviously expensive, American productions—Rich Moranis and Dave Thomas as the McKenzie Brothers on SCTV and Mike Myers with his 'Wayne's World' schtick, from *Saturday Night Live* to Hollywood films, are cases in point.) By 1991, a group like the Barenaked Ladies could create a video for their cover of Bruce Cockburn's 'Lovers in a Dangerous Time' comprised almost entirely of grainy black-and-white footage of the band being spirited around Scarborough, Ontario, on the back of a pickup truck; performing in the parking lots of suburban strip malls and apartment buildings; playing road hockey (a highlight at roughly two minutes into the video involves a group of street hockey players shouting 'Car!' and clearing the road to let the band's pickup pass); looking out over Toronto from the CN Tower observation deck; and, eventually, giving away merchandise to the only two fans who show up to an appearance at a local record store. While viewers from around the world could glean many different meanings from this video, the 'insider' references to Canadian culture abound, making this an early example of the blatantly nationalistic style that groups like the Tragically Hip would exploit with such skill—and much less humour—later in the decade. As the lead singer and lyricist for the Tragically Hip, Gordon Downie, explains, by the mid-1990s he could write an entire album's worth of songs probing 'what it means to be Canadian' without fear of commercial failure. In Downie's words:

> I definitely wasn't aware of it until recently—which may just be selective memory—but I've just sort of watched it evolve in terms of the lyrics. As a young writer from small-town, middle-class Canada I think I started writing about, in my limited scope, Canada, and in a weird way I guess what I'm thinking about is how it all unfolded and how a lot of people might attribute the band's popularity to a blatant nationalism. (theHip.com/theBand.html)

Rough Trade: 'High School Confidential' (1980)

Comprised of lead vocalist Carole Pope, guitarist Kevan Staples, and a rotating cast of backing musicians, Rough Trade remains one of the most controversial rock bands ever to perform in Canada. Based in Toronto, Ontario, Pope and Staples began their careers together in 1969, though they would not secure a record deal until 11 years later, when they signed with Bernie Finkelstein's True North label. The band's first LP, *Rough Trade Live!* (Umbrella, 1977), was more of a demonstration recording made to shop the band to executives at major labels than a full-scale release. Sex and sexuality formed a central focus for the duo from the very beginning, evidenced in the band names they chose for themselves ('O', 'The Bullwhip Brothers', and, eventually, 'Rough Trade'); in their sexually charged live performances (Pope often performed around Toronto in full bondage attire); in videos, which could feature Pope brazenly lusting after scantily clad female high school students; and, finally, in Pope's often unambiguous lyrical celebrations of all sexualities, as in 'All Touch' (1980), the band's best-selling single while they still were a performing entity in the 1980s:

I pushed her tense face, away from me
I pushed her tense face, away from me
The hard smile, the voice going on
Like a razor blade on glass
All touch, but no contact

I pushed his hand away from me
I pushed his hand away from me
Splintering fragments of conversation
Never got down to cold hard facts
All touch, but no contact

In fact, Rough Trade is now best remembered for 'High School Confidential' (1980), the second track from their cheekily titled debut LP, *Avoid Freud* (1980). The song is a fairly straightforward statement of 1980s new wave music, even if it was recorded early in the genre's development. A successful mixture of rock and new wave conventions, the song uses a standard rock form (it features four strophes divided into verses and refrains, with a brief instrumental introduction and conclusion), but is overlaid with two hallmarks of new wave music from the time, namely, Carole Pope's aggressive and slightly dissonant vocals, and the inclusion of synthesizer and digital piano timbres performing the song's introductory hook and a sometimes angular countermelody based on that hook in the final two strophes. The experience of driving lust recounted in the lyrics finds musical expression in the relentless pounding of quarter notes by the left hand of the piano, the electric bass, and the drum kit. The only two instruments that vary from that quarter-note pulse at any point in the song, besides during the introduction and conclusion, are the hi-hat—

which diverges only to provide a constant and equally relentless eighth-note subdivision of the beat—and an overdubbed piano part, which doubles the basic melody with block chords throughout the song (a chorus of male vocals harmonizes with Pope during the song's refrains, effectively setting those sections off from the rest of the song). Finally, Gene Martynec's production for the track reinforces the lyrical narrative, adding a rattle of castanets each time Pope mentions the stiletto heels favoured by her crush, and overdubbed shouting when Pope recalls the '*cat calls*' shouted by the presumably myriad '*teenage Brandos*' who attended her high school.

Tense and sometimes unnerving, Pope's lyrics voice the turmoil many gay and lesbian teens report experiencing in high school, especially those who, for whatever reasons, felt conflicted about, or compelled to hide, their sexualities. For however much critics and historians now claim 'High School Confidential' as an open and unadulterated celebration of lesbian desire, which it undoubtedly is, the song's meanings actually probe much deeper—the narrative Pope constructs recreates the turmoil of a young female high school student fixated on another female student but ultimately unable to express her desires. One could even argue that the object of Pope's lust is secondary to how that lust is experienced—confidential, as the title suggests, and yet bold ('*it makes me cream my jeans when she comes my way*'); impatient ('*if I don't get her soon I'll have a heart attack*'); jealous ('*who's the guy she's with — is he screwing her?*'); and, ultimately, gut-wrenching ('*I want her so much I feel sick*'). The song's narrator can only observe the object of her affections from afar—so far, in fact, that she goes basically unnoticed by her crush, making the song all the more tragic for the almost total absence of any interaction between the narrator and her crush. In the end, the singer's lust remains only a 'high school confidential', as the title suggests.

A controversial video was produced for the song, which made heavy rotation on MuchMusic. If there were any doubts as to the subject matter of 'High School Confidential', Rough Trade's video for the song aggressively quashed them. The video opens with a first-person view, from behind a synthesizer, of a long high school corridor; panning down that corridor, still behind the synthesizer, the performer eventually stops to inspect a young woman, the camera lingering (leering) over her short red-and-white skirt, black nylons, and exposed garter. Throughout the rest of the video, two narratives emerge: the one related in the song's lyrics, and another that retells the telling, as it were, featuring highly stylized performance footage of Pope and Staples performing the song. Pope's performance is as sexually charged as her lyrics, the singer most famously running her hands along her crotch as she sings, '*it makes me cream my jeans when she comes my way.*' After the figure of the '*teenage Brando*' is introduced, however, in the form of a muscular young man in jeans and a white T-shirt, with a package of cigarettes folded into one of his rolled up sleeves, the video increasingly clarifies that only the boy and girl will make contact, leaving Pope to jealously observe from the concert stage. The video concludes with an image of the young coquette exhaling from her cigarette, remembering her '*teenage Brando*', while Pope looks defiantly—and unapologetically—through the camera to the viewer, placing her hands on her hips.

Tina Turner: 'What's Love Got to Do with It' (1984)

By the time Tina Turner (née Annie Mae Bullock, b. 1939 in Tennessee) recorded 'What's Love Got to Do with It', released in 1984, she had been in the popular music limelight for over 20 years. Her recording debut took place in 1960 as a member of the Ike and Tina Turner Revue. Tina's husband, Ike Turner, had begun his recording career much earlier, as a performer on Jackie Brenston's 'Rocket 88' (1951), sometimes credited as the first rock 'n' roll record. Ike and Tina scored big crossover hits in America throughout the 1960s with 'A Fool in Love' (Number 2 R&B and Number 27 pop in 1960), 'It's Gonna Work Out Fine' (Number 2 R&B and Number 14 pop in 1961), and, their first record to chart in Canada, a cover version of Creedence Clearwater Revival's 1969 hit, 'Proud Mary' (Number 4 pop, Number 5 R&B, and Number 3 CHUM in 1971).

As recounted in her 1986 best-selling autobiography—*I, Tina*—Tina Turner eventually tired of the abusive behaviour of her husband, leaving him in 1976 to start her own career. The first years were tough, but by 1981 the Rolling Stones and Rod

Tina Turner in action.
Frank Driggs Collection.

Stewart, old fans of the Ike and Tina Revue, had hired her as an opening act on their concert tours. In 1983 she was offered a contract by Capitol Records. Her first album, entitled *Private Dancer* (1984), reached Number 3 on the album charts, stayed in the Top 40 for 71 weeks, spawned five hit singles, and eventually went on to attain worldwide sales in excess of 11 million copies. In succeeding years Turner continued to build her career, releasing a series of platinum albums and appearing in movies such as the Mel Gibson sci-fi action film *Mad Max Beyond Thunderdome* (1985). Earlier, in 1975, she had a featured role as the Acid Queen in the Who's rock opera film, *Tommy*. In 1993 a film version of her autobiography was produced, entitled *What's Love Got to Do with It*.

The crossover hit 'What's Love Got to Do with It' (Number 1 pop and Number 2 R&B in 1984) stayed on the charts for 28 weeks, and earned Turner Grammy awards in 1984 for Best Female Pop Vocalist, Song of the Year, and Record of the Year. Turner did not like the song at first, and did not hesitate in conveying this sentiment to Terry Britten, its co-author and producer of the *Private Dancer* album. '[Terry] said that when a song is given to an artist it's changed for the artists', Turner reminisced. 'He said for me to make it a bit rougher, a bit more sharp around the edges. All of a sudden, just sitting there with him in the studio, the song became mine' (Wynn, 1985: 132).

The lyric of 'What's Love Got to Do With It' sets up an ambivalent relationship between the overwhelming sexual attraction described in the verses and the singer's cynicism about romantic love, derided in the song's chorus as '*a second-hand emotion*'. This dynamic in the song's text is reinforced by the musical accompaniment. Though the tempo remains fairly constant (a relaxed pace of 98 beats per minute), the instrumental arrangement alternates between the rich, continuous texture—dominated by flute and string synthesizer sounds—that underlies the verses, and a more bouncy, reggae-like groove established by the electric bass and guitars in the chorus, the lyrics of which begin with the song's title.

The whole arrangement itself is carefully constructed—an eight-bar instrumental introduction; an unusual 13-bar verse ('*You must understand . . .*'), comprising seven- and six-bar sections ('A'); an eight-bar chorus ('B'); then another verse ('A') ('*It may seem . . .*'), followed by another chorus ('B'). The middle point of the arrangement in structural terms is a synthesizer solo of seven and a half bars, using the harmonies of the chorus ('B'). This is followed by an eight-bar section ('C') with new harmonies, where the singer reveals her fear of heartbreak more explicitly ('*I've been taking . . .*'). The arrangement concludes with three repetitions of the chorus (minus one bar, thanks to the early entrance of the chorus each time through), fading away at the very end.

For many in her audience, the character in this song—an experienced, cynical, yet still vulnerable woman—was Turner herself, a case where the boundary between the public and private lives of a recording artist seems to have dissolved almost entirely. In the case of a David Bowie or—as we shall see later in this chapter—Madonna, a sense of ironic distance between the celebrity image and the individual behind it is carefully maintained; in Tina Turner's case, this distinction between image and identity remains much less clear. The combination of poignant vulnerability and toughness projected in Turner's recordings and live performances was linked by her fans to the details of her biography, and helps to explain her appeal as the first black woman to attain major status in the predominantly white male field of arena rock music.

Kim Mitchell: 'Patio Lanterns' (1986)

Kim Mitchell is widely admired by fans for his hyperactive performances and the many manic 'party rock' anthems he composed over the course of his more than three-decades-long career ('I Am a Wild Party', 'Go for a Soda', and 'Rock 'N' Roll Duty'), and other of his songs would score higher than 'Patio Lanterns' (1986) on the charts—most notably 'All We Are', which reached Number 1 in Canada in January 1985. Yet, Mitchell's 'Patio Lanterns', a sweetly innocent paean to first loves and long summer nights spent outside in his home town of Sarnia, Ontario, best encapsulates the remarkably down-to-earth Canadian rocker's musical achievements.

Mitchell first came to national prominence in the early 1970s as the lead singer, songwriter, and guitarist for the Sarnia-based rock band, Max Webster. With a rotating cast of band members, Max Webster eventually centred on the work of Mitchell and lyricist Pye Dubois, who did not tour with the group (the duo would continue to work together even after Max Webster disbanded in 1982 and Mitchell began his pursuit of solo success). Producing a number of popular songs—including 'High

Kim Mitchell won over fans with his many 'party rock' anthems. The Canadian Press.

Class in Borrowed Shoes', 'Hangover', 'Paradise Skies', 'A Million Vacations', and 'Let Go the Line'—the band eventually caught the ear of fellow Canadian rockers, Rush, with whom the group toured Canada, Britain, and the United States during the late 1970s. Dubois would go on to pen lyrics for Rush, including for the perennially popular 'Tom Sawyer', and band members Geddy Lee, Alex Lifeson, and Neil Peart appeared on a live recording of 'Battle Scar' for the fifth full-length Max Webster release, *Universal Juveniles* (1980).

Having established his reputation as an imaginative and immensely gifted, if often underestimated, guitar player, and a songwriter of great dexterity and skill, Mitchell 'went solo' in 1982, after working briefly as a session guitarist and producer. His first LP release as a solo artist, *akimbo alogo* (1984), established Mitchell as a musician with his finger on 'the concerns and diversions of the teenaged Canadian male', as Betty Nygard King put it, but two singles from the album—'Go for a Soda' and 'All We Are'—demonstrated that Mitchell's appeal extended well beyond national borders, the often hyperactive singer topping the charts in Canada and entering the *Billboard* Top 40 in the US, thanks largely to multiple plays on both MuchMusic and MTV. That same year Mitchell received a Juno award for Most Promising Male Vocalist, though he had been singing rock music for well over a decade by then.

'Patio Lanterns' appeared on the follow-up to *akimbo alogo*, the triple platinum *Shakin' Like a Human Being* LP, released in 1986 (the album won a Juno for Album of the Year in 1987). The song's simple structure and its 'no muss, no fuss' arrangement testify to Mitchell's maturity as a composer and producer, the singer crafting an appropriately uncomplicated production to match the youthful innocence detailed in Dubois's lyrics for the song:

> *Our house had the biggest patio.*
> *Our house had all the summer shade.*
> *We had patio lanterns.*
> *I'd spend half the night making lemonade*
> *Which we drank a lot*
> *'Cause we were all so shy—*
> *Shy and nervous.*
> *Who was gonna be—*
> *Who would be the first to kiss*
> *Under those patio lanterns?*
>
> *And I was stuck on Joy*
> *That was her name*
> *We didn't talk much*
> *She was a nervous girl*
> *I was a nervous boy*

Divided into a simple verse-chorus structure—with two 'A' sections parsed into a verse and chorus each, with a final iteration of the chorus added before a long fade-out—'Patio Lanterns' features little to distract listeners form Mitchell's vocal performance. Backed by an electric keyboard, a synthesizer, an electric bass, drum kit, and acoustic and electric guitars—a remarkably economical instrumentation compared to many rock records made in the mid-1980s—Mitchell sets off the choruses from the verses via choral harmonization. During the second verse, a call-and-response between himself and multi-instrumentalist Peter Fredette complicates the arrangement (Fredette played electric bass, guitar, keyboard, and drums on Mitchell's best-selling albums from the mid-1980s). In sum, listeners hear only three melodies on 'Patio Lanterns': the song's introductory hook, provided by digital piano and synthesizer; Mitchell's lead vocal line; and Fredette's call-and-response countermelody in the chorus.

The video for 'Patio Lanterns', which peaked at Number 12 on the charts in 1986 thanks to repeated plays on MuchMusic, begins with what could only be the product of Mitchell's famously goofy sense of humour. Two Japanese men in lab coats pack a box of patio lanterns to be shipped to North America (later we learn that they are being shipped to Mitchell's home in Sarnia). Taking a break, one man asks the other, *'Are these going to North America—what do they do with them?'* To which the other responds, *'They use them in the bathroom at Christmas time . . . ha ha!'* Next Mitchell appears dressed in his trademark black-and-gold OPP (Ontario Provincial Police) baseball cap, a white short-sleeved button-up shirt tucked into a pair of stonewashed blue jeans, and an acoustic guitar strapped across his back. Eventually he is joined by his backing band onstage, and Mitchell's layered arrangement calls for each member to perform in turn, after which the video jumps between footage of Mitchell performing the song in the present and flashbacks recounting his tale of first kisses and *'nervous'* adolescent love. Without a hint of embarrassment, 'Patio Lanterns'—both the video and the song—sweetly conjures the awkwardness, and the nervous exhilaration, of first loves and Canadian summers, a time many Canadian teens spent making anxious small talk with future loves under the very same patio lanterns Mitchell remembers so fondly.

The Eurythmics: 'Sweet Dreams (Are Made of This)' (1983)

This Number 1 single from the early 1980s exemplifies one of the directions dance music took in the post-disco era. With its heavy reliance on electronically synthesized sounds, sequenced loops, and what has been described as a cool or austere emotional tone, the Eurythmics' 'Sweet Dreams' points the way towards later technology-centred music styles such as techno. Like some of the most successful techno groups of the 1990s, the Eurythmics consisted of a core of only two musicians—the singer Annie Lennox (b. 1954 in Scotland) and keyboardist and technical whiz Dave Stewart (b. 1952 in England).

The Eurythmics' first chart appearance in North America came with the release of their second album, *Sweet Dreams (Are Made of This)*, in 1983. The title track was released as a single soon after the album release, rocketed to Number 2 on the English charts, and shortly afterwards climbed to Number 1 on the American and Canadian charts. The popularity of 'Sweet Dreams (Are Made of This)' was boosted enormously by a video produced to promote the record, which was placed into heavy rotation by the fledgling MTV channel (it would make heavy rotation on MuchMusic the next year). In particular, the stylishly androgynous image of Annie Lennox—a female David Bowie, in a business suit with close-cropped orange hair—is often identified as an important ingredient in the Eurythmics' success and an icon of gender politics in a rock world completely reshaped by music television.

Alongside the earlier 'High School Confidential', 'Sweet Dreams' is another good example of commercial new wave music made during the early 1980s, an outgrowth of the 1970s new wave/punk scene promoted by major record labels. But it also exemplifies a more specific genre that emerged around this time—so-called 'synth-pop', the first type of popular music explicitly defined by its use of electronic sound synthesis. Although synth-pop had arguably died out by the end of the 1980s, it helped to establish the centrality of the synthesizer in popular dance music.

'Sweet Dreams' is built around a hypnotic digital loop: a repeated pattern established abruptly at the beginning of the record, as though the listener were dropped into the flow of a synthetic river of sound. A booming steady pulse, synthesized on a digital drum machine and reminiscent of disco music, underlies the melodic portion of the loop. Annie Lennox's singing alternates between an R&B and soul-influenced melismatic style and the flatter, more deadpan tone that she adopts on the verses. The verses themselves consist of two four-line blocks of text, sung by Lennox in over-dubbed harmonies. The singer seems to be expressing an unsettling and titillating combination of cynicism, sensuality, and, in the chorus, hope for the future. Some lines of the text ('*some of them want to use you, some of them want to be abused . . .*') hint at sadomasochistic sex practices, suggesting that the singer's sophistication has perhaps been won at some emotional cost. In the call-and-response chorus, which uses multi-tracking technology to simulate a musical dialogue between Lennox as lead singer and Lennox as choir, the mood lifts, the listener now exhorted to '*hold your head up*' while the multi-tracked chorus urges them to '*keep movin' on*'. Combined with Lennox's carefully cultivated sexual ambiguity—in a subsequent music video, 'Who's That Girl', she plays male and female characters, and ends up kissing herself/himself—the lyrics and musical textures of 'Sweet Dreams' suggest a world-weary take on the nature of love shrouded in mystery and experience.

Finally, although 'Sweet Dreams' is sometimes regarded as an example of the emerging technological sophistication of the early 1980s, the recording was made under less than optimum conditions. The studio rented by Stewart was a dingy, V-shaped warehouse attic, without any of the amenities of a professional studio (such as acoustical tiles or isolation booths for recording separate instrumental tracks). Their equipment was rudimentary—an eight-track tape recorder and a cheap mixer, two microphones, an early version of a digital drum machine available in England at the time, and a handful of old sound effects devices. 'It sounded so sophisticated', reported Stewart in a 1983 feature in *Billboard*, 'but often we had to wait for the timber factory downstairs to turn off their machinery before we could record the vocals.' In fact, not all of the instrumental sounds on the recording are electronic in origin:

the clinking counterpoint under the chorus of 'Sweet Dreams' was played on milk bottles pitched to the right notes by filling them with different levels of water. In this sense, 'Sweet Dreams' both hearkens back to the 'do-it-yourself' ethic of 1970s punk and new wave music and points forward to the experiments of 1990s techno musicians, who often introduce natural environmental sounds into their recordings.

Van Halen: 'Jump' (1984)

Heavy metal music, pioneered in the late 1960s and early 1970s by bands such as Led Zeppelin, Black Sabbath, and Deep Purple, went into a period of relative decline during the late 1970s, partly as a result of the disco craze. By the early 1980s most hit singles—particularly those promoted on music television—were oriented more towards post-disco dance music played on keyboard synthesizers than towards the electric guitar virtuosity of heavy metal bands. The music industry tended to ignore heavy metal music, regarding it and its core audience of adolescent white males as something of an embarrassment.

During the 1980s, however, heavy metal 'came back'—with a vengeance. A slew of metal albums topped the singles and album charts, ranging from the pop metal sounds of bands like Van Halen, Bon Jovi, Motley Crüe, and Def Leppard to the harder sound of speed metal bands such as Metallica, Slayer, Anthrax, and Megadeth. One of the most important moments in this process of 'mainstreaming heavy metal' was the release of Van Halen's album *1984*, which featured the Number 2 pop single 'Jump' (the single went to Number 1 in the US), and spawned a video for the song that was rated 'Best of 1984' by viewers in a poll conducted by MuchMusic after it received considerable airplay on the station.

'Jump' was in some ways a remarkable departure from standard heavy metal practice. To begin with, its main instrumental melody was played on a synthesizer rather than an electric guitar. This may seem like a minor detail, but it was an important symbolic and aesthetic issue for hardcore metal fans throughout the late 1970s and early 1980s, many of whom focused closely on the technical virtuosity of guitarists like Eddie Van Halen and tended to associate the timbre of synthesizers with those marginal—largely dance-oriented—genres that embraced the instrument, such as disco, new wave, and certain varieties of funk. From this perspective, the keyboard synthesizer (like disco music itself) appeared as a somewhat questionable instrument. As Philip Bashe, an expert on heavy metal music, explains, the fact that Eddie Van Halen played the bombastic opening theme of 'Jump' on a synthesizer rather than a guitar was 'a brave test of the Van Halen audience's loyalty' (Bashe, 1985: 137). As noted, the success of the single was boosted by its corresponding music video, which was shot in home-movie style and featured the athletic prowess and oddball sense of humour of David Lee Roth, Van Halen's first lead singer.

On 'Jump', the song itself, in the conventional sense of words-plus-melody, is not a core focus of attention for the musicians or their listeners. For his part, when he was asked by an interviewer what his mother would think of the lyrics to his band's songs, Eddie Van Halen said that he had no idea what they even were! The text of 'Jump'—

a casual come-on to a girl from a guy leaning against a jukebox—seems almost an afterthought, apart, perhaps, from the clever '*go ahead and jump!*' hook phrase, which sounds rather as though David Lee Roth were counselling the object of his affections to jump off a high ledge rather than into his arms. The notion of love as risk-taking—so strongly portrayed in Tina Turner's 'What's Love Got to Do with It?'—is present here as well, though from a decidedly male point of view.

The chief significance of a recording like 'Jump', however, lies not in the song per se, but in the musical textures created by the band and their studio engineer, and in the sensibility that they evoke. As noted, one of the main points of attention for heavy metal fans is the practically gymnastic 'shredding' of the genre's virtuoso guitarists, a tradition that they trace back to pioneers such as Jimi Hendrix and Led Zeppelin's Jimmy Page. Eddie Van Halen, widely recognized as a primary innovator in electric guitar performance, is famous for developing widely used techniques—most notably 'pull-offs' and 'tapping'—and for performing various operations on his guitars and amplifiers to modify their sound.

Yet, for however much 'Jump' relies heavily on the keyboard synthesizer for its effect, the sounds generated by Eddie Van Halen on that instrument are in fact closely analogous to his guitar style. Van Halen uses the synthesizer to create something akin to 'power chords', which are two-note combinations that, when played at high volume on an electric guitar, create the massive, distorted, bone-crunching sound associated with heavy metal bands. 'Jump' opens with a synthesized power chord, as if to announce right from the beginning that the sheer sound of the music is more important than the specific instruments used to produce it. Thick textures and a strong pulse, played on keyboards, bass, and drums, propel us through the first two verses of the song. The arrival of the chorus is marked by a sudden opening up, in which the synthesizer plays long sustained chords, the electric guitar plays a sizzling counterpoint to the vocal melody, and the drums and bass play an interesting irregular rhythmic pattern that first suspends the beat and then, after four bars, unleashes it with even greater energy. After another verse-chorus section, we are transported into the midst of a virtuoso guitar solo that showcases Eddie Van Halen's famed 'shredding' techniques. The guitar solo is followed by a longer synthesizer solo, which develops an elaborate melodic improvisation that closely parallels the style of Van Halen's guitar playing.

Although some hardcore metal fans criticized Van Halen for moving away from the guitar-centred model of heavy metal musicianship, the band succeeded in introducing synthesizers into the genre and in helping to spread metal's popularity to a larger and more diverse audience. In 1983, only 8 per cent of records sold in the United States were of heavy metal; a year later that total had risen to 20 per cent, making metal one of the most popular genres of popular music. This process continued through to 1986, when the pop metal band Bon Jovi released the album *Slippery When Wet*, which held the Number 1 spot for eight weeks and went on to sell over 12 million copies worldwide. Thanks largely to successes like these, by the end of the decade heavy metal would account for roughly half of all the Top 20 albums across North America on any given week.

Peter Gabriel: 'Sledgehammer' (1986)

Peter Gabriel (b. 1950 in England) first achieved celebrity as a member of the art rock group Genesis. After leaving Genesis in 1976, Gabriel released four solo albums, all of them titled *Peter Gabriel*. Partly in an effort to clear up the consumer confusion that followed in the wake of this unusual strategy, he gave his next full-length release a distinctive, if brief, title: *So. So* was an interesting and accessible amalgam of various musical styles, reflecting Gabriel's knowledge of the new digital technologies, his budding interest in world music, and his indebtedness to black music, particularly R&B and soul music of the 1960s. The album peaked at Number 2 on the Top LPs chart, sold four million copies, and produced Gabriel's best-selling single to date—'Sledgehammer', which topped the charts in 1986.

Peter Gabriel in a pensive pose. Frank Driggs Collection.

'Sledgehammer' features a horn section led by the trumpet player Wayne Jackson, who, as a member of the Memphis Horns, had played on many of the biggest soul music hits of the 1960s ('Knock on Wood', 'Soul Man', etc.). Jackson had deeply impressed 16-year-old Peter Gabriel during an appearance with the Otis Redding Soul Revue at a London R&B club in 1966. Gabriel described 'Sledgehammer' as:

an attempt to recreate some of the spirit and style of the music that most excited me as a teenager—60s soul. The lyrics of many of those songs were full of play-ful sexual innuendo and this is my contribution to that songwriting tradition. It is also about the use of sex as a means of getting through a breakdown in com-munication. (Bright, 1999: 267)

The lyrics to 'Sledgehammer'—packed with double-entendre references to 'sledge-hammers', 'big dippers', 'steam trains', the female 'fruitcake', and the male 'honeybee'—are, in fact, a G-rated variant of the sexual metaphors that have long been a part of the blues tradition (consider, for instance, the more explicit blues trope 'squeeze my lemon till the juice runs down my leg'). The formal building blocks of 'Sledgehammer' are 12-bar and eight-bar sections, with the former predominating in the first half of the arrangement. While most pop music recordings are concerned to establish the beat or groove as quickly as possible, 'Sledgehammer' opens with an exotic touch— a digital keyboard sample of a Japanese flute, called the shakuhachi—a hint of Gabriel's budding interest in world music, and a vestige of his involvement with the synthesis-obsessed progressive rock genre. The funk-influenced groove—with strong backbeats on the snare drum, the keyboard bass landing strongly on the first beat of each measure, and the guitar playing a bouncy upstroke pattern similar to what the a guitarist would play in the ska genre—is introduced by the horn section and backed by synthesizers. After eight bars the horns drop out and the rhythm takes four meas-ures to establish the groove that will carry us through the rest of the recording.

Following the introduction, Peter Gabriel sings two verses (beginning with the lines 'You could have a steam train' and 'You could have a big dipper'), each of which is 12 bars in length. Though his intent to evoke the blues form seems clear, he does not strictly observe the a-a-b lyric form found often in blues (that is, he does not repeat the first line of the text in the verses). In addition, he dispenses with the tra-ditional approach to blues harmonies, staying on the tonic chord for a full eight measures, moving to a related chord (which musicians call the relative minor) for two bars, and then returning to the tonic for the last two bars. Although many traditional blues linger on the tonic chord in a manner similar to this, they rarely if ever move to the relative minor chord, a harmony more in keeping with Tin Pan Alley music. After singing two of these 12-bar verses, Gabriel moves to the eight-bar chorus ('I want to be your sledgehammer'). Once again, the song takes an interesting turn in harmonic terms, shifting from the major key of the verse to a minor key based on the same tonic note. (More precisely, the 'B' section begins on a chord closely related to the tonic major, and then shifts to the tonic minor chord itself.)

The arrangement continues with a four-bar instrumental section taking us back to the major-key harmonies of the verse; another verse ('Show me round your fruitcakes'), shortened to eight instead of 12 bars; and two presentations of the chorus ('I want to be your sledgehammer'). The last section of the arrangement relies on a minor-key har-monic pattern closely related to that of the chorus, moving back and forth between the tonic minor chord and another, closely related chord; it begins with a keyboard synthesizer solo. Finally, a series of eight-bar sections ('I will show for you') are heard, in which Gabriel's vocal phrases alternate with a choir of gospel-style singers. The arrangement reaches a peak here, with Gabriel improvising solo phrases against the responses of the choir ('*Show for me, Show for you*'). Gabriel's attempt to 'recreate some of the spirit and style' of 1960s soul music may be successful precisely because he does not try to produce an exact copy of the musical styles that inspired him. Rather, he uses fundamental elements such as the 12-bar blues form, call-and-response singing, strong funk-derived polyrhythms, and an R&B horn section as the basis for a performance that reflects his own musical experience and taste, including references to world music and harmonies that take the blues in new directions.

The success of 'Sledgehammer' was in no small part due to the massive exposure it received on MuchMusic in the mid-1980s. The video version of 'Sledgehammer' was an eye-catching, witty, and technically innovative work that pushed the frontiers of the medium. It won nine MTV awards (more than any video in history), including Best Video and the prestigious Video Vanguard Award for career achievement in 1987, and was ranked the fourth best video of all time in a 1999 retrospective aired on the influential station. The making of the video, which combined stop-motion techniques with live-action sequences, required Gabriel to spend eight painful 16-hour days lying under glass with his head supported by a steel pole. Hardman Animations, the outfit that produced the 'Sledgehammer' video, went on to work on the *Wallace and Gromit* videos and the talking car ads aired by Chevron in the late 1990s.

One key to the success of any music video is the relationship it establishes between the sound of the original recording (which, except in the case of live concert videos, is always made first) and the flow of visual images. The video of 'Sledgehammer'—directed by Steven Johnston—opens with enlarged microscopic images of human sperm cells impregnating an egg, which develops into a fetus, accompanied by the exotic sound of the synthesized shakahuchi flute. As the groove is established, we see Gabriel's face in close-up, moving to the groove, wiggling his eyebrows, ears, and mouth in time to the music. The stop-motion technique—in which the camera is halted and restarted to create the illusion of inanimate objects moving under their own power—creates a jerky stop–start effect that establishes a kind of parallel reality, carefully co-ordinated to match the rhythms of the music. The lyrics of the song are also reflected in the video images: when Gabriel sings '*You could have a steam train*', a toy locomotive circles his head on miniature tracks; when he sings '*You could have a bumper car bumping, this amusement never ends*', two smiling (and singing) bumper cars appear next to his ears, mountains of popcorn pile up behind him, and his hair turns to pink cotton candy. After a series of stop-motion sequences featuring everything from singing fruits and vegetables to dancing furniture, Gabriel is transformed into a 'starman' and walks off into the night sky. Thus, the video takes us from the microscopic origins of life to the vastness of the galaxy, with many diverting stops in between. As Gabriel himself admitted some years later, although the recording of 'Sledgehammer' would probably have done well on its own, the ambitious and highly creative video of the song, played endlessly on MuchMusic, introduced the song to millions of Canadians who might not otherwise have purchased a record by Peter Gabriel.

Bruce Cockburn: 'If I Had a Rocket Launcher' (1984)

Though he was one of the best-loved folksingers in Canada throughout the 1970s, it was not until 1984's *Stealing Fire* LP—and more specifically, not until two videos made to promote that album, 'Lovers in a Dangerous Time' and 'If I Had a Rocket Launcher', gained heavy rotation on MuchMusic—that Bruce Cockburn finally entered the pantheon of Canadian rock legends. Born in Ottawa in 1945, Cockburn was a relative latecomer to international pop success, though he has been popular in Canada for over 45 years. Cockburn didn't score a Top 40 charting until 'Wondering Where the Lions Are', from his *Dancing in the Dragon's Jaw* (1979) LP—the song reached Number 39 in Canada and Number 21 in the US, landing the folksinger an appearance on *Saturday Night Live*. Yet, Cockburn had spent almost two decades leading up to that 'overnight' success. He played around Ottawa with such bands as the Children, the Esquires, the Flying Circus, Olivius (which opened a concert in Ottawa headlined by the Jimi Hendrix Experience and Cream in 1968), and 3's A Crowd. He was a regular at the Mariposa Folk Festival as a solo folk artist, developing such an enthusiastic following that, in 1969, when Neil Young cancelled his appearance to appear at the Woodstock festival with the newly formed CSNY, Cockburn was asked to headline. Earlier, he had studied composition for three semesters at the world famous Berklee College of Music in Boston—'I got a lot out of it', he once said, 'but it didn't feel right to continue there.' Eventually, he took up residence in Toronto's Yorkville Village, where he caught the ear of rock entrepreneur Bernie Finkelstein, who made Cockburn the first artist on his soon-to-be massively influential True North label. (The label would eventually record and/or distribute records from such Canadian popular musicians as 54–40, Randy Bachman, the Cowboy Junkies, Murray McLaughlin, Rough Trade, Saga, and many others.)

If Ian Pearson is right to say that, 'to the generation of Canadians that came of age in the late '60s, Cockburn was a pure indigenous alternative to popular music', a 'bearded mystic who crafted fragile melodies on his acoustic guitar and sang with a voice as ephemeral as mist about spirituality and the wonder of the country' (thecanadianencyclopedia.com/BruceCockburn), the folksinger had migrated from the 'alternative' periphery to direct centre of the Top 40 mainstream by the time he recorded 'If I Had a Rocket Launcher' for his fifteenth album. The song reflected not only Cockburn's increasing acceptance of pop convention, evident in his songwriting, throughout the 1980s, but also his politicization as a singer. The albums *Humans* and *The Trouble with Normal* had already begun to reflect Cockburn's political concerns, but it was *Stealing Fire* that introduced the singer to the world stage as a songwriter willing to put his Top 40 songcraft in the service of humanitarian concerns. Written after Cockburn had taken a 'fact-finding' mission to Guatemalan refugee camps in Chiapas, Mexico, which were attacked by Guatemalan military air strikes before and after Cockburn's visit, the song's lyrics betray the singer's outrage in a way that the practically danceable musical setting for those words does not.

'If I Had a Rocket Launcher' begins with an instrumental introduction, comprised of two distinct arpeggiated lines, panned to the left and right of the stereo spectrum, performed by, respectively, an electronic synthesizer and electric guitar (the syncopated synthesizer line vaguely conjures the rhythms and melodies of Latin American folk music). The groove continues unchanged, as Cockburn's vocals enter, setting a scene of terror and carnage in the first verse ('*Here comes a helicopter, second time today/Everybody scatters and hopes it goes away/How many kids they've murdered — only God can say*'). This depiction only intensifies as the song progresses: by the third verse Cockburn sings of Guatemalans on the Rio Lacantun falling down from starvation, '*or some less humane fate*', and of Guatemala itself, '*with a corpse in every gate*'. Drums, electric bass, and a synthesizer enter for the first refrain, which provides Cockburn an opportunity to describe the moral outrage provoked by the scenes he describes, the repeated refrain '*if I had a rocket launcher*' answered by a different response in each of the song's four verses: '*I'd make somebody pay*', '*I would retaliate*', '*I would not hesitate*', and, finally, '*some son of a bitch would die.*' Interrupted only by a brief guitar solo before the final strophe, characterized by Cockburn's hallmark use of echo and digital delay effects, the song features a layered arrangement, with hand percussion layered-in for the second strophe, Cockburn's echo/delay processed guitar and a synthesizer pad added for third strophe, and another pad layered in during the song's final strophe.

The lyrics to 'If I Had a Rocket Launcher' remain among the most intense expressions of political and moral outrage ever penned by a rock singer, and recall such early songs of bitter protest as Bob Dylan's 'Masters of War', from *The Freewheelin' Bob Dylan* (1963), and point to Neil Young's more recent 'Shock and Awe', from his *Living with War* (2006). But Cockburn's video for the song—which made heavy rotation alongside the more arty video for 'Lovers in a Dangerous Time' on MuchMusic in 1984—was even more remarkable than his lyrics. Rather than the usual footage of a band performing live, or the visual pyrotechnics of a video like Peter Gabriel's 'Sledgehammer', the video for 'If I Had a Rocket Launcher' provides visual documentation of the atrocities suffered by numerous Central Americans during the tumultuous period detailed by Cockburn in the song. The video opens with a clear visual metaphor: a raft ambles randomly, and unmanned, over a series of rapids, and wind chimes burn after a bomb detonates. Next appears archival footage of helicopter strikes, followed by documentary footage of corpses, mourning crowds, starving children, and blinded air strike victims. Finally, Cockburn himself appears, playing an electric guitar at the gate of a razed village. The video concludes with a shot of Cockburn walking down Bloor Street, in Toronto.

Though Cockburn has always maintained that 'If I Had a Rocket Launcher' was a 'cry for Guatemala' rather than 'a call to arms', the outrage conjured by the video and lyrics are difficult to deny. Cockburn would continue his new-found activism well into the 1990s, his last Top 40 song, 'If a Tree Falls in the Forest', being an early document of resurgent environmental activism in Canadian pop music, begun by the likes of Joni Mitchell in the late 1960s, with her path-breaking 'Big Yellow Taxi'. Perhaps a testament to his musicianship, and to his importance as a Canadian icon as well as a pop singer, the uncompromising musician has been awarded more honorary doctorates than any other Canadian singer of his generation, including awards from his alma mater, the Berklee College of Music, Queen's University in Kingston, York University in Toronto, St Thomas University in New Brunswick, and Memorial University of Newfoundland.

Northern Lights: 'Tears Are Not Enough' (1985)

The idea for one of the pivotal movements in 1980s rock music came to a British rock singer by the name of Bob Geldoff, then the lead singer of a popular post-punk outfit called the Boomtown Rats ('I Don't Like Mondays'), as he watched a report submitted by Michael Buell to the BBC, following up on reports by CBC correspondent Brian Stewart, about an ongoing famine in Ethiopia. Moved by the horror Buell described and unable to forget the footage of starving children that accompanied Buell's report, Geldoff announced in an interview with BBC Radio One the next day that he planned to create a supergroup of celebrity musicians—called 'Band Aid'— to record a single that would benefit the victims of famine in Ethiopia, even though the interview was scheduled to promote a new Boomtown Rats record. Enlisting the help of Midge Ure, from the new wave group Ultravox, the duo composed 'Do They Know It's Christmas?'—the first charity rock track of the 1980s, a genre that would come to the fore in the rock world for the next few years.

Released on 3 December 1984, in time for the bulge in record sales that occurs every year around Christmas, and featuring a cast of musicians included solely based on their relative fame (Geldoff recently explained that the criterion of celebrity was used to maximize record sales), Band Aid gathered in BBC Studio One on 25 November 1984 to record 'Do They Know It's Christmas?' The song, which featured vocal cameos by a veritable who's who of British pop superstars from the 1980s—including, in order, Paul Young (singing a part initially composed for David Bowie, who could not make the session), Boy George, George Michael, Simon Le Bon, Sting, Bono, Paul Weller, and Glenn Gregory, among others—quickly topped the pop charts in Great Britain (it peaked only at Number 38 in Canada), becoming the best-selling single of all time in the UK (it has since been surpassed by Elton John's tribute to Diana, the ex-Princess of Wales, 'Candle in the Wind 1997', itself an update of John's earlier 'Candle in the Wind' tribute to Marilyn Monroe).

Almost immediately following Band Aid's success, Harry Belafonte, Kenny Rogers, Michael Jackson, and Lionel Richie formed 'USA For Africa', a collective of American pop singers and musicians, to record a distinctly American response to the distinctly British gauntlet thrown down by Geldoff. The product of their efforts, 'We Are the World' (1985), topped the American charts and peaked at Number 3 in Canada. Though the single remains an unequivocal success, the entire USA For Africa episode remains controversial for some as a result of questions about where proceeds from sales of the record actually went (some claim that proceeds went to the sometimes military governments of the affected countries, rather than to the citizens themselves). As with 'Do They Know It's Christmas', the music for 'We Are The World', composed by Michael Jackson and Lionel Richie and produced by Quincy

Jones, provided a fairly straightforward AABA pop backdrop for a series of vocal cameos by ex-Blues Brother Dan Akroyd (the only Canadian present at the session), Harry Belafonte, Ray Charles, Bob Dylan, Sheila E., Bob Geldoff, Huey Lewis, Stevie Wonder, the Jackson Family, including Michael Jackson, Billy Joel, Cyndi Lauper, Bette Midler, Willie Nelson, Kenny Rogers, Tina Turner, Dionne Warwick, Diana Ross, Lionel Richie, Paul Simon, Bruce Springsteen, and many others.

If USA For Africa made the nationalistic overtones of charity rock clear—records in the genre eventually coming to represent a kind of 'rough guide' to the state of pop music in participating countries—Canada's response was no different. Using national citizenship and relative celebrity as the bases for inclusion, long-time Bryan Adams manager, Bruce Allan, convened a supergroup of Canadian pop stars, dubbed 'Northern Lights', in February of 1985 to record a song written by Bryan Adams, Jim Vallance, and David Foster, called 'Tears Are Not Enough'. True to charity rock convention, 'Tears Are Not Enough'—produced by Foster and Vallance, and featuring Paul Dean (Loverboy) on guitar, Steve Denroche on French horn, Doug Johnson (Loverboy) on synthesizer, David Sinclair (Body Electric) on acoustic guitar, and a quartet of engineers (Hayward Parrott, Geoff Turner, Bob Rock, and Humberto Gatica)—basically served as a vehicle for a series of vocal cameos by Canada's rock and pop elite. Solo vocal contributions were provided by, in order of their appearance on the track, Gordon Lightfoot, Burton Cummings, Anne Murray, Joni Mitchell, Dan Hill, Neil Young, Bryan Adams, Corey Hart, Bruce Cockburn, Geddy Lee, and Mike Reno, while duo and trio contributions came from Mike Reno and Liberty Silver; Carroll Baker, Ronnie Hawkins, and Murray McLaughlin; Véronique Bélivaeau, Robert Charlebois, and Claude Dubois, providing a francophone portion of the bilingual song; Bryan Adams and Don Gerrard; Sale Bey, Mark Holmes (Platinum Blonde), and Lorraine Segato (the Parachute Club); Alfie Zappacosta and Lisa Dalbello; and Carole Pope and Paul Hyde. The song's backing chorus featured an even more diverse range of stars, including classical guitarist Liona Boyd, SCTV alumni John Candy and Eugene Levy, Tom Cochrane (then of Red Rider), Tommy Hunter, Oscar Peterson, Kim Mitchell, Paul Schafer, Jane Siberry, and Sylvia Fricker.

The video for 'Tears Are Not Enough', a basic recreation of the song's performance with every vocalist present before a minimal beige backdrop, preceded by an excerpt from a CBC report on the famine in Ethipoia, made it into heavy rotation on MuchMusic in March 1985, helping push the song to Number 1 later that same month (the video was also notable for its footage of Wayne Gretzky and fellow Campbell Conference All Stars providing backing vocals during the song's extended closing). Generating over $3.5 million in profit, Northern Lights differed from its American and British counterparts in that 10 per cent of the proceeds were kept to help fund various domestic charities (primarily food assistance programs).

When more than 1.5 billion viewers from more than 100 countries tuned in to the 'Live Aid' concerts in July of 1985—a one-day multi-venue concert series conceived as a follow-up to Band Aid by Geldoff and Ure, staged at Wembley Stadium in London and JFK Stadium in Philadelphia, with performances in Moscow and Sydney thrown in for good measure—the charity rock genre arguably reached its zenith. The concert was followed shortly after by 'Farm Aid', a benefit concert staged in Champaign, Illinois, in September 1985. Organized by Neil Young, John Mellencamp, and Willie Nelson to benefit family farmers in the United States, the concert had been inspired largely by comments Bob Dylan made at the Live Aid concert:

> I hope some of the money . . . maybe they can just take a little bit of it, maybe . . . one or two million, maybe . . . and use it, say, to pay the mortgages on some of the farms and the money [that] some of the farmers here owe to the banks.

Preceded by pioneering work by the likes of Ravi Shankhar and George Harrison (the Concert for Bangladesh) and propelled to the cultural fore by the pop elite in the 1980s, charity rock continues to thrive—the successful, if controversial, Live 8 and Live Earth benefit concerts constitute the two most recent examples.

Daniel Lanois, Canada's Quiet Giant

In his co-productions with Brian Eno, and alone, French-Canadian producer, engineer, songwriter, and multi-instrumentalist Daniel Lanois has created some of the most influential avant-garde rock and pop records of the 1980s and 1990s. Emphasizing space and ambient non-veridicism in his arrangements, and using a number of techniques to do so—including creative use of microphone placement, equalization, echo and delay lines, and various other forms of signal processing—Lanois played the pivotal role in the creation of what critics call the 'Grant Avenue Sound'. Named for the three-storey Victorian home in Hamilton, Ontario, that Lanois converted into a one-of-a-kind recording studio, with quirky and sometimes unwieldy spaces for tracking, the Grant Avenue Sound that Lanois developed there became notorious for, as historian Mark Prendergast tells it, 'the extensive use of tape loops, washy harmonizer effects and, as early as 1981, one of the earliest uses of digital sampling'. As Lanois puts it, more than simply a space for recording, Grant Avenue was conceived as 'an electronic network of effects and processes'. The house, transformed from domicile to 'sound processing laboratory', served as the musician's base of operations throughout the 1980s and 1990s, alongside another converted house, this time in New Orleans, which Lanois dubbed Kingsway Studio (Lanois recorded the Neville Brothers' *Yellow Moon* and his first solo outing, *Acadie*, there).

In fact, given his generally unassuming, soft-spoken demeanour—all the more remarkable in comparison to the mostly extroverted rock world—Lanois's crucial contributions to the rock tradition during the past three decades have tended to be overshadowed by the immensity of the numerous 'big personality' rock stars who clamour to work with him. But Lanois has clearly, if quietly, stamped his sonic watermark on the Top 40. Highlights of his career would have to include:

Daniel Lanois created some of the most influential avant-garde rock and pop records of the 1980s and 1990s. © Lynn Goldsmith/Corbis.

- productions for his sisters' new wave rock group, Martha & the Muffins (*This Is The Ice Age*, 1981; *Danseparc*, 1982), whose 'off-balance' production style first brought Lanois to Brian Eno's attention;
- various subsequent chart-topping co-productions with Brian Eno, many of which were tracked at Grant Avenue Studios, including U2's *The Unforgettable Fire* (1984), *The Joshua Tree* (1986), *Achtung Baby* (1991), *All That You Can't Leave Behind* (2000), and *How To Dismantle an Atomic Bomb* (2004);
- productions for Peter Gabriel's best-selling albums of the 1980s and 1990s—*Birdy* (1985), *So* (1986), and *Us* (1992);
- 'comeback' albums by aging boomer rockers, including records by Robbie Robertson (*Robbie Robertson*, 1987), the Neville Brothers (*Yellow Moon*, 1989), and Bob Dylan (*Oh Mercy*, 1989, *Time Out Of Mind*, 1997);
- various 'alternative' classics of the late 1980s and 1990s, such as Scott Weiland, *12 Bar Blues* (1998); Ron Sexsmith, *Ron Sexsmith* (1994); Emmylou Harris, *Wrecking Ball* (1995); and Luscious Jackson, *Luscious Jackson* (1996);
- a number of solo albums, his bilingual debut, *Acadie* (1989)—about the Acadian diaspora after their expulsion from the Maritimes region at the hands of the British in 1755—remaining his most remarkable, though *For the Beauty of Wynona* (1993) and *Belladonna* (2005) rank a close second and third.

Twice awarded Grammies for Album of the Year, in recognition of his work with Brian Eno on U2's *The Joshua Tree* (1986) and as sole producer for Bob Dylan's *Time*

Out Of Mind (1997), Lanois also played a pivotal though often overlooked role in the creation of the ambient genre. He had not yet come to Brian Eno's attention when Eno conceived the genre—a genre whose records are designed to be 'as ignorable as they are interesting', according to Eno, capable of being used by listeners as a tool for interior design or for concentrated listening, depending on how they feel. But Lanois co-produced most of its pioneering releases, working with the likes of Harold Budd, John Hassell, Brian Eno, and Roger Eno on such classics of the genre as *Ambient 4/On Land* (1982), *Apollo: Atmospheres and Soundtracks* (1983), *The Pearl* (1984), and *Thursday Afternoon* (1985), many of which were recorded at Grant Avenue Studios. In fact, though Brian Eno tends to get much of the credit, largely given his willingness to speak with reporters and his propensity for theoretical discoursing, Daniel Lanois deserves an equal share for his crucial contributions to the Top 40 during the 1980s, for his work to develop the ambient strain within the rock tradition, and, simultaneously, for the development of the ambient genre's mainstream cousin—New Age. Lanois is, indeed, truly Canada's quiet giant of the rock industry, happy to remain silently ensconced at the mixing board while others receive the accolades for the remarkable records he is able to coax out of them.

A Tale of Three Albums: *Thriller, Born in the U.S.A.*, and *Graceland*

A brief look at three multi-million-selling albums of the 1980s will help document the variety of styles that characterized this period. Each of these albums represents the biggest commercial success in its artist's solo career. *Thriller*, in fact, ranks as the top-selling album in history as of this writing, having achieved worldwide sales in excess of 40 million copies; singles for the album spent more than a year—a combined 58 weeks—on the Top 40 in Canada during 1983 and 1984.

In the case of Michael Jackson, *Thriller* was the zenith of a career as a solo artist that had been gathering momentum throughout the 1970s, even while Jackson continued to be a pivotal member of the tremendously successful group the Jackson Five (who changed their name to the Jacksons with their departure from the Motown organization in 1976, a departure that caused no substantial interruption in their long-running success story). *Thriller* was state-of-the-art pop music for the time, an album dedicated not so much to breaking new ground as to consolidating Michael Jackson's dominance of the contemporary pop scene by showcasing his versatility as a performer of a stylistically wide range of up-to-date material.

Like Jackson, Paul Simon got his start in the 1960s as a member of a group, in this case the famous folk rock duo Simon and Garfunkel (see Chapter 5). When Simon went on to a productive solo career in the 1970s, however, the duo disbanded. *Graceland* revived a career that had seemed to be in decline in the early 1980s (Simon's two preceding albums had neither the critical nor the commercial success that greeted most of his work of the 1970s) and—with its employment of African musicians, African music, and, occasionally, African subject matter, along with other 'exotic' touches—suddenly thrust Simon into the forefront of the new category called 'world' music.

On the other hand, Bruce Springsteen's *Born in the U.S.A.* seemed more concerned with the past in its depiction of adult working-class Americans whose better days are well behind them, and the album's music is drenched appropriately in Springsteen's typical 'trad rock' sound. The glitzy, consciously 'modern' sound and production values of *Thriller* clearly were not for Springsteen; neither was he trying in any way to change the basic direction of his career and his music, as Simon did with in *Graceland*. In *Born in the U.S.A.* Springsteen simply continued to make the kind of music, and voice the kinds of concerns, that had characterized his career from its beginning in the early 1970s. The unexpected mega-success of the album (it sold over 15 million copies, whereas the best-selling album among Springsteen's previous efforts—*Born to Run* from 1975—had sold less than five million) took the artist somewhat by surprise, and left him anxious to ascertain whether his newly enlarged audience was truly understanding the less-than-cheerful messages he wished to convey.

The 'mega-success' of these three albums would seem to indicate a resurgent global prosperity, including in Canada. At the least, the country had pulled out of the global recession of 1982, and many citizens felt comfortable diverting some of their discretionary income to the record industry. In fact, the country that Brian Mulroney inherited in 1984 from John Turner, who had taken over when Trudeau retired, is often remembered for its booming economy, which gave rise to the social phenomenon of Young Urban Professionals—wealthy, young, and, some might say, cynical post-hippie boomers, dubbed 'Yuppies' by the press, who averted their energies from various social causes to the accumulation of material abundance. Commercial and hugely popular music was part of that abundance, though two of the three mega-successes of the eighties—Springsteen's *Born in the U.S.A.* and Simon's *Graceland*—expressed deep social and political concern about the direction in which the United States and the world were heading.

Michael Jackson: *Thriller* (1982)

In fashioning *Thriller*, Michael Jackson (b. 1958) worked with the veteran producer Quincy Jones to create an album that achieved boundary-crossing popularity to an unprecedented degree. At a time when the pop music audience seemed to be fragmenting to a greater extent perhaps than ever before, *Thriller* demonstrated a kind of across-the-board appeal that established new and still unduplicated heights of commercial success. In a sense, Jackson here revived the goal that had animated his old boss at Motown, Berry Gordy Jr, to create an African-American-based pop music aimed squarely at the mainstream centre of the market. That Jackson met his goal in such a mind-boggling fashion proved conclusively that there still was a mainstream in the pop music of the early 1980s, and Jackson had positioned himself unquestionably at the centre.

To do this, Jackson had to be more than just 'the sound of young America', to quote Motown's memorable phrase from the 1960s. It is, of course, true that teenagers, pre-teenagers, and young adults made up a substantial portion of the 1980s market. But baby boomers, along with the many who came to maturity during the 1970s, were also still major consumers of pop music. And age was far from the only basis on which segmentation of the audience seemed to be taking place—fans of soft rock, heavy metal, funk, and new wave music, for instance, appeared to want less and less to do with one another as the decade wore on. A disturbing subtext of all this was a tendency towards increasing re-segregation along racial lines of the various audiences for pop. Heavy metal and new wave fans—and bands—were overwhelmingly white, while funk and the emerging genre of rap were associated with black performers and listeners.

Thriller represented an effort to find ways to mediate among the various, sometimes fractional, subgenres of early 1980s pop music, to create points of effective synthesis from the welter of apparently competing styles, and to bridge the divides—actual or potential—separating different segments of the pop music audience. Jackson confronted the racial divide head on by collaborating with two very popular, and very different, white artists; ex-Beatle Paul McCartney joined Jackson for a lyrical vocal duet on 'The Girl Is Mine', while Eddie Van Halen of the heavy metal group Van Halen contributed the stinging guitar solo on the intense 'Beat It'. Both of these radically different songs, along with two others on *Thriller*, were written by Jackson himself. Indeed, Jackson's massive accomplishments often overshadow the fact that his versatility as a performer, and his gift for crossing genres, extends also into the domain of songwriting.

It is also clear that 'The Girl Is Mine' and 'Beat It' were fashioned to attract different segments of the white audience. The mere presence of Paul McCartney was a draw for many listeners who had been fans of the Beatles in the 1960s, as well as for those who admired McCartney's 1970s band, Wings. As a song, 'The Girl Is Mine' combines a gentle melodic flow with a feeling of rhythmic vitality, effectively echoing the virtues of the best Beatles and Wings ballads. 'The Girl Is Mine' captured this essentially soft rock ambience—and its audience—especially well, the single staying in the Top 10 in Canada for just over seven weeks in 1982. Moreover, 'The Girl Is Mine' had sufficient crossover appeal to top, for three weeks, the American R&B chart—now called 'Hot Black Singles', marking a return to a racialized segregation of the genres first seen in monikers such as 'race records' back in the 1920s, 1930s, and 1940s. As the first single to come out of the *Thriller* album, 'The Girl Is Mine' demonstrated immediately how well Michael Jackson's new music could break down preconceptions about marketability. 'Beat It', on the other hand, has nothing to do with soft rock, and was a gesture obviously extended to 'metal-heads', who must have been struck by the novelty of a collaboration between a celebrated heavy metal guitarist and a black pop icon. But this door also could, and did, swing both ways: 'Beat It' joined 'The Girl Is Mine' on the list of Top 10 singles in 1983, staying in the Top 10 for 18 weeks in Canada.

Much of *Thriller* consists of up-tempo, synthesizer- and bass-driven, danceable music that occupies a conscious middle ground between the heavy funk of an artist like George Clinton and the brighter, but still beat-obsessed, sound that characterized many new wave bands (of which Blondie would be a good example). Perhaps the outstanding—and, in this case, unexpected and highly original—example of the album's successful synthesis of diverse stylistic elements may be found in the title song. 'Thriller' starts out depicting a horror-movie scene, which eventually turns out to be on the television screen being watched by two lovers, providing them with an excuse for cuddling 'close together' and creating their own kind of thrills. In a conclusion that pairs an old white voice with a new black style, horror-movie star Vincent Price comes from out of nowhere to perform a 'rap' about the terrors of the night (this 'rap' describes some typical horror-film situations, but its language is occasionally spiced up with current pop-oriented slang—as when Price refers to 'the funk of forty thousand years').

In the early years of long-playing records, the pop music album was typically a collection of individual songs, several (and sometimes all) of which had previously been released as singles. In our discussions of the 1960s and 1970s, we have remarked on the steadily increasing importance of the album over the single, as pop artists began more and more to conceive of the album as their principal creative medium. *Thriller* is a unique landmark in this evolutionary process. *Thriller* is not a concept album— unless the 'concept' was to demonstrate that an album could be made to engender hit singles, rather than vice versa. Out of the nine songs on *Thriller*, seven were released as singles, one by one, starting with 'The Girl Is Mine' (the only one to be released prior to the album itself), and all seven were Top 10 hits. Both 'Billie Jean' and 'Beat It' went to Number 1, and these two, along with 'Thriller', sold over two million copies each as singles, while 'The Girl Is Mine' sold just over one million copies. In fact, the only songs from *Thriller* that were not turned into hit singles were 'Baby Be Mine' and 'The Lady in My Life'.

Visual media, both old and new, also played a significant role in the *Thriller* saga. In May 1983 Jackson appeared on the television special *25 Years of Motown* and introduced what came to be known as his 'moonwalk' dance while performing 'Billie Jean' from *Thriller*. The performance was a sensation and doubtless added to the continuing popularity of the album. By this time, the videos for *Thriller* songs that Jackson had made were being shown regularly on MuchMusic and MTV. Jackson's embrace of the relatively new medium of music video reflected his foresight in realizing its potential. While bringing his work to the attention of yet another segment of the music public, his videos in turn helped boost the power and prestige of music television itself, because they were so carefully, creatively, and elaborately produced. Because Jackson was the first black artist to be programmed with any degree of frequency on MTV, *Thriller* thus contributed to the breakdown of yet another emerging colour line in pop culture. (Significantly, in this respect, the video for 'Beat It' sees Jackson break up a racially charged gang fight.)

Bruce Springsteen: *Born in the U.S.A.* (1984)

Throughout the 1970s Bruce Springsteen (b. 1949) had been forging a progressively more successful career in pop music while continuing to cast both his music and his personal image in the light of the rebellious rock 'n' rollers of the 1950s and the socially conscious folk rockers of the 1960s. Springsteen's songs reflected his working-class origins and sympathies, relating the stories of still young but aging men and women with dead-end jobs (or no jobs at all), looking for romance and excitement in the face of repeated disappointments, and seeking meaningful outlets for their seething energies and hopes in an America that seems to have no pieces of the American Dream left to offer them. Some of the song titles from his first few albums are indicative—'Born to Run', 'Darkness on the Edge of Town', 'Hungry Heart', 'Racing in the Street', 'Wreck on the Highway'.

Bruce Springsteen. Frank Driggs Collection.

Springsteen performed with his E Street Band, and their music was characterized by a strong, roots rock sound that emphasized Springsteen's connections to 1950s and 1960s rock 'n' roll. The band even included a saxophone—virtually an anachronism in the pop music of this period—to mark the link with the rhythm and blues and rock 'n' roll of earlier eras. In this connection, it is worth noting that one of the songs on *Born in the U.S.A.*, 'Cover Me', is based on a 12-bar blues progression. The 12-bar blues form was also all but an anachronism in the mainstream pop music of the 1980s, but it was part of Springsteen's musical heritage and style, and his continuing employment of this form represented another obvious homage to the roots of rock. Still, the emphasis in Springsteen's music was predominantly on the traditional rock combo of guitars, bass, and drums, with keyboard instruments only occasionally joining in.

The Springsteen album immediately preceding *Born in the U.S.A.*, *Nebraska* (1982), represented a departure for him. Featuring Springsteen in a solo 'unplugged' setting that underlined the particular bleakness of this collection of songs, *Nebraska* was a difficult sell for many of Springsteen's fans, some of whom were clearly alienated by the record. Consequently, many fans may have celebrated *Born in the U.S.A.*, which brought back the E Street Band with an actual as well as a symbolic bang, as a kind of 'return to form' for Springsteen. Certainly, the album is dominated by up-tempo, rocking songs, with Springsteen shouting away in full voice and grand style and the band playing full tilt behind him. Still, listening to the record—or tape or CD—player with the album's lyric sheet in hand, it is hard to see how anybody could have regarded *Born in the U.S.A.* as anything other than a dire commentary by Springsteen on the current 'state of the union'. Indeed, the very first lyrics of the title song, which opens the album, set the tone decisively:

Born down in a dead man's town,
The first kick I took was when I hit the ground.
You end up like a dog that's been beat too much
Till you spend half your life just covering up.

'Born in the U.S.A.' tells the story of a returning Vietnam veteran unable to get a job or to rebuild his life, and its despairing message is characteristic of most of the songs on the album. But maybe many people weren't listening to the words. In the wake of this album's rapid and enormous popularity, Springsteen found himself and his band on tour playing to huge, sold-out stadiums where—given the amplification levels and the crowd noise—most people probably couldn't even hear the words. Confronted with hordes of fans waving American flags and the exploitation of his image in the presidential election year of 1984 by political forces for which he had little sympathy, Springsteen periodically found himself having to explain that he was not associated with 'feel-good' politics or uncritical 'America first' boosterism. Was Springsteen a victim of his own success, forced into a stadium rock culture that ill served the purpose and meaning of his songs? Had rock music gained the world, so to speak, only to lose its soul? Or was there actually some fundamental dichotomy between Springsteen's message and the energetic, crowd-pleasing music in which he was couching it?

There is, of course, no objectively 'correct' answer to such questions. But when we listen to *Born in the U.S.A.*, we find Springsteen's sincerity to be as apparent as his intensity, and it is hard not to sense, and hard not to be affected by, the prevailing dark tone. In a general way, *Born in the U.S.A.* is a concept album—a series of musical snapshots of working-class Americans, all of whom seem to be somewhere around Springsteen's age (he turned 35 the year he released this album, the same age as his protagonist in the song 'My Hometown'), many of whom are having economic or personal difficulties, and all of whom sense the better times of their lives slipping into the past. In the album's original LP form, each of the two sides starts out with a strong, aggressive song and winds down to a final cut that is softer in sound but, if anything, even darker in mood. The first side ends with the low-key but eerie 'I'm on Fire', whose protagonist seems about to explode from the weight and pain of his own 'bad desire'; in terms of the listening experience, the spooky urgency of this song appears to speak to the cumulative hard luck and frustration of all the different characters described in the songs of Side One. Side Two starts off with an extroverted rebound in musical energy and a cry of 'No Surrender'. But disillusionment and resignation come to characterize the songs on this side of the record as well, until the 'fire' image reappears strikingly in the penultimate song, 'Dancing in the Dark'. Finally comes 'My Hometown'; Springsteen, his voice drained of energy, sings of the decay of his place of birth and of possibly 'getting out' with his wife and child, heading towards . . . it isn't clear what. In this poignant finale, Springsteen comes as close as any pop artist ever has to embracing and conveying an authentically tragic vision.

Amazingly, 'My Hometown' was a hit single, reaching Number 22 in Canada in early 1986. The record reached Number 6 on the *Billboard* Top 40 in the US, where the closing of the American Dream was obviously more relevant, and topped the adult contemporary chart. It was the last of seven consecutive singles to be culled from the album, all of which were Top 10 pop hits across North America. In this respect, *Born in the U.S.A.* followed in the footsteps of *Thriller* as an album that spawned a parade of hit singles. The album stayed on the album charts for over two years. Like Michael Jackson, Springsteen produced a series of music videos to go with several of the songs released as singles from *Born in the U.S.A.*; these videos proved popular in their own right, and further enhanced the popularity of the album. Thus, Springsteen stayed abreast of the changing music scene at the same time that he tried to speak, through his songs, to the values and attitudes that for him lay at the core of all that was worthwhile and enduring in rock.

Paul Simon: *Graceland* (1986)

Paul Simon's interest in music that was not indigenous to the United States manifested itself long before he recorded *Graceland*. When he was still singing with Art Garfunkel, Simon (b. 1941) recorded 'El Condor Pasa', a song that paired his own lyrics with a backing instrumental track based on an old Peruvian folk melody, performed in 'native' style by a group called Los Incas. 'El Condor Pasa' appeared on the 1970 Simon and Garfunkel album, *Bridge over Troubled Water*, and was released as a single that same year. The song was indicative of the path Simon would later pursue much more systematically and thoroughly in *Graceland*, in which many of the tracks present Simon's vocals and lyrics over an accompaniment performed in South African style by South African musicians.

A considerable portion of the music for *Graceland* was actually recorded in South Africa, and that resulted in some awkward political issues for Simon. Like *Born in the U.S.A.*, this album became a focus of political attention for fans, skeptics, and, with reluctance, its creator. At the time, a United Nations boycott on performing and recording in South Africa was in effect as part of an international attempt to isolate and ostracize the government of that country, which was still enforcing the widely despised policy of apartheid. Simon could not deny that he broke the boycott, but he claimed that he was in no sense supporting the ideology of the South African government by making music with black South Africans on their native soil. In fact, the success of *Graceland* helped bring black South African musicians and styles to a much wider and racially more diverse audience than they had ever been able to reach before, and this proved true within South Africa as well as in North America. It could well be argued that Simon ultimately made, through his racially integrated music, a forceful statement about the virtues of free intermingling and cultural exchange. In any case, Simon came to a mutual understanding with the United Nations and the opponents of apartheid in relatively short order, and he stopped performing in South Africa until apartheid was dismantled several years later.

A truly 'global' album from a geographical point of view, *Graceland* was recorded in five different locations on three different continents: in addition to Johannesburg, South Africa, tracks were cut in London, England; New York City; Los Angeles; and Crowley, Louisiana. Many of the selections on the album combine elements that were recorded at different times in different places, but others were the result of sessions where all the participants were present. While Simon flew to South Africa to work on several songs with musicians there, at another time he brought South African musicians to New York to work with him, and on yet another occasion Simon and the South African vocal group Ladysmith Black Mambazo recorded together in London.

What ultimately distinguishes *Graceland* from earlier forays into world music, whether by Simon or by other pop musicians, is the extent to which the album explores the concept of collaboration—collaboration among artists of different races, regions, nationalities, and ethnicities that produced, in turn, collaboration among diverse musical styles and approaches to songwriting. This provides a conceptual basis for *Graceland*, to be sure, but Simon's album is quite different from the usual concept album. There is certainly no explicit or implicit story line that connects the songs, nor is there any single, central subject that links them all together—unless one is willing to view collaboration itself (primarily musical collaboration but also, in two instances, collaboration on lyrics as well) as the album's 'subject matter'. But the idea of an album designed to explore collaboration seems a perfectly logical, if unusual, concept to embrace in understanding *Graceland*.

The various approaches to the concept of collaboration that are found among the songs on *Graceland* run a gamut from 'Homeless', in which both the words (in Zulu and English) and the music were co-written by Simon and Joseph Shabalala of Ladysmith Black Mambazo, to a cut like 'I Know What I Know', in which Simon added his own lyrics and vocal melody to pre-existing music by General M.D. Shirinda and the Gaza Sisters. In the case of 'Homeless', the song makes a unified and gently poignant impression; the images of poor people could refer to South Africa or practically anyplace else, and the slow-moving, harmonious vocal music encourages us to take their plight seriously. In 'I Know What I Know', on the other hand, Simon deliberately makes no attempt to match the tone of his lyrics to the culture or to the implied locale of the original South African music. Instead, the lyrics seem to portray an encounter between two world-weary and cynical people at an upper-crust cocktail party (or some such gathering), and their mood and subject stand in remarkable, ironic contrast to the jubilant, uninhibited sound of the danceable South African instrumental music and to the Gaza Sisters' voices. The result is a virtual embodiment, in words and sounds, of a profound clash of cultures—as if some characters typical of Simon's earlier, sophisticated urban songs of late twentieth-century anxiety (such as those found on an album like *Still Crazy After All These Years*, from 1975) were suddenly dropped into the middle of a busy South African village on a day of celebration.

That the uneasy mismatch of music and lyrics in 'I Know What I Know' is neither accidental nor careless on Simon's part is signalled by the presence on the album of songs that, occupying a conscious middle ground between 'Homeless' and 'I Know What I Know', make cultural diversity an aspect of their stated subject matter and of their music. The third verse of 'You Can Call Me Al' describes a man who is uncomfortable in a foreign culture:

> *A man walks down the street*
> *It's a street in a strange world*
> *Maybe it's the Third World*
> *Maybe it's his first time around*
> *He doesn't speak the language*
> *He holds no currency*
> *He is a foreign man*
> *He is surrounded by the sound*
> *The sound*

The 'sound' here is being produced by a group of black South African musicians playing with Simon, and North American session musicians in New York City. Significantly, the multicultural group is joined on this cut by Morris Goldberg, who (Simon's liner notes pointedly inform us) is a *white* South African emigrant based in New York, and who contributes a striking pennywhistle solo. Members of this same diverse ensemble also play on 'Under African Skies', the verses of which actually shift location from Africa to Tucson, Arizona, and back again. Here Simon is joined in vocal duet by Linda Ronstadt—from Tucson, Arizona.

In both the music and the words of *Graceland*, the meanings and implications can be allusive and elusive, often seeming to change colour or to shift in mid-phrase. Yet the lilt of Simon's melodies and the dynamic rhythms provided by his diverse collaborators keep the album from ever sounding 'difficult' or arcane. It is to Simon's credit that he never attempts to sound like anybody but himself, nor does he require his fellow musicians to adapt their style to his; this is why the songs on *Graceland* are true collaborations, and such unusually successful ones. In the largest sense, one might say that *Graceland* is 'about' the joys, complexities, dangers, and perplexities of living in an increasingly diverse, multicultural—and globalizing—world, a subject that also informs the words and music of Simon's next album, *The Rhythm of the Saints*, from 1990.

That one need not venture to other continents, or even to other countries, to find 'other' cultures is a point made, in effect, by the last two cuts on *Graceland*—'That Was Your Mother', in which Simon is joined by the Zydeco band Good Rockin'

Dopsie and the Twisters, from Louisiana, and 'All Around the World, or The Myth of Fingerprints', in which Simon plays with Los Lobos, the well-known Mexican-American band from Los Angeles. On both of these selections, the prominent employment of accordion and saxophone creates aural links with the sounds of South African ensembles on other songs from *Graceland*, demonstrating musically that the world is indeed a shrinking place. Conversely, Simon remarks in his liner notes how the South African instrumentalists he recorded in Johannesburg for the title song, which describes a pilgrimage to Memphis to visit the Elvis Presley mansion/museum/shrine, produced a sound that reminded him in certain ways of American country music. At the end, then, Paul Simon comes home, only to find himself still, and always, a musical 'citizen of the world'.

Graceland, although not exactly the kind of smash-hit album that both *Thriller* and *Born in the U.S.A.* were (it never hit Number 1 on the album chart, and failed to produce a single Top 10 in Canada), eventually sold over five million copies. As the Grammy award winner for Album of the Year in 1986, it spectacularly revived Simon's then-flagging career, and garnered a great deal of attention—not only for Simon, but also for many of the musicians who played on the album with him. *Graceland* did not prove to be a major source of hit singles, but a concert video featuring much of its music, taped in Africa with African musicians, was very popular. It is the album responsible, more than any other, for introducing a wide audience to the idea of world music, and for this reason alone the importance and influence of *Graceland* cannot be underestimated.

▌ Prince, Madonna, and the Production of Celebrity

The production of celebrity may be as central to the workings of the North American music industry as the production of music itself. In the 1910s and 1920s dancers Irene and Vernon Castle were made into stars through a combination of theatre tours, silent film appearances, magazine stories, and mass-produced 'how-to' guides to ballroom dancing. In the 1930s and 1940s crooners such as Bing Crosby and Frank Sinatra were turned into media stars through increasingly sophisticated promotional techniques involving sound film, network radio, and the print media. During the post-war years, network television became an indispensable tool for the promotion of popular music and the production of celebrity—it is, for example, hard to imagine the careers of Elvis Presley or the Beatles without the initial boost provided by network television appearances.

By the 1980s the 'star-making machinery behind the popular song' (to quote a lyric by singer-songwriter Joni Mitchell) had grown to unprecedented proportions. Since the profitability of the music industry depended on the sales generated by a relatively limited number of multi-platinum recordings, the co-ordination of publicity surrounding the release of such recordings was crucial. The release of a potential hit album—and of those individual tracks on the album thought to have potential as hit singles—was cross-promoted in music videos, television talk show appearances, Hollywood films, and newspaper, magazine, and radio interviews, creating the overall appearance of a multi-front military campaign run by a staff of corporate generals.

The power of mass-mediated charisma is rooted in the idea that an individual fan can enter into a personal relationship with a superstar via images and sounds that are simultaneously disseminated to millions of people. The space between the public image of the star and the private life and personality of the musician who fills this role is where the contemporary industry of celebrity magazines, television exposés, 'unauthorized' biographies, and paparazzi photographers flourishes, providing fans with provocative tidbits of information concerning the glamour, habits, and character traits of their favourite celebrities. This field of popular discourse is dominated by certain well-worn narratives. In what is perhaps the most common of these storylines, the artist, born into humble circumstances, rises to fame, is overtaken by the triple demons of greed, lust for power, and self-indulgence, falls into a deep pit (of despair, depression, drug addiction, alcoholism), and then repents his or her sins and is accepted in a newly humbled status by the media and millions of fans. Of course, as we have seen, some who walk this line of fame implode before achieving repentance and redemption. Other celebrities manage to flaunt convention and maintain their 'bad boy' or 'bad girl' image throughout their careers, while still others are portrayed as good-hearted and generous (if a bit bland) from the get-go. Of course, these storylines are as much about the fans themselves—and the combination of admiration and envy they feel towards their favourite celebrities—as about the particular musicians in question.

While stars such as Bing Crosby, the Beatles, and Bob Dylan had played an important role in shaping their own public image, the 1980s saw the rise of a new breed of music superstar particularly adept at manipulating the mass media and at stimulating public fascination with their personal characteristics, as well as with their music. Certainly no analysis of celebrity in late twentieth-century North America would be complete without discussion of Madonna and Prince. Like their contemporary Michael Jackson, Madonna Louise Veronica Ciccone and Prince Rogers Nelson were born in the industrial upper Midwest during the summer of 1958. (All three of these 1980s superstars were only six years old in 1964, when the Beatles stormed America, and barely 10 years old during the first Woodstock festival.) Despite the proximity of their geographical origins, Ciccone and Nelson followed quite distinctive career paths. To begin with, Ciccone was a dancer and photographer's model who moved into music almost by accident, while Nelson had been making music professionally since the age of 13 as an occasional member of his father's jazz trio. Madonna first emerged out of New York's thriving dance club scene, while Prince's career developed in the regional metropolis of Minneapolis, Minnesota. Madonna's hit recordings—like most pop recordings—depended on a high degree of collaborative interaction between the singer, the songwriter(s), the producer, the recording engineers, studio session musicians, and others. But many of Prince's hit recordings, inspired by the early 1970s example of Stevie Wonder, were composed, produced, engineered, and performed solely by Nelson himself, many at his own studio in Minneapolis, Paisley Park Incorporated.

Superstars of the 1980s: **Prince** and **Madonna**. Frank Driggs Collection.

Despite these obvious differences, however, Madonna and Prince have much in common. Both are self-conscious authors of their own celebrity, creators of multiple artistic alter egos, and highly skilled manipulators of the mass media. Both experienced a meteoric rise to fame during the early 1980s and were dependent on mass media such as cable television and film for doing so. And both Madonna and Prince have sought to blur the conventional boundaries of race, religion, and sexuality, and periodically sought to rekindle their fans' interest by shifting shape, changing strategy, and coming up with new and controversial songs and images. Early on in their careers, sexually explicit recordings by Madonna and Prince played a primary role in stimulating the formation of the Parents' Music Resource Center (PMRC), a watchdog organization founded in 1985. During the second half of the 1980s, the PMRC—bolstered by its alliance with the Parent/Teachers Association (PTA)—pressured the recording industry to institute a rating system parallel to that used in the film industry. Although popular musicians ranging from Frank Zappa to John Denver argued against the adoption of a ratings system, the industry began to place parental warning labels on recordings during the late 1980s.

Madonna

From the late 1980s through the 1990s Madonna's worldwide popularity was second only to that of Michael Jackson; and, in Canada, she left Jackson in her dust, spending more time in the Top 10 and producing more Top 10 singles than any other artist in history. Jackson scores fourth on the Top 100 list of best-selling artists in Canada, after Madonna, Elton John, and Rod Stewart. Between 1984 and 1994 Madonna would have 43 Top 40 singles in Canada, 13 of which reached the top spot on the charts; she recorded eight Top 10 albums, including the Number 1 hits *Like a Virgin* (1984), *True Blue* (1986), and *Like a Prayer* (1989). She spent 49 weeks at Number 1, and a staggering 710 weeks in the Top 40. Over the course of her career, Madonna has sold in excess of 50 million albums, and she has been one of the most reliable sources of profit for Warner Entertainment, corporate owner of the Sire record label for which she records. She also paved the way for female dance music superstars of the 1990s, such as Paula Abdul.

As a purposefully controversial figure, Madonna has tended to elicit strongly polarized reactions. The 1987 *Rolling Stone* readers' poll awarded her second place for Best Female Singer and first place for Worst Female Singer (in the same poll she also scored third place for Best-Dressed Female and first place for Worst-Dressed Female). Jacques Chirac, the former president of France, once described Madonna as 'a great and beautiful artist', while the iconoclastic social theorist Camille Paglia asserted that she represented 'the future of feminism'. The author Luc Sante's distaste for Madonna, as articulated in his *New Republic* article, 'Unlike a Virgin' (20 Aug. 1990), was based largely on aesthetic criteria:

> Madonna . . . is a bad actress, a barely adequate singer, a graceless dancer, a boring interview subject, a workmanlike but uninspired (co-)songwriter, and a dynamo of hard work and ferocious ambition.

Other observers are ambivalent about Madonna, perhaps feeling—as the satirist Merrill Markoe once put it—'I keep trying to like her, but she keeps pissing me off!' (Sexton, 1993: 14). In the academic field of popular culture studies, scholars have created a veritable cottage industry out of analyzing Madonna's social significance, variously interpreting her as a reactionary committed to turning back the advances of feminism, a postmodern performance artist, a politically savvy cultural subversive, and a 'container for multiple images'. Whatever one's view, the fact that it is still difficult to find anyone who has never heard of Madonna, or who harbours no opinion of her at all, is an indication that her career strategy, for the most part, has been quite effective.

Madonna Louise Veronica Ciccone was born into an Italian-American family in Rochester, Michigan, a suburb of Detroit. She moved to New York City in 1977, worked as a photographer's model, studied dance, and became a presence at Manhattan discotheques such as Danceteria, where the DJ, Mark Kamins, played her demo tapes. Kamins introduced Madonna to executives at Sire Records, the label of the Ramones and Talking Heads, and in 1982 he produced her first dance club hit, 'Everybody'. In 1983 Madonna's breakthrough single 'Holiday' established certain elements of a distinctive studio sound, rooted in the synthesizer–pop dance music of the early 1980s. In addition, Madonna took a page from Michael Jackson's book, enlisting the services of manager Freddie DeMann, who had guided Jackson's career in the years leading up to the success of *Thriller*. DeMann oversaw the production of Madonna's first two music videos, 'Borderline' and 'Lucky Star', the latter of which featured glimpses of the young star's navel, setting a precedent for subsequent, ever more explicit sexual provocations. The choice of Freddie DeMann also points towards an important aspect of Madonna's modus operandi—the enlistment of a collaborative network of talented professionals, including producers, recording engineers, designers, and videographers.

In 1984 her second album, *Like a Virgin*, produced by Nile Rodgers, who was involved with the writing and production of a number of disco-era hits, including Le Chic's 'Good Times', shot to the top of the charts, eventually selling more than 10 million copies. The album spawned a series of hit singles: 'Like a Virgin' (Number 1 in the US for six weeks in 1984 and early 1985), 'Material Girl' (Number 5 in 1985), 'Angel', and 'Dress You Up' (both Number 5 in 1985). *Like a Virgin* was promoted on MuchMusic with a series of videos, and formed the basis for an elaborately staged concert tour—the 'Virgin Tour'—all carefully co-ordinated as part of a campaign to establish Madonna as a national celebrity. In 1985 Madonna also played a leading role in the film *Desperately Seeking Susan*, receiving generally positive reviews. In an industry where women are often treated as attractive but essentially non-creative 'objects' or 'visual hooks', Madonna began early on in her career to exert an unusual degree of control, not only over her music (writing or co-writing many of the songs on her early albums and playing an active role in the production process), but also over the creation and promulgation of her media image. Even seemingly uncontrollable events—like

Listening To Madonna's 'Like a Virgin' (1984)

The core dichotomy of Madonna's public persona—the innocent, emotionally vulnerable, cheerful girl versus the tough-minded, sexually experienced, self-directed woman—was established in the hit single 'Like a Virgin', which propelled her to superstar status. 'Like a Virgin' was not written by Madonna herself but by a pair of male songwriters, Billy Steinberg and Tom Kelly. As Steinberg himself put it, this is not a song about a virgin in any narrowly technical sense. Rather, it is about the feeling that someone who has grown pessimistic about love gets from a new relationship. We have already encountered this theme in Tina Turner's rendition of 'What's Love Got to Do with It'. 'Like a Virgin' is a good example of the mileage that Madonna and her producer, Nile Rodgers, were able to get out of a fairly simple set of musical elements.

The form of 'Like a Virgin' is straightforward. After a four-bar instrumental introduction that establishes the dance groove, there is an eight-bar verse, which we are calling 'A¹' ('*I made it through the wilderness . . .*'); a 10-bar version of the verse with somewhat different harmonies, which we call A^2 ('*I was beat, incomplete . . .*'); and a chorus featuring the hook of the song, which we call 'B' ('*Like a virgin . . .*'). The only additional structural element is an eight-bar interlude near the middle of the arrangement. The basic structure of the recording is thus

A^1A^2B
A^1A^2B
Eight-bar interlude
A^2BBB (etc., with a gradual fade-out)

As in much popular music, the timbre, texture, and rhythmic momentum of 'Like a Virgin' are more important to the listener's experience than is the song's structure. The studio mix—overseen by Madonna's long-time collaborator, Shep Pettibone—is clean, with clear stereo separation, heavy reliance on synthesized sound textures, and the singer's voice strongly foregrounded over the instruments. As on many dance-oriented hit singles of the 1980s, the characteristic lead guitar sound of rock music is absent here. Thus, synthesizers are indispensable to the overall effect of the recording—this is a studio sound that simply could not have been created 10 years before. Throughout the recording, however, the producer and engineers are careful not to make the instrumental parts too busy or complex, so that Madonna's voice remains the undisputed focus of the listener's attention.

As we have discussed, Madonna's persona on recordings and videos and in concert depends on the ironic manipulation of long-standing stereotypes about females. Her vocal style in 'Like a Virgin' reflects this aspect of her persona clearly and deliberately, ranging from the soft, intimate breathiness associated with Hollywood sex symbols like Marilyn Monroe, to the throaty, tougher sound of 1960s singers like Ronnie Spector, the lead singer on the Ronettes' 'Be My Baby'. This contrast is further reinforced in the video version of 'Like a Virgin' by an alternation between images of one Madonna as a bride dressed in white, about to be taken to bed by her groom, and another Madonna dressed in a tight black skirt and top and blue tights, dancing sexily in a gondola moving down the canals of Venice. During the verses Madonna uses a breathy, somewhat reedy 'little girl' voice, occasionally interspersing little squeals, sighs, and intakes of breath at the ends of phrases. Throughout the recording, Madonna shifts back and forth between the two personas, the innocent virgin and the experienced, worldly wise woman, each signified by a distinctive set of vocal timbres.

Of course, how a song's lyrics are interpreted is strongly influenced by their musical setting and by the visual images that accompany the words and music in a video or live concert. When Madonna revived 'Like a Virgin' for her 1990 *Blonde Ambition* tour, the song was placed in a more complex and provocative context, with Madonna clad like an ancient Egyptian princess, reclining on a huge bed, and framed on either side by black male dancers wearing cone-shaped brassieres. Whatever one's interpretation of the sexual and religious symbolism of Madonna's performances and the relationship to her own experience growing up as a Catholic, it is clear that she has a talent for recycling her repertoire in controversial and thought-provoking ways.

the ubiquitous tabloid accounts of her tempestuous and short-lived marriage to actor Sean Penn—seemed only to feed Madonna's growing notoriety.

During the second half of the 1980s Madonna began to write and record songs with deeper, and more controversial, lyric content. These included 'Papa Don't Preach' (1986), in which a pregnant young woman declares her determination to keep her baby and urges her father to lend his moral support; 'Open Your Heart' (1986), the video version of which portrays Madonna on display at a sleazy peepshow attended by dozens of men; 'Express Yourself' (1989), in which she appears alternatively as a cross-dressing figure, dominating a tableau of male industrial workers, and as a submissive female stereotype, crawling under a table with a collar around her neck; and 'Like a Prayer' (1989), the video of which included images of group and interracial sex, burning crosses, and an eroticized black Jesus. In fact, this last video was censured by the Vatican, and caused Pepsi-Cola to cancel a lucrative endorsement deal with Madonna.

The controversy-and-commercialism ante was upped even further in 1992 with the publication of *Sex*, a 128-page coffee-table book featuring nude and S&M-garbed photographs of Madonna and other celebrities, and the synchronized release of the album *Erotica*, which produced five major hit singles. The year 1994 saw the release of a warmer and more subtly sexual album, *Bedtime Stories*, which spawned 'Take a Bow', her biggest single hit ever (the song peaked at Number 1 after spending 34 weeks in the Top 40 in 1994). Towards the end of the 1990s Madonna once again refined her public image, winning a Golden Globe award for her leading role in the film *Evita* (1996) and releasing an album of love ballads (*Something to Remember*, 1996) aimed at a more mature audience. But in 1998 she returned to the disco-derived synthesizer–pop sound that had dominated her early recordings with the release of *Ray of Light*, which debuted at Number 2 on the album charts.

Madonna has frequently challenged the accusation—levelled at her by critics on both the left and the right—that her recordings, videos, and concert productions reinforce old, negative stereotypes of women. In a 1991 interview Madonna responded to these criticisms:

> I may be dressing like the typical bimbo, whatever, but I'm in charge. You know. I'm in charge of my fantasies. I put myself in these situations with men, you know, and everybody knows, in terms of my image in the public, people don't think of me as a person who's not in charge of my career or my life, okay? And isn't that what feminism is all about, you know, equality for men and women? And aren't I in charge of my life, doing the things I want to do? Making my own decisions? (Sexton, 1993: 286)

Madonna's rhetorical question pulls us into the middle space between the public image and the private life: between the international superstar, Madonna, and Madonna Louise Veronica Ciccone, a talented and ambitious Italian-American woman from the suburbs of industrial Detroit. Throughout her career, Madonna Ciccone has released tidbits of information about her private life, attitudes, and values that invite her fans (and her detractors) to imagine what the woman behind the 'star-making machinery' is really like.

Prince

Between 1982 and 1992 Prince (a.k.a. the Artist) placed nine albums in the Top 10, reaching the top of the charts with three of them (*Purple Rain* in 1984, *Around the World in a Day* in 1985, and *Batman* in 1989). During the same decade he placed 26 singles in the Top 40 and produced five Number 1 hits. Over the course of his career, Prince has sold almost 40 million recordings, making him one of the most popular music superstars of the last two decades of the twentieth century. More importantly, Prince is one of the most talented musicians ever to achieve mass commercial success in the field of popular music.

Prince Rogers Nelson was born in Minneapolis, Minnesota, the child of parents who migrated from Louisiana to the north, and who identify themselves as black with a mixed-race heritage that includes Italian and Native American ancestry. Prince has stated that growing up in a middle-class Minneapolis neighbourhood exposed him to a wide range of music, and that his early influences included everything from James Brown and Santana to Joni Mitchell. As he stated in a 1985 interview on MTV (also transcribed in *Rock & Soul*, Apr. 1986):

> I was brought up in a black-and-white world and, yes, black and white, night and day, rich and poor. I listened to all kinds of music when I was young, and when I was younger, I always said that one day I would play all kinds of music and not be judged for the color of my skin but the quality of my work.

When he was seven his mother and father separated, and Prince spent much of his adolescence being shunted from one home to another. Various statements by Prince suggest that the instability of that period in his life and the ambivalence of his relationships with his estranged parents have formed the source material for some of his best-known songs.

Prince has been remarkably productive during his career. Throughout the 1980s and 1990s, when most superstars released an album every two or three years, Prince's output averaged over an album per year. During the 1980s he composed, performed, and recorded more than 75 songs each year. Only about 300 of these songs have been released; the studio vault at his Paisley Park Studios in Minneapolis is said to contain more than 1,000 unreleased songs, more than 10,000 hours of material. Prince's compositions have been recorded by a wide range of artists, including George Clinton, Miles Davis, Joni Mitchell, Madonna, Bonnie Raitt, Céline Dion, and the Bangles. In addition to recordings released under his own name, Prince has developed a variety of satellite projects, groups, or artists who have served in part as outlets for his music (for example, the Time, Apollonia 6, and Sheila E.).

In stylistic terms, Prince's recorded output has encompassed a wide range of musical inspirations, from funk and guitar-based rock 'n' roll to urban folk music, new wave, and psychedelic rock. While the dominant impression of Prince's musical approach is that of a thoroughgoing open-mindedness, he has from the beginning sought to exert tight control over his music and his business. Prince owns his own studio, Paisley Park, and produces his own recordings; plays most of the instruments on his albums; and struggled for years to wrest control of his music from Warner Brothers, eventually signing an agreement with Capitol-EMI that let him retain control over the master tapes recorded in his studio (the basis of this dispute seems to have been that Warner Brothers could not release and promote Prince's new material as quickly as he wanted). As of this writing, Prince is re-recording and re-releasing all the material that was originally released by Warner. By the late 1990s he was releasing music exclusively—and extensively—on his own independent label, NPG Records, through his website, and via his direct-selling telephone hotline, which receives some 7,000 calls a month.

Descriptions of Prince's personality in the popular press present a series of opposed images—he is portrayed as a flower child and as a dictator; a male chauvinist who can form close personal relationships only with women; an intensely private person and a shrewd self-promoter; a sexual satyr and a steadfastly pious man, who has dedicated many of his albums to God. These discussions of Prince draw many comparisons with earlier figures in the history of popular music, such as the extroverted and sexually ambiguous rock 'n' roll star Little Richard, the guitar virtuoso Jimi Hendrix, the groundbreaking and idiosyncratic band leader Sly Stone, and the brilliant songwriter and multi-instrumentalist Stevie Wonder. Prince has been critical of the tendency of journalists and record company publicists to identify him only with black artists. In response to the question 'What do you think about the comparisons between you and Jimi Hendrix?', he rather testily responded:

It's only because he's black. That's really the only thing we have in common. He plays different guitar than I do. If they really listened to my stuff, they'd hear more of a Santana influence than Jimi Hendrix. (Karlen, 1985)

Prince's British biographer, Barney Hoskyns, christened Prince 'the Imp of the Perverse', referring to his apparent delight in confounding the expectations and assumptions of his audience, music critics, and the record industry. Certainly, Prince's relationship to the 'star-making machinery' of the entertainment industry is as complex as his racial identity, sexual orientation, and musical style. As a public celebrity, Prince occupies a middle ground between the hermit-like reclusiveness of Michael Jackson and the exuberant exhibitionism of Madonna. Throughout his career, Prince has granted few press interviews, yet, for the most part, he has managed to keep himself in the limelight. In the early 1990s Prince changed his name to a cryptic and unpronounceable symbol that blended male and female elements, engaged in a series of public battles with Warner over control of his music, and produced a compact disc recording that could only be played in the order in which it was originally programmed, a reassertion of the principle of the rock album as a complete artistic work. It is hard to imagine another celebrity who would willingly relinquish his nom de plume, publicly (and successfully) defy the will of the transnational corporation that had initially helped to launch his career, and deny his fans the right to consume his songs in whatever order they might choose.

Perhaps the best example of Prince's skill at manipulating the boundary between the public and the private is the film and soundtrack album *Purple Rain* (1984), which established him as a pop superstar. *Purple Rain* was the best-selling album of 1984, bumping Bruce Springsteen's *Born in the U.S.A.* out of the top position and holding the Number 1 position for 24 weeks, and producing five hit singles, including 'When Doves Cry', 'Let's Go Crazy', and 'Purple Rain'. Since 1984 the album has sold more than 13 million copies, making it one of the 10 best-selling albums of all time. The film did reasonably well at the box office, although it did not succeed in establishing Prince as a matinee idol. Reviews varied widely, some critics regarding the film as a self-indulgent, poorly written, badly acted attempt to promote a music album, while *Rolling Stone* numbered it among the best rock movies ever made. The film and the album were cross-promoted by Warner Entertainment, which spent $3.5 million for television ads, and by MTV, which ran footage from the celebrity-packed premiere party in Hollywood. The single of 'When Doves Cry' was released a few weeks before *Purple Rain* appeared in theatres, and helped to boost the film's popularity, which in turn helped several other songs on the soundtrack to reach the Top 40.

The plot and characters of *Purple Rain* draw heavily on the details of Prince's life, both personal and professional. Prince stars as 'the Kid', a young, gifted musician struggling to establish himself in the nightclub scene of Minneapolis. His main competition in the musical arena is Morris Day, the real-life leader of one of Prince's 'satellite' projects, the Time. The Kid is attracted to a beautiful young singer named Apollonia (another of Prince's real-life proteges), who in the film is also being pursued by Morris Day. The Kid's parents—the only characters in the film portrayed by professional actors—are to some degree based on Prince's mother and father. Another subplot has to do with the Kid's inability to accept creative input from the musicians in his band, the Revolution. The film concludes on a relatively upbeat note as the Kid adopts one of his father's compositions, incorporating a rhythm track created by members of the Revolution, and creates the song 'Purple Rain', which wins over his audience, the band, Apollonia, and even Morris Day.

As with any semi-autobiographical work, it is not easy to draw boundaries between the fictional character (the Kid), the celebrity persona (Prince), and the private individual (Prince Rogers Nelson). The character of the Kid—talented, self-absorbed, obsessed with exerting control over his music and his career, troubled by family conflicts and an inability to sustain intimate relationships—seems consonant with the accounts offered by Prince's family and professional associates. Apart from the Academy Award-winning soundtrack, a major source of the film's attraction for Prince's fans no doubt lay in the idea that this was a form of public psychoanalysis (a genre of 'confessional' and 'therapeutic' lyric writing some rock critics humorously dub 'Oedipus Rox'), a tantalizing opportunity to catch a glimpse of the 'man behind the curtain'. If *Purple Rain* is a film with genuinely confessional aspects, it is also a product of the increasingly sophisticated marketing strategies applied by entertainment corporations during the 1980s.

Listening To Prince's 'When Doves Cry' (1984)

'When Doves Cry'—a last-minute addition to the *Purple Rain* soundtrack—is an unusual pop recording in a number of ways. To begin with, the album track runs almost six minutes, a length that, although not without precedent, was much longer than the typical Top 40 hit of the 1980s (a shortened version was released as a single). Pop music recordings of the 1980s—such as Madonna's 'Like a Virgin'—were typically the product of collaboration among the singer, songwriter(s), producer, studio engineers, session musicians, and others. 'When Doves Cry', on the other hand, is essentially the work of a single person— Prince wrote the song, produced the recording, sang all of the vocal parts, and played all of the instruments, including electric guitar, keyboard synthesizers, and the Linn LM-1 digital drum machine. The lyric of 'When Doves Cry', with its striking imagery and psychoanalytical implications, certainly does not conform to the usual formulas of the romantic pop song. In addition, this recording crosses over the boundaries of established pop genres, fusing a funk rhythm with the lead guitar sound of heavy metal, the digitally synthesized and sampled textures of post-disco dance music, and the aesthetic focus and control of progressive rock and the singer-songwriter tradition. In this sense it is a good example both of Prince's desire to avoid being typecast as a traditional R&B artist and of the creative eclecticism that led music critics to come up with labels such as 'dance rock', 'funk rock', and 'new wave funk' to describe his music.

The instrumentation of 'When Doves Cry' is also somewhat unusual, as it lacks a bass part. Usually the bass helps to establish the tonality (or key) of a given piece of music and combines with the drums to provide the rhythmic bedrock of a recording. Prince's decision to 'punch out' (exclude) the bass track that he had already recorded—apparently a spur-of-the-moment experiment during the process of mixing—gives the recording an unusually open feeling. In addition, Prince's composition avoids the tendency, pronounced in many rock and pop recordings, to establish a clear distinction between a verse and a chorus, each having its own distinctive melody and harmonies. 'When Doves Cry' does use the verse-chorus form, but the melody and supporting harmonies are almost identical in the two sections, making the distinction between them much less fixed. While many pop recordings use the verse-chorus structure to build to a final climax, followed by a relatively rapid fade-out, the musical intensity of 'When Doves Cry' rises and falls continuously, creating a complex succession of peaks and valleys (one critic has interpreted this 'ebbing and flowing of pleasure' as embodying a female rather than male pattern of sexual excitement, and has connected this musical approach to Prince's embracing of female qualities in his own personality). Finally, the studio mix is also unusual, relatively spare and dry, and quite unlike the lush, reverb-laden studio sound of most 1980s dance music recordings (including Madonna's hit singles). Prince does use studio effects such as echo and digital processing, but they are tightly controlled and focused.

The arrangement of 'When Doves Cry' can be divided into two major sections. Section One, about three and a half minutes in length, is basically a presentation of the song, with its alternation of verse ('A') and chorus ('B'). Section Two consists of a series of eight-bar phrases in which the background texture is subtly varied while instrumental solos (guitar and keyboard synthesizer), sung phrases (both solo and overdubbed in harmony), and other vocal effects (breathing, screaming, sighing, groaning) are sometimes juxtaposed or layered on top of one another and sometimes alternated one after the other. Perhaps the best analogy for the overall effect of this recording is that of a weaving, made up of patches of subtly shifting textural effects and tone colours, held together by the strong threads of a funk-derived dance groove, and strung on a formal loom made up of eight-bar sections. This is a recording that rewards repeated listening, not least because one musician has created every sound that you hear throughout.

'When Doves Cry' opens abruptly with a virtuoso burst of lead guitar, establishing from the very first moment Prince's mastery of the hard rock idiom. (We could say that Prince was able to do for himself what Michael Jackson needed Eddie Van Halen's help to accomplish on his *Thriller* album.) As the main dance groove is established on the Linn LM-1 digital drum machine, the guitar plays five more bars. We then hear a strange yet recognizably human sound, a pattern created by running Prince's voice through a digital processor and turning it into a repeating loop. As the keyboard synthe-sizer introduces a chord pattern that interlocks rhythmically with the drum machine (completing the basic groove that will carry us through most of the recording), Prince's voice moves across the stereo space of the recording from left to right and then fades out. Only 16 bars into the recording, it is clear that this is not your normal pop single.

The first half of the arrangement (Section One) begins by placing equal weight on the verse and the chorus material (16 bars each) and then gradually de-emphasizes the verse ('A'), which finally disappears altogether. The chorus is always followed by an eight-bar groove section, in which the underlying drum machine-and-synthesizer dance rhythm is brought to the fore. The presentation of the song, with its weakly contrasted verse-chorus structure, makes full use of studio technology and of Prince's remarkable abilities as a singer. In the first verse he sings alone, in a middle-register voice. The second verse introduces a second copy of Prince, another middle-register voice that overlaps slightly with the first one; as this concludes, the two Princes sing together, first in unison, then in overdubbed harmony. In the chorus ('*How can you . . .*') these two voices are joined by a third, low-register, growling voice; eventually ('*Maybe you're . . .*'), we are presented with four Princes singing in harmony with one another, plus a fifth Prince who interjects solo responses.

The second half of 'When Doves Cry' (Section Two) presents an even more complex palette of timbral and textural variations, playing with combinations of the drum machine–synthesizer groove, sustained orchestral sounds, instrumental solos (including a keyboard solo that resembles eighteenth-century music), and an astonishing variety of vocal timbres. If you listen closely you should be able to distinguish as many as a dozen unique voices in the studio mix, positioned to the left, right, and centre, some heavily modified by digital technology and others closer to the natural sound of Prince's singing voice. In addition to the complex patterns of harmony and call-and-response singing, Prince uses a variety of vocal effects, including a James Brown-like scream, rhythmic breathing, sighs, and groans. These sounds lend a sense of physical intimacy to the recording and enhance its aura of sexuality.

If 'Like a Virgin' can be interpreted as a musical analogue to Madonna's 'split personality', 'When Doves Cry' may represent an even more complex set of psychological relations between the public persona and private personality of a pop superstar. In a 1996 television interview, Prince Rogers Nelson revealed that he, like millions of other children, had created an alternative personality, an imaginary companion who had not only helped him through the dislocations of his youth but also continued to offer him guidance as an adult. It may not be too much of a reach to suggest that the 'multiple Princes' of 'When Doves Cry'—a song that wears its Oedipal heart on its sleeve—are not only an experiment in musical polyphony but also a conscious representation of the continuous inner dialogue that has shaped Prince's career (in interviews, Prince has described how his 'spirit' has advised him to change course, abandon projects, and even alter his name). In its rich layering of instrumental textures and vocal personalities, 'When Doves Cry' imparted to the public image of Prince a complexity and psychological depth that is atypical of mass-media celebrities. And in the process, it established his reputation as one of the most creative and influential musicians of the 1980s.

Discussion Questions

1. How has MuchMusic reshaped the rock tradition? Do you watch MuchMusic? Why or why not? If you do watch MuchMusic, which kinds of content (i.e., musical, discrete programming, industry news, etc.) attract your attention?
2. There has yet to be a satisfactory explanation for *why* music television proved to be so popular. Why do you think it was so popular?
3. What are the influences of the MuchMusic era on the rock tradition today? Can a band be popular without releasing a video? Does image trump sound now?
4. Why did fans of heavy metal consider the synthesizer such a controversial instrument, especially given that many fans of the genre were also fans of, say, Pink Floyd, whose records have regularly featured synthesizers since the early 1970s?
5. In your opinion, why has Madonna proven so popular in Canada?
6. What is the legacy of an album like Paul Simon's *Graceland* on today's rock market? What does his decision to work with South African musicians have to say about the rock tradition (i.e., would the record have resonated as well with a rock listenership, in your opinion, if Simon had engaged with, say, First Nations musicians and traditions)?

Chapter Eight

Alternative Currents: Rock in the 1990s

Throughout the 1990s, the marketplace for popular music continued to metastasize into hundreds of named genres, each correlated with a particular segment of the listening audience. Among these were:

- classic rock (Tragically Hip, Tom Cochrane)
- alternative rock (Sloan, Alanis Morissette)
- foxcore (Bif Naked)
- hardcore (D.O.A.)
- country rock (Blue Rodeo)
- new country (Shania Twain)
- alternative country (k.d. lang)
- roots rock (Cowboy Junkies)
- alternative roots (Be Good Tanyas)
- First Nations pop (Kashtin, Susan Aglukark)
- Celtic pop (Great Big Sea)
- alternative Celtic (Ashley MacIsaac)
- techno (DJ Tiga)
- rap (Maestro Fresh Wes)
- novelty pop (Moxy Früvous).

The 1990s saw a splintering of genres that exceeded anything previously experienced in rock. While many of these styles sprang 'from the ground up', as it were, nurtured by local audiences, regional networks of clubs, and low-profit independent labels, by the mid-1990s the entertainment industry had refined its ability to identify such 'alternative' genres and to target their specialized audiences.

In this chapter we examine the emergence of 'alternative' currents in rock music, and in popular music in general, during the 1990s. This will entail an extended look at the emergence of 'alternative' rock as a category of Top 40 rock in the early and mid-1990s, a study of Canadian Top 40 rock group the Tragically Hip, the meteoric transformation of rap into a mainstream pop genre that had become more profitable than any other by 1998, and a brief consideration of a group of female Canadian rock and pop singers who achieved great success in the late 1990s while still maintaining something of an 'outsider' identity (we briefly address the rise of techno dance music in this chapter, though we examine that genre in closer detail in the next chapter).

The Meaning(s) of 'Alternative'

By 1999, almost every major genre of popular music had sprouted an 'alternative' subcategory. The term, famously difficult to define, was generally used to indicate the presence of some degree of experimentalism on a record, even if only in the image adopted by the musicians who made it. Little else can be said to account for the term. Some artists classified under the 'alternative' heading sounded similar, while others seemed to come from entirely different musical planets (compare, for instance, the Barenaked Ladies' 'Grade Nine' to Sloan's 'Underwhelmed', both of which were marketed as 'alternative' in the early 1990s). Some 'alternative' acts recorded for small indie labels as a matter of principle, while others signed contracts with major labels. Still others had an obvious social, moral, or political outlook that informed their musical output—Pearl Jam, for instance, but also the likes of Our Lady Peace and Sarah McLachlan. Some performers created a kind of 'grassroots' version of charity rock for the 1990s, while their peers had no such political aspirations (for a recent example of a 'grassroots' charity rock album, consider Sarah Harmer's *I'm a Mountain* [2005], which was made to raise awareness and funds for protecting rural lands around the Niagara Escarpment). What, then, characterizes something as an example of 'alternative' music?

The difficulty in formulating a one-size-fits-all definition for 'alternative' music in the 1990s stems partly from the use of this term to advance two different, and often conflicting, agendas. On the one hand, the term 'alternative', like the broadly equivalent terms 'underground' and 'independent', was often used throughout the 1990s to set a particular style of music in binary opposition to some putative 'mainstream' variety, chiefly to demonstrate that it was made by critical thinking—as opposed to commercially motivated—musicians who stood in direct opposition to the 'homogenizing' or 'stultifying' influence of a largely disposable consumer culture. Fans who described their preferred music in this way described themselves as 'alternative' listeners in the process, which is to say, skilled—or discerning—enough to differentiate musical wheat from musical chaff. Thus, the term 'alternative' was most often used by critics to describe, and sometimes to positively valorize, music that, in one sense or another, challenged the status quo. From this perspective 'alternative' music was fiercely iconoclastic, anti-commercial, and anti-mainstream, rather than any particular stylistic amalgam; it was 'local' as opposed to 'corporate', 'homemade' as opposed to 'mass-produced' and 'disposable', and 'genuine' or 'authentic' as opposed to 'prefabricated' and 'manipulative'.

However, an entirely different—though no less apt—sense of the term 'alternative' underlies its commercial use in the 1990s. As the concept of an 'alternative' music became ever more profitable in the 1990s, functionaries of the rock industry used the term to denote certain choices available to consumers via record stores, radio, cable television, and, eventually, the Internet. From the perspective of the record industry in the 1990s, then, 'alternative' was a useful means for major and indie labels alike to market records to listeners who demanded 'alternative' product—no more, no less. This sense of the term is bound up with the need of the music business to identify and exploit new trends, styles, and audiences. In an interview conducted during the late 1980s, a senior executive for a major record company revealed that:

> There's a whole indie section [of our company. There are] . . . kids that will only buy records that are on an indie label . . . which is why we sometimes concoct labels to try and fool them. (Negus, 1992: 16)

The notion of a huge entertainment corporation cooking up a fake 'independent' record label to satisfy an audience hungry for musical expressions of authenticity and rebellion may seem a bizarre contradiction at first glance. From our long-term historical perspective, though, we can see this institutional development as the culmination of a decades-old trend within the music business. In the days before rock 'n' roll, genres such as race and hillbilly were predominantly the bailiwick of small independently owned and operated 'specialty' record labels such as Okeh, Brunswick, and Black Swan. By the early 1990s, however, the major record companies had fully internalized the lesson of rock 'n' roll, as they came to consider independent labels the functional equivalent of Junior A hockey teams—small, specialized, close-to-the-ground, and 'grassroots' operations perfectly situated to sniff out 'the next big thing'. In an era when most so-called 'indie' labels were distributed, promoted, and even owned outright by huge entertainment corporations, it became difficult to sustain a purely economic definition of 'alternative music' as 'music that doesn't make money'. To put it another way, the fact that a band's music, song lyrics, appearance, and ideological stance were explicitly anti-commercial didn't mean that they couldn't sell millions of records, and thereby generate huge corporate profits. This was almost certainly the lesson that major record labels had learned from the success of punk rock outfits like the Sex Pistols and the Clash in the late 1970s; and the commercial marketing of anti-commercialism—what Canadian sociologists Andrew Potter and Joseph Heath call 'the rebel sell'—is one of the significant continuities between 1970s punk rock and alternative rock in the 1990s.

Up from the Underground: Hardcore, Indie, and Alternative Rock

In the wake of punk rock's collapse, symbolized most clearly by the acrimonious split of the Sex Pistols in 1978, a number of distinctive streams of 'indie' or 'underground' rock bubbled up in cities and towns across North America. Not expressly American or Canadian as a musical and cultural phenomenon, the triumph of 'underground rock' occurred synchronously on a continental scale, as bands working in cities across North America began playing similarly unconventional rock music and hustled their way onto international media at roughly the same time (many 'underground' bands found an outlet on weekly music television programs devoted to the genre, such as MuchMusic's *The Wedge*, first hosted by Sook-Yin Lee in 1994, as well as on alternative radio, indie film soundtracks, and various fanzines). In fact, most of the cities where indie rock first took shape in Canada—Vancouver, Toronto, Hamilton, Montreal, and Halifax, to name only a few—hosted large populations of college students who tended to listen to student-programmed college radio stations, both of which remain key ingredients for fostering a local underground rock scene. Starting out as local phenomena supported by small but devoted audiences, touring within regional networks of clubs and releasing recordings on tiny, hand-to-mouth independent labels, bands like the Rheostatics, Sloan, R.E.M., Sonic Youth, the Dead Kennedys, D.O.A., and Nirvana came to symbolize the essence of underground or indie rock—each band contributing a staunchly individualistic, and arguably anti-commercial, variant of the guitar-based pop music that eventually came to be known as alternative rock, blending the dissonant 'DIY' (Do It Yourself) sensibility of 1970s punk with the distorted sonic textures of heavy metal music into a sometimes impenetrable, other times irresistibly catchy, sonic stew.

In general, underground and indie rock bands active in the 1990s maintained a defiant stance towards the conformity and commercialism of the music industry, even as many of them came to work within that industry. They were committed to songwriting that explored taboo subjects such as drug abuse, depression, incest, and suicide; they expressed an unambiguous interest in social and political movements such as environmentalism, abortion rights, and AIDS activism; and they identified themselves both with and through an unconventional—and soon to be heavily merchandised—style of self-presentation that included 'dressing down' in torn jeans, flannel shirts, and work boots (this style of fashion, thanks to its widespread adoption by grunge rock musicians and their fans, itself came to be called 'grunge'). Despite their avowed opposition to mainstream rock music, alternative genres such as indie and underground rock, hardcore, and thrash were supported by predominantly white, middle- or working-class young men who themselves came to form their own mainstream, complete with its own unique soundtrack, vocabulary, code of conduct, and dress.

By 1995 many underground rock groups had already begun to taste commercial success on an international scale, signing deals with major record companies and moving towards a more pop-oriented sound. Others, driven by the notion that 'authentic expression' could only be achieved through nonconformity, remained small, intensely local, and close to their fan base. For the underground bands who achieved commercial success—leading to the emergence of alternative rock as a marketing category around 1990—there were many contradictions to face, not least being the problem of maintaining an 'outsider' identity, so crucial to their image, as their albums rose to the top of the Top 40, garnered multiple Grammy awards, and spawned heavy-rotation videos on mainstream music television. For many of these groups, the sensation of being 'on the inside looking out' was new and unnerving. For some, it even proved fatal.

Each of the following songs represents a prevalent strain of alternative rock in the 1990s. Though not all of the songs we examine enjoyed significant sales, each clearly encapsulates one of the various ways that rock musicians negotiated the concept of alternative rock in the 1990s. Whether they were actually successful in their quest to create a mainstream music that somehow maintains a decidedly non-mainstream aesthetic—if such a music is even possible—is really beside the point. What ultimately matters is that each of the following songs demonstrates that, especially during the first half of the 1990s, many musicians and listeners considered alternative rock a distinct possibility; and, in so doing, each song also provides a record of what particular musicians, working in particular contexts, thought alternative rock might sound like.

Dead Kennedys: 'Holidays in Cambodia' (1981)

Hardcore was an extreme variation of punk, pioneered during the early 1980s by bands primarily in San Francisco (the Dead Kennedys), Vancouver (D.O.A., the Young Canadians, Skinny Puppy, and the Dayglo Abortions), and Los Angeles (the Germs, Black Flag, X, and the Circle Jerks). These groups—and others, such as the Texas-based Butthole Surfers—took the frenzied energy of the Ramones and the Sex Pistols to its logical limit, playing simple riff-based songs at impossibly fast tempos, and screaming nihilistic lyrics over a chaotic wall of guitar chords. Audiences at hardcore clubs—typically adorned in tattoos, buzz cuts, and combat boots—developed the practice of *slam dancing* or *moshing*, in which members of the audience pushed their way up to a *mosh pit* (an area situated directly in front of the stage) and smashed into one another, sometimes climbing onto the stage and diving off into the crowd (*stage diving*). Most hardcore recordings were released by independent labels like SST, Alternative Tentacles, and IRS, and the typical hardcore disc was produced to look and sound as though it had been made in someone's basement. Few of these bands managed to score contracts with major labels—a fact proudly touted by many fans as proof of their genuine 'underground' status.

'Holiday in Cambodia' by the Dead Kennedys, released on the independent label Alternative Tentacles in 1981, is a good example of the sensibility of early 1980s hardcore rock. The lyrics—written by lead singer Jello Biafra (a.k.a. Eric Boucher)—brim with merciless sarcasm. The song is directed at the spoiled children of suburban yuppies, who Biafra suggests ought to be sent to forced labour camps in Cambodia, then in the grip of Pol Pot's genocidal regime, to gain some perspective on the magnitude of their own problems. The recording opens with a nightmarish display of guitar pyrotechnics, a series of Hendrix-inspired whoops, slides, scratches, and feedback, meant to evoke the sonic reality of a war zone. The band—comprised of only an electric guitar, electric bass, and drums—gradually builds to an extremely fast tempo (around 208 beats per minute). Over this chaotic din, Jello Biafra's quavering voice sneers out the caustic lyrics:

> So you been to school for a year or two
> And you know you've seen it all
> In daddy's car, thinkin' you'll go far
> Back east your type don't crawl
> Play ethnicky jazz to parade your snazz
> On your five grand stereo
> Braggin' that you know how the niggers feel cold
> And the slums got so much soul . . .
> Well you'll work harder with a gun in your back
> For a bowl of rice a day
> Slave for soldiers till you starve
> Then your head is skewered on a stake . . .
>
> Pol Pot, Pol Pot, Pol Pot, Pol Pot . . .
> And it's a holiday in Cambodia
> Where you'll do what you're told
> A holiday in Cambodia
> Where the slums got so much soul

The Dead Kennedys' variant of hardcore was lent focus by the band's political stance, which opposed American imperialism overseas, the destruction of human rights and the environment, and what the band saw as a hypocritical and soulless suburban lifestyle. Jello Biafra composed songs with such titles as 'California Über Alles', 'Kill the Poor', and 'Chemical Warfare'. As the hardcore scene began to attract right-wing racial supremacists, though, many of whom misunderstood the parodic intent of lyrics such as '*Braggin' that you know how the niggers feel cold/And the slums got so much soul*', many hardcore bands felt compelled to clarify their political allegiances. Thus, the genre's pronounced parodism gave way to a lucent, if sometimes overly 'straight-edged', left-wing earnestness. Biafra penned the song 'Nazi Punks Fuck Off' (1981), for instance, in an unambiguous attempt to distance the progressive hardcore skinheads from their fascist counterparts.

By the mid-1980s the hardcore movement had largely played itself out, though aspects of the music's style and attitude were carried on by bands playing thrash, which blended the fast tempos and rebellious attitude of hardcore with the technical virtuosity of heavy metal guitar playing. Thrash was a harder, faster version of the commercially successful speed metal style, played by bands such as Metallica, Megadeth, and Anthrax. The 1991 album *Metallica*, though with more of a pop

sound than earlier fare such as *Ride the Lightning* and *Master of Puppets*, was the ultimate confirmation of heavy metal's mass popularity and new-found importance to
the music industry: it streaked to Number 1 across the continent, sold over five million copies, and stayed on the record charts for an incredible 266 weeks. Unlike speed
metal, thrash didn't produce any superstars—the Los Angeles band Suicidal
Tendencies was the most recognizable name to emerge from the genre—but it did
exert an influence on alternative rock bands of the 1990s. Although thrash never
developed a mass audience, its fans remained dedicated, keeping the style alive as an
underground club-based phenomenon to this day.

Indie Rock Pioneers: R.E.M. and Sonic Youth

The two most influential indie rock bands of the 1980s were R.E.M., which formed
in 1980 in Athens, Georgia, and Sonic Youth, which formed in New York City in
1981. While both bands were influenced by the 1970s New York punk scene, they
developed this musical impetus in different directions. R.E.M.'s reinterpretation of the
punk aesthetic incorporated aspects of folk rock—particularly a ringing acoustic guitar sound reminiscent of the 1960s group the Byrds—and a propensity for catchy
melodic hooks. Touring almost constantly, and releasing a series of critically
acclaimed, and increasingly profitable, albums from the independent label IRS, R.E.M.
gradually grew from its roots as a regional cult phenomenon to command a large
national audience. This process culminated in the release of *Document*, the band's
first Top 10 album, in 1987. The next year, in 1988, R.E.M. signed a $10 million, five-
album agreement with Warner Brothers, becoming one of the first underground
bands of the 1980s to receive such a deal. By 1991, when alternative rock seemed to
many observers to have suddenly erupted onto the pop music scene, R.E.M. had
already been working steadily at developing the genre for more than a decade. That
year the band released the album *Out of Time*, which shot to Number 1 on the album
chart, sold four million copies, generated two Top 10 singles, and won a Grammy
award for Best Alternative Music LP (the 'alternative' category had been established
just the year before, an indication of the music industry's awakening interest in maintaining an 'underground' rock music market).

Sonic Youth, formed in New York City in 1981, pushed underground rock music
in a quite different direction. Influenced by avant-garde experimentalists such as the
Velvet Underground, Sonic Youth developed a dark, sometimes menacing, feedback-
oriented sound, altering the tuning of their guitars by inserting screwdrivers and
drumsticks under the strings at random intervals, and ignoring the conventional song
structures of rock and pop music. On a series of influential—though commercially
unsuccessful—recordings, released during the mid-1980s on the independent label
SST, Sonic Youth began to experiment with more conventional pop song forms while

maintaining the discordant sound with which they were so closely identified by fans and other musicians. By the early 1990s, Sonic Youth, the former underground phenomenon, had signed with the major label DGC, owned by the media magnate David Geffen, and was being widely hailed as a pioneer of the alternative movement in rock. The magazine *Vanity Fair* went so far as to proclaim Sonic Youth's lead singer, Kim Gordon, the 'godmother of alternative rock', making her the conceptual spouse of Neil Young, who many grunge bands—but especially Pearl Jam, who would eventually record an album with the Canadian rocker—dubbed 'the Godfather of grunge'. The 1994 album *Experimental Jet Set, Trash and No Star*, their third release on DGC, reached Number 34 on the Top 100 album chart, proof that their national audience, like that of R.E.M., had expanded beyond all expectations.

Nirvana: 'Smells Like Teen Spirit' (1991)

Although underground bands began to appear on the charts during the late 1980s, the commercial breakthrough for alternative rock, and the occasion of its enshrinement as a privileged category in the pop music marketplace, was achieved in 1992 by Nirvana, a band from the Pacific Northwest. Between 1992 and 1994, Nirvana—a trio comprised of singer and guitarist Kurt Cobain, bassist Krist Novoselic, and, eventually, drummer Dave Grohl—released two multi-platinum albums that moved alternative rock's blend of hardcore punk and heavy metal out of the back bins of specialty record stores and into the commercial mainstream. The rise of so-called *grunge rock* and the tragic demise of Kurt Cobain, who committed suicide in 1994 at the age of 27, provide some insight into the opportunities, and the pressures, facing alternative rock musicians in the early 1990s.

Cobain and Novoselic met in 1985 in the town of Aberdeen, an economically depressed logging town some 160 kilometres from Seattle. Cobain's parents had divorced when he was eight years old, an event that, by his own account, troubled him deeply and left him shy and introspective. Inspired by the records of underground rock and hardcore bands like R.E.M., Sonic Youth, and the Dead Kennedys and by the pop creativity of the Beatles, and frustrated with the limitations of small-town working-class life, Cobain and Novoselic formed Nirvana in 1987 and began playing gigs at local colleges and clubs. The following year they were signed by the independent label Sub Pop Records, which was formed in 1987 by the entrepreneurs Bruce Pavitt and Jonathan Poneman (*Sub Pop* began as a mimeographed fanzine for local bands before mutating into a record label). Nirvana's debut album, *Bleach* (1989), cost slightly over $600 to record—less than the cost of 30 minutes of recording time at a major New York or Los Angeles recording studio—and sold 35,000 copies, an impressive feat for a regional indie rock release.

In 1991 Nirvana signed with major label DGC. Following a European tour with Sonic Youth, the album *Nevermind* (1991) was released in September, quickly selling out its initial shipment of 50,000 copies and creating a much-ballyhooed shortage in record stores in the process. By the beginning of 1992, *Nevermind* had reached Number 1 on record charts across North America, displacing Michael Jackson's highly publicized 'comeback' album, *Dangerous*. In fact, *Nevermind* would stay on the charts for almost five years, eventually selling more than 10 million copies, making it the alternative rock world's *Sgt. Pepper*.

One source of *Nevermind*'s success was the platinum single 'Smells Like Teen Spirit'—the alternative rock genre's, and the band's, first Top 10 hit (the video for 'Smells Like Teen Spirit' was also the first in the genre to make heavy rotation on MuchMusic). One of the most striking aspects of 'Teen Spirit' is its fusion of heavy metal instrumental textures with straightforward pop songwriting techniques, including a number of memorable verbal and melodic hooks. The band's sound, which had been thick and plodding on its Sub Pop record, is sleek and well focused here, thanks largely to the production of Butch Vig and of mixing engineer Andy Wallace. The song itself combines a four-chord heavy metal harmonic progression with a somewhat conventional formal structure, made up of four-, eight-, and 12-bar sections. The overall structure of the song includes a verse of eight bars ('*Load up on guns . . .*'), which we are calling 'A', and two repeated sections, or choruses, which we have labelled 'B' (eight bars in length) and 'C' (12 bars). These sections are marked off by distinctive instrumental textures, shifting from the quiet, reflective, even somewhat depressed quality of 'A', through the crescendo of 'B', with its spacey one-word mantra and continuous carpet of thick guitar chords, and into the 'C' section, where Cobain bellows his unfocused feelings of discontent and the group slams out heavy metal power chords. This ABC structure is repeated three times over the course of the five-minute recording, with room created between the second and final iterations for a 16-bar guitar solo, which might be considered the bridge of a larger AABA form (true to pop convention, Cobain's solo reiterates the melody from the song's 'A' and 'B' sections).

Nirvana's 'Smells Like Teen Spirit', the first alternative rock single of the 1990s to enter the Top 10, is actually a carefully crafted pop record. Its sleek, lacquered studio sound, Cobain's liberal use of melodic and verbal hooks, the trio's careful attention to textural shifts as a means of marking off formal sections of the song, and the fact that Cobain's guitar solo consists of an almost note-for-note restatement of the melodies of the 'A' and 'B' sections—all basic pop conventions—serve to remind us that the Beatles were just as profound an influence on 1990s alternative rock as were more eagerly dissonant bands like the Dead Kennedys, Sonic Youth, and the Velvet Underground.

Although alternative rock bands like R.E.M. and Sonic Youth handled their rise to fame with relative aplomb, success destroyed Nirvana. The group's attitude towards the music industry appears to have crystallized early on, as this 1989 Sub Pop press release (reproduced at the Sub Pop Records website) indicates:

NIRVANA sees the underground scene as becoming stagnant and more accessible to big league capitalist pig major record labels. But does NIRVANA feel a moral duty to fight this cancerous evil? NO WAY! We want to cash in and suck up to the big wigs in hopes that we too can GET HIGH AND I— . . . SOON we will need groupie repellant. SOON we will be coming to your town and asking if we can stay over at your house and use the stove. SOON we will do encores of 'GLORIA' and 'LOUIE LOUIE' at benefit concerts with all our celebrity friends.

The sardonic humour of this public relations document only partially masks the band's intense ambivalence towards rock celebrity, a kind of 'listen to us but don't listen to us' stance. As *Nevermind* rose up the charts, Nirvana began to attract a mass audience that included millions of fans of hard rock and commercial heavy metal, genres to which they had always thought their own music was explicitly opposed. The realization that this was not actually the case—that they were, in fact, not so different from the 'hair metal sellouts' they so viciously mocked in interviews—impelled the group to ever more outrageous behaviour. Most famously, the band took to baiting their audiences and irritating some fans' outward homophobia by often wearing women's clothing and kissing each other on stage.

In 1992 Cobain married Courtney Love, the leader of an all-female alternative rock (a.k.a. 'foxcore') group called Hole. Rumours concerning the couple's use of heroin began to circulate, and an article in *Vanity Fair* charged that Love had used the narcotic while pregnant with the couple's child, Francis Bean Cobain, leading to a public struggle with the Los Angeles child services bureau over custody of the baby. In the midst of this adverse publicity, Nirvana released their second album for DGC, *In Utero*, a conscious return to the raw sound of Nirvana's debut record for Sub Pop. Despite producer Steve Albini's decidedly 'anti-pop' tweaking, *In Utero* quickly went to Number 1 across North America in 1993, selling four million copies thanks largely to the ragged beauty of tracks such as 'Pennyroyal Tea', 'All Apologies', and 'Heart Shaped Box'.

The 'Seattle Sound'

Regional 'sounds' have played an important part in the history of popular music, from the Chicago blues of Muddy Waters to the Memphis rockabilly style of Elvis Presley and the southern California inflections of gangsta rap. Seattle, where Nirvana honed their sound and built a local fan base, was already home to a thriving alternative rock scene by the late 1980s (the Pacific Northwest, while at somewhat of a remove from the main centres of the recording industry, had 25 years earlier played a role in the development of garage band rock, an important predecessor of punk rock). The group often singled out as an originator of the 'Seattle sound' was Green River (formed in 1983), whose 1988 album *Rehab Doll*, released on Sub Pop, helped to popularize grunge rock, blending heavy metal guitar textures with hardcore punk. Green River was also the training ground for members of later, more widely known Northwest bands such as Mudhoney (formed in 1988 by Green River alumni Mark Arm and Steve Turner), which was Sub Pop's biggest act until Nirvana came along, and Pearl Jam (formed in 1990 by Green River alumni Stone Gossard, Jeff Ament, and Bruce Fairweather), who went on to become one of the most popular rock bands of the 1990s. One of the first bands signed to the fledgling Sub Pop label was Soundgarden (formed 1984), a heavy metal band that many insiders expected to be the first group to break the Seattle grunge sound on the national market. However, Soundgarden's first across-the-boards success, the album *Superunknown*, which reached Number 1 on the charts and sold five million copies, was not released until 1994.

Today, the push to define a regional style often comes as much from the promotion departments of record companies as from the local artists and fans themselves. The documentary video *Hype!* (1996), a revealing portrait of the role of Sub Pop Records in the Seattle alternative rock scene, suggests that many Seattle-based musicians and fans rejected the grunge label as a commercial gimmick, especially when it was adopted by advertising agencies and upscale fashion designers. This tension between commercialism and authenticity continues to play a central role in the creation and promotion of alternative rock music.

In 1994, after the band had interrupted a concert tour of Europe, Kurt Cobain overdosed on champagne and tranquilizers, remaining in a coma for 20 hours. Although the event was initially described as an accident, a suicide note was later discovered. He returned to Seattle and entered a detoxification program, only to check out two days later. On 8 April 1994, Cobain's body was discovered in his home; he had died three days earlier of an allegedly self-inflicted shotgun wound. While there is a diversity of opinion concerning the ultimate meaning of Cobain's death—he is viewed by some as a martyr of alternative rock, while others see Cobain as the hard rock cliché of a self-absorbed, heroin-addicted star incapable of navigating the inevitable compromises and emotional greyness of everyday adult life—his death has widely come to be viewed as the beginning of the end for alternative rock. By the year 2000, in fact, it almost seemed as if alternative rock hadn't happened at all, as teen idols, techno, hip-hop, and other dance-oriented, non-guitar based sounds came to dominate the Top 40.

Sloan: 'Underwhelmed' (1992)

Shortly after Kurt Cobain died, alternative rock entrenched itself as the new mainstream in Canada. Grunge bands slowly came to dominate the Top 40 as the decade wore on, and a number of the country's east coast musicians fused certain aspects of the Maritime region's rich musical heritage with the grunge aesthetic to create a distinctly Canadian variant of the genre—characterized by a sometimes rough-and-tumble admixture of dissonant production values, distorted timbres, and musical instruments and song forms characteristic of the region's Celtic traditions. Ashley

MacIsaac, for one, brought a decidedly alternative edge to the Celtic fiddle tradition, and he even included a few outright grunge rock songs, such as 'What an Idiot He Is', on his major label debut, *Hi™How Are You Today?* (1995). But another east coast band, Halifax's Sloan, most clearly embodied the Canadian contribution to grunge rock in the early and mid-1990s, as well as the tendency of most Canadian grunge bands to interject a decidedly pop sensibility into the normally dour alternative rock genre. Thanks largely to the band's efforts, in fact, Halifax was heralded by critics as 'the New Seattle', if only for a few short weeks in 1992.

Formed by Chris Murphy and Andrew Scott while the pair were students at the Nova Scotia College of Art and Design, with Patrick Pentland and Jay Ferguson added to the mix soon after, Sloan created their own label, Murderecords, in 1992. By the time the group signed with the DGC label later that same year—because they sounded so much like Nirvana, label owner David Geffen would later explain—Sloan had already recorded their debut album, *Smeared* (1992). Geffen took that album, spent a few thousand dollars to remix some of its tracks, and then released it with no further alterations. Thanks to the success of the record's hit single, 'Underwhelmed', Sloan soon was receiving accolades from critics and fans worldwide. As bassist Chris Murphy recalls:

> This was just as grunge was getting going in Seattle. We were all affected by punk and hardcore and British pop groups, and we had a similar sort of timeline to the Nirvana story. There was a lot going on before us—we were the ones that got lucky. We had some degree of popularity in our hometown [Halifax]. But after that, we became international. (Mersereau, 2007: 178)

'Underwhelmed' takes the caustic and self-deprecating humour so popular in the alternative rock genre to its masochistic limit, lyrically detailing the insecure misgivings of a teenage crush in high school with such cynicism that the song arguably verges on 'creep rock' (characterized by self-loathing lyrics set to a grunge beat, 'creep rock' was named by critics for its first hit in 1993, Radiohead's 'Creep'— '*You're so fucking special/I wish I was special/But I'm a creep/I'm a weirdo*'). As such, 'Underwhelmed' provides an excellent example of one way that rock musicians reworked the traditional 'teenage' focus of rock to suit the Gen-X 1990s.

At the outset of 'Underwhelmed', as a distorted guitar—treated with some form of modulation processing, such as flange or phase—slowly fades in, listeners are informed that 'she was underwhelmed, if that's a word.' The remainder of the introductory strophe explains the singer's failure to connect with his crush over a series of grammatical misfortunes, and the former's pronounced capacity for '*missing the point*':

> *She said, 'You is funny.'*
> *I said, 'You are funny.'*
> *She said, 'Thank you.'*
> *And I said 'Never mind'*
> *And she rolled her eyes—*
> *Her beautiful eyes.*

The song's remaining two strophes develop this capacity for '*missing the point*' further, providing two more near-misses between singer and love object. The second strophe has him feeling like '*he just ate his young*' because he once ate meat. Similarly, in strophe three, when given a '*story about her life*' that mentions him in conjunction with the word '*affection*', the singer only corrects her spelling:

She wrote a story about her life
I think it included something about me.
I'm not sure about that
But I'm sure of one thing:
Her spelling's atrocious.
She told me to read between the lines
And tell her exactly what I got out of it.
I told her affection had two Fs
(Especially when you're dealing with me)—
I usually notice all the little things.

One of the few tracks from Sloan's self-produced demo that David Geffen had remixed—initially recorded by Sloan and Terry Pulliam at Soundmarket Studio in Halifax, the released single was remixed by Dave Ogilvie at Light House Recorders in North Hollywood—'Underwhelmed' is a good example of non-veridic production values placed in the service of constructing a veridic recording, which was a hallmark of grunge rock production values. The song's initial fade-in and muted-to-open-stringed eighth note crescendo, for instance, create the illusion of a 'live' performance, as does the obviously imperfect doubling of the song's mumbled lead vocals. Likewise, the whole-note 'tremolo' guitar chords, heard first during the introductory refrain ('*but not in hers . . .*'), sound as though they were captured 'live', though they were clearly overdubbed. And, finally, the many fills from drummer Andrew Scott arguably contribute to the general sense of spontaneity on the recording.

By the time Sloan released their second full-length album—1994's *Twice Removed*—the band had already begun to move beyond the dissonant, decidedly anti-pop sensibilities of their first album for a sound more obviously geared to Top 40 success. As Jay Ferguson explains:

We were signed to an LA record label [Geffen]. We felt we had to make our own thing. We were really conscious of being of the time, and I think we wanted to get away from being on the caboose of the grunge scene. We thought it [grunge] was over, and we wanted to get off the train before it crashed. (Mersereau, 2007: 178)

With a number of large-scale pop productions—characterized by baroque, Beatlesesque arrangements and close vocal harmonies reminiscent of the Beach Boys—*Twice Removed* not only announced Sloan's departure from 'the caboose of the grunge scene', but the album also gave the band their first Top 10 placing in

Canada. Videos released in support of the album put the group in heavy rotation on MuchMusic.

During the next 15 years, Sloan converted these early successes into one of the most successful recording careers in Canadian rock history. The band has released a total of 11 records since forming in 1992—and *Twice Removed* was selected as the best Canadian rock album ever recorded in a reader poll conducted by *Chart!* magazine in 1996. Other honours include a Juno for *One Chord to Another* as Best Alternative Album in 1997, and seven more nominations, including three for Best Rock Album (*Navy Blues*, 1999; *Pretty Together*, 2002; and *Never Hear the End of It*, 2007), one for Best Alternative Album (*Twice Removed*, 1995), and one for Best Rock Single ('If It Feels Good Do It', 2002).

Ani DiFranco: 'Not a Pretty Girl' (1995)

A folksinger dressed in punk rock clothing, Ani DiFranco (b. 1970 in Buffalo, New York) has spent her career resisting the lure of the corporate music business, releasing an album and playing upward of 200 live dates every year, and building up a successful independent record label—Righteous Babe Records—and a substantial grassroots following. DiFranco began performing publicly at nine, performing covers of Beatles songs at a local coffeehouse. By the age of 19, DiFranco had written over 100 original songs and relocated from her native Buffalo to New York City to pursue a musical career. In 1989 she recorded a demo of original songs and pressed 500 copies of an eponymous cassette to sell at shows. The tape—a spare collection of intensely personal songs about failed relationships, sex and sexuality, and gender inequality, accompanied with acoustic guitar—quickly sold out, and in 1990

Ani DiFranco. Courtesy BMI Archives.

DiFranco founded the independent label Righteous Babe Records to distribute her recordings more effectively.

By the mid-1990s the mainstream media had begun to take notice of DiFranco's homespun, low-fi music. Her 1995 album *Not a Pretty Girl* garnered notice from CNN and the *New York Times*, though it did not appear in the *Billboard* charts. But 1996 brought *Dilate*, an eclectic work recounting a love affair with a man, which created a slight, if much discussed, controversy at the time among those of DiFranco's fans who felt she had 'tricked' them into believing that she was a lesbian. *Dilate* debuted in the Top 100 of the *Billboard* charts, an unusual achievement for an independent release. The live album *Living in Clip*, released in 1997, became her first gold album. In 1998 DiFranco released the studio effort *Little Plastic Castle*, her highest-charting album to that date, which debuted at Number 22 on the Top 200 chart. All of these albums were released on the Righteous Babe label, despite many offers from major record companies.

'Not a Pretty Girl', from the album *Not a Pretty Girl* (1995), is a typical Ani DiFranco recording, with self-revealing lyrics and an austere, minimalist studio aesthetic, focused on DiFranco's voice and acoustic guitar. Because, as is often the case in urban folk music, the words are so important to the effect of this song, we must pay particularly close attention to their construction and how they are performed. The lyrics operate on at least two levels: first, as a response to an individual, a man who has wronged the singer in some way; and second, as a more general indictment of society's treatment of women.

The track opens in a reflective mood, with the solo acoustic guitar playing a four-chord progression. The musical form of 'Not a Pretty Girl' is not dissimilar to that of many urban folksongs, and the song's text, as printed on the CD liner notes, suggests the format of a traditional folk ballad, made up of a series of stanzas. However, DiFranco's performance of the lyrics—which escalates from a sung whisper at the beginning to an assertive growl in the middle, then ends with gentle vocalizing—creates an effect entirely different from that of seeing the words laid out on the page. DiFranco lays her lyrics over the structure of the song like ropes, tightening them here, loosening them there, and creating a sense of emotional intensity and musical momentum. Her dislike for the man to whom the song is addressed emerges clearly only on the word 'punk', which she spits out derisively. The way the accents in the text are distributed around the strong waltz rhythm of the music—with its one-two-three, one-two-three pulsations—creates the sense of a woman who is impatient with the injustices of the world and who insists on being treated as a person rather than a stereotype:

I am not a
pretty *girl,*
that is not what **I do**, *I ain't no* **dam-**
sel in **distress**, *and* **I** *don't* **need**
to be rescued, so, so put me dowwwwn,
punk. *Wouldn't you pre-*
fer *a maiden* **fair**? *Isn't there a*
kitten *stuck up a* **tree** *somewhere?*

At this point DiFranco's acoustic guitar is joined by electric guitar, bass, and drums, changing the texture of the recording to a blend of folk music and alternative rock.

In the second verse DiFranco packs more syllables into each four-bar musical phrase, the words rushing out and then being held back, emphasizing the central point of the lyrics (i.e., that women who express themselves forcefully are too often dismissed as merely being 'angry'). In the second half of the verse, the accents of her words coincide with the stressed beats of the music more frequently, creating a sense of urgency.

I am not an
*an**gry girl, but it seems like*
*I've got ev**eryone fooled. Every time I say*
*some**thing they find hard to **hear**, they chalk it up*
*to my **ang**er, and never to their own fear. I-*
*ma**gine you're a girl, just trying to*
*fi**nally come **clean**, knowing full*
*well** they'd prefer you were **dirty***
*and **smi-i-i**ling. And I am*
*sorry**, but **I** am*
*not** a **mai**den fair, and I am not a*
*kit**ten stuck up a tree somewhere*

In the third verse the texture moves even further towards the rock side, and DiFranco further escalates the emotional tension. At the very end of the verse a slight shift in the lyric makes us more aware of the singer's mixture of defiance and vulnerability. In the second verse DiFranco's character states emphatically that she is 'not a kitten up a tree', but at the end of the third verse that claim is pushed a bit off centre when she asks rhetorically, 'Don't you think every kitten figures out how to get down, whether or not you ever show up?' Here we catch a glimpse of a wound that lies beneath the protagonist's emotional armor:

And generally my
*gene**ration wouldn't be caught **dead***
*work**ing for the **man**, And generally I a-*
*gree** with them, **Trouble** is, you've got to **have***
*yourself an **al**ternate plan, And I have **ear** . . .***
*ned** my **dis**illusionment, I have been*
*work**ing all of my **life** And **I** am a pa-*
*triot, **I** have been*
*fight**ing the good **fight**. And **what** if there are no*
*dam**sels in distress? **What** if I knew*
*that**, and I called your **bluff**? Don't you think every*
*kitten figures out how to get **down***
*Whe**ther or not you ever **show up**?*

The final stanza of 'Not a Pretty Girl' reinforces the more general message of the text, a critique of the physical norms by which society, and men in particular, so often judge women:

*I am **not** a pretty girl*
*I don't really **want** to be **pretty** girl*
*I want to be **more** than a **pretty** girl.*

The recording ends gently, with DiFranco's overdubbed voice singing two melodic patterns in a responsorial manner.

The impact of 'Not a Pretty Girl' is closely tied up with its carefully controlled fluctuations in musical texture, verbal density, and emotional colour. DiFranco blends the progressive outlook of urban folk music with the rebellious energy of alternative rock. At the same time, her performance—a song-portrait of a woman whose experience of sexism has had profound emotional consequences—implies that matters of the heart cannot simply be reduced to political positions. This is where music can exceed the power of a speech or slogan—filling in the texture and nuance of emotions and demonstrating that social injustice is registered not only in the mind but also in the heart.

Our Lady Peace: 'Superman's Dead' (1997)

In 1993 DC Comics published a storyline about the death of Superman at the hands of the arch-villain Doomsday. For the first time in the DC Comics universe, evil was allowed the ultimate triumph (only making matters worse for the residents of Metropolis and Gotham, Batman broke his back a few months later). Fans of the comic book and popular culture pundits took the death of Superman as a kind of death knell for the post-war idealism that had so obviously informed boomer politics and culture. The Man of Steel's murder signalled a new-found cynicism in popular culture that could no longer tolerate a hero so earnest, so infallible, and, ultimately, so good-natured as Superman.

It was within this atmosphere that Toronto's Our Lady Peace was born. The Canadian alternative rock outfit sold close to two million records in 1997 alone, based largely on the popularity of such tracks as 'Superman's Dead', which opened their second major label release, *Clumsy* (1997). Established in 1992, when Mike Maida (a.k.a. Raine Maida), then a criminology student at the University of Toronto, answered a 'musicians wanted' ad in *Now Magazine*, Our Lady Peace (OLP) began performing around Oshawa under the moniker As If. Coming to the attention of songwriter and producer Arnold Lanni, who owned Arnyar Records at the time, the band renamed themselves Our Lady Peace in time for their first 'break'—they were added to the bill for a number of concerts throughout eastern Ontario and Quebec with the Tea Party, who were then riding a wave of popularity generated by their debut for EMI Canada, the double-platinum *Splendor Solis* (1993). Eventually represented by Coalition Management—comprised of Lanni and Eric Lawrence—OLP secured **showcase gigs** for a number of major labels in Canada, including Warner Canada, EMI Canada, and Sony Music Canada. But it was Richard Zuckerman, the head of A&R at Sony Music Canada, who finally offered OLP a recording contract in 1993.

The band's debut for the label, *Naveed* (1994), produced two Top 40 hits both in Canada and in the United States, 'Starseed' and 'Naveed'. ('Starseed' would go on to play a prominent role in the soundtrack for the summer blockbuster, *Armageddon*.) OLP next set out to solidify their fan base through 18 months of touring. Between 1994 and 1996, OLP shared the concert stage with the Canadian musicians I Mother Earth, 54–40, and Alanis Morissette and heavy metal superstars Van Halen.

Returning to the studio in late 1996, OLP produced *Clumsy*, the best-selling album of their career. The album spawned four Top 40 singles—'Superman's Dead', '4AM', 'Automatic Flowers', and 'Clumsy'—and it sold more than one million copies both in Canada and in the US (the band would never again sell more than 300,000 copies of an album in the US, but would achieve sales in the millions for their fifth release in Canada, 2002's *Gravity*). Before splitting, OLP reached the Top 10 Canadian record charts six times between 1997 and 2005, sold over five million albums worldwide, won four Juno awards from 20 nominations, and received 10 MuchMusic video awards— including the coveted People's Choice Award for 1997, 1998, and 2000, making Our Lady Peace the most decorated group in the show's two decades of existence.

Maida's trademark jittery vocals, featuring unexpected, and often gymnastic, leaps into the falsetto range, seem perfectly suited for voicing the troubled lyrics to 'Superman's Dead', with its anxious refrain, *'Alone, I'm thinking, "Why is Superman dead?"'* The song's lyrical narrative presents a young man confronted by a world in the midst of transformation by forces beyond his comprehension, and clearly careening out of control. The traditional foundations of culture have come unstuck (*'Superman is dead'*) and, consequently, the traditional means of socialization available to young adults have become obviously bankrupt (*'an ordinary boy/an ordinary name/but ordinary's just not good enough today'*). According to Maida, in the modern world—or, at least, in the post-Superman 1990s—polite exchanges replace meaningful interaction (*'you're happy cause you smile, but how much can you fake?'*), hatred replaces love (*'you're happy you're in love—you need someone to hate'*), and simple obedience replaces spiritual discipline (*'are you worried about your faith? Kneel down and obey'*). And, only making the song's narrator more anxious, nobody seems to notice:

> *Why is Superman dead?*
> *Is it in my head?*
> *We'll just laugh instead.*
> *You worry about the weather*
> *And whether or not you should hate.*

OLP's arrangement of 'Superman's Dead' is typical of the grunge rock genre— even if it was recorded almost a full three years after most critics had already pronounced grunge rock dead. A Top 40 pop song at its core, set in an AABA form,

'Superman's Dead' situates itself within the grunge genre via the dissonant production values Arnold Lanni creates for the track (though Lanni's mix replicates pop convention in that Maida's vocals are pushed clearly to the forefront), the quiet-verses/loud-choruses formula that characterizes both the song and the grunge rock genre in general, and the distorted electric guitar tracks, comprised of strummed eighth-note power chords, which are heard in each of the song's choruses and during its climactic conclusion ('*doesn't anybody know that the world's a subway?*'). The song eventually fades to silence, reinforcing the sensation that whatever the turmoil detailed in 'Superman's Dead', Maida and crew can offer nothing in the way of explanation or respite.

For a clear contrast to OLP's angst at the Man of Steel's demise, one need look no further than the eulogy for Superman that Winnipeg's Crash Test Dummies released in 1991, 'Superman's Song'. The song depicts Clark Kent as 'a real gent', and humorously compares Superman to Tarzan:

Tarzan wasn't a ladies' man
He'd just come along and scoop 'em up under his arm
Like that, quick as a cat in the jungle
But Clark Kent now there was a real gent
He would not be caught sittin' around in no
Junglescape, dumb as an ape doing nothing

Superman never made any money
For saving the world from Solomon Grundy
And sometimes I despair the world will never see
Another man like him

Hey Bob, Supe had a straight job
Even though he could have smashed through any bank
In the United States, he had the strength, but he would not
Folks said his family were all dead
Their planet crumbled but Superman, he forced himself
To carry on, forget Krypton, and keep going

Tarzan was king of the jungle and Lord over all the apes
But he could hardly string together four words:
'I Tarzan, You Jane.'

Sometimes when Supe was stopping crimes
I'll bet that he was tempted to just quit and turn his back
On man, join Tarzan in the forest
But he stayed in the city, and kept on changing clothes
In dirty old phone booths till his work was through
And nothing to do but go on home

Alanis Morissette: 'You Oughta Know' (1995)

Alanis Morissette was the best-selling alternative rock artist of the 1990s. Sales of Morissette's Top 40 alternative rock classic, *Jagged Little Pill* (1995), far eclipsed worldwide sales of records by more canonic American bands like Nirvana, Soundgarden, Hole, or Pearl Jam. But before Morissette topped the charts in the United States, the singer had already enjoyed a three-year stint on the charts in Canada as a teen idol, along the lines of Tiffany and Debby Gibson. Working with producer Leslie Howe, Morissette produced two Top 100 albums for MCA in 1991 (*Alanis*) and 1992 (*Now Is the Time*), and two Top 10 singles ('Too Hot' and 'An Emotion Away'), before receiving a Juno for most promising female vocalist in 1992 and securing a coveted opening slot for rapper Vanilla Ice on tour. Far from apologetic—or even sheepish—about her career as a teen idol, which rock ideology would tend to call for, Morissette simply showed her development as an artist by performing a slowed-down, grunge version of her Top 5 bubblegum hit, 'Too Hot' (Number 4, 1991) on her world support tour for *Jagged Little Pill*.

In early 1993, however, it seemed very unlikely that Morissette would embark on a world tour any time in the near future, let alone release the epochal record that her debut for Maverick Records, *Jagged Little Pill*, would become only two years later. Morissette's contract with MCA expired in 1993 and, despite the two Top 5 hits, neither party sought to renew. With no other contracts on the table, the singer relocated from

Alanis Morissette began her career as a bubblegum pop star but became the best-selling alternative rock artist of the 1990s. © Tim Mosenfelder/Corbis.

Ottawa to Toronto in the hopes of finding musicians to collaborate with. She failed to find anyone who sustained her interest, however, and a trip to Nashville a few months later likewise provoked only frustration. Thus, in late 1993, Morissette began making regular trips to Los Angeles out of desperation, working with as many musicians as she could find there. One of those trips yielded a meeting with producer and songwriter Glen Ballard, who agreed to collaborate with Morissette after only 10 minutes.

After roughly a year of working together, the duo released *Jagged Little Pill* on Maverick Records in 1995 (Maverick was a new venture between Madonna, Frederick DeMann, Ronni Dashev, and Warner Brothers at the time, the name drawn from the pop singer's birth name—*Ma*donna *Ver*on*ica*). *Jagged Little Pill*, which Maverick marketed as a grunge rock record with obvious Top 40 appeal, quickly set records and spawned five Top 40 singles across North America—'You Oughta Know', 'Hand In My Pocket', 'Ironic', 'You Learn', and 'Head Over Feet'—the last four reaching Number 1 on the pop charts. *Jagged Little Pill* charted for more than a year, was the first record of the CD era to achieve double-diamond status, and eventually sold over 30 million copies worldwide, making it the best-selling record of the 1990s and the best-selling international debut of all time (of course, whether or not the record can rightly be called a 'debut' is debatable, especially given the Top 5 status of Morissette's pre-grunge output in Canada). Moreover, especially in her words to 'You Oughta Know', the first single released from *Jagged Little Pill* and widely rumoured to be a poison-pen letter to ex-lover Dave Coullier (from the popular sitcom *Full House*), Morissette struck a shockingly frank, attention-grabbing posture. Over a superbly crafted grunge-cum-pop backing, featuring Dave Navarro on electric guitar, Flea on electric bass, Benmont Tench on organ, Matt Lang on 'live' drums, and sample-programming by producer Glen Ballard, Morissette asks some of the decade's angriest—and most explicit—questions:

> *An older version of me*
> *Is she perverted like me?*
> *Would she go down on you in a theatre?*
> *Does she speak eloquently?*
> *And would she have your baby?*
> *I'm sure she'd make a really excellent mother*
> *. . .*
> *Did you forget about me, Mr. Duplicity?*
> *I hate to bug you in the middle of dinner.*
> *It was a slap in the face, how quickly I was replaced—*
> *Are you thinking of me when you fuck her?*

At the very pinnacle of success, Morissette became extremely disillusioned with the music industry. Bringing along her mother, two aunts, and two female friends, Morissette thus embarked on a six-week trip to India to gather her wits and deepen her Iyengar Yoga practice, after playing the final show of the *Jagged Little Pill* tour in December of 1996. Whatever she did worked—rather than burning out, as so many stars of Morissette's stature tend to do, the singer returned from India rejuvenated and ready to proceed with her career. Popping up for cameos on records by the likes of Ringo Starr ('Drift Away', 1998) and the Dave Matthews Band ('Don't Drink the Water' and 'Spoon'), and scoring a prominent placement on the soundtrack for the film *City of Angels* ('Uninvited'), the latter earning Morissette two Grammies in 1999—for Best Rock Song and Best Female Rock Vocal Performance—the Ottawa native, now relocated to Vancouver, returned to the studio in 1997 to create her second full-length release, *Supposed Former Infatuation Junkie*, again in collaboration with Glen Ballard. Though the album didn't recapture Morissette's former glory in its

---

Listening Chart: 'You Oughta Know'

Music and lyrics by Alanis Morissette and Glen Ballard; performed by Morissette et al.

FORM	LYRICS	DESCRIPTIVE COMMENTS
A-a	*I want you to know . . .*	Close-miked and 'dry' vocals start the song, backed by Ballard's syncopated snare drum sample and high-end guitar frequencies quietly in background.
-b	*An older version of me . . .*	Electric bass enters, followed by a full drum kit; 'breakbeat' sample; lead guitar enters; high-end guitar frequencies continue in background.
-c	*'Cause the love . . .*	Pre-chorus section; rhythm guitar enters; vocals are close-miked and doubled, and panned far left and far right along the stereo spectrum.
Chorus	*And I'm here . . .*	Vocals centred, and treated as in 'A-a' and 'A-b'; distorted electric guitar plays straight eighth notes, and electric bass subdivides the beat with a basic sixteenth-note pulse.
A-a	*You seem very well . . .*	As in 'A-a'.
-b	*Did you forget about me . . .*	As in 'A-b', but with more active accompaniment from the electric bass, which at times plays in the 'slap-and-pop' style.
-c	*'Cause the love . . .*	Pre-chorus section repeats, as in 'A-c'.
Chorus	*And I'm here . . .*	Chorus repeats.
B	*Bridge Ooooooh . . .*	Breakdown section, featuring vocalizations doubling a melody played on electric guitar; strummed whole notes from the electric guitar are panned far left and far right along the stereo spectrum; drums enter to signal return to chorus.
A-c'	*'Cause the joke . . .*	As in 'A-c', with slight variation in lyrics.
Chorus (x2)	*And I'm here . . .*	Chorus repeats twice and fades out.

entirety, and though it featured at times extremely experimental songwriting techniques (some songs being basically harmonically static, and featuring an almost prose-
like barrage of lyrics), the record nonetheless outstripped Maverick's modest hope to
sell roughly one million copies, debuting at Number 1 on both the *RPM* and *Billboard*
charts and generating sales of over 469,000 units during its first week of release.

Bif Naked: 'Chotee' (1998)

If Kurt Cobain wore his emotions on his sleeve, then Bif Naked had hers tattooed on
her arms. Born Beth Torbett in New Delhi, India, the future Juno award-winning
Canadian punk rock star (and actress), who arguably created the template for such
future Canadian 'tween punkers as Avril Lavigne and Fefe Dobson, was raised by
American missionaries in Lexington, Kentucky, and then in The Pas and Winnipeg,
Manitoba. After studying theatre at the University of Winnipeg, she joined the punk
bands Gorilla Gorilla and Chrome Dog before she embarked on a successful solo
career as a poet, actress, and punk rock singer and songwriter. Adopting the stage
name Bif Naked, Torbett has released four full-length albums of original material—
Bif Naked (1995), *I Bificus* (1998), *Purge* (2001), and *Superbeautifulmonster* (2005)—
toured Europe, Canada, and the US as both a headliner and a support act for an
incredibly diverse array of artists (including Snoop Doggy Dogg, Billy Idol, Dido,
Sarah McLachlan, the Cult, Chrissie Hynde, the Foo Fighters, and many others), and
she has scored a number of placements on popular film and TV soundtracks, including for *Ready to Rumble* (with a cover of Twisted Sister's 'We're Not Gonna Take It'),
MTV's *Celebrity Deathmatch* ('Vampire'), and for the immensely popular *Buffy the
Vampire Slayer* TV series ('Moment of Weakness' and 'Lucky'). A testament to her pop-
ularity in the mid- and late 1990s, Bif Naked appeared as herself on an episode of
Buffy in 1999, performing 'Anything', 'Lucky', and 'Moment of Weakness'.

Frankly outspoken about her bisexuality, Torbett penned a number of songs that, following the lead of Carole Pope and other forebears, openly explored her desires for, and
relationships with, both men and women. In fact, taking her cue from Madonna—'*She
was not afraid of anything, man!*' Torbett remembers—the singer became known for her
no-topic-is-taboo approach to songwriting. According to Torbett herself:

> I've written about being raped, my parents' divorce, necking with girls, doing it
> with boys, terminating a pregnancy, my own divorce. I've written a song about my
> bicycle, too. It's all the same to me. I just don't believe in hiding anything. Life's
> too short. I used to sing this song about sexual assault to open the show. And I used
> to get people yelling at me to shut up and get off the stage, or to shut up and show
> them my tits instead. It was almost like self-punishment, but I kept doing it. I did-
> n't care. (musicianguide.com/biographies/1608002659/Bif-Naked.html)

Torbett clearly signalled the unapologetically frank nature of her musical output through the image she presented to fans. As one critic put it, 'with her pitch-black Cleopatra coiffure and heavy-lashed poster-child eyes, Bif Naked would be a dead ringer for '50s icon Betty Page, if only Page had gone on to be a tattooed rock and roller instead of a trailer park born-again Christian' (musicianguide.com/biographies/1608002659/Bif-Naked.html). Typically, Bif Naked has appeared sleeveless in videos and in live appearances, the better for fans to see the many tattooes adorning her arms. Torbett's first tattoo, an Egyptian Eye of Horus, inked when she was 16 years old, has since been supplemented by symbols of the Tao, Japanese writing, Buddhist and Hindu poetry and images. She also prominently featured her muscled midriff in videos well before Britney Spears got credit for exposing hers. Yet for all this attention to image—and, clearly, image was an important part of what Bif Naked sought to convey to her audiences—it was undoubtedly the singer-songwriter's often harrowing lyrics, and the driving music she composed, that captured fans throughout the 1990s.

The song 'Chotee', from the 1998 release *I Bificus*, remains probably Naked's most heartfelt song—and her most heartbreaking. In an apology to her aborted child, Naked explains her reasons for terminating the pregnancy and evokes the emotional turmoil she experienced at the time. Barely out of high school, the singer had married the drummer in her first band and was convinced that their love was everlasting. Things quickly unravelled, however. After only two years of marriage, most of which the couple spent on the road, the now pregnant singer was forced to deal with her husband's infidelity and his almost complete indifference towards being a husband to her, let alone a father to their child. After repeated pleas for forgiveness, Naked ends the song with a sad farewell to the baby that was never born.

Musically, however, 'Chotee' sounds miles away from a troubled confessional. Beginning with an upbeat drum solo that segues into a call-and-response between vocals and electric guitar during the first verse, 'Chotee' sounds more like a Top 40 pop song than anything else, complete with doubled vocals and synthesized brass during its choruses. That said, at roughly two minutes in, 'Chotee' reaches an initial and unorthodox climax, at which point the song becomes basically an extended closure, concluding with Naked repeatedly shouting '*so long my baby!*'—hardly straightforward Top 40 fare.

Hayden: 'Bad As They Seem' (1995)

A staunchly indie singer-songwriter from Toronto, who graduated with a BAA in Radio and Television Arts from Ryerson University in 1993, Hayden Desser managed to convert a fluke hit on MuchMusic—'Bad As They Seem', from his second full-length release, *Everything I Long For* (1995)—into a decades-long career. Recording on a four-track tape machine in the basement of his parents' house, Hayden crafted a low-fidelity production aesthetic on *Everything I Long For* that became the acknowledged ideal for indie folk releases by everyone from Elliot Smith (*Elliot Smith*) to Beck (*Mutations*) later in the decade. Hayden started his own Hardwood Records label in 1994 to carry only his own releases; all seven of Desser's full-length records bear the Hardwood imprint—*In September* (1994), *Everything I Long For* (1995), *The Closer I Get* (1998), *Skyscraper National Park* (2001), *Live at Convocation Hall* (2002), *Elk-Lake Serenade* (2004), and *In Field & Town* (2008), although *Everything I Long For* and *The Closer I Get* were distributed by Universal Music Canada. While Hardwood still serves primarily as an outlet for Desser's own recordings, the lo-fi pioneer has recently begun to expand the label's purview to include records from other bands working in central and southwestern Ontario, including two from Oshawa natives Cuff The Duke (*Cuff The Duke*, 2005, and *Sidelines of the City*, 2007) and one from London-based Basia Bulat (*Oh, My Darling*, 2007).

Even on his 'major' releases, however, Hayden always seems to foreground the technological limitations he faces as a recording artist with limited financial means. In fact, a large part of Hayden's appeal has been in the fact that his records—especially his early releases—sound like they were recorded on a tape machine in somebody's basement, rather than in the expensive confines of a professional recording studio. Almost every song on *Everything I Long For*, for instance, features only four tracks (when songs do feature more than the customary four tracks, embellishments remain generally

Listening Chart: 'Bad As They Seem'

Music and lyrics by Hayden Desser; performed by Hayden Desser; recorded by Joao at Umbrella Sound and the Dubhouse, Toronto; mixed by Joao and Hayden

FORM	DESCRIPTIVE COMMENTS
Intro	Acoustic guitar, spread across the stereo spectrum, accompanied by electric bass, and a basic backbeat provided by kick drum, snare (played with brushes), and eighth notes on hi-hat played softly with regular sticks.
A	Lead vocal line enters, centred and 'pushed' to front.
A	Arrangement continues unchanged.
Chorus	Arrangement continues unchanged, as song shifts to chorus; harmonic rhythm doubles; backing vocal line harmonizes main melody roughly a major sixth above.
Harmonica solo	
A	Arrangement from first verse sounds without alteration.
Chorus	Arrangement from first chorus sounds without alteration.
Ending	Song concludes when all instruments hold the downbeat of the first bar after the second chorus.

small, such as the addition of a snare and ride cymbal, played with brushes, on 'Bad As They Seem'). Two of the four tracks are typically devoted to Hayden's often whispered vocals—one vocal line being delivered in the singer's gruff bass register, and the other in his high, sometimes falsetto range—while the final two tracks are reserved for Hayden's acoustic and/or electric guitar work. The tracks are then typically mixed so that both the high and low vocal takes occupy direct centre, while the guitars are spread to occupy the left and right sides of the stereo spectrum. As Hayden commented, when asked to account for the surprising popularity of *Everything I Long For*:

> Perhaps it's the simplicity, rawness and the subject matter of the songs—relatable stories in strong detail, with not much to get in the way. The songs described things that had happened to me, things that I wanted to happen to me, and things that I didn't want to happen to me. That's it. (Mersereau, 2007: 155)

In Search of Canada: The Tragically Hip

The 1990s were a time of tumult and transformation in Canada. During that decade the country's economic borders grew porous, opening first to the United States, via the Free Trade Agreement of 1989, and then to Mexico, with the establishment of the North American Free Trade Agreement (NAFTA) in 1994. At the same time, Canada became more ethnically diverse than ever before. Whereas the British Isles accounted for more than 80 per cent of immigration to Canada between 1946 and 1970, the country contributed a paltry 3 per cent during the 1990s; the vast majority of new residents came from, in order, Hong Kong, India, and the Philippines. And women came to occupy increasingly prominent positions of power throughout the decade—Kim Campbell replaced Mulroney and became the first female Prime Minister of Canada in June of 1993, though her reign and the federal party she led were short-lived once an election was called; Sheila Copps became the country's first female Deputy Prime Minister, under Jean Chrétien, shortly after; Maureen Kempson-Darkes served as the first female chief executive of General Motors Canada; and Adrienne Clarkson became only the second female Governor General of Canada, after Jean Sauvé.

The sovereignty movement also reawakened in Quebec in the 1990s. The defeat of the Meech Lake and Charlottetown constitutional accords in 1990 and 1992, respectively, and the viciousness surrounding their demise, only fanned nationalist passions in Quebec. At the height of conflict some communities outside of Quebec (Sault Ste Marie, Ontario, most famously) declared themselves 'English only', invoking the ire of at least Gord Downie, the lead singer of the Tragically Hip, who wrote 'Born in the Water', which appeared on the band's second full-length release, *Road Apples* (1991), in response:

> *Smart as trees in Sault Ste Marie*
> *'I can speak my mother tongue.'*
> *Passing laws, just because . . .*
> *How could you do it?*

The Tragically Hip: Reluctant figureheads of a powerful grassroots nationalism.
Adrian Wyld/The Canadian Press.

By 1993, support for sovereignty in Quebec had skyrocketed to a historic high of 65 per cent, a result, in part, of the failed Meech Lake process and of an essentially rudderless Progressive Conservative Party that seemed to be tilting westward and, by now, a hugely unpopular Prime Minister Brian Mulroney. Some of Mulroney's Quebec lieutenants in the federal government bolted the party after the Meech Lake failure to form the Bloc Québécois (BQ), a political party devoted to Quebec independence and the peaceful dissolution of the country. Later, the BQ secured 52 seats in the federal Parliament in the 1993 election that saw Chrétien become Prime Minister and ushered Campbell, Mulroney's short-term replacement, out of politics. (The Conservatives were left with a measly two seats, and never recovered from this defeat until they joined with the right-wing and western-based Canadian Alliance to form the Conservative Party of Canada, in the process losing their 'Progressive' label.) As a consequence of the strong 1993 showing at the polls in Quebec alone—they fielded no candidates outside that province—the BQ became the country's official opposition in Ottawa, an irony not lost on many Canadians.

Two years later, a provincial referendum on Quebec sovereignty, led by the provincial Parti Québécois government and their BQ confreres, was narrowly defeated, with 49.6 per cent voting for the federalist 'Non' side and 48.5 per cent voting 'Oui'. Only further complicating the already complicated issue of Quebec nationalism in officially multicultural Canada, the Premier of Quebec (and Parti Québécois leader),

Jacques Parizeau, famously blamed the loss on what he called 'money and the ethnic vote' in his concession speech.

Like the nation itself, cultural nationalism also came under fire in the 1990s. Commentators described the CRTC as a failed experiment, many suggesting that the Commission had failed even in its most basic task—to foster a national market for Canadian cultural productions. CBC-TV may have adopted an almost exclusively Canadian prime time in the 1990s, critics argued, but eight of the 10 most watched programs in Canada remained American productions. Thus, when Bryan Adams fired the first volley in a campaign to scrap the CRTC in January of 1992, he provoked earnest debate much more than outright outrage. Topping the charts in 17 countries with the hit single '(Everything I Do) I Do It For You' from his *Waking Up the Neighbors* LP—the title a sly jab at American indifference to Canadian culture—Adams was utterly dismayed to discover that, according to CRTC regulations, the song did not qualify as 'Canadian content' because its co-composer, album producer Robert 'Mutt' Lange, was not a citizen. 'You'd never hear Elton John being declared un-British', Adams fumed at a press conference in Nova Scotia, calling the CRTC 'a disgrace, a shame . . . stupidity'.

The notion that Canadian culture was 'under construction'—that Canada seemed to lack any particular identity or meta-narrative except 'the attempt to construct one', as Karen Pegley (2000) put it—re-emerged with renewed vigour in the 1990s. Comedian Rick Mercer humorously probed the depths of American ignorance about Canadian culture on the TV programs *Talking To Americans* and *This Hour Has 22 Minutes*. Mercer famously asked Americans for their opinion on such 'world events' as a Russian invasion of Saskatchewan (for its wheat stores), the controversial legalization of VCRs in Canada, and the country's adoption of the 24-hour day in the mid-1990s—but such humour masked a deep-seated insecurity on the part of many Canadians that there wasn't all that much for Americans to know anyway. Canada was failing as a country, many felt, because it had failed, or perhaps had refused, to establish a viable national mythology. In the wake of this realization many Canadians began to identify themselves as citizens of a nation without identity; the single most pervasive national myth to emerge in the 1990s was that Canada lacked national myths.

Into this void was thrust the Tragically Hip—a trad-rock outfit from Kingston, Ontario, comprised of vocalist and lyricist Gord Downie, guitarists Rob Baker and Paul Langlois (Langlois replaced Davis Manning, a saxophonist, in 1986), bassist and backing vocalist Gord Sinclair, and drummer Johnny Fay. Notoriously ambivalent about the privileged position in the pantheon of Canadian rock that they would quickly secure for themselves, the Tragically Hip nonetheless found themselves the reluctant figureheads of a powerful grassroots nationalism. The fact that the band regularly filled arenas on their annual East–West tours of Canada, but could scarcely fill a nightclub or bar in the United States, was all the proof many needed that such a thing as Canadian rock, let alone Canadian culture, could indeed be said to exist (even as the country seemed destined for irreparable fracture). As music critic Andrea Loera put it in September 1998:

Ask an American to name a Canadian icon and the answer will surely involve a Mountie, beer or back-bacon. Ask most Canadians to single out (oot) a far-reaching symbol of their nationalism, and the Tragically Hip are sure to come. (austin.citysearch.com/feature/19280)

A large part of the Tragically Hip's appeal was not that they embodied an already completed Canadian identity—though the band obviously, and proudly, displayed traditional markers of Canadianness, such as a profound love for hockey and an intimate familiarity with the country's vast tracts of northern wilderness—but, rather, that they invited their fans to (re)construct that identity along with them. The Hip wrote songs about Bill Barilko ('Fifty Mission Cap'), Bobby Orr ('Fireworks'), Jacques Cartier ('Looking for Something to Happen'), Hugh MacLennan ('Courage [For Hugh MacLennan]'), and David Milgaard ('Wheat Kings'). They sang about watching constellations *reveal themselves one star at time* in a provincial park ('Bobcaygeon'), flooding public parks to make hockey rinks during long Canadian winters ('700 Ft. Ceiling'), dangerously debunking American myths ('At the Hundredth Meridian'), loving first girlfriends who shock-ingly *didn't give a fuck about hockey* ('Fireworks'), and national scandals ('Wheat Kings'). They referenced race riots in 1930s Toronto ('Bobcaygeon'), Canadian World War II pilots receiving a commemorative cap, and the right to crease it on the occasion of their fiftieth mission ('Fifty Mission Cap'), the *'worst ice storm in Canadian history'*, which shut down parts of Ontario, Quebec, and New Brunswick for weeks in January 1998 ('Something On'), Bobby Orr scoring the game-winner against the St Louis Blues in 1970 ('Fireworks'), and Paul Henderson scoring the winning goal in the Canada–Soviet Union hockey series in 1972 ('Fireworks'). All the while, many in Canada only cheered all the louder, buoyed by the prospect that they had discovered in the Hip a band capable of making cultural landmarks (or, at the very least, capable of making sense) out of their everyday experience as Canadians. Not every Canadian listener may have caught, or even cared to catch, each obscure reference, but most caught some references—and a Top 40 rock record with at least some Canadian references seemed much more than any other Top 40 rock record save a handful of miraculous exceptions released by Jack Richardson and the Guess Who in the early 1970s and, of course, the myth-mak-ing country songs of Stompin' Tom Connors from the sixties and seventies, as well as some of Gordon Lightfoot's songs from the sixties.

In Downie's capable hands, what was once the detritus of Canadian identity became its most powerful symbols. Hockey games became metaphors for seduction and romantic love ('Fireworks', 'At the Lonely End of the Rink'); portraits of *'our par-ents' Prime Ministers'*, hung on high school walls painted *'yellow, grey and sinister'*, summarized the awful desperation of Saskatchewan native David Milgaard when he spent two decades in jail for a murder he didn't commit ('Wheat Kings'); a book by Canadian novelist Hugh MacLennan anchored a metaphysical treatise on the fick-leness, and utility, of bravery ('Courage [For Hugh MacLennan]'); and a biograph-ical blurb on the back of a hockey card, about doomed Toronto Maple Leafs forward

Bill Barilko, and a World War II bomber's 50 mission cap, became fodder for an extended meditation on the vagaries of mortality ('Fifty Mission Cap'):

> Bill Barilko disappeared that summer
> He was on a fishing trip
> The last goal he ever scored (in overtime)
> Won the Leafs the [Stanley] Cup
> They didn't win another until 1962—
>
> The year he was discovered.
> I stole this from a hockey card
> I keep tucked up under
> My fifty mission cap
> (I worked it in to look like that)

Other of Downie's lyrics were more opaque, providing a history of Canada in metaphor and symbol rather than in chronological detail. The song 'Bobcaygeon', for instance, from the band's 1998 release *Phantom Power* (1998), contains multiple allusions—from Willie Nelson to a sky both *'dull and hypothetical'*—but one of the song's clearer references is to the Christie Pitts race riot of 1933. By the time of *'that riot'*, as Downie constantly refers to it throughout the song, Toronto had became something of a hotbed for anti-Semitism. The Nazi accession to power in 1933 inspired a group of Torontonians to convene the Balmy Beach Swastika Club in July of that year (the group was basically dedicated to maintaining the de facto 'Gentiles Only' policy of most city beaches). At a baseball game held at the Christie Pitts ballpark the next month, members of the Swastika Club responded to the success of the mostly Jewish Harbord Playground team by unfurling a large Nazi flag and shouting 'Heil Hitler!' A riot subsequently erupted, and spread throughout Toronto, eventually involving an estimated 10,000 residents at the height of conflict:

> That night in Toronto, with its checkerboard floors
> Riding on horseback and keeping order restored
> 'Til the men they couldn't hang
> Stepped to the mike and sang
> And their voices rang
> With that Aryan twang
> . . .
> In the middle of that riot
> Couldn't get you off my mind

'Nautical Disaster' provides another good example of Downie's 'creative non-fiction' approach to Canadian history. On the band's second diamond-certified release of the 1990s, *Day for Night* (1994), 'Nautical Disaster' relates the garbled details of a dream Downie had about the disastrous raid by mostly Canadian forces on Dieppe in 1942—ostensibly as a 'test' for a future allied invasion of Western Europe—during which more than 3,600 Canadian soldiers were killed, wounded, or captured in a matter of hours. By song's end, however, the battle has become a metaphor for the emotional wreckage of a failed relationship with an ex-lover named '*Susan, if you like*':

I had this dream where I relished the fray
And the screaming filled my head all day
It was as though I'd been spit here, settled in—
Into the pocket of a lighthouse on some rocky socket—
Off the coast of France, dear.

One afternoon 4,000 men died in the water here
And 500 hundred more were thrashing madly
(as parasites might in your blood).

Now I was in a lifeboat designed for ten and ten only
Anything that systematic will get you hated—
It's not a deal nor a test nor a love of something fated.

The selection was quick— the crew was picked in order
And those left in the water got kicked off our pant legs
And we headed for home.

Then the dream ends when the phone rings
'You doing alright?'
He said, 'It's out there most days and nights,
but only a fool would complain.'

Anyway Susan, if you like, our conversation
Is as faint as a sound in my memory
As those fingernails scratching on my hull.

Even as he flatly rejected the status of cultural nationalist, Downie seemed eager to embrace the identification of Canadians as a literary people. Throughout the 1990s the singer penned a series of increasingly prose-like lyrics, rife with Canadiana, extending the tradition of literary lyric writing of such Canadian songwriters as Lightfoot, Leonard Cohen, and Joni Mitchell from decades earlier. Tragically Hip songs arguably achieve much of their noted 'funkiness' from the syncopated rhythms of Downie's gleefully unconventional lyrics, which more often resemble the phonetic poetry of e.e. cummings than words to a pop song. The chorus of 'Inevitability of Death' (1994) provides an example of Downie's penchant for phonetic wordplay:

But I thought you beat the death of inevitability to death just a little bit
I thought you beat the inevitability of death to death just a little bit.

For all this attention to Downie's lyrics, the recorded version of a Hip song rarely matched what he sang in live performances. Throughout the 1990s, Downie became legendary among fans for his eccentric rants and the weird—one might say absurdist—spur-of-the-moment monologues he improvised during live performances. In some cases, these rants and monologues formed the basis for future songs; more often, however, they served as fodder for a vibrant bootlegging community that sprang up around the band, who not only allowed but encouraged fans to tape their performances. One of the best-known bootlegs is the so-called 'Killerwhaletank' version of 'New Orleans Is Sinking' (1989)—recorded at the Roxy Theatre in Los Angeles on 3 May 1991 and released as the 'B' side of 'Grace, Too' (1991)—which captures Downie detailing his harrowing experiences as a diver in a killer whale tank, and lamenting how that career cost him both of his arms when a killer whale bit them off. Another bootlegged version of 'New Orleans Is Sinking'—dubbed 'The Policeman Frog'—relates a heroic tale about Downie rescuing a family trapped in a car at the bottom of a frozen lake. A number of bootlegged versions of 'Highway Girl' also remain popular, including 'Double Suicide', on which Downie improvises a story about 'accidentally' shooting a girlfriend, and 'Greek Porter', which has Downie detailing an affair he had with a female porter on a luxury cruise ship. A typically odd rant, called 'Japanese Exchange Student', appears on a bootleg of 'At the Hundredth Meridian', in which Downie tells of accidentally shooting a Japanese exchange student in a tragic trick-or-treat accident one Halloween.

For all this distinctiveness, however, the Tragically Hip's recorded output throughout the 1990s remained arguably straightforward, if not unambiguously continentalist, rock 'n' roll fare—despite the fact that they worked with a number of different producers at a number of mostly American recording studios. Regardless of who produced them, or where they recorded, songs by the Tragically Hip rarely strayed very far from veridic ideals in the 1990s. Tracks typically feature a conventional rock 'n' roll instrumentation (two electric guitars, an electric bass, and drums; or, for ballads, an acoustic guitar, electric guitars, electric bass, and drums). Most songs are set in strophic form, with conventional verse-refrain subdivisions and common time. Downie's plaintive voice—often captured extremely dry and close-miked for the rock genre, emphasizing the cracks and frog-in-the-throat imperfections of his singing—perfectly complemented the generally sequential nature of his melodies, which were typically comprised of two or three short three- to five-pitch phrases, descending stepwise through odd 'extended' regions of the harmony and repeated a number of times over the course of a song. This approach to melody writing can be heard on tracks such as: 'Cordelia', 'Fiddler's Green', and 'Little Bones' from *Road Apples* (1991); 'At the Hundredth Meridian' and 'Locked in the Trunk of a Car' from *Fully Completely* (1992); 'Grace, Too', 'So Hard Done By', 'Terrarium', and 'Nautical Disaster' from *Day For Night* (1994); 'Coconut Cream', 'Giftshop', and 'Butts Wiggling' from *Trouble at the Henhouse* (1996); and 'Thomson Girl', 'Escape Is at Hand for the Travellin' Man', 'Save the Planet', and 'The Rules' from *Phantom Power* (1998).

The Tragically Hip remain one of the most celebrated—and hard-working—rock bands in Canadian history. The band has toured extensively across North America,

Europe, and Australia, sharing the stage with pop legends Midnight Oil, World Party, Hothouse Flowers, Spirit of the West, Ziggy Marley, Los Lobos, Ron Sexsmith, and Wilco, among others. In 1993, the Tragically Hip established a series of cross-country charity rock festivals, called 'Another Roadside Attraction', to raise funds and awareness for various international charities. The band has also made a number of appearances on film and television, performing on *Saturday Night Live* in 1995; lending their song 'Butts Wiggling' to the Canadian comedy troupe The Kids In The Hall for their cult classic, *Brain Candy* (1996); composing the soundtrack for, and making a cameo appearance in, one of the first CanCon films to make a significant dent in national box-office receipts, *Men with Brooms* (2002); and, most recently, appearing in an episode of the extremely popular Canadian sitcom, *Corner Gas* (2005).

The Tragically Hip also have received a number of prestigious awards for their work. The Hip secured a Juno for Most Promising Group of the Year in 1990, the same year that their major label debut, *Up To Here* (1989), achieved triple platinum status in Canada. In 1991, 1993, and 1995 the band won the coveted CARAS (Canadian Academy of Recording Arts and Sciences) Canadian Entertainer of the Year award; and, in 1997, they won another Juno for Group of the Year, plus a Juno for Album of the Year and the North Star Rock Album of the Year award, for *Trouble at the Henhouse*. Two years later, in 1999, the Tragically Hip took home a Juno for Best Rock Album for *Phantom Power* (1998); and, in 2000, they won a Juno for Best Single ('Bobcaygeon'). Though the band was inducted into the Canadian Walk of Fame in 2002 and the Canadian Music Hall of Fame in 2005, perhaps no accolade has proved more lasting, or career defining, for the Tragically Hip than the fan-given moniker 'Canada's band'.

Rap City: Rap in the 1990s

Despite the early successes of tracks like 'Rapper's Delight' in Canada, which topped the charts in January 1980, and despite the subsequent success of numerous novelty rap records by groups like Toronto's the Shuffle Demons (i.e., 'Spadina Bus' and 'Get Outta My House, Roach'), rap music remained basically a peripheral genre—confined mostly to black communities in Toronto, Montreal, and Halifax—well into the 1980s. When Wesley Williams (a.k.a. Maestro Fresh Wes) broke into the Top 40 twice in 1990, with videos for his multi-platinum singles 'Let Your Backbone Slide' and 'Drop the Needle' (both tracks were produced by the First Offence team of Peter and Anthony Davis), major labels in Canada began to take notice of the genre; and it didn't hurt that MC Hammer and Vanilla Ice both topped the pop charts with rap tracks of their own—'Can't Touch This' and 'Ice Ice Baby,' respectively—that same year. In fact, so peripheral was the genre, at first, that the work of Canada's 'first wave' rappers (i.e., MCs Supreme, Brother A, and Sunshine and the Ebony Crew) remains basically undocumented, even if it is remembered enthusiastically by fans. By 1991, Maestreo Fresh Wes's *Symphony in Effect* LP had sold over 150,000 copies in Canada, and the Toronto native received the inaugural Juno award for Best Rap Recording.

By 1995, Toronto was regularly hailed in international publications as one of the most important urban centres for rap production in the Western world, as many Canadian rappers had by then begun to enjoy extended stays on Top 40 charts in Europe, if not necessarily in Canada or the United States. Ivan Berry, head of Toronto's Beat Factory Productions, released tracks by Michelle 'Michie Mee' McCulloch and Phillip 'LA Lux' Gayle in 1991. While these were perhaps not as popular in Canada as in the US, they enjoyed their largest success overseas. Toronto's Dream Warriors slowly made their way up the European pop charts at the same time, and they made heavy rotation on MuchMusic with videos for 'Wash Your Face in My Sink', 'My Definition of a Boombastic Jazz Style', and 'Ludi'. Sean Merrick (a.k.a. HDV) added his provocative 'gangsta rap' style to the mix in Toronto with songs such as 'Pimp of the Microphone', which aggressively challenged the prevailing myth that Canada has no ethnically marked underclass or any impoverished inner-city communities.

In Montreal, MCJ and Cool G—both originally from Halifax—mixed R&B with hip-hop breakbeats to create their own unique variant of the genre, exemplified in tracks such as 'So Listen' and 'Smooth As Silk'. At the same time, francophone rap began to expand its popularity. In 1989, Laymen Twist—an interracial trio of MCs from Montreal—produced a popular cover of Lou Reed's 'Walk on the Wild Side', anticipating Marky Mark & the Fresh Bunch's Top 40 cover later in the decade. Meanwhile, francophone 'collectives', like Les French B., comprised of Jean-Robert Bisaillon and Richard Gauthier, updated the *chansons engagés* tradition with their extended meditations on, among other topical concerns, Quebec's language law, Bill 101 ('Je me souviens', 1989). And Kool Rock (Ghislain Proulx) and Jay Tree (Jean Tarzi) , better known as the Mouvement Rap Francophone (MRF), dominated dance clubs across Quebec with tracks like the self-referential 'M.R.F. est arrivé' (1990).

The legacy of all these groups, each of which faced a basically indifferent music industry in Canada, can be heard in the music of rap groups that emerged in Canada in the decades following their pioneering work—in records by Fresh B., Nubian Islamic Force, Sweet Ebony, Nu Black Nation, Sonyalive, R&R, KGB, Organized Rhyme (featuring a young Tom Green), Nase Poet, and Brothers Doing Work, and, more recently, in Top 40 records and videos by the Swollen Members, Kardinall Ofishall, Choclair, and K-os. Indeed, were it not for such pioneers as Maestro Fresh Wes, Michie Mee, the Dream Warriors, and Kish, these later rap groups may not be regularly topping the charts in Canada.

That said, Canadian rappers obviously benefited from the increasing mainstream success of rap in the United States—not to mention strong, if somewhat belated, support for their videos on MuchMusic. Tracks played on MuchMusic's popular *Rap City* show, hosted first by Michael Williams and then by Master P, proved to those in the recording industry that rap could definitely generate sales on par with any rock group in Canada, and that it could even appeal to a broader audience in the process. Though no records exist as to which videos received what number of plays during *Rap City*'s earliest days, each of the recordings we will now examine—Run-D.M.C.'s 'Walk This Way' (1986), Public Enemy's 'Night of the Living Baseheads' (1989), N.W.A.'s *Straight Outta Compton* (1989), Snoop Doggy Dogg's 'What's My Name?'

(1993), and Lauryn Hill's 'Doo Wop (That Thing)' (1998)—received multiple plays both on *Rap City* and on the station's regular programming. As such, they provide historical landmarks of rap's long journey back to the top of the Top 40 after the Sugarhill Gang's chart-topping hit, 'Rapper's Delight' (1979), becoming the most profitable genre of popular music in the world by 1998, and they provide a historical record of the kinds of rap music that many Canadian rock fans heard emanating from their TV sets as it did so.

Run-D.M.C.: 'Walk This Way' (1986)

The year 1986 saw the release of the first two multi-platinum rap albums—Run-D.M.C.'s *Raising Hell* and the Beastie Boys' *Licensed To Ill*. That neither Run-D.M.C. nor the Beastie Boys hailed from the Bronx indicates the expanding appeal of rap music. The key to the commercial success of these albums, however, was the expansion of the audience for rap music in general, which now included millions of young white fans who were exposed to the genre on a daily basis via music television, and who were attracted to its driving rhythms and transgressive, rebellious sensibility. Both *Raising Hell* and *Licensed To Ill* were released on a new independent label, Def Jam, co-founded in 1984 by the hip-hop promoter Russell Simmons and the musician-producer Rick Rubin. During the 1980s Def Jam took up where Sugar Hill Records left off, cross-promoting a new generation of artists, expanding and diversifying the national audience for hip-hop, and, in 1986, becoming the

Run-D.M.C. Courtesy BMI Archives.

first rap-oriented independent label to sign a distribution deal with one of the 'Big Five' record companies, Columbia Records.

A trio consisting of the MCs Run (Joseph Simmons, b. 1964) and D.M.C. (Darryl McDaniels, b. 1964), and the DJ Jam Master Jay (Jason Mizell, 1965–2002), Run-D.M.C. was perhaps the most influential act in the history of rap music. Simmons, McDaniels, and Mizell were college-educated black men, raised in a middle-class neighbourhood in the New York City borough of Queens. Working with Russell Simmons, who was MC Run's older brother, and producer Rick Rubin, the trio established a hard-edged, rock-influenced style that was to influence profoundly the sound and sensibility of later rap music. Their raps were literate and rhythmically skilled, with Run and D.M.C. weaving their phrases together and often completing the last few words of one another's lines. The 'beats', produced by Rubin and Jam Master Jay, were stark and powerful, mixing digitized loops of hard rock drumming with searing guitar sounds from the heavy metal and hardcore genres. Run-D.M.C. was the first rap group to headline a national tour and the first to appear on MTV. They popularized rap among the young, predominantly white audience for rock music, gave the genre a more rebellious image, and introduced hip-hop sartorial style—hats, gold chains, and untied Adidas sports shoes with fat laces—to their millions of fans (the now familiar connection between rap music and athletic wear was arguably established in 1986, when the Adidas corporation and Run-D.M.C. inked a promotional deal worth $1.5 million).

The creative and commercially successful synergy between rock music and hip-hop for which Def Jam Records became so well known is well illustrated in Run-D.M.C.'s 'Walk This Way', the gold single that propelled *Raising Hell* nearly to the top of the album charts. 'Walk This Way', a collaboration between Run-D.M.C. and the popular rock group Aerosmith, was a cover version of a song written and previously recorded by Aerosmith alone. The proposed merger proved both musically and socially meaningful: the meeting of Run-D.M.C. and Aerosmith in song—and in the video—clearly modelled the rapprochement between rock and rap culture that Def Jam intended to inspire and profit from (Aerosmith brought a large portion of the hard rock audience to the table, having sold over 25 million albums since the early 1970s).

'Walk This Way' opens with a sample of rock drumming from the original recording, interrupted by the sound of a turntable scratching and the main riff of the song, played by Aerosmith's guitarist, Joe Perry. Run and D.M.C. then trade lines of the song's verses in an aggressive, shouted style that matches the intensity of the rock rhythm section. The chorus ('*Walk this way, talk this way . . .*') is sung by Aerosmith's Steven Tyler in a high, strained voice—a timbre most readily associated with heavy metal music and hard rock from the time. As the track progresses, Run, D.M.C., and Tyler combine vocal forces, providing a musical analogue for the merging of rock and rap all involved sought to inspire, and the recording ends with a virtuoso guitar solo by Joe Perry.

The video version of 'Walk This Way'—the first rap video to make heavy rotation on MuchMusic—gives visual substance to the musical image of a tense conversation between the worlds of hard rock and rap, unified by the sizzling textures of hip-hop scratching and hard rock guitar, the contrasting but similarly aggressive vocal timbres of Run, D.M.C., and Steven Tyler, and the over-the-top male braggadocio of the song's text. (The lyrics to 'Walk This Way', with references to horny cheerleaders and high school locker room voyeurism, suggest that one of the few things shared by the predominantly male audiences for rap and rock was a decidedly adolescent approach to sex.)

The video for 'Walk This Way' opens with Run-D.M.C. performing in a small sound studio. The amplified sound of turntable scratching penetrates a wall that separates this intimate but restricted musical world from that of a hard rock concert, held on the stage of a huge arena. Disturbed by the noise, the members of Aerosmith use their guitars to punch a hole in the wall, through which Run-D.M.C. run onto the stage of the concert and basically take over the show. Initially met with skeptical scowls from Tyler and Perry, the rappers succeed in winning over the pair, and the video ends in discordant harmony, with the huge, largely white crowd cheering.

It is difficult to think of a more explicit (or more calculated) acting out of the process of black–white crossover in the history of rock. While Run-D.M.C. was not the first rap group to incorporate textures and grooves from rock music—early hip-hop DJs Kool Herc and Afrika Bambaata often used breaks from groups like the Rolling Stones and Led Zeppelin—they were the first to make heavy rotation on MuchMusic and, consequently, the first to reach a majority portion of the rock and pop listening audience.

The Beastie Boys

The Beastie Boys, the rap trio whose album *Licensed To Ill* topped the pop charts a few months after the release of *Raising Hell*, were the first commercially successful white act in hip-hop. Like Run-D.M.C., their recordings were produced by Rick Rubin, released on Def Jam Records, and benefited greatly from a distribution deal brokered by Russell Simmons with industry giant Columbia Records. Although they received a great deal of criticism for 'ripping off' a 'black' style, it is perhaps more accurate—and less racist—to suggest that their early recordings represent a fusion of the youth-oriented rebelliousness of hardcore punk rock, which the band started out playing in 1981, with the sensibility and techniques of hip-hop, producing an authentic 'frat rap' variant of what they helped to make a globally successful Top 40 genre.

In 1985 the Beastie Boys were signed by Def Jam Records, appeared in *Krush Groove*—one of the first films to deal with hip-hop culture—and toured as the opening act for both Madonna and Run-D.M.C. The following year *Licensed To Ill*, the group's debut LP, sold 720,000 copies in six weeks and became the fastest-selling debut album on the Columbia roster up until then. The most popular track on the album, the 'frat rap' anthem '(You Gotta) Fight for Your Right (To Party)', which peaked at Number 10 on the Top 40 in Canada in 1987, established the Beastie Boys' appeal for the most rapidly expanding segment of the rap audience—young, predominantly white males who, although primarily fans of rock music, had developed a taste for rap through repeated exposure on music television. After leaving Def Jam Records in 1988, eventually creating their own label, Grande Royale, in the process, which would release records by Luscious Jackson and Sean Lennon in the mid- and late 1990s, the Beastie Boys continued to experiment with combinations of rap, heavy metal, punk, and psychedelic rock. Throughout the 1990s, the group scored a series of critical and commercial successes, culminating in the release of their 1998 album, *Hello Nasty*, which featured the band's highest charting single to date in Canada, 'Intergalactic' (Number 9, 1998).

Public Enemy: 'Night of the Living Baseheads' (1988)

By 1987 a series of million-selling singles had proven rap's commercial potential. The hits included rap ballads (L.L. Cool J's 'I Need Love'), women's rap (Salt-N-Pepa's 'Push It'), humorous party rap (Tone-Loc's 'Wild Thing'), and novelty rap specifically targeted at a young adolescent audience ('Parents Just Don't Understand' by D.J. Jazzy Jeff and the Fresh Prince). Rap's commercial success was further aided by the decision of a number of the small independent labels that had sprung up to feed the growing demand for rap music—Jive, Cold Chillin', Tommy Boy, and Priority—to follow the lead of Def Jam and negotiate distribution deals with major record labels interested in the emerging rap market.

The 'mainstreaming' of rap music—what some would call the genre's 'commercialization'—had a number of interesting consequences. While some rappers and producers focused their energies on creating multi-platinum crossover hits, others reacted against the commercialism of what they derisively labelled 'pop rap', choosing instead to reanimate the tradition of social realism ('reality rap') that had informed recordings like 'The Message', creating a more 'hardcore' sound that, as it turned out, generated some of the best-selling crossover hits of all time.

The tradition of socially engaged rap, which was dedicated to chronicling the declining fortunes of urban black communities, received its strongest impetus from

Public Enemy. Courtesy BMI Archives.

the New York-based group Public Enemy. Founded in 1982, Public Enemy was organized around a core set of members who met as college students, drawn together by their interest in hip-hop culture and political activism. Clearly conjuring the ghost of the Black Panther Party, which had dissipated in the 1970s due to internal and external pressures, the standard hip-hop configuration of two MCs—Chuck D (a.k.a. Carlton Ridenhour) and Flavor Flav (a.k.a. William Drayton)—plus a DJ, Terminator X (Norman Lee Rogers), was augmented by a 'Minister of Information' (Professor Griff, a.k.a. Richard Griffin) and by the Security of the First World (S1W), a cohort of dancers who dressed in paramilitary uniforms, carried Uzi machine guns, and performed a martial arts-inspired parody of Motown choreography.

The release of Public Enemy's second album in 1988—*It Takes a Nation of Millions to Hold Us Back*—was a breakthrough event for rap music. The album fused the trenchant social and political analyses of Chuck D—delivered in a deep, authoritative voice—with the streetwise interjections of his trickster sidekick Flavor Flav, who wore comical glasses and an oversized clock around his neck. Their complex verbal interplay was situated within a dense, multi-layered sonic web created by the group's production team, the Bomb Squad (Hank Shocklee, Keith Shocklee, and Eric 'Vietnam' Sadler). Tracks like 'Countdown to Armageddon' (an apocalyptic opening instrumental track, taped at a live concert in London), 'Don't Believe the Hype' (a critique of white-dominated mass media), and 'Party for Your Right to Fight' (a parody of the Beastie Boys' 'Fight for Your Right [To Party]' from the previous year) turned the technology of digital sampling to new artistic purposes and insisted, in effect, that rap music continue to engage with the real-life conditions of urban black communities—to the point of becoming, in Chuck D's famous turn of phrase, 'black America's CNN'.

'Night of the Living Baseheads' is an instructive example of the moral authority and musical complexity of many Public Enemy records. The lyrics combine images of corpse-like zombies with a commentary on the crack cocaine epidemic that swept American inner cities during the mid- and late 1980s. The track opens with the voice of the black nationalist leader Louis Farrakhan, sampled from one of his speeches:

Have you forgotten that once we were brought here, we were robbed of our names, robbed of our language, we lost our religion, our culture, our God? And many of us, by the way we act, we even lost our minds.

With these words still ringing in our ears, we are suddenly dropped into the middle of a complexly textured groove. The lead MC of Public Enemy, Chuck D, opens with a verbal explosion, a play on words derived from hip-hop slang:

Here it is—
BAMMM!—
And you say, 'Goddamn,
This is the dope jam!'
But let's define the term called 'dope'
And you think it mean funky now? No!

In hip-hop argot the term 'dope' carries a double meaning. It can function as a positive adjective, broadly equivalent to older terms such as 'cool', 'hip', or 'funky'. Alternatively, 'dope' functions as a reference to psychoactive drugs, ranging from marijuana to crack cocaine, the new, more devastating drug being critiqued by Chuck D in the song. The rhetorical tactic of announcing the arrival of a compelling performance (a 'dope jam') and, thereby, laying claim to the listener's attention is common in rap recordings. Chuck D takes this opening gambit and plays with it, however, redefining the term 'dope jam' as a message about drug use and its effects on the black community. At the end of each stanza of his rap, Chuck D uses another pun, based on the homonyms 'bass' (the deep, booming tones favoured by rap producers) and 'base' (a shorthand reference to 'freebase', i.e., crack cocaine):

> *Sellin', smellin'*
> *Sniffin', riffin'*
> *And brothers try to get swift an'*
> *Sell to their own—rob a home*
> *While some shrivel to bone*
> *Like comatose walkin' around*
> *Please don't confuse this with the sound*
> *I'm talking about . . . BASE*

Throughout the song, Chuck D presents a chilling snapshot of the devastating effects crack cocaine has on the human body ('*Some shrivel to bone, like comatose walkin' around*'), and he uses the bass/base pun to draw a contrast between the aesthetics of hip-hop and the scourge of crack cocaine ('*Please don't confuse this [base] with the sound [bass]*'). After this first occurrence, the bass/base homonym returns periodically in a syncopated, digitally sampled loop that punctuates the thickly layered sonic texture created by the Bomb Squad. Chuck D goes on to scold black drug dealers for victimizing members of their own community ('*Shame on a brother when he dealin' [drugs on] the same block where my [Oldsmobile] 98 be wheelin'*'). A sampled verbal phrase ('*How low can you go?*') is used as a rhythmic and rhetorical device to set up the final sequence of Chuck D's rap, which concludes with the story of a crack addict, a former hip-hop MC fallen on bad times:

> *Daddy-O once said to me*
> *He knew a brother who stayed all day in his jeep*
> *And at night he went to sleep*
> *And in the mornin' all he had was*
> *The sneakers on his feet*
> *The culprit used to jam and rock the mike, yo*
> *He stripped the jeep to fill his pipe*
> *And wander around to find a place*
> *Where they rocked to a different kind of . . . come on, y'all*
> *[Samples of voices]*
> *I'm talkin' 'bout BASE*

The grim message of 'Night' is enveloped in a jagged and stark sonic landscape, layered with fractured words and vocal noises, bits and pieces of sampled music and other 'found sounds' sewn together like a crazy quilt. The producers incorporated digital samples from 13 different recorded sources, among them an early 12-inch rap single, several soul music records, a gospel record, a glam rock record, and the 'found' sound of drums and air-raid sirens. In musical terms, 'Night of the Living Baseheads' is like a complex archaeological dig, a site richly layered with sonic objects, the cumulative meaning of which depends on the cultural and musical expertise of the listener.

Although rap is often regarded primarily as a verbal genre, a recording like 'Night of the Living Baseheads', with its carefully constructed pastiche of sampled sound sources, compels us to consider rap as music as well. Hank Shocklee has argued vociferously for a broader conception of music and musicianship:

> Music is nothing but organized noise. You can take anything—street sounds, us talking, whatever you want—and make it music by organizing it. That's still our philosophy, to show people that this thing you call music is a lot broader than you think it is. (Rose, 1994: 82)

This philosophy is similar to that expressed by certain art music composers throughout the twentieth century, such as Karlheinz Stockhause, Pierre Henry, Terry Riley, and Steve Reich, who have used tape recorders, digital technology, and elements of noise in their works. But it could be argued that the most extensive and creative use of the technology of digital sampling has been made in genres such as ambient, ambient-electronica, hip-hop, R&B, house music, and techno, and in singles such as Public Enemy's 'Night of the Living Baseheads', which still stands as a pioneering example of the creative and social potential of digital audio technology.

N.W.A.: *Straight Outta Compton* (1989)

By the late 1980s a number of distinctive regional variations on the formula of hip-hop music were well established in cities such as Philadelphia, Cleveland, Miami, Atlanta, Houston, Seattle, Oakland, and Los Angeles. The music critic Nelson George noted this process of regionalization:

> The rap that'll flow from down South, the Midwest and the West Coast will not, and should not, feel beholden to what came before. Just as hip-hop spit in the face of disco (and funk too), non-New York hip-hop will have its own accent, its own version of b-boy wisdom, if it's to mean anything. (George, 1998: 132)

During this period southern California became a primary centre of hip-hop innovation, supported by a handful of independent labels and one of the few commercial AM stations nationwide to feature hip-hop programming (KDAY).

The sound of 'new school' west coast rap differed from 'old school' New York hip-hop in a number of regards. The edgy, rapid-fire delivery of Melle Mel and Run-

D.M.C., for instance, remained influential, but it was augmented by a smoother, more laid-back style of rapping. The dialects of rappers from southern California, many of them the offspring of migrants from Louisiana and Texas, also contributed to the distinctive flavour of west coast rap. And if the verbal delivery of west coast rap was sometimes cooler, the content of the MCs' recitations became angrier, darker, and more menacing, the social commitment of Public Enemy supplanted by the outlaw swagger of artists such as Ice-T (Tracy Marrow), who, in 1987, recorded the theme song for *Colors*, Dennis Hopper's violent film about gang-versus-police warfare, and the increasingly fractious issue of police brutality, in south-central Los Angeles. Both the film and Ice-T's raps reflected ongoing changes in southern California's urban communities, including a decline in industrial production and rising rates of joblessness, the continuing effects of crack cocaine, and a concomitant growth of drug-related gang violence.

The emergence of west coast gangsta rap was heralded nationwide by the release of the album *Straight Outta Compton* by N.W.A. (Niggaz with Attitude). While rap artists had previously dealt with aspects of urban street life in brutally straightforward terms, N.W.A. upped the ante with recordings that expressed the gangsta lifestyle, saturated with images of sex and violence straight out of the prison toast tradition. The nucleus of the group was formed in 1986, when O'Shea 'Ice Cube' Jackson (b. 1969), the product of a middle-class home in south-central Los Angeles, met Andre 'Dr Dre' Young (b. 1965), a sometime member of a local funk group called the World Class Wreckin' Cru. Jackson and Young shared an interest in writing rap songs, an ambition that was realized when they teamed up with Eric 'Eazy-E' Wright (1973–95), a former drug dealer who was using the proceeds from dealing to fund a record label, Ruthless Records. Soon, the three began working together as N.W.A., eventually adding D.J. Yella (Antoine Carraby) and MC Ren (Lorenzo Patterson) to the group.

When the group started work on their second album, *Straight Outta Compton*, the idea of establishing a distinctive west coast identity within hip-hop was clearly on their minds. As MC Ren put it in a 1994 interview in *The Source*:

> When we did N.W.A . . . New York had all's the bomb groups. New York was on the map and all we was thinking, man—I ain't gonna lie, no matter what nobody in the group say—I think we was all thinking about making a name for Compton and L.A. (George, 1998: 135)

Released in 1989, the album was more than a local success, selling 750,000 copies in America alone, even before N.W.A. started a promotional tour. The album's attitude, sound, and sensibility were clearly indebted to earlier hip-hop recordings—particularly Public Enemy's *It Takes a Nation of Millions to Hold Us Back*, released the year before—but was in some ways unlike anything heard before, featuring tracks with titles like 'Fuck the Police' and 'Gangsta Gangsta', underlain by a soundtrack that mixed the sound of automatic weapon fire and police sirens with samples from funk masters such as George Clinton and James Brown, a bouncy drum machine-generated dance groove dubbed 'New Jack Swing', and high-pitched, thin-sounding synthesizer lines. The raps themselves were harrowing accounts of gang life, hearkening back to the bleakest aspects of the toast tradition. The cover of the CD—with the posse staring implacably down at, and holding a gun to the head of, the prospective purchaser—reinforced the aura of danger, one of the main appeals of the group for the young suburban audience that pushed the album to multi-platinum sales. And the group's prominent use of the term 'nigga', which caused a still unresolved controversy as more and more rappers and their fans adopted the term throughout the 1990s, signalled N.W.A.'s desire to reclaim traditional elements of

Murder Rap: East Coast versus West Coast

While the conflation of gangsta rhetoric and reality at least temporarily boosted the sales of rap recordings, it also had terrible real-life consequences, as the matrix of conflict between posses—one source of the creative energy that gave birth to hip-hop in the 1970s—turned viciously in on itself during the mid-1990s. Such conflicts—evoked constantly in gangsta rap—can develop at many levels: between members of the same posse ('set trippin"), among posses representing different 'hoods, between gangs of different ethnicity (as, for example, between Chicano and black gangs in Los Angeles), among larger organizations (for example, national gangs like the Crips, Hoods, and Black Gangster Disciples), and between entire cities or regions.

The mid-1990s saw the violent eruption of conflicts between east coast and west coast factions within the hip-hop business. Standing in one corner was Marion 'Suge' Knight, CEO of Los Angeles-based Death Row Records, and Death Row's up-and-coming star, Tupac (2pac) Shakur (1971–96). In the other corner stood the producer and rapper Sean 'Puffy' Combs (a.k.a. Puff Daddy, P. Diddy), CEO of the New York independent label Bad Boy Records, and the rising star the Notorious B.I.G. (Christopher Wallace, a.k.a. Biggie Smalls, 1972–97). By the time the scenario played itself out at the end of the 1990s, Tupac Shakur and Christopher Wallace had been shot to death; Suge Knight, already on parole for a 1992 assault conviction, was reincarcerated after an attack on two rappers in a Las Vegas casino and had come under federal investigation for racketeering; Interscope, a subdivision of Time Warner Entertainment, had severed its formerly lucrative promotion and distribution deal with Death Row Records; Tupac Shakur's mother had sued Death Row for the rights to her dead son's tapes; and Dr Dre and Snoop Doggy Dogg, Death Row's biggest stars, had severed ties with the label. In January 1998 Snoop told the *Long Beach Press-Telegram* (as quoted in RockOnTheNet.com) that he was leaving Death Row Records for fear of his life:

I definitely feel my life is in danger if I stay in Death Row Records. That's part of the reason why I'm leaving . . . there's nothing over there. Suge Knight is in jail, the president; Dr Dre left and 2Pac is dead. It's telling me that I'm either going to be dead or in jail or I'm going to be nothing.

Chillingly, both Tupac Shakur and the Notorious B.I.G. had recorded prophetic raps that ended with the narrator speaking from the grave rather than standing in bloody triumph over his victims. (True to the logic of the popular music business, these voices were manifested in highly profitable posthumous albums with such titles as *Life after Death*, *Born Again*, *Still I Rise*, and *Here After*).

Since the late 1980s the highly stylized narratives of gangsta rap have provided a chronicle of the dilemmas faced by many urban communities—poverty, drug addiction, and violence—from a first-person, present-tense viewpoint. The recordings of artists like Ice-T, N.W.A., Snoop Doggy Dogg, Tupac Shakur, and the Notorious B.I.G. combine a grim, survivalist outlook on life with a gleeful celebration of the gangsta lifestyle. This celebratory nihilism, propelled by funk-derived, digitally sampled grooves, and surrounded in the video versions of rap recordings with a continual flow of images of hip-hop fashion, champagne, expensive cars, and sexy women (often characterized as 'bitches' and 'whores'), provokes an understandable ambivalence towards gangsta rap on the part of observers genuinely sympathetic to the plight of people struggling for economic and cultural survival. How, such critics ask, could a genre of music that presents itself as being committed to 'keeping it real' so deeply indulge itself in the escapism of consumer capitalism and in the exploitation of women as sex objects?

Part of the answer may lie in the fact that rap music is a part not only of African-American culture but also of North American culture as a whole. Rap reflects the positive qualities of North American culture—its creative energy, regional diversity, and technological acumen—just as it expresses the society's dark side: an obsession with guns and violence, material wealth and status symbols, and long-standing traditions of racism, homophobia, and sexism. (And, as a number of observers have pointed out, tales of black outlaws like Stagger Lee have always existed in a dialogue with popular images of white gangsters like Capone and Derringer, and with violent Hollywood films like *Little Caesar*, *Scarface*, and *Natural Born Killers*.)

On the one hand, rap has provided an unvarnished view of the dystopia that infects many urban communities—what Cornel West, the prominent African-American cultural critic, has called 'the lived experience of coping with a life of horrifying meaninglessness, hopelessness, and lovelessness . . . a numbing detachment from others and a self-destructive disposition toward the world' (West, 1993: 14). On the other hand, it is also clear that gangsta recordings, promoted by huge entertainment corporations to a predominantly white mass audience, may have served inadvertently to reinforce some old and pernicious stereotypes of black masculinity, dating back to the knife-toting dandy seen in nineteenth-century minstrel shows. Perhaps this is what Chuck D was referring to in 1998 when he told an interviewer:

Ten years ago, I called rap music black America's CNN. My biggest concern now is keeping it from becoming the Cartoon Network. (Rose, 1994: 183) racial oppression and reconfigure them for the creation of a strong, independent, unapologetic, and defiant new community. N.W.A., however, did not last long in its original configuration. In late 1989 Ice Cube left the group over a royalties dispute to pursue a successful solo career, and he and the remaining members, who recorded the final N.W.A. album in 1991 as well as solo efforts, put the sorry side of rap on full display as they exchanged obscene taunts, death threats, accusations of homosexuality, racist slurs, and the like in their ensuing recordings.

Snoop Doggy Dogg: 'What's My Name?' (1993)

The acrimonious breakup of N.W.A., beginning in 1989, had the effect of disseminating the group's influence over a wider territory. During the 1990s Ice Cube went on to make a series of platinum albums totalling almost six million in sales, including the brilliant *AmeriKKKa's Most Wanted* (1991), a more explicitly political album recorded in New York with Public Enemy and the Bomb Squad, and *The Predator*, which reached Number 1 in 1992. Eazy-E, who died of AIDS in 1995, sold over five million albums in the 1990s, all released on his Ruthless Records label, and MC Ren sold a million copies of his *Kizz My Black Azz* (Number 12 in 1992). But the most influential and economically successful member of N.W.A. turned out to be Andre Young (Dr Dre), who founded an independent record label (Death Row/Interscope), cultivated a number of younger rappers, and continued to develop a distinctive hip-hop production style, christened 'G-Funk' in homage to the P-funk style developed in the 1970s by George Clinton, often sampled on Dre's productions. Dr Dre's 1992 album, *The Chronic*, named after a particularly potent strain of marijuana, sold over three million copies and introduced his protege, Snoop Doggy Dogg (Calvin Broadus), to the world.

   Snoop's soft drawl and laid-back-but-lethal gangster persona were featured on *Doggystyle* (1993), which made its debut at the top of album charts across North America in 1993. The gold single 'What's My Name?'—a so-called 'clean' remix of the opening track on the *Doggystyle* album—will give us a sense of Snoop Doggy Dogg's prowess as a rapper and of Dr Dre's distinctive G-funk production style. (Like many rap records intended to cross over to the pop charts, 'What's My Name' was released on the album in its original, unexpurgated version and in a 'clean' version on a single designed for radio airplay and mass distribution; we will analyze the remix here.) Although the track opens with a dense, scratchy sample reminiscent of a Public Enemy/Bomb Squad recording—actually a brief sequence from an old Parliament track, looped to create a syncopated pattern—the texture soon shifts to a smoother, more dance-oriented sound. A relaxed, medium-tempo dance groove is established by drum machine and keyboard synthesizers (including a weighty and sinuous keyboard bass part), over which a digitally processed, nasal-sounding human voice floats, singing a melismatic phrase:

   Eee-yi-yi-yi-yi-yah, the Dogg Pound's in the hou-ouse

A female choir then enters, repeating the phrase 'Snoop Doggy Dogg' in soul music style, answered by the sampled voice of George Clinton, intoning 'Da Bomb' (a phrase commonly used to describe compelling grooves and other pleasurable experiences). After this brief mood-setting introduction, Snoop's drawling, laconic voice enters:

> *From the depths of the sea, back to the block [the neighbourhood]*
> *Snoop Doggy Dogg, funky as the, the, the Doc [Dr Dre]*
> *Went solo on that ass, but it's still the same*
> *Long Beach is the spot where I served my cane [prison term]*

These two stanzas immediately establish Snoop's local identity, his indebtedness to his mentor Dr Dre, and his street credibility, referring to the time he spent in jail. He then explodes into a rapid-fire, percussively articulated sequence of tongue-twisting wordplay:

> *Follow me, follow me, follow me, follow me, but you betta not slip*
> *'Cause Nine-trizzay's the yizzear [1993's the year]*
> *for me to fuck up shit [make an impact]*
> *So I ain't holdin' nuttin' back*
> *And once again I got 5 on the 20 sack [sentenced to five years in prison for possession of a $20 bag of marijuana]*

Snoop declares his arrival in no uncertain terms, asserting that 1993 is the year for him to make a major impact on the music scene. He refers to a more recent conviction on marijuana possession charges and then shifts to a more threatening posture—aided by Dr Dre's interjection of an automatic weapon-like sound effect:

> *It's like that and as a matter of fact (Dr Dre: rat-tat-tat-tat)*
> *'Cause I never hesitate to put a fool on his back [imitating Muhammad Ali]*
> *(Dr Dre: Yeah, so peep out the manuscript [pay close attention to the words]*
> *You see that it's a must we drop gangsta shit [talk gangster talk])*
> *Hold on, what's my name?*

The female choir re-enters, introducing a bit of hip-hop history—a melodic line from Parliament's 'Give Up the Funk (Tear the Roof off the Sucker)'. Then Snoop continues to add verbal layers to his gangsta persona, boasting about his potential for lethal violence, referring to himself as '*Mr. One Eight Seven*'—a reference to the California penal code for homicide—and departing the scene of a bloody massacre by disappearing mysteriously into the night ('*I step through the fog and I creep through the smog*').

The following interlude between verses introduces a digitally processed voice chanting '*Bow-wow-wow, yippie-yo-yippie-yay*', a sly reference to country and western music and cowboy films (references to cowboys and country music are not at all unknown in rap music; for example, Seattle-based rapper Sir Mix-A-Lot's 'Buttermilk

Biscuits', recorded in 1988, is a parody of square dance music). In the third and final section, Snoop moves on to another favourite subject, his sexual potency. He begins with a catchphrase that goes back to the South Bronx origins of hip-hop and MCs like Kool Herc and Grandmaster Flash:

> *Now just throw your hands way up in the air*
> *And wave them all around like ya just don't care*
> *Yeah roll up the dank [marijuana], and pour the drank*
> *And watch your step (why?) 'cause Doggy's on the gank*
> *My bank roll's on swoll [swollen]*
> *I'm standin' on hit, legit, now I'm on parole, stroll*
> *With the Dogg Pound right behind me*
> *And rollin' with my b [woman], is where ya might find me*
> *Layin' that, playin' that G Thang*
> *She want the G with the biggest sack [testicles], and who's that?*
> *He is I, and I am him, slim with the tilted brim*
> *Wha's yo name?*

Read as words on a page, divorced of their musical context, 'What's My Name?' is simply an updated version of 'Stagger Lee', a traditional African-American ballad about a powerful and amoral black desperado of toast fame. But the commercial success of 'What's My Name?' had as much to do with the musical groove and texture of the recording as with the content and flow (rhyme and rhythm) of Snoop Doggy Dogg's verbal performance. In fact, 'What's My Name?' is a club dance record, more than half of which is taken up by instrumental music or singing. This recording is obviously less musically complex than Public Enemy's 'Night of the Living Baseheads', judged from the viewpoints of textural complexity, tone colour, or historical references. But Dr Dre's G-funk sound, while indebted to the innovations of Public Enemy's production team, the Bomb Squad, has an entirely different aesthetic and commercial goal. Despite its controversial verbal content, 'What's My Name?' is essentially a pop record, bristling with hooks, catchy melodies, riffs, and verbal mottoes, organized around a medium-tempo groove, and carefully calibrated for dance club consumption.

Lauryn Hill, 'Doo Wop (That Thing)' (1998)

Lauryn Hill (b. 1975) is a hip-hop artist whose work provides a self-conscious alternative to the violence and sexism of rap stars such as Dr Dre, the Notorious B.I.G., and Tupac Shakur in the mid- and late 1990s. She also is the long-time partner of Bob Marley's son, Rohan, with whom she has had several children. Hill started her recording career with the Fugees, a New Jersey-based hip-hop trio that scored a Number 1 hit in 1996 with their second album, *The Score* (1995). Hill's debut solo album—*The Miseducation of Lauryn Hill* (1998)—extended the Fugees' successful blend of rap, reggae, and R&B. The album shot to Number 1 on the charts, selling seven million copies in a little over a year and spawning the Number 1 hit, 'Doo Wop (That Thing).'

Hip-Hop, Sampling, and the Law

As we have seen, the tradition of incorporating beats from secondary sources is as old as hip-hop itself. However, the increasing sophistication and affordability of digital sampling technology had, by the late 1980s, made it possible for rap producers to go much farther, weaving entire sound textures out of previously recorded materials. This development triggered some interesting court cases, as some of the artists being sampled sought to protect their rights.

In 1989 the Miami-based rap group 2 Live Crew released a song called 'Pretty Woman', which borrowed from the rock 'n' roll hit 'Oh, Pretty Woman' (1964), written by Roy Orbison and William Dees. Although 2 Live Crew had tried to get permission from the music publisher of the song, Acuff-Rose Music, to make a rap version of the song, permission had been denied. A lawsuit ensued over the raunchy send-up of the song by rapper Luther R. Campbell (a.k.a. Luke Skyywalker), and Campbell took the position that his use of the song was a parody that was legally protected as a fair use. The Supreme Court recognized the satirical intent of Campbell's version and held that 2 Live Crew's copying of portions of the original lyric was not excessive in relation to the song's satirical purpose.

Although the 2 Live Crew decision upheld the rights of rap musicians and producers to parody pre-existing recorded material, control over actual digital sampling tightened up during the 1990s as a result of a few well-publicized court cases. In 1991, the 1960s folk rock group the Turtles sued the hip-hop group De La Soul for using a snippet of the Turtles' song 'You Showed Me' on a track called 'Transmitting Live from Mars'. The Turtles won a costly out-of-court settlement. That same year, an up-and-coming hip-hop artist named Biz Markie recorded a track that sampled the sentimental pop song 'Alone Again (Naturally)', a Number 1 pop hit for the Irish songwriter Gilbert O'Sullivan in 1972. O'Sullivan was not pleased and pursued the case, eventually forcing Warner Brothers to remove Biz Markie's album from the market until the offending track was removed from the album.

These decisions sent a chill through the rap music industry and encouraged producers to be less ambitious in their use of sampled materials. As the hip-hop historian Nelson George puts it, 'The high-intensity sound tapestries of Public Enemy have given way to often simpleminded loops of beats and vocal hooks from familiar songs—a formula that has grossed [MC] Hammer, Coolio, and Puff Daddy millions in sales and made old R&B song catalogs potential gold mines' (George, 1998: 95).

'Doo Wop' combines aspects of 1950s R&B—including a soulful lead vocal, four-part vocal harmony, and a horn section—with Hill's penetrating observations on male and female behaviour. The cut opens with Hill and a few of her friends reminiscing about the good old days. Then the digital drum machine's groove enters, and Hill launches into the first half of her rap, directed to female listeners:

> *It's been three weeks since you were looking for your friend*
> *The one you let hit it [have sex with you] and never called you again*
> *Remember when he told you he was 'bout the benjamins? [interested only in money]*
> *You act like you ain't hear him, then gave him a little trim [had sex with him] . . .*
> *Talkin' out your neck [being hypocritical], sayin' you're a Christian*
> *A Muslim, sleeping with the Gin*
> *Now that was the sin that did Jezebel in . . .*

Hill admonishes the women in her audience to be more selective about their sexual relationships and to avoid being hypocritical about their personal conduct. She then turns to the men in her audience, opening up a rapid-fire volley of wordplay that strips the so-called gangstas of their tough-guy trappings, exposing them as mother-dependent, sneaky, woman-beating, sexually immature hypocrites:

> *The second verse is dedicated to the men . . .*
> *Let's stop pretendin' they wanna-pack-pistol-by-they-waist men*
> *Cristal [champagne]-by-the-case men, still [living] in they Mother's basemen'*
> *The pretty-face-men-claimin'-that-they-did-a-bid [prison time] men*
> *Need-to-take-care-of-their-3-and-4-kids men*
> *But they face a court case when the child support's late*
> *Money-takin', heart-breakin', now you wonder why women hate men*
> *The sneaky-silent men, the punk-domestic-violence men*
> *The quick-to-shoot-the-semen . . . Stop acting like boys and be men!*
> *How you gon' win when you ain't right within?!*

'Doo Wop (That Thing)' is essentially a moral parable, delivered in terms that leaven Hill's righteous anger with light-hearted and thoroughly up-to-date hip-hop jargon. She lowers her audience's potential defensiveness by admitting that she has found herself in similar situations and pleads with them to pay attention to the development of an inner life—*How you gon' win when you ain't right within?*—in order to avoid the twin traps of materialism and easy pleasure. The mixture of sweet soul singing and assertive rapping, R&B horns and a digital groove, moral serious-ness and playful humour not only announced the arrival of a new and distinctive voice but also made the single 'Doo Wop' a unique and important contribution to the hip-hop repertoire.

▌ Techno: Dance Music in the Digital Age

During the 1980s, following on the heels of disco and paralleling the emergence of hip-hop, new forms of up-tempo, repetitive, electronic dance music developed in the club scenes of cities such as New York, Chicago, Montreal, Toronto, Vancouver, and Detroit, cross-fertilized with developments in London, Dusseldorf, and other European cities. These styles, generally traced to early 1980s genres such as garage and house music, and loosely lumped together under the general term 'techno', are quite varied. In fact, the electronica genre remains perhaps the most fractious in all of pop music, with literally dozens of subcategories, including jungle, drum'n'bass, funky breaks, tribal, 'ardcore, gabba, happy hardcore, trance, trip-hop, acid jazz, electro-techno, intelligent techno, ambient, and ever more subtly defined sub-subcategories (ambient house, dark ambient, ambient breakbeat, ambient dub, and so on). Each of these subgenres was patronized by a loyal cadre of fans. As Simon Reynolds puts it in his book, *Generation Ecstasy*:

> For the newcomer to electronic dance music, the profusion of scenes and sub-genres can seem at best bewildering, at worst willful obfuscation. Partly, this is a trick of perspective: kids who've grown up with techno feel it's rock that 'all sounds the same.' The urgent distinctions rock fans take for granted—that Pantera, Pearl Jam, and Pavement operate in separate aesthetic universes—make sense only if you're already a participant in the ongoing rock discourse. The same applies to dance music: step inside and the genre begins to make sense. (Reynolds, 1998: 7)

In essence, techno is the musical dimension of a whole youth culture, within which arguments about the difference between good music and bad music are informed by a set of shared assumptions and shared knowledge of the genre's history. Techno culture is focused on DJ/producers—who, unlike disco and hip-hop DJs, often attempt to remain anonymous, operating their equipment in the dark behind a web of wiring. Most techno 'groups', such as the Orb, Orbital, Prodigy, the Chemical Brothers, and Moby, are, in fact, solo acts, or teams of two or three DJs.

The main venues for techno are dance clubs and semi-public events called raves, partly modelled on the be-ins of the 1960s counterculture. A controversial aspect of raves—which started in England in the late 1980s and spread, in a more limited fashion, to North America soon thereafter—is the prevalent use by participants of a psychoactive drug called ecstasy (MDMA), which creates visceral sensations of warmth and euphoria. Matthew Collin, a British journalist who has written extensively about the drug–rave–music connection that emerged in his country in the 1980s, has described the drug's sensation:

> The world had opened up all around, the blank warehouse somehow changed into a wonderland designed just for us, glistening with a magic iridescence that I couldn't see earlier. New world. New sound. New life. Everything felt so right. A huge, glowing, magical YES. (Collin, 1997: 3)

Unfortunately, this 'YES' eventually mutated into a resounding '*NO*', for one of the documented long-term effects of MDMA (which was initially manufactured and marketed as an appetite suppressant) is an alteration of brain chemistry that makes it harder and harder to get high, leading to severe depression. Added to this was the banning of ecstasy by the FDA in the United States, which drove the drug underground, exacerbated the problem of worse drugs being circulated under the guise of ecstasy, and led to a number of fatal overdoses. In any case, by the mid-1990s increasing numbers of DJs and fans had rejected the use of ecstasy. As one insider put it, 'the *music* drugs the listeners.'

The roots of techno are often traced to the Detroit area—home of Motown, the Stooges, and George Clinton. During the early 1980s a group of young, middle-class black men living in the predominantly white suburban town of Belleville developed a form of electronic dance music that Derrick May, a pioneer of the genre, described as being like George Clinton and Kraftwerk 'stuck in an elevator' with just a sequencer. Detroit techno was grounded in a different cultural scene from that which had spawned the Motown sound; young men like May and Juan Atkins were obsessed with symbols of class mobility, Italian fashions, and European disco recordings, and they developed a form of electronic dance music that featured futuristic imagery, samples from European records, and a dry, minimalist sound, underlain by a subliminal funk pulse.

At around the same time a genre called *house music*—named after the Warehouse, a popular gay dance club—was developing in Chicago. The Chicago house scene was pioneered by Frankie Knuckles, a DJ from New York who worked at the Warehouse from 1979 until 1983. Knuckles introduced New York turntable techniques to Chicago, manipulating disco records to emphasize the dance beat—the drums and bass—even more strongly. Many house recordings were purely instrumental, with elements of European synthesizer-pop, Latin soul, reggae, rap, and jazz grafted over an insistent dance beat. By the mid-1980s house music scenes had emerged in New York and London, and in the late 1980s the genre made its first appearances on the pop charts under the guise of artists like M/A/R/R/S and Madonna.

In the 1990s techno music began to diversify into the dozens of specialized subcategories mentioned above—which we explore in greater detail in the next chapter. These branches of techno were often distinguished by their relative 'hardness', a quality connected with the tempo or beats per minute of recordings. Some forms of techno were influenced by punk rock, others by experimental art music, and still others by black popular music, including funk and hip-hop. The sensual and emotional tone of the music also varied widely, from the stark, futuristic sound of Belgian gabba and the energetic funkiness of jungle to the world music influences of tribal and the otherworldly sonic atmospheres of ambient. Although techno has produced few big commercial hits throughout its history, the recordings of musicians like Prodigy, Orbital, and Moby did make inroads into the charts during the late 1990s, and techno recordings were increasingly being licensed as the soundtracks for technologically oriented television commercials and films.

The Years of the Canadian Women: Shania Twain, Céline Dion, Sarah McLachlan, and k.d. lang

The late 1990s were a boon time for female singers and songwriters in general, and for Canadian women working in the singer-songwriter and pop genres in particular. In fact, though critics have dubbed the last half of the decade 'The Years of the Woman' in pop music, they might just as well have called them 'The Years of the Canadian Woman', as female Canadian pop singers achieved unprecedented world-wide chart dominance during the mid- and late 1990s. To understand just how successful certain Canadian female singers and songwriters were during the late 1990s, one need only realize that of the four double-diamond awards (double-diamond signifies sales of over two million units for a record) awarded by the Canadian Recording Industry Association since CDs were first sold in Canada, three belong to Canadian 'new country' sensation, Shania Twain—for *The Woman in Me* (1995), *Come on Over* (1997), and *Up!* (2002)—while the other belongs to Alanis Morisette, for *Jagged Little Pill* (1995). Two already successful, not to mention extremely eclectic, male producers worked on all four of these double-diamond compact discs— Robert 'Mutt' Lange on Twain's albums (Lange also has produced for such recording artists as Def Leppard, Foreigner, AC/DC, the Cars, Billy Ocean, Bryan Adams, and selected tracks for Céline Dion) and Glenn Ballard (who has worked with Michael Jackson, Wilson Phillips, and Aerosmith, among others) on Morissette's. Yet, both producers remain adamant about the 'collaborative' nature of their work in the studio with the Canadian singers. And Morissette's subsequent successes alone clearly demonstrate her own pop prowess as a producer and songwriter.

The simultaneous success of Québécois chanteuse Céline Dion further solidified the hold of Canadian vocalists on the worldwide Top 40 market during the mid- and late 1990s. The runaway success of Number 1 hits like 'Falling Into You' (1996) and 'Because You Loved Me' (1996) still could not have prepared Dion for the international success she would enjoy with tracks like 'New Day Dawning' (written by fellow Canadian Stephan Moccio) and 'My Heart Will Go On'. Featured prominently on the soundtrack for James Cameron's 1997 blockbuster, *Titanic* (still the most viewed film in history), 'My Heart Will Go On' has sold more than 25 million copies, topped pop charts worldwide, and won Dion two Grammy awards for Best Female Pop Vocal Performance and Record of the Year in 1998. The song was rated fourteenth on the United World Chart's 'most successful songs in music history', and as the second most successful song released by a female musician, behind only Whitney Houston's cover of 'I Will Always Love You'. Though Dion has now sold over 100 million records worldwide, perhaps a better indication of her success in the mid- and late 1990s can be gleaned from her inclusion on VH1's popular *Divas Live* series for 1997, along with such singers as Aretha Franklin, fellow Canadian Shania Twain, Gloria Estefan, and Mariah Carey.

Another Canadian singer-songwriter made strong headway on the rock charts at the same time as Dion, Twain, and Morissette—Halifax native Sarah McLachlan. Tired of concert promoters and radio stations refusing to program two female musicians consecutively, McLachlan established a concert tour and travelling music festival comprised entirely of female solo artists and female-led bands, which she called Lilith Fair, after the apocryphal Lilith (the Biblical Adam's first wife). From 1997 to 1999—on 'main', 'second', and 'village' stages—Lilith Fair combined pop consumerism with social activism, with one dollar from each ticket sold going to a prominent women's charity in the area where the concert was held. The festival brought an estimated two million people together in its three-year history and raised an estimated $7 million for charities, becoming the most successful all-female music festival in rock history.

Almost immediately in the identity-conscious 1990s, Lilith Fair came under fire. Some critics argued that the festival was based on, and perpetuated, a kind of doublethink, discriminating against male front men on the basis of their gender in a misguided effort to combat gender-based discrimination in the rock industry (festival policy allowed men to perform at Lilith Fair, but only as backup musicians). Other critics claimed that McLachlan effectively commodified gender politics through Lilith Fair, that is, that she used gender-based social activism as a marketing tool (as though a rock festival can't, by itself, be a form of activism as well as a marketing tool). What these critics all typically failed to address was that McLachlan's basic aim in establishing the festival was simply to prove to programmers and promoters alike that female pop and rock musicians could sell just as many—if not more—tickets as their male counterparts, and that there was a sizable market for musicians who used rock as a forum for negotiating the increasingly complicated nuances of gender politics in the mid- and late 1990s.

Still other critics focused on the music of Lilith Fair. A vocal contingent of the rock press accused McLachlan of ignoring female artists who didn't fit the singer-songwriter mould; in the process, they claimed, McLachlan had reinforced rather than countered the stereotype of 'the feminine' as 'soft and emotional'. McLachlan often downplayed the inherent gender politicking of Lilith Fair, hoping above all else to demonstrate by the festival that women could command a sizable audience entirely on their own. Furthermore, a glance at a representative sample of 'main stage' performers over the three years would seem to confirm the suspicion that Lilith Fair catered to listeners interested in the singer-songwriter genre. Sarah McLachlan performed alongside the Indigo Girls, Jewel, Paula Cole, Fiona Apple, Cowboy Junkies, the Dixie Chicks, Shawn Colvin, and many others.

That said, the festival also featured a number of hard rock, punk, riot grrrl, and foxcore outfits on its 'second' and 'village' stages, including Cibo Matto and Canadians Kinnie Starr, Bif Naked, and Tegan and Sara. And, of course, critics have tended to conveniently overlook the 'main stage' contributions of R&B and hip-hop singers such as Queen Latifah, Erykah Badu, Missy Elliott, and Me'shell Ndegeocello, as well as hard rock musicians such as Holly McNarland and Antigone Rising.

One of the most unorthodox female vocalists yet to emerge in Canada is k.d. lang, Alberta's own *enfant terrible* of the country world. If lang did anything in her career, it was challenge convention. Born and raised in the 'cattle capital' of Canada, the country-pop singer was an outspoken vegetarian (lang appeared in a number of anti-meat commercials), an 'out-of-the-closet' lesbian (her most famous cover photo, for a *Vanity Fair* magazine shoot, involved receiving a sexually charged shave from super-model Cindy Crawford), and more than a bit of a musical malcontent, as we shall see in lang's 'cow-punk' classic 'Nowhere To Stand' (1989). Yet for all her uniqueness, lang was nothing if not typical of the Canadian country genre in that each of her records—but especially those released in the early and mid-1990s—comfortably straddled a generic middle-ground between country and pop, resulting in a number of 'crossover' hits for the singer.

Shania Twain

Nobody could accuse country-pop superstar Shania Twain (b. 1965 as Eileen Edwards) of being an overnight success—nor of having had an easy life. Her parents divorced in the early 1980s and her mother later married Jerry Twain, an Ojibwa living in Timmins, who subsequently adopted Eilleen, and thus the future country singer became Eilleen Twain. Raised in relative poverty, at eight years old she began performing in local clubs and bars to help support her family. At 13, the singer was invited to perform on CBC-TV's *The Tommy Hunter Show* and, while still attending Timmins High and Vocational School, Twain took up lead-vocal duties for a local Top 40 cover band appropriately called Longshot.

In 1987, however, Twain was forced to put her dreams of pop stardom on hold when her mother and adoptive father were killed in a car accident. The 22-year-old Twain moved her half-brothers, Mark and Darryl, and her half-sister, Carrie-Ann, to Huntsville, Ontario, where she secured a gig singing at Deerhurst Resort. Eventually recording a demonstration tape in 1991 at a local studio in Huntsville, Twain secured a recording contract with entertainment lawyer Richard Frank later that same year. Changing her name to 'Shania', an Ojibwa word meaning 'on my way' chosen in honour of her adoptive father, Twain's first record featured two moderate hits, 'What Made You Say That' and 'Dance with the One That Brought You', the latter peaking at Number 55 on *Billboard*'s country chart (the single failed to dent the Top 40 in Canada). Selling fewer than 250,000 copies by 1993, Twain's debut was considered a moderate success at best.

Her career received the boost it needed in June 1993, when the singer met producer Robert 'Mutt' Lange at Nashville's Fan Fair. Lange, an internationally renowned record producer, was impressed with Twain's singing, and he offered to work with her on another album. Accepting the offer, Twain and Lange would soon marry, becoming perhaps the most successful husband-and-wife production team in pop music history. Their first album, 1995's *The Woman In Me*, scored Twain her first Number 1 single, 'Any Man of Mine'. The album topped the country charts across North America for months, and crossed over to a peak position of Number 5 on the Top 40 pop charts. As of 2007, *The Woman In Me* has sold over 12 million units worldwide.

Twain and Lange's follow-up shot her into the status of country-pop legend—the multi-million selling *Come On Over*. Released in 1997, the record racked up six Top 40 singles—'You're Still the One', 'Don't Be Stupid', 'Honey, I'm Home', 'Man! I Feel Like a Woman!', 'That Don't Impress Me Much', and 'From This Moment On'—propelling the album to sales of over 20 million copies in North America and over 34 million copies worldwide. By 2008, *Come On Over* had become the best-selling album by a female musician, and the best-selling country album, in pop, country, and rock history. The album is a classic example of Canadian country, with its genre-bending and massive crossover success, sitting with equal ease on the country and pop charts.

Come On Over was remixed in 1999 for release in the European market, which tends to display less interest in country music as a rule. The remix involved somewhat less country instrumentation (fiddle tracks were placed much lower in the mix, if not removed entirely), but almost every other feature of the record remained similar if not completely intact. The decision to remix proved worthwhile, as *Come On Over* went to Number 1 in Britain for 11 weeks, becoming the best-selling album of the year there. Germany also provided a receptive audience for the record, *Come On Over* moving over one million units there in 1999 and 2000. The singles 'That Don't Impress Me Much' and 'Man! I Feel Like A Woman!' also did well in the European market, making the Top 10 in Britain, Germany, and France.

Exhausted after a whirlwind of activity, in 2000 Twain decided to take a two-year break. Thus the country-pop singer, now a global superstar, waited five years before releasing her third collaboration with her husband in 2002—*Up!* Reconnecting with her Canadian roots, she chose Hamilton as the launching point for a worldwide tour, and eventually played the halftime show of the Grey Cup as well. After the success of the European remixes for *Come On Over*, Twain decided to release *Up!* as a double album, with three different 'remix' discs available—a red 'pop' disc, a green 'country' disc, and a blue 'Indian' disc, the latter recorded in Mumbai, India. In North American markets the red 'pop' mix was paired with the green 'country' mix; in international markets, it was paired with the blue 'Indian'—once again speaking to the greater interest in country music in North America than elsewhere. *Up!* debuted at Number 1 on the pop charts, and sold over 874,000 copies in its first week of release. The album's pop mix also made the Top 5 in Germany, France, Australia, and Britain.

Céline Dion

Céline Dion was the youngest of 14 children, most of whom have worked in show business at some point during their lives. Born in 1968 in Charlemagne, Quebec, a mostly francophone town just minutes from Montreal, Dion began singing professionally at only seven years of age, performing Ginette Reno songs at her parents' restaurant a couple of nights each week. Recognizing her daughter's extraordinary talent, based on the often rousing applause the young singer received from diners, Dion's mother composed 'Ce n'était qu'un reve' as a showcase for the young singer; she sent a recording to René Angélil, who was then Ginette Reno's manager, a few weeks later. Impressed with the tape, Angélil hired francophone lyricist Eddy Marnay to compose 'La Voix du Bon Dieu' for Dion, and he supervised Dion's recording of the single before eventually agreeing to manage her.

It didn't take long for Dion and Angélil to garner a sizable following both in Quebec and abroad. Almost as soon as she dropped out of high school in 1983 at the age of 15, Dion embarked on a cross-Quebec recital tour; that same year Dion's recording of 'D'amour ou d'amitié' sold more than 500,000 copies in France alone. During the same time Dion won the Musicians' Prize and a Gold Medal for her performance of 'Tellement j'ai d'amour pour toi' at the Tokyo Song Festival in Japan, and she represented Canada at the MIDEM (International Music Market) in Cannes, France. She also secured a spot on CBC-TV's *Les Beaux Dimanches*, a showcase for francophone singers working in Quebec that aired in the spring of 1983, and later in the year Dion won several Félix awards, given by l'Association québécoise de l'industrie du disque, du spectacle et de la vidéo (ADISQ) —including for Best Female Performer and for Discovery of the Year (she would eventually win 15 Félix awards before 1990).

Dion quickly tired of the 'good-girl' image she and Angélil had crafted, however. In 1986, when Dion turned 18, she disappeared from public for roughly 18 months. Once she reappeared, now sporting short hair and tight sequined dresses, she began to sing more obviously danceable songs, though with the same Top 40 approach. The strategy paid off. In 1987, Dion won the coveted Eurovision prize for 'Ne partez pas sans mois', and the singer's recording of the song subsequently sold more than 200,000 copies in just two days across the continent. Securing a deal with CBS (Sony) in 1989, Dion recorded her first English record, *Unison*, later that same year. Produced by David Foster in Los Angeles, Chris Neal in London, and Andy Goldmark in New York, *Unison* sold more than 100,000 copies in Canada and produced the Number 4 hit 'Where Does My Heart Beat' (1989). Winning the Juno for Best Female Performer in 1991, Dion generated a slight controversy when she refused a Félix award for Best Anglophone Artist that same year.

In 1992, Dion broke through as an international pop superstar. That year alone her second English-language album, *Céline* (1992), sold more than two million copies worldwide and gained double-platinum certification in Canada and platinum certification in the United States. Touring Spain, Italy, Britain, New Zealand, Australia, and Japan in support of the album, Dion finished the year with an Academy Award for Best Original Song for 'Beauty and the Beast' (1992), which figured prominently in the Disney film of the same name. Performing for the likes of Prince Charles and President Bill Clinton—at the latter's inaugural party—Dion hosted the Junos early in 1993, winning awards in both French- and English-language categories. That same year her third English-language release, *Colour of My Love* (1993), sold over seven million units. The album's best-known single, 'The Power of Love', another David Foster production, topped the charts in Canada and in the United States and reached Number 4 in England.

True to her francophone roots, and despite all her successes in the anglophone market, Dion continued to record in French throughout the 1990s. In fact, her 1995 French-language album *D'Eux* remains the best-selling French-language album in history; and *Céline Dion à l'Olympia* (1994) made the singer the best-selling French singer around the world.

Sarah McLachlan

Even if she hadn't established Lilith Fair, Sarah McLachlan (b. 1968) would still rank alongside Alanis Morissette, Shania Twain, and Céline Dion as one of the most popular singers and songwriters in the world in the mid- and late 1990s. Raised by her adoptive parents in Halifax, the pop balladeer was already fronting a rock band—October Game—when she was 17 years old . After the group's debut concert, opening for Moev at Dalhousie University, McLachlan caught the ear of band member Mark Jowett, who offered McLachlan a recording contract with the Vancouver-based Nettwerk label despite the fact that she had not yet written a single song. McLachlan accepted, though her parents prevailed upon her to complete the two remaining years for her degree at the Nova Scotia College of Art and Design before moving to Vancouver.

By 1988, McLachlan had released her first record for Nettwerk—*Touch* (1988). Produced by Greg Reely, the album, which spawned the popular single 'Vox', was a moderate seller at first, failing to chart. After a national tour opening for Vancouver's Grapes of Wrath, who were then riding a groundswell of popularity after MuchMusic slotted their video of 'You May Be Right' into heavy rotation, *Touch* went on to sell more than 150,000 copies in Canada, over 500,000 in the United States, and a combined 1.1 million worldwide, earning gold certification in America and platinum certification in Canada.

Returning to the studio in 1990, this time with producer Pierre Marchand, McLachlan produced *Solace* (1991). Basically her breakthrough album in Canada, *Solace* included the hit singles 'The Path of Thorns (Terms)', 'Drawn To the Rhythm', and 'Into the Fire', the videos of the latter two songs also making heavy rotation on MuchMusic. *Solace* sold more than 200,000 copies in Canada, over 700,000 in the US, and a total 1.2 million copies worldwide, gaining another gold certification in America, a double-platinum certification at home, and the status of 'household name' in her native country. For all her successes up to this point in her career, however, *Fumbling Towards Ecstasy* (1993), another Marchand–McLachlan collaboration, secured McLachlan's reputation. The album, which included a number of hit songs and videos—including 'Possession', 'Hold On', and 'Good Enough'—has sold more than 500,000 copies in Canada, three million in the US, and five million worldwide, and has achieved triple-platinum certification in America and, in Canada, quintuple-platinum certification.

McLachlan released her best-selling record to date, *Surfacing*, in 1997—the same year she established Lilith Fair. *Surfacing*, again produced by Pierre Marchand, far eclipsed the already high expectations for it within its first year of release. The album sold more than one million copies in Canada, eight million copies in the United States, and a combined 11 million copies worldwide; it received eight-times platinum certification in America and a coveted diamond certification in Canada; and it earned McLachlan two Grammy awards and four Junos. *Surfacing* also spun off five Top 40 singles—including 'Building a Mystery', 'Sweet Surrender', 'Adia', 'I Love You', and 'Angel'—the latter written in memory of the Smashing Pumpkins' touring keyboardist Jonathan Melvoin, who died of a fatal overdose (controversy surrounding

Sarah McLachlan is one of the most celebrated Canadian pop vocalists in history, having sold over 26 million records worldwide. Nettwerk Music Group. Photo by Kharen Hill.

Pumpkins' drummer Jimmy Chamberlain's role in Melvoin's death, and his own heroin problem, prompted Chamberlain's dismissal from the band).

Marrying her long-time drummer, Ashwin Sood, in February 1997, McLachlan slowly withdrew from recording. For the next six years, from 1997 to 2003, she often performed at various benefits—such as the Neil Young-hosted Bridge School Benefit concert in California in 1997—and on various singles for movie sound-tracks (i.e., 'When She Loved Me' from *Toy Story 2*). McLachlan remains one of the most celebrated Canadian pop vocalists in history, having by now sold over 26 million records worldwide.

k.d. lang

k.d. lang (b. 1961) has always occupied a marginal position in the conservative world of country music. Raised in an isolated town in rural Alberta, lang listened to classical and rock music as a young girl, discovering country music somewhat later, when she played a Patsy Cline-type character in a college play. She began her career in 1982 as a Cline imitator, going so far as to christen her band the Re-clines. During the early 1980s she released two albums on the Edmonton-based independent label, Bumstead Records. But in 1987, when Sire Records (former label of Patti Smith and the Ramones) released her *Angel with a Lariat*, which got airplay on college and progressive country stations, lang came to the attention of a broader audience. Her biggest

Listening To k.d. lang's 'Nowhere To Stand' (1989)

'Nowhere To Stand', from the 1989 album *Absolute Torch and Twang* (1989), is a traditional song in musical terms, with a series of four-line verses and a repeated chorus, all in triple metre. In fact, apart from lang's public image, the only thing that marks this as an alternative country song is the content of the lyrics, which are an indictment of the 'traditional' practice of child abuse. The song begins quietly with lang's country-tinged alto voice, accompanied by acoustic guitar. The message of the song is not explicit in the first two verses, the second of which is accompanied by a solo fiddle:

As things start to surface, tears come on down
Scars of a childhood in a small town
The hurt she pushed inward, starting to show
Now she'll do some talkin', but he'll never know

Tables have turned now, with a child of her own
But she's blind to the difference, what's taught is what's known
Numbed by reaction, and stripped of the trust
A young heart is broken, not aware that it's just

The intensity of lang's performance builds through the second verse, but only in the chorus—which enters suddenly, a measure early—do we become aware that this is not the typical lovelorn country song and that something hidden, and deadly serious, is being revealed to us:

A family tradition, the strength of this land
Where what's right and wrong is the back of a hand
Turns girls into women, and a boy to a man
The rights of the children have nowhere to stand.

The characterization of child abuse as a '*family tradition, the strength of this land*'—in which moral values and gender identity are taught with '*the back of a hand*'—drives lang's message home without resorting to explicit descriptions of violence. The verse that follows sketches the psychological legacy of domestic violence as a deeply buried memory, '*like a seed that's been planted and won't be denied*', and the recording reaches its emotional peak in the second, final chorus. Here, lang's juxtaposition of traditional Anglo-American song form and country music sensibility with a lyric that in essence questions the sanctity of the family—used by politicians and cultural commentators as the ultimate symbol of traditional values—creates a tender but powerful critique of North American culture.

break came that same year, when Roy Orbison, the country and rockabilly legend, sought her for a re-recording of his old hit, 'Crying', as a duet. This earned her the first of four Grammys, for Best Country Collaboration, and later that year she appeared on Orbison's critically acclaimed television special, *Roy Orbison and Friends*, as a backup singer along with Bonnie Raitt and Jennifer Warnes. In later years lang would team up for other collaborative recordings, with crooner Tony Bennett and with her childhood idol, Anne Murray.

Her subsequent albums—*Shadowland* (1988) and *Absolute Torch and Twang* (1989)—moved towards a more traditional honky-tonk sound, producing lang's first appearances on the country Top 40 chart, and a Grammy for Best Female Country Vocal Performance. Even at that stage, however, lang never sat quite right with the Nashville establishment, who found her campy outfits (rhinestone suits and cat-eye glasses) and somewhat androgynous image unsettling.

A scandal over lang's appearance in a commercial for the 'Meat Stinks' campaign of the People for Ethical Treatment of Animals led stations in the cattle-producing areas of the US Midwest and in the prairie regions of Canada (especially Alberta) to boycott her records and generated an impressive volume of hate mail. In 1992 lang officially announced her homosexuality—a move that, rather than hurting her career, led to lang being christened an 'icon of lesbian chic' (*New York* magazine). During the 1990s lang moved in the direction of adult contemporary pop music, becoming

k.d. lang. Courtesy BMI Archives.

an 'alternative' star in that category as well. *Ingenue*, a 1992 album that owed little to country music, sold over a million copies in the United States and over two million in Canada. A single from *Ingenue*, 'Constant Craving', reached the pop Top 40 and won the Grammy award for Best Female Pop Vocal Performance. Although she was not able to repeat this commercial success, lang continued throughout the 1990s to maintain a dedicated following.

Discussion Questions

1. Does the term 'alternative' still have relevance for the rock tradition today? In musical terms, what does 'alternative' currently mean?

2. Alanis Morissette was the best-selling female musician of the 1990s. What in particular about her music resonated with listeners at the time? Does the record *Jagged Little Pill* sound dated today? Why or why not?

3. What do you think accounts for the Tragically Hip's famous ambivalence towards the moniker 'Canada's band'? Is there something distinctly Canadian about their music? Though nobody can say for certain, why do you think the Hip failed to duplicate their Canadian success in the United States? Did the Hip encourage nationalistic readings of their songs in any way?

4. What about the political and social upheavals of the mid- and late 1990s in Canada might account for the widespread consensus that records by the Tragically Hip can be interpreted in nationalistic terms? Why didn't records by such performers as Alanis Morissette, Sloan, Hayden, or Our Lady Peace garner similarly nationalistic interpretations?

5. What is the legacy of rap on today's rock tradition? How have groups like Beck or the Eels interpellated stylistic characteristics of rap into the rock genre? Conversely, how did groups like Run-D.M.C. and the Beastie Boys interpellate stylistic characteristics of rock into the rap genre?

6. Is there something distinctly Canadian about the records made by k.d. lang, Sarah McLachlan, and Céline Dion during the late 1990s? What, in your opinion, accounts for their global success?

Chapter Nine

What Just Happened?
Rock in the 2000s

Rock obviously—and utterly—changed in the 2000s. When the cover of the January 2000 edition of *Rolling Stone* featured the Backstreet Boys with their pants pulled down around their ankles, as the winner of the magazine's annual readers' poll Artists of the Year award, it seemed to many that the rock tradition had clearly entered one of its recurring fallow periods, if it had not entered a terminal phase. This seemed especially true given the tiny notice afforded to the passing of Rick Danko on the cover, who had been the bass player and vocalist for the Band. While nobody could foresee the massive transformations awaiting the genre later in the decade, when the effects of Napster, p2p file-sharing, and the iPod had become apparent in the closure of flagship record stores like Tower Records in Boston and Sam The Record Man in Toronto, it was already clear that the genre was transforming back from an album- to a singles-oriented genre. Bubblegum pop sung by boy bands and girl singers crammed the airwaves, as multi-million-selling Canadian pop-punk performers like Avril Lavigne, SUM 41, and A Simple Plan competed with the likes of 'N Sync, the Backstreet Boys, Britney Spears, and Christina Aguilera for chart dominance.

The first half of the decade also saw Céline Dion return from her brief hiatus from performing and recording. The Québécois singer enjoyed yet another massive world-wide success with the release of her *A New Day Has Come* LP, in March 2002. The record featured the single 'A New Day Has Come'—co-written by Aldo Nova and University of Western Ontario graduate Stephan Moccio—and topped the United World Chart for a full week and the American Hot Adult Contemporary Tracks chart for more than 21 weeks, breaking the previous record set by Phil Collins in 1999 with

'You'll Be in My Heart'. The single would go on to place in the Top 30 in 26 countries, charting in Argentina (Number 27), Australia (Number 19), Belgium (Number 2), Brazil (Number 18), Canada (Number 1), Denmark (Number 1), Holland (Number 19), Finland (Number 17), France (Number 14), Germany (Number 6), Greece (Number 8), Hong Kong (Number 1), Hungary (Number 4), Ireland (Number 10), Italy (Number 10), Japan (Number 1), New Zealand (Number 20), Norway (Number 2), Poland (Number 1), Portugal (Number 2), Spain (Number 12), Sweden (Number 3), Switzerland (Number 2), Taiwan (Number 1), the UK (Number 7), and the US (Number 1).

Only two years before Dion topped the charts around the world, Vancouver native Nelly Furtado did the same with two singles from her debut album, *Whoa Nelly!* (2000)—'Turn Off the Light', which reached Number 3 on the United World Chart, and 'I'm Like a Bird', which reached Number 7 (both singles topped the charts in Canada, and made the Top 10 in the US, Britain, Poland, Australia, Switzerland, and New Zealand). (In 2007, combining forces with producer Timbaland and 'N Sync alumnus Justin Timberlake, Furtado improved on those numbers, reaching Number 3 on the United World Chart with 'Give It To Me'). At the same time, 'prairie soul' bands like Nickelback and the Corb Lund Band enjoyed success with their hard rock and country 'post-grunge' fusions; Nickelback's 'How You Remind Me' reached Number 4 in the US, Number 4 in Britain, and Number 1 in Canada in 2001.

Indeed, for however much critics bemoaned the death of rock in the early 2000s, not to mention the impending demise of the market-oriented dissemination of popular music in general given the pernicious influence of the Internet and peer-to-peer (p2p) file-sharing, rock music continues to sell well. If anything, the Internet rejuvenated the genre's margins, pushing rock into a transitional phase from which it has yet to emerge. By the close of the twentieth century, annual sales of recorded music totalled $14 billion in the United States and $40 billion worldwide, a figure that would drop by almost 30 per cent by 2003. As we have charted the growth of the marketplace for recorded music throughout this book, it has become increasingly difficult to sustain the distinction we initially drew between the 'mainstream' of rock music and its margins. At the outset we were able to conflate two quite different concepts. On the one hand, a musical mainstream and margins, involving cultural, national, regional, and stylistic differences, could be clearly distinguished, but these differences have grown more and more blurry over time. Indeed, the nature of rock, from its inception as rock 'n' roll in the years immediately following World War II, has been to fuse, combine, mix, and borrow from other musical traditions. On the other hand, the market for popular music was seen to have an economic and institutional centre and periphery. In the early twentieth century these two dichotomies fit together rather neatly, for the mainstream of popular music coincided to a great degree with the central institutions of the music business (publishing firms, phonograph companies, and somewhat later, radio networks). But by the end of the century, the two dichotomies, as well as the correlation between them, had broken down almost completely.

What started out as marginal genres—R&B, country and western, urban folk music, soul music, disco, heavy metal, rap, alternative rock, and, ultimately, even rock 'n' roll itself—came in turn to occupy a mainstream or central position, right alongside (and frequently displacing) 'adult contemporary' music more directly descended from the Tin Pan Alley tradition. And this process was mirrored by the economic evolution of the music business. Independent record labels, which once operated on the fringes of the industry, are today more and more closely tied in with (and sometimes even invented by) the major record companies, though the Internet has allowed some indie bands to remain almost entirely independent. At the dawn of the rock 'n' roll era, New York City and Los Angeles, and Toronto and Montreal in Canada, were unquestionably the geographical centres of the music industry. Fifty years later, however, the spread of digital technology seems to be completing a process of total decentralization, as anybody with a computer, anywhere, can produce and market his or her own recordings.

Moreover, the rise of international pop superstars such as Julio Iglesias, Ricky Martin, Céline Dion, Nelly Furtado, and Shakira and the emergence of world music as a distinct category with its own Juno category suggest that the centre–periphery concept must now be recast in truly global terms. That said, not every periphery genre achieves mainstream status; the world music craze, for instance, which was so popular as the year 2000 approached, has by now receded from the Top 40. Although the United States remains the largest market for recorded music in the world, its pre-eminence as the nexus of the music industry is no longer indisputable. In the early twenty-first century five major conglomerates are responsible for as much as 90 per cent of the sales of music worldwide, and only one of these corporations is officially headquartered in the US. With the unification of the European market and ongoing changes in Asia (including the rise of India and China as major centres for the production and consumption of popular music), it seems likely that the US will remain an important, even indispensable, part of the global music system, but not its dominant centre, and a number of Canadian indie bands have stepped in to fill the void this reshaping of the market's geographical boundaries has created.

In this chapter, we examine the margins of the rock genre throughout the 2000s, charting the rise and fall of world music, the seemingly continuous fracturing of the electronica genre, the effects on rock of widespread digitalization and the rise of p2p file-sharing sites on the Internet, and the rise from the margins of the Top 40 to global prominence of Canadian indie and 'post-rock'. Indeed, Leslie Feist's meteoric rise from being a darling of the indie scene in Canada, working with bands like Broken Social Scene and Peaches, to world fame as a pop chanteuse in her own right seems apt. Feist represents the constant movement from margin to core that has constantly reinvigorated the rock tradition since Elvis Presley moved from Sun Records to RCA-Victor in the mid-1950s, just as she provides a Canadian perspective on the rock genre in the 2000s. As Brendan Canning wrote in the March 2005 Canadian edition of *Time* magazine:

> The international music community has spoken: Canada is now the hotbed of indie rock. The latest export, the Arcade Fire, has taken things to an all-time indie high. Before that there were other bands at the forefront, like my own,

Broken Social Scene. And the Dears, Metric, Stars, the New Pornographers, Feist, the Hidden Cameras, the Stills, Do Make Say Think. In other words, this is a great time to be in an indie band, especially a Canadian one.

In many respects, this book has been about how such a state of affairs came to be, that is, it is an explanation of how Canada went from being a small niche market for modest sales of rock records to, in the words of one of its denizens, 'the hotbed' of the genre in the early twenty-first century.

▌The Rise and Fall of World Music

As the year 2000 approached, narratives of economic and cultural globalization became widespread, contributing to a general sense that the nation-state, once the bedrock of social and economic life, was dissipating into the mists of history, leaving behind centuries of often brutal conflict. With the fall of the Berlin Wall in 1989 and the dissolution of the Soviet Union two years later, some scholars began to openly discuss the possibility of a new global order founded on liberal-democratic capitalism. Francis Fukuyama's *The End of History* (1992) famously heralded the emergence of this global order:

> What we may be witnessing is not just the end of the Cold War, or the passing of a particular period of post-war history, but the end of history as such: that is, the end point of mankind's ideological evolution and the universalization of Western liberal democracy as the final form of human government. (Fukuyama, 1992)

As the world was conceptually transformed from a collection of nationalities into a 'global village', as University of Toronto professor Marshall McLuhan prophesied back in the mid-1950s, some in the rock world self-consciously 'globalized' their music in response. Ex-Police front man Sting, for instance, followed the leads of Paul Simon and Peter Gabriel and undertook collaborations with a number of artists from around the world beginning in 1998. Most notably, Sting combined forces with the Algerian Rai singer Cheb Mami to create the Top 40 hit song 'Desert Rose' (1999). Peaking at Number 6 in Canada, 'Desert Rose' benefited greatly from a prominent placement on television commercials for the Jaguar S-Type, which aired throughout 2000 and 2001. The placement was brokered in the wake of ambient-electronica superstar Moby's decision to license songs from *Play* (1999) for use in commercials and on film soundtracks when he could not get Top 40 airplay—a decision that generated more than 1,000 licences in a roughly 24-month span, from 1999 to 2001, prompting more than one critic to call advertisements, movies, and TV the Top 40 of the twenty-first century. In case anyone missed his point, Sting titled his world music LP *Brand New Day* (1999)—besides Cheb Mami, the album also featured contributions from musicians such as Manu Katché (percussion), Mino Cinelu (percussion), Sté (vocal), and Ettarmi Mustapha (darbouka), among others.

Of course, globalization was not without its opponents. In 2000 Canadian journalist Naomi Klein published her dark chronicle of the exploitive underside of globalization, *No Logo: Taking Aim at the Brand Name Bullies*, which implicated numerous Western brands in the rise of child labour and sweatshops around the world, and gave voice to an emerging anti-globalization and anti-corporate movement within North America. Numerous socially conscious pop musicians began to cite the book in interviews, but possibly the most vocal of her supporters was Radiohead's Thom Yorke, who most recently mentioned the book in an interview with David Byrne in the January 2008 issue of *Wired Magazine*. In one chapter of *No Logo*, Klein studied another popular anti-globalization/anti-corporate forum produced in Canada, *Adbusters* magazine, published by Kalle Lasn out of Vancouver. The magazine, with its often hilarious 'subvertisements', was popular among the over 40,000 protestors who assembled in Seattle outside the World Trade Organization Ministerial Conference on 30 November 1999. The WTO meeting was quickly dwarfed by the 'Battle of Seattle'—an at times violent guerrilla confrontation between police and protestors that culminated in the arrest of over 600 protestors in one day and clearly signalled to the world the growing uncertainty about, and opposition to, the emerging global order.

Not surprisingly, then, by the year 2000, the world music craze had already begun to recede, as opposition to globalization and the culture of multinationalism became increasingly widespread throughout youth culture. Only compounding matters were the 9/11 terrorist attacks on New York City and Washington, DC, in 2001; terror attacks in Spain and England in the ensuing years; the American invasions and occupations of Afghanistan and Iraq in response to 9/11; and the strengthening of border security across North America and abroad. These troubling events reinserted national citizenship, and the nation-state, as a basis of modern identity. As happened in the wake of the violent traumas of the late 1960s and early 1970s, a back-to-basics repudiation of experimentalism once more seized the North American Top 40. John Mayer updated the singer-songwriter and soft rock tradition with his *No Room For Squares*; Alicia Keys returned the R&B and soul style of the late 1960s and early 1970s to the Top 40 with her *Songs in A Minor*; bands such as the Strokes channelled mid-1970s punk rock acts like the Ramones with their albums *Is This It?* and *Room On Fire*; and, more recently, singers such as Amy Winehouse and The Pipettes channelled the girl-group magic of 'teen tycoon' Phil Spector, now charged with murder, and Motown impressario Berry Gordy Jr with records like *Back To Black* and *The Pipettes*. Even Sting, once the leader of the world music movement in rock, seemed to be in retreat by the year 2006—releasing an entire album of sixteenth-century English lute music for the Deutsche Grammophon label entitled simply *Labour of Love*.

The Meaning(s) of 'World'

Throughout the last two decades of the twentieth century the boundary between 'mainstream' and 'marginal' music became fuzzier, and the twin pressures to expand the global market for popular music and to create new 'alternative' genres and audiences within the existing popular music market grew stronger. One of the more interesting results of these processes was the emergence of the category called 'world music'. The title was first used in the late 1980s by independent record label owners and concert promoters, and it entered the popular music marketplace as a replacement for older classifications such as 'traditional music', 'international music', and 'ethnic music'. 'World music' records were traditionally positioned at the very back of record stores, in bins containing low-turnover items such as Irish folksong collections, Scottish bagpipe samplers, German polka records, records by tourist bands from the Caribbean and Hawaii, and perhaps a few field recordings of so-called 'primitive' musics from Africa, Native North America, or Asia. These records were generally marketed to immigrants hungry for a taste of home, cross-cultural music scholars and ethnomusicologists, and a handful of other aficionados of non-Top 40 music.

Of course, while transnational entertainment corporations became increasingly successful at marketing records of Western popular music around the globe during the 1980s and 1990s, most of the world's music continued to have little, if any, direct influence on the North American marketplace. That said, we can point to some examples of international influence on the pop mainstream before the 1980s—Cuban rumba, Hawaiian guitar, and Mexican marimba records of the 1920s and 1930s; Indian classical musician Ravi Shankar's album, *Live at the Monterey Pop Festival*, which peaked at Number 43 on the *Billboard* Top 100 albums chart in 1967; 'Grazing in the Grass' (1968), by South African jazz musician Hugh Masekela, which topped the charts across North America in 1968; and 'Soul Makossa' (1973), by the Cameroon pop musician Manu Dibango, which broke the Top 40 in Canada and the US in 1973, setting what most historians agree was a major precedent for the widespread emergence of disco only a few years later. But these 'world' influences were typically filtered through the sensibilities of Western musicians and channelled by the strategies of North American and European record companies and publishing firms.

A quintessential example of the typically unidirectional flow of musical influence between 'the West' and 'the Rest' is the Tokens' rock 'n' roll hit 'The Lion Sleeps Tonight' (1961). The record, which topped the pop charts both in Canada and in the US, was an adaptation of a hit single by the urban folk group the Weavers, entitled 'Wimoweh' (1952), which made Number 14 in the US in 1952. The Weavers' recording, however, was itself an adaptation of a 1939 South African record by a vocal group comprised of Zulu mine workers, called Solomon Linda and the Evening Birds. By the time the Evening Birds' song reached the ears of North Americans, then, it had already undergone several transformations—including the insertion of a Top 40 melodic hook and English lyrics and the careful excision of all royalty rights pertaining to the song's original composers and performers.

This sort of 'rip-off'—a basic operating principle for many years in the rock world—reflected global imbalances of power first created by Western colonialism. When it seemed commercially viable, music from Third World countries and performers was expropriated, often without proper credit or payment, and at the same time music from North America found its way to remote corners of the globe. The film *Good Morning Vietnam* (1987), about Air Force DJ Adrian Cronauer (played by

Robin Williams), who introduces rock 'n' roll to the playlist of the armed forces radio station in Saigon against the orders of his superiors, depicts this imbalance beautifully. In one poignant scene, after Cronauer has gone to great lengths to date a young Vietnamese woman, she tells him that she knows some American music, and proceeds to sing a halting version of Peter, Paul, and Mary's 'Puff the Magic Dragon'. And then she tells him they cannot see each other again—the cultural (and musical) divide was too great. And all the power and control, so it seemed, had been in the hands of the imperial West. This would soon begin to change, at least to an extent.

So-called 'world fusion' or 'world beat' projects, such as Paul Simon's pioneering albums *Graceland* and *The Rhythm of the Saints*, the annual WOMAD (World Music and Dance) festival initiated by Peter Gabriel in 1982, and various records by Ry Cooder, David Byrne, and Brian Eno, among others, helped to redress the imbalance of power. But their Western patrons—i.e., the likes of Simon, Gabriel, Byrne, Cooder, and Eno—nonetheless received most of the credit for the success of their records, making them a kind of new rocker, one whose musical work suddenly had as much to do with their ability to discover interesting and entertaining musics from around the world and introducing these to the Western rock world. Such an imbalance of cultural and economic power between 'the West' and 'the Rest' haunts cross-cultural collaborations between rock and world musicians to this day.

The 1980s and 1990s saw musicians from Africa, South Asia, the Near East, Eastern Europe, and Latin America tour North America with increasing frequency. Some of these groups slowly, if rarely, found their way onto North American pop charts. The first indication that musicians from the Third World might gain increased access to the North American pop market was the release in 1982 of the album *Juju Music*, by a Nigerian group called the African Beats, led by the guitarist King Sunny Adé. Featuring an infectious brand of urban African dance music that blended electric guitars, Christian church hymns, and Afro-Caribbean rhythms with the pulsating sound of the Yoruban 'talking drum', *Juju Music* sold over 100,000 copies and rose to Number 111 on *Billboard*'s album chart in the United States. The African Beats' next album, *Synchro System*, reached Number 91. However, Island Records soon dropped the group—the money they made was obviously not enough to justify marketing and promotion costs—and King Sunny Adé and the African Beats never again graced the pop charts in North America.

In an article published in 1982 in the *Village Voice* entitled 'Are You Ready for Juju?', a clear play on Neil Young's iconic country-rock salvo 'Are You Ready for the Country?' from his *Harvest* (1973) LP, popular music critic Greg Tate identified King Sunny Adé as a potential replacement for Bob Marley, the Jamaican reggae superstar who had recently died. Tate's thinking was, on first gloss, perfectly logical, and it undoubtedly reflected the strategic thinking of Island Records when they agreed to release Adé's albums in the West. In fact, Adé might well have had a shot at equalling Marley's success, but the fact that he sang in Yoruban—a language spoken by precious few North American listeners—rather than Marley's richly spiced patois version of Jamaican English likely doomed Adé to failure from the beginning. Aside from songs aimed at the francophone market in Quebec, few Top 40 hits in North America have featured lyrics in languages other than English. This can be an insurmountable barrier for many international musicians, although this may yet change as Canada and the United States continue to diversify and Canada's official multiculturalism continues to allow funding of a plethora of differently texted rock songs. Despite the language barrier, Adé did succeed in establishing a market for so-called Afro-pop music in the West, opening the door for many of the African popular musicians who followed him, such as Youssou N'dour (Senegal), Salif Keita (Mali), Thomas Mapfumo (Zimbabwe), and Ali Farka Toure (see below).

By 1990, when the heading 'world music' first appeared above a North American record chart, it was as a subcategory of the broader heading 'adult alternative albums'. Interestingly, this latter category also included new age music, a genre of mostly instrumental music designed to facilitate contemplative and mystical moods and sometimes loosely linked with the religious and healing practices of Amerindian, African, and Asian cultures. The larger category 'adult alternative albums' suggests an effort on the industry's part to identify forms of alternative music that would appeal to an affluent baby-boomer audience, rather than to the younger audience attracted to records by rock bands such as Nirvana. Since 1991, in fact, the National Academy of Recording Arts and Sciences (NARAS) has limited its Grammy awards for world music, new age, folk, Latin, reggae, blues, polka, and various other alternative genres to albums only, presumably on the assumption that such genres are unlikely to generate hit singles. And, in this respect, it is interesting to note that 'world music' sections in most record stores usually do not include Latin dance music (salsa) or reggae—two genres that typically sell enough records to justify their own discrete territories both on the pop charts and in record stores.

What, then, is 'world' music? In a strictly musical sense, it is a pseudo-genre, taking into its sweep styles as diverse as African urban pop (*juju*), Pakistani dance club music (*bhangara*), Australian Aboriginal rock music (the band Yothu Yindi), and even the Bulgarian State Radio and Television Female Vocal Choir, whose 1987 release, *Le Mystere des Voix Bulgares* ('The Mystery of the Bulgarian Voices') reached Number 165 in North America in 1988. Best-selling albums on *Billboard*'s world music chart have featured the Celtic group Clannad (whose popularity was boosted in North America by their appearance in the soundtrack for a Volkswagen advertisement, as well as a 'Celtic craze' that swept the culture there throughout the mid-1990s), Spanish flamenco music (played by the Gypsy Kings, for instance, once a lowly hotel band from France), Tibetan Buddhist chant (presented by Mickey Hart, drummer for the Grateful Dead), and diverse collaborations between American and English rock stars and musicians from Africa, Latin America, and South Asia. The overlap among various types of 'adult alternative' music—including new age, world music, techno, and certain forms of European sacred music—is reflected in the commercial success of albums like *Vision* (1994), a mélange of 'twelfth-century chant, world beat rhythms, and electronic soundscapes', as one press release put it (it's hard to imagine better confirmation of the maxim that 'the past is another country'). Moreover, the attraction of world music for its contemporary North American audience is also bound up with stereotyped images of the 'exotic', whether discovered on imaginary pilgrimages to Africa and the Himalayas or in time travel back to the monastic Christianity of medieval Europe. (Of course, there are limits to the degree of musical 'exoticism' most listeners are willing to tolerate, which may explain the almost total absence on 'world' charts of music from East Asia, which many North American listeners find particularly challenging.)

We are all familiar with the assertion that music is a universal language, by which people usually mean to suggest that music can transcend the boundaries separating diverse nations, cultures, or languages (indeed, isn't this the sort of transcendence many present-day scholars of rock 'n' roll argue the genre either did or didn't deliver?). This statement, however comforting, does not stand up to close scrutiny—even within North American culture, one person's music may be another person's noise. Nonetheless, the music industry has wasted no time in chaining the rhetoric of musical universalism to the profit motive, as in this mid-1990s advertisement for the E-mu Proteus/3 World, a digital device programmed with hundreds of samples of world music:

> Enrich Your Music with a Global Texture. As borders dissolve, traditions are shared. And this sharing of cultures is most powerful in the richness of music. . . . E-mu has gathered these sounds and more—192 in all. Use them to emulate traditional world instruments or as raw material for creating one-of-a-kind synthesized sounds of your own. (Théberge, 1997: 201)

With its ability to flow over the boundaries of society and the borders of nations, music holds open the possibility that we may glimpse something familiar and sympathetic in people strange to us—that the inequalities of the world in which we live may, if only for a moment, be suspended, or even undermined, in the act of making or listening to music. Still, the suggestion that installing a digital device in your home studio in order to emulate the 'gathered sounds' of faraway people has anything to do

Listening To Two World Music Collaborations: Ali Farka Toure and Nusrat Fateh Ali Khan

By the 1990s, collaborations between Western and 'world' musicians had become more common, spurred by folk and alternative music fans' search for a broader range of musical experiences and by the globalization of the music industry. Two particularly interesting examples of this sort of transnational collaboration are the album *Talking Timbuktu*, which won the Grammy award for Best World Music Recording in 1994, and a sampler album inspired by the film *Dead Man Walking*, which reached Number 61 on the album charts in 1996.

Talking Timbuktu was produced by the singer and guitarist Ry Cooder (b. 1947 in Los Angeles), whose career as a session musician and bandleader had already encompassed a wide array of styles, including blues, reggae, Tex-Mex music, urban folk, Hawaiian guitar music, Dixieland jazz, and gospel. The sound and sensibility of *Talking Timbuktu* are derived from the music of Ali Farka Toure (b. 1950), a guitarist and traditional praise singer (*griot*) from the West African nation of Mali.

Encountering a track like 'Diaraby', an American listener is likely to be struck by the music's close affinities with the blues. This is no accident. To begin with, the blues styles of the US South were strongly influenced by the traditions of African slaves, many of whom came precisely from the Sahel region of West Africa, homeland of Ali Farka Toure's people, the Bambara. The high-pitched, almost wailing sound of Toure's singing, the percussive, ostinato-driven guitar patterns, and the use of song as a medium for social and personal commentary represent an evolution of centuries-old links between the West African *griot* tradition and the blues created by black musicians in America's Deep South. In fact, it turns out that Toure's style was directly influenced by American blues musicians such as John Lee Hooker, whose records he discovered after his career was established in Africa—a case of the diaspora influencing the homeland.

Talking Timbuktu features contributions by the blues guitarist and fiddler, Clarence 'Gatemouth' Brown, and various prominent session musicians. The result, as exemplified by 'Diaraby', sung in the Bambara language, hews close to its African roots, with the American musicians playing in support of Toure. The lyric of the song is itself reminiscent of the bittersweet emotion of some American blues:

What is wrong my love? It is you I love
Your mother has told you not to marry me, because I have nothing.
But I love you.
Your friends have told you not to marry me, because I have nothing.
But I love you.
Your father has told you not to marry me, because I have nothing.
But I love you.
What is wrong my love? It is you I love.
Do not be angry, do not cry, do not be sad because of love.

Both the lyrics and the sound of 'Diaraby' provide additional evidence, if any were needed, of the deep links between African and North American music. This is not music functioning as a universal language, but rather a conversation between two dialects of a complexly unified Afro-Atlantic musical language.

The track 'The Face of Love' is a different sort of collaboration, featuring the lead singer for the Seattle-based alternative rock band Pearl Jam, Eddie Vedder (b. 1966 in Chicago), and the great Pakistani musician, Nusrat Fatah Ali Khan (1948–97), and produced by Ry Cooder. Khan was a leading performer of *qawwali*, a genre of mystical singing practised by Sufi Muslims in Pakistan and India. (Sufism was founded in Iran between the ninth and twelfth centuries; a response to orthodox Islam, Sufism emphasizes the inner kinship between God and human beings, and seeks to bridge the distance between them through the force of love.) *Qawwali* singing is traditionally accompanied by a double-headed drum called the *dholak* (or a *tabla*, used in Indian classical music), and a portable keyboard instrument called the harmonium, which creates a continuous drone under the singing. In traditional settings the lead singer (or *qawwal*) alternates stanzas of traditional poetic texts, sung in unison with a choir, with spectacular and elaborate melodic improvisations in an attempt to arouse his listeners and move them into emotional proximity with the Divine.

During the 1990s Nusrat Fateh Ali Khan became the first *qawwali* artist to command a large international following, owing to his performances at the annual WOMAD festivals curated by the rock star Peter Gabriel and to a series of recordings released on Gabriel's Real World label. Khan began to experiment with non-traditional instruments and to work with musicians outside the *qawwali* tradition, leading some critics

to charge that the music had moved away from its spiritual roots. 'All these albums are experiments', Khan told the interviewer Ken Hunt in 1993. 'There are some people who do not understand at all but just like my voice. I add new lyrics and modern instruments to attract the audience. This has been very successful' (see the web version of *All Music Guide*).

Most North American listeners first heard Khan in the soundtracks to *The Last Temptation of Christ* and *Natural Born Killers*, though without knowing it, since he was part of the overall blend (Khan was reportedly unhappy about being included in the soundtrack for *Natural Born Killers* since, to his mind, it did not reflect the spiritual goals of *qawwali*). The 1996 film *Dead Man Walking*—the story of a nun's attempt to redeem the soul of a convicted murderer on the verge of execution—was the first to foreground Khan's contributions. Many reviews of *Dead Man Walking* stressed the contribution of Khan's voice

Nusrat Fateh Ali Khan and Ensemble. Photo by S.T. Sakata.

to the haunting, spiritual atmosphere of the film. The song 'The Face of Love' is based on a simple melody, sung first by Khan with lyrics in the Urdu language, and then with English lyrics by Pearl Jam's Eddie Vedder:

Jeena kaisa Pyar bins [What is life without love]—
Is Duniya Mein Aaye ho to [Now that you have come to this world]
(2 times)
Ek Duje se pyar karo [Love each other, one another]
Look in the eyes of the face of love
Look in her eyes, oh, there is peace
No, nothing dies within pure light
Only one hour of this pure love
To last a life of thirty years
Only one hour, so come and go

In this case the sound of the music (particularly the drone of the harmonium) and the mysticism of the Sufi poetic text resonate with the transcendental atmosphere of the film—the contemplative mood of a man sentenced to die by lethal injection. The filmmaker does not make an explicit argument for or against the death penalty, and the music, with its subtly shifting textures, embodies the complexity and ambivalence of the film's subject. Although Eddie Vedder could not be expected to possess the formidable vocal improvisatory technique that Khan unleashes

briefly in the middle of this track, he nonetheless manages to blend the timbre of his voice (and his acoustic guitar playing) with the mood and texture of the *qawwali* ensemble. In addition, Vedder's English lyrics do evoke the theme of mystical love so central to *qawwali* singing. Again, this is not an example of music's functioning as a universal language, for most members of the film's North American audience neither understood the words that Khan sang nor possessed any knowledge of the centuries-long history of Sufi mystical traditions. Nonetheless, it could be argued that this is a case where the well-meaning effort of artists to reach across cultural and musical boundaries does produce something like an aesthetic communion, a common purpose embodied in musical texture and poetry, provisional though it might be.

Khan's appearance on the soundtrack of *Dead Man Walking* led to his being signed by the indie label American Recordings, managed by Rick Rubin, formerly the mastermind behind the rappers Run-D.M.C. and the Beastie Boys. The North American music industry's market positioning of world music as yet another variant of alternative music is indicated by that label's roster of artists, which included not only Nusrat Fateh Ali Khan but also the 'death metal' band Slayer, the rap artist Sir Mix-A-Lot, and the country music icon Johnny Cash.

with 'sharing cultures' reveals a critically impoverished vision of cross-cultural communication. There is no denying that music has the potential to traverse the boundaries of culture and language, and thereby add to our understanding of people very different from us. But the ultimate responsibility for interpreting its meanings, and determining its impact, lies with the listener.

'World' As 'Roots': Canadian Definitions

The definition of 'world music' used by most Canadian media is typically much less elusive than elsewhere. Alongside its traditional 'exotic' references, 'world music' typically refers to any music made by, or which obviously derives from, the musical traditions of an indigenous culture, and which, in so doing, references a particular geographic region apart from Vancouver, Toronto, or Montreal. Thus, Inuit throat-singing can occupy space in a Canadian 'world music' bin alongside albums of traditional Métis and Cape Breton fiddle music, prairie 'cowboy' songs, Acadian and francophone folksongs, and traditional Maritime songs and sea shanties, to name only a few examples. This somewhat loose definition of 'world music' often leads to disjunct programming decisions by national broadcasters, so that Canadian pop musicians who work in a clearly regional idiom often share space on radio and television programs devoted to world music with musicians from outside of the country. During the early and mid-1990s, for instance, the Newfoundland folk-Celtic group Great Big Sea, Maritime fiddler Ashley MacIsaac, and Aboriginal singer Susan Aglukark all made appearances on MuchMusic's *ClipTrip* world music program, alongside francophone pop singers such as Mitsou and roots rockers La Bouttaine Souriante—even though all hailed from Canada.

World music was officially acknowledged as a category of Canadian popular music in 1996, when a world music category was established for Juno awards. Takadja, an ensemble comprised of founder, and Quebec City native, Francis Martel, and musicians from as far afield as Montreal, Chicoutimi, Quebec City, Sénégal, and the Ivory Coast, took home the inaugural award in 1996. However, critics complained that the award was a case of the country's pop establishment doing too little too late. By the time the world music category had been established a number of successful Canadian 'world' musicians were already in the midst of long and internationally successful careers. Nonetheless, the mid- and late 1990s saw something like a world music craze emerge in Canada, which arguably peaked when Susan Aglukark topped the pop charts in 1995 with 'O Siem', a song with lyrics in both English and Inuktitut.

Kashtin

Established in 1984 in Quebec and initially playing for Native communities in northern Quebec and along the lower north shore of the St Lawrence River—including a famous appearance at the Innu Nikamu Festival at Malioten Am—Kashtin ('Tornado on the horizon' in the Innu-aimun language) remains the most successful First Nations pop band of the past two decades. Comprised of singer-songwriters Florent Vollant and Claude McKenzie, the duo's debut album, *Kashtin* (1989), recorded at the prodding of Montreal composer and producer Guy Trépanier, sold over 200,000 copies globally and included the three songs that became hits in Quebec—'E Vassivian' (*'mon enfance'*), 'Tpatshimun' (*'Chanson du diable'*), and 'Tshinanu' (*'Nous autres'*). In fact, Kashtin's 'Tshinanu' now serves as something of an Innu-Canadian anthem.

To facilitate crossover appeal, Kashtin typically included some French and English song titles on their albums. On their second release, *Innu* (1991), the duo recorded a song entirely in English, Willie Dunn's 'Son of the Sun'. Aside from these relatively minor attempts to broaden their market, all of Kashtin's songs feature texts composed in the Innu-aimun language. Characterized by 'simple but spirited refrains sung in throaty harmony over vigorous, acoustic guitar rhythms', according to one reviewer (thecanadianencyclopedia.com/Kashtin), Vollant and McKenzie have performed extensively in Quebec and France, and sporadically across the rest of Canada and the US Northeast, since forming in 1984; and the duo have toured with a number of Top 40 acts such as the Gypsy Kings and Daniel Lanois, touring with the latter as far afield as Switzerland and Belgium. By 1994 the band had also begun to make headway into the increasingly lucrative field of television soundtracks, placing songs on the popular shows *Due South* and *Northern Exposure*. Following the release of their third album, *Akua Tuta* (1994), McKenzie and Vollant went their separate ways, though they have reunited for a number of performances.

Susan Aglukark

Susan Aglukark is another example of a Canadian recording artist whose work was once almost reflexively slotted into 'world music' bins and sequences by programmers, but now she sits comfortably on the pop charts next to records by other Top 40 artists. Born in Churchill, Manitoba, in 1967, but moved to the Keewatin Region of Canada's Northwest Territories (since 1999, part of Nunavut) only a short while later, before finally settling in Arviat in 1978, Susan Aglukark did not begin a career as a professional musician. First she worked in Ottawa as a linguist for the Department of Indian and Northern Affairs and with the lobby group, Inuit Tapirisat (Brotherhood) of Canada. In 1990, after Aglukark met a producer from CBC North in Ottawa, she made her professional record debut, appearing on a collection of songs, *Nitjuatiit* (1991), recorded by Arctic artists and released by CBC Records. Having already independently recorded *Dreams For You* in 1990, Aglukark next recorded two more independently produced albums—*Christmas* (1993) and *Arctic Rose* (1994)—before catching the ears of executives at EMI Music Canada, who signed Aglukark to an exclusive recording contract in late 1993. A testament to Aglukark's abilities in the studio, EMI simply re-released *Arctic Rose* (1994) without any alterations, and the album earned Aglukark Junos that year for Best New Solo Artist and Best Aboriginal Canadian Recording.

Far from simply being a singer of pop confectionaries, Aglukark was often outspoken in her songs about the social hardships that Canadian Native peoples face. Aside from traditional love-song narratives, Aglukark's lyrics include accounts of the alcoholism, suicide, and child abuse that trouble many Canadian Aboriginal communities. Aglukark's 'O Siem', from her first full-length recording for EMI, *This Child* (1995), is typical of her music from this time, fusing contemporary melodies, traditional chant, modern lyrics, and narratives describing traditional Inuit culture and

Susan Aglukark's music has helped to give a voice to First Nations issues. Courtesy of EMI Music Canada.

folklore, all the while decrying the racism and prejudice Aglukark experienced as an Aboriginal Canadian:

> *O Siem—We are all family*
> *O Siem—We're all the same*
> *The fires of freedom dance in the burning flame*
>
> *Siem o siyeya—all people rich and poor*
> *Siem o siyeya—those who do and do not know*
> *Siem o siyeya—take the hand of one close by*
> *Siem o siyeya—of those who know because they try*
> *And watch the walls come tumbling down . . .*
>
> *Siem o siyeya—all people of the world*
> *Siem o siyeya—it's time to make the turn*
> *Siem o siyeya—a chance to share your heart*
> *Siem o siyeya—to make a brand new start*
> *And watch the walls come tumbling down*

In 1995, 'O Siem' reached Number 1 on the Canadian Top 40 pop chart, making Aglukark the first Inuk performer to reach the Top 40—let alone to top it!

Since the unprecedented success of 'O Siem', Aglukark has continued to advocate for Canada's Aboriginal peoples through her music (she also served as a spokesperson for the RCMP National Alcohol and Drug Awareness Program, and has worked as an ambassador for the Northwest Territories). In fact, two years after she topped the Top 40 Aglukark appeared alongside Kashtin on Robbie Robertson's historic compilation album, *Music for 'The Native Americans'* (1997), and, in 1999, she released 'Turn of the Century', from the album *Unsung Heroes* (1999), which detailed the elation felt by many in Canada at the creation of the new northern territory of Nunavut. (Officially separated from the Northwest Territories on 1 April 1999, via the Nunavut Act and the Nunavut Land Claims Agreement Act, the creation of Nunavut represents the first large-scale change to the map of Canada since Newfoundland and Labrador joined Confederation in 1949.) Continuing her career into the present decade, Aglukark won another Juno, this time for Best Aboriginal Recording, for her Ben Mink-produced *Big Feeling* (2004) LP. As an indication of her importance as a musician, as a spokesperson for Canada's northern Aboriginal communities, and, more simply, as a Canadian, Aglukark was named an officer of the Order of Canada in 2005.

Electronica at the Turn of the Century

The mid- and late 1990s and early 2000s saw the electronica genre spin off into a seemingly endless array of different subgenres. Marked off by what, from an out-sider's perspective, can seem very much like musical minutia, the differences between the various subgenres of the electronica movement remain crucially important to many listeners and fans, and the titles given to genres remain hotly contested on Internet chat sites. The best we can do here is to trace the emergence and describe the musical characteristics of some of the more important of these subgenres that have emerged during the past 15 years.

By 1999, for instance, 'house' had become 'ambient house' or 'chill out', a kind of 'House music subtracted of its incessant thumping beats and filled with Ambient samples of nature, extraneous noises, vocal snippets and other people's music', according to critic Mark Prendergast. The genre is exemplified in records like KLF's aptly named *Chill Out* (1990) and the Orb's 'Little Fluffy Clouds' (1991) from *Adventures Beyond the Ultraworld* (1991). Other popular house groups include Enigma, who combined samples of Gregorian chant and world music with industrial beats to create a subgenre known as 'spiritual house'; Mixmaster Morris and the Future Sound of London, both of whom approximated an updated version of German synthesizer rock band Tangerine Dream; and the German DJ Sven Vath, who almost single-handedly invented the so-called 'progressive house' genre with his album *Accident in Paradise* (1993).

Following closely on the heels of 'ambient house', both aesthetically and chrono-logically, was 'intelligent dance music (IDM) or 'ambient techno'. Pete Namlook, a classically trained electronic musician from Germany, established the Fax label to promote the genre, believing that IDM—a slowed down, often beatless variation of 'house', which combined its timbres and compositional practices to create something more akin to electronic chamber music—would become the pre-eminent art music idiom of the twenty-first century. Of all the genre's stars, Britain's Richard James, a.k.a. Aphex Twin, is likely the best known. In 1994, the oddly imaged composer, who emulated the 'rural hippie' rather than the 'urban DJ', released *Selected Ambient Works, Vol. 2*, what many critics still rank as one of the top ambient albums of all time, after only Brian Eno's *Music for Airports* (1978) and *Discreet Music* (1975). Recording at home, live to tape, and entirely on analogue hardware, James sought to document the musical musings of a musician in a state of:

> Lucid dreaming. This was me [the album] basically going asleep, dreaming up a track in my studio or in my imaginary studio with imaginary equipment and then waking myself up and re-creating that track in my studio.

James was only 22 years old when *SAW, Vol. 2* was released, and his debt to work by Brian Eno and Daniel Lanois (see Chapter 7 on such records as *Discreet Music* (1975), *Music for Airports* (1978), *On Land* (1982), *Apollo: Atmospheres* (1983), and *Thursday Afternoon* (1975)—is obvious, despite James's protestations that Eno and Lanois were far from his mind when he recorded the album. Nonetheless, *Selected Ambient Works, Vol. 2* represents perhaps the first post-techno record to gain much traction in the rock community. James, however, sought to create a version of electronica palatable to the interests of Western art music, which makes him analogous to the antics of progressive rock musicians of the 1970s, but in this regard James borrowed more the ideologies of 'the work' and the 'concentrated listener' from the classical tradition rather than any compositional devices and performance techniques, as did progressive rock bands such as Rush and ELP. Despite however much he admired composers such as Michael Nyman and Karlheinz Stockhausen, James's music was seldom welcomed as equal by composers in the art music community. Stockhausen, in fact, scorned James when he was presented with a copy of *SAW, Vol. 2* by a perhaps overeager interviewer for BBC Radio 3 in 1995.

And still electronica spun itself off into ever more esoteric subgenres. In the mid-1990s an ambient extension of hip-hop music called trip-hop, coalesced in Bristol, England. Bands like Massive Attack, Tricky, and Portishead created what one critic, looking back from the year 2002, called 'a form of slow motion breakbeat music that blended Rap with Dub Reggae and soundtrack samples', offering 'a calming response to the visceral highs of ecstasy music—sound loops and vinyl scratching were important ingredients but the overall effect was one of cool film music for the mind.' Though Massive Attack fired the genre's first salvo, with 'Unfinished Sympathy' (1991), the first release from their debut album, it was Portishead's 'Sour Times' (1995) that cracked MuchMusic's heavy-rotation list, exposing the station's primarily rock and rock-rap listenership to the slowed-down beats and sampled sounds of trip-hop music. In 1998, Massive Attack, with *Mezzanine*, what some consider trip-hop's *Sgt. Pepper*, would ultimately top Portishead, which failed to capitalize on the momentum of 'Sour Times'. Featuring lushly orchestrated ballads like 'Teardrop' and such slow-motion dance tracks as 'Sunshine', *Mezzanine* cracked the Top 100 album charts in Britain and North America, and proved exceedingly popular among rock listeners.

'Jungle', a similarly slowed-down music, but based in London rather than Bristol, emerged in the wake of trip-hop. More fragmented than trip-hop and popular among a predominantly urban and black club-going listenership in London, and featuring more syncopation than other genres of electronica, 'jungle' produced a number of stars in its earliest years but Goldie remains probably the best known, thanks largely to his work with Icelandic ambient-electronica singer Bjork on her second album, *Post* (1995). Given the genre's popularity among black youth in London, the term 'jungle' was considered to have racist overtones, and thus the genre was renamed 'drum'n'bass' later in the decade. As with every other subgenre of electronica, the sound of drum'n'bass became ever more complicated, and ever more abstract, so that the genre spun off a subgenre known as 'intelligent drum'n'bass', headed by the fractal beats of LTJ Bukem.

By the year 2000, yet another subgenre—'trance'—assumed the mantle of 'next big thing' in the world of electronic music. As one critic described the genre:

> The ultimate Acid House and Techno computer-sampling hybrid, Trance was a music tailor-made for club nirvana as millions the world over danced to slithery mixes full of synthesizer riffs, drum-machine rolls, long, suspenseful buildups and even lengthier breakdowns. (Prendergast, 2000: 372)

Originating in Frankfurt and Berlin in the early 1990s in live sets played by Jame & Spoon, Pete Namlook, and Sven Vath, the genre became miraculously popular in Goa, in the south of India, birthing a psychedelicized rendition of the genre called 'Goa trance'. Championed by perhaps the two most popular DJs to perform in the 1990s and early 2000s, Paul Van Dyke and Paul Oakenfold, trance made its furthest inroads into the pop Top 40 with William Orbit, in his production work on Madonna's 1998 'comeback' album, *Ray of Light* (1998), which included the Top 40 hits 'Ray of Light' and 'Frozen'.

The year 2000 saw the emergence of the closest thing to a rock–electronica fusion yet: so-called 'big beat'. A beat-oriented, synthesizer-heavy, sample-based fusion of rock 'n' roll song forms with funk music's relentless grooving, big beat had a number of Top 40 acts, not to mention a series of DJ-cum-rock-group celebrities, many of whom would collaborate with the rock world elite (members of Oasis, Mazzy Star, and the Flaming Lips, for instance, have all appeared on Chemical Brothers albums). Fat Boy Slim gained heavy rotation on MuchMusic with the Spike Jonze-produced anti-video, 'Praise You' (1999), precisely as the song made heavy rotation on traditional rock stations ('Rockafeller Skank' likewise proved popular). The Chemical Brothers, another big beat band, made strong headway into the pop charts with 'Block Rockin' Beats' (1998) and their *Surrender* (1997) album. Finally, the French duo Air created a slowed-down version of big beat for the soundtrack to Sofia Copolla's debut film, *The Virgin Suicides*, in 1998.

Music and Technology in the Twenty-First Century

Throughout this book, we have traced innovations in technology for the recording, reproduction, and mass dissemination of music, from magnetic tape and the long-playing disc (1940s), through FM radio and 45s (1950s), to the innovations of the 1970s and 1980s (i.e., home video, cable television, portable tape players, digital recording, and the compact disc). At each stage in rock's historical development, new technologies have opened up creative possibilities for musicians and created a wider range of choices for consumers. Of course, there is no guarantee that a given techno-logical innovation will automatically provide greater freedom and flexibility for musi-cians and consumers, or that it will lead to more creative, interesting, and satisfying music. Whole genres of rock are, in fact, predicated on a rejection of certain music technologies, or on a nostalgia for older, more 'human' technologies—a sentiment that animates many 'alternative' rock scenes and the contemporary 'lo-fi' movement. But listeners, nonetheless, are generally accustomed to thinking of technology as an agent of change. In some cases, however, the new digital technologies have allowed musicians to excavate the musical past; Moby, for instance, on his album *Play*, sam-pled segments of performances by Georgia Sea Islands singer Bessie Jones, Texas blues singer Boy Blue, and the Shining Light Gospel Choir, recorded in the field some 40 years earlier by the folk music scholar Alan Lomax.

ADATs and DAWs: The Future of Recording

Technology continues to affect how popular music is made, recorded, reproduced, marketed, and enjoyed. A new standard for digital music-making was introduced in 1992 with the ADAT system. The core of the ADAT (Alesis Digital Audio Tape) system was an eight-track digital synthesizer/recorder that could expand to 128 tracks by adding additional units. This meant that anyone could set up a basic home studio at relatively small expense, while professionals could use the same technology to build highly sophisticated digital sound facilities. So popular was the technology that, in 1992, *Electronic Musician* magazine declared that 'ADAT is more than a technological innovation; it's a social force.' Obviously, the magazine had not foreseen the transfor-mations awaiting not just rock musicians, but musicians in general, in the wake of the Internet and computer music revolutions that would occur a few years later.

Indeed, the 1990s and early 2000s are likely most important in the history of rock because, during this time, digital-audio programs such as ProTools, Logic, and Propellerhead Reason, designed to run on personal computers, were introduced on a mass scale. Called digital-audio workstations (DAWs), these programs combined audio, MIDI, and virtual synthesis capabilities to create a kind of studio-in-a-box, most of which retailed for less than $1,500 by 2002. This software allowed recording engineers and musicians control over almost every aspect of musical sound, includ-ing not only pitch and tempo but also the quality of a singer's voice or an instrumen-talist's timbre. One of the most obvious examples of this control was Cher's Number

1 hit, 'Believe' (1998)—the best-selling single of 1998—which prominently featured a vocal sound obviously processed via an autotuner set to instantaneous attack times. Interestingly, the same sort of experimentation and voice modulation had been achieved with a synthesizer 30 years earlier by Buffy Sainte-Marie in her remarkable album, *Illuminations* (1969), which included the haunting 'God Is Alive, Magic Is Afoot', the lyrics for which she took from Leonard Cohen's novel, *Beautiful Losers*.

Yet, while those involved in making recordings applauded digitalization, many rock musicians bristled, sensing that they were losing control over the recording process. In fact, one of the complaints voiced against digital-audio practices by rock musicians was that it allowed for the correction of musical errors—including not only the erasure and substitution of individual notes and phrases, but also the alteration of musicians' sonic identity, the very aspect of their sound that makes them recognizable and unique. This position derived from a complete lack of understanding about the recording process; basically, digital recording technologies and processors are modelled on what analogue generations did for decades before digitalization became widespread. Nonetheless, the reaction against digital-audio has been particularly vocal in rock circles since the mid-1990s. As the drummer Matt Cameron put it in an interview about Pearl Jam's 2002 album *Riot Act*, recorded 'live' in a studio:

> This is definitely our anti-ProTools record . . . it's more interesting hearing musicians in a room playing hard, with the tempo fluctuating slightly as the band heats up. Perfection is boring. (*Philadelphia Inquirer*, 10 Nov. 2002)

Broadcasting and Promotions: Vertical Integration

In the arena of radio broadcasting and concert promotion, intense debates have arisen in response to the increasing integration of aspects of the music business by corporations. Much of the controversy has centred on Clear Channel, a publicly traded corporation that owns over 1,200 radio stations, 39 television stations, more than 100,000 advertising billboards, and over 100 live performance venues, ranging from huge amphitheatres to dance clubs, allowing it to present more than 70 per cent of all live events in the United States. This strategy is typically referred to as 'vertical integration', whereby a corporation gains control over all aspects of the production of a commodity and of its promotion and delivery to consumers.

Critics have asserted that Clear Channel's use of its radio stations and billboards to advertise Clear Channel-booked shows at Clear Channel-owned venues is basically a monopoly. The corporation has also drawn criticism for using 'voice tracking', in which DJs at the company's headquarters in Texas record radio shows that are played on Clear Channel stations nationwide but presented as though they were being broadcast locally. It is argued that this dominance of radio markets makes it harder for local musicians and artists to get their music played on local stations, leading to a homogenization of music broadcasting nationwide. Clear Channel defends itself with the claim that it simply gives consumers what they want. Whatever one's viewpoint on the matter, it seems undeniable that this controversy is a direct descendant of the introduction of standardized Top 40 playlists and the payola scandals of the 1950s, only on a much larger scale.

The Internet and the MP3

Despite this evidence of a trend towards corporate consolidation in the music business, it can be argued that the most profound transformations in rock's dissemination and consumption has come about through the ubiquity of the Internet, a vast concatenation of millions of computers linked together by a global network. In musical terms, the most influential new medium associated with the Internet is MP3, a variant of MPEG, which was a digital file compression system originally applied in the development of DVDs (digital video discs). MP3 allows sound files to be compressed to as little as one-twelfth of their original size. Let's assume that you would like to download a four-minute track of music from a website featuring original music. In its uncompressed, digitally encoded form, this track would require 40 megabytes of data, creating a file that could take hours to download. With MP3 compression, the file could be squeezed down to only four megabytes, while still retaining something approaching the sound quality of a CD.

The introduction of MP3 technology spurred a series of bitter struggles between entertainment corporations and small-scale entrepreneurs, echoing past conflicts between major and indie record labels, though, again, on a larger scale. In 1997 a firm called MP3.com was founded by Michael Robertson, who started by making 3,000 songs available for free downloading over the Internet. By the year 2000, MP3.com had become by far the most successful music site on the World Wide Web, with over 10 million registered members. As with digital sampling, this new way of disseminating musical materials raised a host of thorny legal problems centred on the issue of copyright. While MP3 files are not inherently illegal, the practice of digitally reproducing music from a copyrighted compact disc and giving it away for free without the artist's or record company's permission rather obviously breaks intellectual property rights concerning the reproduction of songs (if not of their recorded performances).

In January 2000 a lawsuit was filed against MP3.com by the Recording Industry Association of America (RIAA). The trade association's member companies—Universal, Sony, Warner Brothers, Arista, Atlantic, BMG, RCA, Capitol, Elektra, Interscope, and Sire Records—controlled the sale and distribution of approximately 90 per cent of the off-line music in the United States. The suit charged Robertson with copying 45,000 compact discs produced by these companies and making them available for free. MP3.com immediately issued a countersuit against the RIAA, but a court injunction forced it to remove all files owned by the corporations.

The year before, in 1999, an 18-year-old college dropout named Shawn Fanning had developed Napster, an Internet-based software program that allowed computer users to share and swap files—specifically music files—through a centralized file server. Once again, the RIAA filed suit, charging Napster with tributary copyright infringement (meaning that the firm was accused not of violating copyright itself but of contributing to and facilitating other people's violation of the law). In its countersuit the firm argued that because the actual files were not permanently stored on its servers but rather transferred from user to user, Napster was not acting illegally. A federal court injunction finally forced Napster to shut down operations in February 2001, and users exchanged some 2.79 billion files in the closing days of Napster's existence as a free service.

In the wake of Napster's closure a number of companies specializing in 'peer-to-peer' (p2p) file-sharing networks were established, including FastTrack, Gnutella, Audio Galaxy, and Grokster. These services claimed exemption from copyright law based on the fact that in a peer-to-peer network there is no central server on which files are even temporarily stored, and thus no 'place' in cyberspace to which the act of copyright violation can be traced, apart from the millions of computers of the network's users. From the viewpoint of these users—including many musicians attempting to promote their recordings outside the corporate framework—p2p is the ultimate expression of musical democracy, a decentralized system made up of millions of individuals expressing free choice. From the RIAA's viewpoint, peer-to-peer music sharing is a case of mass theft, a maddeningly complex cyber network that challenges the ability of corporations (and of courts) to apply traditional conceptions of music as a form of property.

In Canada, similar charges were brought against five Internet service providers in 2004 and 2005 in an effort to compel them to disclose the identity of 29 of their customers, each of whom, according to Justice Von Finckenstein's judgement, 'used file-sharing software and pseudonyms to download more than 1,000 songs over which the plaintiffs had copyright' (Von Finckenstein, 31 Mar. 2004). Nonetheless, this case, *BMG Canada Inc. v. Jon Doe*, could not stop major file-sharing because of technicalities in copyright laws developed before widespread digitalization. BMG Canada and a number of other major labels with interests in Canada had sued Shaw Communications, Roger Cable Communications, Bell Canada, Telus, and Videotron. The charges were dismissed and many Canadian news outlets announced open season for p2p file-sharing, based on the initial judgement, announced on 31 March 2004:

> there was no evidence of copyright infringement. Downloading a song for personal use did not constitute infringement. It had not been established that the defendants either distributed or authorized the reproduction of sound recordings. They merely placed personal copies into their shared directories, which were accessible by other internet users. Before such an activity could amount to distribution, there had to be some positive act by the owner of the shared directory, such as sending out copies or advertising that they were available for copying. *No such evidence was presented in this case*. (Von Finckenstein, 31 Mar. 2004)

On appeal, announced on 19 May 2005, it was held that 'BMG's motion for an order to compel the internet service providers to disclose the file sharers' identities was dismissed because there was no clear evidence linking the IP addresses to the pseudonyms' (*Richard, Noel, and Sexton*, 19 May 2005). Moreover, it was held that 'the trial judge should not have made a finding regarding whether or not BMG's copyright had been infringed at such an early stage in the proceedings', in which case 'BMG had the right to pursue a further application for disclosure of the identities of the file sharers' (*Richard, Noel, and Sexton*, 19 May 2005). The possibility of future prosecution thus remains open in Canada.

iPod, Therefore I Am

The development of new personal listening devices appeared at the same time as the rise of file-sharing on the Internet. In 2001 Apple Computers introduced the first-generation iPod player, a digital walkman of sorts, which could store up to 1,000 CD-quality songs on its up to 40 gigabyte internal hard drive (the iPod was also 'hubbed' with Apple's iTunes personal music program).

The iPod and other MP3 players have come to dominate the market for portable listening devices, in part because they provide the listener with the ability to build a unique library of music reflecting his or her personal tastes. As noted, though, this trend was initiated half a century earlier with the introduction of the 45 rpm record changer, which allowed consumers to play their favourite songs in whatever order they chose—portability, however, clearly was not part of the equation. The ability of the iPod to 'shuffle' music—that is, to play tracks in random order, mixing genres, performers, and historical periods—has not only exerted an influence on personal listening habits but also provided a metaphor for the contemporary state of consumer culture. Ever attuned to the culture surrounding it, in 2005 Apple echoed this sentiment when it introduced a device called the iPod Shuffle with the advertising slogans 'Random Is the New Order' and 'Lose Control. Love It.'

Studies of the intimate relationship between the iPod and its users suggest that for many listeners the device functions as a kind of aural prosthetic—an extension of their ears and minds, and a point of connection to wider circuits for the circulation of digital information. Through these portable devices contemporary consumers of popular music are connected to a global entertainment matrix that includes home computers, the Internet, p2p and legitimate download services such as the new Napster, and new services that are beginning to supplant the traditional functions of broadcasting, such as Myspace.com, GarageBand.com, Macjams.com, and Youtube.com. And, for a brief while, the rise of 'podcasting'—a method of on-line audio distribution in which digital sound files are uploaded to a website, and listeners can automatically load files onto a portable player as they're made available—even had some cultural observers forecasting the demise of radio, though satellite radio seems, for the moment, to have rejuvenated the industry, even if only slightly.

Of course, there is no way for us to provide the final word on the rapidly shifting landscape of music technology. At present, Napster has 'gone legit', paying a multi-million-dollar settlement to music publishers for past copyright infringements, signing licensing agreements with the corporations represented by the RIAA, and reopening as a fee-based service. More recently, in June 2005, the US Supreme Court handed down a ruling in the case *MGM Studios v. Grokster* that only furthered the rights of culture industry workers in the digital age. MGM was supported in its cause by other film studios, the RIAA, Major League Baseball, and intellectual property advocates. Grokster and allied software companies contended they should not be held responsible for the illegal acts of their customers, since their software is intended to download and share legal or non-protected files, and therefore meets the legal standard for protection from liability. In the end, the Supreme Court sided unanimously with the music and film corporations, holding that the software companies had, in fact, actively encouraged copyright infringement. While the ruling provided immediate support for the battle against file-sharing, many 'insiders' agreed that the entertainment industry was simply staving off inevitable changes in the business model for selling popular music.

As one might expect, the *MGM Studios v. Grokster* case provoked intense responses among musicians and music fans as well as corporate lawyers. Speaking on the steps of the Supreme Court, Lamont Dozier, the great Motown songwriter and producer, said:

> If I was back in Detroit, if we had this problem then, in the sixties there never would have been a Motown, I would have been at Ford's car factory, because I couldn't make a living in the music business. (Money.CNN.com, 29 Mar. 2005)

At the same time that Dozier was defending the rights of composers, musicians, and record companies to profit by their labour, hundreds of mostly young people gathered to support the p2p file-sharing companies, chanting and carrying signs. Some camped out overnight to attend the oral arguments, and it is easy to imagine that they passed the time listening to and exchanging music on their iPods—perhaps even some of Dozier's classic Motown tracks! One thing seems clear: the *MGM Studios v. Grokster* decision will not end the struggle between the entertainment conglomerates, on the one hand, and Internet entrepreneurs, fans, and independent musicians, on the other.

The Fall of CDs: Redefining the Concept of Record Label

It is worth returning to the basic issue that underlies these controversies and others surely yet to come—digital technology allows the content of a recording to be seemingly liberated from its physical medium. To be clear, a record is not actually liberated from time and space by digitalization, as the sequences of ones and zeros that comprise a digital recording must nonetheless be stored on some playback device to ever be heard. But digitalization allows for an unprecedented degree of mobility—once digitized, a recording can be transmitted, reproduced, and manipulated in a 'virtual' form, free of the constraints of all technology save computers. This development has raised questions that will no doubt shape the course of rock and pop music for years to come: What does it mean when a consumer licenses the right to use the contents of an album, rather than buying a single copy of it in a store? How can copyright be enforced—indeed, what is the meaning of the term 'copyright'—when thousands of consumers can download the same piece of music simultaneously over the Internet? If 'Video Killed the Radio Star', as the Buggles claimed, will the Internet kill the CD store? What will the music industry of tomorrow look like?

Whatever answers analysts propose, by 2008 it was clear to almost everyone that record labels would have to change their business models to survive digitalization, regardless of the legality of file-sharing. More than 500 million downloads of p2p software had occurred in North America by 2005, and an estimated 60 million users had downloaded more than one song by 2007. Indeed, by 2008 it was fairly clear that, for all intents and purposes, the CD was likely dead. The International Federation of the Phonographic Industry (IFPI) estimated in 2004 that the number of illegally copied or 'pirated' CDs climbed 14 per cent in 2002, and another 4.3 per cent in 2003, to total over 1.1 billion units on a worldwide scale by 2004. Most experts agreed that over 35 per cent of all CDs sold around the world were illegal copies, creating a trade of upward of $4.6 billion per year. And those numbers do not even account for the considerable growth of computer-only listeners, who only procure their music from on-line sources and who listen to music primarily via portable MP3 devices.

In 2002 the worldwide recorded music market dropped by 7 per cent, to a total of $32 billion, and then it dropped another 7.6 per cent in 2003. From 2000 to 2005, overall record sales plummeted by a total of 26 per cent, resulting in the loss of over $2 billion in revenue worldwide. Not surprisingly, then, the early years of the twenty-first century saw a complete reshuffling of the traditional hierarchies of power within the rock and pop industry, with touring and publishing becoming the primary locus of profits. In fact, when the valuation for the acquisition of Warner Music Group was set in the mid-decade, for instance, the corporation's music publishing arm was valued at just over $2 billion, while its recorded music operation had fallen to a value of only $1.5 billion. As rock industry analysts David Kusek and Gerd Leonhard note:

> the record industry is a mere slice of the overall music industry pie, and many of the other slices are not even known to the average music fan. Music and event merchandising, concerts and touring, and live entertainment in general account for some $25 billion globally, while music publishing is a $12 billion business, approximately. Further, according to sources in *Pollstar, Billboard,* and *Music Week*, record companies make nearly $2 billion every year in 'special products', such as giveaway CD sets, corporate marketing items, and various business-to-business licensing activities.

Marketing to the Internet Generation

Sales of recorded music have been a driving factor in the rock industry since the industry first took recognizable shape in the mid-1950s. Thus, many musicians have had to completely retool their release strategies to reach an ever-elusive generation of listeners who were raised to think of music as something available for free on-line, albeit via illegal p2p programs. Trent Reznor, of the Nine Inch Nails, has come up with a relatively novel idea, targeting millions of new amateur digital-audio enthusiasts in the process. Since deciding to make GarageBand available free of charge with the purchase of any new Macintosh computer in 2002, Apple has sold more than 300 million legally acquired copies of the program. Keen to tap this emerging market, Reznor decided to release tracks from his *With Teeth* (2004) and *Year Zero* (2007) albums on-line as GarageBand multi-track files, which fans can download without charge to remix and play with as they like. Though this release strategy did not necessarily lead to any immediate boosts in record sales for Reznor, it certainly increased his visibility, as numerous articles about the unorthodox marketing strategy were published in widely read magazines such as *Wired*, even though Reznor's public standing as an artist had been obviously slumping since the late 1990s; aside from increased visibility, the strategy also garnered simple gratitude from many of Reznor's fans, who appreciated the gesture of a gift from the musician. A similar strategy was adopted by David Byrne and Brian Eno for the 25-year anniversary release of their *My Life in the Bush of Ghosts* (1981) LP in 2006, and by Radiohead, who released an EP single of the track 'Nude' (2008), from *In Rainbows* (2007), on iTunes, purchase of which allowed users to download the song in the form of a GarageBand multi-track file.

Another relatively innovative strategy—since dubbed 'pay-what-you-will'—was devised by Radiohead to market their album, *In Rainbows*. Initially only available on-line, the record netted more than one million downloads in its first month of release. Priced at whatever listeners chose to pay (hence 'pay-what-you-will'), an esti-mated 40 per cent of downloaders gave an average of $6 dollars per download. Thus, Radiohead made more than $3 million on a record that they had at least theoreti-cally given away for free—prompting critics to dub the entire episode 'the Radiohead revolution'.

If anything, the Radiohead revolution speaks to the continued relevance of intel-lectual property rights to rock musicians, even as a vocal minority of theorists cele-brate the demise of copyright, some going so far as to claim copyright to be an old or outdated concept. What was so exciting about the release strategy of *In Rainbows* to Radiohead, at least according to lead singer and songwriter Thom Yorke, was that for the first time in the band's history the group was able to retain 100 per cent own-ership of the master recording, which allowed them subsequently to license the record to TBD Records/ATO Records Group for a traditional CD release in January 2008. As Yorke summarized in an interview with ex-Talking Heads lead singer David Byrne:

> We've made more money out of this record than out of all the other Radiohead albums put together, forever—in terms of anything on the Net. And that's nuts. It's partly due to the fact that EMI wasn't giving us any money for digital sales. All the contracts signed in a certain era have none of that stuff. (Byrne, 2007: 115)

Other groups, lacking the brand-name recognition of a band like Radiohead, exploited the Internet to their advantage by luring potential listeners to Myspace.com and Youtube.com, for instance, and allowing them to download songs free of charge in the hopes of generating enough interest to allow them to profitably charge at a later date. Similarly, many bands have benefited from the attention and hyperbolic praise of new indie review sites; Montreal's Arcade Fire, for instance, sold out the entire Merge Records inventory of its full-length debut, *Funeral* (2003), after the record received a 9.7 rating from the massively influential Pitchfork website. Since then, after appearing on the cover of *Time* in April 2005 as 'the band who helped put Canadian music on the world map', Arcade Fire was nominated for a Grammy in 2006 (Best Alternative Music Album) and again in 2008 (Best Alternative Music Album, this time for *Neon Bible*). Indeed, for all the talk of changing priorities and values, and widespread industry transformation, the goal of professional rock musicians remains unchanged—to become known and to profit by their craft. That said, it nonetheless remains indisputable that rock music has changed, and is still changing, in the wake of widespread digitalization; a band like Arcade Fire would likely remain unknown to most in the Top 40 world were it not for the Internet. Interestingly, one group of musicians has thrived despite the erosion of the rock market by p2p file-sharing—Canadian indie and post-rock bands, thanks largely to the continued patronage of Canadian granting agencies for the production and manufacture of CD recordings, and the work of two important indie labels, Constellation Records and Arts & Crafts.

▎Canadian Indie and Post-Rock

Likely the strongest and clearest statement of an ethical rationale for bands to maintain indie status came from Godspeed You! Black Emperor, an extremely influential post-rock band headquartered in Montreal and signed to the Montreal-based post-rock label Constellation Records. 'Post-rock', largely agreed to have been named by critic Simon Reynolds in an interview with the English post-punk band Bark Psychosis in the March 1994 issue of *Mojo* magazine, is a relatively new genre characterized by the use of rock instruments performing instrumental music marked by rhythms, harmonies, and melodies drawn from a variety of classical and free jazz traditions; post-rock songs are generally long for the rock genre, most clocking in at more than seven minutes, and they typically feature a seemingly endless series of layered riffs and motifs arranged into long, crescendoing waves.

The artwork for Godspeed You! Black Emperor's 2002 release for Constellation Records, *Yanqui u.x.o.*, made a bold statement about the ethics of record production. A flow chart on the back cover of the album implicates basically every 'major' record label still in existence in 2002 with a number of military–industrial endeavours. The band claimed, for instance, that Atlantic, Rhino, Elektra/Sire, Asylum, Reprise, Warner Brothers, American, Maverick, and EMI were all related, through a series of co-ventures and mergers, with Raytheon Industries, a company responsible for the manufacture of 'general dynamics missile systems' and 'tomahawk cruise missiles, etc.' BMG, Arista, and RCA, on the other hand, were directly linked with Hutchinson Worldwide and Barry Controls, both of which, the band alleged, manufacture 'ring mounts, shock/vibration isolators for fighter jets, military tyres'. Likewise Sony, Columbia, and Epic all were implicated in parent company Sony's co-venture with the US Army and the University of Southern California, which resulted in the creation of Future Combat Technologies, Inc. And, finally, Vivendi Universal, MCA, Polygram, Motown, Geffen-DGC, Interscope, and Universal all bore a direct relation to Lockheed-Martin and, thus, the creation of 'mission planning systems for P-3 Orion Patrol Aircraft' (the band would later have to apologize for certain extensions on this flow chart, conceding that some—though by no means all—of their research had been inaccurate).

Constellation Records

Godspeed You! Black Emperor's label mates at Constellation Record were only slightly less political, as was Constellation Records itself. Initially conceived in 1997 to provide a live performance space for Montreal's growing post-rock community, with the label itself to follow, hiccups in planning forced the founders of Constellation Records to launch both their performance series, called 'Musique fragile', and the label concurrently. Openly anti-corporate and anti-globalization, many of the label's written missives betrayed more than a passing familiarity with Marxist and post-Marxist theory, the label presenting itself in the press as much less anticapitalist—indeed, Constellation Records is a for-profit venture—than an advocate of artisanal rather than industrial modes of production. Sending handwritten thank-you notes with mail orders and hiring local artists to produce hand-designed packages for CDs, Constellation still operates with the stated objective that running a label as it does 'enacts a mode of cultural production that critiques the worst tendencies of the music industry, artistic commodification, and perhaps in some tiny way, the world at large.' Not surprisingly, Constellation has had to compromise a fair bit to make ends meet, now agreeing to sell its records in corporate chains such as HMV, Virgin Records, and Amazon.com. Artists on the Constellation label include a who's who of the Canadian post-rock elite, including Godspeed You! Black Emperor, Do Make Say Think, A Silver Mt. Zion, Fly Pan Am, Sofa, and 1-Speed Bike (other popular post-rock bands include Explosions in the Sky and Mogwai).

Broken Social Scene

Eventually winding up much more on the Top 40 end of the rock spectrum than any band on the Constellation Records roster, Toronto's Broken Social Scene—the collective that launched the Canadian indie rock explosion, which has characterized rock both in Canada and around the world since 2002—actually started off with a decidedly post-rock, if not ambient, recording aesthetic. A massive collective of musicians who participate in performances and recordings whenever time permits, Broken Social Scene's core members, Kevin Drew and Brendan Canning, recorded and released the band's debut album, *Feel Good Lost* (2001), for Noise Factory Records in 2001. Basically a lo-fi, ambient record, *Feel Good Lost* did not translate well at live performances, and thus the pair recruited a number of musicians from the burgeoning indie rock scene in Toronto, including Jason Collett, Leslie Feist, and Metric's Emily Haines (between then and 2005, records by Broken Social Scene have featured contributions from K-os, Murray Lightburn, Ohad Benchetrit, Charles Spearin, Jason Tait, Jessica Moss, James Shaw, Torquil Campbell, and Amy Millan, among many others).

Broken Social Scene: A collective that launched the Canadian indie rock explosion and is in part responsible for the success of the renowned indie label, Arts & Crafts. Chris Weeks/WireImages.

The band's second release, the David Newfeld-produced *You Forgot It In People* (2003), proved their breakthrough. Including the hit song 'Stars and Sons', eventually featured on the Academy Award-nominated film *Half Nelson* (with a breakout performance by London, Ontario, native Ryan Gosling), the record received the 2003 Juno for Alternative Album of the Year. Later that year, a collection of 'B' sides, entitled *Bee Hives*, was released. Two years later the band released their third record, *Broken Social Scene*, which prompted a slight breakthrough in the US. To promote the album, the band performed on *Late Night with Conan O'Brien*, performing '7/4 (shoreline)'. This album garnered another Juno for Alternative Album in 2006, after which point the group said they were going on hiatus following the end of their US tour in November. Since then, the group has spun off into numerous solo projects, the collective's best known alumnus now being Leslie Feist, whose second release, *The Reminder* (2007), ranked as one of the best-selling and most critically acclaimed albums of 2007.

Arts & Crafts

Most subsequent releases by ex-members of Broken Social Scene, and all of the group's albums save their debut, have been released on the Arts & Crafts label, which was established by Jeffrey Remedios in 2002, a friend of the band then working as the head of promotions for Virgin Music. Certain that Broken Social Scene and other

Canadian indie rock groups could sell just as easily in the US as in Canada, Remedios made the unprecedented move of incorporating the Arts & Crafts label both in Canada and in the United States. He brokered a distribution deal with Universal Music Canada and EMI, the former now contracted to distribute more than 25 indie labels across Canada, and recently opened an office for the label in Europe, officially launching Arts & Crafts Europe in partnership with City Slang Records in 2006. Every group on the Arts & Crafts roster except the Most Serene Republic features an alumnus of the Broken Social Scene collective; these include: the American Analog Set, Apostle of Hustle, Broken Social Scene, Jason Collett, the Constantines, the Dears, Feist, the Hidden Cameras, Los Campesinos!, Amy Millan, New Buffalo, Pheonix, Stars, the Stills, Valley of the Giants, and Young Galaxy.

Leslie Feist

Likely the best-known graduate of Broken Social Scene is currently Leslie Feist. Born in Amherst, Nova Scotia, but soon thereafter moving to western Canada with her family, Feist began her musical career in 1991 at the age of 15 as the lead vocalist for the Calgary punk band Placebo. After the group won an opening slot for the Ramones at a local 'battle of the bands' contest in 1993, Feist met future Broken Social Scene members Brendan Canning and Kevin Drew backstage, though it would be 10 years before she officially worked with the group. She learned bass to perform with Noah's Arkweld in 1996 and later joined the band By Divine Right as a rhythm guitarist, touring with the group from 1998 to 2000. In 1999 Feist moved in with a musical acquaintance named Merrill Nisker, who was then performing with an electro-punk group, Peaches, a friendship that led Feist to provide guest vocals on Peaches' hugely successful *Teaches of Peaches*.

Feist recorded a now out-of-print debut, *Monarch (Lay Your Jewelled Head Down)*, in 1999 and worked on-again, off-again in the interim with Broken Social Scene. Her second solo release and first for Arts & Crafts, *Let It Die* (2004), saw the singer-songwriter finally break into the Top 40, the album reaching Number 38 on *Billboard*'s Heatseeker album chart; 'Mushaboom' (2004), the second track on the album, broke the Top 100 in both Britain and France but failed to chart anywhere in North America. Following the success of European tours with fellow Canadian musician Gonzales, and for personal reasons, Feist relocated to Paris, France, in the wake of *Let It Die*'s success. With a support tour running across North America, Europe, Asia, and Australia from 2004 to 2006, *Let It Die* eventually sold more than 500,000 copies worldwide, earning Feist her first platinum certification in Canada, gold certification in France, and Juno awards for Best New Artist and Best Alternative Rock Album in 2004.

Feist's third solo release, *The Reminder* (2007), established her as a singer of international importance. The album sold close to one million copies worldwide, peaking at Number 2 in Canada and Number 16 in the United States. It received a strong boost when the track '1234', co-written by Feist with New Buffalo's Sally Seltmann, was prominently featured on a commercial for the iPod nano and subsequently reached the Top 10 in Canada and the US. *Time* named the song the second best of 2007. 'My Moon My Man', another track from *The Reminder*, was featured on a commercial for Verizon Wireless's new LG Chocolate VX8550 phone in 2007, but this failed to produce the same results as the iPod nano commercial did. Feist was the featured musical guest on *Saturday Night Live* in November 2007, continues to perform with alumni of Broken Social Scene, and made a cameo appearance on 'Give Er' for the Peaches' album, *Impeach My Bush* (2006). In 2008 she was nominated for four Grammys but won none, while in Canada she won five Junos, for single, album, artist, songwriter, and pop album. It certainly would appear that Feist has transcended her indie roots to become the pre-eminent female pop vocalist currently at work in Canada.

We have reached the end point of our journey, but there is every reason to expect that the energy and creativity, and the crassness and commercialism, of the rock tradition—that messy product of centuries of cultural miscegenation—will continue to have a significant impact on the world's consciousness, provoking equal measures of admiration and disapproval. Whether one views this process as an extension of cultural imperialism or as proof positive of the unique value of North American musical culture, there can be no denying that popular music—forged by the sons and daughters of Africa and Europe, shaped by the diverse musical cultures of the first peoples of the Americas, hustled and hyped by generations of entrepreneurs, moulded and remoulded by the force fields of identity, technology, and the music industry—constitutes an epochal contribution not only to North American culture but also to a wider, still-emerging world culture. As for the present moment in Canada, we'll let Brendan Canning of Broken Social Scene have the final say:

> Why is this Canada's . . . moment? It's partly because there are now so many talented Canadian bands, but it's also because it has taken some of our musicians and labels until now to realize that competing on an international level is very much within our reach. And success feeds on itself: there is now a worldwide audience hungry for the latest independent Canadian musical exports. Our ideas are simple enough to understand, and we're not pushing anything ridiculous or pretentious. We are Canadian. We are successful. And we have our dignity intact. (Canning, 2005)

Discussion Questions

1. How has rock music changed since 9/11?
2. What accounts for the rise and fall of world music? Why do Canadians tend to lump traditional musics in with 'world' music? What does this categorization tell us about the ongoing stratification of Canadian culture and society?
3. How might ambient music, particularly the ambient recordings of Aphex Twin, be situated vis-à-vis progressive rock and the Western art music tradition?
4. Why have rock musicians traditionally been so resistant to digitalization? Can you hear the difference between digital and analog?
5. Do you engage in p2p file-sharing? Do you consider sharing an act of theft or copyright infringement? How do you think p2p file-sharing will change the rock tradition?

APPENDIX: INTERNET RESOURCES

Students should take great care when evaluating information offered on the Internet; more often than not, information requires substantiation by external print texts, where the process of verification is typically more transparent. That said, the sites listed below should provide researchers with a good means of orienting themselves towards any particular subject having to do with the historical development of a rock tradition in Canada.

By no means is this list exhaustive. It is offered as a starting point for researchers who wish to pursue further research on subjects considered in this text. The list is organized according to topic, rather than by chapter, for greater ease of use. Certain sites are listed with a keyword or two appearing in brackets beside the web address. In these cases, the site has its own internal search engine. Researchers should input the keyword into the internal search engine *exactly* as it appears below, since many of these engines are case-sensitive. These keyword searches will yield multiple entries, each of which is related to the general topic and, as such, is worth consulting on its own and in conjunction with all the other entries that appear.

To provide entries on specific musicians, bands, or records would be unwieldy. I recommend that researchers start their studies of particular bands, musicians, or records by consulting the *Encyclopedia of Music in Canada* (see 'General Information' below). Also, sites for the various Canadian awards programs are excellent sources for general information about various nominees and songs.

▌General Information

Encyclopedia of Music in Canada: thecanadianencyclopedia.com
A searchable database of entries, available free of charge, for the *Encyclopedia of Music in Canada*. Also available are a database of articles published in *Maclean's* magazine, a *Youth Encyclopedia*, and *The Canadian Encyclopedia*. A regularly updated list of feature articles is also provided, organized according to general subject. Searching this site is a good place for students to begin research on particular artists, labels, industry personnel, etc.

Rock's Backpages: www.rocksbackpages.com
A subscription archive of critical writings—i.e., interviews, reviews, and feature articles—on rock bands (over 12,000 articles as of this writing), records, performances, and industry personalities. Many university libraries now maintain subscriptions to this site.

The History of Rock 'n' Roll: www.history-of-rock.com
Provides survey information on the development of crucial subgenres of the rock tradition for the years 1954–63.

Canoe.ca: www.canoe.ca
An Internet archive of past and current articles on a variety of searchable subjects. Follow the link to 'Jam! Showbiz' for entertainment news and biographical entries.

▌Chart Listings

Historical overview: thecanadianencyclopedia.com (keyword: 'charts')
Provides a historical overview of the development of national chart listings in Canada, a list of Canadians appearing on the *Billboard* Top 100 from September 1957 (Paul Anka, 'Diana') to July 1991 (Bryan Adams, '[Everything I Do] I Do It for You'), and a list of Canadian singers and musicians who have topped the *Billboard* country charts from 1950 to 1974. Finally, the site provides a useful bibliography and links to other sites.

CHUM charts: www.1050chum.com/index_chumcharts.aspx
This site provides a brief history of the development of the CHUM singles charts and a searchable database of every chart published from 27 May 1957 to the last week of June 1986. The database can be searched by both artist and track name.

***RPM* charts: www.collectionscanada.gc.ca/rpm/index-e.html**
This site provides a brief history of the development of the *RPM* album charts, biographical sketches of the lives of Walter Grealis and Stan Klees, an interview with Grealis and Klees about their time at *RPM*, an overview of *RPM*'s impact on the development of a rock music industry in Canada, and a searchable database of every chart published from 24 February 1964 to the year 2000. The database can be searched by artist name or keyword.

***Billboard* charts: www.billboard.com/bbcom/charts/genre_index.jsp**
This site provides a searchable database of numerous historical and current *Billboard* charts, including Hot/Pop, Digital & Mobile, Historical, R&B/Hip-Hop, Country, Latin, Rock, Top 40/Adult Contemporary, Heatseekers/Independent, Christian/

Gospel, Dance/Electronic, Classical/Jazz, International, Video, Boxscore, Top Compilation Albums, Top Blues Albums, Buzz 100, Top New Age Albums, Top World Albums, Top Soundtracks, Top Comedy Albums, Top Reggae Albums, Top Kid Audio, Top Cast Albums, Top Holiday Albums, and a Comprehensive Albums Chart. A pay subscription is required to search many of these databases.

Awards and Institutions

The Canadian Music Hall of Fame: www.junoawards.ca/vhof/index.php
A searchable database with information on every inductee, generally announced at annual Juno awards ceremonies. Inductees include Triumph, Bob Rock, Bryan Adams, the Tragically Hip, Bob Ezrin, Tom Cochrane, Daniel Lanois, Bruce Cockburn, the Guess Who, Neil Young, and many others.

Historical overview: thecanadianencyclopedia.com (keyword: 'Awards')
Provides links to a number of articles on various awards programs for Canadian pop and rock musicians, including the Juno awards, the Félix awards, and the Big Country awards.

Polaris Prize: polarismusicprize.ca
Provides information on the annual Polaris Prize, including information on current and past nominees, jury members, rules, and links to related articles.

ECMA Awards (East Coast Music Awards): www.ecma.ca/splash.asp
Provides information on the East Coast Music Awards, nominees, and award winners, and an archive of media releases.

Juno Awards: www.juno-awards.ca
Provides an overview of the development of the Juno awards and an archive with information on past Juno award winners and nominees. This archive is searchable by a number of different categories, including by year (provides a summary of all winners by year), category (provides a summary of all winners by category), artist (provides a summary of all awards won by particular artists, as well as nominations), and top winners, which divides artists by number of awards won. The site also has a link to a 'Virtual Hall of Fame' with information on current and past inductees, as well as an archive for current and past winners of the Walter Grealis Special Achievement Award.

Félix Awards: thecanadianencyclopedia.com (keyword: 'Félix Awards')
Provides an overview of the development of the Félix awards from 1979 to present, as well as links to articles on related topics and people. No listing is given of winners or nominees.

Big Country Awards: thecanadianencyclopedia.com (keyword: 'BigCountry Awards')
Provides an overview of the development of the Big Country awards, established in 1975 by Walter Grealis and Stan Klees, and held annually until 1981, when they were replaced by the Canadian Country Music Assocation awards. No listing is given of winners or nominees. Links to related sites are given.

Canadian Songwriters Hall of Fame: www.cansong.ca/en/default.aspx
Provides an overview of the development of the Canadian Songwriters' Hall of Fame and a searchable database of inductees organized according to either when a hit song was first released (i.e., during the 'Radio Era, 1921–1955' or the 'Modern Era, 1957 to 25 Years Prior to Present'), or the singers themselves, depending upon which was inducted (the Canadian Songwriters' Hall of Fame inducts both songwriters and songs, though it is rare that songwriters are inducted). The site claims to be divided according to anglophone and francophone repertory, but the anglophone and francophone listings are identical. A brief overview of each inducted song is provided, as is a biographical sketch of the inducted songwriters, which thus far number only four: Alex Kramer, André Lejeune, Paul Anka, and Claude Dubois.

▌Recording Industry and CanCon Regulations

Historical overview: thecanadianencyclopedia.com (keyword: 'ADISQ'/'CARAS')
Accesses entries that span the development of sound reproduction and popular music broadcasting industries in Canada.

ADISQ (Association québécoise de l'industrie du disque, du spectacle et de la vidéo): www.adisq.com/doc/assoc-profil.html
Provides an overview of the organization's mandates, information on its various members, an archive of press releases, and access to annual reports.

CARAS (Canadian Academy of Recording Arts and Sciences): www.carasonline.ca
Provides information on the academy itself, as well as links to various academy initiatives, including MusiCan, Juno awards, and the Canadian Music Hall of Fame. Also available is information on how to become a member.

SOCAN (Society of Composers, Authors and Music Publishers of Canada): socan.ca
Provides information on the workings of SOCAN, which administers performance and communication rights of copyrighted music when it is performed in Canada. Under 'Music Creators & Publishers' researchers can find useful information on how royal-

ties are earned and collected in Canada, as well as links to performance rights organizations around the world with which SOCAN maintains reciprocal agreements.

CIRPA (Canadian Independent Record Production Association): www.cirpa.ca
Provides a history of the record industry in Canada, the Canadian Independent Record Production Association itself, and links to 'member' sites (divided by function: accountants, managers, creative services, distributors, lawyers, record labels, record producers, others, studios, etc.).

CMPA (Canadian Music Publishers Association): www.musicpublishercanada.ca
Provides information on the activities of the CMPA, the music publishing industry in Canada and abroad (under 'Industry Issues'), an FAQ, and contact information.

Canadian Country Music Hall of Fame: www.ccma.org/pastinduct.html
Provides a listing of all inductees divided by categories of induction (artists, builders, and broadcasters), as well as an overview of the Canadian Country Music Association and the Canadian Country Music Hall of Fame.

Disc-O-Logue: www.collectionscanada.gc.ca/discologue/index-e.html
An on-line catalogue of francophone pop music recordings from Library and Archives Canada.

History of Recorded Sound in Canada: www.capsnews.org/barrcan
This site is an attempt by one author, Steve Barr, to narrate the historical development of sound reproduction in Canada. Separate articles are also available on the work of various record labels both in Canada and abroad, including Berliner, Victor, RCA, Columbia, and Brunswick. Also provides a number of useful links to resources on 'Phonograph and Recording History, Vintage Phonographs, Radios and Automated Musical Instruments', collections of vintage records, and various other related topics.

**The Berliner Gram-o-phone Company of Canada:
www.collectionscanada.gc.ca/gramophone/m2-3005-e.html**
A history of the Berliner Gram-o-phone Company's Canadian operations, from Library and Archives Canada.

**The Virtual Gramophone: The First World War Era:
www.collectionscanada.gc.ca/gramophone/m2-3010-e.html**
A wonderful site with clips of popular songs produced in Canada during the World War I period. Also available are digitized sheet music and related archival resources from Library and Archives Canada. Also provides information on 'the music scene in Quebec, 1915–1920', and biographies of many World War I era musicians.

Government Arts Institutions

CRTC: **www.crtc.gc.ca/eng/welcome.htm**
Provides a number of useful links. An explanation of how the MAPL system works is provided (crtc.gc.ca/eng/INFO_SHT/R1.htm). Researchers can also gain access to an on-line repository of related decisions, notices, and orders; news releases; and speeches given (crtc.ca/eng/documents/htm). Useful information concerning government regulations for the implementation of Canadian content laws can be found on the same site (crtc.gc.ca/eng/cancon.htm). Finally, under 'Statutes & Regulations' (crtc.gc.ca/eng/statues.htm), researchers can find text for a number of statutes and regulations, helpfully organized according to 'Acts', 'Regulations (Broadcasting)', 'Regulations (Telecommunications)', and 'Directions to the CRTC'.

Canadian Heritage Fund: www.canadianheritage.gc.ca/index_e.cfm
An overview of the policies established and enforced by the Canadian Heritage program. The site can be difficult to navigate but provides useful information on funding policy under the heading 'Arts and Culture'. Provides links to information on a number of funding programs for Canadian music, including: Canada Council for the Arts, Canada Music Fund, Canadian Broadcasting Corporation, Music Policy and Programs, etc.

FACTOR **(Foundation Assisting Canadian Talent on Recordings): www.factor.ca**
Provides information on the historical development of FACTOR, its programs, composition of competition juries, information on applications, and an advertisement for upcoming live events.

Country, R&B, and Traditional Music

Canadian Country Music Association: www.ccma.org
Provides an overview of the Association, information on Country Music Week, the Canadian Country Music Hall of Fame (see above), and information for members. Also provides links to the official sites for country music stars, and listings for upcoming country music events.

CJTM: Canadian Journal of Traditional Music: cjtm.icaap.org
Provides an on-line collection of all current and past issues of the *Canadian Journal of Traditional Music*. Also provides submission guidelines for interested authors.

Canadian Musician: www.canadianmusician.com
A magazine that covers Canadian musicians and the pop music industry in Canada. Provides an on-line directory of artist websites and an archive of articles. Also offers a classified section, geared specifically for Canadian musicians.

Nova Scotia Country Music Hall of Fame: www.nscmhf.ca
Provides an overview of the association, including listings of the Hall of Fame executive and of all inductees divided by year, event listings, and related external links.

Country Music News: www.countrymusicnews.ca/home_ihtml
An on-line magazine that covers the Canadian country music scene. Includes an archive of articles dating back to the magazine's inception in 1980.

Toronto Blues Society: www.torontobluessociety.com
Official society website, with links to event listings, musicians and blues groups, and Canadian and American record labels that specialize in blues music.

The Rock Tradition

Sites listed below typically present general survey information on the development of subgenres of the rock tradition, and entries on important players and records within each subgenre. They are offered as starting points for further research; it is recommended that researchers read the information offered on each site and follow the links provided for more detailed information on particular bands, performances, records, labels, etc. Sites are divided according to subject below.

Doo Wop

Doo Wop Sound: www.history-of-rock.com/DooWopSound.htm
Doo Wop Preservation League: www.doowopusa.org/index/.html
Doo Wop Society of Southern California: www.electricearl.com/dws/origin.html
Doo Wop Dreams: www.doowopdreams.com/principal.htm
Doo Wop Nation Ezine: www.home.earthlink.net/~jaymar41/doowopTP.html

Rockabilly

The Rockabilly Saga, A Brief History: www.rockabilly.nl/rockabilly1.htm
Official Rockabilly Hall of Fame: www.rockabillyhall.com
Rockabilly Central: www.rockabilly.net
Rockabilly Magazine: www.rockabillymagazine.com

Rock 'n' Roll

Rock and Roll Hall of Fame: www.rockhall.com
The History of Rock and Roll: www.history-of-rock.com
Rock 'n' Roll Music: 42explore.com/rocnroll.htm

Urban Folk

1960s Folk Rock Links: www.richieunterberger.com/turnlinks.html
Folk Alliance Canada: folkalliance.ca/fac
Songs of Atlantic Canada: www.mun.ca/folklore/leach
History of Folk Music in English Canada: folkmusichistory.com/intro.shtml
Ottawa Folklore Centre: ottawafolklore.com
Canadian Folk Music Awards: canadianfolkmusicawards.ca

Music of Quebec

Phonoteque québécoise: www.phonotheque.org
Disc-O-Logue: www.collectionscanada.gc.ca/discologue/index-e.html
Traditions and Musical Instruments of the Francophonie:
    www.virtualmuseum.ca/Exhibitions/Instruments
Musique du Québec: www.audio-archives.com/en/catalogue/e_th_world-music_
    quebec.htm

Punk

Punk101: punkmusic.about.com/od/punk101/u/Punk101.htm
A Brief History of Punk: punkmusic.about.com/od/punk101/a/punhistory2.htm
A History of Punk: www.fastnbulbous.com/punk.htm
The History of Punk Rock: www.scaruffi.com/history/cpt42.html
Punk77! Punk in the UK: www.punk77.co.uk
Punk Music Community: www.punkmusic.com
Punk Rock Confidential Fanzine: www.punkrockcon.com

Disco

Relive the Disco Era!: www.discomusic.com
History of Disco: www.soul-patrol.com/funk/disco1.htm
American Heritage: Disco: www.americanheritage.com/articles/magazine/ah/1999/
    7/1999_7_43.shtml

New Wave

New Wave Outpost: www.nwoutpost.com/default.asp
What Is New Wave Music?: www.wisegeek.com/what-is-new-wave-music.htm
New Wave Music: www.silver-dragon-records.com/new_wave.htm

Electronica

CanEhdian Electronic Dance Music: canehdian.com/genre/electronica.html
Resource for the Electronic Music Lifestyle: Dub.ca
The Electronica Primer: www.plato.bl/e-primer
What Is Electronica?: cec.concordia.ca/econtact/issues_in_ea/Digs.htm

Rap

Hip-Hop Pioneers and the History of Rap: www.associatedcontent.com/article/
  23806/hiphop_pioneers_and_the_history_of.html
A Brief History of Rap: rap.about.com/od/rootsofraphiphop/p/RootsOfRap.htm
Music History: Rap/Hip-Hop: www.digital-daydreams.com/enc/history/show_
  history.php?id=44

Grunge

Grunge Music History: www.silver-dragon-records.com/grunge.htm
History of Rock: The 90s: www.scaruffi.com/history/cpt512.html
History of Grunge, 1988–1995: www.history-of-rock-music/com/age/
  Grunge-1988–1995.php

GLOSSARY

a cappella Vocal singing that involves no instrumental accompaniment.

A&R ('artists and repertoire') The department of a record company whose responsibility it is to discover and cultivate new musical talent and to find material for the artists to perform—naturally, with an eye towards commercial potential. Since many artists today write and record their own material, the latter function of A&R has atrophied to some extent.

arranger A person who adapts (or arranges) the melody and chords of a song to exploit the capabilities and instrumental resources of a particular musical ensemble. For example, a simple pop tune originally written for voice and piano may be arranged for a jazz 'big band' with many horns and a rhythm section.

backbeat A characteristic beat in early rock 'n' roll music. The 'classic' backbeat consists of quarter-note hits on the kick-drum on beats 1 and 3, and on the snare drum on beats 2 and 4, of a 4/4 bar, often accompanied by straight eighth notes on hi-hat or ride cymbal subdividing the beat. The backbeat has proven remarkably resilient, still comprising a core component of much popular music produced today.

ballad A type of song consisting usually of verses set to a repeating melody (see *strophic*) in which a story, often romantic, historic, or tragic, is sung in narrative fashion.

blue notes Expressive notes or scalar inflections found primarily in blues and jazz music. The blue notes derive from African musical practice; although they do not correspond exactly to the Western system of major and minor scales, it is helpful to imagine them as 'flatter' or 'lower' versions of the scale degrees to which they are related, and thus one speaks of 'blue' thirds, fifths, and sevenths.

blues A genre of music originating principally from the field hollers and work songs of rural blacks in the southern United States during the latter half of the nineteenth century. Themes treated by blues lyrics included the oppressive conditions suffered by African Americans; love gone wrong; alienation; misery; and the supernatural. The lyrics are often obscured by a coded, metaphorical language. The music of the blues is rich in Africanisms and earthy rhythms. Originally an acoustic music, the blues moved to the urban North in the mid-twentieth century, becoming electrified in the process.

bottleneck A euphemism for slide guitar technique referencing the necks of glass bottles that pioneers of the technique first employed. Slide guitar is particularly characteristic of blues and blues-based subgenres of rock.

breakbeats (breaks) Initially the name given to the highly syncopated beats sampled by hip-hop DJs in the late 1970s, 'breakbeat' now refers to any beat punctuated by numerous off-beat syncopations. Break-beats were often sampled from moments on dance-oriented records, called 'breaks', when all harmonic and melodic activity ceased, leaving just the rhythm section or drums exposed. Once the purview of hip-hop DJs, breakbeats have become common in almost every subgenre of rock, save the more veridically oriented subgenres (i.e., punk, folk, and heavy metal).

bridge A passage consisting of new, contrasting material that serves as a link between repeated sections of melodic material. A bridge is sometimes called a 'release' (see discussion of AABA song form in Chapter 2).

cadence A melodic or harmonic event that signals the end of a musical line or section, or of the piece as a whole.

call-and-response A musical form in which a phrase performed by a single musician (the 'call') is answered by a contrasting phrase performed by a group of musicians (the 'response'), as was done, for example, among field workers and on prison chain gangs. In African-American music and related genres the call is typically improvised, while the response is repeated more or less exactly.

Canadian country A style of country music performance, typically particular to musicians born and raised in Canada. The genre typically reflects Canada's regional dialects and manners of speaking, and is generally sung in a lower-pitched, less nasal, and more clearly enunciated style than American country music. Most Canadian country songs also tend to be clearly based in folk styles of composition and performance, and thus typically enjoy greater crossover success than other varieties of country music.

CanCon A shorthand reference for Canadian content regulations, first established in 1970, whereby radio and music TV stations are required to play a certain percentage of Canadian songs, 'Canadian' being defined according to several criteria, including music and lyric composition, producer, and artist(s) (see Chapter 5).

chansonnier A singer of French songs, often of a social or political nature, with minimal instrumental accompaniment, i.e., only guitar or piano.

chansons engagés Urban folksongs with topical lyrics in French.

chord The simultaneous sounding of different pitches.

chorus A repeating section within a song consisting of a fixed melody *and* lyric that is repeated each time that it occurs, typically following one or more verses.

coda The 'tail end' of a musical composition, typically a brief passage after the last complete section that serves to bring the piece to its conclusion.

composer A person who creates a piece of music. Although the term may be, and often is, used to describe the creators of popular songs, it is more commonly applied to those who create more extended, formally notated works of music.

counterculture A subculture existing in opposition to and espousing values contrary to that of the dominant culture. The term is most often used to describe the values and lifestyle of young people during the late 1960s and early 1970s (see Chapter 5).

counterpoint The sounding of two independent melodic lines or voices against one another.

cover version The term 'cover' or 'cover version' refers to the second version, and all subsequent versions, of a song, performed by either another act than the one that originally recorded it or by anyone except its composer(s). In the early days of rock 'n' roll, white singers and groups frequently covered rhythm and blues hits by black artists. Because the white performers had easier access to radio airplay, the cover versions often outsold the original recordings.

cracks A vocal technique common in much early R&B, rockabilly, and country music. Singers allow 'cracks' to punctuate their vocal performances, often to signal emotional intensity or to interject rhythmic syncopation into an otherwise 'straight' melodic line.

dialect A regional speech variant; one may allude to regional musical 'dialects' to describe stylistic variants of the same basic musical genre, as with Mississippi Delta blues or east Texas blues.

dissonance A harsh or grating sound. (The perception of dissonance is culturally conditioned. For example, the smaller intervals employed in certain Asian and Middle Eastern musics may sound 'out of tune' and dissonant to Western ears; within their original context, however, they are regarded as perfectly consonant.)

distortion A buzzing, crunchy, or 'fuzzy' tone colour originally achieved by overdriving the vacuum tubes of a guitar amplifier. This effect can be simulated today by solid state and digital sound processors. Distortion is often heard in a hard rock or heavy metal context.

DJ (disc jockey or deejay) One who plays recordings (as on a radio program).

dominant A chord, or harmony, built upon the fifth degree of a major or minor scale.

feedback Technically, an out-of-control sound oscillation that occurs when the output of a loudspeaker finds its way back into a microphone or electric instrument pickup and is reamplified, creating a sound loop that grows in intensity and continues until deliberately broken. Although feedback can be difficult to manage, it becomes a powerful expressive device in the hands of certain blues and rock musicians, most notably the guitarist Jimi Hendrix. Feedback can be recognized as a 'screaming' or 'crying' sound.

Félix awards Annual music awards, named in honour of *chansonnier* Félix Leclerc, given out by l'Association québécoise de l'industrie du disque, du spectacle et de la vidéo (ADISQ).

groove A term originally employed by jazz, rhythm and blues, and funk musicians to describe the channelled flow of swinging, 'funky', or 'phat' rhythms.

hiccupping A vocal technique characteristic of rockabilly, R&B, and certain other subgenres of rock. Singers produce small, short 'hiccups' to rhythmically punctuate their performances and to signal emotional intensity.

hillbilly music An early term for what now would be called country music: music made by rural southerners that developed out of traditions originating in the British Isles.

hook A 'catchy' or otherwise memorable musical phrase or pattern.

licks Short, recurring riff-like phrases, heard often in blues and blues-based music. Licks often form the basis of solo improvisations in blues and blues-based subgenres of rock.

lyricist A person who supplies a poetic text (lyrics) to a piece of vocal music; not necessarily the composer.

major One of the two scale systems central to Western music (see *minor*); a major scale is arranged in the following order of whole- and half-step intervals: $1–1–{}^1/_2–1–1–1–{}^1/_2$. (This pattern is easy to see if one begins at the pitch C on the piano keyboard and plays the next seven white notes in succession, which yields the C major scale: CDEFGABC.) A song is said to be in a major tonality or key if it uses melodies and chords that are constructed from the major scale. Of course, a song may (and frequently does) 'borrow' notes and chords from outside a particular major scale, and it may 'modulate' or shift from key to key within the course of the song.

melisma One syllable of text spread out over many musical tones.

melody The sequence of pitches that comprise the crucial focus of harmonized music. Far from a universal attribute of all music, different genres value melody differently.

minor One of the two scale systems central to Western music (see *major*); a minor scale is arranged in the following order of whole- and half-step intervals: $1–\frac{1}{2}–1–1–\frac{1}{2}–1–1$. (This pattern represents the so-called natural minor scale, often found in blues and blues-based popular music; it is easy to see if one begins at the pitch A on the piano keyboard and plays the next seven white notes in succession, which yields the A minor scale: ABCDEFGA. The two other minor scales in common usage—the melodic minor and harmonic minor scales—have ascending and descending forms that differ somewhat from the natural minor scale.) A song is said to be in a minor tonality or key if it uses melodies and chords constructed from the minor scale. Of course, a song may (and frequently does) 'borrow' notes and chords from outside a particular minor scale, and it may 'modulate' or shift from key to key within the course of the song. In comparison to the major scale, the minor scale is often described as having a 'sad' or 'melancholy' sound.

MP3 A variant of the MPEG compression system, which allows sound files to be compressed to as little as one-twelfth of their original size.

payola The illegal and historically widespread practice of offering money or other inducements to a radio station or DJ to ensure the prominent airplay of a particular recording.

polyrhythm The simultaneous sounding of rhythms in two or more contrasting metres, such as three against two, or five against four. Polyrhythms are found in abundance in African and Asian musics and their derivatives.

producer A person engaged either by a recording artist or, more often, a record company, who directs and assists the recording process. The producer's duties may include securing the services of session musicians; deciding on arrangements; making technical decisions; motivating the artist creatively; helping to realize the artistic vision in a commercially viable way; and, not unimportantly, ensuring that the project comes in under budget. A good producer often develops a distinctive signature sound, and successful producers are always in great demand. They are often rewarded handsomely for their efforts, garnering a substantial share of a recording's earnings in addition to a commission.

R&B (rhythm and blues) An African-American musical genre emerging after World War II. It consisted of a loose cluster of styles derived from black musical traditions, characterized by energetic and hard-swinging rhythms. At first performed exclusively by black musicians and aimed at black audiences, R&B came to replace the older category of 'race records' (see Chapter 2).

refrain In the verse-refrain song, the refrain is the 'main part' of the song, usually constructed in AABA or ABAC form (see discussion of 'Love and Marriage' in Chapter 1).

reverb Short for 'reverberation'—a prolongation of a sound by virtue of an ambient acoustical space created by hard, reflective surfaces. The sound bounces off these surfaces and recombines with the original sound, slightly delayed (reverb is measured in terms of seconds and fractions of seconds). Reverberation can occur naturally or be simulated either electronically or by digital sound processors.

riff A simple, repeating melodic idea or pattern that generates rhythmic momentum; typically played by the horns or the piano in a jazz ensemble, or by an electric guitar in a rock 'n' roll context.

rockabilly A vigorous form of country and western music ('hillbilly' music) informed by the rhythms of black R&B and electric blues. It is exemplified by such artists as Carl Perkins and the young Elvis Presley.

sampling A digital recording process wherein a sound source is recorded or 'sampled' with a microphone, converted into a stream of binary numbers that represent the profile of the sound, quantized, and stored in computer memory. The digitized sound sample may then be retrieved in any number of ways, including 'virtual recording studio' programs for the computer, or by activating the sound from an electronic keyboard or drum machine.

scat singing A technique that involves the use of nonsense syllables as a vehicle for wordless vocal improvisation. It is most often found in a jazz context.

showcase gig An industry term for a performance deliberately booked so that label representatives can watch the band perform in a 'live' setting.

slap-back A distinctive short reverberation with few repetitions, often heard in the recordings of rockabilly artists, such as the Sun Records recordings of Elvis Presley.

sock-rhythm A dance rhythm characteristic of honky-tonk music in particular.

sound system The name given to travelling public address systems used by DJs in Jamaica since the mid-1960s. Sound systems are considered by most historians to have played a crucial role in the development of dub and, eventually, of hip-hop.

strophes Poetic stanzas; often, a pair of stanzas of alternating form that constitute the structure of a poem. These could become the *verse* and *chorus* of a *strophic* song.

strophic A song form that employs the same music for each poetic unit in the lyrics.

subdominant A chord, or harmony, built upon the fourth degree of a major or minor scale.

syncopation Rhythmic patterns in which the stresses occur on what are ordinarily weak beats, thus displacing or suspending the sense of metric regularity.

tempo Literally, 'time' (from Italian). The rate at which a musical composition proceeds, regulated by the speed of the beat or pulse to which it is performed.

timbre The 'tone colour' or characteristic sound of an instrument or voice, determined by its frequency and overtone components. Timbre is the aspect of sound that allows us, for example, to differentiate between the sound of a violin and a flute when both instruments are playing the same pitch.

Tin Pan Alley Originally a name for the area in New York City where music publishing was centred, this phrase came to refer to the extremely popular style of music that was produced there during the first half of the twentieth century—and to later popular music obviously indebted to that style.

tonic Refers to the central or 'home' pitch, or chord, of a musical piece—or sometimes of just a section of the piece. Also a chord, or harmony, built upon the first scale degree.

tremolo The rapid reiteration of a single pitch to create a vibrating sound texture. This effect can be produced by acoustic instruments or by electronic means.

verse In general usage, this term refers to a group of lines of poetic text, often rhyming, that usually exhibit regularly recurring metrical patterns. In the verse-refrain song, the verse refers to an introductory section that precedes the main body of the song, the *refrain* (see discussion of 'Love and Marriage' in Chapter 1).

vibrato An expressive musical technique that involves minute wavering or fluctuation of a pitch.

waltz A dance in triple metre with a strong emphasis on the first beat of each bar.

BIBLIOGRAPHY

This list includes all works cited in the body of this book, along with a small number of others that were consulted or that we recommend for further reading on individual topics and issues central to the material covered in the preceding pages. No attempt has been made to offer a comprehensive bibliography here, or to list books of a general introductory nature in the area of rock.

Anderson, Kyle. *Accidental Revolution: The Story of Grunge.* New York, 2007.

Angus, Ian. *A Border Within: National Identity, Cultural Plurality and Wilderness.* Montreal, 1997.

Archbold, Rick. *I Stand For Canada—The Story of the Maple Leaf Flag.* Toronto, 2002.

Atwood, Margaret. *Survival: A Thematic Guide to Canadian Literature.* Toronto, 1972.

Bachman, Randy, and John Einarson. *Still Takin' Care of Business: The Randy Bachman Story.* Toronto, 2007.

Barlow, Maude. *Too Close for Comfort: Canada's Future within Fortress North America.* Toronto, 2005.

Bashe, Philip. *Heavy Metal Thunder.* Garden City, NY, 1985.

Beatey, Bart, and Rebecca Sullivan. *Canadian Television Today.* Calgary, 2006.

Beatles, the. *Anthology.* San Francisco, 2000.

Berry, Chuck. *The Autobiography.* New York, 1987.

Bickerton, James, Stephen Brooks, and Alain Gagnon. *Freedom, Equality, Community: The Political Philosophy of Six Influential Canadians.* Montreal, 2006.

Bothwell, Robert. *The Penguin History of Canada.* Toronto, 2006.

——— and J.L. Granatstein. *Our Century: The Canadian Journey.* Toronto, 2000.

——— et al. *Canada Since 1945.* Toronto, 1993.

Bright, Spencer. *Peter Gabriel: An Authorized Biography.* London, 1999.

Bromell, Nick. *Tomorrow Never Knows: Rock and Psychedelics in the 1960s.* Chicago, 2000.

Bronson, Fred. *Billboard's Hottest Hot 100 Hits.* New York, 2007.

Byrne, David. 'David Byrne and Thom Yorke on the Real Value of Music', *Wired* 16, 1 (2008): 115–16.

Canning, Brendan. In *Time*, Canadian edn (Mar. 2005).

Champ, Hamish. *The 100 Best Selling Albums of the 70s.* Singapore, 2004.

Chang, Jeff. *Can't Stop Won't Stop: A History of the Hip Hop Generation.* New York, 2005.

Chapple, Steve, and Reebee Garofalo. *Rock 'n' Roll Is Here to Pay: The History and Politics of the Music Industry.* Chicago, 1977.

Charles, Ray, and David Ritz. *Brother Ray: Ray Charles' Own Story.* New York, 1978.

Chilton, John. *Let the Good Times Roll: The Story of Louis Jordan and His Music.* Ann Arbor, MI, 1994.

Clarke, Donald. *The Rise and Fall of Popular Music*. New York, 1995.

Coleman, Mark. *Playback: From the Victrola to MP3, 100 Years of Music, Machines and Money*. New York, 2003.

Collin, Matthew. *Altered State: The Story of Ecstasy Culture and Acid House*. London, 1997.

Cott, Jonathan. *Bob Dylan: The Essential Interviews*. New York, 2006.

Cummings, Burton. *Bachman Cummings Songbook*. New York, 2006.

Deffaa, Chip. *Blue Rhythms: Six Lives in Rhythm and Blues*. Urbana, IL, 1996.

Echard, William. *Neil Young and the Poetics of Energy*. Bloomington, IN, 2005.

Einarson, John. *Neil Young: Don't Be Denied*. Kingston, ON, 1992.

———. *American Woman: The Story of the Guess Who*. Kingston, ON, 1995.

———. *Made in Manitoba: A Musical Legacy*. Winnipeg, 2005.

English, John. *Citizen of the World: The Life of Pierre Elliott Trudeau, Volume One, 1919–1968*. Toronto, 2006.

Fast, Susan. *In the Houses of the Holy: Led Zeppelin and the Power of Rock Music*. New York, 2001.

Freeman, Philip. *Runnin the Voodoo Down: The Electric Music of Miles Davis*. San Francisco, 2005.

Fricke, Jim, and Charlie Ahearn. *Yes Yes Y'All: Oral History of Hip Hop's First Decade*. New York, 2002.

Frith, Simon. *Sound Effects: Youth, Leisure, and the Politics of Rock 'n' Roll*. New York, 1981.

Fukuyama, Francis. *The End of History and the Last Man*. Toronto, 1992.

Furay, Ritchie, and John Einarson. *For What It's Worth: The Story of Buffalo Springfield*. New York, 1997.

George, Nelson. *Hip Hop America*. New York, 1998.

——— et al., eds. *Fresh: Hip-Hop Don't Stop*. New York, 1985.

Gillett, Charlie. *The Sound of the City: The Rise of Rock and Roll*. New York, 1996.

Gillmor, Don, Achille Michaud, and Pierre Turgeon. *Canada: A People's History*, vol. 2. Toronto, 2001.

Goffman, Ken, and Dan Joy. *Counterculture through the Ages: From Abraham to Acid House*. New York, 2004.

Goodwin, Andrew. *Dancing in the Distraction Factory: Music Television and Popular Culture*. Minneapolis, 1992.

Granatstein, J.L. *Who Killed Canadian History?* Toronto, 1998.

Grant, George. *Lament for a Nation: The Defeat of Canadian Nationalism*. Toronto, 1965.

Greenfield, Robert. *Exile on Main Street: A Season in Hell with the Rolling Stones*. New York, 2007.

Guralnick, Peter. *Sweet Soul Music: Rhythm and Blues and the Southern Dream of Freedom*. New York, 1986.

———. *Last Train to Memphis: The Rise of Elvis Presley*. Boston, 1994.

———. *Careless Love: The Unmaking of Elvis Presley*. Boston, 1999.

Gwyn, Richard. *The Northern Magus: Pierre Trudeau and Canadians*. Toronto, 1980.

Hager, Steven. *Hip Hop: The Illustrated History of Break Dancing, Rap Music, and Graffiti*. New York, 1984.

Harris, John. *The Dark Side of the Moon: The Making of the Pink Floyd Masterpiece*. New York, 2007.

Hemphill, Paul. *Lovesick Blues: The Life of Hank Williams*. Toronto, 2005.

Igartu, José E. *The Other Quiet Revolution: National Identities in English Canada, 1945–71*. Vancouver, 2006.

Inglis, Sam. 'Harvest', in David Barker, ed., *33 1/3 Greatest Hits*, vol. 1. New York, 2006, pp. 34–45.

Jackson, Mahalia, and E.M. Wylie. *Movin' On Up*. New York, 1966.

Jennings, Nicholas. *Before the Gold Rush: Flashbacks to the Dawn of the Canadian Sound*. Toronto, 1997.

Joplin, Laura. *Love Janis: An Intimate Biography of Janis Joplin with Never-Before Published Letters*. New York, 1992.

Karlen, Neal. 'Prince Talks', *Rolling Stone*, Apr. 1985.

Kay, John, and John Einarson. *Magic Carpet Ride: The Autobiography of John Kay and Steppenwolf*. Kingston, ON, 1994.

Keil, Charles. *Urban Blues*. Chicago, 1966.

———— and Steven Feld. *Music Grooves*. Chicago, 1994.

Keillor, Elaine. *Music in Canada: Capturing Landscape and Diversity*. Montreal, 2006.

Kernerman, Gerald. *Multicultural Nationalism: Civilizing Difference, Constituting Community*. Vancouver, 2005.

Krims, Adam. *Rap Music and the Poetics of Identity*. Cambridge, UK, 2000.

Kusek, David, and Gerd Leonhard. *The Future of Music: Manifesto for the Digital Music Revolution*. Boston, 2005.

Laing, Dave. *One-Chord Wonders*. Philadelphia, 1985.

Lawrence, Sharon. *Jimi Hendrix: The Intimate Story of a Betrayed Musical Legend*. New York, 2004.

Levine, Lawrence. *Black Culture and Black Consciousness: Afro-American Folk Thought from Slavery to Freedom*. New York, 1977.

Lhamon, W.T., Jr. *Raising Cain: Blackface Performance from Jim Crow to Hip Hop*. Cambridge, MA, 1998.

Light, Alan. *The Skills to Pay the Bills: The Story of the Beastie Boys*. New York, 2005.

MacDonald, Ian. *Revolution in the Head: The Beatles' Records and the Sixties*. London, 1998.

McDonough, Jimmy. *Shakey: Neil Young's Biography*. Toronto, 2002.

McLean, Steve. *Hot Canadian Bands*. Toronto, 2005.

McQuillar, Tayannah Lee. *When Rap Music Had a Conscience*. New York, 2007.

Malone, Bill C. *Country Music, U.S.A.*, rev. edn. Austin, TX, 1985.

Marcus, Greil. *Stranded: Rock and Roll for a Desert Island*. New York, 1979.

————. *Invisible Republic: Bob Dylan's Basement Tapes*. New York, 1997.

————. *Mystery Train: Images of America in Rock 'n' Roll Music*. Toronto, 1997.

————. *Double Trouble: Bill Clinton and Elvis Presley in a Land of No Alternatives*. New York, 2000.

————. *Like a Rolling Stone: Bob Dylan at the Crossroads*. New York, 2005.

Martin, George, and Jeremy Hornsby. *All You Need Is Ears: The Inside Personal Story of the Genius Who Created the Beatles*. New York, 1979.

Melhuish, Martin. *Heart of Gold: 30 Years of Canadian Pop Music*. Toronto, 1983.

————. *Oh What a Feeling: A Vital History of Canadian Music*. Kingston, ON, 1996.

Mersereau, Bob. *The Top 100 Canadian Albums*. Fredericton, NB, 2007.

Millard, Andre. *America on Record: A History of Recorded Sound*. Cambridge, UK, 2005.

Moorfield, Virgil. *The Producer as Composer: Shaping the Sounds of Popular Music*. Cambridge, UK, 2005.

Morse, Dave. *Motown and the Arrival of Black Music*. New York, 1971.

Morton, David. *Sound Recording: The Life Story of a Technology*. Baltimore, 2007.

Nadel, Ira B. *Various Positions—A Life of Leonard Cohen*. Toronto, 1996.

Negus, Keith. *Producing Pop: Culture and Conflict in the Popular Music Industry*. London, 1992.

Oliver, Paul. *Blues Fell This Morning: Meaning in the Blues*. Cambridge, UK, 1990.

Owram, Douglas. *Born at the Right Time: A History of the Baby Boom Generation*. Toronto, 1996.

Palmer, Robert. *Deep Blues*. New York, 1981.

————. *Rock & Roll: An Unruly History*. New York, 1995.

Pegley, Karen. 'Toronto 2000: Local, National, and Global Intersections', *Discourses in Music* 1, 1 (2000). At: <discourses.ca>.

Peterson, Richard A. *Creating Country Music: Fabricating Authenticity*. Chicago, 1997.

Petkov, Steven, and Leonard Mustazza, eds. *The Frank Sinatra Reader*. New York, 1995.

Pleasants, Henry. *The Great American Popular Singers*. New York, 1974.

Pound, Richard W. *Fitzhenry and Whiteside Book of Canadian Facts and Dates*, 3rd edn. Markham, ON, 2005.

Potter, Greg. *Hand Me Down World: The Canadian Pop–Rock Paradox*. Toronto, 1999.

Prendergast, Mark. *The Ambient Century: From Mahler to Moby—The Evolution of Sound in the Electronic Age*. London, 2000.

Pritchard, David, and Alan Lysaght. *The Beatles: An Oral History*. Toronto, 1998.

Reynolds, Simon. *Generation Ecstasy: Into the World of Techno and Rave Culture*. New York, 1998.

———. *Rip It Up and Start Again: Postpunk 1978–1984*. New York, 2005.

Ribowsku, Mark. *He's a Rebel—Phil Spector, Rock & Roll's Legendary Producer*. New York, 2006.

Robbins, Li. *Don Messer's Violin: Canada's Fiddle*. Toronto, 2005.

Roberts, John Storm. *The Latin Tinge: The Impact of Latin American Music on the United States*. New York, 1979.

Rose, Tricia. *Black Noise: Rap Music and Black Culture in Contemporary America*. Middletown, CT, 1994.

Savage, John. *England's Dreaming: Sex Pistols and Punk Rock*. London, 1991.

Schaffner, Nicholas. *Saucerful of Secrets: The Pink Floyd Odyssey*. New York, 1991.

Scobie, Stephen. *Alias: Bob Dylan Revisited*. Calgary, 2003.

Sexton, Adam, ed. *Desperately Seeking Madonna*. New York, 1993.

Shaw, Arnold. *Honkers and Shouters: The Golden Years of Rhythm and Blues*. New York, 1986.

Stafford, Peter. *Psychedelics*. Oakland, 2003.

Southall, Brian. *Sex Pistols: 90 Days at EMI*. London, 2007.

——— and Rupert Perry. *Northern Songs: The True Story of the Beatles' Song Publishing Empire*. New York, 2007.

Taylor, Timothy D. *Global Pop: World Music, World Markets*. New York, 1997.

———. *Strange Sounds: Music, Technology & Culture*. New York, 2001.

Tetley, William. *The October Crisis, 1970: An Insider's View*. Montreal, 2007.

Théberge, Paul. *Any Sound You Can Imagine: Making Music/Consuming Technology*. Middletown, CT, 1997.

Tingen, Paul. *Miles Beyond: The Electric Explorations of Miles Davis, 1967–1991*. New York, 2001.

Toop, David. *The Rap Attack 2: African Rap to Global Hip Hop*. London, 2000.

Unterberger, Richie. *Eight Miles High: Folk Rock's Flight from Haight-Ashbury to Woodstock*. San Francisco, 2003.

Vance, Jonathan. *Building Canada: People and Projects That Shaped the Nation*. Toronto, 2006.

Walser, Robert. *Running with the Devil: Power, Gender, and Madness in Heavy Metal Music*. Middletown, CT, 1993.

Werner, Craig. *Higher Ground: Stevie Wonder, Aretha Franklin, Curtis Mayfield and the Rise and Fall of American Soul*. New York, 2004.

West, Cornel. *Race Matters*. Boston, 1993.

Whitaker, Reg. *Canadian Immigration Policy Since Confederation*. Toronto, 1991.

Whitburn, Joel. *The Billboard Book of Top 40 Hits*, 8th edn. New York, 2004.

Wilkinson, Paul. *Rat Salad: Black Sabbath, the Classic Years, 1969–1975*. London, 2006.

Williamson, Nigel. *The Rough Guide to Bob Dylan: The Man, the Music, the Myth*. New York, 2006.

Wilson, Carl. *Let's Talk about Love: A Journey to the End of Taste*. New York, 2007.

Witts, Richard. *The Velvet Underground*. Bloomington, IN, 2006.

Wynn, Ron. *Tina: The Tina Turner Story*. New York, 1985.

Yetnikoff, Walter, and David Ritz. *Howlin' at the Moon*. New York, 2004.

Zimmer, Dave, ed. *4 Way Street: The Crosby, Stills, Nash & Young Reader*. New York, 2004.

INDEX

Select Milestones in Canadian Rock and Popular Music History 1950s – 2000s

1986
- The Department of Communication establishes the Sound Recording Development Program to support Canadian music
- The last CHUM chart is published on 14 June, featuring Madonna's 'Live to Tell' at Number One
- Launch of MusiquePlus, a francophone version of MuchMusic aimed at Québécois viewers
- Alan Cross begins work as an overnight announcer at CFNY in Toronto
- Producer Daniel Lanois receives a Grammy for his work on U2's *The Joshua Tree*
- Glass Tiger, *The Thin Red Line* ('Don't Forget Me (When I'm Gone)', 'Someday')
- Kim Mitchell, *Shakin' Like a Human Being* ('Patio Lanterns')
- The Shuffle Demons, *Streetniks* ('Spadina Bus', 'Out of My House, Roach')
- Ian Tyson, *Cowboyography*
- 54-40, *54-40* ('I Go Blind')

1987
- Bryan Adams, *Into the Fire*
- Blue Rodeo, *Outskirts* ('Try')
- Skinny Puppy, *Cleanse Fold & Manipulate*

1988
- Leonard Cohen, *I'm Your Man* ('First We Take Manhattan', 'Everybody Knows')
- The Cowboy Junkies, *The Trinity Sessions* ('Misguided Angel')
- The Jeff Healey Band, *See the Light* ('Angel Eyes', 'See the Light')
- Mitsou, 'Bye Bye Mon Cowboy'
- The Pursuit of Happiness, *Love Junk* ('I'm an Adult Now')

1989
- Kashtin, *Kashtin* ('E Uassiuian' ['mon enfance], 'Tpatshimun' ['Chanson du diable'], 'Tshinanu' ['Nous autres'])
- Daniel Lanois, *Acadie*
- Alannah Myles, *Alannah Myles* ('Black Velvet', 'Love Is')
- The Tragically Hip, *Up to Here* ('Blow at High Dough', 'New Orleans Is Sinking')

1990
- Jean Leloup, *L'amour est sans pitié*

1991
- Bryan Adams, *Waking Up the Neighbours* ('(Everything I Do) I Do It for You')
- Tom Cochrane, *Mad Mad World* ('Life Is a Highway')
- Crash Test Dummies, *The Ghosts That Haunt Me* ('Superman's Song')
- The Lowest of the Low, *Shakespeare My Butt*
- Maestreo Fresh Wes, *Symphony in Effect* ('Let Your Backbone Slide', 'Drop the Needle')
- The Rheostatics, *Melville* ('Record Body Count')
- The Tragically Hip, *Road Apples* ('Little Bones', 'Twist My Arm')

1992
- Bryan Adams calls the CRTC 'stupidity' and suggests that 'CanCon' regulations be scrapped after his album, *Waking Up the Neighbours*, fails to qualify as 'Canadian' content
- Jann Arden, *Time for Mercy* ('I Would Die for You')
- The Barenaked Ladies, *Gordon* ('Enid', 'Be My Yoko Ono', 'If I Had a Million Dollars', 'Brian Wilson')
- k.d. lang, *Ingénue* ('Constant Craving', 'Miss Chatelaine')

- Alannah Myles, 'Song Instead of a Kiss'
- Sloan, *Smeared* ('Underwhelmed')
- The Tragically Hip, *Fully Completely* ('Courage (For Hugh MacLennan)', 'Wheat Kings', 'Locked in the Trunk of a Car', 'At the 100th Meridian', 'Fifty-Mission Cap')
- The Rheostatics, *Whale Music*
- Neil Young, *Harvest Moon* ('Harvest Moon')

1993
- The first Another Roadside Attraction tour is launched
- Blue Rodeo, *Five Days in July* ('5 Days in May', 'Hasn't Hit Me Yet', 'Bad Timing')
- Snow, 'Informer'

1994
- Jann Arden, *Living under June* ('Good Mother', 'Living under June')
- Sarah McLachlan, *Fumbling towards Ecstasy* ('Possession', 'Hold On', 'Good Enough')
- The Tragically Hip, *Day for Night* ('Nautical Disaster', 'Scared', 'Grace, Too')

1995
- Task Force on the Future of the Canadian Music Industry releases its report
- Bryan Adams, 'Have You Ever Really Loved a Woman?'
- Susan Aglukark, *This Child* ('O Siem')
- Hayden, *Everything I Long For* ('Bad as They Seem')
- Ashley MacIsaac, *Hi How Are You Today?*
- Alanis Morissette, *Jagged Little Pill* ('You Oughta Know', 'Hand in My Pocket', 'Ironic', 'You Learn')
- Ron Sexsmith, *Ron Sexsmith*
- Shania Twain, *The Woman in Me*

1996
- Alanis Morissette receives the Grammy for Album of the Year for *Jagged Little Pill*
- The Tragically Hip, *Trouble at the Henhouse* ('Ahead by a Century', '100 Ft. Ceiling')

1997
- The first Lilith Fair tour launches
- Céline Dion, 'My Heart Will Go On'
- Matthew Good Band, Underdogs ('Everything is Automatic', 'Apparitions')
- Sarah McLachlan, *Surfacing* ('Building a Mystery', 'Sweet Surrender', 'Angel')
- Our Lady Peace, *Clumsy* ('Superman's Dead', 'Automatic Flowers')
- The Tea Party, *Transmission*
- Shania Twain, *Come on Over* ('You're Still the One', 'From This Moment On', 'That Don't Impress Me Much', 'Man! I Feel Like a Woman')

1998
- Bob Dylan's *Time Out of Mind*, produced by Daniel Lanois, receives the Grammy for Album of the Year
- The Barenaked Ladies, 'One Week'
- Bif Naked, *I Bificus*
- Hayden, *The Closer I Get* ('The Hazards of Sitting Beneath Palm Trees', 'Two Doors')
- Alanis Morissette, *Supposed Former Infatuation Junkie* ('Thank U')
- The Tragically Hip, *Phantom Power* ('Bobcaygeon', 'Poets')
- Rufus Wainwright, *Rufus Wainwright*